The Mathematics of
Financial Modeling
and Investment
Management

SERGIO M. FOCARDI

FRANK J. FABOZZI

WILEY
John Wiley & Sons, Inc.

SMF

To Dominique, Leila, Guillaume, and Richard

FJF

To my beautiful wife Donna and my children,
Francesco, Patricia, and Karly

Contents

Preface

Since the pioneering work of Harry Markowitz in the 1950s, sophisticated statistical and mathematical techniques have increasingly made their way into finance and investment management. One might question whether all this mathematics is justified, given the present state of economics as a science. However, a number of laws of economics and finance theory with a bearing on investment management can be considered empirically well established and scientifically sound. This knowledge can be expressed only in the language of statistics and mathematics. As a result, practitioners must now be familiar with a vast body of statistical and mathematical techniques.

Different areas of finance call for different mathematics. Investment management is primarily concerned with understanding hard facts about financial processes. Ultimately the performance of investment management is linked to an understanding of risk and return. This implies the ability to extract information from time series that are highly noisy and appear nearly random. Mathematical models must be simple, but with a deep economic meaning.

In other areas, the complexity of instruments is the key driver behind the growing use of sophisticated mathematics in finance. There is the need to understand how relatively simple assumptions on the probabilistic behavior of basic quantities translate into the potentially very complex probabilistic behavior of financial products. Derivatives are the typical example.

This book is designed to be a working tool for the investment management practitioner, student, and researcher. We cover the process of financial decision-making and its economic foundations. We present financial models and theories, including CAPM, APT, factor models, models of the term structure of interest rates, and optimization methodologies. Special emphasis is put on the new mathematical tools that allow a deeper understanding of financial econometrics and financial economics. For example, tools for estimating and representing the tails of the distributions, the analysis of correlation phenomena, and dimensionality reduction through factor analysis and cointegration are recent advances in financial economics that we discuss in depth.

Special emphasis has been put on describing concepts and mathematical techniques, leaving aside lengthy demonstrations, which, while the substance of mathematics, are of limited interest to the practitioner and student of financial economics. From the practitioner's point of view, what is important is to have a firm grasp of the concepts and techniques, which will allow one to interpret the results of simulations and analyses that are now an integral part of finance.

There is no prerequisite mathematical knowledge for reading this book: all mathematical concepts used in the book are explained, starting from ordinary calculus and matrix algebra. It is, however, a demanding book given the breadth and depth of concepts covered. Mathematical concepts are in bolded type when they appear for the first time in the book, economic and finance concepts are italicized when they appear for the first time.

In writing this book, special attention was given to bridging the gap between the intuition of the practitioner and academic mathematical analysis. Often there are simple compelling reasons for adopting sophisticated concepts and techniques that are obscured by mathematical details; whenever possible, we tried to give the reader an understanding of the reasoning behind these concepts. The book has many examples of how quantitative analysis is used in practice. These examples help the reader appreciate the connection between quantitative analysis and financial decision-making. A distinctive feature of this book is the integration of notions deeply rooted in the practice of investment management with methods based on finance theory and statistical analysis.

Sergio M. Focardi
Frank J. Fabozzi

Acknowledgments

We are grateful to Professor Ren-Raw Chen of Rutgers University for coauthoring Chapter 22 ("Credit Risk Modeling and Credit Default Swaps").

The application of mean-variance analysis to asset allocation in Chapter 16 is from the coauthored work of Frank Fabozzi with Harry Markowitz and Francis Gupta. The discussion of tracking error and risk decomposition in Chapter 18 draws from the coauthored work of Frank Fabozzi with Frank Jones and Raman Vardharaj.

In writing a book that covers a wide range of technical topics in mathematics and finance, we were fortunate enough to receive assistance from the following individuals:

- Caroline Jonas of The Intertek Group read and commented on most chapters in the book.
- Dr. Petter Kolm of Goldman Sachs Asset Management reviewed Chapters 4, 6, 7, 9, and 20.
- Dr. Bernd Hanke of Goldman Sachs Asset Management reviewed Chapters 14, 15, and 16.
- Dr. Lisa Goldberg of Barra reviewed Chapter 13.
- Professor Martijn Cremers of Yale University reviewed the first draft of the financial econometrics material.
- Hafize Gaye Erkan, a Post-General Ph.D. Candidate in the Department of Operations Research and Financial Engineering at Princeton University, reviewed the chapters on stochastic calculus (Chapters 8 and 10).
- Professor Antti Petajisto of Yale University reviewed Chapter 14.
- Dr. Christopher Maloney of Citigroup reviewed Chapter 5.
- Dr. Marco Raberto of the University of Genoa reviewed Chapter 13 and provided helpful support for the preparation of illustrations.
- Dr. Mehmet Gokcedag of the Istanbul Bilgi University reviewed Chapter 22 and provided helpful comments on the organization and structure of the book.
- Professor Silvano Cincotti of the University of Genoa provided insightful comments on a range of topics.

- Dr. Lev Dynkin and members of the Fixed Income Research Group at Lehman Brothers reviewed Chapter 21.
- Dr. Srichander Ramaswamy of the Bank for International Settlement prepared the illustration in Chapter 13 to show the importance of fat-tailed processes in credit risk management based on his book *Managing Credit Risk in Corporate Bond Portfolios: A Practitioner's Guide.*
- Hemant Bhangale of Morgan Stanley reviewed Chapter 23.

Finally, Megan Orem typeset the book and provided editorial assistance. We appreciate her patience and understanding in working through several revisions of the chapters and several reorganizations of the table of contents.

About the Authors

Sergio Focardi is a founding partner of the Paris-based consulting firm The Intertek Group. Sergio lectures at CINEF (Center for Interdisciplinary Research in Economics and Finance) at the University of Genoa and is a member of the Editorial Board of the *Journal of Portfolio Management*. He has published numerous articles on econophysics and coauthored two books, *Modeling the Markets: New Theories and Techniques* and *Risk Management: Framework, Methods and Practice*. His research interests include modeling the interaction between multiple heterogeneous agents and the econometrics of large equity portfolios based on cointegration and dynamic factor analysis. Sergio holds a degree in Electronic Engineering from the University of Genoa and a postgraduate degree in Communications from the Galileo Ferraris Electrotechnical Institute (Turin).

Frank J. Fabozzi, Ph.D., CFA, CPA is the Frederick Frank Adjunct Professor of Finance in the School of Management at Yale University. Prior to joining the Yale faculty, he was a Visiting Professor of Finance in the Sloan School of Management at MIT. Frank is a Fellow of the International Center for Finance at Yale University, the editor of the *Journal of Portfolio Management*, a member of Princeton University's Advisory Council for the Department of Operations Research and Financial Engineering, and a trustee of the BlackRock complex of closed-end funds and Guardian Life sponsored open-end mutual funds. He has authored several books in investment management and in 2002 was inducted into the Fixed Income Analysts Society's Hall of Fame. Frank earned a doctorate in economics from the City University of New York in 1972.

Commonly Used Symbols

$A(L)$	polynomial in the lag operator L
β	k-vector $[\beta_1...\beta_k]'$
Δ	difference operator
ε_t	error, usually white noise
$\cdot$	vector scalar product $\mathbf{x} \cdot \mathbf{y}$ also written $\mathbf{xy}$
$+$	sum of vector or matrices $\mathbf{A} + \mathbf{B}$
T	transpose of a vector or matrix $\mathbf{A}^T$
adj	adjoint of a matrix
$|\mathbf{A}|$	determinant of a matrix
$\mathfrak{B}$	Borel σ-algebra
$\mathfrak{I}$	Filtration
$\mathfrak{R}_\alpha$	regularly varying functions of index α
$\cup$	union of sets
$\cap$	intersection of sets
$\in$	belongs to
$\notin$	does not belong to
$\rightarrow$	tends to
$\sum$	summation with implicit range
$\sum_{i=1}^{N}$	summation over range shown
$\prod$	product with implicit range
$\prod_{i=1}^{N}$	product over range shown
$\Phi(x)$	cdf of the standardized normal
Ω	sample space
$E[X]$	expectation
$E[X|Z]$	conditional expectation

Abbreviations and Acronyms

ABS	asset-backed securities
ADF	augmented Dickey-Fuller
a.e.	almost everywhere
AIC	Akaike information criterion
AMEX	American Stock Exchange
APT	asset pricing theory
AR	auto regressive
ARCH	autoregressive conditional heteroschedastic
ARDL	auto regressive distributed lag
ARIMA	auto regressive integrated moving average
ARMA	auto regressive moving average
a.s.	almost surely
ASE	American Stock Exchange
BET	bond equivalent yield
BGM	Brace-Gatarek-Musiela model
BIC	Bayesian information criterion
CAPM	capital asset pricing model
C(CAPM)	conditional capital asset pricing model
CD	certificate of deposit
CFM	cash flow matching
CFTC	Commodity Futures Trading Commission
CLT	central limit theorem
CML	capital market line
CrVaR	credit risk value-at-risk
CvaR	conditional value-at-risk
DAX	Geman stock index
d.f	(cumulative) distribution functions
DF	Dickey-Fuller
DGP	data generation process
DJIA	Dow Jones Industrial Average

EAFE Index   Europe, Australia, and Far East Index
EC   error correction
ECM   error correction model
ECN   electronic communication network
EM   expectation maximization
ERISA   Employee Retirement Income Security Act
ES   expected shortfall
ESR   expected shortfall risk
EVT   extreme value theory

FLOPS   floating point operations per second

GAAP   generally accepted accounting principles
GARCH   generalized autoregressive conditional heteroschedastic
GET   general equilibrium theory
GEV   generalized extreme value
GMM   generalized method of moments
GNP   gross national product

HFD   high frequency data
HJM   Heath, Jarrow, Morton model

IC   information criteria
IGRACH   integrated GARCH
IID   independent and identically distributed
IIN   independent identically normal
IN   independent normal
IR   information ratio
ISO   International Standards Organization

L   lag operator
LIBOR   London Interbank Offered Rate
LLN   law of large numbers
LP   linear program, linear programming

MA   moving average
MDA   maximum domain of attraction
MBS   mortgage-backed securities
MIP   mixed integer programming
ML   maximum likelihood
MLE   maximum likelihood estimator
MPT   modern portfolio theory

MSCI-EM	Morgan Stanley Composite Index-Emerging Markets
MSCI-EME	Morgan Stanley Composite Index-Emerging Markets Equity
M-V analysis	mean-variance analysis
NASDAQ	National Association of Securities Dealers Automated Quotation System
NAV	net asset value
NYSE	New York Stock Exchange
ODE	ordinary differential equation
OLS	ordinary least squares
OTC	over-the-counter
P/B	price-to-book ratio
P&C	property & casualty
PCA	principal component analysis
PDE	partial differential equation
pdf	probability density function
QP	quadratic program, quadratic programming
RAP	regulatory accounting principles
RDF	resource description framework
RMT	random matrix theory
ROI	return on investment
SDE	stochastic differential equation
S&L	savings & loan
S&P 500	Standard & Poor's 500 Index
SML	security market line
ss	self similar
SSB BIG Index	Salomon Smith Barney Broad Investment Grade Index
sssi	self similar with stationary increments
UL	unexpected loss
VaR	value-at-risk
VAR	vector auto regressive
VC theory	Vapnik-Chervonenkis theory
VLCA	Value Line Composite Average
XML	eXtensible markup language

CHAPTER 1

From Art to Engineering in Finance

It is often said that investment management is an art, not a science. However since early 1990s the market has witnessed a progressive shift towards a more industrial view of the investment management process. There are several reasons for this change. First, with globalization the universe of investable assets has grown many times over. Asset managers might have to choose from among several thousand possible investments from around the globe. The S&P 500 index is itself chosen from a pool of 8,000 investable U.S. stocks. Second, institutional investors, often together with their investment consultants, have encouraged asset management firms to adopt an increasingly structured process with documented steps and measurable results. Pressure from regulators and the media is another factor. Lastly, the sheer size of the markets makes it imperative to adopt safe and repeatable methodologies. The volumes are staggering. With the recent growth of the world's stock markets, total market capitalization is now in the range of tens of trillions of dollars[1] while derivatives held by U. S. commercial banks topped $65.8 trillion in the second quarter of 2003.[2]

---

[1] Exact numbers are difficult to come up with as information about many markets is missing and price fluctuations remain large.

[2] Office of the Comptroller of the Currency, *Quarterly Derivatives Report*, Second Quarter 2003.

INVESTMENT MANAGEMENT PROCESS

The investment management process involves the following five steps:

Step 1: Setting investment objectives
Step 2: Establishing an investment policy
Step 3: Selecting an investment strategy
Step 4: Selecting the specific assets
Step 5: Measuring and evaluating investment performance

The overview of the investment management process described below should help in understanding the activities that the portfolio manager faces and the need for the analytical tools that are described in the chapters that follow in this book.

Step 1: Setting Investment Objectives

The first step in the investment management process, setting investment objectives, begins with a thorough analysis of the investment objectives of the entity whose funds are being managed. These entities can be classified as *individual investors* and *institutional investors*. Within each of these broad classifications is a wide range of investment objectives.

The objectives of an individual investor may be to accumulate funds to purchase a home or other major acquisitions, to have sufficient funds to be able to retire at a specified age, or to accumulate funds to pay for college tuition for children. An individual investor may engage the services of a financial advisor/consultant in establishing investment objectives.

In Chapter 3 we review the different types of institutional investors. We will also see that in general we can classify institutional investors into two broad categories—those that must meet contractually specified liabilities and those that do not. We can classify those in the first category as institutions with "liability-driven objectives" and those in the second category as institutions with "nonliability driven objectives." Some institutions have a wide range of investment products that they offer investors, some of which are liability driven and others that are nonliability driven. Once the investment objective is understood, it will then be possible to (1) establish a "benchmark" or "bogey" by which to evaluate the performance of the investment manager and (2) evaluate alternative investment strategies to assess the potential for realizing the specified investment objective.

Step 2: Establishing an Investment Policy

The second step in the investment management process is establishing policy guidelines to satisfy the investment objectives. Setting policy begins with the asset allocation decision. That is, a decision must be made as to how the funds to be invested should be distributed among the major classes of assets.

Asset Classes

Throughout this book we refer to certain categories of investment products as an "asset class." From the perspective of a U.S. investor, the convention is to refer the following as *traditional asset classes*:

- U.S. common stocks
- Non-U.S. (or foreign) common stocks
- U.S. bonds
- Non-U.S. (or foreign) bonds
- Cash equivalents
- Real estate

Cash equivalents are defined as short-term debt obligations that have little price volatility and are covered in Chapter 2.

Common stocks and bonds are further divided into asset classes. For U.S. common stocks (also referred to as U.S. equities), the following are classified as asset classes:

- Large capitalization stocks
- Mid-capitalization stocks
- Small capitalization stocks
- Growth stocks
- Value stocks

By "capitalization," it is meant the market capitalization of the company's common stock. This is equal to the total market value of all of the common stock outstanding for that company. For example, suppose that a company has 100 million shares of common stock outstanding and each share has a market value of $10. Then the capitalization of this company is $1 billion (100 million shares times $10 per share). The market capitalization of a company is commonly referred to as the "market cap" or simply "cap."

For U.S. bonds, also referred to as fixed-income securities, the following are classified as asset classes:

- U.S. government bonds
- Investment-grade corporate bonds
- High-yield corporate bonds

- U.S. municipal bonds (i.e., state and local bonds)
- Mortgage-backed securities
- Asset-backed securities

All of these securities are described in Chapter 2, where what is meant by "investment grade" and "high yield" are also explained. Sometimes, the first three bond asset classes listed above are further divided into "long term" and "short term."

For non-U.S. stocks and bonds, the following are classified as asset classes:

- Developed market foreign stocks
- Emerging market foreign stocks
- Developed market foreign bonds
- Emerging market foreign bonds

In addition to the traditional asset classes, there are asset classes commonly referred to as *alternative investments*. Two of the more popular ones are hedge funds and private equity.

How does one define an asset class? One investment manager, Mark Kritzman, describes how this is done as follows:

> ... some investments take on the status of an asset class simply because the managers of these assets promote them as an asset class. They believe that investors will be more inclined to allocate funds to their products if they are viewed as an asset class rather than merely as an investment strategy.[3]

He then goes on to propose criteria for determining asset class status. We won't review the criteria he proposed here. They involve concepts that are explained in later chapters. After these concepts are explained it will become clear how asset class status is determined. However, it should not come as any surprise that the criteria proposed by Kritzman involve the risk, return, and the correlation of the return of a potential asset class with that of other asset classes.

Along with the designation of an investment as an asset class comes a barometer to be able to quantify performance—the risk, return, and the correlation of the return of the asset class with that of another asset class. The barometer is called a "benchmark index," "market index," or simply "index."

---

[3] Mark Kritzman, "Toward Defining an Asset Class," *The Journal of Alternative Investments* (Summer 1999), p. 79.

Constraints

There are some institutional investors that make the asset allocation decision based purely on their understanding of the risk-return characteristics of the various asset classes and expected returns. The asset allocation will take into consideration any investment constraints or restrictions. Asset allocation models are commercially available for assisting those individuals responsible for making this decision.

In the development of an investment policy, the following factors must be considered:

- Client constraints
- Regulatory constraints
- Tax and accounting issues

Client-Imposed Constraints Examples of client-imposed constraints would be restrictions that specify the types of securities in which a manager may invest and concentration limits on how much or little may be invested in a particular asset class or in a particular issuer. Where the objective is to meet the performance of a particular market or customized benchmark, there may be a restriction as to the degree to which the manager may deviate from some key characteristics of the benchmark.

Regulatory Constraints There are many types of regulatory constraints. These involve constraints on the asset classes that are permissible and concentration limits on investments. Moreover, in making the asset allocation decision, consideration must be given to any risk-based capital requirements. For depository institutions and insurance companies, the amount of statutory capital required is related to the quality of the assets in which the institution has invested. There are two types of risk-based capital requirements: credit risk-based capital requirements and interest rate-risk based capital requirements. The former relates statutory capital requirements to the credit-risk associated with the assets in the portfolio. The greater the credit risk, the greater the statutory capital required. Interest rate-risk based capital requirements relate the statutory capital to how sensitive the asset or portfolio is to changes in interest rates. The greater the sensitivity, the higher the statutory capital required.

Tax and Accounting Issues Tax considerations are important for several reasons. First, in the United States, certain institutional investors such as pension funds, endowments, and foundations are exempt from federal income taxation. Consequently, the assets in which they invest will not be those that are tax-advantaged investments. Second, there are tax factors that must be incorporated into the investment policy. For example, while a pension fund might be tax-exempt, there may be certain assets or the use of some investment vehicles in which it invests whose earnings may be taxed.

Generally accepted accounting principles (GAAP) and regulatory accounting principles (RAP) are important considerations in developing investment policies. An excellent example is a defined benefit plan for a corporation. GAAP specifies that a corporate pension fund's surplus is equal to the difference between the market value of the assets and the present value of the liabilities. If the surplus is negative, the corporate sponsor must record the negative balance as a liability on its balance sheet. Consequently, in establishing its investment policies, recognition must be given to the volatility of the market value of the fund's portfolio relative to the volatility of the present value of the liabilities.

Step 3: Selecting a Portfolio Strategy

Selecting a portfolio strategy that is consistent with the investment objectives and investment policy guidelines of the client or institution is the third step in the investment management process. Portfolio strategies can be classified as either active or passive.

An *active portfolio strategy* uses available information and forecasting techniques to seek a better performance than a portfolio that is simply diversified broadly. Essential to all active strategies are expectations about the factors that have been found to influence the performance of an asset class. For example, with active common stock strategies this may include forecasts of future earnings, dividends, or price-earnings ratios. With bond portfolios that are actively managed, expectations may involve forecasts of future interest rates and sector spreads. Active portfolio strategies involving foreign securities may require forecasts of local interest rates and exchange rates.

A *passive portfolio strategy* involves minimal expectational input, and instead relies on diversification to match the performance of some market index. In effect, a passive strategy assumes that the marketplace will reflect all available information in the price paid for securities. Between these extremes of active and passive strategies, several strategies have sprung up that have elements of both. For example, the core of a portfolio may be passively managed with the balance actively managed.

In the bond area, several strategies classified as *structured portfolio strategies* have been commonly used. A structured portfolio strategy is one in which a portfolio is designed to achieve the performance of some predetermined liabilities that must be paid out. These strategies are frequently used when trying to match the funds received from an investment portfolio to the future liabilities that must be paid.

Given the choice among active and passive management, which should be selected? The answer depends on (1) the client's or money manager's view of how "price-efficient" the market is, (2) the client's risk tolerance, and (3) the nature of the client's liabilities. By marketplace price efficiency we mean how difficult it would be to earn a greater return than passive management after adjusting for the risk associated with a strategy and the transaction costs associated with implementing that strategy. Market efficiency is explained in Chapter 3.

Step 4: Selecting the Specific Assets

Once a portfolio strategy is selected, the next step is to select the specific assets to be included in the portfolio. It is in this phase of the investment management process that the investor attempts to construct an *efficient portfolio*. An efficient portfolio is one that provides the greatest expected return for a given level of risk or, equivalently, the lowest risk for a given expected return.

Inputs Required

To construct an efficient portfolio, the investor must be able to quantify risk and provide the necessary inputs. As will be explained in the next chapter, there are three key inputs that are needed: future expected return (or simply expected return), variance of asset returns, and correlation (or covariance) of asset returns. All of the investment tools described in the chapters that follow in this book are intended to provide the investor with information with which to estimate these three inputs.

There are a wide range of approaches to obtain the expected return of assets. Investors can employ various analytical tools that will be discussed throughout this book to derive the future expected return of an asset. For example, we will see in Chapter 18 that there are various asset pricing models that provide expected return estimates based on factors that historically have been found to systematically affect the return on all assets. Investors can use historical average returns as their estimate of future expected returns. Investors can modify historical average returns with their judgment of the future to obtain a future expected return. Another approach is for investors to simply use their intuition without any formal analysis to come up with the future expected return.

In Chapter 16, the reason why the variance of asset returns should be used as a measure of an asset's risk will be explained. This input can be obtained for each asset by calculating the historical variance of asset returns. There are sophisticated time series statistical techniques that can be used to improve the estimated variance of asset returns that are discussed in Chapter 18. Some investors calculate the historical variance of asset returns and adjust them based on their intuition.

The covariance (or correlation) of returns is a measure of how the return of two assets vary together. Typically, investors use historical covariances of asset returns as an estimate of future covariances. But why is a covariance of asset returns needed? As will be explained in Chapter 16, the covariance is important because the variance of a portfolio's return depends on it and the key to diversification is the covariance of asset returns.

Approaches to Portfolio Construction

Constructing an efficient portfolio based on the expected return for a portfolio (which depends on the expected return of all the asset returns in the portfolio) and the variance of the portfolio's return (which depends on the variance of the return of all of the assets in the portfolio and the covariance of returns between all pairs of assets in the portfolio) are referred to as "mean-variance" portfolio management. The term "mean" is used because the expected return is equivalent to the "mean" or "average value" of returns. This approach also allows for the inclusion of constraints such as lower and upper bounds on particular assets or assets in particular industries or sectors. The end result of the analysis is a set of efficient portfolios—alternative portfolios from which the investor can select—that offer the maximum expected portfolio return for a given level of portfolio risk.

There are variations on this approach to portfolio construction. Mean-variance analysis can be employed by estimating risk factors that historically have explained the variance of asset returns. The basic principle is that the value of an asset is driven by a number of systematic factors (or, equivalently, risk exposures) plus a component unique to a particular company or industry. A set of efficient portfolios can be identified based on the risk factors and the sensitivity of assets to these risk factors. This approach is referred to the "multifactor risk approach" to portfolio construction and is explained in Chapter 19 for common stock portfolio management and Chapter 21 for fixed-income portfolio management.

With either the full mean-variance approach or the multifactor risk approach there are two variations. First, the analysis can be performed by investors using individual assets (or securities) or the analysis can be performed on asset classes.

The second variation is one in which the input used to measure risk is the tracking error of a portfolio relative to a benchmark index, rather than the variance of the portfolio return. By a benchmark index it is meant the benchmark that the investor's performance is compared against.

As explained in Chapter 19, tracking error is the variance of the difference in the return on the portfolio and the return on the benchmark index. When this "tracking error multifactor risk approach" to portfolio construction is applied to individual assets, the investor can identify the set of efficient portfolios in terms of a portfolio that matches the risk profile of the benchmark index for each level of tracking error. Selecting assets that intentionally cause the portfolio's risk profile to differ from that of the benchmark index is the way a manager actively manages a portfolio. In contrast, indexing means matching the risk profile. "Enhanced" indexing basically means that the assets selected for the portfolio do not cause the risk profile of the portfolio constructed to depart materially from the risk profile of the benchmark. This tracking error multifactor risk approach to common stock and fixed-income portfolio construction will be explained and illustrated in Chapters 19 and 21, respectively.

At the other extreme of the full mean-variance approach to portfolio management is the assembling of a portfolio in which investors ignore all of the inputs—expected returns, variance of asset returns, and covariance of asset returns—and use their intuition to construct a portfolio. We refer to this approach as the "seat-of-the-pants approach" to portfolio construction. In a rising stock market, for example, this approach is too often confused with investment skill. It is not an approach we recommend.

Step 5: Measuring and Evaluating Performance

The measurement and evaluation of investment performance is the last step in the investment management process. Actually, it is misleading to say that it is the last step since the investment management process is an ongoing process. This step involves measuring the performance of the portfolio and then evaluating that performance relative to some benchmark.

Although a portfolio manager may have performed better than a benchmark, this does not necessarily mean that the portfolio manager satisfied the client's investment objective. For example, suppose that a financial institution established as its investment objective the maximization of portfolio return and allocated 75% of its funds to common stock and the balance to bonds. Suppose further that the manager responsible for the common stock portfolio realized a 1-year return that was 150 basis points greater than the benchmark.[4] Assuming that the risk of the portfolio was similar to that of the benchmark, it would appear that the manager outperformed the benchmark. However, suppose that in spite of this performance, the financial institution cannot

---

[4] A basis point is equal to 0.0001 or 0.01%. This means that 1% is equal to 100 basis points.

meet its liabilities. Then the failure was in establishing the investment objectives and setting policy, not the failure of the manager.

FINANCIAL ENGINEERING IN HISTORICAL PERSPECTIVE

In its modern sense, financial engineering is the design (or engineering) of contracts and portfolios of contracts that result in predetermined cash flows contingent to different events. Broadly speaking, financial engineering is used to manage investments and risk. The objective is the transfer of risk from one entity to another via appropriate contracts. Though the aggregate risk is a quantity that cannot be altered, risk can be transferred if there is a willing counterparty. Just why and how risk transfer is possible will be discussed in Chapter 23 on risk management.

Financial engineering came to the forefront of finance in the 1980s, with the broad diffusion of derivative instruments. However the concept and practice of financial engineering are quite old. Evidence of the use of sophisticated cross-border instruments of credit and payment dating from the time of the First Crusade (1095–1099) has come down to us from the letters of Jewish merchants in Cairo. The notion of the diversification of risk (central to modern risk management) and the quantification of insurance risk (a requisite for pricing insurance policies) were already understood, at least in practical terms, in the 14th century. The rich epistolary of Francesco Datini, a 14th century merchant, banker and insurer from Prato (Tuscany, Italy), contains detailed instructions to his agents on how to diversify risk and insure cargo.[5] It also gives us an idea of insurance costs: Datini charged 3.5% to insure a cargo of wool from Malaga to Pisa and 8% to insure a cargo of malmsey (sweet wine) from Genoa to Southampton, England. These, according to one of Datini's agents, were low rates: He considered 12–15% a fair insurance premium for similar cargo.

What is specific to modern financial engineering is the quantitative management of uncertainty. Both the pricing of contracts and the optimization of investments require some basic capabilities of statistical modeling of financial contingencies. It is the size, diversity, and efficiency of modern competitive markets that makes the use of modeling imperative.

---

[5] Datini wrote the richest medieval epistolary that has come down to us. It includes 500 ledgers and account books, 300 deeds of partnership, 400 insurance policies, and 120,000 letters. For a fascinating portrait of the business and private life of a medieval Italian merchant, see Iris Onigo, *The Merchant of Prato* (London: Penguin Books, 1963).

THE ROLE OF INFORMATION TECHNOLOGY

Advances in information technology are behind the widespread adoption of modeling in finance. The most important advance has been the enormous increase in the amount of computing power, concurrent with a steep fall in prices. Government agencies have long been using computers for economic modeling, but private firms found it economically justifiable only as of the 1980s. Back then, economic modeling was considered one of the "Grand Challenges" of computational science.[6]

In the late 1980s, firms such as Merrill Lynch began to acquire supercomputers to perform derivative pricing computations. The overall cost of these supercomputing facilities, in the range of several million dollars, limited their diffusion to the largest firms. Today, computational facilities ten times more powerful cost only of a few thousand dollars.

To place today's computing power in perspective, consider that a 1990 run-of-the-mill Cray supercomputer cost several million U.S. dollars and had a clock cycle of 4 nanoseconds (i.e., 4 billionths of a second or 250 million cycles per second, notated as 250 MHz). Today's fast laptop computers are 10 times faster with a clock cycle of 2.5 GHz and, at a few thousand dollars, cost only a fraction of the price. Supercomputer performance has itself improved significantly, with top computing speed in the range of several teraflops[7] compared to the several megaflops of a Cray supercomputer in the 1990s. In the space of 15 years, sheer performance has increased 1,000 times while the price-performance ratio has decreased by a factor of 10,000. Storage capacity has followed similar dynamics.

The diffusion of low-cost high-performance computers has allowed the broad use of numerical methods. Computations that were once performed by supercomputers in air-conditioned rooms are now routinely

---

[6] Kenneth Wilson, "Grand Challenges to Computational Science," *Future Generation Computer Systems 5* (1989), p. 171. The term "Grand Challenges" was coined by Kenneth Wilson, recipient of the 1982 Nobel Prize in Physics, and later adopted by the U.S. Department Of Energy (DOE) in its High Performance Communications and Computing Program which included economic modeling among the grand challenges. Wilson was awarded the Nobel Prize in Physics for discoveries he made in understanding how bulk matter undergoes "phase transition," i.e., sudden and profound structural changes. The mathematical techniques he introduced—the renormalization group theory—is one of the tools used to understand economic phase transitions. Wilson is an advocate of computational science as the "third way" of doing science, after theory and experiment.

[7] A flops (Floating Point Operations Per Second) is a measure of computational speed. A Teraflop computer is a computer able to perform a trillion floating point operations per second.

performed on desk-top machines. This has changed the landscape of financial modeling. The importance of finding closed-form solutions and the consequent search for simple models has been dramatically reduced. Computationally-intensive methods such as Monte Carlo simulations and the numerical solution of differential equations are now widely used. As a consequence, it has become feasible to represent prices and returns with relatively complex models. Nonnormal probability distributions have become commonplace in many sectors of financial modeling. It is fair to say that the key limitation of financial econometrics is now the size of available data samples or training sets, not the computations; it is the data that limits the complexity of estimates.

Mathematical modeling has also undergone major changes. Techniques such as equivalent martingale methods are being used in derivative pricing (Chapter 15) and cointegration (Chapter 11), the theory of fat-tailed processes (Chapter 13), and state-space modeling (including ARCH/GARCH and stochastic volatility models) are being used in econometrics (Chapter 11).

Powerful specialized mathematical languages and vast statistical software libraries have been developed. The ability to program sequences of statistical operations within a single programming language has been a big step forward. Software firms such as Mathematica and Mathworks, and major suppliers of statistical tools such as SAS, have created simple computer languages for the programming of complex sequences of statistical operations. This ability is key to financial econometrics which entails the analysis of large portfolios.[8]

Presently only large or specialized firms write complex applications from scratch; this is typically done to solve specific problems, often in the derivatives area. The majority of financial modelers make use of high-level software programming tools and statistical libraries. It is difficult to overestimate the advantage brought by these software tools; they cut development time and costs by orders of magnitude.

In addition, there is a wide range of off-the-shelf financial applications that can be used directly by operators who have a general understanding of the problem but no advanced statistical or mathematical training. For example, powerful complete applications from firms such as Barra and component applications from firms such as FEA make sophisticated analytical methods available to a large number of professionals.

Data have, however, remained a significant expense. The diffusion of electronic transactions has made available large amounts of data,

---

[8] A number of highly sophisticated statistical packages are available to economists. These packages, however, do not serve the needs of the financial econometrician who has to analyze a large number of time series.

including high-frequency data (HFD) which gives us information at the transaction level. As a result, in budgeting for financial modeling, data have become an important factor in deciding whether or not to undertake a new modeling effort.

A lot of data are now available free on the Internet. If the required granularity of data is not high, these data allow one to study the viability of models and to perform rough tuning. However, real-life applications, especially applications based on finely grained data, require data streams of a higher quality than those typically available free on the Internet.

INDUSTRY'S EVALUATION OF MODELING TOOLS

A recent study by The Intertek Group[9] tried to assess how the use of financial modeling in asset management had changed over the highly volatile period from 2000 to 2002. Participants in the study included 44 heads of asset management firms in Europe and North America; more than half were from the biggest firms in their home markets.

The study found that the role of quantitative methods in the investment decision-making process had increased at almost 75% of the firms while it had remained stable at about 15% of the firms; five reported that their process was already essentially quantitative. Demand pull and management push were among the reasons cited for the growing role of models. The head of risk management and product control at an international firm said, "There is genuinely a portfolio manager demand pull plus a top-down management push for a more systematic, robust process." Many reported that fund managers have become more eager consumers of modeling. "Fund managers now perceive that they gain increased insights from the models," the head of quantitative research at a large northern European firm commented.

In another finding, over one half of the participants evaluated that models had performed better in 2002 than two years ago; some 20% evaluated 2002 model performance to be stable with respect to the previous two years while another 20% considered that performance worsened. Performance was widely considered to be model-dependent. Among those that believed that model performance had improved, many attributed better performance to a better understanding of models and the modeling process at asset management firms. Some firms reported hav-

---

[9] Caroline Jonas and Sergio Focardi, *Trends in Quantitative Methods in Asset Management, 2003*, The Intertek Group, Paris, 2003.

ing in place a formal process in which management was systematically trained in modeling and mathematical methods.

The search for a silver bullet typical of the early days of "rocket science" in finance has passed; modeling is now widely perceived as an approximation, with the various models shedding different light on the same phenomena. Just under 60% of the participants in the 2002 study indicated having made significant changes to their modeling approach from 2000 to 2002; for many others, it was a question of continuously recalibrating and adapting the models to the changing environment.[10]

Much of the recent attention on quantitative methods has been focused on risk management—a relatively new function at asset management firms. More than 80% of the firms participating in the Intertek study reported a significant evolution of the role of risk management from 2000 to 2002. Some of the trends revealed by the study included daily or real-time risk measurement and the splitting of the role of risk management into two separate functions, one a support function to the fund managers, the other a central control function reporting to top management. These issues will be discussed in Chapter 23.

In another area which is a measure of an increasingly systematic process, more than 60% of the firms in the 2002 study reported having formalized procedures for integrating quantitative and qualitative input, though half mentioned that the process had not gone very far and 30% reported no formalization at all. One way the integration is being handled is through management structures for decision-making. A source at a large player in the bond market said, "We have regularly scheduled meetings where views are expressed. There is a good combination of views and numbers crunched. The mix between quantitative and qualitative input will depend on the particular situation. For example, if models are showing a 4 or 5 standard deviation event, fundamental analysis would have to be very strong before overriding the models."

Many firms have cast integration in a quantitative framework. The head of research at a large European firm said, "One year ago, the integration was totally fuzzy, but during the past year we have made the integration extremely rigorous. All managers now need to justify their statements and methods in a quantitative sense." Some firms are prioritizing the inputs from various sources. A business manager at a Swiss firm said, "We have recently put in place a scoring framework which pulls together the gut feeling of the fund manager and the quantitative

---

[10] Financial models are typically statistical models that have to be estimated and calibrated. The estimation and calibration of models will be discussed in Chapter 23. The above remarks reflect the fact that financial models are not "laws of nature" but relationships valid only for a limited span of time.

models. We will be taking this further. The objective is to more tightly link the various inputs, be they judgmental or model results."

Some firms see the problem as one of model performance evaluation. "The integration process is becoming more and more institutionalized," said the head of quantitative research at a big northern European firm. "Models are weighted in terms of their performance: if a model has not performed so well, its output is less influential than that of models which have performed better."

In some cases, it is the portfolio manager himself who assigns weights to the various inputs. A source at a large firm active in the bond markets said, "Portfolio managers weight the relative importance of quantitative and qualitative input in function of the security. The more complex the security, the greater the quantitative weighting; the more macro, long-term, the less the quantitative input counts: Models don't really help here." Other firms have a fixed percentage, such as 50/50, as corporate policy. Outside of quantitatively run funds, the feeling is that there is a weight limit in the range of 60–80% for quantitative input. "There will always be a technical and a tactical element," said one source.

Virtually all firms reported a partial automation in the handling of qualitative information, with some 30% planning to add functionality over and above the filtering and search functionality now typically provided by the suppliers of analyst research, consensus data and news. About 25% of the participants said that they would further automate the handling of information in 2003. The automatic summarization and analysis of news and other information available electronically was the next step for several firms that had already largely automated the investment process.

INTEGRATING QUALITATIVE AND QUANTITATIVE INFORMATION

Textual information has remained largely outside the domain of quantitative modeling, having long been considered the domain of judgment. This is now changing as financial firms begin to tackle the problem of what is commonly called *information overload*; advances in computer technology are again behind the change.[11]

Reuters publishes the equivalent of three bibles of (mostly financial) news daily; it is estimated that five new research documents come out of Wall Street every minute; asset managers at medium-sized firms report receiving up to 1,000 e-mails daily and work with as many as five

---

[11] Caroline Jonas and Sergio Focardi, *Leveraging Unstructured Data in Investment Management*, The Intertek Group, Paris, 2002.

screens on their desk. Conversely, there is also a lack of "digested" information. It has been estimated that only one third of the roughly 10,000 U.S. public companies are covered by meaningful Wall Street research; there are thousands of companies quoted on the U.S. exchanges with no Wall Street research at all. It is unlikely the situation is better relative to the tens of thousands of firms quoted on other exchanges throughout the world. Yet increasingly companies are providing information, including press releases and financial results, on their Web sites, adding to the more than 3.3 billion pages on the World Wide Web as of mid-2003.

Such unstructured (textual) information is progressively being transformed into self-describing, semistructured information that can be automatically categorized and searched by computers. A number of developments are making this possible. These include:

■ The development of XML (eXtensible Markup Language) standards for tagging textual data. This is taking us from free text search to queries on semi-structured data.
■ The development of RDF (Resource Description Framework) standards for appending metadata. This provides a description of the content of documents.
■ The development of algorithms and software that generate taxonomies and perform automatic categorization and indexation.
■ The development of database query functions with a high level of expressive power.
■ The development of high-level text mining functionality that allows "discovery."

The emergence of standards for the handling of "meaning" is a major development. It implies that unstructured textual information, which some estimates put at 80% of all content stored in computers, will be largely replaced by semistructured information ready for machine handling at a semantic level. Today's standard structured databases store data in a prespecified format so that the position of all elementary information is known. For example, in a trading transaction, the date, the amount exchanged, the names of the stocks traded and so on are all stored in predefined fields. However, textual data such as news or research reports, do not allow such a strict structuring. To enable the computer to handle such information, a descriptive metafile is appended to each unstructured file. The descriptive metafile is a structured file that contains the description of the key information stored in the unstructured data. The result is a semistructured database made up of unstructured data plus descriptive metafiles.

Industry-specific and application-specific standards are being developed around the general-purpose XML. At the time of this writing, there are numerous initiatives established with the objective of defining XML standards for applications in finance, from time series to analyst and corporate reports and news. While it is not yet clear which of the competing efforts will emerge as the de facto standards, attempts are now being made to coordinate standardization efforts, eventually adopting the ISO 15022 central data repository as an integration point.

Technology for handling unstructured data has already made its way into the industry. Factiva, a Dow Jones-Reuters company, uses commercially available text mining software to automatically code and categorize more than 400,000 news items daily, in real time (prior to adopting the software, they manually coded and categorized some 50,000 news articles daily). Users can search the Factiva database which covers 118 countries and includes some 8,000 publications, and more than 30,000 company reports with simple intuitive queries expressed in a language close to the natural language. Suppliers such as Multex use text mining technology in their Web-based research portals for clients on the buy and sell sides. Such services typically offer classification, indexation, tagging, filtering, navigation, and search.

These technologies are helping to organize research flows. They allow to automatically aggregate, sort, and simplify information and provide the tools to compare and analyze the information. In serving to pull together material from myriad sources, these technologies will not only form the basis of an internal knowledge management system but allow to better structure the whole investment management process. Ultimately, the goal is to integrate data and text mining in applications such as fundamental research and event analysis, linking news, and financial time series.

PRINCIPLES FOR ENGINEERING A SUITE OF MODELS

Creating a suite of models to satisfy the needs of a financial firm is engineering in full earnest. It begins with a clear statement of the objectives. In the case of financial modeling, the objective is identified by the type of decision-making process that a firm wants to implement. The engineering of a suite of financial models requires that the process on which decisions are made is fully specified and that the appropriate information is supplied at every step. This statement is not as banal as it might seem.

We have now reached the stage where, in some markets, financial decision-making can be completely automated through optimizers. As we will see in the following chapters, one can define models able to construct a conditional probability distribution of returns. An optimizer will then translate the forecast into a tradable portfolio. The manager becomes a kind of high-level supervisor of an otherwise automated process.

However, not all financial decision-making applications are, or can be, fully automated. In many cases, it is the human operator who makes the decision, with models supplying the information needed to arrive at the decision. Building an effective suite of financial models requires explicit decisions as to (1) what level of automation is feasible and desirable and (2) what information or knowledge is required.

The integration of different models and of qualitative and quantitative information is a fundamental need. This calls for integration of different statistical measures and points of view. For example, an asset management firm might want to complement a portfolio optimization methodology based on Gaussian forecasting with a risk management process based on Extreme Value Theory (see Chapter 13). The two processes offer complementary views. In many cases, however, different methodologies give different results though they work on similar principles and use the same data. In these cases, integration is delicate and might run against statistical principles.

In deciding which modeling efforts to invest in, many firms have in place a sophisticated evaluation system. "We look at the return on investment [ROI] of a model: How much will it cost to buy the data necessary to run the model? Then we ask ourselves: What are the factors that are remunerated? Our decision on what data to buy and where to spend on models is made in function of what indicators are the most 'remunerated,'" commented the head of quantitative management at a major European asset management firm.

SUMMARY

- The investment management process is becoming increasingly structured; the objective is a well-defined, repeatable investment process.
- This requires measurable objectives and measurable results, financial engineering, risk control, feedback processes and, increasingly, knowledge management.
- In general, the five steps in the investment management process are setting investment objectives, establishing an investment policy, selecting an investment strategy, selecting the specific assets, and measuring and evaluating investment performance.

■ Changes in the investment management business are being driven by the explosion in the universe of investable assets brought about by globalization, investors, and especially institutional investors and their consultants, pressure from regulators and the media, and the sheer size of the markets.

■ Given the size, diversity, and efficiency of modern markets, a more disciplined process can be achieved only in a quantitative framework.

■ Key to a quantitative framework is the measurement and management of uncertainty (i.e., risk) and financial engineering.

■ Modeling is the tool to achieve these objectives; advances in information technology are the enabler.

■ Unstructured textual information is progressively being transformed into self-describing, semistructured information, allowing a better structuring of the research process.

■ After nearly two decades of experience with quantitative methods, market participants now more clearly perceive the benefits and the limits of modeling; given today's technology and markets, the need to better integrate qualitative and quantitative information is clearly felt.

CHAPTER 2

Overview of Financial Markets, Financial Assets, and Market Participants

In a market economy, the allocation of economic resources is driven by the outcome of many private decisions. Prices are the signals that direct economic resources to their best use. The types of markets in an economy can be divided into (1) the market for products (manufactured goods and services), or the *product market;* and (2) the market for the factors of production (labor and capital), or the *factor market.* Our primary application of the mathematical techniques presented in this book is to one part of the factor market, the market for financial assets, or, more simply, the *financial market.* In this chapter we review the basic characteristics and functions of financial assets and financial markets, the major players in the financial market, and the major financial assets (common stock, bonds, and derivatives).

FINANCIAL ASSETS

An *asset* is any possession that has value in an exchange. Assets can be classified as tangible or intangible. The value of a tangible asset depends on particular physical properties—examples include buildings, land, or machinery. Tangible assets may be classified further into reproducible assets such as machinery, or nonreproducible assets such as land, a mine, or a work of art. *Intangible assets,* by contrast, represent legal claims to some future benefit. Their value bears no relation to the form, physical or otherwise, in which the claims are recorded.

Financial assets (also referred to as financial instruments, or securities) are intangible assets. For these instruments, the typical future benefit comes in the form of a claim to future cash. The entity that agrees to make future cash payments is called the *issuer* of the financial asset; the owner of the financial asset is referred to as the *investor*.

The claims of the holder of a financial asset may be either a fixed dollar amount or a varying, or residual, amount. In the former case, the financial asset is referred to as a *debt instrument*. Bonds and bank loans are examples of debt instruments. An *equity claim* (also called a *residual claim*) obligates the issuer of the financial asset to pay the holder an amount based on earnings, if any, after holders of debt instruments have been paid. Common stock is an example of an equity claim. A partnership share in a business is another example. Some financial assets fall into both categories. Preferred stock, for example, represents an equity claim that entitles the investor to receive a fixed dollar amount. This payment is contingent, however, due only after payments to debt instrument holders are made. Another instrument is convertible bonds, which allow the investor to convert debt into equity under certain circumstances. Both debt and preferred stock that pays a fixed dollar amount are called *fixed income instruments*.

Financial assets serve two principal economic functions. First, financial assets transfer funds from those parties who have surplus funds to invest to those who need funds to invest in tangible assets. As their second function, they transfer funds in such a way as to redistribute the unavoidable risk associated with the cash flow generated by tangible assets among those seeking and those providing the funds. However, the claims held by the final wealth holders generally differ from the liabilities issued by the final demanders of funds because of the activity of entities operating in financial markets, called *financial intermediaries*, who seek to transform the final liabilities into different financial assets preferred by the public. We discuss financial intermediaries later in this chapter.

Financial assets possess the following properties that determine or influence their attractiveness to different classes of investors: (1) moneyness; (2) divisibility and denomination; (3) reversibility; (4) term to maturity; (5) liquidity; (6) convertibility; (7) currency; (8) cash flow and return predictability; and (9) tax status.[1]

---

[1] Some of these properties are taken from James Tobin, "Properties of Assets," undated manuscript, Yale University.

Some financial assets act as a medium of exchange or in settlement of transactions. These assets are called *money*. Other financial assets, although not money, closely approximate money in that they can be transformed into money at little cost, delay, or risk. Moneyness clearly offers a desirable property for investors. Divisibility and denomination divisibility relates to the minimum size at which a financial asset can be liquidated and exchanged for money. The smaller the size, the more the financial asset is divisible.

Reversibility, also called round-trip cost, refers to the cost of investing in a financial asset and then getting out of it and back into cash again. For financial assets traded in organized markets or with "market makers," the most relevant component of round-trip cost is the so-called bid-ask spread, to which might be added commissions and the time and cost, if any, of delivering the asset. The bid-ask spread consists of the difference between the price at which a market maker is willing to sell a financial asset (i.e., the price it is asking) and the price at which a market maker is willing to buy the financial asset (i.e., the price it is bidding). The spread charged by a market maker varies sharply from one financial asset to another, reflecting primarily the amount of risk the market maker assumes by "making" a market. This market-making risk can be related to two main forces.

One is the variability of the price as measured, say, by some measure of dispersion of the relative price over time. The greater the variability, the greater the probability of the market maker incurring a loss in excess of a stated bound between the time of buying and reselling the financial asset. The variability of prices differs widely across financial assets. The second determining factor of the bid-ask spread charged by a market maker is what is commonly referred to as the thickness of the market, which is essentially the prevailing rate at which buying and selling orders reach the market maker (i.e., the frequency of transactions). A "thin market" sees few trades on a regular or continuing basis. Clearly, the greater the frequency of orders coming into the market for the financial asset (referred to as the "order flow"), the shorter the time that the financial asset must be held in the market maker's inventory, and hence the smaller the probability of an unfavorable price movement while held. Thickness also varies from market to market. A low round-trip cost is clearly a desirable property of a financial asset, and as a result thickness itself is a valuable property. This attribute explains the potential advantage of large over smaller markets (economies of scale), and a market's endeavor to standardize the instruments offered to the public.

The term to maturity, or simply maturity, is the length of the interval until the date when the instrument is scheduled to make its final payment, or the owner is entitled to demand liquidation. Maturity is an important characteristic of financial assets such as debt instruments. Equities set no maturity and are thus a form of perpetual instrument. Liquidity serves an important and widely used function, although no uniformly accepted definition of liquidity is presently available. A useful way to think of liquidity and illiquidity, proposed by James Tobin, is in terms of how much sellers stand to lose if they wish to sell immediately against engaging in a costly and time consuming search.[2] Liquidity may depend not only on the financial asset but also on the quantity one wishes to sell (or buy). Even though a small quantity may be quite liquid, a large lot may run into illiquidity problems. Note that liquidity again closely relates to whether a market is thick or thin. Thinness always increases the round-trip cost, even of a liquid financial asset. But beyond some point it becomes an obstacle to the formation of a market, and directly affects the illiquidity of the financial asset.

An important property of some financial assets is their convertibility into other financial assets. In some cases, the conversion takes place within one class of financial assets, as when a bond is converted into another bond. In other situations, the conversion spans classes. For example, with a corporate convertible bond the bondholder can change it into equity shares. Most financial assets are denominated in one currency, such as U.S. dollars or yen or euros, and investors must choose them with that feature in mind. Some issuers have issued dual-currency securities with certain cash flows paid in one currency and other cash flows in another currency.

The return that an investor will realize by holding a financial asset depends on the cash flow expected to be received, which includes dividend payments on stock and interest payments on debt instruments, as well as the repayment of principal for a debt instrument and the expected sale price of a stock. Therefore, the predictability of the expected return depends on the predictability of the cash flow. Return predictability, a basic property of financial assets, provides the major determinant of their value. Assuming investors are risk averse, as we will see in later chapters, the riskiness of an asset can be equated with the uncertainty or unpredictability of its return.

An important feature of any financial asset is its tax status. Governmental codes for taxing the income from the ownership or sale of financial assets vary widely if not wildly. Tax rates differ from year to year, country to country, and even among municipalities or provinces within a country. Moreover, tax rates may differ from financial asset to financial asset, depending on the type of issuer, the length of time the asset is held, the nature of the owner, and so on.

---

[2] Tobin, "Properties of Assets."

FINANCIAL MARKETS

Financial assets are traded in a financial market. Below we discuss how financial markets can be classified and the functions of financial markets.

Classification of Financial Markets

There are five ways that one can classify financial markets: (1) nature of the claim, (2) maturity of the claims, (3) new versus seasoned claims, (4) cash versus derivative instruments, and (5) organizational structure of the market.

The claims traded in a financial market may be either for a fixed dollar amount or a residual amount and financial markets can be classified according to the nature of the claim. As explained earlier, the former financial assets are referred to as debt instruments, and the financial market in which such instruments are traded is referred to as the *debt market*. The latter financial assets are called equity instruments and the financial market where such instruments are traded is referred to as the *equity market* or *stock market*. Preferred stock represents an equity claim that entitles the investor to receive a fixed dollar amount. Consequently, preferred stock has in common characteristics of instruments classified as part of the debt market and the equity market. Generally, debt instruments and preferred stock are classified as part of the *fixed income market*.

A second way to classify financial markets is by the maturity of the claims. For example, a financial market for short-term financial assets is called the *money market*, and the one for longer maturity financial assets is called the *capital market*. The traditional cutoff between short term and long term is one year. That is, a financial asset with a maturity of one year or less is considered short term and therefore part of the money market. A financial asset with a maturity of more than one year is part of the *capital market*. Thus, the debt market can be divided into debt instruments that are part of the money market, and those that are part of the capital market, depending on the number of years to maturity. Because equity instruments are generally perpetual, a third way to classify financial markets is by whether the financial claims are newly issued. When an issuer sells a new financial asset to the public, it is said to "issue" the financial asset. The market for newly issued financial assets is called the *primary market*. After a certain period of time, the financial asset is bought and sold (i.e., exchanged or traded) among investors. The market where this activity takes place is referred to as the *secondary market*.

Some financial assets are contracts that either obligate the investor to buy or sell another financial asset or grant the investor the choice to buy or sell another financial asset. Such contracts derive their value from the price of the financial asset that may be bought or sold. These contracts are called *derivative instruments* and the markets in which they trade are referred to as *derivative markets*. The array of derivative instruments includes options contracts, futures contracts, forward contracts, swap agreements, and cap and floor agreements.

Although the existence of a financial market is not a necessary condition for the creation and exchange of a financial asset, in most economies financial assets are created and subsequently traded in some type of organized financial market structure. A financial market can be classified by its organizational structure. These organizational structures can be classified as auction markets and over-the-counter markets. We describe each type later in this chapter.

Economic Functions of Financial Markets

The two primary economic functions of financial assets were already discussed. Financial markets provide three additional economic functions.

First, the interactions of buyers and sellers in a financial market determine the price of the traded asset; or, equivalently, the required return on a financial asset is determined. The inducement for firms to acquire funds depends on the required return that investors demand, and this feature of financial markets signals how the funds in the economy should be allocated among financial assets. It is called the *price discovery process*. Whether these signals are correct is an issue that we discuss when we examine the question of the efficiency of financial markets.

Second, financial markets provide a mechanism for an investor to sell a financial asset. This feature offers liquidity in financial markets, an attractive characteristic when circumstances either force or motivate an investor to sell. In the absence of liquidity, the owner must hold a debt instrument until it matures and an equity instrument until the company either voluntarily or involuntarily liquidates. Although all financial markets provide some form of liquidity, the degree of liquidity is one of the factors that differentiates various markets.

The third economic function of a financial market reduces the search and information costs of transacting. *Search costs* represent explicit costs, such as the money spent to advertise the desire to sell or purchase a financial asset, and implicit costs, such as the value of time spent in locating a counterparty. The presence of some form of organized financial market reduces search costs. *Information costs* are incurred in assessing the investment merits of a financial asset, that is, the amount and the likelihood of the cash flow expected to be generated. In an efficient market, prices reflect the aggregate information collected by all market participants.

Secondary Markets

The secondary market is where already-issued financial assets are traded. The key distinction between a primary market and a secondary market is that in the secondary market the issuer of the asset does not receive funds from the buyer. Rather, the existing issue changes hands in the secondary market, and funds flow from the buyer of the asset to the seller. Below we explain the various features of secondary markets. These features are common to any type of financial instrument traded.

It is in the secondary market where an issuer of securities, whether the issuer is a corporation or a governmental unit, may be provided with regular information about the value of the security. The periodic trading of the asset reveals to the issuer the consensus price that the asset commands in an open market. Thus, firms can discover what value investors attach to their stocks, and firms and noncorporate issuers can observe the prices of their bonds and the implied interest rates investors expect and demand from them. Such information helps issuers assess how well they are using the funds acquired from earlier primary market activities, and it also indicates how receptive investors would be to new offerings.

The other service a secondary market offers issuers is that it provides the opportunity for the original buyers of the asset to reverse their investment by selling it for cash. Unless investors are confident that they can shift from one financial asset to another as they may deem necessary, they would naturally be reluctant to buy any financial asset. Such reluctance would harm potential issuers in one of two ways: either issuers would be unable to sell new securities at all or they would have to pay a high rate of return, as investors would demand greater compensation for the expected illiquidity of the securities.

Investors in financial assets receive several benefits from a secondary market. Such a market obviously offers them liquidity for their assets as well as information about the assets' fair or consensus values. Further, secondary markets bring together many interested parties and so can reduce the costs of searching for likely buyers and sellers of assets. Moreover, by accommodating many trades, secondary markets keep the cost of transactions low. By keeping the costs of both searching and transacting low, secondary markets encourage investors to purchase financial assets.

Perfect Market

In order to explain the characteristics of secondary markets, we will first describe a "perfect market" for a financial asset. Then we can show how common occurrences in real markets keep them from being theoretically perfect.

In general, a perfect market results when the number of buyers and sellers is sufficiently large, and all participants are small enough relative to the market so that no individual market agent can influence the commodity's price. Consequently, all buyers and sellers are price takers, and the market price is determined where there is equality of supply and demand. This condition is more likely to be satisfied if the commodity traded is fairly homogeneous (for example, corn or wheat).

There is more to a perfect market than market agents being price takers. It is also required that there are no transaction costs or impediments that interfere with the supply and demand of the commodity. Economists refer to these various costs and impediments as "frictions." The costs associated with frictions generally result in buyers paying more than in the absence of frictions, and/or sellers receiving less.

In the case of financial markets, frictions would include:

- Commissions charged by brokers.
- Bid-ask spreads charged by dealers.
- Order handling and clearance charges.
- Taxes (notably on capital gains) and government-imposed transfer fees.
- Costs of acquiring information about the financial asset.
- Trading restrictions, such as exchange-imposed restrictions on the size of a position in the financial asset that a buyer or seller may take.
- Restrictions on market makers.
- Halts to trading that may be imposed by regulators where the financial asset is traded.

Role of Brokers and Dealers in Real Markets

Common occurrences in real markets keep them from being theoretically perfect. Because of these occurrences, brokers and dealers are necessary to the smooth functioning of a secondary market.

One way in which a real market might not meet all the exacting standards of a theoretically perfect market is that many investors may not be present at all times in the marketplace. Further, a typical investor may not be skilled in the art of the deal or completely informed about every facet of trading in the asset. Clearly, most investors in even smoothly functioning markets need professional assistance. Investors need someone to receive and keep track of their orders for buying or selling, to find other parties wishing to sell or buy, to negotiate for good prices, to serve as a focal point for trading, and to execute the orders. The broker performs all of these functions. Obviously, these functions are more important for the complicated trades, such as the small or large trades, than for simple transactions or those of typical size.

A broker is an entity that acts on behalf of an investor who wishes to execute orders. In economic and legal terms, a broker is said to be an "agent" of the investor. It is important to realize that the brokerage activity does not require the broker to buy and hold in inventory or sell from inventory the financial asset that is the subject of the trade. (Such activity is termed "taking a position" in the asset, and it is the role of the dealer.) Rather, the broker receives, transmits, and executes investors' orders with other investors. The broker receives an explicit commission for these services, and the commission is a "transaction cost" of the capital markets.

A real market might also differ from the perfect market because of the possibly frequent event of a temporary imbalance in the number of buy and sell orders that investors may place for any security at any one time. Such unmatched or unbalanced flow causes two problems. First, the security's price may change abruptly even if there has been no shift in either supply or demand for the security. Second, buyers may have to pay higher than market-clearing prices (or sellers accept lower ones) if they want to make their trade immediately.

For example, suppose the consensus price for ABC security is $50, which was determined in several recent trades. Also suppose that a flow of buy orders from investors who suddenly have cash arrives in the market, but there is no accompanying supply of sell orders. This temporary imbalance could be sufficient to push the price of ABC security to, say, $55. Thus, the price has changed sharply even though there has been no change in any fundamental financial aspect of the issuer. Buyers who want to buy immediately must pay $55 rather than $50, and this difference can be viewed as the price of "immediacy." By immediacy, we mean that buyers and sellers do not want to wait for the arrival of sufficient orders on the other side of the trade, which would bring the price closer to the level of recent transactions.

The fact of imbalances explains the need for the dealer or market maker, who stands ready and willing to buy a financial asset for its own account (add to an inventory of the security) or sell from its own account (reduce the inventory of the security). At a given time, dealers are willing to buy a security at a price (the bid price) that is less than what they are willing to sell the same security for (the ask price).

In the 1960s, economists George Stigler[3] and Harold Demsetz[4] analyzed the role of dealers in securities markets. They viewed dealers as the suppliers of immediacy—the ability to trade promptly—to the market.

The bid-ask spread can be viewed in turn as the price charged by dealers for supplying immediacy, together with short-run price stability (continuity or smoothness) in the presence of short-term order imbalances. There are two other roles that dealers play: they provide better price information to market participants, and in certain market structures they provide the services of an auctioneer in bringing order and fairness to a market.[5]

The price-stabilization role relates to our earlier example of what may happen to the price of a particular transaction in the absence of any intervention when there is a temporary imbalance of order. By taking the opposite side of a trade when there are no other orders, the dealer prevents the price from materially diverging from the price at which a recent trade was consummated.

Investors are concerned with immediacy, and they also want to trade at prices that are reasonable, given prevailing conditions in the market. While dealers cannot know with certainty the true price of a security, they do have a privileged position in some market structures with respect to the flow of market orders. They also have a privileged position regarding "limit" orders, the special orders that can be executed only if the market price of the security changes in a specified way.

Finally, the dealer acts as an auctioneer in some market structures, thereby providing order and fairness in the operations of the market. For example, the market maker on organized stock exchanges in the United States performs this function by organizing trading to make sure that the exchange rules for the priority of trading are followed. The role of a market maker in a call market structure is that of an auctioneer. The market maker does not take a position in the traded security, as a dealer does in a continuous market.

One of the most important factors that determine the price dealers should charge for the services they provide (i.e., the bid-ask spread) is the order processing costs incurred by dealers, such as the costs of equipment necessary to do business and the administrative and operations staff. The lower these costs, the narrower the bid-ask spread. With the reduced cost of computing and better-trained personnel, these costs have declined over time.

Dealers also have to be compensated for bearing risk. A dealer's position may involve carrying inventory of a security (along position) or

[3] George Stigler, "Public Regulation of Securities Markets," *Journal of Business* (April 1964), pp. 117–34.

[4] Harold Demsetz, "The Cost of Transacting," *Quarterly Journal of Economics* (October 1968), pp. 35–6.

[5] Robert A. Schwartz, *Equity Markets: Structure, Trading, and Performance* (New York: Harper & Row Publishers, 1988), pp. 389–397.

selling a security that is not in inventory (a short position). There are three types of risks associated with maintaining a long or short position in a given security. First, there is the uncertainty about the future price of the security. A dealer who has a long position in the security is concerned that the price will decline in the future; a dealer who is in a short position is concerned that the price will rise.

The second type of risk has to do with the expected time it will take the dealer to unwind a position and its uncertainty. And this, in turn, depends primarily on the rate at which buy and sell orders for the security reaches the market (i.e., the thickness of the market). Finally, while a dealer may have access to better information about order flows than the general public, there are some trades where the dealer takes the risk of trading with someone who has better information[6] This results in the better-informed trader obtaining a better price at the expense of the dealer. Consequently, in establishing the bid-ask spread for a trade, a dealer will assess whether the trader might have better information. Some trades that we will discuss below can be viewed as "information-less trades." This means that the dealer knows or believes a trade is being requested to accomplish an investment objective that is not motivated by the potential future price movement of the security.

Market Price Efficiency

The term "efficient" capital market has been used in several contexts to describe the operating characteristics of a capital market. There is a distinction, however, between an operationally (or internally) efficient market and a pricing (or externally) efficient capital market.[7] In this section we describe pricing efficiency.

Pricing efficiency refers to a market where prices at all times fully reflect all available information that is relevant to the valuation of securities. That is, relevant information about the security is quickly impounded into the price of securities. In his seminal review article on pricing efficiency, Eugene Fama points out that in order to test whether a market is price efficient, two definitions are necessary.[8] First, it is necessary to define what it means that prices "fully reflect" information. Second, the "relevant" set of information that is assumed to be "fully reflected" in prices must be defined.

---

[6] Walter Bagehot, "The Only Game in Town," *Financial Analysts Journal* (March–April 1971), pp. 12–14, 22.

[7] Richard R. West, "Two Kinds of Market Efficiency," *Financial Analysts Journal* (November–December 1975), pp. 30–34.

[8] Eugene F. Fama, "Efficient Capital Markets: A Review of Theory and Empirical Work," *Journal of Finance* (May 1970), pp. 383–417.

Fama, as well as others, defines "fully reflects" in terms of the expected return from holding a security. The expected return over some holding period is equal to expected cash distributions plus the expected price change, all divided by the initial price. The price formation process defined by Fama and others is that the expected return one period from now is a stochastic (i.e., random) variable that already takes into account the "relevant" information set.

In defining the "relevant" information set that prices should reflect, Fama classified the pricing efficiency of a market into three forms: weak, semistrong, and strong. The distinction between these forms lies in the relevant information that is hypothesized to be impounded in the price of the security. *Weak efficiency* means that the price of the security reflects the past price and trading history of the security. *Semistrong efficiency* means that the price of the security fully reflects all public information (which, of course, includes but is not limited to historical price and trading patterns). *Strong-form efficiency* exists in a market where the price of a security reflects all information, whether or not it is publicly available.

A price-efficient market has implications for the investment strategy that investors may wish to pursue. Throughout this book, we shall refer to various active strategies employed by investors. In an active strategy, investors seek to capitalize on what they perceive to be the mispricing of a security or securities. In a market that is price efficient, active strategies will not consistently generate a return after taking into consideration transaction costs and the risks associated with a strategy that is greater than simply buying and holding securities. This has lead investors in certain markets that empirical evidence suggests are price efficient to pursue a strategy of indexing, which simply seeks to match the performance of some financial index.

Operational Efficiency

In an operationally efficient market, investors can obtain transaction services as cheaply as possible, given the costs associated with furnishing those services. Commissions are only part of the cost of transacting as we noted above. The other part is the dealer spread. Bid-ask spreads for bonds vary by type of bond. Other components of transaction costs are discussed below.

In an investment era where one-half of one percentage point can make a difference when an asset manager is compared against a performance benchmark, an important aspect of the investment process is the cost of implementing an investment strategy. Transaction costs are more than merely brokerage commissions—they consist of commissions, fees, execution costs, and opportunity costs.[9]

Commissions are the fees paid to brokers to trade securities. *Execution costs* represent the difference between the execution price of a security and the price that would have existed in the absence of the trade. Execution costs can be further decomposed into market (or price) impact and market-timing costs. *Market impact* cost is the result of the bid-ask spread and a price concession extracted by dealers to mitigate their risk that an investor's demand for liquidity is information-motivated. *Market-timing cost* arises when an adverse price movement of the security during the time of the transaction can be attributed in part to other activity in the security and is not the result of a particular transaction. Execution costs, then, are related to both the demand for liquidity and the trading activity on the trade date.

There is a distinction between information-motivated trades and informationless trades. Information-motivated trading occurs when investors believe they possess pertinent information not currently reflected in the security's price. This style of trading tends to increase market impact because it emphasizes the speed of execution, or because the market maker believes a desired trade is driven by information and increases the bid-ask spread to provide some protection. It can involve the sale of one security in favor of another. Informationless trades are the result of either a reallocation of wealth or implementation of an investment strategy that utilizes only existing information. An example of the former is a pension fund's decision to invest cash in the stock market. Other examples of informationless trades include portfolio rebalances, investment of new money, or liquidations. In these circumstances, the demand for liquidity alone should not lead the market maker to demand the significant price concessions associated with new information.

The problem with measuring execution costs is that the true measure—which is the difference between the price of the security in the absence of the investor's trade and the execution price—is not observable. Furthermore, the execution prices are dependent on supply and demand conditions at the margin. Thus, the execution price may be influenced by competitive traders who demand immediate execution, or other investors with similar motives for trading. This means that the execution price realized by an investor is the consequence of the structure of the market mechanism, the demand for liquidity by the marginal

---

[9] For a further discussion of these costs, see Bruce M. Collins and Frank J. Fabozzi, "A Methodology for Measuring Transaction Costs," *Financial Analysts Journal* (March-April 1991), pp. 27–36.

investor, and the competitive forces of investors with similar motivations for trading.

The cost of not transacting represents an opportunity cost. Opportunity costs may arise when a desired trade fails to be executed. This component of costs represents the difference in performance between an investor's desired investment and the same investor's actual investment after adjusting for execution costs, commissions, and fees. Opportunity costs have been characterized as the hidden cost of trading, and it has been suggested that the shortfall in performance of many actively managed portfolios is the consequence of failing to execute all desired trades.[14] Measurement of opportunity costs is subject to the same problems as measurement of execution costs. The true measure of opportunity cost depends on knowing what the performance of a security would have been if all desired trades had been executed at the desired time across an investment horizon. As these are the desired trades that the investor could not execute, the benchmark is inherently unobservable

OVERVIEW OF MARKET PARTICIPANTS

With an understanding of what financial assets are and the role of financial assets and financial markets, we can now identify who the players are in the financial markets. By this we mean the entities that issue financial assets and the entities that invest in financial assets. We will focus on one particular group of market players, called financial intermediaries, because of the key economic functions that they perform in financial markets. In addition to reviewing their economic function, we will set forth the basic asset/liability problem faced by managers of financial intermediaries.

There are entities that issue financial assets, both debt instruments and equity instruments. There are investors who purchase these financial assets. This does not mean that these two groups are mutually exclusive—it is common for an entity to both issue a financial asset and at the same time invest in a different financial asset.

A simple classification of these entities is as follows: (1) central governments; (2) agencies of central governments; (3) municipal governments; (4) supranationals; (5) nonfinancial businesses; (6) financial enterprises; and (7) households. Central governments borrow funds for a wide variety of reasons. Many central governments establish agencies to raise funds to perform specific functions. Most countries have municipalities or provinces that raise funds in the capital market. A supranational institution is an organization that is formed by two or more central governments through international treaties. Businesses are classified into nonfinancial and financial businesses. These entities borrow funds in the debt market and raise funds in the equity market. Nonfinancial businesses are divided into three categories: corporations, farms, and nonfarm/noncorporate businesses. The first category includes corporations that manufacture products (e.g., cars, steel, computers) and/or provide nonfinancial services (e.g., transportation, utilities, computer programming). In the last category are businesses that produce the same products or provide the same services but are not incorporated.

Financial businesses, more popularly referred to as *financial institutions*, provide services related to one or more of the following:

1. Transforming financial assets acquired through the market and constituting them into a different and more preferable type of asset—which becomes their liability. This is the function performed by *financial intermediaries*, the most important type of financial institution.
2. Exchanging financial assets on behalf of customers.
3. Exchanging financial assets for their own account.
4. Assisting in the creation of financial assets for their customers and then selling those financial assets to other market participants.
5. Providing investment advice to other market participants.
6. Managing the portfolios of other market participants.

Financial intermediaries include: depository institutions that acquire the bulk of their funds by offering their liabilities to the public mostly in the form of deposits; insurance companies (life and property and casualty companies); pension funds; and finance companies. Later in this chapter we will discuss these entities. The second and third services in the list above are the broker and dealer functions. The fourth service is referred to as *securities underwriting*. Typically, a financial institution that provides an underwriting service also provides a brokerage and/or dealer service.

Some nonfinancial businesses have subsidiaries that provide financial services. For example, many large manufacturing firms have subsidiaries that provide financing for the parent company's customer. These financial institutions are called *captive finance companies*.

Role of Financial Intermediaries

Financial intermediaries obtain funds by issuing financial claims against themselves to market participants and then investing those funds. The investments made by financial intermediaries—their assets—can be in loans and/or securities. These investments are referred to as *direct investments*. As just noted, financial intermediaries play the basic role of transforming financial assets that are less desirable for a large part of the public into other financial assets—their own liabilities—which are preferred more by the public. This transformation involves at least one of four economic functions: (1) providing maturity intermediation; (2) risk reduction via diversification; (3) reducing the costs of contracting and information processing; and (4) providing a payments mechanism.

Maturity intermediation involves a financial intermediary issuing liabilities against itself that have a maturity different from the assets it acquires with the fund raised. An example is a commercial bank that issues short-term liabilities (i.e., deposits) and invests in assets with a longer maturity than those liabilities. Maturity intermediation has two implications for financial markets. First, investors have more choices concerning maturity for their investments; borrowers have more choices for the length of their debt obligations. Second, because investors are reluctant to commit funds for a long period of time, they will require that long-term borrowers pay a higher interest rate than on short-term borrowing. In contrast, a financial intermediary will be willing to make longer-term loans, and at a lower cost to the borrower than an individual investor would, by counting on successive deposits providing the funds until maturity (although at some risk as discussed below). Thus, the second implication is that the cost of longer-term borrowing is likely to be reduced.

To illustrate the economic function of risk reduction via diversification, consider an investor who invests in a mutual fund. Suppose that the mutual fund invests the funds received in the stock of a large number of companies. By doing so, the mutual fund has diversified and reduced its risk. Investors who have a small sum to invest would find it difficult to achieve the same degree of diversification because they would not have sufficient funds to buy shares of a large number of companies. Yet by investing in the investment company for the same sum of money, investors can accomplish this diversification, thereby reducing risk. This economic function of financial intermediaries—transforming more risky assets into less risky ones—is called *diversification*. While individual investors can do it on their own, they may not be able to do it as cost effectively as a financial intermediary, depending on the amount of funds they have to invest. Attaining cost-effective diversification in order to reduce risk by purchasing the financial assets of a financial intermediary is an important economic benefit for financial markets.

Investors purchasing financial assets should develop skills necessary to understand how to evaluate an investment. Once those skills are developed, investors should apply them to the analysis of specific financial assets that are candidates for purchase (or subsequent sale). Investors who want to make a loan to a consumer or business will need to write the loan contract (or hire an attorney to do so). While there are some people who enjoy devoting leisure time to this task, most of us find that leisure time is in short supply, so to sacrifice it, we have to be compensated. The form of compensation could be a higher return obtained from an investment. In addition to the opportunity cost of the time to process the information about the financial asset and its issuer, there is the cost of acquiring that information. All these costs are called *information processing costs*. The costs of writing loan contracts are referred to as *contracting costs*. Another dimension to contracting costs is the cost of enforcing the terms of the loan agreement. There are economies of scale in contracting and processing information about financial assets, because of the amount of funds managed by financial intermediaries. The lower costs accrue to the benefit of the investor who purchases a financial claim of the financial intermediary and to the issuers of financial assets, who benefit from a lower borrowing cost.

While the previous three economic functions may not have been immediately obvious, this last function should be. Most transactions made today are not done with cash. Instead, payments are made using checks, credit cards, debit cards, and electronic transfers of funds. These methods for making payments are provided by certain financial intermediaries. The ability to make payments without the use of cash is critical for the functioning of a financial market. In short, depository institutions transform assets that cannot be used to make payments into other assets that offer that property.

Institutional Investors

Managers of the funds of financial entities manage those funds to meet specified investment objectives. For many institutional investors (insurance companies, pension funds, investment companies, depository institutions, and endowments and foundations), those objectives are dictated by the nature of their liabilities. It is within the context of the asset/liability problem faced by managers of institutional funds that investment vehicles and investment strategies make any sense. Therefore, in this section we provide an overview of the investment objectives of institutional investors and the constraints imposed on managers of the funds of these entities.

Nature of Liabilities

The nature of an institutional investor's liabilities will dictate the general investment strategy to pursue. Depository institutions, for example, seek to generate income by the spread between the return that they earn on their assets and the cost of their funds. Life insurance companies are in the spread business. Pension funds are not in the spread business, in that they themselves do not raise funds in the market. Certain types of pension funds seek to cover the cost of pension obligations at a minimum cost to the plan sponsor. Most investment companies face no explicit costs for the funds they acquire and must satisfy no specific liability obligations, the exception being target-term trusts.

A liability is a cash outlay that must be made at a specific time to satisfy the contractual terms of an obligation. An institutional investor is concerned with both the amount and timing of liabilities, because its assets must produce the cash flow to meet any payments it has promised to make in a timely way. In fact, liabilities are classified according to the degree of certainty of their amount and timing, as shown in Exhibit 2.1. This exhibit assumes that the holder of the obligation will not cancel it prior to any actual or projected payout date.

The descriptions of cash outlays as either known or uncertain are undoubtedly broad. When we refer to a cash outlay as being uncertain, we do not mean that it cannot be predicted. There are some liabilities where the "law of large numbers" makes it easier to predict the timing and/or amount of cash outlays. This work is typically done by actuaries, but even actuaries have difficulty predicting natural catastrophes such as floods and earthquakes.

In our description of each type of risk category, it is important to note that, just like assets, there are risks associated with liabilities. Some of these risks are affected by the same factors that affect asset risks.

A Type I liability is one for which both the amount and timing of the liabilities are known with certainty. An example would be when an institution knows that it must pay $8 million six months from now. Banks and thrifts know the amount that they are committed to pay (principal plus interest) on the maturity date of a fixed-rate certificate of deposit (CD), assuming that the depositor does not withdraw funds prior to the maturity date. Type I liabilities, however, are not limited to depository institutions. A product sold by life insurance companies is a guaranteed investment contract, popularly referred to as a GIC (discussed below). The obligation of the life insurance company under this contract is that, for a sum of money (called a premium), it will guarantee an interest rate up to some specified maturity date.

EXHIBIT 2.1   Classification of Liabilities of Institutional Investors

Liability Type	Amount of Outlay	Timing of Cash Outlay
Type I	Known	Known
Type II	Known	Uncertain
Type III	Uncertain	Known
Type IV	Uncertain	Uncertain

A Type II liability is one for which the amount of the cash outlay is known, but the timing of the cash outlay is uncertain. The most obvious example of a Type II liability is a life insurance policy. There are many types of life insurance policies, but the most basic type provides that, for an annual premium, a life insurance company agrees to make a specified dollar payment to policy beneficiaries upon the death of the insured. Naturally, the timing of the insured's death is uncertain.

A Type III liability is one for which the timing of the cash outlay is known, but the amount is uncertain. A 2-year, floating-rate CD for which the interest rate resets quarterly, based on some market interest rate, is an example.

A Type IV liability is one for which there is uncertainty as to both the amount and the timing of the cash outlay. There are numerous insurance products and pension obligations in this category. Probably the most obvious examples are automobile and home insurance policies issued by property and casualty insurance companies. When, and if, a payment will have to be made to the policyholder is uncertain. Whenever damage is done to an insured asset, the amount of the payment that must be made is uncertain. The liabilities of pension plans can also be Type IV liabilities. In defined benefit plans, retirement benefits depend on the participant's income for a specified number of years before retirement and the total number of years the participant worked. This will affect the amount of the cash outlay. The timing of the cash outlay depends on when the employee elects to retire, and whether the employee remains with the sponsoring plan until retirement. Moreover, both the amount and the timing will depend on how the employee elects to have payments made— over only the employee's life or those of the employee and spouse.

Overview of Asset/liability Management

The two goals of a financial institution are (1) to earn an adequate return on funds invested and (2) to maintain a comfortable surplus of assets beyond liabilities. The task of managing funds of a financial institution to accomplish these goals is referred to as asset/liability management or surplus management. This task involves a trade-off between controlling the risk of a decline in the surplus and taking on acceptable risks in order to earn an adequate return on the funds invested. With respect to the risks, the manager must consider the risks of both the assets and the liabilities.

Institutions may calculate three types of surpluses: economic, accounting, and regulatory. The method of valuing assets and liabilities greatly affects the apparent health of a financial institution. Unrealistic valuation, although sometimes allowable under accounting procedures and regulations, is not sound investment practice.

The *economic surplus* of any entity is the difference between the market value of all its assets and the market value of its liabilities. That is,

Economic surplus = Market value of assets – Market value of liabilities

The market value of the liabilities is simply the present value of the liabilities, where the liabilities are discounted at an appropriate interest rate.

Institutional investors must prepare periodic financial statements. These financial statements must be prepared in accordance with "generally accepted accounting principles" (GAAP). Thus, the assets and liabilities reported are based on GAAP accounting and the resulting surplus is referred to as *accounting surplus*.

Institutional investors that are regulated at the state or federal levels must also provide financial reports to regulators based on regulatory accounting principles (RAP). RAP accounting for a regulated institution need not use the same rules as set forth in GAAP accounting. Liabilities may or may not be reported at their present value, depending on the type of institution and the type of liability. The surplus, as measured using RAP accounting, is called *regulatory surplus* or *statutory surplus*, and, as in the case of accounting surplus, may be materially different from economic surplus.

Benchmarks for Nonliability Driven Entities

Thus far, our discussion has focused on institutional investors that face liabilities. However, not all financial institutions face liabilities. An investment company (discussed later) is an example. Also, while an entity such as a pension plan may face liabilities, it may engage external asset managers and set for those managers an objective that is unrelated to the pension fund's liabilities. For such asset managers who do not face liabilities, the objective is to outperform some client-designated benchmark. In bond portfolio management, the benchmark may be one of the bond indexes described in Chapter 21. In general, the performance of the money manager will be measured as follows:

Return on the portfolio – Return on the benchmark

Active money management involves creating a portfolio that will earn a return (after adjusting for risk) greater than the benchmark. In contrast, a strategy of indexing is one in which an asset manager creates a portfolio that only seeks to match the return on the benchmark.

From our discussion of asset/liability management and the management of funds in the absence of liabilities, we can see that the investment strategy of one institutional investor may be inappropriate for another. As with investment strategies, a security or asset class that may be attractive for one institutional investor may be inappropriate for the portfolio of another.

In the remainder of this section we look at the investment objective of the major institutional investors. For each entity, the nature of the liabilities and the strategies they use to accomplish their investment objectives are also reviewed, as well as regulations that influence investment decisions.

Insurance Companies

Insurance companies are financial intermediaries that, for a price, will make a payment if a certain event occurs. They function as risk bearers. There are two types of insurance companies: life insurance companies ("life companies") and property and casualty insurance companies ("P&C companies"). The principal event that the former insures against is death. Upon the death of a policyholder, a life insurance company agrees to make either a lump sum payment or a series of payments to the beneficiary of the policy. Life insurance protection is not the only financial product sold by these companies; a major portion of the business of life companies is in the area of providing retirement benefits. In contrast, P&C companies insure against a wide variety of occurrences. Two examples are automobile insurance and home insurance.

The key distinction between life and P&C companies lies in the difficulty of projecting whether a policyholder will be paid off and, if so, how much the payment will be. While this is no simple task for either type of insurance company, from an actuarial perspective it is easier for a life company. The amount and timing of claims on P&C companies are more difficult to predict because of the randomness of natural catastrophes and the unpredictability of court awards in liability cases. This uncertainty about the timing and amount of cash outlays to satisfy claims affects the investment strategies used by the managers of P&C companies' funds.

Pension Funds

A pension plan is a fund that is established for the payment of retirement benefits. The entities that establish pension plans—called *plan sponsors*—are private business entities acting for their employees, state and local entities on behalf of their employees, unions on behalf of their members, and individuals for themselves. In the United States, corporate pension plans are governed by the Employee Retirement Income Security Act of 1974 (ERISA). Pension funds are exempt from taxation.

There are two basic and widely used types of pension plans: defined contribution plans and defined benefit plans. In a defined contribution plan, the plan sponsor is responsible only for making specified contributions into the plan on behalf of qualifying participants. The payments that will be made to qualifying participants upon retirement will depend on the growth of the plan assets; that is, payment is determined by the investment performance of the assets in which the pension fund is invested. Therefore, in a defined contribution plan, the employee bears all the investment risk. In a defined benefit plan, the plan sponsor agrees to make specified dollar payments to qualifying employees at retirement (and some payments to beneficiaries in case of death before retirement). The retirement payments are determined by a formula that usually takes into account both the length of service and the earnings of the employee. The pension obligations are effectively the liability of the plan sponsor, who assumes the risk of having insufficient funds in the plan to satisfy the contractual payments that must be made to retired employees. Thus, unlike a defined contribution plan, in a defined benefit plan, all the investment risks are borne by the plan sponsor.

Investment Companies

Investment companies sell shares to the public and invest the proceeds in a diversified portfolio of securities. Each share they sell represents a proportionate interest in a portfolio of securities. The securities purchased could be restricted to specific types of assets such as common stock, government bonds, corporate bonds, or money market instruments. The investment strategies followed by investment companies range from high-risk active portfolio strategies to low-risk passive portfolio strategies.

There are two types of managed investment companies: open-end funds and closed-end funds. An open-end fund, more popularly referred to as a *mutual fund*, continually stands ready to sell new shares to the public and to redeem its outstanding shares on demand at a price equal to an appropriate share of the value of its portfolio, which is computed daily at the close of the market. A mutual fund's share price is based on its net asset value (NAV) per share, which is found by subtracting from the market value of the portfolio the mutual fund's liabilities and then dividing by the number of mutual fund shares outstanding.

In contrast to mutual funds, closed-end funds sell shares like any other corporation and usually do not redeem their shares. Shares of closed-end funds sell on either an organized exchange, such as the New

York Stock Exchange, or in the over-the-counter market. The price of a share in a closed-end fund is determined by supply and demand, so the price can fall below or rise above the net asset value per share.

Depository Institutions

Depository institutions are financial intermediaries that accept deposits. They include commercial banks (or simply banks), savings and loan associations (S&Ls), savings banks, and credit unions. It is common to refer to depository institutions other than banks as "thrifts." Depository institutions are highly regulated and supervised because of the important role that they play in the financial system.

The asset/liability problem that depository institutions face is quite simple to explain—although not necessarily easy to solve. A depository institution seeks to earn a positive spread between the assets it invests in (loans and securities) and the cost of its funds (deposits and other sources). This difference between income and cost is referred to as spread income or margin income. The spread income should allow the institution to meet operating expenses and earn a fair profit on its capital.

In generating spread income a depository institution faces several risks. These include credit risk, regulatory risk, and interest rate risk. Regulatory risk is the risk that regulators will change the rules so as to adversely impact the earnings of the institution. Simply put, interest rate risk is the risk that a depository institution's spread income and capital will suffer because of changes in interest rates. This kind of risk can be explained best by an illustration. To illustrate the impact on spread income, suppose that a depository institution raises $100 million by issuing a certificate of deposit that has a maturity of one year and by agreeing to pay an interest rate of 7%. Ignoring for the time being the fact that the depository institution cannot invest the entire $100 million because of reserve requirements, suppose that $100 million is invested in a U.S. Treasury security that matures in 15 years paying an interest rate of 9%. Because the funds are invested in a U.S. Treasury security, there is no credit risk.

It seems at first that the depository institution has locked in a spread of 2% (9% minus 7%). This spread can be counted on only for the first year, though, because the spread in future years will depend on the interest rate this depository institution will have to pay depositors in order to raise $100 million after the 1-year certificate of deposit matures. If interest rates decline, the spread income will increase because the depository institution has locked in the 9% rate. If interest rates rise, however, the spread income will decline. In fact, if this depository institution must pay more than 9% to depositors for the next 14 years, the spread income will be negative. That is, it will cost the depository institution more to finance the purchase of the Treasury security than it will earn on the funds invested in that security.

In our example, the depository institution has "borrowed short" (borrowed for one year) and "lent long" (invested for 15 years). This investment policy will benefit from a decline in interest rates, but suffer if interest rates rise. Suppose the institution could have borrowed funds for 15 years at 7% and invested in a U.S. Treasury security maturing in one year earning 9%—borrowing long (15 years) and lending short (one year). A rise in interest rates will benefit the depository institution because it can then reinvest the proceeds from the maturing 1-year government security in a new 1-year government security offering a higher interest rate. In this case a decline in interest rates will reduce the spread income. If interest rates fall below 7%, there will be a negative spread income.

All depository institutions face this interest rate risk problem. Managers of a depository institution who have particular expectations about the future direction of interest rates will seek to benefit from these expectations. Those who expect interest rates to rise may pursue a policy to borrow funds long term and lend funds short term. If interest rates are expected to drop, managers may elect to borrow short and lend long.

The problem of pursuing a strategy of positioning a depository institution based on expectations is that considerable adverse financial consequences will result if those expectations are not realized. The evidence on interest rate forecasting suggests that it is a risky business. We doubt if there are managers of depository institutions who have the ability to forecast interest rate moves so consistently that the institution can benefit with any regularity. The goal of management should be to lock in a spread as best as possible, not to wager on interest rate movements.

Some interest rate risk, however, is inherent in any balance sheet of a depository institution. Managers must be willing to accept some interest rate risk, but they can take various measures to address the interest rate sensitivity of the institution's liabilities and its assets. A depository institution should have an asset/liability committee that is responsible for monitoring the exposure to interest rate risk. There are several asset/liability strategies for controlling interest rate risk.

Because of the special role that depository institutions play in the financial system, they are highly regulated and supervised by either federal and/or state government entities. Regulators have placed restrictions on the types of securities that depository institutions can take a position in for their investment portfolio. There are risk-based capital requirements for depository institutions that specify capital requirements based on their credit risk and the interest rate risk exposures.

Endowments and Foundations

Endowments and foundations include colleges, private schools, museums, and hospitals. The investment income generated from the funds invested by endowments and foundations is used for the operation of the entity. In the case of a college, the investment income is used to meet current operating expenses and capital expenditures (i.e., the construction of new buildings or sports facilities).

As with pension funds, qualified endowments and foundations are exempt from taxation. The board of trustees, just like the plan sponsor for a pension fund, specifies the investment objectives and the acceptable investment alternatives. Typically, the managers of endowments and foundations invest in long-term assets and have the primary goal of safeguarding the principal of the entity. The second goal, and an important one, is to generate a stream of earnings that allow the endowment or foundation to perform its functions of supporting certain operations. There is a constraint imposed on an endowment or foundation in that it must maintain its tax-exempt status.

COMMON STOCK

Common stocks are also called *equity securities*. Equity securities represent an ownership interest in a corporation. Holders of equity securities are entitled to the earnings of the corporation when those earnings are distributed in the form of *dividends*; they are also entitled to a pro rata share of the remaining equity in case of liquidation.

Trading Locations

In the United States, the secondary market that trades in common stocks has occurred in two ways. The first is on organized exchanges, which are specific geographical locations called trading floors, where representatives of buyers and sellers physically meet. The trading mechanism on exchanges is the auction system, which results from the presence of many competing buyers and sellers assembled in one place. The second type is via over-the-counter (OTC) trading, which results from geographically dispersed traders or market-makers linked to one another via telecommunication systems. That is, there is no trading floor. This trading mechanism is a negotiated system whereby individual buyers negotiate with individual sellers.

Exchange markets are called *central auction specialist systems* and OTC markets are called *multiple market maker systems*. In recent years a new method of trading common stocks via independently owned and

operated electronic communications networks (ECNs) has developed
and is growing quickly.

In the United States there are two national stock exchanges: the New
York Stock Exchange (NYSE) and the American Stock Exchange (AMEX
or ASE). In addition to the national exchanges, there are regional stock
exchanges in Boston, Chicago (called the Midwest Exchange), Cincinnati,
San Francisco (called the Pacific Coast Exchange) and Philadelphia.
Regional exchanges primarily trade stocks from corporations based within
their region. The major OTC market in the United States is NASDAQ (the
National Association of Securities Dealers Automated Quotation System.
In 1998, NASDAQ and AMEX merged to form the NASDAQ-AMEX
Market Group, Inc.

Stock Market Indicators

Stock market indicators have come to perform a variety of functions,
from serving as benchmarks for evaluating the performance of professional money managers to answering the question, "How did the market do today?" Thus, stock market indicators (indexes or averages) have
become a part of everyday life. Even though many of the stock market
indicators are used interchangeably, it is important to realize that each
indicator applies to, and measures, a different facet of the stock market.

The most commonly quoted stock market indicator is the Dow
Jones Industrial Average (DJIA). Other popular stock market indicators
cited in the financial press are the Standard & Poor's 500 Composite
(S&P 500), the New York Stock Exchange Composite Index (NYSE
Composite), the NASDAQ Composite Index, and the Value Line Composite Average (VLCA). There are a myriad of other stock market indicators such as the Wilshire stock indexes and the Russell stock indexes,
which are followed primarily by institutional money managers.

In general, market indexes rise and fall in fairly similar patterns.
Although the correlations among indexes are high, the indexes do not
move in exactly the same way at all times. The differences in movement
reflect the different manner in which the indexes are constructed. Three
factors enter into that construction: the universe of stocks represented by
the sample underlying the index, the relative weights assigned to the stocks
included in the index, and the method of averaging across all the stocks.

Some indexes represent only stocks listed on an exchange. Examples
are the DJIA and the NYSE Composite, which represent only stocks
listed on the NYSE or Big Board. By contrast, the NASDAQ includes
only stocks traded over the counter. A favorite of professionals is the
S&P 500 because it is a broader index containing both NYSE-listed and
OTC-traded shares. Each index relies on a sample of stocks from its

universe, and that sample may be small or quite large. The DJIA uses only 30 of the NYSE-traded shares, while the NYSE Composite includes every one of the listed shares. The NASDAQ also includes all shares in its universe, while the S&P 500 has a sample that contains only 500 of the more than 8,000 shares in the universe it represents.

The stocks included in a stock market index must be combined in certain proportions, and each stock must be given a weight. The three main approaches to weighting are: (1) weighting by the market capitalization, which is the value of the number of shares times price per share; (2) weighting by the price of the stock; and (3) equal weighting for each stock, regardless of its price or its firm's market value. With the exception of the Dow Jones averages (such as the DJIA) and the VLCA, nearly all of the most widely used indexes are market-value weighted. The DJIA is a price-weighted average, and the VLCA is an equally weighted index.

Stock market indicators can be classified into three groups: (1) those produced by stock exchanges based on all stocks traded on the exchanges; (2) those produced by organizations that subjectively select the stocks to be included in indexes; and (3) those where stock selection is based on an objective measure, such as the market capitalization of the company. The first group includes the New York Stock Exchange Composite Index, which reflects the market value of all stocks traded on the NYSE. While it is not an exchange, the NASDAQ Composite Index falls into this category because the index represents all stocks traded on the NASDAQ system.

The three most popular stock market indicators in the second group are the Dow Jones Industrial Average, the Standard & Poor's 500, and the Value Line Composite Average. The DJIA is constructed from 30 of the largest blue chip industrial companies traded on the NYSE. The companies included in the average are those selected by Dow Jones & Company, publisher of the *Wall Street Journal*. The S&P 500 represents stocks chosen from the two major national stock exchanges and the over-the-counter market. The stocks in the index at any given time are determined by a committee of Standard & Poor's Corporation, which may occasionally add or delete individual stocks or the stocks of entire industry groups. The aim of the committee is to capture present overall stock market conditions as reflected in a very broad range of economic indicators. The VLCA, produced by Value Line Inc., covers a broad range of widely held and actively traded NYSE, AMEX, and OTC issues selected by Value Line.

In the third group we have the Wilshire indexes produced by Wilshire Associates (Santa Monica, California) and Russell indexes produced by the Frank Russell Company (Tacoma, Washington), a consultant to pension funds and other institutional investors. The criterion for inclusion in each of these indexes is solely a firm's market capitalization. The most comprehensive index is the Wilshire 5000, which actually includes more than 6,700 stocks now, up from 5,000 at its inception. The Wilshire 4500 includes all stocks in the Wilshire 5000 except for those in the S&P 500. Thus, the shares in the Wilshire 4500 have smaller capitalization than those in the Wilshire 5000. The Russell 3000 encompasses the 3,000 largest companies in terms of their market capitalization. The Russell 1000 is limited to the largest 1,000 of those, and the Russell 2000 has the remaining smaller firms.

Two methods of averaging may be used. The first and most common is the arithmetic average. An arithmetic mean is just a simple average of the stocks, calculated by summing them (after weighting, if appropriate) and dividing by the sum of the weights. The second method is the geometric mean, which involves multiplication of the components, after which the product is raised to the power of 1 divided by the number of components.

Trading Arrangements

Below we describe the key features involved in trading stocks.

Types of Orders

When an investor wants to buy or sell a share of common stock, the price and conditions under which the order is to be executed must be communicated to a broker. The simplest type of order is the *market order*, an order to be executed at the best price available in the market.

The danger of a market order is that an adverse move may take place between the time the investor places the order and the time the order is executed. To avoid this danger, the investor can place a *limit order* that designates a price threshold for the execution of the trade. The key disadvantage of a limit order is that there is no guarantee that it will be executed at all; the designated price may simply not be obtainable. The limit order is a *conditional order*: It is executed only if the limit price or a better price can be obtained.

Another type of conditional order is the *stop order*, which specifies that the order is not to be executed until the market moves to a designated price, at which time it becomes a market order. There are two dangers associated with stop orders. Stock prices sometimes exhibit abrupt price changes, so the direction of a change in a stock price may be quite temporary, resulting in the premature trading of a stock. Also, once the designated price is reached, the stop order becomes a market order and is subject to the uncertainty of the execution price noted earlier for market orders. A *stop-limit order*, a hybrid of a stop order and a limit order, is a stop order that designates a price limit. In contrast to the stop order, which becomes a market order if the stop is reached, the stop-limit order becomes a limit order if the stop is reached. The stop-limit order can be used to cushion the market impact of a stop order. The investor may limit the possible execution price after the activation of the stop. As with a limit order, the limit price may never be reached after the order is activated, which therefore defeats one purpose of the stop order—to protect a profit or limit a loss.

Short Selling

Short selling involves the sale of a security not owned by the investor at the time of sale. The investor can arrange to have her broker borrow the stock from someone else, and the borrowed stock is delivered to implement the sale. To cover her short position, the investor must subsequently purchase the stock and return it to the party that lent the stock. The investor benefits if the price of the of the security sold short declines. Two costs will reduce the profit on a short sale. First, a fee will be charged by the lender of the stock. Second, if there are any dividends paid, the short seller must pay those dividends to the lender of the security.

Exchanges impose restrictions as to when a short sale may be executed; these so-called *tick-test rules* are intended to prevent investors from destabilizing the price of a stock when the market price is falling. A short sale can be made only when either (1) the sale price of the particular stock is higher than the last trade price (referred to as an "uptick trade"), or (2) if there is no change in the last trade price of the particular stock (referred to as a "zero uptick"), the previous trade price must be higher than the trade price that preceded it.

Margin Transactions

Investors can borrow cash to buy securities and use the securities themselves as collateral. A transaction in which an investor borrows to buy shares using the shares themselves as collateral is called buying on margin. By borrowing funds, an investor creates financial leverage. The funds borrowed to buy the additional stock will be provided by the broker, and the broker gets the money from a bank. The interest rate that banks charge brokers for these funds is the *call money rate* (also labeled the *broker loan rate*). The broker charges the borrowing investor the call money rate plus a service charge.

The brokerage firm is not free to lend as much as it wishes to the investor to buy securities. The Securities Exchange Act of 1934 prohibits brokers from lending more than a specified percentage of the market value of the securities. The *initial margin requirement* is the proportion of the total market value of the securities that the investor must pay as an equity share, and the remainder is borrowed from the broker. The 1934 act gives the Board of Governors of the Federal Reserve (the Fed) the responsibility to set initial margin requirements. The initial margin requirement has been below 40% and is 50% as of this writing.

The Fed also establishes a maintenance margin requirement. This is the minimum proportion of (1) the equity in the investor's margin account to (2) the total market value. If the investor's margin account falls below the minimum maintenance margin (which would happen if the share price fell), the investor is required to put up additional cash. The investor receives a margin call from the broker specifying the additional cash to be put into the investor's margin account. If the investor fails to put up the additional cash, the broker has the authority to sell the securities in the investor's account.

Trading Arrangements Used by Institutional Investors

With the increase in trading by institutional investors, trading arrangements more suitable to these investors were developed. Institutional needs included trading in large size and trading groups of stocks, both at a low commission and with low market impact. This has resulted in the evolution of special arrangements for the execution of certain types of orders commonly sought by institutional investors: (1) orders requiring the execution of a trade of a large number of shares of a given stock and (2) orders requiring the execution of trades in a large number of different stocks at as near the same time as possible. The former types of trades are called *block trades*; the latter are called *program trades*.

On the NYSE, block trades are defined as either trades of at least 10,000 shares of a given stock, or trades of shares with a market value of at least $200,000, whichever is less. Program trades involve the buying and/or selling of a large number of names simultaneously. Such trades are also called basket trades because effectively a "basket" of stocks is being traded. The NYSE defines a program trade as any trade involving the purchase or sale of a basket of at least 15 stocks with a total value of $1 million or more.

The institutional arrangement that has evolved to accommodate these two types of institutional trades is the development of a network of trading desks of the major securities firms and other institutional investors that communicate with each other by means of electronic display systems and telephones. This network is referred to as the "upstairs market." Participants in the upstairs market play a key role by (1) providing liquidity to the market so that such institutional trades can be executed, and (2) by arbitrage activities that help to integrate the fragmented stock market.

BONDS

In its simplest form, a bond is a financial obligation of an entity that promises to pay a specified sum of money at specified future dates. The entity that promises to make the payment is called the *bond issuer* and is referred to as the borrower. Bond issuers include central governments, municipal/provincial governments, supranational (e.g., the World Bank), and corporations. The investor who purchases bond is said to be the *lender* or *creditor*. The promised payments that the bond issuer agrees to make at the specified dates consist of two components: interest payments and repayment of the amount borrowed.

Prior to the 1980s, bonds were simple investment vehicles. Holding aside default by the bond issuer, the investor knew how much interest would be received periodically and when the amount borrowed would be repaid. Moreover, most investors purchased bonds with the intent of holding them to their maturity date. Beginning in the 1980s, the bond world changed. First, bond structures became more complex. There are features in many bonds that make it difficult to determine when the amount borrowed will be repaid. For some bonds it is difficult to project the amount of interest that will be received periodically. Second, the hold-to-maturity investor has been replaced by the institutional investor who actively trades bonds. These new product design features in bonds and the shift in trading strategies have lead to the increased use of the mathematical techniques described in later chapters.

Maturity

The *term to maturity* of a bond is the number of years over which the issuer has promised to meet the conditions of the obligation. The maturity of a bond refers to the date that the debt will cease to exist, at which time the bond issuer will redeem the bond by paying the amount borrowed. The maturity date of a bond is always identified when describing a bond. For example, a description of a bond might state "due 12/1/2020." The practice in the bond market is to refer to the "term to maturity" of a bond as simply its "maturity" or "term." As we explain later, there may be provisions in the bond agreement that allow either the bond issuer or bondholder to alter a bond's term to maturity.

There are three reasons why the term to maturity of a bond is important. The most obvious is that it indicates the time period over which the bondholder can expect to receive interest payments and the number of years before the principal will be paid in full. The second reason is that the yield on a bond depends on it. Finally, the price of a bond will fluctuate over its life as interest rates in the market change. The price volatility of a bond is dependent on its maturity. More specifically, with all other factors constant, the longer the maturity of a bond, the greater the price volatility resulting from a change in interest rates. We will demonstrate these two properties in Chapter 4 as an application of calculus.

Par Value

The *par value* of a bond is the amount that the issuer agrees to repay the bondholder by the maturity date. This amount is also referred to as the *principal, face value, redemption value,* or *maturity value.* Bonds can have any par value.

Because bonds can have a different par value and currency (e.g., U.S. dollar, euro, pound sterling), the practice is to quote the price of a bond as a percentage of its par value. A value of 100 means 100% of par value. So, for example, if a bond has a par value of $1,000 and the issue is selling for $900, this bond would be said to be selling at 90. If a bond with a par value of Eur 5,000 is selling for Eur 5,500, the bond is said to be selling for 110.

Coupon Rate

The *coupon rate,* also called the *nominal rate,* is the interest rate that the bond issuer agrees to pay each year. The annual amount of the interest payment made to bondholders during the term of the bond is called the *coupon.* The coupon is determined by multiplying the coupon rate by the par value of the bond. For example, a bond with an 8% coupon rate and a par value of $1,000 will pay annual interest of $80.

When describing a bond of an issuer, the coupon rate is indicated along with the maturity date. For example, the expression "6s of 12/1/2020" means a bond with a 6% coupon rate maturing on 12/1/2020.

In the United States, the usual practice is for the issuer to pay the coupon in two semiannual installments. Outside the U.S., bond payments with semiannual and annual payments are found. For certain sectors of the bond market—mortgage-backed and asset-backed securities—payments are made monthly. If the bondholder sells a bond between coupon payments and the buyer holds it until the next coupon payment, then the entire coupon interest earned for the period will be paid to the buyer of the bond since the buyer will be the holder of record. The seller of the bond gives up the interest from the time of the last coupon payment to the time until the bond is sold. The amount of interest over this period that will be received by the buyer, even though it was earned by the seller, is called *accrued interest*. In the United States and in many countries, the bond buyer must pay the bond seller the accrued interest. The amount that the buyer pays the seller is the agreed-upon price for the bond plus accrued interest. This amount is called the *dirty price*. The agreed-upon bond price without accrued interest is called the *clean price*.

In addition to indicating the coupon payments that the investor should expect to receive over the term of the bond, the coupon rate also affects the bond's price sensitivity to changes in market interest rates. As illustrated later, all other factors constant, the higher the coupon rate, the less the price will change in response to a change in market interest rates. Again, this property will be demonstrated as an application of calculus in Chapter 4.

Not all bonds make periodic coupon payments. Bonds that are not contracted to make periodic coupon payments are called *zero-coupon bonds*. The holder of a zero-coupon bond realizes interest by buying the bond substantially below its par value. Interest then is paid at the maturity date, with the interest being the difference between the par value and the price paid for the bond. So, for example, if an investor purchases a zero-coupon bond for 70, the interest is 30. This is the difference between the par value (100) and the price paid (70).

The coupon rate on a bond need not be fixed over the bond's term. *Floating-rate securities* have coupon payments that reset periodically according to some reference rate. The typical formula for the coupon rate at the dates when the coupon rate is reset is:

Reference rate + Quoted margin

The quoted margin is the additional amount that the issuer agrees to pay above the reference rate. For example, suppose that the reference rate is the 1-month London interbank offered rate (LIBOR). Suppose that the quoted margin is 100 basis points. Then the coupon reset formula is:

1-month LIBOR + 100 basis points

So, if 1-month LIBOR on the coupon reset date is 5%, the coupon rate is reset for that period at 6% (5% plus 100 basis points).

The reference rate for most floating-rate securities is an interest rate or an interest rate index. There are some issues where this is not the case. Instead, the reference rate is some financial index such as the return on the Standard & Poor's 500 or a nonfinancial index such as the price of a commodity. Through financial engineering, issuers have been able to structure floating-rate securities with almost any reference rate. In several countries, there are government bonds whose coupon reset formula is tied to an inflation index.

A floating-rate security may have a restriction on the maximum coupon rate that will be paid at a reset date. The maximum coupon rate is called a *cap*. Because a cap restricts the coupon rate from increasing, a cap is an unattractive feature for the investor. In contrast, there could be a minimum coupon rate specified for a floating-rate security. The minimum coupon rate is called a *floor*. If the coupon reset formula produces a coupon rate that is below the floor, the floor is paid instead. Thus, a floor is an attractive feature for the investor.

Financial engineering has also allowed bond issuers to create interesting floating-rate structures. These include the following:

■ *Inverse floaters.* Typically, the coupon reset formula on floating-rate securities is such that the coupon rate increases when the reference rate increases, and decreases when the reference rate decreases. With an inverse floater the coupon rate moves in the opposite direction from the change in the reference rate. A general formula for an inverse floater is $K - L$ (Reference rate) with a floor of zero.

■ *Range notes.* A range note is a bond whose coupon rate is equal to the reference rate as long as the reference rate is within a certain range at the reset date. If the reference rate is outside of the range, the coupon rate is zero for that period. For example, a 3-year range note might specify that the reference rate is 1-year LIBOR and that the coupon rate resets every year. The coupon rate for the year will be 1-year LIBOR as long as 1-year LIBOR at the coupon reset date falls within the range as specified below:

	Year 1	Year 2	Year 3
Lower limit of range	4.5%	5.25%	6.00%
Upper limit of range	5.5%	6.75%	7.50%

If 1-year LIBOR is outside of the range, the coupon rate is zero.

■ *Stepup notes.* There are bonds whose coupon rate increases over time. These securities are called *stepup notes* because the coupon rate "steps up" over time. For example, a 5-year stepup note might have a coupon rate that is 5% for the first 2 years and 6% for the last 3 years. Or, the stepup note could call for a 5% coupon rate for the first 2 years, 5.5%

for the third and fourth years, and 6% for the fifth year. When there is only one change (or stepup), as in our first example, the issue is referred to as a *single stepup note*. When there is more than one increase, as in our second example, the issue is referred to as a *multiple stepup note*.

Provisions for Paying off Bonds

The bond issuer of a bond agrees to repay the principal by the stated maturity date. The issuer can agree to repay the entire amount borrowed in one lump sum payment at the maturity date. That is, the issuer is not required to make any principal repayments prior to the maturity date. Such bonds are said to have a *bullet maturity*. Bonds backed by pools of loans (mortgage-backed securities and asset-backed securities) often have a schedule of principal repayments. Such bonds are said to be amortizing securities. For many loans, the payments are structured so that when the last loan payment is made, the entire amount owed is fully paid off.

There are bond issues that have a provision granting the bond issuer an option to retire all or part of the issue prior to the stated maturity date. This feature is referred to as a *call feature* and a bond with this feature is said to be a *callable bond*. If the issuer exercises this right, the issuer is said to "call the bond." The price that the bond issuer must pay to retire the issue is referred to as the *call price*. Typically, there is not one call price but a call schedule, which sets forth a call price based on when the issuer can exercise the call option. When a bond is issued, typically the issuer may not call the bond for a number of years. That is, the issue is said to have a *deferred call*.

A bond issuer generally wants the right to retire a bond issue prior to the stated maturity date because it recognizes that at some time in the future the general level of interest rates may fall sufficiently below the issue's coupon rate so that redeeming the issue and replacing it with another issue with a lower coupon rate would be economically beneficial. This right is a disadvantage to the bondholder since proceeds received must be reinvested at a lower interest rate. As a result, an issuer who wants to include this right as part of a bond offering must compensate the bondholder when the issue is sold by offering a higher coupon rate, or equivalently, accepting a lower price than if the right is not included.

If a bond issue does not have any protection against early call, then it is said to be a *currently callable issue*. But most new bond issues, even if currently callable, usually have some restrictions against certain types of early redemption. The most common restriction is prohibiting the refunding of the bonds for a certain number of years. *Refunding* a bond issue means redeeming bonds with funds obtained through the sale of a new bond issue. Call protection is much more absolute than refunding protection. While there may be certain exceptions to absolute or complete call protection in some cases, it still provides greater assurance against premature and unwanted redemption than does refunding protection. Refunding prohibition merely prevents redemption only from certain sources of funds, namely the proceeds of other debt issues sold at a lower cost of money. The bondholder is only protected if interest rates decline, and the borrower can obtain lower-cost money to pay off the debt.

For amortizing securities that are backed by loans and have a schedule of principal repayments, individual borrowers typically have the option to pay off all or part of their loan prior to the scheduled date. Any principal repayment prior to the scheduled date is called a *prepayment*. The right of borrowers to prepay is called the *prepayment option*. Basically, the prepayment option is the same as a call option. However, unlike a call option, there is not a call price that depends on when the borrower pays off the issue. Typically, the price at which a loan is prepaid is par value.

Options Granted to Bondholders

A bond issue may include a provision that gives either the bondholder and/or the issuer an option to take some action against the other party. The most common type of option embedded in a bond is a call feature, which was discussed earlier. This option is granted to the issuer. There are two options that can be granted to the bondholder: the right to put the issue and the right to convert the issue.

An issue with a put provision grants the bondholder the right to sell the issue back to the issuer at a specified price on designated dates. The bond with this feature is called a *putable bond* and the specified price is called the *put price*. The advantage of the put provision to the bondholder is that if after the issue date market rates rise above the issue's coupon rate, the bondholder can force the issuer to redeem the bond at the put price and then reinvest the proceeds at the prevailing higher rate.

A *convertible bond* is an issue giving the bondholder the right to exchange the bond for a specified number of shares of common stock. Such a feature allows the bondholder to take advantage of favorable movements in the price of the bond issuer's common stock. An *exchangeable bond* allows the bondholder to exchange the issue for a specified number of shares of common stock of a corporation different from the issuer of the bond.

FUTURES AND FORWARD CONTRACTS

A futures contract is an agreement that requires a party to the agreement either to buy or sell something at a designated future date at a predetermined price. Futures contracts are products created by exchanges. To create a particular futures contract, an exchange must obtain approval from the Commodity Futures Trading Commission (CFTC), a government regulatory agency. When applying to the CFTC for approval to create a futures contract, the exchange must demonstrate that there is an economic purpose for the contract. Futures contracts are categorized as either commodity futures or financial futures. *Commodity futures* involve traditional agricultural commodities (such as grain and livestock), imported foodstuffs (such as coffee, cocoa, and sugar), and industrial commodities. Futures contracts based on a financial instrument or a financial index are known as *financial futures*. Financial futures can be classified as (1) stock index futures, (2) interest rate futures, and (3) currency futures.

A party to a futures contract has two choices on liquidation of the position. First, the position can be liquidated prior to the settlement date. For this purpose, the party must take an offsetting position in the same contract. For the buyer of a futures contract, this means selling the same number of identical futures contracts; for the seller of a futures contract, this means buying the same number of identical futures contracts. The alternative is to wait until the settlement date. At that time the party purchasing a futures contract accepts delivery of the underlying (financial instrument, currency, or commodity) at the agreed-upon price; the party that sells a futures contract liquidates the position by delivering the underlying at the agreed-upon price. For some futures contracts settlement is made in cash only. Such contracts are referred to as cash-settlement contracts.

Associated with every futures exchange is a clearinghouse, which performs two key functions. First, the clearinghouse guarantees that the two parties to the transaction will perform. It does so as follows. When an investor takes a position in the futures market, the clearinghouse takes the opposite position and agrees to satisfy the terms set forth in the contract. Because of the clearinghouse, the investor need not worry about the financial strength and integrity of the party taking the opposite side of the contract. After initial execution of an order, the relationship between the two parties ends. The clearinghouse interposes itself as the buyer for every sale and the seller for every purchase. Thus investors are free to liquidate their positions without involving the other party in the original contract, and without worry that the other party may default. In addition to the guarantee function, the clearinghouse makes it simple for parties to a futures contract to unwind their positions prior to the settlement date.

When a position is first taken in a futures contract, the investor must deposit a minimum dollar amount per contract as specified by the exchange. This amount is called the *initial margin* and is required as deposit for the contract. The initial margin may be in the form of an interest-bearing security such as a Treasury bill. As the price of the futures contract fluctuates, the value of the investor's equity in the position changes. At the end of each trading day, the exchange determines the settlement price for the futures contract. This price is used to mark to market the investor's position, so that any gain or loss from the position is reflected in the investor's equity account.

Maintenance margin is the minimum level (specified by the exchange) by which an investor's equity position may fall as a result of an unfavorable price movement before the investor is required to deposit additional margin. The additional margin deposited is called *variation margin*, and it is an amount necessary to bring the equity in the account back to its initial margin level. Unlike initial margin, variation margin must be in cash not interest-bearing instruments. Any excess margin in the account may be withdrawn by the investor. If a party to a futures contract who is required to deposit variation margin fails to do so within 24 hours, the futures position is closed out.

Although there are initial and maintenance margin requirements for buying securities on margin, the concept of margin differs for securities and futures. When securities are acquired on margin, the difference between the price of the security and the initial margin is borrowed from the broker. The security purchased serves as collateral for the loan, and the investor pays interest. For futures contracts, the initial margin, in effect, serves as "good faith" money, an indication that the investor will satisfy the obligation of the contract. Normally no money is borrowed by the investor.

Futures versus Forward Contracts

A *forward contract*, just like a futures contract, is an agreement for the future delivery of something at a specified price at the end of a designated period of time. Futures contracts are standardized agreements as to the delivery date (or month) and quality of the deliverable, and are traded on organized exchanges. A forward contract differs in that it is usually nonstandardized (that is, the terms of each contract are negotiated individually between buyer and seller), there is no clearinghouse, and secondary markets are often nonexistent or extremely thin. Unlike a futures contract, which is an exchange-traded product, a forward contract is an over-the-counter instrument.

Futures contracts are marked to market at the end of each trading day. Consequently, futures contracts are subject to interim cash flows as additional margin may be required in the case of adverse price movements, or as cash is withdrawn in the case of favorable price movements. A forward contract may or may not be marked to market, depending on the wishes of the two parties. For a forward contract that is not marked to market, there are no interim cash flow effects because no additional margin is required.

Finally, the parties in a forward contract are exposed to credit risk because either party may default on the obligation. Credit risk is minimal in the case of futures contracts because the clearinghouse associated with the exchange guarantees the other side of the transaction.

Other than these differences, most of what we say about futures contracts applies equally to forward contracts.

Risk and Return Characteristics of Futures Contracts

When an investor takes a position in the market by buying a futures contract, the investor is said to be in a *long position* or to be *long futures*. If, instead, the investor's opening position is the sale of a futures contract, the investor is said to be in a short position or short futures. The buyer of a futures contract will realize a profit if the futures price increases; the seller of a futures contract will realize a profit if the futures price decreases; if the futures price decreases, the buyer of the futures contract realizes a loss while the seller of a futures contract realizes a profit. Notice that the risk-return is symmetrical for a favorable and adverse price movement.

When a position is taken in a futures contract, the party need not put up the entire amount of the investment. Instead, only initial margin must be put up. Thus a futures contract, as with other derivatives, allows a market participant to create leverage. While the degree of leverage available in the futures market varies from contract to contract, the leverage attainable is considerably greater than in the cash market by buying on margin. While at first the leverage available in the futures market may suggest that the market benefits only those who want to only speculate on price movements. This is not true. Futures markets can be used to reduce price risk. Without the leverage possible in futures transactions, the cost of reducing price risk using futures would be too high for many market participants.

Pricing of Futures Contracts

In later chapters we will see how the mathematical tools presented in this book can be applied to valuing complex financial instruments.

However, the pricing of futures contracts does not require any high level mathematical analysis. Rather it is based on simple arbitrage arguments discussed in Chapter 14. To see this, let's derive the theoretical price of a futures contract using simple algebra. All we need to know is the following:

- The price that the underlying asset for the futures contract is selling for in the cash market.
- The cash yield earned on the underlying asset until the settlement date.
- The interest rate for borrowing and lending until the settlement date.

Let

r = financing cost
y = cash yield on underlying asset
P = cash market price (\$) of the underlying asset
F = futures price (\$)

Now consider the following strategy, referred to as a *cash and carry trade*:

- Sell the futures contract at F
- Purchase the underlying asset in the cash market for P
- Borrow P until the settlement date at the financing cost of r

The outcome at the settlement date then is:

1. From Settlement of the Futures Contract

Proceeds from sale of the underlying asset to settle the futures contract	$= F$
Payment received from investing in the underlying asset for 3 months	$= yP$
Total proceeds	$= F + yP$

2. From the Loan

Repayment of the principal of loan	$= P$
Interest on loan	$= rP$
Total outlay	$= P + rP$

The profit will equal:

$$\text{Profit} = \text{Total proceeds} - \text{Total outlay}$$
$$= F + yP - (P + rP)$$

The theoretical futures price is where the profit from this strategy is zero. Thus, to have equilibrium, the following must hold:

$$0 = F + yP - (P + rP)$$

Solving for the theoretical futures price, we have:

$$F = P + P\,(r - y)$$

Alternatively, consider the following strategy called a *reverse cash and carry trade*:

■ Buy the futures contract at F
■ Sell (short) the underlying asset for P
■ Invest (lend) P at r until the settlement date

The outcome at the settlement date would be:

1. From Settlement of the Futures Contract

Price paid for purchase of the underlying asset to settle futures contract	$= F$
Payment to lender of the underlying asset in order to borrow the asset	$= yP$
Total outlay	$= F + yP$

2. From the Loan

Proceeds received from maturing of the loan investment	$= P$
Interest earned	$= rP$
Total proceeds	$= P + rP$

The profit will equal:

$$\text{Profit} = \text{Total proceeds} - \text{Total outlay}$$
$$= P + rP - (F + yP)$$

Setting the profit equal to zero so that there will be no arbitrage profit and solving for the futures price, we would obtain the same equation for the theoretical futures price as given from the cash and carry trade.

The theoretical futures price may be at a premium to the cash market price (higher than the cash market price) or at a discount from the cash market price (lower than the cash market price) depending on $P(r - y)$. The term $r - y$, which reflects the difference between the cost of financing and the asset's cash yield, is called the *net financing cost*. The net financing cost is more commonly called the *cost of carry* or, simply, *carry*. Positive carry means that the yield earned is greater than the financing cost; negative carry means that the financing cost exceeds the yield earned.

At the delivery date, the futures price must be equal to the cash market price. Thus, as the delivery date approaches, the futures price will converge to the cash market price. This can be seen by looking at the equation for the theoretical futures price. As the delivery date approaches, the financing cost approaches zero, and the yield that can be earned by holding the investment approaches zero. Hence the cost of carry approaches zero, and the futures price will approach the cash market price.

To derive the theoretical futures price using the arbitrage argument, several assumptions are made. When the assumptions are violated, there will be a divergence between the actual futures price and the theoretical futures price as derived above; that is, the difference between the two prices will differ from carry. The reasons for the deviation of the actual futures price from the theoretical futures price are as follows.

First, no interim cash flows due to variation margin are assumed. In addition, any cash flows payments from the underlying asset are assumed to be paid at the delivery date rather than at an interim date. However, we know that interim cash flows can occur for both of these reasons. Because we assume no variation margin, the theoretical price for the contract is technically the theoretical price for a forward contract that is not marked to market, not the theoretical price for a futures contract. This is because, unlike a futures contract, a forward contract that is not marked to market at the end of each trading day does not require additional margin.

Second, in deriving the theoretical futures price it is assumed that the borrowing rate and lending rate are equal. Typically, however, the borrowing rate is greater than the lending rate. Letting r_B denote the borrowing rate and r_L denote the lending rate, then the following boundaries would exist for the theoretical futures price:

$$Upper\ boundary:\ F = P + P(r_B - y)$$

$$Lower\ boundary:\ F = P + P(r_L - y)$$

Third, in determining the theoretical futures price, transaction costs involved in establishing the positions are ignored. In actuality, there are transaction costs of entering into and closing the cash position as well as round-trip transactions costs for the futures contract that do affect the theoretical futures price. Transaction costs widen the boundaries for the theoretical futures price.

In the strategy involving short-selling of the underlying asset, it is assumed that the proceeds from the short sale are received and reinvested. In practice, for individual investors, the proceeds are not received, and, in fact, the individual investor is required to put up margin (securities margin not futures margin) to short-sell. For institutional investors, the asset may be borrowed, but there is a cost to borrowing. This cost of borrowing can be incorporated into the model by reducing the yield on the asset.

In our derivation, we assumed that only one asset is deliverable. There are futures contracts, such as the government bond futures contract in the United States and other countries, where the short has the option of delivering one of several acceptable issues to satisfy the futures contract. Thus, the buyer of a futures contract with this feature does not know what the deliverable asset will be. This leads to the notion of the "cheapest to deliver asset." It is not difficult to value this option granted to the short.

Finally, the underlying for some futures contracts is not a single asset but a basket of assets, or an index. Stock index futures contracts are an example. The problem in arbitraging these futures contracts on an index is that it is too expensive to buy or sell every asset included in the index. Instead, a portfolio containing a smaller number of assets may be constructed to "track" the index. The arbitrage, however, is no longer risk-free because there is the risk that the portfolio will not track the index exactly. All of this leads to higher transaction costs and uncertainty about the outcome of the arbitrage.

The Role of Futures in Financial Markets

Without financial futures, investors would have only one trading location to alter portfolio positions when they get new information that is expected to influence the value of assets—the cash market. If economic news that is expected to impact the value of an asset adversely is received, investors can reduce their price risk exposure to that asset. The opposite is true if the new information is expected to impact the value of that asset favorably: an investor would increase price-risk exposure to that asset. There are, of course, transaction costs associated with altering exposure to an asset—explicit costs (commissions), and hidden or execution costs (bid-ask spreads and market impact costs).

Futures provide another market that investors can use to alter their risk exposure to an asset when new information is acquired. An investor will transact in the market that is the more efficient to use in order to achieve the objective. The factors to consider are liquidity, transaction costs, taxes, and leverage advantages of the futures contract. The market that investors feel is the one that is more efficient to use to achieve their investment objective should be the one where prices will be established that reflect the new economic information. That is, this will be the market where price discovery takes place. Price information is then transmitted to the other market. It is in the futures market that it is easier and less costly to alter a portfolio position. Therefore, it is the futures market that will be the market of choice and will serve as the price discovery market. It is in the futures market that investors send a collective message about how any new information is expected to impact the cash market.

How is this message sent to the cash market? We know that the futures price and the cash market price are tied together by the cost of carry. If the futures price deviates from the cash market price by more than the cost of carry, arbitrageurs (in attempting to obtain arbitrage profits) would pursue a strategy to bring them back into line. Arbitrage brings the cash market price into line with the futures price. It is this mechanism that assures that the cash market price will reflect the information that has been collected in the futures market.

OPTIONS

An option is a contract in which the writer of the option grants the buyer of the option the right, but not the obligation, to purchase from or sell to the writer something at a specified price within a specified period of time (or at a specified date). The writer, also referred to as the *seller*, grants this right to the buyer in exchange for a certain sum of money, which is called the *option price* or *option premium*. The price at which the asset may be bought or sold is called the *exercise* or *strike price*. The date after which an option is void is called the expiration date.

When an option grants the buyer the right to purchase the designated instrument from the writer (seller), it is referred to as a *call option*, or call. When the option buyer has the right to sell the designated instrument to the writer, the option is called a *put option*, or put. Buying calls or selling puts allows the investor to gain if the price of the underlying asset rises. Selling calls and buying puts allows the investor to gain if the price of the underlying asset falls.

An option is also categorized according to when the option buyer may exercise the option. There are options that may be exercised at any time up to and including the expiration date. Such an option is referred to as an *American option*. There are options that may be exercised only at the expiration date. An option with this feature is called a *European option*.

There are no margin requirements for the buyer of an option once the option price has been paid in full. Because the option price is the maximum amount that the investor can lose, no matter how adverse the price movement of the underlying asset, there is no need for margin. Because the writer of an option has agreed to accept all of the risk (and none of the reward) of the position in the underlying asset, the writer is generally required to put up the option price received as margin. In addition, as price changes occur that adversely affect the writer's position, the writer is required to deposit additional margin (with some exceptions) as the position is marked to market.

Options, like other financial instruments, may be traded either on an organized exchange or in the over-the-counter market. An exchange that wants to create an options contract must obtain approval from either the Commodities Futures Trading Commission or the Securities and Exchange Commission. Exchange-traded options have three advantages. First, the exercise price and expiration date of the contract are standardized. Second, as in the case of futures contracts, the direct link between buyer and seller is severed after the order is executed because of the interchangeability of exchange-traded options. The clearinghouse associated with the exchange where the option trades performs the same function in the options market that it does in the futures market. Finally, the transaction costs are lower for exchange-traded options than for OTC options. The higher cost of an OTC option reflects the cost of customizing the option for the many situations where an institutional investor needs to have a tailor-made option because the standardized exchange-traded option does not satisfy its investment objectives. Some commercial and investment and banking firms act as principals as well as brokers in the OTC options market. OTC options are sometimes referred to as *dealer options*.

OTC options can be customized in any manner sought by an institutional investor. Basically, if a dealer can reasonably hedge the risk associated with the opposite side of the option sought, it will create the option desired by a customer. OTC options are not limited to European or American type expiration designs. An option can be created in which the option can be exercised at several specified dates as well as the expiration date of the option. Such options are referred to as limited exercise options, *Bermuda options*, and *Atlantic options*.

Risk-Return for Options

The maximum amount that an option buyer can lose is the option price. The maximum profit that the option writer can realize is the option price. The option buyer has substantial upside return potential, while the option writer has substantial downside risk.

Notice that, unlike in a futures contract, one party to an option contract is not obligated to transact—specifically, the option buyer has the right but not the obligation to transact. The option writer does have the obligation to perform. In the case of a futures contract, both buyer and seller are obligated to perform. Of course, a futures buyer does not pay the seller to accept the obligation, while an option buyer pays the seller an option price.

Consequently, the risk/reward characteristics of the two contracts are also different. In the case of a futures contract, the buyer of the contract realizes a dollar-for-dollar gain when the price of the futures contract increases and suffers a dollar-for-dollar loss when the price of the futures contract drops. The opposite occurs for the seller of a futures contract. Options do not provide this symmetric risk/reward relationship. The most that the buyer of an option can lose is the option price. While the buyer of an option retains all the potential benefits, the gain is always reduced by the amount of the option price. The maximum profit that the writer may realize is the option price; this is offset against substantial downside risk. This difference is extremely important because investors can use futures to protect against symmetric risk and options to protect against asymmetric risk.

The Option Price

Determining the value of an option is not as simple as the value of a futures contract. In Chapter 15 we will present a model employing stochastic calculus and arbitrage arguments to determine the theoretical price of an option. In this section we simply present the factors that affect the valuation of an option.

Basic Components of the Option Price

The option price is a reflection of the option's intrinsic value and any additional amount over its intrinsic value. The premium over intrinsic value is often referred to as the time premium.

The *intrinsic value* of an option is the economic value of the option if it is exercised immediately, except that if there is no positive economic value that will result from exercising immediately then the intrinsic value is zero. The intrinsic value of a call option is the difference between the current price of the underlying asset and the strike price if positive; it is otherwise zero. For example, if the strike price for a call option is $100 and the current asset price is $105, the intrinsic value is $5. That is, an option buyer exercising the option and simultaneously selling the underlying asset would realize $105 from the sale of the asset, which would be covered by acquiring the asset from the option writer for $100, thereby netting a $5 gain.

When an option has intrinsic value, it is said to be "in the money." When the strike price of a call option exceeds the current asset price, the call option is said to be "out of the money"; it has no intrinsic value. An option for which the strike price is equal to the current asset price is said to be "at the money." Both at-the-money and out-of-the-money options have an intrinsic value of zero because it is not profitable to exercise the option. Our call option with a strike price of $100 would be: (1) in the money when the current asset price is greater than $100; (2) out of the money when the current asset price is less than $100; and (3) at the money when the current asset price is equal to $100.

For a put option, the intrinsic value is equal to the amount by which the current asset price is below the strike price. For example, if the strike price of a put option is $100 and the current asset price is $92, the intrinsic value is $8. That is, the buyer of the put option who exercises the put option and simultaneously sells the underlying asset will net $8 by exercising. The asset will be sold to the writer for $100 and purchased in the market for $92. For our put option with a strike price of $100, the option would be: (1) in the money when the asset price is less than $100; (2) out of the money when the current asset price exceeds the strike price; and (3) at the money when the strike price is equal to the asset's price.

The *time premium* of an option is the amount by which the option price exceeds its intrinsic value. The option buyer hopes that, at some time prior to expiration, changes in the market price of the underlying asset will increase the value of the rights conveyed by the option. For this prospect, the option buyer is willing to pay a premium above the intrinsic value. For example, if the price of a call option with a strike price of $100 is $9 when the current asset price is $105, the time premium of this option is $4 ($9 minus its intrinsic value of $5). Had the current asset price been $90 instead of $105, then the time premium of this option would be the entire $9 because the option has no intrinsic value. Clearly, other things being equal, the time premium of an option will increase with the amount of time remaining to expiration.

There are two ways in which an option buyer may realize the value of a position taken in the option. First is to exercise the option. The second is by selling the call option for $9. In the first example above, selling the call is preferable because the exercise of an option will realize a gain of only $5—it will cause the immediate loss of any time premium. There are circumstances under which an option may be exercised prior to the expiration date; they depend on whether the total proceeds at the expiration date would be greater by holding the option or exercising and reinvesting any cash proceeds received until the expiration date.

Factors that Influence the Option Price

There are six factors that influence the option price:

1. Current price of the underlying asset.
2. Strike price.
3. Time to expiration of the option.
4. Expected return volatility of the underlying asset over the life of the option.
5. Short-term risk-free interest rate over the life of the option.
6. Anticipated cash payments on the underlying asset over the life of the option.

The impact of each of these factors may depend on whether the option is a call or a put, and whether the option is an American option or a European option. A summary of the effect of each factor on put and call option prices is presented in Exhibit 2.2.

Option Pricing Models

Earlier we illustrated that the theoretical price of a futures contract can be determined on the basis of arbitrage arguments. Theoretical boundary conditions for the price of an option also can be derived through arbitrage arguments. For example, using arbitrage arguments it can be shown that the minimum price for an American call option is its intrinsic value; that is:

EXHIBIT 2.2 Summary of Factors that Affect the Price of an Option

Factor	Effect of an Increase of Factor on	
	Call Price	Put Price
Current price of underlying asset	Increase	Decrease
Strike price	Decrease	Increase
Time to expiration of option	Increase	Increase
Expected price volatility	Increase	Increase
Short-term interest rate	Increase	Decrease
Anticipated cash payments	Decrease	Increase

Call option price = $\geq$ Max (0, Price of asset – Strike price)

This expression says that the call option price will be greater than or equal to the difference between the price of the underlying asset and the strike price (intrinsic value), or zero, whichever is higher.

The boundary conditions can be "tightened" by using arbitrage arguments coupled with certain assumptions about the cash distribution of the asset.[10] The extreme case is an option pricing model that uses a set of assumptions to derive a single theoretical price, rather than a range. Deriving a theoretical option price is much more complicated than deriving a theoretical futures price, because the option price depends on the expected return volatility of the underlying asset over the life of the option.

Several models have been developed to determine the theoretical value of an option. The most popular one was developed by Fischer Black and Myron Scholes in 1973 for valuing European call options.[11] Several modifications to their model have followed since then. We shall discuss the Black-Scholes model and its assumptions in Chapter 15. Basically, the idea behind the arbitrage argument is that if the payoff from owning a call option can be replicated by purchasing the asset underlying the call option and borrowing funds, the price of the option is then (at most) the cost of creating the replicating strategy.

SWAPS

A swap is an agreement whereby two parties (called counterparties) agree to exchange periodic payments. The dollar amount of the payments exchanged is based on some predetermined dollar principal, which is called the *notional principal amount* or *notional amount*. The dollar amount each counterparty pays to the other is the agreed-upon periodic rate times the notional principal amount. The only dollars that are exchanged between the parties are the agreed-upon payments, not the notional principal amount. In a swap, there is the risk that one of the parties will fail to meet its obligation to make payments (default). This is referred to as *counterparty risk*.

Swaps are classified based on the characteristics of the swap payments. There are four types of swaps: interest rate swaps, interest rate-equity swaps, equity swaps, and currency swaps. In an *interest rate swap*, the

---

[10] See Chapter 4 in John C. Cox and Mark Rubinstein, *Option Markets* (Englewood Cliffs, N.J.: Prentice Hall, 1985), Chapter 4.

[11] Fischer Black and Myron Scholes, "The Pricing of Corporate Liabilities," *Journal of Political Economy* (May–June 1973), pp. 637–659.

counterparties swap payments in the same currency based on an interest rate. For example, one of the counterparties can pay a fixed-interest rate and the other party a floating interest rate. The floating-interest rate is commonly referred to as the reference rate. In an *interest rate-equity swap*, one party is exchanging a payment based on an interest rate and the other party based on the return of some equity index. The payments are made in the same currency. In an *equity swap*, both parties exchange payments in the same currency based on some equity index. Finally, in a *currency swap*, two parties agree to swap payments based on different currencies.

A swap is not a new derivative instrument. Rather, it can be decomposed into a package of forward contracts. While a swap may be nothing more than a package of forward contracts, it is not a redundant contract for several reasons. First, in many markets where there are forward and futures contracts, the longest maturity does not extend out as far as that of a typical swap. Second, a swap is a more transactionally efficient instrument. By this we mean that in one transaction an entity can effectively establish a payoff equivalent to a package of forward contracts. The forward contracts would each have to be negotiated separately. Third, the liquidity of some swap markets is now better than many forward contracts, particularly long-dated (i.e., long-term) forward contracts.

CAPS AND FLOORS

There are agreements available in the financial market whereby one party, for a fee (premium), agrees to compensate the other if a designated reference is different from a predetermined level. The party that will receive payment if the designated reference differs from a predetermined level and pays a premium to enter into the agreement is called the buyer. The party that agrees to make the payment if the designated reference differs from a predetermined level is called the seller.

When the seller agrees to pay the buyer if the designated reference exceeds a predetermined level, the agreement is referred to as a *cap*. The agreement is referred to as a *floor* when the seller agrees to pay the buyer if a designated reference falls below a predetermined level. The designated reference could be a specific interest rate such as LIBOR or the prime rate, the rate of return on some domestic or foreign stock market index such as the S&P 500 or the DAX, or an exchange rate such as the exchange rate between the U.S. dollar and the Japanese yen. The predetermined level is called the strike. As with a swap, a cap and a floor have a notional principal amount. Only the buyer of a cap or a floor is exposed to counterparty risk.

In general, the payment made by the seller of the cap to the buyer on a specific date is determined by the relationship between the designated reference and the strike. If the former is greater that the latter, then the seller pays the buyer:

Notional principal amount × [Actual value of designated reference − Strike]

If the designated reference is less than or equal to the strike, then the seller pays the buyer nothing.

For a floor, the payment made by the seller to the buyer on a specific date is determined as follows. If the designated reference is less than the strike, then the seller pays the buyer:

Notional principal amount × [Strike − Actual value of designated reference]

If the designated reference is greater than or equal to the strike, then the seller pays the buyer nothing.

In a cap or floor, the buyer pays a fee which represents the maximum amount that the buyer can lose and the maximum amount that the seller of the agreement can gain. The only party that is required to perform is the seller. The buyer of a cap benefits if the designated reference rises above the strike because the seller must compensate the buyer. The buyer of a floor benefits if the designated reference falls below the strike because the seller must compensate the buyer.

In essence the payoff of these contracts is the same as that of an option. A call option buyer pays a fee and benefits if the value of the option's underlying asset (or equivalently, designated reference) is higher than the strike price at the expiration date. A cap has a similar payoff. A put option buyer pays a fee and benefits if the value of the option's underlying asset (or equivalently, designated reference) is less than the strike price at the expiration date. A floor has a similar payoff. An option seller is only entitled to the option price. The seller of a cap or floor is only entitled to the fee. Thus, a cap and a floor can be viewed as simply a package of options. As with a swap, a complex contract can be seen to be a package of basic contracts (forward contracts in the case of swaps and options in the case of caps and floors).

SUMMARY

- The claims of the holder of a financial asset may be either a fixed dollar amount (fixed income instrument or bond) or a varying, or residual, amount (common stock).

- The two principal economic functions of financial assets are to (1) transfer funds from those parties who have surplus funds to invest to those who need funds to invest in tangible assets; and (2) transfer funds in such a way as to redistribute the unavoidable risk associated with the cash flow generated by tangible assets among those seeking and those providing the funds.
- Financial assets possess the following properties that determine or influence their attractiveness to different classes of investors: (1) moneyness; (2) divisibility and denomination; (3) reversibility; (4) term to maturity; (5) liquidity; (6) convertibility; (7) currency; (8) cash flow and return predictability; and (9) tax status.
- There are five ways to classify financial markets: (1) nature of the claim; (2) maturity of the claims; (3) new versus seasoned claims; (4) cash versus derivative instruments; and (5) organizational structure of the market.
- Financial markets provide the following economic functions: (1) They signal how the funds in the economy should be allocated among financial assets (i.e., price discovery); (2) they provide a mechanism for an investor to sell a financial asset (i.e., provide liquidity); and (3) they reduce search and information costs of transacting.
- Pricing efficiency refers to a market where prices at all times fully reflect all available information that is relevant to the valuation of securities.
- Financial intermediaries obtain funds by issuing financial claims against themselves to market participants, then investing those funds.
- Asset managers manage funds to meet specified investment objectives—either based on a market benchmark or based on liabilities.
- Common stocks, also called equity securities, represent an ownership interest in a corporation; holders of this types of security are entitled to the earnings of the corporation when those earnings are distributed in the form of dividends.
- A bond is a financial obligation of an entity that promises to pay a specified sum of money at specified future dates; a bond may include a provision that grants the issuer or the investor an option to alter the effective maturity.
- A futures contract and forward contract are agreements that require a party to the agreement either to buy or sell the underlying at a designated future date at a predetermined price.
- Futures contracts are standardized agreements as to the delivery date and quality of the deliverable, and are traded on organized exchanges; a forward contract differs in that it is usually nonstandardized, there is no clearinghouse (and therefore counterparty risk), and secondary markets are often nonexistent or extremely thin.

- ◾ An option is a contract in which the writer of the option grants the buyer of the option the right, but not the obligation, to purchase from the writer (a call option) or sell to the writer (a put option) the underlying at the strike (or exercise) price within a specified period of time (or at a specified date); the option price is a reflection of the option's intrinsic value and any additional amount over its intrinsic value.
- ◾ A swap is an agreement whereby the counterparties agree to exchange periodic payments; the dollar amount of the payments exchanged is based on a notional amount.
- ◾ A cap and a floor are agreements whereby one party, for a fee (premium), agrees to compensate the other if a designated reference is different from a predetermined level.

CHAPTER 3

Milestones in Financial Modeling and Investment Management

The mathematical development of present-day economic and finance theory began in Lausanne, Switzerland at the end of the nineteenth century, with the development of the mathematical equilibrium theory by Leon Walras and Wilfredo Pareto.[1] Shortly thereafter, at the beginning of the twentieth century, Louis Bachelier in Paris and Filip Lundberg in Uppsala (Sweden) made two seminal contributions: they developed sophisticated mathematical tools to describe uncertain price and risk processes.

These developments were well in advance of their time. Further progress was to be made only much later in the twentieth century, thanks to the development of digital computers. By making it possible to compute approximate solutions to complex problems, digital computers enabled the large-scale application of mathematics to business problems.

A first round of innovation occurred in the 1950s and 1960s. Kenneth Arrow and Georges Debreu introduced a probabilistic model of markets and the notion of contingent claims. (We discuss their contributions in Chapter 6.) In 1952, Harry Markowitz described mathematically the principles of the investment process in terms of utility optimization. In 1961, Franco Modigliani and Merton Miller clarified the nature of economic value, working out the implications of absence of arbitrage. Between 1964 and 1966, William Sharpe, John Lintner,

---

[1] References for some of the works cited in this chapter will be provided in later chapters in this book. For an engaging description of the history of capital markets see Peter L. Bernstein, *Capital Ideas* (New York: The Free Press, 1992). For a history of the role of risk in business and investment management, see Peter L. Bernstein, *Against the Gods* (New York: John Wiley & Sons, 1996).

and Jan Mossin developed a theoretical model of market prices based on the principles of financial decision-making laid down by Markowitz. The notion of efficient markets was introduced by Paul Samuelson in 1965, and five years later, further developed by Eugene Fama.

The second round of innovation started at the end of the 1970s. In 1973, Fischer Black, Myron Scholes, and Robert Merton discovered how to determine option prices using continuous hedging. Three years later, Stephen Ross introduced arbitrage pricing theory (APT). Both were major developments that were to result in a comprehensive mathematical methodology for investment management and the valuation of derivative financial products. At about the same time, Merton introduced a continuous-time intertemporal, dynamic optimization model of asset allocation. Major refinements in the methodology of mathematical optimization and new econometric tools were to change the way investments are managed.

More recently, the diffusion of electronic transactions has made available a huge amount of empirical data. The availability of this data created the hope that economics could be given a more solid scientific grounding. A new field—*econophysics*—opened with the expectation that the proven methods of the physical sciences and the newly born science of complex systems could be applied with benefit to economics. It was hypothesized that economic systems could be studied as physical systems with only minimal *a priori* economic assumptions. Classical econometrics is based on a similar approach; but while the scope of classical econometrics is limited to dynamic models of time series, econophysics uses all the tools of statistical physics and complex systems analysis, including the theory of interacting multiagent systems.

THE PRECURSORS: PARETO, WALRAS, AND THE LAUSANNE SCHOOL

The idea of formulating quantitative laws of economic behavior in ways similar to the physical sciences started in earnest at the end of the nineteenth century. Though quite accurate economic accounting on a large scale dates back to Assyro-Babylonian times, a scientific approach to economics is a recent endeavor.

Leon Walras and Wilfredo Pareto, founders of the so-called Lausanne School at the University of Lausanne in Switzerland, were among the first to explicitly formulate quantitative principles of market economies, stating the principle of economic equilibrium as a mathematical theory. Both worked at a time of great social and economic change. In Pareto's work in particular, pure economics and political science occupy a central place.

Convinced that economics should become a mathematical science, Walras set himself the task of writing the first mathematical *general equilibrium system*. The British economist Stanley Jevons and the Austrian economist Carl Menger had already formulated the idea of economic equilibrium as a situation where supply and demand match in interrelated markets. Walras's objective—to prove that equilibrium was indeed possible—required the explicit formulation of the equations of supply-and-demand equilibrium.

Walras introduced the idea of *tatonemment* (French for groping) as a process of exploration by which a central auctioneer determines equilibrium prices. A century before, in 1776, in his book *An Inquiry into the Nature and Causes of the Wealth of Nations*, Adam Smith had introduced the notion of the "invisible hand" that coordinates the activity of independent competitive agents to achieve desirable global goals.[2] Walras was to make the hand "visible" by defining the process of price discovery.

Pareto followed Walras in the Chair of Economics at the University of Lausanne. Pareto's focus was the process of economic decision-making. He replaced the idea of supply-and-demand equilibrium with a more general idea of the ordering of preferences through *utility functions*.[3] Equilibrium is reached where marginal utilities are zero. The Pareto system hypothesized that agents are able to order their preferences and take into account constraints in such a way that a numerical index—"utility" in today's terminology—can be associated to each choice.[4] Economic decision-making is therefore based on the maximization of utility. As Pareto assumed utility to be a differentiable function, global equilibrium is reached where marginal utilities (i.e., the partial derivatives of utility) vanish.

Pareto was especially interested in the problem of the global optimum of utility. The Pareto optimum is a state in which nobody can be better off without making others worse off. A Pareto optimum does not imply the equal division of resources; quite the contrary, a Pareto optimum might be a maximally unequal distribution of wealth.

---

[2] In the modern parlance of complex systems, the "invisible hand" would be called an "emerging property" of competitive markets. Much recent work on complex systems and artificial life has focused on understanding how the local interaction of individuals might result in complex and purposeful global behavior.

[3] Pareto used the word "ophelimity" to designate what we would now call utility. The concept of ophelimity is slightly different from the concept of utility insofar as ophelimity includes constraints on people's preferences.

[4] It was not until 1944 that utility theory was formalized in a set of necessary and sufficient axioms by von Neumann and Morgenstern and applied to decision-making under risk and uncertainty. See John von Neumann and Oskar Morgenstern, *Theory of Games and Economic Behavior* (Princeton, NJ: Princeton University Press, 1944).

A lasting contribution of Pareto is the formulation of a law of income distribution. Known as the *Pareto law*, this law states that there is a linear relationship between the logarithm of the income I and the number N of people that earn more than this income:

$$\text{Log } N = A + s \log I$$

where A and s are appropriate constants.

The importance of the works of Walras and Pareto were not appreciated at the time. Without digital computers, the equilibrium systems they conceived were purely abstract: There was no way to compute solutions to economic equilibrium problems. In addition, the climate at the turn of the century did not allow a serene evaluation of the scientific merit of their work. The idea of free markets was at the center of heated political debates; competing systems included mercantile economies based on trade restrictions and privileges as well as the emerging centrally planned Marxist economies.

PRICE DIFFUSION: BACHELIER

In 1900, the Sorbonne University student Louis Bachelier presented a doctoral dissertation, *Théorie de la Spéculation,* that was to anticipate much of today's work in finance theory. Bachelier's advisor was the great French mathematician Henri Poincaré. There were three notable aspects in Bachelier's thesis:

- He argued that in a purely speculative market stock prices should be random.
- He developed the mathematics of Brownian motion.
- He computed the prices of several options.

To appreciate the importance of Bachelier's work, it should be remarked that at the beginning of the 20th century, the notion of probability was not yet rigorous; the formal mathematical theory of probability was developed only in the 1930s (see Chapter 6). In particular, the precise notion of the propagation of information essential for the definition of conditional probabilities in continuous time had not yet been formulated.

Anticipating the development of the theory of efficient markets 60 years later, the key economic idea of Bachelier was that asset prices in a speculative market should be a fair game, that is, a martingale process such that the expected return is zero (see Chapter 15). According to Bachelier, "The expectation of the speculator is zero." The formal concept of a martingale (i.e., of a process such that its expected value at any moment coincides with the present value) had not yet been introduced in probability theory. In fact, the rigorous notion of conditional probability and filtration (see Chapter 6) were developed only in the 1930s. In formulating his hypothesis on market behavior, Bachelier relied on intuition.

Bachelier actually went much further. He assumed that stock prices evolve as a continuous-time Markov process. This was a brilliant intuition: Markov was to start working on these problems only in 1906. Bachelier established the differential equation for the time evolution of the probability distribution of prices, noting that this equation was the same as the heat diffusion equation. Five years later, in 1905, Albert Einstein used the same diffusion equation for the Brownian motion (i.e., the motion of a small particle suspended in a fluid). Bachelier also made the connection with the continuous limit of random walks, thus anticipating the work of the Japanese mathematician Kiyosi Itô at the end of the 1940s and the Russian mathematician and physicist Ruslan L. Stratonovich on stochastic integrals at the end of the 1950s.

By computing the extremes of Brownian motion, Bachelier computed the price of several options. He also computed the distributions of a number of functionals of Brownian motion. These were remarkable mathematical results in themselves. Formal proof was given only much later. Even more remarkable, Bachelier established option pricing formulas well before the formal notion of absence of arbitrage was formulated.

Though the work of Bachelier was correctly assessed by his advisor Poincaré, it did not bring him much recognition at the time. Bachelier succeeded in getting several books on probability theory published, but his academic career was not very successful. He was offered only minor positions in provincial towns and suffered a major blow when in 1926, at the age of 56, he was refused a permanent chair at the University of Dijon under the pretext (false) that his 1900 thesis contained an error.[5]

Bachelier's work was outside the mainstream of contemporary mathematics but was too mathematically complex for the economists of his time. It wasn't until the formal development of probability theory in 1930s that his ideas became mainstream mathematics and only in the 1960s, with the development of the theory of efficient markets, that his ideas became part of mainstream finance theory. In an efficient market, asset prices should, in each instant, reflect all the information available at the time, and any event that causes prices to move must be unex-

---

[5] The famous mathematician Paul Levy who, apparently in *bona fide*, initially endorsed the claim that Bachelier's thesis contained an error, later wrote a letter of apology to Bachelier.

pected (i.e., a random disturbance). As a consequence, prices move as martingales, as argued by Bachelier. Bachelier was, in fact, the first to give a precise mathematical structure in continuous time to price processes subject to competitive pressure by many agents.

THE RUIN PROBLEM IN INSURANCE: LUNDBERG

In Uppsala, Sweden, in 1903, three years after Bachelier defended his doctoral dissertation in Paris, Filip Lundberg defended a thesis that was to become a milestone in actuarial mathematics: He was the first to define a collective theory of risk and to apply a sophisticated probabilistic formulation to the insurance ruin problem. The ruin problem of an insurance company in a nonlife sector can be defined as follows. Suppose that an insurance company receives a stream of sure payments (premiums) and is subject to claims of random size that occur at random times. What is the probability that the insurer will not be able to meet its obligations (i.e., the probability of ruin)?

Lundberg solved the problem as a collective risk problem, pooling together the risk of claims. To define collective risk processes, he introduced marked Poisson processes. Marked Poisson processes are processes where the random time between two events is exponentially distributed. The magnitude of events is random with a distribution independent of the time of the event. Based on this representation, Lundberg computed an estimate of the probability of ruin.

Lundberg's work anticipated many future developments of probability theory, including what was later to be known as the *theory of point processes*. In the 1930s, the Swedish mathematician and probabilist Harald Cramer gave a rigorous mathematical formulation to Lundberg's work. A more comprehensive formal theory of insurance risk was later developed. This theory now includes Cox processes—point processes more general than Poisson processes—and fat-tailed distributions of claim size.

A strong connection between actuarial mathematics and asset pricing theory has since been established.[6] In well-behaved, complete markets (see Chapter 23), establishing insurance premiums entails principles that mirror asset prices. In the presence of complete markets, insurance would be a risk-free business: There is always the possibility of reinsurance. In markets that are not complete—essentially because they make unpredictable jumps—hedging is not possible; risk can only be diversi-

---

[6] Paul Embrechts, Claudia Klüppelberg, and Thomas Mikosch, *Modelling Extremal Events for Insurance and Finance* (Berlin: Springer, 1996).

fied and options are inherently risky. Option pricing theory again mirrors the setting of insurance premiums.

Lundberg's work went unnoticed by the actuarial community for nearly 30 years, though this did not stop him from enjoying a successful career as an insurer. Both Bachelier and Lundberg were in advance of their time; they anticipated, and probably inspired, the subsequent development of probability theory. But the type of mathematics implied by their work could not be employed in full earnest prior to the development of digital computers. It was only with digital computers that we were able to tackle complex mathematical problems whose solutions go beyond closed-form formulas.

THE PRINCIPLES OF INVESTMENT: MARKOWITZ

Just how an investor should allocate his resources has long been debated. Classical wisdom suggested that investments should be allocated to those assets yielding the highest returns, without the consideration of correlations. Before the modern formulation of efficient markets, speculators widely acted on the belief that positions should be taken only if they had a competitive advantage in terms of information. A large amount of resources were therefore spent on analyzing financial information. John Maynard Keynes suggested that investors should carefully evaluate all available information and then make a calculated bet. The idea of diversification was anathema to Keynes, who was actually quite a successful investor.

In 1952, Harry Markowitz, then a graduate student at the University of Chicago, and a student member of the Cowles Commission,[7] published a seminal article on optimal portfolio selection that upset established wisdom. He advocated that, being risk adverse, investors should diversify their portfolios.[8] The idea of making risk bearable through risk diversification was not new: It was widely used by medieval merchants. Markowitz understood that the risk-return trade-off of investments could be improved by diversification and cast diversification in the framework of optimization.

---

[7] The Cowles Commission is a research institute founded by Alfred Cowles in 1932. Originally based in Colorado Springs, the Commission later moved to the University of Chicago and thereafter to Yale University. Many prominent American economists have been associated with the Commission.

[8] See Harry M. Markowitz, "Portfolio Selection," *Journal of Finance* (March 1952), pp. 77–91. The principles in Markowitz's article were then expanded in his book *Portfolio Selection*, Cowles Foundation Monograph 16 (New York: John Wiley, 1959).

Markowitz was interested in the investment decision-making process. Along the lines set forth by Pareto 60 years earlier, Markowitz assumed that investors order their preferences according to a *utility index*, with utility as a convex function that takes into account investors' risk-return preferences. Markowitz assumed that stock returns are jointly normal. As a consequence, the return of any portfolio is a normal distribution, which can be characterized by two parameters: the mean and the variance. Utility functions are therefore defined on two variables—mean and variance—and the Markowitz framework for portfolio selection is commonly referred to as *mean-variance analysis*. The mean and variance of portfolio returns are in turn a function of a portfolio's weights. Given the variance-covariance matrix, utility is a function of portfolio weights. The investment decision-making process involves maximizing utility in the space of portfolio weights.

After writing his seminal article, Markowitz joined the Rand Corporation, where he met George Dantzig. Dantzig introduced Markowitz to computer-based optimization technology.[9] The latter was quick to appreciate the role that computers would have in bringing mathematics to bear on business problems. Optimization and simulation were on the way to becoming the tools of the future, replacing the quest for closed-form solutions of mathematical problems.

In the following years, Markowitz developed a full theory of the investment management process based on optimization. His optimization theory had the merit of being applicable to practical problems, even outside of the realm of finance. With the progressive diffusion of high-speed computers, the practice of financial optimization has found broad application.[10]

---

[9] The inputs to the mean-variance analysis include expected returns, variance of returns, and either covariance or correlation of returns between each pair of securities. For example, an analysis that allows 200 securities as possible candidates for portfolio selection requires 200 expected returns, 200 variances of return, and 19,900 correlations or covariances. An investment team tracking 200 securities may reasonably be expected to summarize their analyses in terms of 200 means and variances, but it is clearly unreasonable for them to produce 19,900 carefully considered correlation coefficients or covariances. It was clear to Markowitz that some kind of model of the covariance structure was needed for the practical application of the model. He did little more than point out the problem and suggest some possible models of covariance for research to large portfolios. In 1963, William Sharpe suggested the single index market model as a proxy for the covariance structure of security returns ("A Simplified Model for Portfolio Analysis," *Management Science* (January 1963), pp. 277–293).

[10] In Chapter 16 we illustrate one application. For a more detailed discussion, see Frank J. Fabozzi, Francis Gupta, and Harry M. Markowitz, "The Legacy of Modern Portfolio Theory," *Journal of Investing* (Summer 2002), pp. 7–22.

UNDERSTANDING VALUE: MODIGLIANI AND MILLER

At about the same time that Markowitz was tackling the problem of how investors should behave, taking asset price processes as a given, other economists were trying to understand how markets determine value. Adam Smith had introduced the notion of perfect competition (and therefore perfect markets) in the second half of the eighteenth century. In a perfect market, there are no impediments to trading: Agents are price takers who can buy or sell as many units as they wish. The neoclassical economists of the 1960s took the idea of perfect markets as a useful idealization of real free markets. In particular, they argued that financial markets are very close to being perfect markets. The theory of asset pricing was subsequently developed to explain how prices are set in a perfect market.

In general, a *perfect market* results when the number of buyers and sellers is sufficiently large, and all participants are small enough relative to the market so that no individual market agent can influence a commodity's price. Consequently, all buyers and sellers are price takers, and the market price is determined where there is equality of supply and demand. This condition is more likely to be satisfied if the commodity traded is fairly homogeneous (for example, corn or wheat).

There is more to a perfect market than market agents being price takers. It is also required that there are no transaction costs or impediments that interfere with the supply and demand of the commodity. Economists refer to these various costs and impediments as "frictions." The costs associated with frictions generally result in buyers paying more than in the absence of frictions, and/or sellers receiving less. In the case of financial markets, frictions include:

- Commissions charged by brokers.
- Bid-ask spreads charged by dealers.
- Order handling and clearance charges.
- Taxes (notably on capital gains) and government-imposed transfer fees.
- Costs of acquiring information about the financial asset.
- Trading restrictions, such as exchange-imposed restrictions on the size of a position in the financial asset that a buyer or seller may take.
- Restrictions on market makers.
- Halts to trading that may be imposed by regulators where the financial asset is traded.

Modigliani-Miller Irrelevance Theorems and the Absence of Arbitrage

A major step was taken in 1958 when Franco Modigliani and Merton Miller published a then-controversial article in which they maintained that the value of a company does not depend on the capital structure of the firm.[11] (The *capital structure* of a firm is the mix of debt and equity.) The traditional view prior to the publication of the article by Modigliani and Miller was that there existed a capital structure that maximized the value of the firm (i.e., there is an optimal capital structure). Modigliani and Miller demonstrated that in the absence of taxes and in a perfect capital market, the capital structure was irrelevant (i.e., the capital structure does not affect the value of a firm).[12]

In 1961, Modigliani and Miller published yet another controversial article where they argued that the value of a company does not depend on the dividends it pays but on its earnings.[13] The basis for valuing a firm—earnings or dividends—had always attracted considerable attention. Because dividends provide the hard cash which remunerates investors, they were considered by many as key to a firm's value.

Modigliani and Miller's challenge to the traditional view that capital structure and dividends matter when determining a firm's value was founded on the principle that the traditional views were inconsistent with the workings of competitive markets where securities are freely traded. In their view, the value of a company is independent of its financial structure: from a valuation standpoint, it does not matter whether the firm keeps its earnings or distributes them to shareholders.

Known as the *Modigliani-Miller theorems*, these theorems paved the way for the development of arbitrage pricing theory. In fact, to establish their theorems, Modigliani and Miller made use of the notion of *absence of arbitrage*. Absence of arbitrage means that there is no possibility of making a risk-free profit without an investment. This implies that the same stream of cash flows should be priced in the same way across dif-

---

[11] Franco Modigliani and Merton H. Miller, "The Cost of Capital, Corporation Finance, and the Theory of Investment," *American Economic Review* (June 1958), pp. 261–297. In a later article, they corrected their analysis for the impact of corporate taxes: Franco Modigliani and Merton H. Miller, "Corporate Income Taxes and the Cost of Capital: A Correction," *American Economic Review* (June 1963), pp. 433–443.

[12] By extension, the irrelevance principle applies to the type of debt a firm may select (e.g., senior, subordinated, secured, and unsecured).

[13] Merton H. Miller and Franco Modigliani, "Dividend Policy, Growth, and the Valuation of Shares," *Journal of Business* (October 1961), pp. 411–433.

ferent markets. Absence of arbitrage is the fundamental principle for relative asset pricing; it is the pillar on which derivative pricing rests.

EFFICIENT MARKETS: FAMA AND SAMUELSON

Absence of arbitrage entails market efficiency. Shortly after the Modigliani-Miller theorems had been established, Paul Samuelson in 1965[14] and Eugene Fama in 1970[15] developed the notion of efficient markets: A market is efficient if prices reflect all available information. Bachelier had argued that prices in a competitive market should be random conditionally to the present state of affairs. Fama and Samuelson put this concept into a theoretical framework, linking prices to information.

As explained in the previous chapter, in general, an efficient market refers to a market where prices at all times fully reflect all available information that is relevant to the valuation of securities. That is, relevant information about the security is quickly impounded into the price of securities.

Fama and Samuelson define "fully reflects" in terms of the expected return from holding a security. The expected return over some holding period is equal to expected cash distributions plus the expected price change, all divided by the initial price. The price formation process defined by Fama and Samuelson is that the expected return one period from now is a stochastic variable that already takes into account the "relevant" information set. They argued that in a market where information is shared by all market participants, prices should fluctuate randomly.

A price-efficient market has implications for the investment strategy that investors may wish to pursue. In an active strategy, investors seek to capitalize on what they perceive to be the mispricing of financial instruments (cash instruments or derivative instruments). In a market that is price efficient, active strategies will not consistently generate a return after taking into consideration transaction costs and the risks associated with a strategy that is greater than simply buying and holding securities. This has lead investors in certain sectors of the capital market where empirical evidence suggests the sector is price efficient to pursue a strategy of *indexing*, which simply seeks to match the performance of some financial index. However Samuelson was careful to remark that the notion of efficient markets does not make investment analysis useless; rather, it is a condition for efficient markets.

---

[14] Paul A. Samuelson, "Proof the Properly Anticipated Prices Fluctuate Randomly," *Industrial Management Review* (Spring 1965), pp. 41–50.
[15] Eugene F. Fama, "The Behavior of Stock Market Prices," *Journal of Business* (January 1965), pp. 34–105.

Another facet in this apparent contradiction of the pursuit of active strategies despite empirical evidence on market efficiency was soon to be clarified. Agents optimize a risk-return trade-off based on the stochastic features of price processes. Price processes are not simply random but exhibit a rich stochastic behavior. The objective of investment analysis is to reveal this behavior (see Chapters 16 and 19).

CAPITAL ASSET PRICING MODEL: SHARPE, LINTNER, AND MOSSIN

Absence of arbitrage is a powerful economic principle for establishing relative pricing. In itself, however, it is not a market equilibrium model. William Sharpe (in 1964),[16] John Lintner (in 1965),[17] and Jan Mossin (in 1966),[18] developed a theoretical equilibrium model of market prices called the *Capital Asset Pricing Model* (CAPM). As anticipated 60 years earlier by Walras and Pareto, Sharpe, Lintner, and Mossin developed the consequences of Markowitz's portfolio selection into a full-fledged stochastic general equilibrium theory.

Asset pricing models categorize risk factors into two types. The first type is risk factors that cannot be diversified away via the Markowitz framework. That is, no matter what the investor does, the investor cannot eliminate these risk factors. These risk factors are referred to as *systematic risk factors* or *nondiversifiable risk factors*. The second type is risk factors that can be eliminated via diversification. These risk factors are unique to the asset and are referred to as *unsystematic risk factors* or *diversifiable risk factors*.

The CAPM has only one systematic risk factor—the risk of the overall movement of the market. This risk factor is referred to as "market risk." This is the risk associated with holding a portfolio consisting of all assets, called the "market portfolio." In the market portfolio, an asset is held in proportion to its market value. So, for example, if the total market value of all assets is $\$X$ and the market value of asset j is $\$Y$, then asset j will comprise $\$Y/\$X$ of the market portfolio.

---

[16] William F. Sharpe, "Capital Asset Prices," *Journal of Finance* (September 1964), pp. 425–442.

[17] John Lintner, "The Valuation of Risk Assets and the Selection of Risky Investments in Stock Portfolio and Capital Budgets," *Review of Economics and Statistics* (February 1965), pp. 13–37.

[18] Jan Mossin, "Equilibrium in a Capital Asset Market," *Econometrica* (October 1966), pp. 768–783.

The expected return for an asset *i* according to the CAPM is equal to the risk-free rate plus a risk premium. The risk premium is the product of (1) the sensitivity of the return of asset *i* to the return of the market portfolio and (2) the difference between the expected return on the market portfolio and the risk-free rate. It measures the potential reward for taking on the risk of the market above what can be earned by investing in an asset that offers a risk-free rate. Taken together, the risk premium is a product of the quantity of market risk and the potential compensation of taking on market risk (as measured by the second component).

The CAPM was highly appealing from the theoretical point of view. It was the first general-equilibrium model of a market that admitted testing with econometric tools. A critical challenge to the empirical testing of the CAPM is the identification of the market portfolio.[19]

THE MULTIFACTOR CAPM: MERTON

The CAPM assumes that the only risk that an investor is concerned with is uncertainty about the future price of a security. Investors, however, are usually concerned with other risks that will affect their ability to consume goods and services in the future. Three examples would be the risks associated with future labor income, the future relative prices of consumer goods, and future investment opportunities.

Recognizing these other risks that investors face, in 1976 Robert Merton extended the CAPM based on consumers deriving their optimal lifetime consumption when they face these "extra-market" sources of risk.[20] These extra-market sources of risk are also referred to as "factors," hence the model derived by Merton is called a *multifactor CAPM*.

The multifactor CAPM says that investors want to be compensated for the risk associated with each source of extra-market risk, in addition to market risk. In the case of the CAPM, investors hedge the uncertainty associated with future security prices by diversifying. This is done by holding the market portfolio. In the multifactor CAPM, in addition to investing in the market portfolio, investors will also allocate funds to something equivalent to a mutual fund that hedges a particular extra-market risk. While not all investors are concerned with the same sources of extra-market risk, those that are concerned with a specific extra-market risk will basically hedge them in the same way.

---

[19] Richard R. Roll, "A Critique of the Asset Pricing Theory's Tests," *Journal of Financial Economics* (March 1977), pp. 129–176.

[20] Robert C. Merton, "An Intertemporal Capital Asset Pricing Model," *Econometrica* (September 1973), pp. 867–888.

88   The Mathematics of Financial Modeling and Investment Management

The multifactor CAPM is an attractive model because it recognizes nonmarket risks. The pricing of an asset by the marketplace, then, must reflect risk premiums to compensate for these extra-market risks. Unfortunately, it may be difficult to identify all the extra-market risks and to value each of these risks empirically. Furthermore, when these risks are taken together, the multifactor CAPM begins to resemble the arbitrage pricing theory model described next.

ARBITRAGE PRICING THEORY: ROSS

An alternative to the equilibrium asset pricing model just discussed, an asset pricing model based purely on arbitrage arguments, was derived by Stephen Ross.[21] The model, called the *Arbitrage Pricing Theory* (APT) *Model*, postulates that an asset's expected return is influenced by a variety of risk factors, as opposed to just market risk as assumed by the CAPM. The APT model states that the return on a security is linearly related to H systematic risk factors. However, the APT model does not specify what the systematic risk factors are, but it is assumed that the relationship between asset returns and the risk factors is linear.

The APT model as given asserts that investors want to be compensated for all the risk factors that systematically affect the return of a security. The compensation is the sum of the products of each risk factor's systematic risk and the risk premium assigned to it by the capital market.

Proponents of the APT model argue that it has several major advantages over the CAPM. First, it makes less restrictive assumptions about investor preferences toward risk and return. As explained earlier, the CAPM theory assumes investors trade off between risk and return solely on the basis of the expected returns and standard deviations of prospective investments. The APT model, in contrast, simply requires that some rather unobtrusive bounds be placed on potential investor utility functions. Second, no assumptions are made about the distribution of asset returns. Finally, since the APT model does not rely on the identification of the true market portfolio, the theory is potentially testable. The model simply assumes that no arbitrage is possible. That is, using no additional funds (wealth) and without increasing risk, it is not possible for an investor to create a portfolio to increase return.

The APT model provides theoretical support for an asset pricing model where there is more than one risk factor. Consequently, models of

---

[21] Stephen A. Ross, "The Arbitrage Theory of Capital Asset Pricing," *Journal of Economic Theory* (December 1976), pp. 343–362.

this type are referred to as *multifactor risk models*. These models are applied to portfolio management.

ARBITRAGE, HEDGING, AND OPTION THEORY: BLACK, SCHOLES, AND MERTON

The idea of arbitrage pricing can be extended to any price process. A general model of asset pricing will include a number of independent price processes plus a number of price processes that depend on the first process by arbitrage. The entire pricing structure may or may not be cast in a general equilibrium framework.

Arbitrage pricing allowed derivative pricing. With the development of derivatives trading, the requirement of a derivative valuation and pricing model made itself felt. The first formal solution of the option pricing model was developed independently by Fisher Black and Myron Scholes in 1976,[22] working together, and in the same year by Robert Merton.[23]

The solution of the option pricing problem proposed by Black, Scholes, and Merton was simple and elegant. Suppose that a market contains a risk-free bond, a stock, and an option. Suppose also that the market is arbitrage-free and that stock price processes follow a continuous-time geometric Brownian motion (see Chapter 8). Black, Scholes, and Merton demonstrated that it is possible to construct a portfolio made up of the stock plus the bond that perfectly replicates the option. The replicating portfolio can be exactly determined, without anticipation, solving a partial differential equation.

The idea of replicating portfolios has important consequences. Whenever a financial instrument (security or derivative instrument) process can be exactly replicated by a portfolio of other securities, absence of arbitrage requires that the price of the original financial instrument coincide with the price of the replicating portfolio. Most derivative pricing algorithms are based on this principle: to price a derivative instrument, one must identify a replicating portfolio whose price is known.

Pricing by portfolio replication received a powerful boost with the discovery that calculations can be performed in a risk-neutral probability space where processes assume a simplified form. The foundation was thus laid for the notion of **equivalent martingales**, developed by Michael

---

[22] Fischer Black and Myron Scholes, "The Pricing of Options and Corporate Liabilities," *Journal of Political Economy* (1973), pp. 637–654.

[23] Robert C. Merton, "Theory of Rational Option Pricing," *Bell Journal of Economics and Management Science* (1973), pp. 141–183.

Harrison and David Kreps[24] and Michael Harrison and Stanley Pliska[25] in the late 1970s and early 1980s. Not all price processes can be reduced in this way: if price processes do not behave sufficiently well (i.e., if the risk does not vanish with the vanishing time interval), then replicating portfolios cannot be found. In these cases, risk can be minimized but not hedged.

SUMMARY

- The development of mathematical finance began at the end of the nineteenth century with work on general equilibrium theory by Walras and Pareto.
- At the beginning of the twentieth century, Bachelier and Lundberg made a seminal contribution, introducing respectively Brownian motion price processes and Markov Poisson processes for collective risk events.
- The advent of digital computers enabled the large-scale application of advanced mathematics to finance theory, ushering in optimization and simulation.
- In 1952, Markowitz introduced the theory of portfolio optimization which advocates the strategy of portfolio diversification.
- In 1961, Modigliani and Miller argued that the value of a company is based not on its dividends and capital structure, but on its earnings; their formulation was to be called the Modigliani-Miller theorem.
- In the 1960s, major developments include the efficient market hypothesis (Samuelson and Fama), the capital asset pricing model (Sharpe, Lintner, and Mossin), and the multifactor CAPM (Merton).
- In the 1970s, major developments include the arbitrage pricing theory (Ross) that lead to multifactor models and option pricing formulas (Black, Scholes, and Merton) based on replicating portfolios which are used to price derivatives if the underlying price processes are known.

---

[24] J. Michael Harrison and David M. Kreps, "Martingale and Arbitrage in Multiperiod Securities Markets," *Journal of Economic Theory* 20 (1979), pp. 381–408.
[25] Michael Harrison and Stanley Pliska, "Martingales and Stochastic Integrals in the Theory of Continuous Trading," *Stochastic Processes and Their Applications* (1981), pp. 313–316.

CHAPTER 4

Principles of Calculus

Invented in the seventeenth century independently by the British physicist Isaac Newton and the German philosopher G.W. Leibnitz, (infinitesimal) calculus was a major mathematical breakthrough; it was to make possible the modern development of the physical sciences. Calculus introduced two key ideas:

- The concept of instantaneous rate of change.
- A framework and rules for linking together quantities and their instantaneous rates of change.

Suppose that a quantity such as the price of a financial instrument varies as a function of time. Given a finite interval, the rate of change of that quantity is the ratio between the amount of change and the length of the time interval. Graphically, the rate of change is the steepness of the straight line that approximates the given curve.[1] In general, the rate of change will vary as a function of the length of the time interval.

What happens when the length of the time interval gets smaller and smaller? Calculus made the concept of infinitely small quantities precise with the notion of **limit**. If the rate of change can get arbitrarily close to a definite number by making the time interval sufficiently small, that number is the instantaneous rate of change. The **instantaneous rate of change** is the limit of the rate of change when the length of the interval gets infinitely small. This limit is referred to as the **derivative of a function,** or simply, **derivative.** Graphically, the derivative is the steepness of the tangent to a curve.

Starting from this definition and with the help of a number of rules for computing a derivative, it was shown that the instantaneous rate of

---

[1] The rate of change should not be confused with the return on an asset, which is the asset's percentage price change.

change of a number of functions—such as polynomials, exponentials, logarithms, and many more—can be explicitly computed as a closed formula. For example, the rate of change of a polynomial is another polynomial of a lower degree.

The process of computing a derivative, referred to as **differentiation,** solves the problem of finding the steepness of the tangent to a curve; the process of **integration** solves the problem of finding the area below a given curve. The reasoning is similar. The area below a curve is approximated as the sum of rectangles and is defined as the limit of these sums when the rectangles get arbitrarily small.

A key result of calculus is the discovery that integration and derivation are inverse operations: Integrating the derivative of a function yields the function itself. What was to prove even more important to the development of modern science was the possibility of linking together a quantity and its various instantaneous rates of change, thus forming **differential equations,** the subject of Chapter 9.

A **solution to a differential equation** is any function that satisfies it. A differential equation is generally satisfied by an infinite family of functions; however, if a number of initial values of the solutions are imposed, the solution can be uniquely identified. This means that if physical laws are expressed as differential equations, it is possible to exactly forecast the future development of a system. For example, knowing the differential equations of the motion of bodies in empty space, it is possible to predict the motion of a projectile knowing its initial position and speed. It is difficult to overestimate the importance of this principle. The fact that most laws of physics can be expressed as relationships between quantities and their instantaneous rates of change prompted the physicist Eugene Wigner's remark on the "unreasonable effectiveness of mathematics in the natural sciences."[2]

Mathematics has, however, been less successful in describing human artifacts such as the economy or financial markets. The problem is that no simple mathematical law can faithfully represent the evolution of observed quantities. A description of economic behavior requires the introduction of a certain amount of uncertainty in economic laws.

Uncertainty can be represented in various ways. It can, for example, be represented with concepts such as fuzziness and imprecision or more quantitatively as probability. In economics, uncertainty is usually represented within the **framework of probability.** Probabilistic laws can be cast in two mathematically equivalent ways:

---

[2] Eugene Wigner, "The Unreasonable Effectiveness of Mathematics in the Natural Sciences," *Communications in Pure and Applied Mathematics* 13, no. 1 (February 1960).

■ The evolution of probability distributions is represented through differential equations. This is the case within the framework of calculus.

■ The evolution of random phenomena is represented through direct relationships between stochastic processes. This is the case within the framework of stochastic calculus.

Stochastic calculus has been adopted as the preferred framework in finance and economics. We will start with a review of the key concepts of calculus and then introduce the concepts of its stochastic evolution.

SETS AND SET OPERATIONS

The basic concept in calculus (and in the theory of probability) is that of a **set**. A set is a collection of objects called elements. The notions of both element and set should be considered primitive. Following a common convention, let's denote sets with capital Latin or Greek letters: A,B,C,Ω... and elements with small Latin or Greek letters: a,b,ω. Let's then consider collections of sets. In this context, a set is regarded as an element at a higher level of aggregation. In some instances, it might be useful to use different alphabets to distinguish between sets and collections of sets.

Piling up sets and sets of sets is not as innocuous as it might seem; it is effectively the source of subtle and basic fundamental logical contradictions called **antinomies**. Mathematics requires that a distinction be made between **naive set theory,** which deals with basic set operations, and **axiomatic set theory,** which deals with the logical structure of set theory. In working with calculus, we can stay within the framework of naive set theory and thus consider only basic set operations.

Proper Subsets

An element a of a set A is said to belong to the set A written as $a \in A$. If every element that belongs to a set A also belongs to a set B, we say that A is contained in B and write: $A \subset B$. We will distinguish whether A is a **proper subset** of B (i.e., whether there is at least one element that belongs to B but not to A) or if the two sets might eventually coincide. In the latter case we write $A \subseteq B$.

For example, as explained in Chapter 2, in the United States there are indexes that are constructed based on the price of a subset of common stocks from the universe of all common stock in the country. There are three types of common stock (equity) indexes:

1. Produced by stock exchanges based on all stocks traded on the particular exchanges (the most well known being the New York Stock Exchange Composite Index).
2. Produced by organizations that subjectively select the stocks included in the index (the most popular being the Standard & Poor's 500).
3. Produced by organizations where the selection process is based on an objective measure such as market capitalization.

The Russell equity indexes, produced by Frank Russell Company, are examples of the third type of index. The Russell 3000 Index includes the 3,000 largest U.S. companies based on total market capitalization. It represents approximately 98% of the investable U.S. equity market. The Russell 1000 Index includes 1,000 of the largest companies in the Russell 3000 Index while the Russell 2000 Index includes the 2,000 smallest companies in the Russell 3000 Index. The Russell Top 200 Index includes the 200 largest companies in the Russell 1000 Index and the Russell Midcap Index includes the 800 smallest companies in the Russell 1000 Index. None of the indexes include non-U.S. common stocks.

Let us introduce the notation:

A = all companies in the United States that have issued common stock

I_{3000} = companies included in the Russell 3000 Index

I_{1000} = companies included in the Russell 1000 Index

I_{2000} = companies included in the Russell 2000 Index

I_{Top200} = companies included in the Russell Top 200 Index

I_{Micap} = companies included in the Russell Midcap200 Index

We can then write the following:

$I_{3000} \subset A$ (every company that is contained in the Russell 3000 Index is contained in the set of all companies in the United States that have issued common stock)

$I_{1000} \subset I_{3000}$ (the largest 1,000 companies contained in the Russell 1000 Index are contained in the Russell 3000 Index)

$I_{Micap} \subset I_{1000}$ (the 800 smallest companies in the Russell Midcap Index are contained in the Russell 1000 Index)

$I_{Top200} \subset I_{1000} \subset I_{3000} \subset A$

$I_{Micap} \subset I_{1000} \subset I_{3000} \subset A$

Throughout this book we will make use of the convenient logic symbols ∀ and ∃ that mean respectively, "for any element" and "an element exists such that." We will also use the symbol ⇒ that means "implies." For instance, if A is a set of real numbers and $a \in A$, the notation $\forall a$: $a < x$ means "for any number a smaller than x" and $\exists a$: $a < x$ means "there exists a number a smaller than x."

Empty Sets

Given a subset B of a set A, the complement of B with respect to A written as B^C is formed by all elements of A that do not belong to B. It is useful to consider sets that do not contain any elements called **empty sets**. The empty set is usually denoted by $\emptyset$. For example, using the Russell Indexes, the set of non-U.S. companies in the Russell 3000 Index whose stock is not traded in the United States is an empty set.

Union of Sets

Given two sets A and B, their **union** is formed by all individuals that belong to either A or B. This is written as $C = A \cup B$. For example,

$$I_{1000} \cup I_{2000} = I_{3000}$$ (the union of the companies contained in the Russell 1000 Index and the Russell 2000 Index is the set of all companies contained in the Russell 3000 Index)

$$I_{Micap} \cup I_{Top200} = I_{1000}$$ (the union of the companies contained in the Russell Midcap Index and the Russell Top 200 Index is the set of all companies contained in the Russell 1000 Index)

Intersection of Sets

Given two sets A and B, their **intersection** is formed by all elements that belong to both A and B. This is written as $C = A \cap B$. For example, let

$$I_{S\&P} = \text{companies included in the S\&P 500 Index}$$

The S&P 500 is a stock market index that includes 500 widely held common stocks representing about 77% of the New York Stock Exchange market capitalization. (*Market capitalization* for a company is the product of the market value of a share and the number of shares outstanding.) Then

$I_{S\&P} \cap I_{Top200} = C$ (the stocks contained in the S&P 500 Index that are the largest 200 companies in the Russell Index)

We can also write:

$I_{1000} \cap I_{2000} = \varnothing$ (companies included in both the Russell 2000 and the Russell 1000 Index is the empty set since there are no companies that are in both indexes)

Elementary Properties of Sets

Suppose that the set Ω includes all elements that we are presently considering (i.e., that it is the total set). Three elementary properties of sets are given below:

■ *Property 1.* The complement of the empty set is the total set:

$$\Omega^C = \varnothing, \varnothing^C = \Omega$$

■ *Property 2.* If A,B,C are subsets of Ω, then the distribution properties of union and intersection hold:

$$A \cup (B \cap C) = (A \cup B) \cap (A \cup C)$$

$$A \cap (B \cup C) = (A \cap B) \cup (A \cap C)$$

■ *Property 3.* The complement of the union is the intersection of the complements and the complement of the intersection is the union of the complements:

$$(B \cup C)^C = B^C \cap C^C$$

$$(B \cap C)^C = B^C \cup C^C$$

DISTANCES AND QUANTITIES

Calculus describes the dynamics of quantitative phenomena. This calls for equipping sets with a metric that defines distances between elements. Though many results of calculus can be derived in abstract metric spaces, standard calculus deals with sets of **n-tuples** of real numbers. In a quantitative framework, real numbers represent the result of observations (or measurements) in a simple and natural way.

n-tuples

An *n*-tuple, also called an **n-dimensional vector,** includes *n* components: $(a_1, a_2, ..., a_n)$. The set of all *n*-tuples of real numbers is denoted by R^n. The R stands for real numbers.[3]

For example, suppose the monthly rates of return on a portfolio in 2002 are as shown below along with the actual return for the S&P 500 (the benchmark index for the portfolio manager):[4]

Month	Portfolio	S&P 500
January	1.10%	−1.46%
February	1.37%	1.93%
March	2.95%	3.76%
April	5.78%	6.06%
May	0.51%	0.74%
June	7.32%	7.09%
July	7.13%	7.80%
August	1.47%	0.66%
September	9.54%	10.87%
October	7.32%	8.80%
November	6.19%	5.89%
December	−4.92%	−5.88%

Then the monthly returns r_{port} for the portfolio can be written as a 12-tuple and has the following 12 components:

$$r_{\text{port}} = \begin{bmatrix} 1.10\%, 1.37\%, 2.95\%, 5.78\%, 0.51\%, 7.32\%, \\ 7.13\%, 1.47\%, 9.54\%, 7.32\%, 6.19\%, -4.92\% \end{bmatrix}$$

Similarly, the return $r_{\text{S\&P}}$ on the S&P 500 can be expressed as a 12-tuple as follows:

---

[3] Where the components of an *n*-tuple are only integers, the set of *n*-tuples is denoted by Z^n, Z representing *zahlen,* which is German for integer.

[4] The monthly rate of return on the S&P 500 is computed as follows

$$\frac{\text{Dividends paid on all} + \text{Change in the index}}{\text{the stock in the index}} - 1$$
$$\frac{}{\text{Value of the index at the beginning of the period}}$$

$$r_{S\&P} = \begin{bmatrix} -1.46\%, \ 1.93\%, \ 3.76\%, \ 6.06\%, \ 0.74\%, \ 7.09\%, \\ 7.80\%, \ 0.66\%, \ 10.87\%, \ 8.80\%, \ 5.89\%, \ -5.88\% \end{bmatrix}$$

One can perform standard operations on n-tuples. For example, consider the portfolio returns in the two 12-tuples. The 12-tuple that expresses the deviation of the portfolio's performance from the benchmark index is computed by subtracting from each component of the return 12-tuple from the corresponding return on the S&P 500. That is,

$$r_{port} - r_{S\&P}$$

$$= \begin{bmatrix} 1.10\%, \ 1.37\%, \ 2.95\%, \ 5.78\%, \ 0.51\%, \ 7.32\%, \\ 7.13\%, \ 1.47\%, \ 9.54\%, \ 7.32\%, \ 6.19\%, \ -4.92\% \end{bmatrix}$$

$$- \begin{bmatrix} -1.46\%, \ 1.93\%, \ 3.76\%, \ 6.06\%, \ 0.74\%, \ 7.09\%, \\ 7.80\%, \ 0.66\%, \ 10.87\%, \ 8.80\%, \ 5.89\%, \ -5.88\% \end{bmatrix}$$

$$= \begin{bmatrix} 2.56\%, \ -0.56\%, \ -0.81\%, \ -0.28\%, \ -0.23\%, \ 0.23\%, \\ -0.67\%, \ 0.81\%, \ -1.33\%, \ -1.48\%, \ 0.30\%, \ 1.26\% \end{bmatrix}$$

It is the resulting 12-tuple that is used to compute the *tracking error* of a portfolio—the standard deviation of the variation of the portfolio's return from its benchmark index's return described in Chapter 19.

Coming back to the portfolio return, one can compute a logarithmic return for each month by adding 1 to each component of the 12-tuple and then taking the natural logarithm of each component. One can then obtain a geometric average, called the **geometric return**, by multiplying each component of the resulting vector and taking the 12th root.

Distance

Consider the real line R^1 (i.e., the set of real numbers). Real numbers include rational numbers and irrational numbers. A **rational number** is one that can be expressed as a fraction, c/d, where c and d are integers and $d \neq 0$. An **irrational number** is one that cannot be expressed as a fraction. Three examples of irrational numbers are

$$\sqrt{2} \cong 1.4142136$$

Ratio between diameter and circumference
$$= \pi \cong 3.1415926535897932384626$$

Natural logarithm $= e \cong 2.718281828459045235360287471352$

On the real line, distance is simply the absolute value of the difference between two numbers $|a - b|$ which also can be written as

$$\sqrt{(a-b)^2}$$

R^n is equipped with a natural metric provided by the Euclidean distance between any two points

$$d[(a_1, a_2, ..., a_n), (b_1, b_2, ..., b_n)] = \sqrt{\sum (a_i - b_i)^2}$$

Given a set of numbers A, we can define the least upper bound of the set. This is the smallest number s such that no number contained in the set exceeds s. The quantity s is called the **supremum** and written as s = sup$A$. More formally, the supremum is that number, if it exists, that satisfies the following properties:

$$\forall a: a \in A, s \geq a$$

$$\forall \varepsilon > 0, \exists a: s - a \leq \varepsilon$$

The supremum need not to belong to the set A. If it does, it is called the **maximum**.

Similarly, **infimum** is the greatest lower bound of a set A, defined as the greatest number s such that no number contained in the set is less than s. If infimum belongs to the set it is called the **minimum.**

Density of Points

A key concept of set theory with a fundamental bearing on calculus is that of the **density of points**. In fact, in financial economics we distinguish between discrete and continuous quantities. **Discrete quantities** have the property that admissible values are separated by finite distances. **Continuous quantities** are such that one might go from one to any of two possible values passing through every possible intermediate value. For instance, the passing of time between two dates is considered to occupy every possible instant without any gap.

The fundamental continuum is the set of real numbers. A **continuum** can be defined as any set that can be placed in a one-to-one relationship with the set of real numbers. Any continuum is an **infinite noncountable set**; a proper subset of a continuum can be a continuum. It can be demonstrated that a finite interval is a continuum as it can be placed in a one-to-one relationship with the set of all real numbers.

EXHIBIT 4.1   Bernoulli's Construction to Enumerate Rational Numbers

1/1	1/2	1/3	1/4
2/1	2/2	2/3	2/4
3/1	3/2	3/3	3/4
4/1	4/2	4/3	4/4

The intuition of a continuum can be misleading. To appreciate this, consider that the set of all rational numbers (i.e., the set of all fractions with integer numerator and denominator) has a dense ordering, i.e., has the property that given any two different rational numbers a,b with $a < b$, there are infinite other rational numbers in between. However, rational numbers have the cardinality of natural numbers. That is to say rational numbers can be put into a one-to-one relationship with natural numbers. This can be seen using a clever construction that we owe to the seventeenth century Swiss mathematician Jacob Bernoulli.

Using Bernoulli's construction, we can represent rational numbers as fractions of natural numbers arranged in an infinite two-dimensional table in which columns grow with the denominators and rows grow with the numerators. A one-to-one relationship with the natural numbers can be established following the path: (1,1) (1,2) (2,1) (3,1) (2,2) (1,3) (1,4) (2,3) (3,2) (4,1) and so on (see Exhibit 4.1).

Bernoulli thus demonstrated that there are as many rational numbers as there are natural numbers. Though the set of rational numbers has a dense ordering, rational numbers do not form a continuum as they cannot be put in a one-to-one correspondence with real numbers.

Given a subset A of R^n, a point $a \in A$ is said to be an **accumulation point** if any sphere centered in a contains an infinite number of points that belong to A. A set is said to be "closed" if it contains all of its own accumulation points and "open" if it does not.

FUNCTIONS

The mathematical notion of a function translates the intuitive notion of a relationship between two quantities. For example, the price of a security is a function of time: to each instant of time corresponds a price of that security.

Formally, a **function** f is a mapping of the elements of a set A into the elements of a set B. The set A is called the **domain** of the function. The subset $R = f(A) \subseteq B$ of all elements of B that are the mapping of some element in A is called the **range** R of the function f. R might be a proper subset of B or coincide with B.

The concept of function is general: the sets A and B might be any two sets, not necessarily sets of numbers. When the range of a function is real numbers, the function is said to be a **real function** or a **real-valued function**.

Two or more elements of A might be mapped into the same element of B. Should this situation never occur, that is, if distinct elements of A are mapped into distinct elements of B, the function is called an **injection**. If a function is an injection and $R = f(A) = B$, then f represents a one-to-one relationship between A and B. In this case the function f is invertible and we can define the **inverse function** $g = f^{-1}$ such that $f(g(a)) = a$.

Suppose that a function f assigns to each element x of set A some element y of set B. Suppose further that a function g assigns an element z of set C to each element y of set B. Combining functions f and g, an element z in set C corresponds to an element x in set A. This process results in a new function, function h, and that function takes an element in set A and assigns it to set C. The function h is called the composite of functions g and f, or simply a **composite function**, and is denoted by $h(x) = g[f(x)]$.

VARIABLES

In calculus one usually deals with functions of numerical variables. Some distinctions are in order. A **variable** is a symbol that represents any element in a given set. For example, if we denote time with a variable t, the letter t represents any possible moment of time. **Numerical variables** are symbols that represent numbers. These numbers might, in turn, represent the elements of another set. They might be thought of as numerical indexes which are in a one-to-one relationship with the elements of a set. For example, if we represent time over a given interval with a variable t, the letter t represents any of the numbers in the given interval. Each of these numbers in turn represents an instant of time. These distinctions might look pedantic but they are important for the following two reasons.

First, we need to consider **numeraire** or units of measure. Suppose, for instance, that we represent the price P of a security as a function of time t: $P = f(t)$. The function f links two sets of numbers that represent the physical quantities price and time. If we change the time scale or the currency, the numerical function f will change accordingly though the abstract function that links time and price will remain unchanged.

Second, in probability theory we will have to introduce random variables which are functions from states of the world to real numbers and not from real numbers to real numbers.

One important type of function is a sequence. A **sequence** is a mapping of the set of natural numbers into another set. For example a discrete-time, real-valued time series maps discrete instants of time into real numbers.

LIMITS

The notion of **limit** is fundamental in calculus. It applies to both functions and sequences. Consider an infinite sequence S of real numbers

$$S \equiv (a_1, a_2, ..., a_i, ...)$$

If, given any real number $\varepsilon > 0$, it is always possible to find a natural number $i(\varepsilon)$ such that

$$i \geq i(\varepsilon) \text{ implies } |a_i - a| < \varepsilon$$

then we write

$$\lim_{n \to \infty} a_n = a$$

and say that the sequence S tends to a when n tends to infinity, or that a is the limit of the sequence S.

Two aspects of this definition should be noted. First, ε can be chosen arbitrarily small. Second, for every choice of ε the difference, in absolute value, between the elements of the sequence S and the limit a is smaller than ε for every index i above $i(\varepsilon)$. This translates the notion that the sequence S gets arbitrarily close to a as the index i grows.

We can now define the concept of limit for functions. Suppose that a real function $y = f(x)$ is defined over an open interval (a,b), i.e., an interval that excludes its end points. If, given any real number $\varepsilon > 0$, it is always possible to find a positive real number $r(\varepsilon)$ such that

$$|x - c| < r(\varepsilon) \text{ implies } |y - d| < \varepsilon$$

then we write

$$\lim_{x \to c} f(x) = d$$

and say that the function f tends to the limit d when x tends to c.

These basic definitions can be easily modified to cover all possible cases of limits: infinite limits, limits from the left or from the right or finite limits when the variable tends to infinity. Exhibit 4.2 presents in graphical form these cases. Exhibit 4.3 lists the most common definitions, associating the relevant condition to each limit.

EXHIBIT 4.2   Graphical Presentation of Infinite Limits, Limits from the Left or Right, and Finite Limits

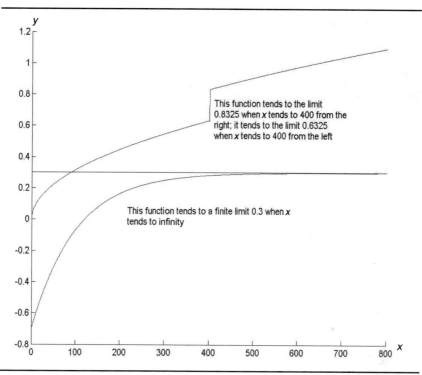

Note that the notion of limit can be defined only in a continuum. In fact, the limit of a sequence of rational numbers is not necessarily a rational number.

CONTINUITY

Continuity is a property of functions, a continuous function being a function that does not make jumps. Intuitively, a continuous function might be considered one that can be represented through an uninterrupted line in a Cartesian diagram. Its formal definition relies on limits.

A function f is said to be **continuous** at the point c if

$$\lim_{x \to c} f(x) = f(c)$$

EXHIBIT 4.3　Most Common Definitions Associating the Relevant Condition to Each Limit

The sequence tends to a finite limit	$\lim_{n \to \infty} a_n = a$	$\forall \varepsilon > 0, \exists i(\varepsilon): |a_n - a| < \varepsilon$ for $n > i(\varepsilon)$
The sequence tends to plus infinity	$\lim_{n \to \infty} a_n = +\infty$	$\forall D > 0, \exists i(D): a_n > D$ for $n > i(\varepsilon)$
The sequence tends to minus infinity	$\lim_{n \to \infty} a_n = -\infty$	$\forall D < 0, \exists i(D): a_n < D$ for $n > i(\varepsilon)$
Finite limit of a function	$\lim_{x \to c} f(x) = d$	$\forall \varepsilon > 0, \exists r(\varepsilon): |f(x) - d| < \varepsilon$ for $|x - c| < r(\varepsilon)$
Finite left limit of a function	$\lim_{x \to c^-} f(x) = d$	$\forall \varepsilon > 0, \exists r(\varepsilon): |f(x) - d| < \varepsilon$ for $|x - c| < r(\varepsilon), x < c$
Finite right limit of a function	$\lim_{x \to c^+} f(x) = d$	$\forall \varepsilon > 0, \exists r(\varepsilon): |f(x) - d| < \varepsilon$ for $|x - c| < r(\varepsilon), x > c$
Finite limit of a function when x tends to plus infinity	$\lim_{x \to +\infty} f(x) = d$	$\forall \varepsilon > 0, \exists R(\varepsilon) > 0: |f(x) - a| < \varepsilon$ for $x > R(\varepsilon)$
Finite limit of a function when x tends to minus infinity	$\lim_{x \to -\infty} f(x) = d$	$\forall \varepsilon > 0, \exists R(\varepsilon) > 0: |f(x) - a| < \varepsilon$ for $x < -R(\varepsilon)$
Infinite limit of a function	$\lim_{x \to c} |f(x)| = \infty$	$\forall D > 0, \exists r(D): |f(x)| > D$ for $|x - c| < r(D)$
Infinite limit of a function when x tends to plus infinity	$\lim_{x \to +\infty} f(x) = +\infty$	$\forall D > 0, \exists R(D): f(x) > D$ for $x > r(D)$

This definition does not imply that the function f is defined in an interval; it requires only that c be an accumulation point for the domain of the function f.

A function can be **right continuous** or **left continuous** at a given point if the value of the function at the point c is equal to its right or left limit respectively. A function f that is right or left continuous at the point c can make a jump provided that its value coincides with one of the two right or left limits. (See Exhibit 4.4.) A function $y = f(x)$ defined on an open interval (a,b) is said to be continuous on (a,b) if it is continuous for all $x \in (a,b)$.

A function can be **discontinuous** at a given point for one of two reasons: (1) either its value does not coincide with any of its limits at that point or (2) the limits do not exist. For example, consider a function f defined in the interval $[0,1]$ that assumes the value 0 at all rational points in that interval, and the value 1 at all other points. Such a func-

EXHIBIT 4.4   Graphical Illustration of Right Continuous and Left Continuous

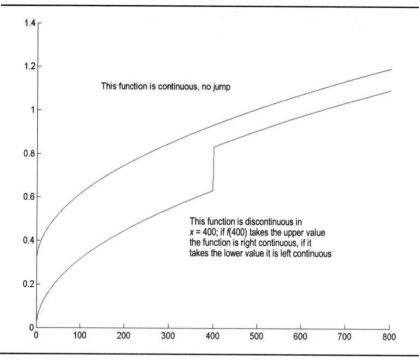

This function is continuous, no jump

This function is discontinuous in
x = 400; if f(400) takes the upper value
the function is right continuous, if it
takes the lower value it is left continuous

tion is not continuous at any point of [0,1] as its limit does not exist at any point of its domain.

TOTAL VARIATION

Consider a function $f(x)$ defined over a closed interval $[a,b]$. Then consider a partition of the interval $[a,b]$ into n disjoint subintervals defined by $n + 1$ points: $a = x_0 < x_1 < \ldots < x_{n-1} < x_n = b$ and form the sum

$$T = \sum_{i=1}^{n} |f(x_i) - f(x_{i-1})|$$

The supremum of the sum T over all possible partitions is called the **total variation** of the function f on the interval $[a,b]$. If the total variation is finite, the function f is said to have **bounded variation** or **finite variation**. Note that a function can be of infinite variation even if the function itself remains bounded. For example, the function that assumes the value 1 on rational numbers and 0 elsewhere is of infinite variation in any interval, though the function itself is finite.

Continuous functions might also exhibit infinite variation. The following function is continuous but with infinite variation in the interval [0,1]:

$$f(x) = \begin{cases} 0 \text{ for } x = 0 \\ x \sin\left(\dfrac{\pi}{x}\right) \text{ for } 0 < x \le 1 \end{cases}$$

DIFFERENTIATION

Given a function $y = f(x)$ defined on the open interval (a,b), consider its increments around a generic point x consequent to an increment h of the variable $x \in (a,b)$

$$\Delta y = f(x + h) - f(x)$$

Consider now the ratio $\Delta y/h$ between the increments of the dependent variable y and the independent variable x. Called the **difference quotient**, this quantity measures the average rate of change of y in some interval around x. For instance, if y is the price of a security and t is time, the difference quotient

$$\Delta y = \frac{y(t + h) - y(t)}{h}$$

represents the average price change per unit time over the interval $[t,t+h]$. The ratio $\Delta y/h$ is a function of h. We can therefore consider its limit when h tends to zero.

If the limit

$$f'(x) = \lim_{h \to 0} \frac{f(x + h) - f(x)}{h}$$

exists, we say that the function f is differentiable at x and that its derivative is f', also written as

$$\frac{df}{dx} \text{ or } \frac{dy}{dx}$$

The derivative of a function represents its instantaneous rate of change. If the function f is differentiable for all $x \in (a,b)$, then we say that f is differentiable in the open interval (a,b).

Introduced by Leibnitz, the notation dy/dx has proved useful; it suggests that the derivative is the ratio between two infinitesimal quantities and that calculations can be performed with infinitesimal quantities as well as with discrete quantities. When first invented, calculus was thought of as the "calculus of infinitesimal quantities" and was therefore called "infinitesimal calculus." Only at the end of the nineteenth century was calculus given a sound logical basis with the notion of the limit.[5] The infinitesimal notation remained, however, as a useful mechanical device to perform calculations. The danger in using the infinitesimal notation and computing with infinitesimal quantities is that limits might not exist. Should this be the case, the notation would be meaningless.

In fact, not all functions are differentiable; that is to say, not all functions possess a derivative. A function might be differentiable in some domain and not in others or be differentiable in a given domain with the exception of a few singular points. A prerequisite for a function to be differentiable at a point x is that it is continuous at the point.

However, continuity is not sufficient to ensure differentiability. This can be easily illustrated. Consider the Cartesian plot of a function f. Derivatives have a simple geometric interpretation: The value of the derivative of f at a point x equals the angular coefficient of the tangent of its plot in the same point (see Exhibit 4.5). A continuous function does not make jumps, while a differentiable function does not change direction by discrete amounts (i.e., it does not have cusps). A function can be continuous but not differentiable at some points. For example, the function $y = |x|$ at $x = 0$ is continuous but not differentiable. However, there are examples of functions that defy visual intuition; in fact, it is possible to demonstrate that there are functions that are continuous in a given interval but never differentiable. One such example is the path of a Brownian motion which we will discuss in Chapter 8.

Commonly Used Rules for Computing Derivatives

There are rules for computing derivatives. These rules are mechanical rules that apply provided that all derivatives exist. The proofs are provided in all standard calculus books. The *basic rules* are:

---

[5] In the 1970s the mathematician Abraham Robinson reintroduced on a sound logical basis the notion of infinitesimal quantities as the basis of a generalized calculus called "nonstandard analysis." See Abraham Robinson, *Non-Standard Analysis* (Princeton, NJ: Princeton University Press, 1996).

EXHIBIT 4.5   Geometric Interpretation of a Derivative

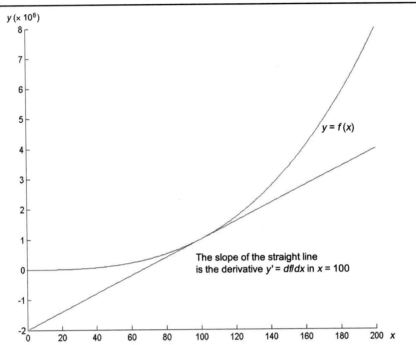

- *Rule 1:* $\dfrac{d}{dx}(c) = 0$, where c is a real constant.

- *Rule 2:* $\dfrac{d}{dx}(bx^n) = nbx^{n-1}$, where b is a real constant.

- *Rule 3:* $\dfrac{d}{dx}(af(x) + bg(x)) = a\dfrac{d}{dx}f(x) + b\dfrac{d}{dx}g(x)$, where a and b are real constants.

Rule 3 is called the rule of termwise differentiation and shows that differentiation is a linear operation.

Let's apply the basic rules to the following function:

$$y = a + b_1x + b_2x^2 + b_3x^3 + \ldots + b_kx^k$$

where a, b_1, b_2, b_3, ..., b_k are the constants.

The first term is just a and as per Rule 1 the derivative is zero. The derivative of $b_1 x$ by Rule 2 is b_1. For each term $b_n x^n$ by Rule 2 the derivative is $n b_n x^{n-1}$. Thus, the derivative of

$b_2 x^2$ is $2 b_2 x^1$

$b_3 x^3$ is $3 b_3 x^2$

$b_4 x^4$ is $4 b_4 x^3$

etc.

Therefore, the derivative of y is

$$\frac{dy}{dx} = b_1 + 2 b_2 x^1 + 3 b_3 x^2 + 4 b_4 x^3 + \ldots + n b_n x^{n-1}$$

There is a special rule for a **composite function**. Consider a composite function: $h(x) = f[g(x)]$. Provided that h and g are differentiable at the point x and that f is derivable at the point $s = g(x)$, then the following rule, called the **chain rule**, applies:

$$h'(x) = f'(g(x))g'(x)$$

$$h(x) = f(g(x))$$

$$\frac{dh}{dx} = \left(\frac{df}{dg}\right)\left(\frac{dg}{dx}\right)$$

Exhibit 4.6 shows the **sum rule, product rule, quotient rule,** and chain rule for calculating derivatives in both standard and infinitesimal notation. In Exhibit 4.6 it is assumed that a,b are real constants (i.e., fixed real numbers), that f, g, and h are functions defined in the same domain, and that all functions are differentiable at the point x. Exhibit 4.7 lists (without proof) a number of commonly used derivatives.

Given a function $f(x)$, its derivative $f'(x)$ represents its instantaneous rate of change. The logarithmic derivative

$$\frac{d}{dx} \ln P(x) = \frac{f'(x)}{f(x)}$$

for all x such that $P(x) \neq 0$, represents the instantaneous percentage change. In finance, the function $p = p(t)$ represents prices; its logarithmic derivative represents the instantaneous returns.

EXHIBIT 4.6   Commonly Used Rules of Derivation

	Function	Standard Notation		Infinitesimal Notation
Termwise differentiation	$h(x) = af(x) + bg(x)$	$h'(x) = af'(x) + bg'(x)$	or	$\dfrac{dh}{dx} = a\dfrac{df}{dx} + b\dfrac{dg}{dx}$
Product rule	$h(x) = f(x)g(x)$	$h'(x) = f'(x)g(x) + f(x)g'(x)$	or	$\dfrac{dh}{dx} = \dfrac{df}{dx}g + f\dfrac{dg}{dx}$
Quotient rule	$h(x) = \dfrac{1}{g(x)}$	$h'(x) = -\dfrac{g'(x)}{\left(g(x)\right)^2}$	or	$\dfrac{dh}{dx} = -\dfrac{1}{\left(g(x)\right)^2}\dfrac{dg}{dx}$
Chain rule	$h(x) = f(g(x))$	$h'(x) = f'(g(x))g'(x)$		$\dfrac{dh}{dx} = \dfrac{df}{dg}\dfrac{dg}{dx}$

EXHIBIT 4.7 Commonly Used Derivatives

$f(x)$	$\dfrac{df}{dx}$	Domain of P
x^n	nx^{n-1}	$R, x \neq 0$ if $n < 0$
x^α	$ax^{\alpha-1}$	$x > 0$
$\sin x$	$\cos x$	R
$\cos x$	$-\sin x$	R
$\tan x$	$\dfrac{1}{\cos^2(x)}$	$-\dfrac{\pi}{2} + n\dfrac{\pi}{2} < x < \dfrac{\pi}{2} + n\dfrac{\pi}{2}$
$\ln x$	$\dfrac{1}{x}$	$x > 0$
e^x	e^x	R
$\log (f(x))$	$\dfrac{f'(x)}{f(x)}$	$f(x) \neq 0$

Note: Where R denotes real numbers.

Given a function $y = f(x)$, its increments $\Delta f = f(x + \Delta x) - f(x)$ can be approximated by

$$\Delta f(x) = f'(x)\Delta x$$

The quality of this approximation depends on the function itself.

HIGHER ORDER DERIVATIVES

Suppose that a function $f(x)$ is differentiable in an interval D and its derivative is given by

$$f'(x) = \frac{df(x)}{dx}$$

The derivative might in turn be differentiable. The derivative of a derivative of a function is called a **second-order derivative** and is denoted by

$$f''(x) = \frac{d^2 f(x)}{dx^2} = \frac{d\left(\frac{df(x)}{dx}\right)}{dx}$$

Provided that the derivatives exist, this process can be iterated, producing derivatives of any order. A derivative of order n is written in the following way:

$$f^{(n)}(x) = \frac{d^n f(x)}{dx^n} = \frac{d\left(\frac{df^{n-1}(x)}{dx^{n-1}}\right)}{dx}$$

Application to Bond Analysis

Two concepts used in bond portfolio management, duration and convexity, provide an illustration of derivatives. A bond is a contract that provides a predetermined stream of positive cash flows at fixed dates assuming that the issuer does not default nor prepay the bond issue prior to the stated maturity date. If the interest rate is the same for each period, the present value of a risk-free bond has the following expression:

$$V = \frac{C}{(1+i)^1} + \frac{C}{(1+i)^2} + \dots + \frac{C+M}{(1+i)^N}, i = 1,\dots,N$$

If interest rates are different for each period, the previous formula becomes

$$V = \frac{C}{(1+i_1)^1} + \frac{C}{(1+i_2)^2} + \dots + \frac{C+M}{(1+i_N)^N}, i = 1,\dots,N$$

In Chapter 8, we introduce the concept of continuous compounding. With continuous compounding, if the short-term interest rate is constant, the bond valuation formula becomes[6]

---

[6] If the short-term rate is variable:

$$V = Ce^{-\int_0^1 i(s)ds} + Ce^{-\int_0^2 i(s)ds} + \dots + (C+M)e^{-\int_0^N i(s)ds}$$

$$V = \frac{C}{e^{1i}} + \frac{C}{e^{2i}} + \ldots + \frac{C+M}{e^{Ni}}$$

Application of the First Derivative

The sensitivity of the bond price V to a change in interest rates is given by the first derivative of V with respect to the interest rate i. The first derivative of V with respect to the interest rate i is called *dollar duration*. We can compute dollar duration in each case using the derivation formulas defined thus far. In the discrete-time case we can write

$$
\begin{aligned}
\frac{dV(i)}{di} &= \frac{d}{di}\left(\frac{C}{(1+i)^1} + \frac{C}{(1+i)^2} + \ldots + \frac{C+M}{(1+i)^N} \right) \\
&= \frac{d}{di}\left[\frac{C}{(1+i)^1} \right] + \ldots + \frac{d}{di}\left[\frac{C+M}{(1+i)^N} \right] \\
&= C\frac{d}{di}\left[\frac{1}{(1+i)^1} \right] + \ldots + (C+M)\frac{d}{di}\left[\frac{1}{(1+i)^N} \right]
\end{aligned}
$$

We can use the quotient rule

$$\frac{d}{dx}\left[\frac{1}{f(x)} \right] = -\frac{1}{f^2(x)}f'(x)$$

to compute the derivatives of the generic summand as follows:

$$\frac{d}{di}\left[\frac{1}{(1+i)^i} \right] = -\frac{1}{(1+i)^{2i}}i(1+i)^{i-1} = -i\frac{1}{(1+i)^{i+1}}$$

Therefore, the derivative of the bond value V with respect to the interest rates is

$$\frac{dV}{di} = -(1+i)^{-1}[C(1+i)^{-1} + 2C(1+i)^{-2} + \ldots + N(C+M)(1+i)^{-N}]$$

Using a similar reasoning, we can slightly generalize this formula, allowing the interest rates to be different for each period. Call i_t the interest rate for period t. The sequence of values is called the yield curve. We will have more to say about the yield curve in Chapter 20.

Now suppose that interest rates are subject to a parallel shift. In other words, let's assume that the interest rate for period t is $(i_t + x)$. If we compute the first derivative with respect to x for $x = 0$, we obtain

$$\left. \frac{dV(i)}{dx} \right|_{x=0} = \left. \frac{d}{dx}\left(\frac{C}{(1+i_1+x)^1} + \frac{C}{(1+i_2+x)^2} + \dots + \frac{C}{(1+i_N+x)^N} \right) \right|_{x=0}$$

$$= -[C(1+i_1)^{-2} + 2C(1+i_2)^{-3} + \dots + N(C+M)(1+i_N)^{-N-1}]$$

In this case we cannot factorize any term as interest rates are different in each period. Obviously, if interest rates are constant, the yield curve is a straight line and a change in the interest rates can be thought of as a parallel shift of the yield curve.

In the continuous-time case, assuming that interest rates are constant, the dollar duration is[7]

$$\frac{dV}{di} = \frac{d[Ce^{-1i} + Ce^{-2i} + \dots + (C+M)e^{-Ni}]}{di}$$

$$= -1Ce^{-1i} - 2Ce^{-2i} - \dots - N(C+M)e^{-Ni}$$

where we make use of the rule

---

[7] When interest rates are deterministic but time-dependent, the derivative dV/di is computed as follows. Assume that interest rates experience a parallel shift $i(t) + x$ and compute the derivative with respect to x evaluated at $x = 0$. To do this, we need to compute the following derivative:

$$\frac{d}{dx}e^{-\int_0^t [i(s)+x]ds} = \frac{d}{dx}\left[e^{-\int_0^t i(s)ds} e^{-\int_0^t x ds} \right] = e^{-\int_0^t i(s)ds} \frac{d}{dx}(e^{-xt})$$

$$= -te^{-xt}e^{-\int_0^t i(s)ds}$$

$$\left. \frac{d}{dx}e^{-\int_0^t [i(s)+x]ds} \right|_{x=0} = \left. -te^{-xt}e^{-\int_0^t i(s)ds} \right|_{x=0} = -te^{-\int_0^t i(s)ds}$$

Therefore, we can write the following:

$$\left. \frac{dV}{dx} \right|_{x=0} = -Ce^{-\int_0^1 i(s)ds} - 2Ce^{-\int_0^2 i(s)ds} - \dots - N(C+M)e^{-\int_0^N i(s)ds}$$

For i = constant we find again the formula established above.

$$\frac{d}{dx}(e^x) = e^x$$

Application of the Chain Rule

The above formulas express dollar duration which is the derivative of the price of a bond with respect with the interest rate and which approximates price changes due to small parallel interest rate shifts. Practitioners, however, are more interested in the percentage change of a bond price with respect to small parallel changes in interest rates. The percentage change is the price change divided by the bond value:

$$\frac{dV}{di}\frac{1}{V}$$

The percentage price change is approximated by *duration,* which is the derivative of a bond's value with respect to interest rates divided by the value itself. Recall from the formulas for derivatives that the latter is the logarithmic derivative of a bond's price with respect to interest rates:

$$\text{Duration} = \frac{dV}{di}\frac{1}{V} = \frac{d(\log V)}{di}$$

Based on the above formulas, we can write the following formulas for duration:

Duration for constant interest rates in discrete time:

$$\frac{dV}{di}\frac{1}{V} = -\frac{1}{V(1+i)}\left[\frac{C}{(1+i)} + \frac{2C}{(1+i)^2} + \ldots + \frac{N(C+M)}{(1+i)^N}\right]$$

Duration for variable interest rates in discrete time:

$$\frac{dV}{dx}\frac{1}{V} = -\frac{1}{V}\left[\frac{C}{(1+i_1)^2} + \frac{2C}{(1+i_2)^3} + \ldots + \frac{N(C+M)}{(1+i_N)^{N+1}}\right]$$

Duration for continuously compounding constant interest rate in discrete time:[8]

$$\frac{dV}{di}\frac{1}{V} = -\frac{1}{V}[Ce^{-i} + 2Ce^{-2i} + \dots + N(C+M)e^{-Ni}]$$

We will now illustrate the chain rule of derivation by introducing the concept of effective duration. In Chapter 2, we described the different features of bonds. The bond valuation we presented earlier is for an option-free bond. But when a bond has an embedded option, such as a call option as discussed in Chapter 2, it is more complicated to value. Similarly, the sensitivity of the value of a bond to changes in interest rates is more complicated to assess when there is an embedded call option. Intuitively, we know that the sensitivity of the value of a bond with an embedded option would be sensitive to not only how changes in interest rates affect the present value of the cash flows as shown above for an option-free bond, but also how they would affect the value of the embedded option.

We will use the following notation to assess the sensitivity of a callable bond's value (i.e., a bond with an embedded call option) to a change in interest rates. The value of an option-free bond can be decomposed as follows:

$$V_{ofb} = V_{cb} + V_{co}$$

where

V_{ofb} = value of an option-free bond
V_{cb} = value of a callable bond
V_{co} = value of a call option on the bond

The above equation says that an option-free bond's value depends on the sum of the value of a callable bond's value and a call option on that option-free bond. The equation can be rewritten as follows:

$$V_{cb} = V_{ofb} - V_{co}$$

---

[8] The duration for continuously compounding variable interest rate in discrete time is

$$\frac{dV}{di}\frac{1}{V} = -\frac{1}{V}\left[Ce^{-\int_0^1 i(s)ds} + 2Ce^{-\int_0^2 i(s)ds} + \dots + N(C+M)e^{-\int_0^N i(s)ds}\right]$$

That is, the value of a callable bond is found by subtracting the value of the call option from the value of the option-free bond. Both components on the right side of the valuation equation depend on the interest rate i. Using linearity to compute the first derivative of the valuation equation with respect to i and dividing both sides of the equation by the callable bond's value gives

$$\frac{dV_{cb}}{di}\frac{1}{V_{cb}} = \frac{dV_{ofb}}{di}\frac{1}{V_{cb}} - \frac{dV_{co}}{di}\frac{1}{V_{cb}}$$

Multiplying the numerator and denominator of the right-hand side by the value of the option-free bond and rearranging terms gives

$$\frac{dV_{cb}}{di}\frac{1}{V_{cb}} = \frac{dV_{ofb}}{di}\frac{1}{V_{ofb}}\frac{V_{ofb}}{V_{cb}} - \frac{dV_{co}}{di}\frac{1}{V_{ofb}}\frac{V_{ofb}}{V_{cb}}$$

The above equation is the sensitivity of a callable bond's value to changes in interest rates. That is, it is the duration of a callable bond, which we denote by Dur_{CB}.[9] The component given by

$$\frac{dV_{ofb}}{di}\frac{1}{V_{ofb}}$$

is the duration of an option-free bond's value to changes in interest rates, which we denote by Dur_{ofb}. Thus, we can have

$$Dur_{cb} = Dur_{ofb}\frac{V_{ofb}}{V_{cb}} - \frac{dV_{co}}{di}\frac{1}{V_{ofb}}\frac{V_{ofb}}{V_{cb}}$$

Now let's look at the derivative, which is the second term in the above equation. The change in the value of an option when the price of the underlying changes is called the option's *delta*. In the case of an option on a bond, as explained above, changes in interest rates change the value of a bond. In turn, the change in the value of the bond changes the value of the embedded option. Here is where we see a function of a function and the need to apply the chain rule. That is,

---

[9] Actually, it is equal to $-Dur_{cb}$, but because we will be omitting the negative sign for the durations on the right-hand side, this will not affect our derivation.

$$V_{co}(i) = f[V_{ofb}(i)]$$

This tells us that the value of the call option on an option-free bond depends on the value of the option-free bond and the value of the option-free bond depends on the interest rate. Now let's apply the chain rule. We get

$$\frac{dV_{co}(i)}{di} = \frac{df}{dV_{ofb}}\frac{dV_{ofb}}{di}$$

The first term on the right-hand side of the equation is the change in the value of the call option for a change in the value of the option-free bond. This is the delta of the call option, Δ_{co}. Thus,

$$\frac{dV_{co}(i)}{di} = -\Delta_{co}\frac{dV_{ofb}}{di}$$

Substituting this equation into the equation for the duration and rearranging terms we get

$$Dur_{cb} = Dur_{ofb}\frac{V_{ofb}}{V_{cb}}(1 - \Delta_{co})$$

This equation tells us that the duration of the callable bond depends on the following three quantities. The first quantity is the duration of the corresponding option-free bond. The second quantity is the ratio of the value of the option-free bond to the value of the callable bond. The difference between the value of an option-free bond and the value of a callable bond is equal to the value of the call option. The greater (smaller) the value of the call option, the higher (lower) the ratio. Thus, we see that the duration of the callable bond will depend on the value of the call option. Basically, this ratio indicates the leverage effectively associated with the position. The third and final quantity is the delta of the call option. The duration of the callable bond as given by the above equation is called the *option-adjusted duration* or *effective duration*.

Application of the Second Derivative

We can now compute the second derivative of the bond value with respect to interest rates. Assuming cash flows do not depend on interest rates, this second derivative is called *dollar convexity*. Dollar convexity divided by the bond's value is called *convexity*. In the discrete-time fixed interest rate case, the computation of convexity is based on the second derivatives of the generic summand:

$$\frac{d^2}{di^2}\left[\frac{1}{(1+i)^t}\right] = \frac{d}{di}\left\{\frac{d}{di}\left[\frac{1}{(1+i)^t}\right]\right\} = \frac{d}{di}\left[-t\frac{1}{(1+i)^{t+1}}\right]$$

$$= -t\frac{d}{di}\left[\frac{1}{(1+i)^{t+1}}\right] = t(1+t)\frac{1}{(1+i)^{t+2}}$$

Therefore, dollar convexity assumes the following expression:

$$\frac{d^2 V(i)}{di^2} = \frac{d^2}{di^2}\left[\frac{C}{(1+i)^1} + \frac{C}{(1+i)^2} + \dots + \frac{C+M}{(1+i)^N}\right]$$

$$= C\frac{d^2}{di^2}\left[\frac{1}{(1+i)^1}\right] + \dots + (C+M)\frac{d^2}{di^2}\left[\frac{1}{(1+i)^N}\right]$$

$$= [2C(1+i)^{-3} + 2\cdot 3C(1+i)^{-4} + \dots$$
$$+ N(N+1)(C+M)(1+i)^{-(N+2)}]$$

Using the same reasoning as before, in the variable interest rate case, dollar convexity assumes the following expression:

$$\left.\frac{d^2 V(i)}{dx^2}\right|_{x=0} = [2C(1+i_1)^{-3} + 2\cdot 3\cdot C(1+i_2)^{-4} + \dots$$

$$+ N(N+1)(C+M)(1+i_N)^{-N-2}]$$

This scheme changes slightly in the continuous-time case, where, assuming that interest rates are constant, the expression for convexity is[10]

---

[10] For variable interest rates this expression becomes

$$\left.\frac{dV}{dx}\right|_{x=0} = 1^2 Ce^{-\int_0^1 i(s)ds} + 2^2 Ce^{-\int_0^2 i(s)ds} + \dots + N^2(C+M)e^{-\int_0^N i(s)ds}$$

$$\frac{d^2V}{di^2} = \frac{d^2[Ce^{-i} + Ce^{-2i} + \ldots + (C+M)e^{-Ni}]}{di^2}$$

$$= 1^2 \cdot Ce^{-i} + 2^2 \cdot Ce^{-2i} + \ldots + N^2 \cdot (C+M)e^{-Ni}$$

where we make use of the rule

$$\frac{d^2}{dx^2}(e^x) = e^x$$

We can now write the following formulas for convexity:

Convexity for constant interest rates in discrete time:

$$\frac{dV^2}{di^2}\frac{1}{V} = \frac{1}{V(1+i)^2}\left[\frac{2C}{(1+i)} + \frac{(3)(2)C}{(1+i)^2} + \ldots + \frac{N(N+1)(C+M)}{(1+i)^N}\right]$$

Convexity for variable interest rates in discrete time:

$$\frac{d^2V}{dx^2}\frac{1}{V} = \frac{1}{V}\left[\frac{2C}{(1+i_1)^3} + \frac{(3)(2)C}{(1+i_2)^4} + \ldots + \frac{N(N+1)(C+M)}{(1+i_N)^{N+2}}\right]$$

Convexity for continuously compounding constant interest rate in discrete time:[11]

$$\frac{d^2V}{di^2}\frac{1}{V} = \frac{1}{V}[Ce^{-i} + 2^2Ce^{-2i} + \ldots + N^2(C+M)e^{-Ni}]$$

---

[11] The convexity for continuously compounding variable interest rate in discrete time is

$$\frac{d^2V}{di^2}\frac{1}{V} = \frac{1}{V}\left[Ce^{-\int_0^1 i(s)ds} + 2^2Ce^{-\int_0^2 i(s)ds} + \ldots + N^2(C+M)e^{-\int_0^N i(s)ds}\right]$$

TAYLOR SERIES EXPANSION

An important relationship used in economics and finance theory to approximate how the value of a function, such as a price function, will change is the **Taylor series expansion**. We begin by establishing **Taylor's theorem**. Consider a continuous function with continuous derivatives up to order n in the closed interval $[a,b]$ and differentiable with continuous derivatives in the open interval (a,b) up to order $n + 1$. It can be demonstrated that there exists a point $\xi \in (a,b)$ such that

$$f(b) = f(a) + f'(a)(b - a) + \frac{f''(a)(b-a)^2}{2!} + \dots + \frac{f^{(n)}(a)(b-a)^n}{n!} + R_n$$

where the residual R_n can be written in either of the following forms:

$$\textit{Lagrange's form: } R_n = \frac{f^{(n+1)}(\xi)(b-a)^{n+1}}{(n+1)!}$$

$$\textit{Cauchy's form: } R_n = \frac{f^{(n+1)}(\xi)(b-\xi)^n(b-a)}{n!}$$

In general, the point $\xi \in (a,b)$ is different in the two forms. This result can be written in an alternative form as follows. Suppose x and x_0 are in (a,b). Then, using Lagrange's form of the residual, we can write

$$f(x) = f(x_0) + f'(x)(x - x_0) + \frac{f''(x)(x-x_0)^2}{2!} + \dots + \frac{f^{(n)}(x)(x-x_0)^n}{n!}$$
$$+ \frac{f^{(n+1)}(\xi)(x-x_0)^{n+1}}{(n+1)!}$$

If the function f is infinitely differentiable, i.e., it admits derivatives of every order and if

$$\lim_{n \to \infty} R_n = 0$$

the infinite series obtained is called a **Taylor series expansion** (or **simply Taylor series**) for $f(x)$. If $x_0 = 0$, the series is called a **Maclaurin series**.

Such series, called **power series**, generally converge in some interval, called **interval of convergence**, and diverge elsewhere.

The Taylor series expansion is a powerful analytical tool. To appreciate its importance, consider that a function that can be expanded in a power series is represented by a denumerable set of numbers even if it is a continuous function. Consider also that the action of any linear operator on the function f can be represented in terms of its action on powers of x.

The Maclaurin expansion of the exponential and of trigonometric functions are given by:

$$e^x = 1 + x + \frac{x^2}{2!} + \dots + \frac{x^n}{n!} + R_n$$

$$\sin x = x - \frac{x^3}{3!} + \frac{x^5}{5!} + \dots + \frac{(-1)^n x^{2n+1}}{(2n+1)!} + R_n$$

$$\cos x = 1 - \frac{x^2}{2!} + \frac{x^4}{4!} + \dots + \frac{(-1)^n x^{2n}}{(2n)!} + R_n$$

Application to Bond Analysis

Let's illustrate Taylor and Maclaurin power series by computing a second-order approximation of the changes in the present value of a bond due to a parallel shift of the yield curve. This information is important to portfolio managers and risk managers to control the interest rate risk exposure of a position in bonds. In bond portfolio management, the first two terms of the Taylor expansion series are used to approximate the change in an option-free bond's value when interest rates change. An approximation based on the first two terms of the Taylor series is called a **second order approximation**, because it considers only first and second powers of the variable.

We begin with the bond valuation equation, again assuming a single discount rate. We first compute dollar duration and convexity, i.e., the first and second derivatives with respect to x evaluated at $x = 0$, and we expand in Maclaurin power series. We obtain

$$V(x) = V(0) - (\text{Dollar duration})x + \frac{1}{2}(\text{Dollar convexity})x^2 + R_3$$

We can write this expression explicitly as:

$$V(x) = \frac{C}{(1+i)^1} + \frac{C}{(1+i)^2} + \dots + \frac{C+M}{(1+i)^N}$$

$$-x\left[\frac{C}{(1+i)^2} + \frac{C}{(1+i)^3} + \dots + \frac{N(C+M)}{(1+i)^{N+1}}\right]$$

$$+\frac{1}{2}x^2\left[\frac{2C}{(1+i)^3} + \frac{3\cdot 2\cdot C}{(1+i)^4} + \dots + \frac{(N(N+1))(C+M)}{(1+i)^{N+2}}\right]$$

$$-\frac{1}{3\cdot 2}x^3\left[\frac{3\cdot 2\cdot C}{(1+i+\xi)^4} + \frac{4\cdot 3\cdot 2\cdot C}{(1+i+\xi)^5} + \dots\right.$$

$$+\frac{N(N+1)(N+2)(C+M)}{(1+i+\xi)^{N+3}}$$

Asset managers, however, are primarily interested in percentage price change. We can now compute the percentage price change as follows:

$$\frac{\Delta V}{V} = \frac{V(x)-V(0)}{V(0)}$$

$$= -x\left[\left[\frac{C}{(1+i)^2} + \frac{C}{(1+i)^3} + \dots + \frac{N(C+M)}{(1+i)^{N+1}}\right]\right.$$

$$\times \frac{1}{\left[\dfrac{C}{(1+i)^1} + \dfrac{C}{(1+i)^2} + \dots + \dfrac{C+M}{(1+i)^N}\right]}$$

$$+\frac{1}{2}x^2\left[\left[\frac{2\cdot C}{(1+i)^3} + \frac{3\cdot 2\cdot C}{(1+i)^4} + \dots + \frac{N(N+1)(C+M)}{(1+i)^{N+2}}\right]\right.$$

$$\times \frac{1}{\left[\dfrac{C}{(1+i)^1} + \dfrac{C}{(1+i)^2} + \dots + \dfrac{C+M}{(1+i)^N}\right]}$$

$$-\frac{1}{3 \cdot 2}x^3 \left[\left[\frac{3 \cdot 2 \cdot C}{(1+i+\xi)^4} + \cdots + \frac{N(N+1)(N+2)(C+M)}{(1+i+\xi)^{N+3}}\right]\right]$$

$$\frac{1}{\left[\frac{C}{(1+i)^1} + \frac{C}{(1+i)^2} + \cdots + \frac{C+M}{(1+i)^N}\right]}$$

The first term in the square brackets on the right-hand side of the equation is the first approximation and is the approximation based on the duration of the bond. The second term in the square brackets on the right-hand side is the second derivative, the convexity measure, multiplied by one half. The third term is the residual. Its size is responsible for the quality of the approximation.

The residual is proportional to the third power of the interest rate shift x. The term in the square bracket of the residual is a rather complex function of $C, M, N,$ and i. A rough approximation of this term is $N(N+1)(N+2)$. In fact, in the case of zero-coupon bonds, i.e., $C = 0$, the residual can be written as

$$R_3 = -\frac{1}{3 \times 2}x^3 \left[\left(\frac{N(N+1)(N+2)M}{(1+i+\xi)^{N+3}}\right)\frac{1}{\left[\frac{M}{(1+i)^N}\right]}\right]$$

$$= N(N+1)(N+2)\frac{(1+i)^N}{(1+i+\xi)^{N+3}}$$

which is a third order polynomial in N.

Therefore, the error of the second order approximation is of the order $[1/(3 \times 2)](xN)^3$. For instance, if $x = 0.01$ and $N = 20$ years, the approximation error is of the order 0.001. The following numerical example will clarify these derivations.

In Chapter 2 we discussed the features of bonds. In our illustration to demonstrate how to use the Taylor series, we will use an option-free bond with a coupon rate of 9% that pays interest semiannually and has 20 years to maturity. Suppose that the initial yield is 6%. In terms of our bond valuation equation, this means C = \$4.5, M = \$100, and i = 0.06. Substituting these values into the bond valuation equation, the price of the bond is \$134.6722.

Suppose that we want to know the approximate percentage price change if the interest rate (i.e., i) increases instantaneously from 6% to 8%. In the bond market, a change in interest rates is referred to in terms of *basis points*. One basis point is equal to 0.0001 and therefore 1 percentage point is 100 basis points. In our illustration we are looking at an instantaneous change in interest rates of 200 basis points. We will use the two terms of the Taylor expansion series to show the approximate percentage change in the bond's value for a 200 basis point increase in interest rates.

We do know what the answer is already. The initial value for this bond is \$134.6722. If the interest rate is 8%, the value of this bond would be \$109.8964. This means that the bond's value declines by 18.4%. Let's see how well the Taylor expansion series using only two terms approximates this change.

The first approximation is the estimate using duration. The duration for this bond is 10.66 found by using the formula above for duration. The convexity measure for this bond is 164.11 The change in interest rates, di, is 200 basis points. Expressed in decimal it is 0.02. The first term of the Taylor expansion series gives

$$-10.66 \times (0.02) = -0.2132 = -21.32\%$$

Notice that this approximation overestimates the actual change in value, which is −18.4% and means that the estimated new value for the bond is underestimated.

Now we add the second approximation. The second term of the Taylor series gives

$$\tfrac{1}{2}(164.11) \times (0.02)^2 = 3.28\%$$

The approximate percentage change in the bond's value found by using the first term of the Taylor series and the second term of the Taylor series is −21.32% + 3.28% = −18.0%. The actual percentage change in value is −18.4%. Thus the two terms of the Taylor series do an excellent job of approximating the percentage change in value.

Let's look at what would happen if the change in interest rates is a decline from 6% to 4%. The exact percentage change in value is +25.04% (from 134.6722 to 168.3887). Now the change in interest rates di is −0.02. Notice that the approximate change in value due to duration is the same except for a change in sign. That is, the approximate change based on the first term (duration) is +21.32%. Since the percentage price change is underestimated, the new value of the bond is underestimated. The change due to the second term of the Taylor series is the same in magnitude and sign since when –0.02 is squared, it gives a positive value. Thus, the approximate change is 21.32% + 3.28% = 24.6%. Using the terms of the Taylor series does a good job of estimating the change in the bond's value.

We used a relatively large change in interest rates to see how well the two terms of the Taylor series approximate the percentage change in a bond's value. For a small change in interest rates, duration does an effective job. For example, suppose that the change in interest rates is 10 basis points. That is, di is 0.001. For an increase in interest rates from 6% to 6.1% the actual change in the bond's value would be –1.06% ($134.6722 to $133.2472). Using just the first term of the Taylor series, the approximate change in the bond's value gives the precise change:

$$-10.66 \times 0.001 = -1.066\%$$

For a decrease in interest rates by 10 basis points, the result would be 1.066%.

What this illustration shows is that for a small change in a variable, a linear approximation does a good job of estimating the change in the value of the price function of a bond. A different interpretation, however, is possible. Note that in general convexity is computed as a number, which is a function of the term structure of interest rates as follows:

$$\text{Dollar convexity} = [2C(1+i_1)^{-3} + 2 \cdot 3 \cdot C(1+i_2)^{-4} + \ldots$$
$$+ N \cdot (N+1) \cdot (C+M)(1+i_N)^{-N-2}]$$

This expression is a nonlinear function of all the yields. It is sensitive to changes of the curvature of the term structure. In this sense it is a measure of the convexity of the term structure.

Let's suppose now that the term structure experiences a change that can be represented as a parallel shift plus a change in slope and curvature. In general both duration and convexity will change. The previous Maclaurin expansion, which is valid for parallel shifts of the term structure, will not hold. However, we can still attempt to represent the change in a bond's value as a function of duration and convexity. In particular, we could represent the changes in a bond's value as a linear function of duration and convexity. This idea is exploited in more general terms by assuming that the term structure changes are a linear combination of factors.

INTEGRATION

Differentiation addresses the problem of defining the instantaneous rate of change, whereas **integration** addresses the problem of calculating the area of an arbitrary figure. Areas are easily defined for rectangles and triangles, and any plane figure that can be decomposed into these objects. While formulas for computing the area of polygons have been known since antiquity, a general solution of the problem was arrived at first in the seventeenth century, with the development of calculus.

Riemann Integrals

Let's begin by defining the integral in the sense of Riemann, so called after the German mathematician Bernhard Riemann who introduced it. Consider a bounded function $y = f(x)$ defined in some domain which includes the interval $[a,b]$. Consider the partition of the interval $[a,b]$ into n disjoint subintervals $a = x_0 < x_1 < ... < x_{n-1} < x_n = b$, and form the sums:

$$S_n^U = \sum_{i=1}^n f^M(x_i)(x_i - x_{i-1})$$

where $f^M(x_i) = \sup f(x), x \in [x_{i-1}, x_i]$ and

$$S_n^L = \sum_{i=1}^n f_m(x_i)(x_i - x_{i-1})$$

where $f_m(x_i) = \inf f(x), x \in [x_{i-1}, x_i]$.

Exhibit 4.8 illustrates this construction. S_n^U, S_n^L are called, respectively, the **upper Riemann sum** and **lower Riemann sum**. Clearly an infinite number of different sums, S_n^U, S_n^L can be formed depending on the choice of the partition. Intuitively, each of these sums approximates the area below the curve $y = f(x)$, the upper sums from above, the lower sums from below. Generally speaking, the more refined the partition the more accurate the approximation.

Consider the sets of all the possible sums $\{S_n^U\}$ and $\{S_n^L\}$ for every possible partition. If the supremum of the set $\{S_n^L\}$ (which in general will not be a maximum) and the infimum of the set $\{S_n^U\}$ (which in general will not be a minimum) exist, respectively, and if the minimum and the supremum coincide, the function f is said to be "Riemann integrable in the interval (a,b)."

If the function f is Riemann integrable in $[a,b]$, then

EXHIBIT 4.8   Riemann Sums

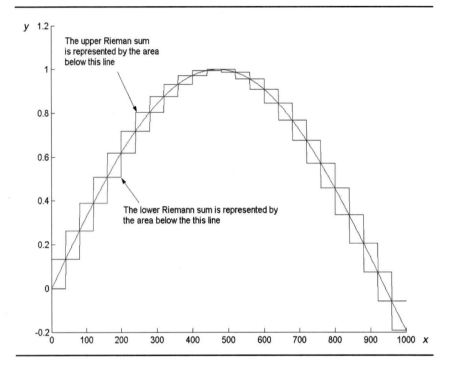

$$I = \int_a^b f(x)dx = \sup\{S_n^L\} = \inf\{S_n^U\}$$

is called the proper integral of f on $[a,b]$ in the sense of Riemann.

An alternative definition of the proper integral in the sense of Riemann is often given as follows. Consider the Riemann sums:

$$S_n = \sum_{i=1}^n f(x_i^*)(x_i - x_{x-1})$$

where x_i^* is an arbitrary point in the interval $[x_1, x_{i-1}]$. Call $\Delta x_i = (x_i - x_{i-1})$ the length of the i-th interval. The proper integral I between a and b in the sense of Riemann can then be defined as the limit (if the limit exists) of the sums S_n when the maximum length of the subintervals tends to zero:

$$I = \lim_{\max\Delta x_i \to 0} S_n$$

In the above, the limit operation has to be defined as the limit for any sequence of sums S_n as for each n there are infinitely many sums. Note that the function f need not be continuous to be integrable. It might, for instance, make a finite number of jumps. However every function that is integrable must be of bounded variation.

Properties of Riemann Integrals

Let's now introduce a number of properties of the integrals (we will state these without proof). These properties are simple mechanical rules that apply provided that all integrals exist. Suppose that a,b,c are fixed real numbers, that f,g,h are functions defined in the same domain, and that they are all integrable on the same interval (a,b). The following properties apply:

Properties of Riemann Integrals

Property 1 $\int_a^a f(x)dx = 0$

Property 2 $\int_a^c f(x)dx = \int_a^b f(x)dx + \int_b^c f(x)dx, \quad a \le b \le c$

Property 3 $h(x) = \alpha f(x) + \beta g(x) \Rightarrow \int_a^b h(x)dx = \alpha \int_a^b f(x)dx + \beta \int_a^b g(x)dx$

Property 4 $\int_a^b f'(x)g(x)dx = f(x)g(x)\big|_a^b - \int_a^b f(x)g'(x)dx$

- Properties 1 and 2 establish that integrals are additive with respect to integration limits.
- Property 3 is the statement of the linearity of the operation of integration.
- Property 4 is the rule of integration by parts.

Now consider a composite function: $h(x) = f(g(x))$. Provided that g is integrable on the interval (a,b) and that f is integrable on the interval corresponding to all the points $s = g(x)$, the following rule, known as the **chain rule of integration**, applies:

$$\int_a^b f(y)dy = \int_{g^{-1}(a)}^{g^{-1}(b)} f(g(x))g'(x)dx$$

Lebesgue-Stieltjes Integrals

Most applications of calculus require only the integral in the sense of Riemann. However, a number of results in probability theory with a bearing on economics and finance theory can be properly established only in the framework of **Lebesgue-Stieltjes integral**. Let's therefore extend the definition of integrals by introducing the Lebesgue-Stieltjes integral.

The integral in the sense of Riemann takes as a measure of an interval its length, also called the **Jordan measure**. The definition of the integral can be extended in the sense of Lebesgue-Stieltjes by defining the integral with respect to a more general **Lebesgue-Stieltjes measure**.

Consider a non-decreasing, left-continuous function $g(x)$ defined on a domain which includes the interval $[x_i - x_{i-1}]$ and form the differences $m_{L_i} = g(x_i) - g(x_{i-1})$. These quantities are a generalization of the concept of length. They are called **Lebesgue measures**. Suppose that the interval (a,b) is divided into a partition of n disjoint subintervals by the points $a = x_0 < x_1 < \ldots < x_n = b$ and form the Lebesgue-Stieltjes sums

$$S_n = \sum_{i=1}^{n} f(x_i^*)m_{L_i}, \; x_i^* \in (x_i, x_{i-1})$$

where x_i^* is any point in i-th subinterval of the partition.

Consider the set of all possible sums $\{S_n\}$. These sums depend on the partition and the choice of the midpoint in each subinterval. We define the integral of $f(x)$ in the sense of Lebesgue-Stieltjes as the limit, if the limit exists, of the Lebesgue-Stieltjes sums $\{S_n\}$ when the maximum length of the intervals in the partition tends to zero. We write, as in the case of the Riemann integral:

$$I = \int_a^b f(x)dg(x) = \lim S_n$$

The integral in the sense of Lebesgue-Stieltjes can be defined for a broader class of functions than the integral in the sense of Riemann. If f is an integrable function and g is a differentiable function, the two integrals coincide. In the following chapters, all integrals are in the sense of Riemann unless explicitly stated to be in the sense of Lebesgue-Stieltjes.

INDEFINITE AND IMPROPER INTEGRALS

In the previous section we defined the integral as a real number associated with a function on an interval (a,b). If we allow the upper limit b to vary, then the integral defines a function:

$$F(x) = \int_a^x f(u)\,du$$

which is called an **indefinite integral**.

Given a function f, there is an indefinite integral for each starting point. From the definition of integral, it is immediate to see that any two indefinite integrals of the same function differ only by a constant. In fact, given a function f, consider the two indefinite integrals:

$$F_a(x) = \int_a^x f(u)\,du, \; F_b(x) = \int_b^x f(u)\,du$$

If $a < b$, we can write

$$F_a(x) = \int_a^x f(u)\,du = \int_a^b f(u)\,du + \int_b^x f(u)\,du = \text{constant} + F_b(x)$$

We can now extend the definition of proper integrals by introducing improper integrals. **Improper integrals** are defined as limits of indefinite integrals either when the integration limits are infinite or when the integrand diverges to infinity at a given point. Consider the improper integral

$$\int_a^\infty f(x)\,dx$$

This integral is defined as the limit

$$\int_a^\infty f(x)\,dx = \lim_{x \to \infty} \int_a^x f(u)\,du$$

if the limit exists. Consider now a function f that goes to infinity as x approaches the upper integration limit b. We define the improper integral

$$\int_a^b f(x)\,dx$$

as the left limit

$$\int_a^b f(x)\,dx = \lim_{x \to b^-} \int_a^x f(u)\,du$$

A similar definition can be established for the lower integration limit. Improper integrals exist only if these limits exist. For instance, the integral

$$\int_0^1 \frac{1}{x}\,dx = \lim_{x \to 0^+}\left[-\frac{1}{x^2}\right]_0^1 = \lim_{x \to 0^+}\left(\frac{1}{x^2} - 1\right) = \infty$$

does not exist.

THE FUNDAMENTAL THEOREM OF CALCULUS

The **fundamental theorem of calculus** shows that integration is the inverse operation of derivation; it states that, given a continuous function f, any of its indefinite integrals F is a differentiable function and the following relationship holds:

$$\frac{dF(x)}{dx} = \frac{d\int_a^x f(u)\,du}{dx} = f(x)$$

If the function f is not continuous, then the fundamental theorem still holds, but in any point of discontinuity the derivative has to be replaced with the left or right derivative dependent on whether or not the function f is left or right continuous at that point.

Given a continuous function f, any function F such that

$$\frac{dF(x)}{dx} = f(x)$$

is called a **primitive** or an **indefinite integral of the function** f. It can be demonstrated that any two primitives of a function f differ only by a constant. Any primitive of a function f can therefore be represented generically as an indefinite integral plus a constant.

As an immediate consequence of the fundamental theorem of calculus we can now state that, given a primitive F of a function f, the definite integral

$$\int_a^b f(x)\,dx$$

can be computed as

$$\int_a^b f(x)\,dx = F(b) - F(a)$$

All three properties—the linearity of the integration operation, the chain rule, and the rule of integration by parts—hold for indefinite integrals:

$$h(x) = af(x) + bg(x) \Rightarrow \int h(x)\,dx = a\int f(x)\,dx + b\int g(x)\,dx$$

$$\int f'(x)g(x)\,dx = f(x)g(x) - \int f(x)g'(x)\,dx$$

$$y = g(x) \Rightarrow \int f(y)\,dy = \int f(x)g'(x)\,dx$$

The differentiation formulas established in the previous section can now be applied to integration. Exhibit 4.9 lists a number of commonly used integrals.

EXHIBIT 4.9   Commonly Used Integrals

$f(x)$	$\int f(x)\,dx$	Domain
x^n	$\dfrac{1}{n+1}x^{n+1}$	$n \neq -1,\ R,\ x \neq 0$ if $n < 0$
x^α	$\dfrac{1}{\alpha+1}x^{\alpha+1}$	$x > 0$
$\sin x$	$-\cos x$	R
$\cos x$	$\sin x$	R
$\dfrac{1}{x}$	$\log x$	$x > 0$
e^x	e^x	R
$\dfrac{f'(x)}{f(x)}$	$\log[f(x)]$	$f(x) > 0$

INTEGRAL TRANSFORMS

Integral transforms are operations that take any function $f(x)$ into another function $F(s)$ of a different variable s through an improper integral

$$F(s) = \int_{-\infty}^{\infty} G(s, x)f(x)dx$$

The function $G(s,x)$ is referred to as the kernel of the transform. The association is one-to-one so that f can be uniquely recovered from its transform F. For example, linear processes can be studied in the time domain or in the frequency domain: The two are linked by integral transforms. We will see how integral transforms are applied to several applications in finance. The two most important types of integral transforms are the **Laplace transform** and **Fourier transform**. We discuss both in this section.

Laplace Transform

Given a real-valued function f, its **one-sided Laplace transform** is an operator that maps f to the function $L(s) = \mathcal{L}(f(x))$ defined by the improper integral

$$L(s) = \mathcal{L}[f(x)] = \int_{0}^{\infty} e^{-sx}f(x)dx$$

if it exists.

The Laplace transform of a real-valued function is thus a real-valued function. The one-sided transform is the most common type of Laplace transform used in physics and engineering. However in probability theory Laplace transforms are applied to density functions. As these functions are defined on the entire real axis, the two-sided Laplace transforms are used. In probability theory, the two-sided Laplace transform is called the moment generating function. **The two-sided Laplace transform** is defined by

$$L(s) = \mathcal{L}[f(x)] = \int_{-\infty}^{\infty} e^{-sx}f(x)dx$$

if the improper integral exists.

Laplace transforms "project" a function into a different function space, that of their transforms. Laplace transforms exist only for functions that are sufficiently smooth and decay to zero sufficiently rapidly when $x \to \infty$. The following conditions ensure the existence of the Laplace transform:

- $f(x)$ is piecewise continuous.
- $f(x)$ is of exponential order as $x \to \infty$, that is, there exist positive real constants K, a, and T, such that $|f(x)| \le Ke^{ax}$, for $x > T$.

Note that the above conditions are sufficient but not necessary for Laplace transforms to exist. It can be demonstrated that, if they exist, Laplace transforms are unique in the sense that if two functions have the same Laplace transform they coincide pointwise. As a consequence, the Laplace transforms are invertible in the sense that the original function can be fully recovered from its transform. In fact, it is possible to define the **inverse Laplace transform** as the operator $\mathcal{L}^{-1}(F(s))$ such that

$$\mathcal{L}^{-1}[L(s)] = f(x)$$

The inverse Laplace transform can be represented as a **Bromwich integral**, that is, an integral defined on a contour in the complex plane that leaves all singularities of the transform to the left:

$$f(X) = \frac{1}{2\pi i} \int_{\gamma - i\infty}^{\gamma + i\infty} e^{sx} L(s) ds$$

The following conditions ensure the existence of an inverse Laplace transform:

$$\lim_{s \to \infty} F(s) = 0$$
$$\lim_{s \to \infty} sF(s) \text{ is finite}$$

We will now list (without proof) some key properties of Laplace transforms; both the one-sided and two-sided Laplace transforms have similar properties. The Laplace transform is a linear operator in the sense that, if f,g are real-valued functions that have Laplace transforms and a,b are real-valued constants, then the following property holds:

$$L[af(x) + bg(x)] = \int_{-\infty}^{\infty} e^{-sx}(af(x) + bg(x))dx$$

$$= a\int_{-\infty}^{\infty} e^{-sx}f(x)dx + b\int_{-\infty}^{\infty} e^{-sx}g(x)dx$$

$$= a\mathcal{L}[f(x)] + b\mathcal{L}[g(x)]$$

Laplace transforms turn differentiation, integration, and convolution (defined below) into algebraic operations. For derivatives the following property holds for the two-sided transform:

$$\mathcal{L}\left[\frac{df(x)}{dx}\right] = s\mathcal{L}[f(x)]$$

and

$$\mathcal{L}\left[\frac{df(x)}{dx}\right] = s\mathcal{L}[f(x)] - f(0)$$

for the one-sided transform. For higher derivatives the following formula holds for the two-sided transform

$$\mathcal{L}[f^{(n)}(x)] = s^n\mathcal{L}[f(x)] - s^{n-1}f(0) - s^{n-2}f'(0) - \dots - f^{(n-1)}(0)$$

An analogous property holds for integration for one-sided transforms

$$\mathcal{L}\left[\int_0^t f(x)\right] = \frac{1}{s}\mathcal{L}[f(x)] \text{ for the one-sided transform}$$

$$\mathcal{L}\left[\int_0^t f(x)\right] = \frac{1}{s}\mathcal{L}[f(x)] \text{ for the two-sided transform}$$

Consider now the convolution. Given two functions f and g, their **convolution** $h(x) = f(x) * g(x)$ is defined as the integral

$$h(x) = (f * g)(x) = \int_{-\infty}^{\infty} f(x - t)g(t)dt$$

It can be demonstrated that the following property holds:

$$\mathcal{L}[h(x)] = \mathcal{L}[f * g] = \mathcal{L}[f(x)]\mathcal{L}[g(x)]$$

As we will see in Chapter 9, when we cover differential equations, these properties are useful in solving differential equations, turning the latter into algebraic equations. These properties are also used in representing probability distributions of sums of variables.

Fourier Transforms

Fourier transforms are similar in many respects to Laplace transforms. Given a function f, its Fourier transform $\hat{f}(\omega) = \mathcal{F}[f(x)]$ is defined as the integral

$$\hat{f}(\omega) = \mathcal{F}[f(x)] = \int_{-\infty}^{+\infty} e^{-2\pi i \omega x} f(x)dx$$

if the improper integral exists, where i is the imaginary unity. The Fourier transform of a real-valued function is thus a complex-valued function. For a large class of functions the Fourier transform exists and is unique, so that the original function, f, can be recovered from its transform, $\hat{f}$.

The following conditions are sufficient but not necessary for a function to have a forward and inverse Fourier transform:

- $\int_{-\infty}^{\infty} |f(x)|dx$ exists.
- The function $f(x)$ is piecewise continuous.
- The function $f(x)$ has bounded variation.

The inverse Fourier transform can be represented as:

$$f(x) = \mathcal{F}^{-1}[\hat{f}(\omega)] = \int_{-\infty}^{\infty} e^{2\pi i \omega x} \hat{f}(\omega)d\omega$$

Fourier transforms are linear operators. The Fourier transform of the convolutions is the product of Fourier transforms; the Fourier transform of derivatives and integrals have similar properties to the Laplace transform.

CALCULUS IN MORE THAN ONE VARIABLE

The previous concepts of calculus can be extended in a multivariate environment, that is, they can be extended to functions of several variables. Given a function of n variables, $y = f(x_1,...,x_n)$, we can define n **partial derivatives**

$$\frac{\partial f(x_1, ..., x_n)}{\partial x_i}$$

$i = 1,...,n$ holding constant $n - 1$ variables and then using the definition for derivatives of univariate functions:

$$\frac{\partial f(x_1, ..., x_n)}{\partial x_i} = \lim_{h \to 0} \frac{f(x_1, ..., x_i + h, ..., x_n) - f(x_1, ..., x_i, ..., x_n)}{h}$$

Repeating this process we can define partial derivatives of any order. Consider, for example, the following function of two variables:

$$f(x, y) = e^{-(x^2 + \sigma xy + y^2)}$$

Its partial derivatives up to order 2 are given by the following formulas

$$\frac{\partial f}{\partial x} = -(2x + \sigma y)e^{-(x^2 + \sigma xy + y^2)}$$

$$\frac{\partial f}{\partial y} = -(2y + \sigma x)e^{-(x^2 + \sigma xy + y^2)}$$

$$\frac{\partial^2 f}{\partial x^2} = -2e^{-(x^2 + \sigma xy + y^2)} + (2x + \sigma y)^2 e^{-(x^2 + \sigma xy + y^2)}$$

$$\frac{\partial^2 f}{\partial y^2} = -2e^{-(x^2 + \sigma xy + y^2)} + (2y + \sigma x)^2 e^{-(x^2 + \sigma xy + y^2)}$$

$$\frac{\partial^2 f}{\partial x \partial y} = (2x + \sigma y)(2y + \sigma x)e^{-(x^2 + \sigma xy + y^2)} - \sigma e^{-(x^2 + \sigma xy + y^2)}$$

In bond analysis, we can also compute partial derivatives in the case where each interest rate is not the same for each time period in the bond valuation formula. In that case, derivatives can be computed for each time period's interest rate. When the percentage price sensitivity of a bond to a change in the interest rate for a particular time period is computed, the resulting measure is called *rate duration* or *partial duration*.[12]

The definition of the integral can be obtained in the same way as in the one variable case. The integral is defined as the limit of sums of multidimensional rectangles. Multidimensional integrals represent the ordinary concept of volume in three dimensions and *n*-dimensional hypervolume in more that three dimensions. A more general definition of integral that includes both the Riemann and the Riemann-Stieltjes as special cases, will be considered in the chapter on probability.

SUMMARY

We can now summarize our discussion of calculus as follows:

- *The infinitesimally small and infinitely large.* Through the concept of the limit, calculus has rendered precise the notion of infinitesimally small and infinitely large.
- *Rules for computing limits.* A sequence or a function tends to a finite limit if there is a number to which the sequence or the function can get arbitrarily close; a sequence or a function tends to infinity if it can exceed any given quantity. Starting from these simple concepts, rules for computing limits can be established and limits computed.
- *Derivatives.* A derivative of a function is the limit of its incremental ratio when the interval tends to zero. Derivatives represent the rate of change of quantities.
- *Integrals.* Integrals represent the area below a curve; they are the limit of sums of rectangles that approximate the area below the curve. More

---

[12] There is a technical difference between rate duration and partial duration but the difference is not important here.

in general, integrals can be used to represent cumulated quantities such as cumulated gains.

■ *Integrals and derivatives.* The fundamental theorem of calculus proves that integrals and derivatives are inverse operations, insofar as the derivative of the integral of a function returns the function.

■ The derivative of the product of a constant and a function is the product of the constant and the derivative of the function.

■ The integral of the product of a constant and a function is the product of the constant and the integral of the function.

■ The derivative and the integral of a sum of functions is the sum of derivatives or integrals.

■ Derivation and integration are linear operations.

■ The derivative of a product of functions is the derivative of the first function times the second plus the first function times the derivative of the second.

■ The derivative of a function of function is the product of outer function with respect to the inner function times the derivative of the inner function.

■ A derivative of order n of a function is defined as the function that results from applying the operation of derivation n times.

■ A function that is differentiable to any order at a given point a can be represented as a series of the powers of $(x - a)$ times the n-th derivative at a times the reciprocal of $n!$; this expansion is called a Taylor series expansion.

■ Taylor series truncated to the first or second terms are called first and second order approximations, respectively.

■ Laplace and Fourier transforms of a function are the integral of that function times an exponential.

■ Laplace and Fourier transforms are useful because they transform differentiation and integration into algebraic operations, thereby providing a method for solving linear differential equations.

■ Differentiation and integration can be extended to functions of more than one variable.

■ A function of n variables has n first derivatives, n-square second derivatives and so on.

CHAPTER 5

Matrix Algebra

Ordinary algebra deals with operations such as addition and multiplication performed on individual numbers. In many applications, however, it is useful to consider operations performed on ordered **arrays** of numbers. This is the domain of matrix algebra. Ordered arrays of numbers are called **vectors** and **matrices** while individual numbers are called **scalars**. In this chapter, we will discuss the basic operations of matrix algebra.

VECTORS AND MATRICES DEFINED

Let's now define precisely the concepts of vector and matrix. Though vectors can be thought of as particular matrices, in many cases it is useful to keep the two concepts—vectors and matrices—distinct. In particular, a number of important concepts and properties can be defined for vectors but do not generalize easily to matrices.[1]

Vectors

An *n*-**dimensional vector** is an ordered array of n numbers. Vectors are generally indicated with bold-face lower case letters. Thus a vector **x** is an array of the form

$$\mathbf{x} = [x_1 ... x_n]$$

The numbers x_i are called the **components** of the vector **x**.

A vector is identified by the set of its components. Consider the vectors $\mathbf{x} = [x_1 ... x_n]$ and $\mathbf{y} = [y_1 ... y_m]$. Two vectors are said to be **equal** if

---

[1] Vectors can be thought as the elements of an abstract linear space while matrices are operators that operate on linear spaces.

and only if they have the same dimensions $n = m$ and the same components:

$$\mathbf{x} = \mathbf{y} \Leftrightarrow x_i = y_i, i = 1, \ldots, n$$

Vectors can be **row vectors** or **column vectors**. If the vector components appear in a horizontal row, then the vector is called a row vector, as for instance the vector

$$\mathbf{x} = [1 \quad 2 \quad 8 \quad 7]$$

Here are two examples. Suppose that we let w_n be a risky asset's weight in a portfolio. Assume that there are N risky assets. Then the following vector, **w**, is a row vector that represents a portfolio's holdings of the N risky assets:

$$\mathbf{w} = \begin{bmatrix} w_1 & w_2 & \ldots\ldots & w_N \end{bmatrix}$$

As a second example of a row vector, suppose that we let r_n be the *excess return* for a risky asset. (The excess return is the difference between the return on a risky asset and the risk-free rate.) Then the following row vector is the excess return vector:

$$\mathbf{r} = \begin{bmatrix} r_1 & r_2 & \ldots\ldots & r_N \end{bmatrix}$$

If the vector components are arranged in a column, then the vector is called a column vector as, for instance, the vector

$$\mathbf{x} = \begin{bmatrix} 1 \\ 2 \\ 8 \\ 7 \end{bmatrix}$$

For example, as explained in Chapter 19, a portfolio's excess return will be affected by what can be different *characteristics* or *attributes* that affect all asset prices. A few examples would be the price-earnings ratio, market capitalization, and industry. We can denote for a particular attribute a column vector, **a**, that shows the exposure of each risky asset to that attribute:

$$\mathbf{a} = \begin{bmatrix} a_1 \\ a_2 \\ \cdot \\ \cdot \\ \cdot \\ a_N \end{bmatrix}$$

where a_n is the exposure of asset n to attribute a.

Vector components can be either real or complex numbers. Returning to the row vector **w** of a portfolio of holdings, a positive value for w_n would mean that some of the risky asset n is held in the portfolio; a value of zero would mean that the risky asset n is not held in the portfolio. If the value of w_n is negative, this means that there is a short position in risky asset n.

While in most applications in economics and finance vector components are real numbers, recall that a complex number is a number which can be represented in the form

$$c = a + bi$$

where i is the **imaginary unit**. One can operate on complex numbers[2] as if they were real numbers but with the additional rule: $i^2 = -1$. In the following we will assume that vectors have real components unless we explicitly state the contrary.

Vectors admit a simple graphic representation. Consider an n-dimensional Cartesian space. An n-dimensional vector is represented by a segment that starts from the origin and such that its projections on the n-th axis are equal to the n-th component of the vector. The direction of the vector is assumed to be from the origin to the tip of the segment. Exhibit 5.1 illustrates this representation in the case of the usual three spatial dimensions x,y,z.

The (Euclidean) **length** of a vector **x**, also called the **norm** of a vector, denoted as $\|\mathbf{x}\|$, is defined as the square root of the sum of the squares of its components:

$$\|\mathbf{x}\| = \sqrt{x_1^2 + \ldots + x_n^2}$$

---

[2] In rigorous mathematical terms, complex numbers are defined as ordered pairs of real numbers. Operations on complex numbers are defined as operations on pairs of real numbers. The representation with the imaginary unit is a shorthand based on a rigorous definition of complex numbers.

EXHIBIT 5.1   Graphical Representation of Vectors

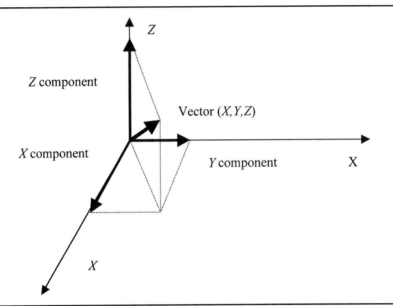

Matrices

An *n×m* **matrix** is a bidimensional ordered array of *n×m* numbers. Matrices are usually indicated with bold-face upper case letters. Thus, the generic matrix **A** is an *n×m* array of the form

$$
\mathbf{A} = \begin{bmatrix} a_{1,1} & \cdot & a_{1,j} & \cdot & a_{1,m} \\ \cdot & \cdot & \cdot & \cdot & \cdot \\ a_{i,1} & \cdot & a_{i,j} & \cdot & a_{i,m} \\ \cdot & \cdot & \cdot & \cdot & \cdot \\ a_{n,1} & \cdot & a_{n,j} & \cdot & a_{n,m} \end{bmatrix}
$$

Note that the first subscript indicates rows while the second subscript indicates columns. The entries a_{ij}—called the **elements** of the matrix **A**—are the numbers at the crossing of the *i*-th row and the *j*-th column. The commas between the subscripts of the matrix entries are omitted when there is no risk of confusion: $a_{i,j} \equiv a_{ij}$. A matrix **A** is often indicated by its generic element between brackets:

$$
\mathbf{A} = \{a_{ij}\}_{nm} \text{ or } \mathbf{A} = [a_{ij}]_{nm}
$$

where the subscripts *nm* are the **dimensions** of the matrix.

The elements of a matrix can be either real numbers or complex numbers. In the following, we will assume that elements are real numbers unless explicitly stated otherwise. If the matrix entries are real numbers, the matrix is called a **real matrix**; if the a_{ij} are complex numbers, the matrix is called a **complex matrix**.

Two matrices are said to be equal if they are of the same dimensions and have the same elements. Consider two matrices $\mathbf{A} = \{a_{ij}\}_{nm}$ and $\mathbf{B} = \{b_{ij}\}_{nm}$ of the same order $n{\times}m$:

$$\mathbf{A} = \mathbf{B} \text{ means } \{a_{ij}\}_{nm} = \{b_{ij}\}_{nm}$$

Vectors are matrices with only one column or only one row. An *n*-dimensional row vector is an $n{\times}1$ matrix, an *n*-dimensional column vector is a $1{\times}n$ matrix. A matrix can be thought of as an array of vectors. Denote by $\mathbf{a}_j$ the column vector formed by the *j*-th column of the matrix **A**. The matrix **A** can then be written as $\mathbf{A} = [\mathbf{a}_j]$. This notation can be generalized. Suppose that the two matrices **B**, **C** have the same number *n* of rows and m_B, m_C columns respectively. The matrix $\mathbf{A} = [\mathbf{B}\ \mathbf{C}]$ is the matrix whose first m_B columns are formed by the matrix **B** and the following m_C columns are formed by the matrix **C**.

SQUARE MATRICES

There are several types of matrices. First there is a broad classification of square and rectangular matrices. A **rectangular matrix** can have different numbers of rows and columns; a **square matrix** is a rectangular matrix with the same number *n* of rows as of columns.

Diagonals and Antidiagonals

An important concept for a square matrix is the **diagonal**. The diagonal includes the elements that run from the first row, first column to the last row, last column. For example, consider the following square matrix:

$$\mathbf{A} = \begin{bmatrix} a_{1,1} & \cdot & a_{1,j} & \cdot & a_{1,n} \\ \cdot & \cdot & \cdot & \cdot & \cdot \\ a_{i,1} & \cdot & a_{i,j} & \cdot & a_{i,n} \\ \cdot & \cdot & \cdot & \cdot & \cdot \\ a_{n,1} & \cdot & a_{n,j} & \cdot & a_{n,n} \end{bmatrix}$$

The diagonal terms are the $a_{j,j}$ terms.

The **antidiagonals** of a square matrix are the other diagonals that do not run from the first row, first column to the last row, last column. For example, consider the following 4×4 square matrix:

$$\begin{bmatrix} 5 & 9 & 14 & 8 \\ 2 & 6 & 12 & 11 \\ 17 & 21 & 42 & 2 \\ 19 & 73 & 7 & 8 \end{bmatrix}$$

The diagonal terms include 5, 6, 42, 8. One antidiagonal is 2, 9. Another antidiagonal is 17, 6, 14. Note that there are antidiagonal terms in rectangular matrices.

Identity Matrix

The $n \times n$ **identity matrix,** indicated as the matrix I_n, is a square matrix whose diagonal elements (i.e., the entries with the same row and column suffix) are equal to one while all other entries are zero:

$$I_n = \begin{bmatrix} 1 & 0 & \cdots & 0 \\ 0 & 1 & \cdots & 0 \\ \cdot & \cdot & \cdot & \cdot \\ \cdot & \cdot & \cdot & \cdot \\ \cdot & \cdot & \cdot & \cdot \\ 0 & 0 & \cdots & 1 \end{bmatrix}$$

A matrix whose entries are all zero is called a **zero matrix.**

Diagonal Matrix

A **diagonal matrix** is a square matrix whose elements are all zero except the ones on the diagonal:

$$A = \begin{bmatrix} a_{11} & 0 & \cdots & 0 \\ 0 & a_{22} & \cdots & 0 \\ \cdot & \cdot & \cdot & \cdot \\ \cdot & \cdot & \cdot & \cdot \\ \cdot & \cdot & \cdot & \cdot \\ 0 & 0 & \cdots & a_{nn} \end{bmatrix}$$

Given a square $n \times n$ matrix A, the matrix dg A is the diagonal matrix extracted from A. The diagonal matrix dg A is a matrix whose elements are all zero except the elements on the diagonal that coincide with those of the matrix **A**:

$$
\mathbf{A} = \begin{bmatrix} a_{11} & a_{12} & \cdot & \cdot & a_{1n} \\ a_{21} & a_{22} & \cdot & \cdot & a_{2n} \\ \cdot & & \cdot & & \cdot \\ \cdot & \cdot & & \cdot & \cdot \\ \cdot & & & \cdot & \cdot \\ a_{n1} & a_{n2} & \cdot & \cdot & a_{nn} \end{bmatrix} \Rightarrow \mathrm{dg}\,\mathbf{A} = \begin{bmatrix} a_{11} & 0 & \cdot & \cdot & 0 \\ 0 & a_{22} & \cdot & \cdot & 0 \\ \cdot & & \cdot & & \cdot \\ \cdot & \cdot & & \cdot & \cdot \\ \cdot & & & \cdot & \cdot \\ 0 & 0 & \cdot & \cdot & a_{nn} \end{bmatrix}
$$

The **trace** of a square matrix **A** is the sum of its diagonal elements:

$$
\mathrm{tr}\,\mathbf{A} = \sum_{i=1}^{n} a_{ii}
$$

A square matrix is called **symmetric** if the elements above the diagonal are equal to the corresponding elements below the diagonal: $a_{ij} = a_{ji}$. A matrix is called **skew-symmetric** if the diagonal elements are zero and the elements above the diagonal are the opposite of the corresponding elements below the diagonal: $a_{ij} = -a_{ji}$, $i \neq j$, $a_{ii} = 0$.

The most commonly used symmetric matrix in finance and econometrics is the **covariance matrix**, also referred to as the **variance-covariance matrix**. (See Chapter 6 for a detailed explanation of variances and covariances.) For example, suppose that there are N risky assets and that the variance of the excess return for each risky asset and the covariances between each pair of risky assets are estimated. As the number of credit risky assets is N there are N^2 elements, consisting of N variances (along the diagonal) and $N^2 - N$ covariances. Symmetry restrictions reduce the number of independent elements. In fact the covariance $\sigma_{ij}(t)$ between risky asset i and risky asset j will be equal to the covariance between risky asset j and risky asset i. We can therefore arrange the variances and covariances in the following square matrix **V**:

$$
\mathbf{V} = \begin{bmatrix} \sigma_{1,1} & \cdot & \sigma_{1,i} & \cdot & \sigma_{1,N} \\ \cdot & \cdot & \cdot & \cdot & \cdot \\ \sigma_{1,i} & \cdot & \sigma_{i,i} & \cdot & \sigma_{i,N} \\ \cdot & \cdot & \cdot & \cdot & \cdot \\ \sigma_{1,N} & \cdot & \sigma_{i,N} & \cdot & \sigma_{N,N} \end{bmatrix}
$$

Notice that **V** is a symmetric matrix.

Upper and Lower Triangular Matrix

A matrix **A** is called **upper triangular** if $a_{ij} = 0$, $i > j$. In other words, an upper triangular matrix is a matrix whose elements in the triangle below the diagonal are all zero as is illustrated below:

$$\mathbf{A} = \begin{bmatrix} a_{1,1} \cdot a_{1,i} \cdot a_{1,n} \\ \cdot \quad \cdot \quad \cdot \quad \cdot \\ 0 \cdot a_{i,i} \cdot a_{i,n} \\ \cdot \quad \cdot \quad \cdot \quad \cdot \\ 0 \cdot 0 \cdot a_{n,n} \end{bmatrix} \text{ [upper triangular]}$$

A matrix **A** is called **lower triangular** if $a_{ij} = 0$, $i < j$. In other words, a lower triangular matrix is a matrix whose elements in the triangle above the diagonal are zero as is illustrated below:

$$\mathbf{A} = \begin{bmatrix} a_{1,1} \cdot 0 \cdot 0 \\ \cdot \quad \cdot \quad \cdot \quad \cdot \\ \cdot \quad a_{i,i} \cdot 0 \\ \cdot \quad \cdot \quad \cdot \quad \cdot \\ a_{n,1} \cdot a_{n,i} \cdot a_{n,n} \end{bmatrix} \text{ [lower triangular]}$$

DETERMINANTS

Consider a square, $n \times n$, matrix **A**. The **determinant** of **A**, denoted $|\mathbf{A}|$, is defined as follows:

$$|\mathbf{A}| = \sum (-1)^{t(j_1, \ldots, j_n)} \prod_{i=1}^{n} a_{ij}$$

where the sum is extended over all permutations $(j_1, \ldots, j_n)$ of the set $(1, 2, \ldots, n)$ and $t(j_1, \ldots, j_n)$ is the number of transpositions (or inversions of positions) required to go from $(1, 2, \ldots, n)$ to $(j_1, \ldots, j_n)$.

Otherwise stated, a determinant is the sum of all different products formed taking exactly one element from each row with each product multiplied by

$$(-1)^{t(j_1, \ldots, j_n)}$$

Consider, for instance, the case $n = 2$, where there is only one possible transposition: $1,2 \Rightarrow 2,1$. The determinant of a 2×2 matrix is therefore computed as follows:

$$|\mathbf{A}| = (-1)^0 a_{11} a_{22} + (-1)^1 a_{12} a_{21} = a_{11} a_{22} - a_{12} a_{21}$$

Consider a square matrix $\mathbf{A}$ of order n. Consider the matrix $\mathbf{M}_{ij}$ obtained by removing the ith row and the jth column. The matrix $\mathbf{M}_{ij}$ is a square matrix of order $(n - 1)$. The determinant $|\mathbf{M}_{ij}|$ of the matrix $\mathbf{M}_{ij}$ is called the **minor** of a_{ij}. The signed minor

$$(-1)^{(i+j)} |\mathbf{M}_{ij}|$$

is called the **cofactor** of a_{ij} and is generally denoted as α_{ij}. The r-minors of the $n \times m$ rectangular matrix $\mathbf{A}$ are the determinants of the matrices formed by the elements at the crossing of r different rows and r different columns of $\mathbf{A}$.

A square matrix $\mathbf{A}$ is called **singular** if its determinant is equal to zero. An $n \times m$ matrix $\mathbf{A}$ is of **rank** r if at least one of its (square) r-minors is different from zero while all $(r + 1)$-minors, if any, are zero. A nonsingular square matrix is said to be of **full rank** if its rank r is equal to its order n.

SYSTEMS OF LINEAR EQUATIONS

A system of n linear equations in m unknown variables is a set of n simultaneous equations of the following form:

$$a_{1,1} x_1 + \ldots + a_{1,m} x_m = b_1$$

$$\ldots\ldots\ldots\ldots\ldots\ldots\ldots$$

$$a_{n,1} x_1 + \ldots + a_{1,m} x_m = b_m$$

The $n \times m$ matrix

$$\mathbf{A} = \begin{bmatrix} a_{1,1} & \cdot & a_{1,j} & \cdot & a_{1,m} \\ \cdot & \cdot & \cdot & \cdot & \cdot \\ a_{i,1} & \cdot & a_{i,j} & \cdot & a_{i,m} \\ \cdot & \cdot & \cdot & \cdot & \cdot \\ a_{n,1} & \cdot & a_{n,j} & \cdot & a_{n,m} \end{bmatrix}$$

formed with the coefficients of the variables is called the **coefficient matrix**. The terms b_i are called the **constant terms**. The **augmented matrix** [**A b**]—formed by adding to the coefficient matrix a column formed with the constant term—is represented below:

$$[\mathbf{A}\ \mathbf{b}] = \begin{bmatrix} a_{1,1} \cdot a_{1,j} \cdot a_{1,m}\, b_1 \\ \cdot\quad\cdot\quad\cdot\quad\cdot \\ a_{i,1} \cdot a_{i,j} \cdot a_{i,m}\, b_i \\ \cdot\quad\cdot\quad\cdot\quad\cdot \\ a_{n,1} \cdot a_{n,j} \cdot a_{n,m}\, b_n \end{bmatrix}$$

If the constant terms on the right side of the equations are all zero, the system is called **homogeneous**. If at least one of the constant terms is different from zero, the system is called **nonhomogeneous**. A system is called **consistent** if it admits a solution, i.e., if there is a set of values of the variables that simultaneously satisfy all the equations. A system is called **inconsistent** if there is no set of numbers that satisfy the system equations.

Let's first consider the case of nonhomogeneous linear systems. The fundamental theorems of linear systems state that:

- ■ *Theorem 1.* A system of n linear equations in m unknowns is consistent (i.e., it admits a solution) if and only if the coefficient matrix and the augmented matrix have the same rank.

- ■ *Theorem 2.* If a consistent system of n equations in m variables is of rank $r < m$, it is possible to choose $n-r$ unknowns so that the coefficient matrix of the remaining r unknowns is of rank r. When these $m-r$ variables are assigned any arbitrary value, the value of the remaining variables is uniquely determined.

An immediate consequence of the fundamental theorems is that (1) a system of n equations in n unknown variables admits a solution and (2) the solution is unique if and only if both the coefficient matrix and the augmented matrix are of rank n.

Let's now examine homogeneous systems. The coefficient matrix and the augmented matrix of a homogeneous system always have the same rank and thus a homogeneous system is always consistent. In fact, the trivial solution $x_1 = \ldots = x_m = 0$ always satisfies a homogeneous system.

Consider now a homogeneous system of n equations in n unknowns. If the rank of the coefficient matrix is n, the system has only the trivial solution. If the rank of the coefficient matrix is $r < n$, then Theorem 2 ensures that the system has a solution other than the trivial solution.

LINEAR INDEPENDENCE AND RANK

Consider an $n \times m$ matrix $\mathbf{A}$. A set of p columns extracted from the matrix $\mathbf{A}$

$$
\begin{bmatrix}
\cdot & a_{1, i_1} & \cdot & a_{1, i_p} & \cdot \\
\cdot & \cdot & \cdot & \cdot & \\
\cdot & \cdot & \cdot & \cdot & \\
\cdot & \cdot & \cdot & \cdot & \\
\cdot & a_{n, i_1} & \cdot & a_{n, i_p} & \cdot
\end{bmatrix}
$$

are said to be linearly independent if it is not possible to find p constants β_s, $s = 1, \ldots, p$ such that the following n equations are simultaneously satisfied:

$$\beta_1 a_{1, i_1} + \ldots + \beta_p a_{1, i_p} = 0$$

$$\ldots\ldots\ldots\ldots\ldots\ldots\ldots\ldots$$

$$\beta_1 a_{n, i_1} + \ldots + \beta_p a_{n, i_p} = 0$$

Analogously, a set of q rows extracted from the matrix $\mathbf{A}$ are said to be linearly independent if it is not possible to find q constants λ_s, $s = 1, \ldots, q$, such that the following m equations are simultaneously satisfied:

$$\lambda_1 a_{i_1, 1} + \ldots + \lambda_q a_{i_q, 1} = 0$$

$$\ldots\ldots\ldots\ldots\ldots\ldots\ldots\ldots$$

$$\lambda_1 a_{i_1, m} + \ldots + \lambda_q a_{i_q, m} = 0$$

It can be demonstrated that in any matrix the number p of linearly independent columns is the same as the number q of linearly independent rows. This number is equal, in turn, to the rank r of the matrix. Recall that an $n \times m$ matrix $\mathbf{A}$ is said to be of **rank r** if at least one of its (square) r-minors is different from zero while all $(r+1)$-minors, if any, are zero. The constant, p, is the same for rows and for columns. We can now give an alternative definition of the rank of a matrix:

Given an $n \times m$ matrix $\mathbf{A}$, its **rank**, denoted rank($\mathbf{A}$), is the number r of linearly independent rows or columns. This definition is meaningful because the row rank is always equal to the column rank.

HANKEL MATRIX

For the theoretical analysis of the autoregressive integrated moving averages (ARMA) processes described in Chapter 11, it is important to understand a special type of matrix, a Hankel matrix. A **Hankel matrix** is a matrix where for each antidiagonal the element is the same. For example, consider the following square Hankel matrix:

$$\begin{bmatrix} 17 & 16 & 15 & 24 \\ 16 & 15 & 24 & 33 \\ 15 & 24 & 33 & 72 \\ 24 & 33 & 72 & 41 \end{bmatrix}$$

Each antidiagonal has the same value. Now consider the elements of the antidiagonal running from the second row, first column and first row, second column. Both elements have the value 16. Consider another antidiagonal running from the fourth row, second column to the second row, fourth column. All of the elements have the value 33.

An example of a rectangular Hankel matrix would be

$$\begin{bmatrix} 72 & 60 & 55 & 43 & 30 & 21 \\ 60 & 55 & 43 & 30 & 21 & 10 \\ 55 & 43 & 30 & 21 & 10 & 80 \end{bmatrix}$$

Notice that a Hankel matrix is a symmetric matrix.[3]

Consider an infinite sequence of square $n \times n$ matrices:

$$H_0, H_1, \ldots, H_i, \ldots$$

The infinite Hankel matrix H is the following matrix:

---

[3] A special case of a Hankel matrix is when the values for the elements in the first row of the matrix are repeated in each successive row such that its value appears one column to the left. For example, consider the following square Hankel matrix:

$$\begin{bmatrix} 41 & 32 & 23 & 14 \\ 32 & 23 & 14 & 41 \\ 23 & 14 & 41 & 32 \\ 14 & 41 & 32 & 23 \end{bmatrix}$$

This type of Hankel matrix is called an **anticirculant matrix**.

$$
H = \begin{bmatrix} H_0 & H_1 & H_2 & \cdots \\ H_1 & H_2 & \cdots & \cdots \\ H_2 & \cdots & \cdots & \cdots \\ \cdots & & & \\ \cdots & & & \end{bmatrix}
$$

The rank of a Hankel matrix can be defined in three different ways:

1. The **column rank** is the largest number of linearly independent sequence columns.
2. The **row rank** is the largest number of linearly independent sequence rows.
3. The **rank** is the superior of the ranks of all finite matrices of the type:

$$
H_{N,\,N'} = \begin{bmatrix} H_0 & H_1 & \cdot & H_{N'} \\ H_1 & H_2 & \cdot & \cdot \\ \cdot & \cdot & \cdot & \cdot \\ H_N & \cdot & \cdot & H_{N+N'} \end{bmatrix}
$$

As in the finite-dimensional case, the three definitions are equivalent in the sense that the three numbers are equal, if finite, or they are all three infinite.

VECTOR AND MATRIX OPERATIONS

Let's now introduce the most common operations performed on vectors and matrices. An **operation** is a mapping that operates on scalars, vectors, and matrices to produce new scalars, vectors, or matrices. The notion of operations performed on a set of objects to produce another object of the same set is the key concept of algebra. Let's start with vector operations.

Vector Operations

The following operations are usually defined on vectors: (1) transpose, (2) addition, and (3) multiplication.

Transpose

The **transpose** operation transforms a row vector into a column vector and vice versa. Given the row vector $\mathbf{x} = [x_1 \ldots x_n]$ its transpose, denoted as $\mathbf{x}^T$ or $\mathbf{x}'$, is the column vector:

$$x^T = \begin{bmatrix} x_1 \\ \cdot \\ \cdot \\ \cdot \\ x_n \end{bmatrix}$$

Clearly the transpose of the transpose is the original vector:

$$(\mathbf{x}^T)^T = \mathbf{x}$$

Addition

Two row (or column) vectors $\mathbf{x} = [x_1...x_n]$, $\mathbf{y} = [y_1...y_n]$ with the same number n of components can be added. The **addition** of two vectors is a new vector whose components are the sums of the components:

$$\mathbf{x} + \mathbf{y} = [x_1 + y_1 ... x_n + y_n]$$

This definition can be generalized to any number N of summands:

$$\sum_{i=1}^{N} \mathbf{x}_i = \left[\sum_{i=1}^{N} x_{1i} ... \sum_{i=1}^{N} y_{ni} \right]$$

The summands must be both column or row vectors; it is not possible to add row vectors to column vectors.

It is clear from the definition of addition that addition is a commutative operation in the sense that the order of the summands does not matter: $\mathbf{x} + \mathbf{y} = \mathbf{y} + \mathbf{x}$. Addition is also an associative operation in the sense that $\mathbf{x} + (\mathbf{y} + \mathbf{z}) = (\mathbf{x} + \mathbf{y}) + \mathbf{z}$.

Multiplication

We define two types of multiplication: (1) multiplication of a scalar and a vector and (2) scalar multiplication of two vectors (inner product).[4]

The multiplication of a scalar λ and a row (or column) vector $\mathbf{x}$, denoted as $\lambda\mathbf{x}$, is defined as the multiplication of each component of the vector by the scalar:

---

[4] Different types of products between vectors can be defined: the vector product between vectors produces a third vector and the outer product produces a matrix. We do not define them here, as, though widely used in the physical sciences, they are not typically used in economics.

$$\lambda \mathbf{x} = [\lambda x_1 ... \lambda x_n]$$

As an example of the multiplication of a vector by a scalar, consider the vector of portfolio weights $\mathbf{w} = [w_1...w_n]$. If the total portfolio value at a given moment is P, then the holding in each asset is the product of the value by the vector of weights:

$$P\mathbf{w} = [Pw_1...Pw_n]$$

A similar definition holds for column vectors. It is clear from this definition that

$$\|a\mathbf{x}\| = |a|\|\mathbf{x}\|$$

and that multiplication by a scalar is associative as

$$\|a(\mathbf{x} + \mathbf{y})\| = \|a\mathbf{x}\| + \|a\mathbf{y}\|$$

The **scalar** (or **inner**) **product** of two vectors of the same dimensions $\mathbf{x}$, $\mathbf{y}$, denoted as $\mathbf{x} \cdot \mathbf{y}$, is defined between a row vector and a column vector. The scalar product between two vectors produces a scalar according to the following rule:

$$\mathbf{x} \cdot \mathbf{y} = \sum_{i=1}^{n} x_i y_i$$

For example, consider the column vector $\mathbf{a}$ of a particular attribute discussed earlier and the row vector $\mathbf{w}$ of portfolio weights. Then $\mathbf{a} \cdot \mathbf{w}$ is a scalar that shows the exposure of the portfolio to the particular attribute. That is,

$$\mathbf{a} \cdot \mathbf{w} = \begin{bmatrix} a_1 \\ a_2 \\ \cdot \\ \cdot \\ a_N \end{bmatrix} \begin{bmatrix} w_1 & w_2 & ...... & w_N \end{bmatrix}$$

$$= \sum_{n=1}^{N} a_n w_N$$

As another example, a portfolio's excess return is found by taking the transpose of the excess return vector, **r**, and multiplying it by the vector of portfolio weights, **w**. That is,

$$\mathbf{r}^T \cdot \mathbf{w} = \begin{bmatrix} r_1 \\ r_2 \\ . \\ . \\ . \\ r_N \end{bmatrix} \begin{bmatrix} w_1 & w_2 & \dots\dots & w_N \end{bmatrix}$$

$$= \sum_{n=1}^{N} r_n w_N$$

Two vectors **x**, **y** are said to be **orthogonal** if their scalar product is zero. The scalar product of two vectors can be interpreted geometrically as an orthogonal projection. In fact, the inner product of vectors **x** and **y**, divided by the square norm of **y**, can be interpreted as the orthogonal projection of **x** onto **y**. The following two properties are an immediate consequence of the definitions:

$$\|\mathbf{x}\| = \sqrt{\mathbf{x} \cdot \mathbf{x}}$$

$$(a\mathbf{x}) \cdot (b\mathbf{y}) = ab\mathbf{x} \cdot \mathbf{y}$$

Matrix Operations

The following five operations on matrices are usually defined: (1) transpose, (2) addition, (3) multiplication, (4) inverse, and (5) adjoint.

Transpose

The definition of the **transpose of a matrix** is an extension of the transpose of a vector. The transpose operation consists in exchanging rows with columns. Consider the $n \times m$ matrix

$$\mathbf{A} = \{a_{ij}\}_{nm}$$

The transpose of **A**, denoted $\mathbf{A}^T$ or $\mathbf{A}'$ is the $m \times n$ matrix whose ith row is the ith column of **A**:

$$\mathbf{A}^T = \{a_{ji}\}_{mn}$$

The following should be clear from this definition:

$$(\mathbf{A}^T)^T = \mathbf{A}$$

and that a matrix is symmetric if and only if

$$\mathbf{A}^T = \mathbf{A}$$

Addition

Consider two $n \times m$ matrices

$$\mathbf{A} = \{a_{ij}\}_{nm}$$

and

$$\mathbf{B} = \{b_{ij}\}_{nm}$$

The **sum** of the matrices $\mathbf{A}$ and $\mathbf{B}$ is defined as the $n \times m$ matrix obtained by adding the respective elements:

$$\mathbf{A} + \mathbf{B} = \{a_{ij} + b_{ij}\}_{nm}$$

Note that it is essential for the definition of addition that the two matrices have the same order $n \times m$.

The operation of addition can be extended to any number N of summands as follows:

$$\sum_{s=1}^{N} \mathbf{A}_i = \left\{ \sum_{s=1}^{N} a_{s_{ij}} \right\}_{nm}$$

where $a_{s_{ij}}$ is the generic i,j element of the sth summand.

The following properties of addition are immediate from the definition of addition:

$$\mathbf{A} + \mathbf{B} = \mathbf{B} + \mathbf{A}$$

$$\mathbf{A} + (\mathbf{B} + \mathbf{C}) = (\mathbf{A} + \mathbf{B}) + \mathbf{C} = \mathbf{A} + \mathbf{B} + \mathbf{C}$$

$$\mathrm{tr}(\mathbf{A} + \mathbf{B}) = \mathrm{tr}\mathbf{A} + \mathrm{tr}\mathbf{B}$$

The operation of addition of vectors defined above is clearly a special case of the more general operation of addition of matrices.

Multiplication
Consider a scalar c and a matrix:

$$\mathbf{A} = \{a_{ij}\}_{nm}$$

The **product** $c\mathbf{A} = \mathbf{A}c$ is the $n{\times}m$ matrix obtained by multiplying each element of the matrix by c:

$$c\mathbf{A} = \mathbf{A}c = \{ca_{ij}\}_{nm}$$

Multiplication of a matrix by a scalar is associative with respect to matrix addition:

$$c(\mathbf{A} + \mathbf{B}) = c\mathbf{A} + c\mathbf{B}$$

Let's now define the **product of two matrices**. Consider two matrices:

$$\mathbf{A} = \{a_{it}\}_{np}$$

and

$$\mathbf{B} = \{b_{sj}\}_{pm}$$

The product $\mathbf{C} = \mathbf{AB}$ is defined as follows:

$$\mathbf{C} = \mathbf{AB} = \{c_{ij}\} = \left\{ \sum_{t=1}^{p} a_{it} b_{tj} \right\}$$

The product $\mathbf{C} = \mathbf{AB}$ is therefore a matrix whose generic element $\{c_{ij}\}$ is the scalar product of the ith row of the matrix $\mathbf{A}$ and the jth column of the matrix $\mathbf{B}$. This definition generalizes the definition of scalar product of vectors: The scalar product of two n-dimensional vectors is the product of an $n{\times}1$ matrix (a row vector) for a $1{\times}n$ matrix (the column vector).

Following the above definition, the matrix product operation is performed rows by columns. Therefore, two matrices can be multiplied only if the number of columns (i.e., the number of elements in each row) of the first matrix equals the number of rows (i.e., the number of elements in each column) of the second matrix.

The following two **distributive properties** hold:

$$C(A + B) = CA + CB$$

$$(A + B)C = AC + BC$$

The **associative property** also holds:

$$(AB)C = A(BC)$$

However, the matrix product operation is not commutative. In fact, if **A** and **B** are two square matrices, in general $AB \neq BA$. Also $AB = 0$ does not imply $A = 0$ or $B = 0$.

Inverse and Adjoint

Consider two square matrices of order n, **A** and **B**. If $AB = BA = I$, then the matrix **B** is called the **inverse** of **A** and is denoted as A^{-1}. It can be demonstrated that the two following properties hold:

■ *Property 1.* A square matrix **A** admits an inverse A^{-1} if and only if it is nonsingular, i.e., if and only if its determinant is different from zero. Otherwise stated, a matrix **A** admits an inverse if and only if it is of full rank.

■ *Property 2.* The inverse of a square matrix, if it exists, is unique. This property is a consequence of the property that, if **A** is nonsingular, then $AB = AC$ implies $B = C$.

Consider now a square matrix of order n $A = \{a_{ij}\}$ and consider its cofactors α_{ij}. Recall that the cofactors α_{ij} are the signed minors $(-1)^{(i+j)}|M_{ij}|$ of the matrix **A**. The **adjoint** of the matrix **A**, denoted as Adj(**A**), is the following matrix:

$$\mathrm{Adj}(A) = \begin{bmatrix} \alpha_{1,1} & \cdot & \alpha_{1,j} & \cdot & \alpha_{1,n} \\ \cdot & \cdot & \cdot & \cdot & \cdot \\ \alpha_{i,1} & \cdot & \alpha_{i,j} & \cdot & \alpha_{i,n} \\ \cdot & \cdot & \cdot & \cdot & \cdot \\ \alpha_{n,1} & \cdot & \alpha_{n,j} & \cdot & \alpha_{n,n} \end{bmatrix}^T = \begin{bmatrix} \alpha_{1,1} & \cdot & \alpha_{2,1} & \cdot & \alpha_{n,1} \\ \cdot & \cdot & \cdot & \cdot & \cdot \\ \alpha_{1,i} & \cdot & \alpha_{2,i} & \cdot & \alpha_{n,i} \\ \cdot & \cdot & \cdot & \cdot & \cdot \\ \alpha_{1,n} & \cdot & \alpha_{2,n} & \cdot & \alpha_{n,n} \end{bmatrix}$$

The adjoint of a matrix $\mathbf{A}$ is therefore the transpose of the matrix obtained by replacing the elements of $\mathbf{A}$ with their cofactors.

If the matrix $\mathbf{A}$ is nonsingular, and therefore admits an inverse, it can be demonstrated that

$$\mathbf{A}^{-1} = \frac{\mathrm{Adj}(A)}{|\mathbf{A}|}$$

A square matrix $\mathbf{A}$ of order n is said to be orthogonal if the following property holds:

$$\mathbf{A}\mathbf{A}' = \mathbf{A}'\mathbf{A} = \mathbf{I}_n$$

Because in this case $\mathbf{A}$ must be of full rank, the transpose of an orthogonal matrix coincides with its inverse: $\mathbf{A}^{-1} = \mathbf{A}'$.

EIGENVALUES AND EIGENVECTORS

Consider a square matrix $\mathbf{A}$ of order n and the set of all n-dimensional vectors. The matrix $\mathbf{A}$ is a linear operator on the space of vectors. This means that $\mathbf{A}$ operates on each vector producing another vector and that the following property holds:

$$\mathbf{A}(a\mathbf{x} + b\mathbf{y}) = a\mathbf{A}\mathbf{x} + b\mathbf{A}\mathbf{y}$$

Consider now the set of vectors $\mathbf{x}$ such that the following property holds:

$$\mathbf{A}\mathbf{x} = \lambda\mathbf{x}$$

Any vector such that the above property holds is called an **eigenvector** of the matrix $\mathbf{A}$ and the corresponding value of λ is called an **eigenvalue**.

To determine the eigenvectors of a matrix and the relative eigenvalues, consider that the equation $\mathbf{A}\mathbf{x} = \lambda\mathbf{x}$ can be written as follows:

$$(\mathbf{A} - \lambda\mathbf{I})\mathbf{x} = 0$$

which can, in turn, be written as a system of linear equations:

$$(\mathbf{A} - \lambda\mathbf{I})\mathbf{x} = \begin{bmatrix} a_{1,1}-\lambda & \cdot & a_{1,j} & \cdot & a_{1,n} \\ & \cdot & & & \\ a_{i,1} & \cdot & a_{i,i}-\lambda & \cdot & a_{i,n} \\ & \cdot & & \cdot & \\ a_{n,1} & \cdot & a_{n,j} & \cdot & a_{n,n}-\lambda \end{bmatrix} \begin{bmatrix} x_1 \\ \cdot \\ x_i \\ \cdot \\ x_n \end{bmatrix} = 0$$

This system of equations has nontrivial solutions only if the matrix $\mathbf{A} - \lambda\mathbf{I}$ is singular. To determine the eigenvectors and the eigenvalues of the matrix $\mathbf{A}$ we must therefore solve the equation

$$|\mathbf{A} - \lambda\mathbf{I}| = \begin{vmatrix} a_{1,1}-\lambda & \cdot & a_{1,j} & \cdot & a_{1,n} \\ & \cdot & \cdot & \cdot & \\ a_{i,1} & \cdot & a_{i,i}-\lambda & \cdot & a_{i,n} \\ & \cdot & \cdot & \cdot & \\ a_{n,1} & \cdot & a_{n,j} & \cdot & a_{n,n}-\lambda \end{vmatrix} = 0$$

The expansion of this determinant yields a polynomial $\phi(\lambda)$ of degree n known as the **characteristic polynomial** of the matrix $\mathbf{A}$. The equation $\phi(\lambda) = 0$ is known as the **characteristic equation** of the matrix $\mathbf{A}$. In general, this equation will have n roots λ_s which are the eigenvalues of the matrix $\mathbf{A}$. To each of these eigenvalues corresponds a solution of the system of linear equations as illustrated below:

$$\begin{bmatrix} a_{1,1}-\lambda_s & \cdot & a_{1,j} & \cdot & a_{1,n} \\ & \cdot & \cdot & \cdot & \\ a_{i,1} & \cdot & a_{i,i}-\lambda_s & \cdot & a_{i,n} \\ & \cdot & \cdot & \cdot & \\ a_{n,1} & \cdot & a_{n,j} & \cdot & a_{n,n}-\lambda_s \end{bmatrix} \begin{bmatrix} x_{1_s} \\ \cdot \\ x_{i_s} \\ \cdot \\ x_{n_s} \end{bmatrix} = 0$$

Each solution represents the eigenvector $\mathbf{x}_s$ corresponding to the eigenvector λ_s. As we will see in Chapter 12, the determination of eigenvalues and eigenvectors is the basis for principal component analysis.

DIAGONALIZATION AND SIMILARITY

Diagonal matrices are much easier to handle than fully populated matrices. It is therefore important to create diagonal matrices equivalent (in a sense to be precisely defined) to a given matrix. Consider two square matrices $\mathbf{A}$ and $\mathbf{B}$. The matrices $\mathbf{A}$ and $\mathbf{B}$ are called **similar** if there exists a nonsingular matrix $\mathbf{R}$ such that

$$\mathbf{B} = \mathbf{R}^{-1}\mathbf{A}\mathbf{R}$$

The following two theorems can be demonstrated:

■ *Theorem 1.* Two similar matrices have the same eigenvalues.

■ *Theorem 2.* If $\mathbf{y}_i$ is an eigenvector of the matrix $\mathbf{B} = \mathbf{R}^{-1}\mathbf{A}\mathbf{R}$ corresponding to the eigenvalue λ_i, then the vector $\mathbf{x}_i = \mathbf{R}\mathbf{y}_i$ is an eigenvector of the matrix $\mathbf{A}$ corresponding to the same eigenvalue λ_i.

A diagonal matrix of order n always has n linearly independent eigenvectors. Consequently, a square matrix of order n has n linearly independent eigenvectors if and only if it is similar to a diagonal matrix.

Suppose the square matrix of order n has n linearly independent eigenvectors $\mathbf{x}_i$ and n distinct eigenvalues λ_i. This is true, for instance, if $\mathbf{A}$ is a real, symmetric matrix of order n. Arrange the eigenvectors, which are column vectors, in a square matrix: $\mathbf{P} = \{\mathbf{x}_i\}$. It can be demonstrated that $\mathbf{P}^{-1}\mathbf{A}\mathbf{P}$ is a diagonal matrix where the diagonal is made up of the eigenvalues:

$$\mathbf{P}^{-1}\mathbf{A}\mathbf{P} = \begin{bmatrix} \lambda_1 & 0 & 0 & 0 & 0 \\ 0 & \cdot & 0 & 0 & 0 \\ 0 & 0 & \lambda_i & 0 & 0 \\ 0 & 0 & 0 & \cdot & 0 \\ 0 & 0 & 0 & 0 & \lambda_n \end{bmatrix}$$

SINGULAR VALUE DECOMPOSITION

Suppose that the $n \times m$ matrix $\mathbf{A}$ with $m \geq n$ has $\mathrm{rank}(\mathbf{A}) = r > 0$. It can be demonstrated that there exists three matrices $\mathbf{U}, \mathbf{W}, \mathbf{V}$ such that the following decomposition, called **singular value decomposition**, holds:

$$\mathbf{A} = \mathbf{U}\mathbf{W}\mathbf{V}'$$

and such that $\mathbf{U}$ is $n \times r$ with $\mathbf{U}'\mathbf{U} = \mathbf{I}_r$; $\mathbf{W}$ is diagonal, with non-negative diagonal elements; and $\mathbf{V}$ is $m \times r$ with $\mathbf{V}'\mathbf{V} = \mathbf{I}_r$.

SUMMARY

■ In representing and modeling economic and financial phenomena it is useful to consider ordered arrays of numbers as a single mathematical object.

■ Ordered arrays of numbers are called vectors and matrices; vectors are a particular type of matrix.

■ It is possible to consistently define operations on vectors and matrices including the multiplication of matrices by scalars, sum of matrices, product of matrices, and inversion of matrices.

■ Determinants are numbers associated with square matrices defined as the sum of signed products of elements chosen from different rows and columns.

■ A matrix can be inverted only if its determinant is not zero.

■ The eigenvectors of a square matrix are those vectors that do not change direction when multiplied by the matrix.

CHAPTER 6

Concepts of Probability

Probability is the standard mathematical representation of uncertainty in finance. In this chapter we present concepts in probability theory that are applied in many areas in financial modeling and investment management. Here are just a few applications: The set of possible economic states is represented as a probability space; prices, cash flows, and other economic quantities subject to uncertainty are represented as time-dependent random variables (i.e., stochastic processes); conditional probabilities are used in representing the dynamics of asset prices; and, probability distributions are used in finding the optimal risk-return tradeoff.

REPRESENTING UNCERTAINTY WITH MATHEMATICS

Because we cannot build purely deterministic models of the economy, we need a mathematical representation of uncertainty. **Probability theory** is the mathematical description of uncertainty that presently enjoys the broadest diffusion. It is the paradigm of choice for mainstream finance theory. But it is by no means the only way to describe uncertainty. Other mathematical paradigms for uncertainty include, for example, fuzzy measures.[1]

Though probability as a mathematical axiomatic theory is well known, its interpretation is still the subject of debate. There are three basic interpretations of probability:

■ Probability as "intensity of belief" as suggested by John Maynard Keynes.[2]

---

[1] Lotfi A. Zadeh, "Fuzzy Sets," *Information and Control* 8 (1965), pp. 338–353.
[2] John Maynard Keynes, *Treatise on Probability* (McMillan Publishing, 1921).

- Probability as "relative frequency" as formulated by Richard von Mises.[3]
- Probability as an axiomatic system as formulated by Andrei N. Kolmogorov.[4]

The idea of probability as intensity of belief was introduced by John Maynard Keynes in his *Treatise on Probability*. In science as in our daily lives, we have beliefs that we cannot strictly prove but to which we attribute various degrees of likelihood. We judge not only the likelihood of individual events but also the plausibility of explanations. If we espouse probability as intensity of belief, probability theory is then a set of rules for making consistent probability statements. The obvious difficulty here is that one can judge only the consistency of probability reasoning, not its truth. Bayesian probability theory (which we will discuss later in the chapter) is based on the interpretation of probability as intensity of belief.

Probability as relative frequency is the standard interpretation of probability in the physical sciences. Introduced by Richard Von Mises in 1928, probability as relative frequency was subsequently extended by Hans Reichenbach.[5] Essentially, it equates probability statements with statements about the frequency of events in large samples; an unlikely event is an event that occurs only a small number of times. The difficulty with this interpretation is that relative frequencies are themselves uncertain. If we accept a probability interpretation of reality, there is no way to leap to certainty. In practice, in the physical sciences we usually deal with very large numbers—so large that nobody expects probabilities to deviate from their relative frequency. Nevertheless, the conceptual difficulty exists. As the present state of affairs might be a very unlikely one, probability statements can never be proved empirically.

The two interpretations of probability—as intensity of belief and as relative frequency—are therefore complementary. We make probability statements such as statements of relative frequency that are, ultimately, based on an *a priori* evaluation of probability insofar as we rule out, in practice, highly unlikely events. This is evident in most procedures of statistical estimation. A statistical estimate is a rule to choose the probability scheme in which one has the greatest faith. In performing statistical estimation, one chooses the probabilistic model that yields the

[3] Richard von Mises, *Wahrscheinlichkeitsrechnung, Statistik unt Wahrheit* (Vienna: Verlag von Julius Spring, 1928). (English edition published in 1939, *Probability, Statistics and Truth*.)
[4] Andrei N. Kolmogorov, *Grundbegriffe der Wahrscheinlichkeitsrechnung* (Berlin: Springer, 1933). (English edition published in 1950, *Foundations of the Theory of Probability*.)
[5] At the time, both were German professors working in Constantinople.

highest probability on the observed sample. This is strictly evident in maximum likelihood estimates but it is implicit in every statistical estimate. Bayesian statistics allow one to complement such estimates with additional *a priori* probabilistic judgment.

The axiomatic theory of probability avoids the above problems by interpreting probability as an abstract mathematical quantity. Developed primarily by the Russian mathematician Andrei Kolmogorov, the axiomatic theory of probability eliminated the logical ambiguities that had plagued probabilistic reasoning prior to his work. The application of the axiomatic theory is, however, a matter of interpretation.

In economics and finance theory, probability might have two different meanings: (1) as a descriptive concept and (2) as a determinant of the agent decision-making process. As a descriptive concept, probability is used in the sense of relative frequency, similar to its use in the physical sciences: the probability of an event is assumed to be approximately equal to the relative frequency of its occurrence in a large number of experiments. There is one difficulty with this interpretation, which is peculiar to economics: empirical data (i.e., financial and economic time series) have only one realization. Every estimate is made on a single time-evolving series. If stationarity (or a well-defined time process) is not assumed, performing statistical estimation is impossible.

PROBABILITY IN A NUTSHELL

In making probability statements we must distinguish between outcomes and events. **Outcomes** are the possible results of an experiment or an observation, such as the price of a security at a given moment. However, probability statements are not made on outcomes but on **events**, which are sets of possible outcomes. Consider, for example, the probability that the price of a security be in a given range, say from $10 to $12, in a given period.

In a discrete probability model (i.e., a model based on a finite or at most a countable number of individual events), the distinction between outcomes and events is not essential as the probability of an event is the sum of the probabilities of its outcomes. If, as happens in practice, prices can vary by only one-hundredth of a dollar, there are only a countable number of possible prices and the probability of each event will be the sum of the individual probabilities of each admissible price.

However, the distinction between outcomes and events is essential when dealing with continuous probability models. In a continuous probability model, the probability of each individual outcome is zero though the probability of an event might be a finite number. For example, if we represent prices as continuous functions, the probability that a price assumes any particular real number is strictly zero, though the probability that prices fall in a given interval might be other than zero.

Probability theory is a set of rules for inferring the probability of an event from the probability of other events. The basic rules are surprisingly simple. The entire theory is based on a few simple assumptions. First, the universe of possible outcomes or measurements must be fixed. This is a conceptually important point. If we are dealing with the prices of an asset, the universe is all possible prices; if we are dealing with n assets, the universe is the set of all possible n-tuples of prices. If we want to link n asset prices with k economic quantities, the universe is all possible $(n + k)$-tuples made up of asset prices and values of economic quantities.

Second, as our objective is to interpret probability as relative frequencies (i.e., percentages), the scale of probability is set to the interval $[0,1]$. The maximum possible probability is one, which is the probability that any of the possible outcomes occurs. The probability that none of the outcomes occurs is 0. In continuous probability models, the converse is not true as there are nonempty sets of measure zero. In other words, in continuous probability models, a probability of one is not equal to certainty.

Third, and last, the probability of the union of disjoint events is the sum of the probabilities of individual events.

All statements of probability theory are logical consequences of these basic rules. The simplicity of the logical structure of probability theory might be deceptive. In fact, the practical difficulty of probability theory consists in the description of events. For instance, derivative contracts link in possibly complex ways the events of the underlying with the events of the derivative contract. Though the probabilistic "dynamics" of the underlying phenomena can be simple, expressing the links between all possible contingencies renders the subject mathematically complex.

Probability theory is based on the possibility of assigning a precise uncertainty index to each event. This is a stringent requirement that might be too strong in many instances. In a number of cases we are simply uncertain without being able to quantify uncertainty. It might also happen that we can quantify uncertainty for some but not all events. There are representations of uncertainty that drop the strict requirement of a precise uncertainty index assigned to each event. Examples include fuzzy measures and the Dempster-Schafer theory of uncertainty.[6] The latter representations of uncertainty have been widely used in Artificial

[6] See G. Schafer, *A Mathematical Theory of Evidence* (Princeton, NJ: Princeton University Press, 1976); Judea Pearl, *Probabilistic Reasoning in Intelligent Systems: Networks of Plausible Beliefs* (San Mateo, CA: Morgan Kaufmann, 1988); and, Zadeh, "Fuzzy Sets."

Intelligence and engineering applications, but their use in economics and finance has so far been limited.

Let's now examine probability as the key representation of uncertainty, starting with a more formal account of probability theory.

OUTCOMES AND EVENTS

The axiomatic theory of probability is based on three fundamental concepts: (1) outcomes, (2) events, and (3) measure. The outcomes are the set of all possible results of an experiment or an observation. The set of all possible outcomes is often written as the set Ω. For instance, in the dice game a possible outcome is a pair of numbers, one for each face, such as 6 + 6 or 3 + 2. The space Ω is the set of all 36 possible outcomes.

Events are sets of outcomes. Continuing with the example of the dice game, a possible event is the set of all outcomes such that the sum of the numbers is 10. Probabilities are defined on events, not on outcomes. To render definitions consistent, events must be a class $\Im$ of subsets of Ω with the following properties:

- *Property 1.* $\Im$ is not empty

- *Property 2.* If $A \in \Im$ then $A^C \in \Im$; A^C is the complement of A with respect to Ω, made up of all those elements of Ω that do not belong to A

- *Property 3.* If $A_i \in \Im$ for $i = 1, 2, \ldots$ then $\bigcup_{i=1}^{\infty} A_i \in \Im$

Every such class is called a σ-algebra. Any class for which Property 3 is valid only for a finite number of sets is called an **algebra**.

Given a set Ω and a σ-algebra $\mathfrak{G}$ of subsets of Ω, any set $A \in \mathfrak{G}$ is said to be **measurable** with respect to $\mathfrak{G}$. The pair $(\Omega, \mathfrak{G})$ is said to be a **measurable space** (not to be confused with a measure space, defined later in this chapter). Consider a class $\mathfrak{G}$ of subsets of Ω and consider the smallest σ-algebra that contains $\mathfrak{G}$, defined as the intersection of all the σ-algebras that contain $\mathfrak{G}$. That σ-algebra is denoted by $\sigma\{\mathfrak{G}\}$ and is said to be the σ-algebra generated by $\mathfrak{G}$.

A particularly important space in probability is the **Euclidean space**. Consider first the real axis R (i.e., the Euclidean space R^1 in one dimension). Consider the collection formed by all intervals open to the left and closed to the right, for example, $(a, b]$. The σ-algebra generated by this set is called the 1-dimensional Borel σ-algebra and is denoted by $\mathfrak{B}$. The sets that belong to $\mathfrak{B}$ are called **Borel sets**.

Now consider the n-dimensional Euclidean space R^n, formed by n-tuples of real numbers. Consider the collection of all generalized rectangles open to the left and closed to the right, for example, $((a_1,b_1] \times \ldots \times (a_n,b_n])$. The σ-algebra generated by this collection is called the n-dimensional Borel σ-algebra and is denoted by $\mathfrak{B}^n$. The sets that belong to $\mathfrak{B}^n$ are called n-dimensional Borel sets.

The above construction is not the only possible one. The $\mathfrak{B}^n$, for any value of n, can also be generated by open or closed sets. As we will see later in this chapter, $\mathfrak{B}^n$ is fundamental to defining random variables. It defines a class of subsets of the Euclidean space on which it is reasonable to impose a probability structure: the class of every subset would be too big while the class of, say, generalized rectangles would be too small. The $\mathfrak{B}^n$ is a sufficiently rich class.

PROBABILITY

Intuitively speaking, probability is a set function that associates to every event a number between 0 and 1. Probability is formally defined by a triple $(\Omega,\mathfrak{J},P)$ called a **probability space**, where Ω is the set of all possible outcomes, $\mathfrak{J}$ the event σ-algebra, and P a probability measure.

A probability measure P is a set function from $\mathfrak{J}$ to R (the set of real numbers) that satisfies three conditions:

■ *Condition 1.* $0 \le P(A)$, for all $A \in \mathfrak{J}$

■ *Condition 2.* $P(\Omega) = 1$

■ *Condition 3.* $P(\cup A_i) = \Sigma P(A_i)$ for every finite or countable collection of disjoint events $\{A_i\}$ such that $A_i \in \mathfrak{J}$

$\mathfrak{J}$ does not have to be a σ-algebra. The definition of a probability space can be limited to algebras of events. However it is possible to demonstrate that a probability defined over an algebra of events $\aleph$ can be extended in a unique way to the σ-algebra generated by $\aleph$.

Two events are said to be independent if:

$$P(A \cap B) = P(A)P(B)$$

The (conditional) probability of event A given event B, written as $P(A|B)$, is defined as follows:

$$P(A|B) = \frac{P(A \cap B)}{P(B)}$$

It is possible to deduct from simple properties of set theory and from the disjoint additivity of probability that

$$P(A \cup B) = P(A) + P(B) - P(A \cap B) \leq P(A) + P(B)$$

$$P(A) = 1 - P(A^C)$$

Bayes theorem is a rule that links conditional probabilities. It can be stated in the following way:

$$P(A|B) = \frac{P(A \cap B)}{P(B)} = \frac{P(A \cap B)P(A)}{P(B)P(A)} = P(B|A)\frac{P(A)}{P(B)}$$

Bayes theorem allows one to recover the probability of the event A given B from the probability of the individual events A, B, and the probability of B given A.

Discrete probabilities are a special instance of probabilities. Defined over a finite or countable set of outcomes, discrete probabilities are non-zero over each outcome. The probability of an event is the sum of the probabilities of its outcomes. In the finite case, discrete probabilities are the usual combinatorial probabilities.

MEASURE

A **measure** is a set function defined over an algebra or σ-algebra of sets, denumerably additive, and such that it takes value zero on the empty set but can otherwise assume any positive value including, conventionally, an infinite value. A probability is thus a measure of total mass 1 (i.e., it takes value 1 on the set Ω).

A measure can be formally defined as a function $M(A)$ from an algebra or a σ-algebra $\mathfrak{I}$ to R (the set of real numbers) that satisfies the following three properties:

■ *Property 1.* $0 \leq M(A)$, for every $A \in \mathfrak{I}$

■ *Property 2.* $M(\varnothing) = 0$

■ *Property 3.* $M(\cup\, A_i) = \Sigma M(A_i)$ for every finite or countable collection of disjoint events $\{A_i\}$ such that $A_i \in \Im$

If M is a measure defined over a σ-algebra $\Im$, the triple $(\Omega,\Im,M)$ is called a **measure space** (this term is not used if $\Im$ is an algebra). Recall that the pair $(\Omega,\Im)$ is a **measurable space** if $\Im$ is a σ-algebra. Measures in general, and not only probabilities, can be uniquely extended from an algebra to the generated σ-algebra.

RANDOM VARIABLES

Probability is a set function defined over a space of events; **random variables** transfer probability from the original space Ω into the space of real numbers. Given a probability space $(\Omega,\Im,P)$, a random variable X is a function $X(\omega)$ defined over the set Ω that takes values in the set R of real numbers such that

$$(\omega: X(\omega) \le x) \in \Im$$

for every real number x. In other words, the inverse image of any interval $(-\infty, x]$ is an event. It can be demonstrated that the inverse image of any Borel set is also an event.

A real-valued set function defined over Ω is said to be measurable with respect to a σ-algebra $\Im$ if the inverse image of any Borel set belongs to $\Im$. Random variables are real-valued measurable functions. A random variable that is measurable with respect to a σ-algebra cannot discriminate between events that are not in that σ-algebra. This is the primary reason why the abstract and rather difficult concept of measurability is important in probability theory. By restricting the set of events that can be identified by a random variable, measurability defines the "coarse graining" of information relative to that variable. A random variable X is said to generate $\mathfrak{G}$ if $\mathfrak{G}$ is the smallest σ-algebra in which it is measurable.

INTEGRALS

In Chapter 4 on calculus we defined the integral of a real-valued function on the real line. However, the notion of the integral can be generalized to a general measure space. Though a bit technical, these definitions are important in the context of probability theory.

For each measure M, the **integral** is a number that is associated to every integrable function f. It is defined in the following two steps:

■ *Step 1.* Suppose that f is a measurable, non-negative function and consider a finite decomposition of the space Ω, that is to say a finite collection of disjoint subsets $A_i \subset \Omega$ whose union is Ω:

$$A_i \subset \Omega \text{ such that } A_i \cap A_j = \varnothing \text{ for } i \neq j \text{ and } \cup A_i = \Omega$$

Consider the sum

$$\sum_i \inf(f(\omega): \omega \in A_i) M(A_i)$$

The integral

$$\int_\Omega f dM$$

is defined as the supremum, if it exists, of all these sums over all possible decompositions of Ω. Suppose that f is bounded and non-negative and $M(\Omega) < \infty$. Let's call

$$S_- = \sup\left(\sum_i (\inf_{\omega \in A_i} f(\omega) M(A_i))\right)$$

the lower integral and

$$S^+ = \inf\left(\sum_i (\sup_{\omega \in A_i} f(\omega) M(A_i))\right)$$

the upper integral. It can be demonstrated that if the integral exists then $S^+ = S_-$. It is possible to define the integral as the common value $S = S^+ = S_-$. This approach is the Darboux-Young approach to integration.[7]

■ *Step 2.* Given a measurable function f not necessarily non-negative, consider its decomposition in its positive and negative parts $f = f^+ - f^-$. The integral of f is defined as the difference, if a difference exists, between the integrals of its positive and negative parts.

---

[7] See Patrick Billingsley, *Probability and Measure*, Second edition (New York: Wiley, 1985).

The integral can be defined not only on Ω but on any measurable set G. In order to define the integral over a measurable set G, consider the indicator function I_G, which assumes value 1 on each point of the set G and 0 elsewhere. Consider now the function $f \cdot I_G$. The integral over the set G is defined as

$$\int_G f dM = \int_\Omega f \cdot I_G dM$$

The integral $\int_G f dM$ is called the indefinite integral of f.

Given a σ-algebra $\mathfrak{I}$, suppose that G and M are two measures and that a function f exists such that for $A \in \mathfrak{I}$

$$G(A) = \int_A f dM$$

In this case G is said to have density f with respect to M.

The integrals in the sense of Riemann and in the sense of Lebesgue-Stieltjes (see Chapter 4 on calculus) are special instances of this more general definition of the integral. Note that the Lebesgue-Stieltjes integral was defined in Chapter 4 in one dimension. Its definition can be extended to n-dimensional spaces. In particular, it is always possible to define the Lebesgue-Stieltjes integral with respect to a n-dimensional distribution function. We omit the definitions which are rather technical.[8]

Given a probability space $(\Omega,\mathfrak{I},P)$ and a random variable X, the expected value of X is its integral with respect to the probability measure P

$$E[X] = \int_\Omega X dP$$

where integration is extended to the entire space.

DISTRIBUTIONS AND DISTRIBUTION FUNCTIONS

Given a probability space $(\Omega,\mathfrak{I},P)$ and a random variable X, consider a set $A \in \mathfrak{B}^1$. Recall that a random variable is a real-valued measurable func-

---

[8] For details, see Yuan Shih Chow and Henry Teicher, *Probability Theory: Second Edition* (New York: Springer, 1988).

tion defined over the set of outcomes. Therefore, the inverse image of A, $X^{-1}(A)$ belongs to $\mathfrak{S}$ and has a well-defined probability $P(X^{-1}(A))$.

The measure P thus induces another measure on the real axis called **distribution** or **distribution law** of the random variable X given by: $\mu_X(A) = P(X^{-1}(A))$. It is easy to see that this measure is a probability measure on the Borel sets. A random variable therefore transfers the probability originally defined over the space Ω to the set of real numbers.

The function F defined by: $F(x) = P(X \leq x)$ for $x \in R$ is the **cumulative distribution function (c.d.f.)**, or simply **distribution function (d.f.)**, of the random variable X. Suppose that there is a function f such that

$$F(x) = \int_{-\infty}^{x} f \, dy$$

or $F'(x) = f(x)$, then the function f is called the **probability density function** of the random variable X.

RANDOM VECTORS

After considering a single random variable, the next step is to consider not only one but a set of random variables referred to as **random vectors**. Random vectors are formed by n-tuples of random variables. Consider a probability space $(\Omega, \mathfrak{S}, P)$. A random variable is a measurable function from Ω to R^1; a random vector is a measurable function from Ω to R^n.

We can therefore write a random vector $\mathbf{X}$ as a vector-valued function

$$f(\omega) = [f_1(\omega) \; f_2(\omega) \; ... \; f_n(\omega)]$$

Measurability is defined with respect to the Borel σ-algebra $\mathfrak{B}^n$. It can be demonstrated that the function f is measurable $\mathfrak{S}$ if and only if each component function $f_i(\omega)$ is measurable $\mathfrak{S}$.

Conceptually, the key issue is to define joint probabilities (i.e., the probabilities that the n variables are in a given set). For example, consider the joint probability that the inflation rate is in a given interval *and* the economic growth rate in another given interval.

Consider the Borel σ-algebra $\mathfrak{B}^n$ on the real n-dimensional space R^n. It can be demonstrated that a random vector formed by n random variables X_i, $i = 1,2,...,n$ induces a probability measure over $\mathfrak{B}^n$. In fact, the set $(\omega \in \Omega: (X_1(\omega), X_2(\omega),...,X_n(\omega)) \in H; H \in \mathfrak{B}^n) \in \mathfrak{S}$ (i.e., the inverse image of every set of the σ-algebra $\mathfrak{B}^n$ belongs to the σ-algebra $\mathfrak{S}$). It is therefore possible to induce over every set H that belongs to $\mathfrak{B}^n$ a probability measure, which is the joint probability of the n random variables X_i. The function

$$F(x_1, \ldots, x_n) = P(X_1 \leq x_1, \ldots, X_n \leq x_n)$$

where $x_i \in R$ is called the **n-dimensional cumulative distribution function** or simply **n-dimensional distribution function (c.d.f. or d.f.)**. Suppose there exists a function $f(x_1, \ldots, x_n)$ for which the following relationship holds:

$$F(x_1, \ldots, x_n) = \int_{-\infty}^{x_1} \cdots \int_{-\infty}^{x_n} f(u_1, \ldots, u_n) du_1 \ldots du_n$$

The function $f(x_1, \ldots, x_n)$ is called the **n-dimensional probability density function (p.d.f.)** of the random vector X. Given a n-dimensional probability density function $f(x_1, \ldots, x_n)$, if we integrate with respect to all variables except the j-th variable, we obtain the **marginal density** of that variable:

$$f_{X_j}(y) = \int_{-\infty}^{\infty} \cdots \int_{-\infty}^{\infty} f(u_1, \ldots, u_n) du_1 \cdot du_{j-1} du_{j+1} \cdot du_n$$

Given a n-dimensional d.f. we define the **marginal distribution function** with respect to the j-th variable, $F_{X_j}(y) = P(X_j \leq y)$ as follows:

$$F_{x_j}(y) = \lim_{\substack{x_i \to \infty \\ i \neq j}} F(x_1, \ldots, x_{j-1}, y, x_{j+1}, \ldots, x_n)$$

If the distribution admits a density we can also write

$$F_{X_j}(y) = \int_{-\infty}^{y} f_{X_j}(u) du$$

These definitions can be extended to any number of variables. Given a n-dimensional p.d.f., if we integrate with respect to k variables $(x_{i_1}, \ldots, x_{i_k})$ over R^k, we obtain the marginal density functions with respect to the remaining variables. Marginal distribution functions with respect to any subset of variables can be defined taking the infinite limit with respect to all other variables.

Any d.f. $F_X(y)$ defines a Lebesgue-Stieltjes measure and a Lebesgue-Stieltjes integral. For example, as we have seen in Chapter 4, in the 1-dimensional case, the measure is defined by the differences $F_{X_j}(x_i) - F_{X_j}(x_{i-1})$. We can now write expectations in two different, and more useful, ways. In an earlier section in this chapter, given a probability space $(\Omega, \mathfrak{I}, P)$, we defined the expectation of a random variable X as the following integral

$$E[X] = \int_\Omega X dP$$

Suppose now that the random variable X has a d.f. $F_X(u)$. It can be demonstrated that the following relationship holds:

$$E[X] = \int_\Omega X dP = \int_{-\infty}^{\infty} u dF_X(u)$$

where the last integral is intended in the sense of Riemann-Stieltjes. If, in addition, the d.f. $F_{X_j}(u)$ has a density $f_X(u) = F'_X(u)$, then we can write the expectation as follows:

$$E[X] = \int_\Omega X dP = \int_{-\infty}^{\infty} u dF_X(u) = \int_{-\infty}^{\infty} u f(u) du$$

where the last integral is intended in the sense of Riemann. More in general, given a measurable function g the following relationship holds:

$$E[g(X)] = \int_{-\infty}^{\infty} g(u) dF_X(u) = \int_{-\infty}^{\infty} g(u) f(u) du$$

This latter expression of expectation is the most widely used in practice.

In general, however, knowledge of the distributions and of distribution functions of each random variable is not sufficient to determine the joint probability distribution function. As we will see later in this chapter, the joint distribution is determined by the marginal distributions plus the copula function.

Two random variables X, Y are said to be independent if

$$P(X \in A, Y \in B) = P(X \in A)P(Y \in B)$$

for all $A \in \mathfrak{B}$, $B \in \mathfrak{B}$. This definition generalizes in obvious ways to any number of variables and therefore to the components of a random vector. It can be shown that if the components of a random vector are independent, the joint probability distribution is the product of distributions. Therefore, if the variables $(X_1,...,X_n)$ are all mutually independent, we can write the joint d.f. as a product of marginal distribution functions:

$$F(x_1, ..., x_n) = \prod_{j=1}^{n} F_{X_j}(x_j)$$

It can also be demonstrated that if a d.f. admits a joint p.d.f., the joint p.d.f. factorizes as follows:

$$f(x_1, ..., x_n) = \prod_{j=1}^{n} f_{X_j}(x_j)$$

Given the marginal p.d.f.s the joint d.f. can be recovered as follows:

$$F(x_1, ..., x_n) = \int_{-\infty}^{x_1} ... \int_{-\infty}^{x_n} f(u_1, ..., u_n) du_1 ... du_n$$

$$= \int_{-\infty}^{x_1} ... \int_{-\infty}^{x_n} \left[\prod_{j=1}^{n} f_{X_j}(u_j) \right] du_1 ... du_n$$

$$= \prod_{j=1}^{n} \int_{-\infty}^{x_j} f_{X_j}(u_j) du_j$$

$$= \prod_{j=1}^{n} F_{X_j}(x_j)$$

STOCHASTIC PROCESSES

Given a probability space $(\Omega, \mathfrak{S}, P)$ a stochastic process is a parameterized collection of random variables $\{X_t\}$, $t \in [0,T]$ that are measurable with respect to $\mathfrak{S}$. The parameter t is often interpreted as time. The interval in which a stochastic process is defined might extend to infinity in both directions.

When it is necessary to emphasize the dependence of the random variable from both time t and the element ω, a stochastic process is explicitly written as a function of two variables: $X = X(t,\omega)$. Given ω, the function $X = X_t(\omega)$ is a function of time that is referred to as the **path** of the stochastic process.

The variable X might be a single random variable or a multidimensional random vector. A stochastic process is therefore a function $X = X(t,\omega)$ from the product space $[0,T] \times \Omega$ into the n-dimensional real space R^n. Because to each ω corresponds a time path of the process—in general formed by a set of functions $X = X_t(\omega)$—it is possible to identify the space Ω with a subset of the real functions defined over an interval $[0,T]$.

Let's now discuss how to represent a stochastic process $X = X(t,\omega)$ and the conditions of identity of two stochastic processes. As a stochastic process is a function of two variables, we can define equality as pointwise identity for each couple (t,ω). However, as processes are defined over probability spaces, pointwise identity is seldom used. It is more fruitful to define equality modulo sets of measure zero or equality with respect to probability distributions. In general, two random variables X,Y will be considered equal if the equality $X(\omega) = Y(\omega)$ holds for every ω with the exception of a set of probability zero. In this case, it is said that the equality holds almost everywhere (denoted *a.e.*).

A rather general (but not complete) representation is given by the finite dimensional probability distributions. Given any set of indices $t_1,...,t_m$, consider the distributions

$$\mu_{t_1, ..., t_m}(H) = P[(X_{t_1}, ..., X_{t_m}) \in H, H \in \mathfrak{B}^n]$$

These probability measures are, for any choice of the t_i, the finite-dimensional joint probabilities of the process. They determine many, but not all, properties of a stochastic process. For example, the finite dimensional distributions of a Brownian motion do not determine whether or not the process paths are continuous.

In general, the various concepts of equality between stochastic processes can be described as follows:

■ *Property 1.* Two stochastic processes are weakly equivalent if they have the same finite-dimensional distributions. This is the weakest form of equality.

■ *Property 2.* The process $X = X(t,\omega)$ is said to be equivalent or to be a modification of the process $Y = Y(t,\omega)$ if, for all t,

$$P(X_t = Y_t) = 1$$

■ *Property 3.* The process $X = X(t,\omega)$ is said to be strongly equivalent to or indistinguishable from the process $Y = Y(t,\omega)$ if

$$P(X_t = Y_t, \text{ for all } t) = 1$$

Property 3 implies Property 2, which in turn implies Property 1. Implications do not hold in the opposite direction. Two processes having the same finite distributions might have completely different paths. However it is possible to demonstrate that if one assumes that paths are continuous functions of time, Properties 2 and 3 become equivalent.

PROBABILISTIC REPRESENTATION OF FINANCIAL MARKETS

We are now in the position to summarize the probabilistic representation of financial markets. From a financial point of view, an *asset* is a contract which gives the right to receive a distribution of future cash flows. In the case of a common stock, the stream of cash flows will be uncertain. It includes the common stock dividends and the proceeds of the eventual liquidation of the firm. A *debt instrument* is a contract that gives its owner the right to receive periodic interest payments and the repayment of the principal by the maturity date. Except in the case of debt instruments of governments whose risk of default is perceived as extremely low, payments are uncertain as the issuing entity might default.

Suppose that all payments are made at the trading dates and that no transactions take place between trading dates. Let's assume that all assets are traded (i.e., exchanged on the market) at either discrete fixed dates, variable dates or continuously. At each trading date there is a market price for each asset. Each asset is therefore modeled with two time series, a series of market prices and a series of cash flows. As both series are subject to uncertainty, cash flows and prices are time-dependent random variables (i.e., they are stochastic processes). The time dependence of random variables in this probabilistic setting is a delicate question and will be examined shortly.

Following Kenneth Arrow[9] and using a framework now standard, the economy and the financial markets in a situation of uncertainty are described with the following basic concepts:

---

[9] Kenneth Arrow, "The Role of Securities in the Optimal Allocation of Risk Bearing," *Review of Economic Studies* (April 1964), pp. 91–96.

- It is assumed that the economy is in one of the states of a probability space $(\Omega, \Im, P)$.

- Every security is described by two stochastic processes formed by two time-dependent random variables $S_t(\omega)$ and $d_t(\omega)$ representing prices and cash flows of the asset.

This representation is completely general and is not linked to the assumption that the space of states is finite.

INFORMATION STRUCTURES

Let's now turn our attention to the question of time. The previous discussion considered a space formed by states in an abstract sense. We must now introduce an appropriate representation of time as well as rules that describe the evolution of information, that is, **information propagation**, over time. The concepts of information and information propagation are fundamental in economics and finance theory.

The concept of information in finance is different from both the intuitive notion of information and that of information theory in which information is a quantitative measure related to the *a priori* probability of messages.[10] In our context, information means the (progressive) revelation of the set of events to which the current state of the economy belongs. Though somewhat technical, this concept of information sheds light on the probabilistic structure of finance theory. The point is the following. Assets are represented by stochastic processes, that is, time-dependent random variables. But the probabilistic states on which these random variables are defined represent entire histories of the economy. To embed time into the probabilistic structure of states in a coherent way calls for information structures and filtrations (a concept we explain in the next section).

Recall that it is assumed that the economy is in one of many possible states and that there is uncertainty on the state that has been realized. Consider a time period of the economy. At the beginning of the period, there is complete uncertainty on the state of the economy (i.e., there is complete uncertainty on what path the economy will take). Different events have different probabilities, but there is no certainty. As time passes, uncertainty is reduced as the number of states to which the econ-

---

[10] There is indeed a deep link between information theory and econometrics embodied in concepts such as the Fisher Information Matrix, see Chapter 12.

omy can belong is progressively reduced. Intuitively, revelation of information means the progressive reduction of the number of possible states; at the end of the period, the realized state is fully revealed. In continuous time and continuous states, the number of events is infinite at each instant. Thus its cardinality remains the same. We cannot properly say that the number of events shrinks. A more formal definition is required.

The progressive reduction of the set of possible states is formally expressed in the concepts of information structure and filtration. Let's start with **information structures**. Information structures apply only to discrete probabilities defined over a discrete set of states. At the initial instant T_0, there is complete uncertainty on the state of the economy; the actual state is known only to belong to the largest possible event (that is, the entire space Ω). At the following instant T_1, assuming that instants are discrete, the states are separated into a **partition**, a partition being a denumerable class of disjoint sets whose union is the space itself. The actual state belongs to one of the sets of the partitions. The revelation of information consists in ruling out all sets but one. For all the states of each partition, and only for these, random variables assume the same values.

Suppose, to exemplify, that only two assets exist in the economy and that each can assume only two possible prices and pay only two possible cash flows. At every moment there are 16 possible price-cash flow combinations. We can thus see that at the moment T_1 all the states are partitioned into 16 sets, each containing only one state. Each partition includes all the states that have a given set of prices and cash distributions at the moment T_1. The same reasoning can be applied to each instant. The evolution of information can thus be represented by a tree structure in which every path represents a state and every point a partition. Obviously the tree structure does not have to develop as symmetrically as in the above example; the tree might have a very generic structure of branches.

FILTRATION

The concept of information structure based on partitions provides a rather intuitive representation of the propagation of information through a tree of progressively finer partitions. However, this structure is not sufficient to describe the propagation of information in a general probabilistic context. In fact, the set of possible events is much richer than the set of partitions. It is therefore necessary to identify not only partitions but also a structure of events. The structure of events used to define the propagation of information is called a **filtration**. In the discrete case, however, the two concepts—information structure and filtration—are equivalent.

The concept of filtration is based on identifying all events that are known at any given instant. It is assumed that it is possible to associate to each trading moment t a σ-algebra of events $\Im_t \subset \Im$ formed by all events that are known prior to or at time t. It is assumed that events are never "forgotten," that is, that $\Im_t \subset \Im_s$, if $t < s$. An ordering of time is thus created. This ordering is formed by an increasing sequence of σ-algebras, each associated to the time at which all its events are known. This sequence is a filtration. Indicated as $\{\Im_t\}$, a filtration is therefore an increasing sequence of all σ-algebras $\Im_t$, each associated to an instant t.

In the finite case, it is possible to create a mutual correspondence between filtrations and information structures. In fact, given an information structure, it is possible to associate to each partition the algebra generated by the same partition. Observe that a tree information structure is formed by partitions that create increasing refinement: By going from one instant to the next, every set of the partition is decomposed. One can then conclude that the algebras generated by an information structure form a filtration.

On the other hand, given a filtration $\{\Im_t\}$, it is possible to associate a partition to each $\Im_t$. In fact, given any element that belongs to Ω, consider any other element that belongs to Ω such that, for each set of $\Im_t$, both either belong to or are outside this set. It is easy to see that classes of equivalence are thus formed, that these create a partition, and that the algebra generated by each such partition is precisely the $\Im_t$ that has generated the partition.

A stochastic process is said to be adapted to the filtration $\{\Im_t\}$ if the variable X_t is measurable with respect to the σ-algebra $\Im_t$. It is assumed that the price and cash distribution processes $S_t(\omega)$ and $d_t(\omega)$ of every asset are adapted to $\{\Im_t\}$. This means that, for each t, no measurement of any price or cash distribution variable can identify events not included in the respective algebra or σ-algebra. Every random variable is a partial image of the set of states seen from a given point of view and at a given moment.

The concepts of filtration and of processes adapted to a filtration are fundamental. They ensure that information is revealed without anticipation. Consider the economy and associate at every instant a partition and an algebra generated by the partition. Every random variable defined at that moment assumes a value constant on each set of the partition. The knowledge of the realized values of the random variables does not allow identifying sets of events finer than partitions.

One might well ask: Why introduce the complex structure of σ-algebras as opposed to simply defining random variables? The point is that, from a logical point of view, the primitive concept is that of states and events. The evolution of time has to be defined on the primitive structure—it cannot simply be imposed on random variables. In practice, filtrations become an important concept when dealing with conditional probabilities in a continuous environment. As the probability that a continuous random variable assumes a specific value is zero, the definition of conditional probabilities requires the machinery of filtration.

CONDITIONAL PROBABILITY AND CONDITIONAL EXPECTATION

Conditional probabilities and conditional averages are fundamental in the stochastic description of financial markets. For instance, one is generally interested in the probability distribution of the price of an asset at some date given its price at an earlier date. The widely used regression models are an example of conditional expectation models.

The **conditional probability** of event A given event B was defined earlier as

$$P(A|B) = \frac{P(A \cap B)}{P(B)}$$

This simple definition cannot be used in the context of continuous random variables because the conditioning event (i.e., one variable assuming a given value) has probability zero. To avoid this problem, we condition on σ-algebras and not on single zero-probability events. In general, as each instant is characterized by a σ-algebra $\Im_t$, the conditioning elements are the $\Im_t$.

The general definition of conditional expectation is the following. Consider a probability space $(\Omega, \Im, P)$ and a σ-algebra $\mathfrak{G}$ contained in $\Im$ and suppose that X is an integrable random variable on $(\Omega, \Im, P)$. We define the conditional expectation of X with respect to $\mathfrak{G}$, written as $E[X|\mathfrak{G}]$, as a random variable measurable with respect to $\mathfrak{G}$ such that

$$\int_G E[X|\mathfrak{G}]dP = \int_G XdP$$

for every set $G \in \mathfrak{G}$. In other words, the **conditional expectation** is a random variable whose average on every event that belongs to $\mathfrak{G}$ is equal to the average of X over those same events, but it is $\mathfrak{G}$-measurable while X is not. It is possible to demonstrate that such variables exist and are unique up to a set of measure zero.

Econometric models usually condition a random variable given another variable. In the previous framework, conditioning one random variable X with respect to another random variable Y means conditioning X given $\sigma\{Y\}$ (i.e., given the σ-algebra generated by Y). Thus $E[X|Y]$ means $E[X|\sigma\{Y\}]$.

This notion might seem to be abstract and to miss a key aspect of conditioning: intuitively, conditional expectation is a function of the conditioning variable. For example, given a stochastic price process, X_t, one would like to visualize conditional expectation $E[X_t|X_s]$, $s < t$ as a **function** of X_s that yields the expected price at a future date given the present price. This intuition is not wrong insofar as the conditional expectation $E[X|Y]$ of X given Y is a random variable function of Y. For example, the regression function that will be explained later in this chapter is indeed a function that yields the conditional expectation.

However, we need to specify how conditional expectations are formed, given that the usual conditional probabilities cannot be applied as the conditioning event has probability zero. Here is where the above definition comes into play. The conditional expectation of a variable X given a variable Y is defined in full generality as a variable that is measurable with respect to the σ-algebra $\sigma(Y)$ generated by the conditioning variable Y and has the same expected value of Y on each set of $\sigma(Y)$. Later in this section we will see how conditional expectations can be expressed in terms of the joint p.d.f. of the conditioning and conditioned variables.

One can define conditional probabilities starting from the concept of conditional expectations. Consider a probability space $(\Omega, \mathfrak{I}, P)$, a sub-$\sigma$-algebra $\mathfrak{G}$ of $\mathfrak{I}$, and two events $A \in \mathfrak{I}$, $B \in \mathfrak{I}$. If I_A, I_B are the indicator functions of the sets A, B (the indicator function of a set assumes value 1 on the set, 0 elsewhere), we can define conditional probabilities of the event A, respectively, given $\mathfrak{G}$ or given the event B as

$$P(A|\mathfrak{G}) = E[I_A|\mathfrak{G}] \qquad P(A|B) = E[I_A|I_B]$$

Using these definitions, it is possible to demonstrate that given two random variables X and Y with joint density $f(x,y)$, the conditional density of X given Y is

$$f(x|y) = \frac{f(x, y)}{f_Y(y)}$$

where the marginal density, defined as

$$f_Y(y) = \int\limits_{-\infty}^{\infty} f(x, y)dx$$

is assumed to be strictly positive.

In the discrete case, the conditional expectation is a random variable that takes a constant value over the sets of the finite partition associated to $\Im_t$. Its value for each element of Ω is defined by the classical concept of conditional probability. Conditional expectation is simply the average over a partition assuming the classical conditional probabilities.

An important econometric concept related to conditional expectations is that of a **martingale**. Given a probability space $(\Omega,\Im,P)$ and a filtration $\{\Im_t\}$, a sequence of $\Im_i$-measurable random variables X_i is called a martingale if the following condition holds:

$$E[X_{i+1}|\Im_i] = X_i$$

A martingale translates the idea of a "fair game" as the expected value of the variable at the next period is the present value of the same value.

MOMENTS AND CORRELATION

If X is a random variable on a probability space $(\Omega,\Im,P)$, the quantity $E[|X|^p]$, $p > 0$ is called the **p-th absolute moment** of X. If k is any positive integer, $E[X^k]$, if it exists, is called the **k-th moment**. In the general case of a probability measure P we can therefore write:

- $E[|X|^p] = \int\limits_{\Omega}|X|^p dP$, $p > 0$, is the p-th absolute moment.

- $E[X^k] = \int\limits_{\Omega}X^k dP$, if it exists for k positive integer, is the k-th moment.

In the case of discrete probabilities p_i, $\Sigma p_i = 1$ the above expressions become

$$E[|X|^p] = \sum|x_i|^p p_i$$

and

$$E[X^k] = \sum x_i^k p_i$$

respectively. If the variable X is continuous and has a density $p(x)$ such that

$$\int_{-\infty}^{\infty} p(x)dx = 1$$

we can write

$$E[|X|^p] = \int_{-\infty}^{\infty} |x|^p p(x)dx$$

and

$$E[X^k] = \int_{-\infty}^{\infty} x^k p(x)dx$$

respectively.

The centered moments are the moments of the fluctuations of the variables around its mean. For example, the **variance** of a variable X is defined as the centered moment of second order:

$$\text{var}(X) = \sigma_x^2 = \sigma^2(X) = E[(X - \overline{X})^2]$$

$$= \int_{-\infty}^{\infty} (x - \overline{X})^2 p(x)dx = \int_{-\infty}^{\infty} x^2 p(x)dx - \left[\int_{-\infty}^{\infty} xp(x)dx \right]^2$$

where $\overline{X} = E[X]$.

The positive square root of the variance, σ_x is called the **standard deviation** of the variable.

We can now define the covariance and the correlation coefficient of a variable. **Correlation** is a quantitative measure of the strength of the dependence between two variables. Intuitively, two variables are dependent if they move together. If they move together, they will be above or below their respective means in the same state. Therefore, in this case, the product of their respective deviations from the means will have a positive mean. We call this mean the **covariance** of the two variables.

The covariance divided by the product of the standard deviations is a dimensionless number called the **correlation coefficient**.

Given two random variables X, Y with finite expected values and finite variances, we can write the following definitions:

■ $\text{cov}(X, Y) = \sigma_{X,Y} = E[(X - \overline{X})(Y - \overline{Y})]$ is the covariance of X, Y.

■ $\rho_{X,Y} = \dfrac{\sigma_{X,Y}}{\sigma_X \sigma_Y}$ is the correlation coefficient of X, Y.

The correlation coefficient can assume values in the interval $[-1,1]$. If two variables X, Y are independent, their correlation coefficient vanishes. However, uncorrelated variables, that is, variables whose correlation coefficient is zero, are not necessarily independent.

It can be demonstrated that the following property of variances holds:

$$\text{var}\left(\sum_i X_i\right) = \sum_i \text{var}(X_i) + \sum_{i \neq j} \text{cov}(X_i, X_j)$$

Further, it can be demonstrated that the following properties hold:

$$\sigma_{X,Y} = E[XY] - E[X]E[Y]$$

$$\sigma_{X,Y} = \sigma_{Y,X}$$

$$\sigma_{aX,bY} = ab\sigma_{Y,X}$$

$$\sigma_{X+Y,Z} = \sigma_{X,Z} + \sigma_{Y,Z}$$

$$\text{cov}\left(\sum_i a_i X_i, \sum_i b_j Y_j\right) = \sum_i \sum_j a_i b_j \text{cov}(X_i, Y_j)$$

COPULA FUNCTIONS

Understanding dependences or functional links between variables is a key theme of modern econometrics. In general terms, functional dependences are represented by dynamic models. As we will see in Chapter 11, many important models are linear models whose coefficients are correlations coefficients. In many instances, in particular in risk management, it is important to arrive at a quantitative measure of the strength of dependencies.

The correlation coefficient provides such a measure. In many instances, however, the correlation coefficient might be misleading. In particular, there are cases of nonlinear dependencies that result in a zero correlation coefficient. From the point of view of risk management this situation is particularly dangerous as it leads to substantially underestimated risk.

Different measures of dependence have been proposed, in particular **copula functions**. We will give only a brief introduction to copula functions.[11] Copula functions are based on the Theorem of Sklar. Sklar demonstrated[12] that any joint probability distribution can be written as a functional link, i.e., a copula function, between its marginal distributions. Let's suppose that $F(x_1, x_2, ..., x_n)$ is a joint multivariate distribution function with marginal distribution functions $F_1(x_1)$, $F_2(x_2)$, ..., $F_n(x_n)$. Then there is a copula function C such that the following relationship holds:

$$F(x_1, x_2, ..., x_n) = C[F_1(x_1), F_2(x_2), ..., F_n(x_n)]$$

The joint probability distribution contains all the information related to the co-movement of the variables. The copula function allows to capture this information in a synthetic way as a link between marginal distributions. We will see an application of the concept of copula functions in Chapter 22 on credit risk modeling.

SEQUENCES OF RANDOM VARIABLES

Consider a probability space $(\Omega, \mathfrak{I}, P)$. A sequence of random variables is an infinite family of random variables X_i on $(\Omega, \mathfrak{I}, P)$ indexed by integer numbers: $i = 0,1,2,...,n...$ If the sequence extends to infinity in both directions, it is indexed by positive and negative integers: $i = ...,-n,..., 0,1,2,...,n....$

A sequence of random variables can **converge** to a **limit random variable**. Several different notions of the limit of a sequence of random variables can be defined. The simplest definition of convergence is that

---

[11] The interested reader might consult the following reference: P. Embrechts, F. Lindskog, and A. McNeil, "Modelling Dependence with Copulas and Applications to Risk Management," Chapter 8 in S.T. Rachev (ed.), *Handbook of Heavy Tailed Distributions in Finance* (Amsterdam: North Holland, 2003).

[12] A. Sklar, "Random Variables, Joint Distribution Functions and Copulas," *Kybernetika 9* (1973), pp. 449–460.

of pointwise convergence. A sequence of random variables X_i, $i \geq 1$ on $(\Omega, \Im, P)$, is said to **converge almost surely to a random variable** X, denoted

$$X_i \xrightarrow{a.s.} X$$

if the following relationship holds:

$$P\{\omega: \lim_{i \to \infty} X_i(\omega) = X(\omega)\} = 1$$

In other words, a sequence of random variables converges almost surely to a random variable X if the sequence of real numbers $X_i(\omega)$ converges to $X(\omega)$ for all ω except a set of measure zero.

A sequence of random variables X_i, $i \geq 1$ on $(\Omega, \Im, P)$, is said to **converge in mean of order p to a random variable X** if

$$\lim_{i \to \infty} E[|X_i(\omega) - X(\omega)|^p] = 0$$

provided that all expectations exist. Convergence in mean of order one and two are called convergence in mean and convergence in mean square, respectively.

A weaker concept of convergence is that of convergence in probability. A sequence of random variables X_i, $i \geq 1$ on $(\Omega, \Im, P)$, is said to **converge in probability to a random variable** X, denoted

$$X_i \xrightarrow{P} X$$

if the following relationship holds:

$$\lim_{i \to \infty} P\{\omega: |X_i(\omega) - X(\omega)| \leq \varepsilon\} = 1, \ \forall \varepsilon > 0$$

It can be demonstrated that if a sequence converges almost surely then it also convergences in probability while the converse is not generally true. It can also be demonstrated that if a sequence converges in mean of order $p > 0$, then it also convergences in probability while the converse is not generally true.

A sequence of random variables X_i, $i \geq 1$ on $(\Omega, \Im, P)$ with distribution functions F_{X_i} is said to **converge in distribution to a random variable** X with distribution function F_X, denoted

$$X_i \xrightarrow{d} X$$

if

$$\lim_{i \to \infty} F_{X_i}(x) = F_X(x), x \in C$$

where C is the set of points where all the functions F_{X_i} and F_X are continuous.

It can be demonstrated that if a sequence converges almost surely (and thus converges in probability) it also converges in distribution while the converse is not true in general.

INDEPENDENT AND IDENTICALLY DISTRIBUTED SEQUENCES

Consider a probability space $(\Omega,\Im,P)$. A sequence of random variables X_i on $(\Omega,\Im,P)$ is called a sequence of **independent and identically distributed** (IID) **sequence** if the variables X_i have all the same distribution and are all mutually independent. An IID sequence is the strongest form of white noise, that is, of a completely random sequence of variables. Note that in many applications white noise is defined as a sequence of uncorrelated variables. This is a weaker definition as an uncorrelated sequence might be forecastable.

An IID sequence is completely unforecastable in the sense that the past does not influence the present or the future in any possible sense. In an IID sequence all conditional distributions are identical to unconditional distributions. Note, however, that an IID sequence presents a simple form of reversion to the mean. In fact, suppose that a sequence X_i assumes at a given time t a value larger than the common mean of all variables: $X_t > E[X]$. By definition of mean it is more likely that X_t be followed by a smaller value: $P(X_{t+1} < X_t) > P(X_{t+1} > X_t)$.

Note that this type of mean reversion does not imply forecastability as the probability distribution of asset returns at time $t + 1$ is independent from the distribution at time t.

SUM OF VARIABLES

Given two random variables $X(\omega)$, $Y(\omega)$ on the same probability space $(\Omega,\Im,P)$, the **sum of variables** $Z(\omega) = X(\omega) + Y(\omega)$ is another random variable. The sum associates to each state ω a value $Z(\omega)$ equal to the sum of the values taken by the two variables X, Y. Let's suppose that the two variables $X(\omega)$, $Y(\omega)$ have a joint density $p(x,y)$ and marginal densities $p_X(x)$ and $p_Y(x)$, respectively. Let's call H the cumulative distribution of the variable Z. The following relationship holds

$$H(u) = P[Z(\omega) \le u] = \iint_A p(x, y)\,dx\,dy$$

$$A = \{y \le -x + u\}$$

In other words, the probability that the sum $X + Y$ be less than or equal to a real number u is given by the integral of the joint probability distribution function in the region A. The region A can be described as the region of the x,y plane below the straight line $y = -x + u$.

If we assume that the two variables are independent, then the distribution of the sum admits a simple representation. In fact, under the assumption of independence, the joint density is the product of the marginal densities: $p(x,y) = p_X(x)p_Y(x)$. Therefore, we can write

$$H(u) = P[Z(\omega) \le u] = \iint_A p(x, y)\,dx\,dy = \int_{-\infty}^{\infty} \left\{ \int_{-\infty}^{u-y} p_X(x)\,dx \right\} p_Y(y)\,dy$$

We can now use a property of integrals called the **Leibnitz rule**, which allows one to write the following relationship:

$$\frac{dH}{du} = p_Z(u) = \int_{-\infty}^{\infty} p_X(u - y)p_Y(y)\,dy$$

Recall from Chapter 4 that the above formula is a convolution of the two marginal distributions. This formula can be reiterated for any number of summands: the density of the sum of n random variables is the convolution of their densities.

Computing directly the convolution of a number of functions might be very difficult or impossible. However, if we take the Fourier transforms of the densities, $P_Z(s)$, $P_X(s)$, $P_Y(s)$ computations are substantially simplified as the transform of the convolution is the product of the transforms:

$$p_Z(u) = \int_{-\infty}^{\infty} p_X(u - y)p_Y(y)\,dy \Rightarrow P_Z(s) = P_X(s) \times P_Y(s)$$

This relationship can be extended to any number of variables.

In probability theory, given a random variable X, the following expectation is called the **characteristic function (c.f.) of the variable X**

$$\varphi_X(t) = E[e^{itX}] = E[\cos tX] + iE[\sin tX]$$

If the variable X admits a d.f. $F_X(y)$, it can be demonstrated that the following relationship holds:

$$\varphi_X(t) = E[e^{itX}] = \int_{-\infty}^{\infty} e^{itX} dF_X(x) = \int_{-\infty}^{\infty} \cos tx \ dF_X(x) + \int_{-\infty}^{\infty} \sin tx \ dF_X(x)$$

In this case, the characteristic function therefore coincides with the Fourier-Stieltjes transform. It can be demonstrated that there is a one-to-one correspondence between c.d.s and d.f.s. In fact, it is well known that the Fourier-Stieltjes transform can be uniquely inverted.

In probability theory convolution is defined, in a more general way, as follows. Given two d.f.s $F_X(y)$ and $F_Y(y)$, their convolution is defined as:

$$F^*(u) = (F_X * F_Y)(u) = \int_{-\infty}^{\infty} F_X(u - y) dF_Y(y)$$

It can be demonstrated that the d.f. of the sum of two variables X, Y with d.f.s $F_X(y)$ and $F_Y(y)$ is the convolution of their respective d.f.s:

$$P(X + Y \le u) = F_{X+Y}(u) = F^*(u) = (F_X * F_Y)(u) = \int_{-\infty}^{\infty} F_X(u - y) dF_Y(y)$$

If the d.f.s admits p.d.f.s, then the inversion formulas are those established earlier. Inversion formulas also exist in the case that the d.f.s do not admit densities but these are more complex and will not be given here.[13]

We can therefore establish the following property: the characteristic function of the sum of n independent random variables is the product of the characteristic functions of each of the summands.

---

[13] See Chow and Teicher, *Probability Theory*.

GAUSSIAN VARIABLES

Gaussian random variables are extremely important in probability theory and statistics. Their importance stems from the fact that any phenomenon made up of a large number of independent or weakly dependent variables has a **Gaussian distribution**. Gaussian distributions are also known as **normal distributions**. The name Gaussian derives from the German mathematician Gauss who introduced them.

Let's start with univariate variables. A **normal variable** is a variable whose probability distribution function has the following form:

$$f(x|\mu, \sigma^2) = \frac{1}{\sigma\sqrt{2\pi}} \exp\left\{-\frac{(x-\mu)^2}{2\sigma^2}\right\}$$

The **univariate normal distribution** is a distribution characterized by only two parameters, (μ,σ^2), which represent, respectively, the mean and the variance of the distribution. We write $X \sim N(\mu,\sigma^2)$ to indicate that the variable X has a normal distribution with parameters (μ,σ^2). We define the **standard normal distribution** as the normal distribution with zero mean and unit variance. It can be demonstrated by direct calculation that if $X \sim N(\mu,\sigma^2)$ then the variable

$$Z = \frac{X-\mu}{\sigma}$$

is standard normal. The variable Z is called the **score** or **Z-score**. The cumulative distribution of a normal variable is generally indicated as

$$F(x) = \Phi\left(\frac{x-\mu}{\sigma}\right)$$

where $\Phi(x)$ is the cumulative distribution of the standard normal.

It can be demonstrated that the sum of n independent normal distributions is another normal distribution whose expected value is the sum of the expected values of the summands and whose variance is the sum of the variances of the summands.

The normal distribution has a typical bell-shaped graph symmetrical around the mean. Exhibit 6.1 shows the graph of a normal distribution.

EXHIBIT 6.1　　Graph of a Normal Variable with Zero Mean and $\sigma = 100$

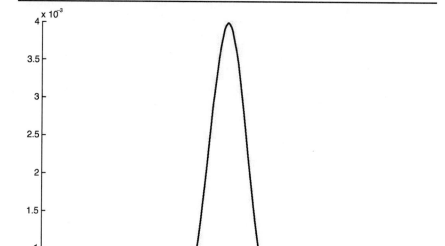

Multivariate normal distributions are characterized by the same exponential functional form. However, a multivariate normal distribution in n variables is identified by n means, one for each axis, and by a $n \times n$ symmetrical variance-covariance matrix. For instance, a bivariate normal distribution is characterized by two expected values, two variances and one covariance. We can write the general expression of a bivariate normal distribution as follows:

$$f(x, y) = \frac{\exp\left\{-\frac{1}{2}Q\right\}}{2\pi\sigma_X\sigma_Y\sqrt{1-\rho^2}}$$

$$Q = \frac{1}{1-\rho^2}\left\{\left(\frac{x-\mu_X}{\sigma_X}\right)^2 - 2\rho\left(\frac{x-\mu_X}{\sigma_X}\right)\left(\frac{y-\mu_Y}{\sigma_Y}\right) + \left(\frac{y-\mu_Y}{\sigma_Y}\right)^2\right\}$$

where ρ is the correlation coefficient.

This expression generalizes to the case of n random variables. Using matrix notation, the joint normal probability distributions of the random n vector $V = \{X_i\}$, $i = 1,2,\ldots,n$ has the following expression:

$$V = \{X_i\} \sim N_n(\mathbf{\mu}, \mathbf{\Sigma})$$

where

$$\mu_i = E[X_i]$$

and $\mathbf{\Sigma}$ is the variance-covariance matrix of the $\{X_i\}$

$$\mathbf{\Sigma} = E[(\mathbf{V} - \mathbf{\mu})(\mathbf{V} - \mathbf{\mu})^T]$$

$$f(\mathbf{v}) = [(2\pi)^n |\mathbf{\Sigma}|]^{-\frac{1}{2}} \exp[(-\tfrac{1}{2})(\mathbf{v} - \mathbf{\mu})^T \mathbf{\Sigma}^{-1}(\mathbf{v} - \mathbf{\mu})]$$

where $|\mathbf{\Sigma}| = \det\mathbf{\Sigma}$, the determinant of $\mathbf{\Sigma}$.

For $n = 2$ we find the previous expression for bivariate normal, taking into account that variances and correlation coefficients have the following relationship

$$\sigma_{ij} = \rho_{ij}\sigma_i\sigma_j$$

It can be demonstrated that a linear combination

$$W = \sum_{i=1}^{n} \alpha_i X_i$$

of n jointly normal random variables $X_i \sim N(\mu_i, \sigma_i^2)$ with $\text{cov}(X_i, X_j) = \sigma_{ij}$ is a normal random variable $W \sim N(\mu_W, \sigma_W^2)$ where

$$\mu_W = \sum_{i=1}^{n} \alpha_i \mu_i$$

$$\sigma_W^2 = \sum_{i=1}^{n} \sum_{j=1}^{n} \alpha_i \alpha_j \sigma_{ij}$$

THE REGRESSION FUNCTION

Given a probability space $(\Omega, \Im, P)$, consider a set of $p + 1$ random variables. Let's suppose that the random vector $\{X\, Z_1 \ldots Z_p\} \equiv \{X\, \mathbf{Z}\}$, $\mathbf{Z} = \{Z_1 \ldots Z_p\}$ has the joint multivariate probability density function:

$$f(xz_1 \ldots z_p) = f(x, \mathbf{z}), \ \mathbf{z} = \{z_1 \ldots z_p\}$$

Let's consider the conditional density

$$f(x|z_1, \ldots, z_p) = f(x, |\mathbf{z})$$

and the marginal density of $\mathbf{Z}$,

$$f_{\mathbf{z}}(\mathbf{z}) = \int_{-\infty}^{\infty} f(x, \mathbf{z}) dx$$

Recall from an earlier section that the joint multivariate density $f(x,\mathbf{z})$ factorizes as

$$f(x, \mathbf{z}) = f(x|\mathbf{z}) f_{\mathbf{z}}(\mathbf{z})$$

Let's consider now the conditional expectation of the variable X given $\mathbf{Z} = \mathbf{z} = \{z_1 \ldots z_p\}$:

$$g(\mathbf{z}) = E[X|\mathbf{Z} = \mathbf{z}] = \int_{-\infty}^{\infty} v f(v|\mathbf{z}) dv$$

The function g, that is, the function which gives the conditional expectation of X given the variables $\mathbf{Z}$, is called the **regression function**. Otherwise stated, the regression function is a real function of real variables which is the locus of the expectation of the random variable X given that the variables $\mathbf{Z}$ assume the values $\mathbf{z}$.

Linear Regression

In general, the regression function depends on the joint distribution of $[X\, Z_1 \ldots Z_p]$. In financial econometrics it is important to determine what joint distributions produce a linear regression function. It can be demonstrated that joint normal distributions produce a linear regression function. Consider the joint normal distribution

$$f(\mathbf{v}) = [(2\pi)^n |\boldsymbol{\Sigma}|]^{-\frac{1}{2}} \exp\left[-\frac{1}{2}(\mathbf{v}-\boldsymbol{\mu})^T \boldsymbol{\Sigma}^{-1}(\mathbf{v}-\boldsymbol{\mu})\right]$$

where parameters are those defined in an earlier section in this chapter. Let's partition the parameters as follows:

$$v = \begin{pmatrix} x \\ z \end{pmatrix}, \; \mu = \begin{pmatrix} \mu_x \\ \mu_z \end{pmatrix}, \; \Sigma = \begin{pmatrix} \sigma_{x,x} & \sigma_{z,x} \\ \sigma_{x,z} & \Sigma_z \end{pmatrix}$$

where μ_x, μ_z are respectively a scalar and a p-vector of expected values, $\sigma_{x,x}$, $\sigma_{x,z}$, $\sigma_{z,x}$, and Σ_z are respectively a scalar, p-vectors and a $p \times p$ matrix of variances and covariances and $\sigma_{x,x} = \sigma_x^2$, $\sigma_{z_i, z_i} = \sigma_{z_i}^2$. It can be demonstrated that the variable $(X|Z = z)$ is normally distributed with the following parameters:

$$(X|Z = z) \sim N[\mu_x - (\Sigma_z^{-1}\sigma_{z,x})'(\mu_z - z), \sigma_{x,x} - \sigma_{x,z}\Sigma_z^{-1}\sigma_{z,x}+]$$

From the above expression we can conclude that the conditional expectation is linear in the conditioning variables. Let's call

$$\alpha = \mu_x - (\Sigma_z^{-1}\sigma_{z,x})'\mu_z \text{ and } \beta = \Sigma_z^{-1}\sigma_{z,x}$$

We can therefore write

$$g(\mathbf{z}) = E[X|Z = z] = \alpha + \beta' z$$

If the matrix Σ is diagonal, the random variables $(X, Z_1,...,Z_p)$ are independent, such that $\sigma_{z,x} = 0$ and $\beta = \Sigma_z^{-1}\sigma_{z,x} = 0$ and therefore the regression function is a constant that does not depend on the conditioning variables. If the matrix Σ_z is diagonal but $\sigma_{x,z}$, $\sigma_{z,x}$ do not vanish, then the linear regression takes the following form

$$g(\mathbf{z}) = E[X|Z = z] = \mu_x - \sum_{i=1}^{p} \frac{\sigma_{x,z_i}}{\sigma_{z_i}^2}\mu_{z_i} + \sum_{i=1}^{p} \frac{\sigma_{x,z_i}}{\sigma_{z_i}^2}z_i$$

In particular, a bivariate normal distribution factorizes in a linear regression as follows:

$$(X|Z = z) \sim N\left[\mu_x - \frac{\sigma_{x,z}}{\sigma_z^2}(\mu_z - z),\ \sigma_x^2 - \frac{(\sigma_{x,z})^2}{\sigma_z^2}\right]$$

$$g(z) = E[X|Z = z] = \mu_x - \frac{\sigma_{x,z}}{\sigma_z^2}\mu_z + \frac{\sigma_{x,z}}{\sigma_z^2}z$$

SUMMARY

■ Probability is a set function defined over a class of events where events are sets of possible outcomes of an experiment. A probability space is a triple formed by a set of outcomes, a σ-algebra of events, and a probability measure.

■ A random variable is a real-valued function defined over the set of outcomes such that the inverse image of any interval is an event. n-dimensional random vectors are functions from the set of outcomes into the n-dimensional Euclidean space with the property that the inverse image of n-dimensional generalized rectangles is an event.

■ Stochastic processes are time-dependent random variables.

■ An information structure is a collection of partitions of events associated to each instant of time that become progressively finer with the evolution of time. A filtration is an increasing collection of σ-algebras associated to each instant of time.

■ The states of the economy, intended as full histories of the economy, are represented as a probability space. The revelation of information with time is represented by information structures or filtrations. Prices and other financial quantities are represented by adapted stochastic processes.

■ By conditioning is meant the change in probabilities due to the acquisition of some information. It is possible to condition with respect to an event if the event has nonzero probability. In general terms, conditioning means conditioning with respect to a filtration or an information structure.

■ A martingale is a stochastic process such that the conditional expected value is always equal to its present value. It embodies the idea of a fair game where today's wealth is the best forecast of future wealth.

■ The variance of a random variable measures the average size of its fluctuations around the mean.

■ The correlation coefficient between two variables is a number that measures how the two variables move together. It is zero for independent variables, plus/minus one for linearly dependent deterministic variables.

■ An infinite sequence of random variables might converge to a limit random variable. Different types of convergence can be defined: pointwise convergence, convergence in probability, or convergence in distribution.

■ Random variables can be added to produce another random variable.

■ The characteristic function of the sum of two random variables is the product of the characteristic functions of each random variable.

■ Given a multivariate distribution, the regression function of one random variable with respect to the others is the conditional expectation of that random variable given the values of the others.

■ Joint normal distributions admits a linear regression function.

CHAPTER 7

Optimization

The concept of optimization is intrinsic to finance theory. The seminal work of Harry Markowitz demonstrated that financial decision-making is essentially a question of an optimal trade-off between risk and returns. While Markowitz was developing his theory of investment in the 1950s, as we will see in Chapter 16, Georg Dantzig, the father of linear programming, was laying down the foundations of the modern computerized approach to optimization.[1]

Purely mathematical solutions to optimization problems were proposed early in the history of calculus. In the eighteenth century, the French mathematician Lagrange introduced a general methodology for finding the maxima or minima of a multivariate function subject to constraints; the Swiss-born mathematician Euler[2] introduced the mathematics of the calculus of variations.[3] Nevertheless, no matter how important from the conceptual point of view, optimization had limited practical applications in engineering, business, and financial planning until the recent development of high-performance computing.

In modern terminology, an optimization problem is called a **mathematical programming** problem. From an analytical perspective, a static mathematical program attempts to identify the maxima or minima of a function $f(x_1,...,x_n)$ of n real-valued variables, called the **objective function**, in a domain identified by a set of constraints. The latter might take the general form of inequalities $g_i(x_1,...,x_n) \geq b_i$. **Linear programming** is the specialization of mathematical programming to instances where

---

[1] Dantzig and Markowitz worked together at the Rand Corporation in the 1950s.

[2] Euler was born in Basel, Switzerland, but spent a large part of his long career in Russia.

[3] The calculus of variations played a fundamental role in the development of modern science.

both f and the constraints are linear. **Quadratic programming** is the specialization of mathematical programming to instances where f is a quadratic function. The Markowitz mean-variance approach leads to a quadratic programming problem.

A different, and more difficult, problem is the optimization of a dynamic process. In this case, the objective function depends on the entire realization of a process, which is often not deterministic but stochastic. Decisions might be taken at intermediate steps on the basis of information revealed up to that point. This is the concept of **recourse**, that is, revision of past decisions. This area of optimization is called **stochastic programming**.

From an application perspective, mathematical programming is an optimization tool that allows the rationalization of many business or technological decisions. The computational tractability of the resulting analytical models is a key issue in mathematical programming. The simplex algorithm, developed in 1947 by George Dantzig, was one of the first tractable mathematical programming algorithms to be developed for linear programming. Its subsequent successful implementation contributed to the acceptance of optimization as a scientific approach to decision-making and initiated the field known as operations research.

Optimization is a highly technical subject, which we will not fully develop in this chapter. Instead, our objective is to give the reader a general understanding of the technology. We begin with an explanation of maxima or minima of a multivariate function subject to constraints. We then discuss the basic tools for static optimization: linear programming and quadratic programming. After introducing the idea of optimizing a process and defining the concepts of the **calculus of variations** and **control theory**, we briefly cover the techniques of stochastic programming.[4]

MAXIMA AND MINIMA

Consider a multivariate function $f(x_1,...,x_n)$ of n real-valued variables. Suppose that f is twice differentiable. Define the gradient of f, grad$f$, also written ∇f, as the vector whose components are the first order partial derivatives of f

$$\text{grad}[f(x_1, ..., x_n)] = \nabla f = \left(\frac{\partial f}{\partial x_1}, ..., \frac{\partial f}{\partial x_n} \right)$$

---

[4] For a good introduction to stochastic programming, see, among others, J.R. Birge and F. Louveaux, *Introduction to Stochastic Programming* (Heidelberg: Springer, 1997) and Peter Kall and Stein W. Wallace, *Stochastic Programming* (Chichester, West Sussex: Wiley, 1995).

Given a multivariate function $f(x_1,...,x_n)$, consider the matrix formed by the second order partial derivatives. This matrix is called the **Hessian matrix** and its determinant, denoted by H, is called the **Hessian determinant** (see Chapter 5 for definition of matrix and determinants):

$$H = \begin{vmatrix} \dfrac{\partial^2 f}{\partial x_1^2} & \cdots & \dfrac{\partial^2 f}{\partial x_1 \partial x_n} \\ \cdot & \cdot & \cdot \\ \cdot & \cdot & \cdot \\ \cdot & \cdot & \cdot \\ \dfrac{\partial^2 f}{\partial x_1 \partial x_n} & \cdots & \dfrac{\partial^2 f}{\partial x_n^2} \end{vmatrix}$$

A point $(a_1,...,a_n)$ is called a **relative local maxima** or a **relative local minima** of the function f if the relationship

$$f(a_1 + h_1, ..., x_n + h_n) \le f(a_1, ..., a_n), \ |h| \le d > 0$$

or, respectively,

$$f(a_1 + h_1, ..., x_n + h_n) \ge f(a_1, ..., a_n), \ |h| \le d > 0$$

holds for any real positive number $d > 0$.

A necessary, but not sufficient, condition for a point $(x_1,...,x_n)$ to be a relative maximum or minimum is that all first order partial derivatives evaluated at that point vanish, that is, that the following relationship holds:

$$\text{grad}[f(x_1, ..., x_n)] = \left(\frac{\partial f}{\partial x_1} \cdots \frac{\partial f}{\partial x_n} \right) = (0, ..., 0)$$

A point where the gradient vanishes is called a **critical point.**

A critical point can be a maximum, a minimum or a **saddle point.** For functions of one variable, the following sufficient conditions hold:

■ If the first derivative evaluated at a point a vanishes and the second derivative evaluated at a is positive, then the point a is a (relative) minimum.

■ If the first derivative evaluated at a point a vanishes and the second derivative evaluated at a is negative, then the point a is a (relative) maximum.

■ If the first derivative evaluated at a point a vanishes and the second derivative evaluated at a also vanishes, then the point a is a saddle point.

In the case of a function $f(x,y)$ of two variables x,y, the following conditions hold:

■ If $\nabla f = 0$ at a given point a and if the Hessian determinant evaluated at a is positive, then the function f has a relative maximum in a if $f_{xx} < 0$ or $f_{yy} < 0$ and a relative minimum if $f_{xx} > 0$ or $f_{yy} > 0$. Note that if the Hessian is positive the two second derivatives f_{xx} and f_{yy} must have the same sign.

■ If $\nabla f = 0$ at a given point a and if the Hessian determinant evaluated at a is negative, then the function f has a saddle point in a.

■ If $\nabla f = 0$ at a given point a and if the Hessian determinant evaluated at a vanishes, then the point a is degenerate and no conclusion can be drawn in this case.

The above conditions can be expressed in a more compact way if we consider the eigenvalues (see Chapter 5) of the Hessian matrix. If both eigenvalues are positive at a critical point a, the function has a local minimum at a; if both are negative the function has a local maximum; if they have opposite signs, the function has a saddle point; and if at least one of them is 0, the critical point is degenerate. Recall that the product of the eigenvalues is equal to the Hessian determinant.

This analysis can be carried over in the three-dimensional case. In this case there will be three eigenvalues, all of which are positive at a local minimum and negative at a local maximum. A critical point of a function of three variables is degenerate if at least one of the eigenvalues of the Hessian determinant is 0 and has a saddle point if at least one eigenvalue is positive, at least one is negative, and none is 0.

In higher dimensions, the situation is more complex and goes beyond the scope of our introduction to optimization.

LAGRANGE MULTIPLIERS

Consider a multivariate function $f(x_1,...,x_n)$ of n real-valued variables. In the previous section we saw that, if the n variables are unconstrained, a local optimum of f can be found by solving the n equations:

$$\nabla f = \left(\frac{\partial f}{\partial x_1}, \, ..., \, \frac{\partial f}{\partial x_n} \right) = (0, \, ..., \, 0)$$

Let's now discuss how to find maxima and minima when the optimization problem has equality constraints. Suppose that the n variables $(x_1,...,x_n)$ are not independent, but satisfy $m < n$ constraint equations

$$g_1(x_1,...,x_n) = 0$$

.

.

.

$$g_m(x_1,...,x_n) = 0$$

These equations define, in general, an $(n-m)$-dimensional surface. For instance, in the case of two variables, a constraint $g_1(x,y) = 0$ defines a line. In the case of three variables, one constraint $g_1(x,y,z) = 0$ defines a two-dimensional surface while two constraints $g_1(x,y,z) = 0$, $g_2(x,y,z) = 0$ define a line in the three-dimensional space, and so on.

Our objective is to find the maxima or minima of the function f for the set of points that also satisfy the constraints. It can be demonstrated that, under this restriction, the gradient ∇f of f need not vanish at the maxima or minima, but need only be orthogonal to the $(n-m)$-dimensional surface described by the constraint equations. That is, the following relationships must hold

$$\nabla f = \lambda^T \nabla g, \text{ for some } \lambda = (\lambda_1, \, ..., \, \lambda_m)$$

or, in the usual notation

$$\frac{\partial f}{\partial x_i} = \sum_{j=1}^{m} \lambda_j \frac{\partial g_j}{\partial x_i}, \, i = 1,...,n$$

The coefficients $(\lambda_1,...,\lambda_m)$ are called **Lagrange multipliers.** If we define the function

$$F(x_1, \, ..., \, x_n, \lambda_1, \, ..., \, \lambda_m) = f(x_1, \, ..., \, x_n) - \sum_{j=1}^{m} \lambda_j g_j$$

the above equations together may be written as

$$\nabla F = 0$$

or

$$\frac{\partial F}{\partial x_1} = \ldots = \frac{\partial F}{\partial x_n} = \frac{\partial F}{\partial \lambda_1} = \ldots = \frac{\partial F}{\partial \lambda_m} = 0$$

In other words, the method of Lagrange multipliers transforms a constrained optimization problem into an unconstrained optimization problem. The method consists in replacing the original objective function f to be optimized subject to the constraints g with another objective function

$$F = f - \sum_{j=1}^{m} \lambda_j g_j$$

to be optimized without constraints in the variables $(x_1,\ldots,x_n,\lambda_1,\ldots,\lambda_m)$. The Lagrange multipliers are not only a mathematical device. In many applications they have a useful physical or economic interpretation.

NUMERICAL ALGORITHMS

The method of Lagrange multiplers works with equality constraints, that is, when the solution is constrained to stay on the surface defined by the constraints. Optimization problems become more difficult if inequality constraints are allowed. This means that the admissible solutions must stay within the boundary defined by the constraints. In this case, approximate numerical methods are often needed. Numerical algorithms or "solvers" to many standard optimization problems are available in many computer packages.

Linear Programming

The general form for a linear programming (LP) problem is as follows. Minimize a **linear objective function**

$$f(x_1, \ldots, x_n) = c_1 x_1 + \ldots + c_n x_n$$

or, in vector notation,

$$f(x_1, \ldots, x_n) = \mathbf{c}^T \mathbf{x}, \ \mathbf{c} = (c_1, \ldots, c_n), \ \mathbf{x} = (x_1, \ldots, x_n)$$

subject to the constraints

$$a_{i,1} x_1 + \ldots + a_{i,n} x_n \begin{pmatrix} \leq \\ = \\ \geq \end{pmatrix} b_i, \ i = 1, 2, \ldots, m$$

or, in matrix notation

$$\mathbf{A}\mathbf{x} \begin{pmatrix} \leq \\ = \\ \geq \end{pmatrix} \mathbf{b}$$

with additional **sign restrictions** such as $x_i \leq 0$, $x_i \geq 0$, or x_i unrestricted in sign.

The largest or smallest value of the objective function is called the **optimal value,** and a vector $[x_1 \ldots x_n]$ that gives the optimal value constitutes an **optimal solution.** The variables $x_1, \ldots, x_n$ are called the **decision variables.** The **feasible region** determined by a collection of linear inequalities is the collection of points that satisfy all of the inequalities. The optimal solution belongs to the feasible region.

The above formulation has the general structure of a mathematical programming problem as outlined in the introduction to the chapter, but is characterized, in addition, by the fact that the objective function and the constraints are *linear.*

LP problems can be transformed into **standard form.** An LP is said to be in *standard form* if (1) all *constraints* are *equality* constraints and (2) all the variables have a *nonnegativity sign restriction.* An LP problem in standard form can therefore be written as follows

$$\min \mathbf{c}^T \mathbf{x}$$

subject to constraints

$$\left. \begin{array}{c} \mathbf{A}\mathbf{x} = \mathbf{b} \\ \mathbf{x} \geq 0 \end{array} \right\}$$

where $\mathbf{A}$ is an $m \times n$ matrix and $\mathbf{b}$ is an m-vector.

Every LP can be brought into standard form through the following transformations:

1. An inequality constraint

$$a_{i,1}x_1 + \ldots + a_{i,n}x_n \begin{pmatrix} \leq \\ = \\ \geq \end{pmatrix} b_i$$

can be converted into an equality constraint through the introduction of a **slack variable**, denoted by S, or an **excess variable**, denoted by E, such that

$$a_{i,1}x_1 + \ldots + a_{i,n}x_n + S = b_i$$

or

$$a_{i,1}x_1 + \ldots + a_{i,n}x_n - E = b_i$$

2. A variable with negative sign restriction $x_i \leq 0$ can be substituted by $x_i = -x_i'$, $x_i' \geq 0$ while an unrestricted variable can be substituted by $x_i = x_i' - x_i''$, $x_i', x_i'' \geq 0$.

There are two major techniques for solving an LP problem: the **simplex method** and the **interior-point method**. The simplex method was discovered by Dantzig in the 1940s. Although the number of iterations may be exponential in the number of unknowns, the simplex method proved very useful and was unrivaled until the late 1980s. The exponential computational complexity of the simplex method led to a search for algorithms with better computational complexity features, in particular polynomial complexity. Khachiyan's ellipsoid method—the first polynomial-time algorithm—appeared in the 1970s. Most interior-point methods also have polynomial complexity. We will briefly describe both the simplex and the interior-point methods.

The Simplex Algorithm

Linear constraints identify a region called a **simplex**. The simplex method searches for optima on the vertices of the simplex. Recall from Chapter 5 on matrix algebra that the system $\mathbf{Ax} = \mathbf{b}$ admits solutions if and only if rank $[\mathbf{Ab}]$ = rank $\mathbf{A}$. We can assume without loss of generality that rank $\mathbf{A} = m$, otherwise we drop redundant equations. The **feasible set** is the set B of points that satisfy the constraints

$$B = \{\mathbf{x}: \mathbf{Ax} = \mathbf{b}, \mathbf{x} \geq 0\}$$

A **feasible basic solution** is a solution $\hat{\mathbf{x}} \equiv (\hat{x}_1 \ldots \hat{x}_n) \in B$ with the following additional properties. For each solution $\mathbf{x}$ consider the set I of indices such that the respective variables are strictly positive: $I(\mathbf{x}) \equiv (i: x_i > 0)$, with $\mathbf{x} \in B$. A feasible basic solution $\mathbf{x}$ is a feasible solution such that the set $\{A_i: i \in I(\hat{\mathbf{x}})\}$ of columns of the matrix $\mathbf{A}$ are linearly independent. Therefore, the components $\hat{x}_i$, $i \in I(\hat{\mathbf{x}})$ are the unique solutions of the system

$$\sum_{i \in I(\hat{\mathbf{x}})} A_i x_i = b_i$$

In fact, it is possible to demonstrate the following two important results:

■ If an LP has a bounded optimal solution, then there exists an *extreme point*, that is, a *minimum* or *maximum,* of the feasible (on one of the vertices) region, which is optimal.
■ Extreme points of the feasible region of an LP correspond to *basic feasible solutions* of the standard form representation of the problem.

The first result implies that in order to obtain an optimal solution of an LP, we can constrain our search on the set of the extreme points of its feasible region. The second result implies that each of these points is determined by selecting a set of basic variables, with cardinality equal to the number of the constraints of the LP and the additional requirement that the (uniquely determined) values of these variables are nonnegative.

This further implies that the set of extreme points for an LP with m constraints and N variables in its standard form representation can have only a *finite* number of extreme points. A naive approach to the problem would be to enumerate the entire set of extreme points and select one which minimizes the objective function over this set. However, for reasonably sized LP problems, the set of extreme points, even though finite, can become extremely large. Hence a more systematic approach to organize the search is needed. The simplex algorithm provides such a systematic approach.

The algorithm starts with an initial basic feasible solution and tests its optimality. If an optimality condition is verified, then the algorithm terminates. Otherwise, the algorithm identifies an adjacent feasible solution with a better objective value. The optimality of this new solution is tested again and the entire scheme is repeated until an optimal solution is found. The algorithm will terminate in a finite number of steps except in special pathological cases. In other words, the simplex algorithm starts from some initial extreme point and follows a path along the edges of the feasible region towards an optimal extreme point, such that all the intermediate extreme points visited improve the objective function. Many standard optimization software packages contain the simplex algorithm. However, the simplex method exhibits exponential complexity. This means that the number of steps required for finding a solution grows exponentially with the number of unknowns.

Interior-Point Methods

The exponential complexity of the simplex method was behind the search for more computationally efficient methods. The 1980s saw the introduction of the first fast algorithms that generate iterates lying in the interior of the feasible set rather than on the boundary, as simplex methods do. The primal-dual class of interior-points algorithms is today considered the state-of-the-art technique for the practical solution of LP problems. Furthermore, this class of methods are also very amenable to theoretical analysis, and has opened up a new area of research within optimization. We will limit our brief discussion to this class of interior-point algorithms.

Let's begin by formulating the concept of duality. Every problem of the type

$$\text{maximize } c_1 x_1 + \ldots + c_n x_n$$

subject to

$$a_{i,1} x_1 + \ldots + a_{i,n} x_n \geq b_i, \, i = 1,2,\ldots,m$$

$$x_j \geq 0, \, j = 1,2,\ldots,n$$

has a **dual problem**

$$\text{minimize } b_1 y_1 + \ldots + b_m y_m$$

subject to

$$y_1 a_{1,i} + \ldots + y_m a_{m,i} \leq c_i, \, i = 1,2,\ldots,n$$

$$y_j \geq 0, \, j = 1,2,\ldots,m$$

The original problem is called the **primal problem**. The primal-dual gap is the difference, if it exists, between the largest primal value and the smallest dual value. The **Strong Duality Theorem** states that, if the primal problem has an optimal solution $\mathbf{x}^* = (x_1,\ldots,x_n)$, the dual also has an optimal solution $\mathbf{y}^* = (y_1,\ldots,y_m)$ and there is no primal-dual gap in the sense that

$$\sum_i c_i x_i = \sum_j b_j y_j$$

Interior-point algorithms generate iterates such that the duality gap is driven to zero, yielding a limiting point that solves the primal and dual linear programs. Commercial software packages that contain primal-dual interior-point solvers are available.

Quadratic Programming

The general quadratic programming (QP) problem is a mathematical programming problem where the objective function is quadratic and constraints are linear as follows:

$$\text{minimize } f(x_1, \ldots, x_n) = \mathbf{c}^T \mathbf{x} + \frac{1}{2} \mathbf{x}^T \mathbf{D} \mathbf{x}$$

where $\mathbf{c} = (c_1, \ldots, c_n)$, $\mathbf{x} = (x_1, \ldots, x_n)$ are n-vectors and $\mathbf{D}$ is a $n \times n$ matrix, subject to

$$\mathbf{a}_i \mathbf{x} \le b_i, i \in I$$

$$\mathbf{a}_i \mathbf{x} = b_i, i \in E$$

$$\mathbf{x} \ge 0$$

where $\mathbf{b}$ is an m-vector $\mathbf{b} = (b_1, \ldots, b_m)$, $\mathbf{A} = [\mathbf{a}_i]$ is an $m \times n$ matrix, and I and E specify the nonequality and equality constraints respectively.

The major classification criteria for these problems come from the characteristics of the matrix $\mathbf{D}$ as follow:

- If the matrix $\mathbf{D}$ is positive semidefinite or positive definite, then the QP problem is a convex quadratic problem. For convex quadratic problems, every local maximum is a global maximum. Algorithms exist for solving this problem in polynomial time.[5] The Markowitz mean-variance optimization problem is of this type.
- If the matrix $\mathbf{D}$ is negative semidefinite, that is, its eigenvalues are all nonpositive, then the QP problem is a concave quadratic problem. All solutions lie at some vertex of the feasible regions. There are efficient algorithms for solving this problem.

---

[5] A problem is said to be solvable in polynomial time if the time needed to solve the problem scales with the number of variables as a polynomial.

■ If the matrix **D** is such that the problem is bilinear, that is, the variables **x** can be split into two subvectors such that the problem is linear when one of the two subvectors is fixed, then the QP problem is bilinear. There are efficient algorithms for solving this problem.

■ If the matrix **D** is indefinite, that is, it has both positive and negative eigenvalues, then the QP problem is very difficult to solve. Depending on the matrix **D**, the complexity of the problem might grow exponentially with the number of variables.

Many modern software optimization packages have solvers for several of these problems.

CALCULUS OF VARIATIONS AND OPTIMAL CONTROL THEORY

We have thus far discussed the problem of finding the maxima or minima of a function of n real variables. The solution to these problems is typically one point in a domain. This formulation is sufficient for problems such as finding the optimal composition of a portfolio for a single period of a finite horizon: An investment is made at the initial time and a payoff is received at the end of the period. However, many other important optimization problems in finance require finding an optimal function or path throughout time and over multiple periods. The mathematical foundation for problems whose solution requires finding an optimal function or path of this kind is the **calculus of variations**. The basic setting of the calculus of variations is the following. An infinite set of admissible functions $y = f(x)$, $x_0 \leq x \leq x_1$ is given. The end points might vary from curve to curve. Let's assume all curves are differentiable in the given interval $[x_0,x_1]$. A function of three variables $F(x,y,z)$ is given such that the integral

$$J_y = \int_{x_0}^{x_1} F(x, y, y')dx$$

is well defined where $y' = dy/dx$. The value of J depends on the curve y. The basic problem of the calculus of variations is to find the curve $y = f(x)$ that minimizes J. This problem could be easily reformulated in many variables.

One strategy for solving this problem is the following. Any solution $y = f(x)$ has the property that, if we slightly displace the curve y, the integral assumes higher values. Therefore if we parameterize parallel displacements with a variable ε (denoting by $\{y_\varepsilon\}$ the collection of all such displacements from the optimal y such that $y_\varepsilon\big|_{\varepsilon=0} = y$), the derivative of J with respect to ε must vanish for $\varepsilon = 0$.

If we compute this derivative, we arrive at the following differential equation that must be satisfied by the optimal solution y

$$\frac{\partial F(x, y, y')}{\partial y} - \frac{d}{dx}\frac{\partial F(x, y, y')}{\partial y'} = 0$$

First established by Leonard Euler in 1744, this differential equation is known as the Euler equation or the Euler-Lagrange equation.[6]

Though fundamental in the physical sciences, this formulation of variational principles, is rarely encountered in finance theory. In finance theory, as in engineering, one is primarily interested in controlling the evolution of a process. For instance, in investment management, one is interested in controlling the composition of a portfolio in order to attain some objective. This is the realm of control theory. Let's now define control theory in a deterministic setting. The following section will discuss stochastic programming—a computational implementation of control theory in a stochastic setting.

Consider a dynamic process which starts at a given initial time t_0 and ends at a given terminal time t_1. Let's suppose that the state of the system is described by only one variable $x(t)$ called the state variable. The state of the system is influenced by a set of control variables that we represent as a vector $\mathbf{u}(t) = [u_1(t),...,u_n(t)]$. The control vector must lie inside a given subset of a Euclidean r-dimensional space, U which is assumed to be closed and time-invariant. An entire path of the control vector is called a control. A control is admissible if it stays in U and satisfies some regularity conditions.

The dynamics of the state variables are specified through the differential equation

$$\frac{dx}{dt} = f_1[x(t), \mathbf{u}(t)]$$

where f_1 is assumed to be continuously differentiable with respect to both arguments. Suppose that the initial state is given but the terminal state is unrestricted.

The problem to be solved is that of maximizing the objective functional:

---

[6] Lagrange himself attributed the equation to Euler.

$$J_y = \int_{t_0}^{t_1} f_0[t, x(t), \mathbf{u}(t)]dt + S[t_1, x(t_1)]$$

A **functional** is a mapping from a set of functions into the set of real numbers; it associates a number to each function. The definite integral is an example of a functional.

To solve the above optimal control problem, a useful strategy is to find a set of differential equations that must be satisfied by the control. Two major approaches for solving this problem are available: **Bellman's Dynamic Programming**[7] and **Pontryagin's Maximum Principle**.[8] The former approach is based on the fact that the value of the state variable at time t captures all the necessary information for the decision-making from time t and onward: The paths of the control vector and the state variable up to time t do not make any difference as long as the state variable at time t is the same. Bellmann showed how to derive from this observation a partial differential equation that uniquely determines the control. Pontryagin's Maximum Principle introduces additional auxiliary variables and derives differential equations via the calculus of variations that might be simpler to solve than those of Bellmann's dynamic programming.

STOCHASTIC PROGRAMMING

The model formulations discussed thus far assume that the data for the given problem are known precisely. However, in financial economics, data are stochastic and cannot be known with certainty. Stochastic programming can be used to make optimal decisions under uncertainty. The fundamental idea behind stochastic programming is the concept of stages and **recourse**. Recourse is the ability to take corrective action at a future time, that is, a decision stage, after a random event has taken place.

To formulate problems of dynamic decision-making under uncertainty as a stochastic program, we must first characterize the uncertainty in the model. The most common method is to formulate scenarios and to assign to each scenario a probability. A scenario is a complete path of data. To illustrate the problem of stochastic programming, let's consider

---

[7] R. Bellman, *Dynamic Programming* (Princeton, NJ: Princeton University Press, 1957).

[8] For a discussion of Pontryagin's Maximum Principle see, for instance: E.B. Lee, and L. Marcus, *Foundations of Optimal Control Theory* (New York: John Wiley & Sons, 1967).

a two-stage program that seeks to minimize the cost of the first-period decision plus the expected cost of the second-period recourse decision. In Chapter 21 we provide an example related to bond portfolio management.

To cast the stochastic programming problem in the framework of LP, we need to create a deterministic equivalent of the stochastic problem. This is obtained introducing a new set of variables at each stage and taking expectations. The first-period direct cost is $\mathbf{c}^T \mathbf{x}$ while the recourse cost at the second stage is $\mathbf{d}_i^T \mathbf{y}_i$ where $i = 1,...,S$ represents the different states. The first-period constraints are represented as $\mathbf{Ax} = \mathbf{b}$. At each stage, recourse is subject to some recourse function $\mathbf{Tx} + \mathbf{Wy} = \mathbf{h}$. This constraint can be, for example, self-financing conditions in portfolio management. It should be noted that in stochastic programs the first-period decision is independent of which second-period scenario actually occurs. This is called the **nonanticipativity property**.

A two-stage problem can be formulated as follows

$$\text{minimize } \mathbf{c}^T \mathbf{x} + \sum_{i=1}^{S} p_i \mathbf{d}_i^T \mathbf{y}_i$$

subject to

$$\mathbf{Ax} = \mathbf{b}$$

$$\mathbf{T}_i \mathbf{x} + \mathbf{W}_i \mathbf{y}_i = \mathbf{h}_i, \quad i = 1,...,S$$

$$\mathbf{x} \geq 0$$

$$\mathbf{y}_i \geq 0$$

where S is the number of states and p_i is the probability of each state such that

$$\sum_{i=1}^{S} p_i = 1$$

Notice that the nonanticipativity constraint is met. There is only one first-period decision whereas there are S second-period decisions, one for each scenario. In this formulation, the stochastic programming problem has been reduced to an LP problem. This formulation can be extended to any number of intermediate stages.

SUMMARY

- Optimizing means finding the maxima or minima of a function or of a functional.
- Optimization is a fundamental principle of financial decision-making insofar as financial decisions are an optimal trade-off between risk and return.
- The partial derivatives of an unconstrained function vanish at maxima and minima.
- The maxima and minima of a function subject to equality constraints can be found equating to zero the derivatives of the corresponding Lagrangian function, which is the sum of the original function and of a linear combination of the constraints.
- If constraints are linear inequalities, the problem can be solved numerically with the techniques of linear programming, quadratic programming, or nonlinear mathematical programming.
- There are two major solution strategies for a linear programming problem: the simplex method and the interior points method.
- The simplex method searches for a solution by moving on the vertices of the simplex, that is, the area identified by the constraint equations.
- The interior points method allows movement in the interior points of the area identified by the constraint equations.
- Quadratic and, more in general, nonlinear optimization problems are more difficult to solve and more computationally intensive.
- Functionals are functions defined on other functions.
- Calculus of variations deals with the problem of finding those functions that optimize a functional.
- Control theory deals with the problem of optimizing a functional by controlling some of the variables while other variables are subject to exogenous dynamics.
- Bellmann's Dynamic Programming and Pontryagin's Maximum Principle are the key mathematical tools of control theory.
- Multistage stochastic programming is a set of numerical techniques for finding the maxima and minima of a functional defined on a stochastic process.
- Multistage stochastic optimization is based on formalizing the rules for recourse, that is, how decisions are made at each stage and on describing possible scenarios.

CHAPTER 8

Stochastic Integrals

In Chapter 4, we explained definite and indefinite integrals for deterministic functions. Recall that integration is an operation performed on *single*, *deterministic* functions; the end product is another single, deterministic function. Integration defines a process of **cumulation**: The integral of a function represents the area below the function. However, the usefulness of deterministic functions in economics and finance theory is limited. Given the amount of uncertainty, few laws in economics and finance theory can be expressed through them. It is necessary to adopt an ensemble view, where *the path of economic variables must be considered a realization of a stochastic process, not a deterministic path*. We must therefore move from deterministic integration to **stochastic integration**. In doing so we have to define how to **cumulate random shocks in a continuous-time environment**. These concepts require rigorous definition. This chapter defines the concept and the properties of stochastic integration. Based on the concept of stochastic integration, Chapter 10 defines **stochastic differential equations**.

Two observations are in order:

■ While ordinary integrals and derivatives operate on functions and yield either individual numbers or other functions, stochastic integration operates on stochastic processes and yield either random variables or other stochastic processes. Therefore, while a definite integral is a number and an indefinite integral is a function, a stochastic integral is a random variable or a stochastic process. A differential equation—when equipped with suitable initial or boundary conditions—admits as a solution a single function while a stochastic differential equations admits as a solution a stochastic process.

■ Moving from a deterministic to a stochastic environment does not necessarily require leaving the realm of standard calculus. In fact, all the stochastic laws of economics and finance theory could be expressed as laws that govern the distribution of transition probabilities. We will see an example of this mathematical strategy when we introduce the Fokker-Planck differential equations (Chapter 20). The latter are deterministic partial differential equations that govern the probability distributions of prices. Nevertheless it is often convenient to represent uncertainty directly through stochastic integration and stochastic differential equations. This approach is not limited to economics and finance theory: it is also used in the domain of the physical sciences. In economics and finance theory, stochastic differential equations have the advantage of being intuitive: thinking in terms of a deterministic path plus an uncertain term is easier than thinking in terms of abstract probability distributions. There are other reasons why stochastic calculus is the methodology of choice in economics and finance but easy intuition plays a key role.

For example, a risk-free bank account, which earns a deterministic instantaneous interest rate $f(t)$, evolves according to the deterministic law:

$$y = A\exp\left(\int f(t)dt\right)$$

which is the general solution of the differential equation:

$$\frac{dy}{y} = f(t)dt$$

The solution of this differential equation tells us how the bank account cumulates over time.

However if the rate is not deterministic but is subject to volatility—that is, at any instant the rate is $f(t)$ plus a random disturbance—then the bank account evolves as a stochastic process. That is to say, the bank account might follow any of an infinite number of different paths: each path cumulates the rate $f(t)$ plus the random disturbance. In a sense that will be made precise in this chapter and in Chapter 10 on stochastic differential equations, we must solve the following equation:

$$\frac{dy}{y} = f(t)dt \text{ plus random disturbance}$$

Here is where stochastic integration comes into play: It defines how the stochastic rate process is transformed into the stochastic account process. This is the direct stochastic integration approach.

It is possible to take a different approach. At any instant t, the instantaneous interest rate and the cumulated bank account have two probability distributions. We could use a partial differential equation to describe how the probability distribution of the cumulated bank account is linked to the interest rate probability distribution.

Similar reasoning applies to stock and derivative price processes. In continuous-time finance, these processes are defined as stochastic processes which are the solution of a stochastic differential equation. Hence, the importance of stochastic integrals in continuous-time finance theory should be clear.

Following some remarks on the informal intuition behind stochastic integrals, this chapter proceeds to define Brownian motions and outlines the formal mathematical process through which stochastic integrals are defined. A number of properties of stochastic integrals are then established. After introducing stochastic integrals informally, we go on to define more rigorously the mathematical process for defining stochastic integrals.

THE INTUITION BEHIND STOCHASTIC INTEGRALS

Let's first contrast ordinary integration with stochastic integration. A definite integral

$$A = \int_a^b f(x)dx$$

is a number A associated to each function $f(x)$ while an indefinite integral

$$y(x) = \int_a^x f(s)ds$$

is a function y associated to another function f. The integral represents the cumulation of the infinite terms $f(s)ds$ over the integration interval.

A **stochastic integral,** that we will denote by

$$W = \int_a^b X_t dB_t$$

or

$$W = \int_a^b X_t \circ dB_t$$

is a random variable W associated to a stochastic process if the time interval is fixed or, if the time interval is variable, is another stochastic process W_t. The stochastic integral represents the cumulation of the stochastic products $X_t dB_t$. As we will see in Chapter 10, the rationale for this approach is that we need to represent *how random shocks feed back into the evolution of a process*. We can cumulate separately the deterministic increments and the random shocks only for linear processes. In nonlinear cases, as in the simple example of the bank account, random shocks feed back into the process. For this reason we define stochastic integrals as the cumulation of the product of a process X by the random increments of a Brownian motion.

Consider a stochastic process X_t over an interval $[S,T]$. Recall that a stochastic process is a real variable $X(\omega)_t$ that depends on both time and the state of the economy ω. For any given ω, $X(\cdot)_t$ is a path of the process from the origin S to time T. A stochastic process can be identified with the set of its paths equipped with an appropriate probability measure. A stochastic integral is an integral associated to each path; it is a random variable that associates a real number, obtained as a limit of a sum, to each path. If we fix the origin and let the interval vary, then the stochastic integral is another stochastic process.

It would seem reasonable, *prima facie*, to define the stochastic integral of a process $X(\omega)_t$ as the definite integral in the sense of Rieman-Stieltjes associated to each path $X(\cdot)_t$ of the process. If the process $X(\omega)_t$ has continuous paths $X(\cdot,\omega)$, the integrals

$$W(\omega) = \int_S^T X(s, \omega) ds$$

exist for each path. However, as discussed in the previous section, this is not the quantity we want to represent. In fact, we want to represent the cumulation of the stochastic products $X_t dB_t$. Defining the integral

$$W = \int_a^b X_t dB_t$$

pathwise in the sense of Rieman-Stieltjes would be meaningless because the paths of a Brownian motion are not of **finite variation**. If we define stochastic integrals simply as the limit of $X_t dB_t$ sums, the stochastic integral would be infinite (and therefore useless) for most processes.

However, Brownian motions have bounded **quadratic variation**. Using this property, we can define stochastic integrals pathwise through an approximation procedure. The approximation procedure to arrive at such a definition is far more complicated than the definition of the Rieman-Stieltjes integrals. Two similar but not equivalent definitions of stochastic integral have been proposed, the first by the Japanese mathematician Kyosi Itô in the 1940s, the second by the Russian physicist Ruslan Stratonovich in the 1960s. The definition of stochastic integral in the sense of Itô or of Stratonovich replaces the increments Δx_i with the increments ΔB_i of a fundamental stochastic process called Brownian motion. The increments ΔB_i represent the "noise" of the process.[1] The definition proceeds in the following three steps:

- *Step 1.* The first step consists in defining a fundamental stochastic process—the **Brownian motion**. In intuitive terms, a Brownian motion $B_t(\omega)$ is a continuous limit (in a sense that will be made precise in the following sections) of a simple **random walk**. A simple random walk is a discrete-time stochastic process defined as follows. A point can move one step to the right or to the left. Movement takes place only at discrete instants of time, say at time 1,2,3,.... At each discrete instant, the point moves to the right or to the left with probability ½.

    The random walk represents the cumulation of completely uncertain random shocks. At each point in time, the movement of the point is completely independent from its past movements. Hence, the Brownian motion represents the cumulation of random shocks in the limit of continuous time and of continuous states. It can be demonstrated that a.s. each path of the Brownian motion is not of bounded total variation but it has bounded quadratic variation.

---

[1] The definition of stochastic integrals can be generalized by taking a generic square integrable martingale instead of a Brownian motion. Itô defined stochastic integrals with respect to a Brownian motion. In 1967 H. Kunita and S. Watanabe extended the definition of stochastic integrals to square integrable martingales.

Recall that the total variation of a function $f(x)$ is the limit of the sums

supremum

$$\sum |f(x_i) - f(x_{i-1})|$$

while the quadratic variation is defined as the limit of the sums

supremum

$$\sum |f(x_i) - f(x_{i-1})|^2$$

Quadratic variation can be interpreted as the **absolute volatility** of a process. Thanks to this property, the ΔB_i of the Brownian motion provides the basic increments of the stochastic integral, replacing the Δx_i of the Rieman-Stieltjes integral.

■ *Step 2.* The second step consists in defining the stochastic integral for a class of simple functions called **elementary functions**. Consider the time interval $[S,T]$ and any partition of the interval $[S,T]$ in N subintervals: $S \equiv t_0 < t_1 < ...t_i < ...t_N \equiv T$. An elementary function ϕ is a function defined on the time t and the outcome ω such that it assumes a constant value on the i-th subinterval. Call $I[t_{i+1},t_i)$ the indicator function of the interval $[t_{i+1},t_i)$. The indicator function of a given set is a function that assumes value 1 on the points of the set and 0 elsewhere. We can then write an elementary function ϕ as follows:

$$\phi(t, \omega) = \sum_i \varepsilon_i(\omega) I[t_{i+1}, t_i)$$

In other words, the constants $\varepsilon_i(\omega)$ are random variables and the function $\phi(t,\omega)$ is a stochastic process made up of paths that are constant on each i-th interval.

We can now define the stochastic integral, in the sense of Itô, of elementary functions $\phi(t,\omega)$ as follows:

$$W = \int_S^T \phi(t, \omega) dB_t(\omega) = \sum_i \varepsilon_i(\omega)[B_{i+1}(\omega) - B_i(\omega)]$$

where B is a Brownian motion.

It is clear from this definition that W is a random variable $\omega \rightarrow W(\omega)$. Note that the Itô integral thus defined for elementary functions cumulates the products of the elementary functions $\phi(t,\omega)$ and of the increments of the Brownian motion $B_t(\omega)$.

It can be demonstrated that the following property, called **Itô isometry**, holds for Itô stochastic integrals defined for bounded elementary functions as above:

$$E\left[\left(\int_S^T \phi(t,\omega)dB_t(\omega)\right)^2\right] = E\left[\int_S^T \phi(t,\omega)^2 dt\right]$$

The Itô isometry will play a fundamental role in Step 3.

■ *Step 3.* The third step consists in using the Itô isometry to show that each function g which is square-integrable (plus other conditions that will be made precise in the next section) can be approximated by a sequence of elementary functions $\phi_n(t,\omega)$ in the sense that

$$E\left[\int_S^T [g - \phi_n(t,\omega)]^2 dt\right] \to 0$$

If g is bounded and has a continuous time-path, the functions $\phi_n(t,\omega)$ can be defined as follows:

$$\phi_n(t,\omega) = \sum_i g(t_i,\omega)I[t_{i+1}, t_i)$$

where I is the indicator function. We can now use the Itô isometry to define the stochastic integral of a generic function $f(t,\omega)$ as follows:

$$\int_S^T f(t,\omega)dB_t(\omega) = \lim_{n \to \infty} \int_S^T \phi_n(t,\omega)dB_t(\omega)$$

The Itô isometry insures that the Cauchy condition is satisfied and that the above sequence thus converges.

In outlining the above definition, we omitted an important point that will be dealt with in the next section: The definition of the stochastic integral in the sense of Itô requires that the elementary functions be *without anticipation*—that is, they depend only on the past history of the Brownian motion. In fact, in the case of continuous paths, we wrote the approximating functions as follows:

$$\phi_n(t, \omega) = \sum_i g(t_i, \omega)[B_{i+1}(\omega) - B_i(\omega)]$$

taking the function g in the left extreme of each subinterval.

However, the definition of stochastic integrals in the sense of Stratonovich *admits anticipation*. In fact, the stochastic integral in the sense of Stratonovich, written as follows:

$$\int_S^T f(t, \omega) \circ dB_t(\omega)$$

uses the following approximation under the assumption of continuous paths:

$$\phi_n(t, \omega) = \sum_i g(t_i^*, \omega)[B_{i+1}(\omega) - B_i(\omega)]$$

where

$$t_i^* = \frac{t_{i+1} - t_i}{2}$$

is the midpoint of the i-th subinterval.

Whose definition—Itô's or Stratonovich's—is preferable? Note that neither can be said to be correct or incorrect. The choice of the one over the other is a question of which one best represents the phenomena under study. The lack of anticipation is one reason why the Itô integral is generally preferred in finance theory.

We have just outlined the definition of stochastic integrals leaving aside mathematical details and rigor. The following two sections will make the above process mathematically rigorous and will discuss the question of anticipation of information. While these sections are a bit technical and might be skipped by those not interested in the mathematical details of stochastic calculus, they explain a number of concepts that are *key* to the modern development of finance theory.

BROWNIAN MOTION DEFINED

The previous section introduced Brownian motion informally as the limit of a simple random walk when the step size goes to zero. This section defines Brownian motion formally. The term "Brownian motion" is due to the Scottish botanist Robert Brown who in 1828 observed that pollen grains suspended in a liquid move irregularly. This irregular motion was later explained by the random collision of the molecules of the liquid with the pollen grains. It is therefore natural to represent Brownian motion as a continuous-time stochastic process that is the limit of a discrete random walk.

Let's now formally define Brownian motion and demonstrate its existence. Let's first go back to the probabilistic representation of the economy. Recall from Chapter 6 that the economy is represented as a probability space $(\Omega, \Im, P)$, where Ω is the set of all possible economic states, $\Im$ is the event σ-algebra, and P is a probability measure. Recall that the economic states $\omega \in \Omega$ are not instantaneous states but represent full histories of the economy for the time horizon considered, which can be a finite or infinite interval of time. In other words, the economic states are the possible realization outcomes of the economy.

Recall also that, in this probabilistic representation of the economy, time-variable economic quantities—such as interest rates, security prices or cash flows as well as aggregate quantities such as economic output—are represented as stochastic processes $X_t(\omega)$. In particular, the price and dividend of each stock are represented as two stochastic processes $S_t(\omega)$ and $d_t(\omega)$.

Stochastic processes are time-dependent random variables defined over the set Ω. It is critical to define stochastic processes so that there is no anticipation of information, i.e., at time t no process depends on variables that will be realized later. Anticipation of information is possible only within a deterministic framework. However the space Ω in itself does not contain any coherent specification of time. If we associate random variables $X_t(\omega)$ to a time index without any additional restriction, we might incur in the problem of anticipation of information. Consider, for instance, an arbitrary family of time-indexed random variables $X_t(\omega)$ and suppose that, for some instant t, the relationship $X_t(\omega) = X_{t+1}(\omega)$ holds. In this case there is clearly anticipation of information as the value of the variable $X_{t+1}(\omega)$ at time $t+1$ is known at an earlier time t. All relationships that lead to anticipation of information must be treated as deterministic.

The formal way to specify in full generality the evolution of time and the propagation of information without anticipation is through the concept of **filtration**. Recall from Chapter 6 that the concept of filtration is based on identifying all events that are known at any given instant. It is assumed that it is possible to associate to each moment t a σ-algebra of events $\Im_t \subset \Im$ formed by all events that are known prior to or at time t. It is assumed that events are never "forgotten," i.e., that $\Im_t \subset \Im_s$, if $t < s$. An increasing sequence of σ-algebras, each associated to the time at which all its events are known, represents the propagation of information. This sequence (called a filtration) is typically indicated as $\Im_t$.

The economy is therefore represented as a probability space $(\Omega, \Im, P)$ equipped with a filtration $\{\Im_t\}$. The key point is that every process $X_t(\omega)$ that represents economic or financial quantities must be **adapted** to the filtration $\{\Im_t\}$, that is, the random variable $X_t(\omega)$ must be measurable with respect to the σ-algebras $\Im_t$. In simple terms, this means that each event of the type $X_t(\omega) \le x$ belongs to $\Im_t$ while each event of the type $X_s(\omega) \le y$ for $t \le s$ belongs to $\Im_s$. For instance, consider a process $P_t(\omega)$ which might represent the price of a stock. Any coherent representation of the economy must ensure that events such as $\{\omega: P_s(\omega) \le c\}$ are not known at any time $t < s$. The filtration $\{\Im_t\}$ prescribes all events admissible at time t.

Why do we have to use the complex concept of filtration? Why can't we simply identify information at time t with the values of all the variables known at time t as opposed to identifying a set of events? The principal reason is that in a continuous-time continuous-state environment any individual value has probability zero; we cannot condition on single values as the standard definition of conditional probability would become meaningless. In fact, in the standard definition of conditional probability (see Chapter 6) the probability of the conditioning event appears in the denominator and cannot be zero.

It is possible, however, to reverse this reasoning and construct a filtration starting from a process. Suppose that a process $X_t(\omega)$ does not admit any anticipation of information, for instance because the $X_t(\omega)$ are all mutually independent. We can therefore construct a filtration $\Im_t$ as the strictly increasing sequence of σ-algebras generated by the process $X_t(\omega)$. Any other process must be adapted to $\Im_t$.

Let's now go back to the definition of the Brownian motion. Suppose that a probability space $(\Omega, \Im, P)$ equipped with a filtration $\Im_t$ is given. A **one-dimensional standard Brownian motion** is a stochastic process $B_t(\omega)$ with the following properties:

- $B_t(\omega)$ is defined over the probability space $(\Omega, \Im, P)$.
- $B_t(\omega)$ is continuous for $0 \le t < \infty$.
- $B_0(\omega) = 0$.
- $B_t(\omega)$ is adapted to the filtration $\Im_t$.
- The increments $B_t(\omega) - B_s(\omega)$ are independent and normally distributed with variance $(t-s)$ and zero mean.

The above conditions[2] state that the standard Brownian motion is a stochastic process that starts at zero, has continuous paths and normally distributed increments whose variance grows linearly with time. Note that in the last condition the increments are independent of the σ-algebra $\mathfrak{I}_s$ and not of the previous values of the process. As noted above, this is because any single realization of the process has probability zero and it is therefore impossible to use the standard concept of conditional probability: conditioning must be with respect to a σ-algebra $\mathfrak{I}_s$. Once this concept has been firmly established, one might speak loosely of independence of the present values of a process from its previous values. It should be clear, however, that what is meant is independence with respect to a σ-algebra $\mathfrak{I}_s$.

Note also that the filtration $\mathfrak{I}_t$ is an integral part of the above definition of the Brownian motion. This does not mean that, given any probability space and any filtration, a standard Brownian motion with these characteristics exists. For instance, the filtration generated by a discrete-time continuous-state random walk is insufficient to support a Brownian motion. The definition states only that we call a one-dimensional standard Brownian motion a mathematical object (if it exists) made up of a probability space, a filtration and a time dependent random variable with the properties specified in the definition

However it can be demonstrated that Brownian motions exist by constructing them. Several construction methodologies have been proposed, including methodologies based on the Kolmogorov extension theorem or on constructing the Brownian motion as the limit of a sequence of discrete random walks. To prove the existence of the standard Brownian motion, we will use the **Kolmogorov extension theorem**.

The Kolmogorov theorem can be summarized as follows. Consider the following family of probability measures

$$\mu_{t_1, \dots, t_m}(H_1 \times \dots \times H_m) = P[(X_{t_1} \in H_1, \dots, X_{t_m} \in H_m), H_i \in \mathfrak{B}^n]$$

for all $t_1, \dots, t_k \in [0, \infty)$, $k \in N$ and where the Hs are n-dimensional Borel sets. Suppose that the following two consistency conditions are satisfied

---

[2] The set of conditions defining a Brownian motion can be more parsimonious. If a process has stationary, independent increments and continuous paths a.s. it must have normally distributed increments. A process with stationary independent increments and with paths that are continuous to the right and limited to the left (the *cadlag* functions), is called a Levy process. In Chapter 13 we will generalize Brownian motion to α-stable Levy processes that admit distributions with infinite variance and/or infinite mean.

$$\mu_{t_{\sigma(1)}, \ldots, t_{\sigma(m)}}(H_1 \times \ldots \times H_m) = \mu_{t_1, \ldots, t_m}(H_{\sigma^{-1}(1)} \times \ldots \times H_{\sigma^{-1}(m)})$$

for all permutations σ on $\{1,2,\ldots,k\}$, and

$$\mu_{t_1, \ldots, t_k}(H_1 \times \ldots \times H_k) = \mu_{t_1, \ldots, t_k, t_{k+1}, \ldots, t_m}(H_1 \times \ldots \times H_k \times R^n \times \ldots \times R^n)$$

for all m. The Kolmogorov extension theorem states that, if the above conditions are satisfied, then there is (1) a probability space $(\Omega, \mathfrak{I}, P)$ and (2) a stochastic process that admits the probability measures

$$\mu_{t_1, \ldots, t_m}(H_1 \times \ldots \times H_m) = P[(X_{t_1} \in H_1, \ldots, X_{tm} \in H_m), H_i \in \mathfrak{B}^n]$$

as finite dimensional distributions.

The construction is lengthy and technical and we omit it here, but it should be clear how, with an appropriate selection of finite-dimensional distributions, the Kolmogorov extension theorem can be used to prove the existence of Brownian motions. The finite-dimensional distributions of a one-dimensional Brownian motion are distributions of the type

$$\mu_{t_1, \ldots, t_k}(H_1 \times \ldots \times H_k)$$
$$= \int_{H_1 \times \ldots \times H_k} p(t, x, x_1) p(t_2 - t_1, x_1, x_2) \ldots p(t_k - t_{k-1}, x_{k-1}, x_k) dx_1 \ldots dx_k$$

where

$$p(t, x, y) = (2\pi t)^{-\frac{1}{2}} \exp\left(-\frac{|x - y|^2}{2t}\right)$$

and with the convention that the integrals are taken with respect to the Lebesgue measure. The distribution $p(t,x,x_1)$ in the integral is the initial distribution. If the process starts at zero, $p(t,x,x_1)$ is a Dirac delta, that is, it is a distribution of mass 1 concentrated in one point.

It can be verified that these distributions satisfy the above consistency conditions; the Kolmogorov extension theorem therefore ensures that a stochastic process with the above finite dimensional distributions exists. It can be demonstrated that this process has normally distributed independent increments with variance that grows linearly with time. It is therefore a one-dimensional Brownian motion. These definitions can be easily extended to a n-dimensional Brownian motion.

In the initial definition of a Brownian motion, we assumed that a filtration $\Im_t$ was given and that the Brownian motion was adapted to the filtration. In the present construction, however, we reverse this process. Given that the process we construct has normally distributed, stationary, independent increments, we can define the filtration $\Im_t$ as the filtration $\Im_t^B$ generated by $B_t(\omega)$. The independence of the increments of the Brownian motion guarantee the absence of anticipation of information. Note that if we were given a filtration $\Im_t$ larger than the filtration $\Im_t^B$, $B_t(\omega)$ would still be a Brownian motion with respect to $\Im_t$.

As we will see in Chapter 10 when we cover stochastic differential equations, there are two types of solutions of stochastic differential equations—strong and weak—depending on whether the filtration is given or generated by the Brownian motion. The implications of these differences for economics and finance will be discussed in the same section.

The above construction does not specify uniquely the Brownian motion. In fact, there are infinite stochastic processes that start from the same point and have the same finite dimensional distributions but have totally different paths. However it can be demonstrated that only one Brownian motion has continuous paths a.s. Recall that **a.s.** means almost surely, that is, for all paths except a set of measure zero. This process is called the **canonical Brownian motion**. Its paths can be identified with the space of continuous functions.

The Brownian motion can also be constructed as the continuous limit of a discrete random walk. Consider a simple random walk W_i where i are discrete time points. The random walk is the motion of a point that moves Δx to the right or to the left with equal probability ½ at each time increment Δx. The total displacement X_i at time i is the sum of i independent increments each distributed as a Bernoulli variable. Therefore the random variable X has a binomial distribution with mean zero and variance:

$$\frac{\Delta^2 x}{\Delta t}$$

Suppose that both the time increment and the space increment approach zero: $\Delta t \to 0$ and $\Delta x \to 0$. Note that this is a very informal statement. In fact what we mean is that we can construct a sequence of random walk processes W_i^n, each characterized by a time step and by a time displacement. It can be demonstrated that if

$$\frac{\Delta^2 x}{\Delta t} \to \sigma$$

(i.e., the square of the spaced interval and the time interval are of the same order) then the sequence of random walks approaches a Brownian motion. Though this is intuitive as the binomial distributions approach normal distributions, it should be clear that it is far from being mathematically obvious.

Exhibit 8.1 illustrates 100 realizations of a Brownian motion approximated as a random walk. The exhibit clearly illustrates that the standard deviation grows with the square root of the time as the variance grows linearly with time. In fact, as illustrated, most paths remain confined within a parabolic region.

PROPERTIES OF BROWNIAN MOTION

The paths of a Brownian motion are rich structures with a number of surprising properties. It can be demonstrated that the paths of a canonical Brownian motion, though continuous, are nowhere differentiable. It can also be demonstrated that they are fractals of fractal dimension ½.

EXHIBIT 8.1   Illustration of 100 Paths of a Brownian Motion Generated as an Arithmetic Random Walk

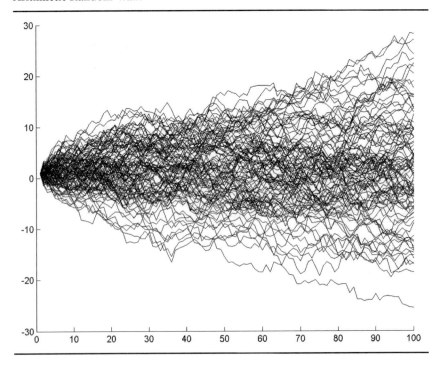

The fractal dimension is a concept that measures quantitatively how a geometric object occupies space. A straight line has fractal dimension one, a plane has fractal dimension two, and so on. Fractal objects might also have intermediate dimensions. This is the case, for example of the path of a Brownian motion which is so jagged that, in a sense, it occupies more space than a straight line.

The fractal nature of Brownian motion paths implies that each path is a self-similar object. This property can be illustrated graphically. If we generate random walks with different time steps, we obtain jagged paths. If we allow paths to be graphically magnified, all paths look alike regardless of the time step with which they have been generated. In Exhibit 8.2, samples paths are generated with different time steps and then portions of the paths are magnified. Note that they all look perfectly similar.

This property was first observed by Benoit Mandelbrot in sequences of cotton prices in the 1960s. In general, if one looks at asset or commodity price time series, it is difficult to recognize their time scale. For

EXHIBIT 8.2   Illustration of the Fractal Properties of the Paths of a Brownian Motion[a]

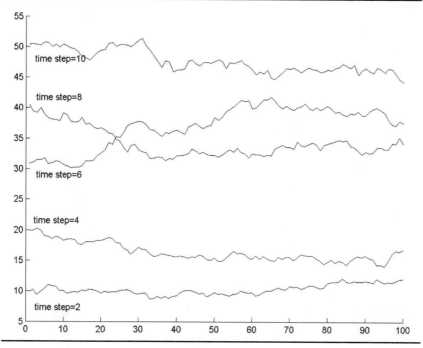

[a] Five paths of a Brownian motion are generated as random walks with different time steps and then magnified.

instance, weekly or monthly time series look alike. Recent empirical and theoretical research work has made this claim more precise as we will see in Chapter 13.

Let's consider a one-dimensional standard Brownian motion. If we wait a sufficiently long period of time, every path except a set of paths of measure zero will return to the origin. The path between two consecutive passages through zero is called an **excursion** of the Brownian motion. The distribution of the maximum height attained by an excursion and of the time between two passages through zero or through any level have interesting properties. The distribution of the time between two passages through zero has infinite mean. This is at the origin of the so-called St. Petersburg paradox described by the Swiss mathematician Bernoulli. The paradox consists of the following. Suppose a player bets increasing sums on a game which can be considered a realization of a random walk. As the return to zero of a random walk is a sure event, the player is certain to win—but while the probability of winning is one, the average time before winning is infinite. To stay the game, the capital required is also infinite. Difficult to imagine a banker ready to put up the money to back the player.

The distribution of the time to the first passage through zero of a Brownian motion is not Gaussian. In fact, the probability of a very long waiting time before the first return to zero is much higher than in a normal distribution. It is a fat-tailed distribution in the sense that it has more weight in the tail regions than a normal distribution. The distribution of the time to the first passage through zero of a Brownian motion is an example of how fat-tailed distributions can be generated from Gaussian variables. We will come back on this subject in Chapter 13 where we deal with the question of how the fat-tailed distributions observed in financial markets are generated from a large number of apparently independent events.

STOCHASTIC INTEGRALS DEFINED

Let's now go back to the definition of stochastic integrals, starting with one-dimensional stochastic integrals. Suppose that a probability space $(\Omega, \mathfrak{I}, P)$ equipped with a filtration $\mathfrak{I}_t$ is given. Suppose also that a Brownian motion $B_t(\omega)$ adapted to the filtration $\mathfrak{I}_t$ is given. We will define Itô integrals following the three-step procedure outlined earlier in this chapter. We have just completed the first step defining Brownian motion. The second step consists in defining the Itô integral for elementary functions.

Let's first define the set $\Phi(S,T)$ of functions $\Phi(S,T) \equiv \{f(t,\omega): [(0,\infty) \times \Omega \to R]\}$ with the following properties:

- Each f is jointly $\mathcal{B} \times \mathfrak{I}$ measurable.
- Each $f(t,\omega)$ is adapted to $\mathfrak{I}_t$.
- $E\left[\int_S^T f^2(t,\omega)dt\right] < \infty.$ [3]

This is the set of paths for which we define the Itô integral.

Consider the time interval $[S,T]$ and, for each integer n, partition the interval $[S,T]$ in subintervals: $S \equiv t_0 < t_1 < ... t_i < ... t_n < ... t_N \equiv T$ in this way:

$$t_k = t_k^n = \begin{cases} k2^{-n} & \text{if } S \leq k2^{-n} \leq T \\ S & \text{if } k2^{-n} < S \\ T & \text{if } k2^{-n} > T \end{cases}$$

This rule provides a family of partitions of the interval $[S,T]$ which can be arbitrarily refined.

Consider the elementary functions $\phi(t,\omega) \in \Phi$ which we write as

$$\phi(t,\omega) = \sum_i \varepsilon_i(\omega) I[t_{i+1} - t_i)$$

As $\phi(t,\omega) \in \Phi$, $\varepsilon_i(\omega)$ are $\mathfrak{I}_{t_i}$ measurable random variables.

We can now define the stochastic integral, in the sense of Itô, of elementary functions $\phi(t,\omega)$ as

$$W = \int_S^T \phi(t,\omega)dB_t(\omega) = \sum_{i \geq 0} \varepsilon_i(\omega)[B_{i+1}(\omega) - B_i(\omega)]$$

where B is a Brownian motion. Note that the $\varepsilon_i(\omega)$ and the increments $B_j(\omega) - B_i(\omega)$ are independent for $j > i$. The key aspect of this definition that was not included in the informal outline is the condition that the $\varepsilon_i(\omega)$ are $\mathfrak{I}_{t_i}$ measurable.

For bounded elementary functions $\phi(t,\omega) \in \Phi$ the Itô isometry holds

---

[3] This condition can be weakened.

$$E\left[\left(\int_S^T \phi(t,\omega)dB_t(\omega)\right)^2\right] = E\left[\int_S^T \phi(t,\omega)^2 dt\right]$$

The demonstration of the Itô isometry rests on the fact that

$$E[\varepsilon_i\varepsilon_j(B_{t_{i+1}} - B_{t_i})(B_{t_{j+1}} - B_{t_j})] = \begin{cases} 0 \text{ if } i \neq j \\ E(\varepsilon_i^2) \text{ if } i = j \end{cases}$$

This completes the definition of the stochastic integral for elementary functions.

We have now completed the introduction of Brownian motions and defined the Itô integral for elementary functions. Let's next introduce the approximation procedure that allows to define the stochastic integral for any $\phi(t,\omega)$. We will develop the approximation procedure in the following three additional steps that we will state without demonstration:

■ *Step 1.* Any function $g(t,\omega) \in \Phi$ that is bounded and such that all its time paths $\phi(\cdot,\omega)$ are continuous functions of time can be approximated by

$$\phi_n(t,\omega) = \sum_i g(t_i,\omega)I[t_{i+1} - t_i)$$

in the sense that:

$$E\int_S^T [(g - \phi_n)^2 dt] \to 0, n \to \infty, \forall\omega$$

where the intervals are those of the partition defined above. Note that $\phi_n(t,\omega) \in \Phi$ given that $g(t,\omega) \in \Phi$.

■ *Step 2.* We release the condition of time-path continuity of the $\phi_n(t,\omega)$. It can be demonstrated that any function $h(t,\omega) \in \Phi$ which is bounded but not necessarily continuous can be approximated by functions $g_n(t,\omega) \in \Phi$ which are bounded and continuous in the sense that

$$E\left[\int_S^T (h - g_n)^2 dt\right] \to 0$$

■ *Step 3.* It can be demonstrated that any function $f(t, \omega) \in \Phi$, not necessarily bounded or continuous, can be approximated by a sequence of bounded functions $h_n(t, \omega) \in \Phi$ in the sense that

$$E\left[\int_S^T (f - h_n)^2 dt\right] \to 0$$

We now have all the building blocks to complete the definition of Itô stochastic integrals. In fact, by virtue of the above three-step approximation procedure, given any function $f(t, \omega) \in \Phi$, we can choose a sequence of elementary functions $\phi_n(t, \omega) \in \Phi$ such that the following property holds:

$$E\left[\int_S^T (f - \phi_n)^2 dt\right] \to 0$$

Hence we can define the Itô stochastic integral as follows:

$$I[f](w) = \int_S^T f(t, \omega) dB_t(\omega) = \lim_{n \to \infty} \left[\int_S^T \phi_n(t, \omega) dt\right]$$

The limit exists as

$$\int_S^T \phi_n(t, \omega) dB_t(\omega)$$

forms a Cauchy sequence by the Itô isometry, which holds for every bounded elementary function.

Let's now summarize the definition of the Itô stochastic integral:

Given any function $f(t, \omega) \in \Phi$, we define the Itô stochastic integral by

$$I[f](w) \,=\, \int_S^T f(t, \omega)dB_t(\omega) \,=\, \lim_{n \to \infty} \left[\int_S^T \phi_n(t, \omega)dt \right]$$

where the functions $\phi_n(t, \omega) \in \Phi$ are a sequence of elementary functions such that

$$E \left[\int_S^T (f - \phi_n)^2 dt \right] \to 0$$

The multistep procedure outlined above ensures that the sequence $\phi_n(t, \omega) \in \Phi$ exists. In addition, it can be demonstrated that the Itô isometry holds in general for every $f(t, \omega) \in \Phi$

$$E \left[\left(\int_S^T f(t, \omega)dB_t(\omega) \right)^2 \right] \,=\, E \left[\int_S^T f(t, \omega)^2 dt \right]$$

SOME PROPERTIES OF ITÔ STOCHASTIC INTEGRALS

Suppose that $f, g \in \Phi(S, T)$ and let $0 < S < U < T$. It can be demonstrated that the following properties of Itô stochastic integrals hold:

$$\int_S^T fdB_t \,=\, \int_S^U fdB_t + \int_U^T fdB_t \text{ for a.a. } \omega$$

$$E \left[\int_S^T fdB_t \right] \,=\, 0$$

$$\int_S^T (cf + dg)dB_t \,=\, c\int_S^T fdB_t + d\int_S^T gdB_t, \text{ for a.a. } \omega, c, d \text{ constants}$$

If we let the time interval vary, say $(0,t)$, then the stochastic integral becomes a stochastic process:

$$I_t(\omega) = \int_0^t f dB_t$$

It can be demonstrated that a continuous version of this process exists. The following three properties can be demonstrated from the definition of integral:

$$\int_0^t dB_s = B_t$$

$$\int_0^t s dB_s = tB_t - \int_0^t B_s ds$$

$$\int_0^t B_s dB_s = \frac{1}{2}B_t^2 - \frac{1}{2}t$$

The last two properties show that, after performing stochastic integration, deterministic terms might appear.

SUMMARY

- Stochastic integration provides a coherent way to represent that instantaneous uncertainty (or volatility) cumulates over time. It is thus fundamental to the representation of financial processes such as interest rates, security prices or cash flows as well as aggregate quantities such as economic output.
- Stochastic integration operates on stochastic processes and produces random variables or other stochastic processes.
- Stochastic integration is a process defined on each path as the limit of a sum. However, these sums are different from the sums of the Riemann-Lebesgue integrals because the paths of stochastic processes are generally not of bounded variation.
- Stochastic integrals in the sense of Itô are defined through a process of approximation.
- Step 1 consists in defining Brownian motion, which is the continuous limit of a random walk.

■ Step 2 consists in defining stochastic integrals for elementary functions as the sums of the products of the elementary functions multiplied by the increments of the Brownian motion.
■ Step 3 extends this definition to any function through approximating sequences.

CHAPTER 9

Differential Equations and Difference Equations

In Chapter 4, we explained how to obtain the derivative of a function. In this chapter we will introduce differential equations. In nontechnical terms, differential equations are equations that express a relationship between a function and one or more derivatives (or differentials) of that function.

It would be difficult to overemphasize the importance of differential equations in modern science: they are used to express the vast majority of the laws of physics and engineering principles. In economics and finance, differential equations are used to express various laws and conditions including the following:

■ The laws of deterministic quantities such as the accumulation of risk-free bank deposits.
■ The laws that govern the evolution of price probability distributions.
■ The solution of economic variational problems, such as intertemporal optimization.
■ Conditions of continuous hedging, such as the Black-Scholes equation that we will describe in Chapter 15.

A large number of properties of differential equations have been established over the last three centuries. This chapter provides only a brief introduction to the concept of differential equations and their properties, limiting our discussion to the principal concepts.

DIFFERENTIAL EQUATIONS DEFINED

A **differential equation** is a condition expressed as a functional link between one or more functions and their derivatives. It is expressed as an equation (that is, as an equality between two terms).

A solution of a differential equation is a function that satisfies the given condition. For example, the condition

$$Y''(x) + \alpha Y'(x) + \beta Y(x) - b(x) = 0$$

equates to zero a linear relationship between an unknown function $Y(x)$, its first and second derivatives $Y'(x), Y''(x)$, and a known function $b(x)$.[1] The unknown function $Y(x)$ is the solution of the equation that is to be determined.

There are two broad types of differential equations: ordinary differential equations and partial differential equations. **Ordinary differential equations** are equations or systems of equations involving only one independent variable. Another way of saying this is that ordinary differential equations involve only total derivatives. In contrast, **partial differential equations** are differential equations or systems of equations involving partial derivatives. That is, there is more than one independent variable.

As we move from deterministic equations to stochastic equations, we introduce **stochastic differential equations**. In these differential equations, a random or stochastic term is included.

ORDINARY DIFFERENTIAL EQUATIONS

In full generality, an ordinary differential equation (ODE) can be expressed as the following relationship:

$$F[x, Y(x), Y^1(x), ..., Y^{(n)}(x)] = 0$$

where $Y^{(m)}(x)$ denotes the m-th derivative of an unknown function $Y(x)$. If the equation can be solved for the n-th derivative, it can be put in the form:

$$Y^{(n)}(x) = G[x, Y(x), Y^{(1)}(x), ..., Y^{(n-1)}(x)]$$

---

[1] In some equations we will denote the first and second derivatives by a single and double prime, respectively.

Order and Degree of an ODE

A differential equation is classified in terms of its order and its degree. The **order** of a differential equation is the order of the highest derivative in the equation. For example, the above differential equation is of order n since the highest order derivative is $Y^{(n)}(x)$. The **degree** of a differential equation is determined by looking at the highest derivative in the differential equation. The degree is the power to which that derivative is raised.

For example, the following ordinary differential equations are first degree differential equations of different orders:

$$Y^{(1)}(x) - 10Y(x) + 40 = 0 \qquad \text{(order 1)}$$

$$4Y^{(3)}(x) + Y^{(2)}(x) + Y^{(1)}(x) - 0.5Y(x) + 100 = 0 \qquad \text{(order 3)}$$

The following ordinary differential equations are of order 3 and fifth degree:

$$4\,[Y^{(3)}(x)]^5 + [Y^{(2)}(x)]^2 + Y^{(1)}(x) - 0.5Y(x) + 100 = 0$$

$$4\,[Y^{(3)}(x)]^5 + [Y^{(2)}(x)]^3 + Y^{(1)}(x) - 0.5Y(x) + 100 = 0$$

When an ordinary differential equation is of the first degree, it is said to be a **linear ordinary differential equation.**

Solution to an ODE

Let's return to the general ODE. A solution of this equation is any function $y(x)$ such that:

$$F[x, y(x), y^{(1)}(x), ..., y^{(n)}(x)] = 0$$

In general there will be not one but an infinite family of solutions. For example, the equation

$$Y^{(1)}(x) = \alpha Y(x)$$

admits, as a solution, all the functions of the form

$$y(x) = C\,\exp(\alpha x)$$

To identify one specific solution among the possible infinite solutions that satisfy a differential equation, additional restrictions must be imposed. Restrictions that uniquely identify a solution to a differential equation can be of various types. For instance, one could impose that a solution of an n-th order differential equation passes through n given points. A common type of restriction—called an **initial condition**—is obtained by imposing that the solution and some of its derivatives assume given initial values at some initial point.

Given an ODE of order n, to ensure the uniqueness of solutions it will generally be necessary to specify a starting point and the initial value of $n-1$ derivatives. It can be demonstrated, given the differential equation

$$F[x, Y(x), Y^{(1)}(x), ..., Y^{(n)}(x)] = 0$$

that if the function F is continuous and all of its partial derivatives up to order n are continuous in some region containing the values $y_0,...,$ $y_0^{(n-1)}$, then there is a unique solution $y(x)$ of the equation in some interval $I = (M \le x \le L)$ such that $y_0 = Y(x_0),...,y_0^{(n-1)} = Y^{(n-1)}(x_0)$.[2] Note that this theorem states that there is an interval in which the solution exists. Existence and uniqueness of solutions in a given interval is a more delicate matter and must be examined for different classes of equations.

The **general solution** of a differential equation of order n is a function of the form

$$y = \varphi(x, C_1, ..., C_n)$$

that satisfies the following two conditions:

■ *Condition 1.* The function $y = \varphi(x,C_1,...,C_n)$ satisfies the differential equation for any n-tuple of values $(C_1,...,C_n)$.

■ *Condition 2.* Given a set of initial conditions $y(x_0) = y_0,...,y^{(n-1)}(x_0) = y_0^{(n-1)}$ that belong to the region where solutions of the equation exist, it is possible to determine n constants in such a way that the function $y = \varphi(x,C_1,...,C_n)$ satisfies these conditions.

The coupling of differential equations with initial conditions embodies the notion of universal determinism of classical physics. Given initial

---

[2] The condition of existence and continuity of derivatives is stronger than necessary. The Lipschitz condition, which requires that the incremental ratio be uniformly bounded in a given interval, would suffice.

conditions, the future evolution of a system that obeys those equations is completely determined. This notion was forcefully expressed by Pierre-Simon Laplace in the eighteenth century: a supernatural mind who knows the laws of physics and the initial conditions of each atom could perfectly predict the future evolution of the universe with unlimited precision.

In the twentieth century, the notion of universal determinism was challenged twice in the physical sciences. First in the 1920s the development of quantum mechanics introduced the so called **indeterminacy principle** which established explicit bounds to the precision of measurements.[3] Later, in the 1970s, the development of nonlinear dynamics and chaos theory showed how arbitrarily small initial differences might become arbitrarily large: the flapping of a butterfly's wings in the southern hemisphere might cause a tornado in northern hemisphere.

SYSTEMS OF ORDINARY DIFFERENTIAL EQUATIONS

Differential equations can be combined to form **systems of differential equations**. These are sets of differential conditions that must be satisfied simultaneously. A first-order system of differential equations is a system of the following type:

$$\begin{cases} \dfrac{dy_1}{dx} = f_1(x, y_1, \ldots, y_n) \\[2mm] \dfrac{dy_2}{dx} = f_2(x, y_1, \ldots, y_n) \\[2mm] \quad\vdots \\[2mm] \dfrac{dy_n}{dx} = f_n(x, y_1, \ldots, y_n) \end{cases}$$

---

[3] Actually quantum mechanics is a much deeper conceptual revolution: it challenges the very notion of physical reality. According to the standard interpretation of quantum mechanics, physical laws are mathematical recipes that link measurements in a strictly probabilistic sense. According to quantum mechanics, physical states are pure abstractions: they can be superposed, as the celebrated "Schrodinger's cat" which can be both dead and alive.

Solving this system means finding a set of functions $y_1,...,y_n$ that satisfy the system as well as the initial conditions:

$$y_1(x_0) = y_{10}, ..., y_n(x_0) = y_{n0}$$

Systems of orders higher than one can be reduced to first-order systems in a straightforward way by adding new variables defined as the derivatives of existing variables. As a consequence, an n-th order differential equation can be transformed into a first-order system of n equations. Conversely, a system of first-order differential equations is equivalent to a single n-th order equation.

To illustrate this point, let's differentiate the first equation to obtain

$$\frac{d^2 y_1}{dx^2} = \frac{\partial f_1}{\partial x} + \frac{\partial f_1}{\partial y_1}\frac{dy_1}{dx} + ... + \frac{\partial f_1}{\partial y_n}\frac{dy_n}{dx}$$

Replacing the derivatives

$$\frac{dy_1}{dx}, ..., \frac{dy_n}{dx}$$

with their expressions $f_1,...,f_n$ from the system's equations, we obtain

$$\frac{d^2 y_1}{dx^2} = F_2(x, y_1, ..., y_n)$$

If we now reiterate this process, we arrive at the n-th order equation:

$$\frac{d^{(n)} y_1}{dx^{(n)}} = F_n(x, y_1, ..., y_n)$$

We can thus write the following system:

$$\begin{cases} \dfrac{dy_1}{dx} = f_1(x, y_1, \ldots, y_n) \\[2mm] \dfrac{d^2 y_1}{dx^2} = F_2(x, y_1, \ldots, y_n) \\[2mm] \vdots \\[2mm] \dfrac{d^{(n)} y_1}{dx^{(n)}} = F_n(x, y_1, \ldots, y_n) \end{cases}$$

We can express $y_2,\ldots,y_n$ as functions of $x, y_1, y'_1, \ldots, y_1^{(n-1)}$ by solving, if possible, the system formed with the first $n - 1$ equations:

$$\begin{cases} y_2 = \varphi_2(x, y_1, y'_1, \ldots, y_1^{(n-1)}) \\[2mm] y_3 = \varphi_3(x, y_1, y'_1, \ldots, y_1^{(n-1)}) \\[2mm] \vdots \\[2mm] y_n = \varphi_n(x, y_1, y'_1, \ldots, y_1^{(n-1)}) \end{cases}$$

Substituting these expressions into the n-th equation of the previous system, we arrive at the single equation:

$$\frac{d^{(n)} y_1}{dx^{(n)}} = \Phi(x, y'_1, \ldots, y_1^{(n-1)})$$

Solving, if possible, this equation, we find the general solution

$$y_1 = y_1(x, C_1, \ldots, C_n)$$

Substituting this expression for y_1 into the previous system, $y_2,\ldots,y_n$ can be computed.

CLOSED-FORM SOLUTIONS OF ORDINARY DIFFERENTIAL EQUATIONS

Let's now consider the methods for solving two types of common differential equations: equations with separable variables and equations of linear type. Let's start with equations with separable variables. Consider the equation

$$\frac{dy}{dx} = f(x)g(y)$$

This equation is said to have **separable variables** because it can be written as an equality between two sides, each depending on only y or only x. We can rewrite our equation in the following way:

$$\frac{dy}{g(y)} = f(x)dx$$

This equation can be regarded as an equality between two differentials in y and x respectively. Their indefinite integrals can differ only by a constant. Integrating the left side with respect to y and the right side with respect to x, we obtain the general solution of the equation:

$$\int \frac{dy}{g(y)} = \int f(x)dx + C$$

For example, if $g(y) \equiv y$, the previous equation becomes

$$\frac{dy}{y} = f(x)dx$$

whose solution is

$$\int \frac{dy}{y} = \int f(x)dx + C \Rightarrow \log y = \int f(x)dx + C \Rightarrow y = A \, \exp\left(\int f(x)dx\right)$$

where $A = \exp(C)$.

A differential equation of this type describes the continuous compounding of time-varying interest rates. Consider, for example, the growth of capital C deposited in a bank account that earns the variable but deterministic rate $r = f(t)$. When interest rates R_i are constant for discrete periods of time Δt_i, compounding is obtained by purely algebraic formulas as follows:

$$R_i \Delta t_i = \frac{C(t_i) - C(t_{i-\Delta t_i})}{C(t_{i-\Delta t_i})}$$

Solving for $C(t_i)$:

$$C(t_i) = (1 + R_i \Delta t_i)C(t_{i-\Delta t_i})$$

By recursive substitution we obtain

$$C(t_i) = (1 + R_i \Delta t_i)(1 + R_{i-1}\Delta t_{i-1})\ldots(1 + R_1 \Delta t_1)C(t_0)$$

However, market interest rates are subject to rapid change. In the limit of very short time intervals, the instantaneous rate $r(t)$ would be defined as the limit, if it exists, of the discrete interest rate:

$$r(t) = \lim_{\Delta t \to 0} \frac{C(t + \Delta t) - C(t)}{\Delta t C(t)}$$

The above expression can be rewritten as a simple first-order differential equation in C:

$$r(t)C(t) = \frac{dC(t)}{dt}$$

In a simple intuitive way, the above equation can be obtained considering that in the elementary time dt the bank account increments by the amount $dC = C(t)r(t)dt$. In this equation, variables are separable. It admits the family of solutions:

$$C = A \exp\left(\int r(t)dt\right)$$

where A is the initial capital.

Linear Differential Equation
Linear differential equations are equations of the following type:

$$a_n(x)y^{(n)} + a_{n-1}(x)y^{(n-1)} + \ldots + a_1(x)y^{(1)} + a_0(x)y + b(x) = 0$$

If the function b is identically zero, the equation is said to be **homogeneous**.

In cases where the coefficients a's are constant, Laplace transforms provide a powerful method for solving linear differential equation. Consider, without loss of generality, the following linear equation with constant coefficients:

$$a_n y^{(n)} + a_{n-1}y^{(n-1)} + \ldots + a_1 y^{(1)} + a_0 y = b(x)$$

together with the initial conditions: $y(0) = y_0,\ldots,y^{(n-1)}(0) = y_0^{(n-1)}$. In cases in which the initial point is not the origin, by a variable transformation we can shift the origin.

Let's recall the formula to Laplace-transform derivatives presented in Chapter 4. For one-sided Laplace transforms the following formulas hold:

$$\mathcal{L}\left(\frac{df(x)}{dx}\right) = s\mathcal{L}[f(x)] - f(0)$$

$$\mathcal{L}\left(\frac{d^n f(x)}{dx^n}\right) = s^n\mathcal{L}[f(x)] - s^{n-1}f(0) - \ldots - f^{(n-1)}(0)$$

Suppose that a function $y = y(x)$ satisfies the previous linear equation with constant coefficients and that it admits a Laplace transform. Apply one-sided Laplace-transform to both sides of the equation. If $Y(s) = \mathcal{L}[y(x)]$, the following relationships hold:

$$L(a_n y^{(n)} + a_{n-1}y^{(n-1)} + \ldots + a_1 y^{(1)} + a_0 y) = L[b(x)]$$

$$a_n[s^n Y(s) - s^{n-1}y^{(1)}(0) - \ldots - y^{(n-1)}(0)]$$
$$+ a_{n-1}[s^{n-1}Y(s) - s^{n-2}y^{(1)}(0) - \ldots - y^{(n-2)}(0)]$$
$$+ \ldots + a_0 Y(s) = B(s)$$

Solving this equation for $Y(s)$, that is, $Y(s) = g[s, y^{(t)}(0),...,y^{(n-1)}(0)]$ the inverse Laplace transform $y(t) = \mathscr{L}^{-1}[Y(s)]$ uniquely determines the solution of the equation.

Because inverse Laplace transforms are integrals, with this method, when applicable, the solution of a differential equation is reduced to the determination of integrals. Laplace transforms and inverse Laplace transforms are known for large classes of functions. Because of the important role that Laplace transforms play in solving ordinary differential equations in engineering problems, there are published reference tables.[4] Laplace transform methods also yield closed-form solutions of many ordinary differential equations of interest in economics and finance.

NUMERICAL SOLUTIONS OF ORDINARY DIFFERENTIAL EQUATIONS

Closed-form solutions are solutions that can be expressed in terms of known functions such as polynomials or exponential functions. Before the advent of fast digital computers, the search for closed-form solutions of differential equations was an important task. Today, thanks to the availability of high-performance computing, most problems are solved numerically. This section looks at methods for solving ordinary differential equations numerically.

The Finite Difference Method

Among the methods used to numerically solve ordinary differential equations subject to initial conditions, the most common is the **finite difference method**. The finite difference method is based on replacing derivatives with difference equations; differential equations are thereby transformed into **recursive difference equations**.

Key to this method of numerical solution is the fact that ODEs subject to initial conditions describe phenomena that evolve from some starting point. In this case, the differential equation can be approximated with a system of difference equations that compute the next point based on previous points. This would not be possible should we impose boundary conditions instead of initial conditions. In this latter case, we have to solve a system of linear equations.

---

[4] See, for example, "Laplace Transforms," Chapter 29 in Milton Abramowitz and Irene A. Stegun (eds.), *Handbook of Mathematical Functions with Formulas, Graphs, and Mathematical Tables* (New York: Dover, 1972).

To illustrate the finite difference method, consider the following simple ordinary differential equation and its solution in a finite interval:

$$f'(x) = f(x)$$

$$\frac{df}{f} = dx$$

$$\log f(x) = x + C$$

$$f(x) = \exp(x + C)$$

As shown, the closed-form solution of the equation is obtained by separation of variables, that is, by transforming the original equation into another equation where the function f appears only on the left side and the variable x only on the right side.

Suppose that we replace the derivative with its forward finite difference approximation and solve

$$\frac{f(x_{i+1}) - f(x_i)}{x_{i+1} - x_i} = f(x_i)$$

$$f(x_{i+1}) = [1 + (x_{i+1} - x_i)]f(x_i)$$

If we assume that the step size is constant for all i:

$$f(x_i) = [1 + \Delta x]^i f(x_0)$$

The replacement of derivatives with finite differences is often called the **Euler approximation**. The differential equation is replaced by a recursive formula based on approximating the derivative with a finite difference. The i-th value of the solution is computed from the $i-1$-th value. Given the initial value of the function f, the solution of the differential equation can be arbitrarily approximated by choosing a sufficiently small interval. Exhibit 9.1 illustrates this computation for different values of Δx.

In the previous example of a first-order linear equation, only one initial condition was involved. Let's now consider a second-order equation:

$$f''(x) + kf(x) = 0$$

EXHIBIT 9.1 Numerical Solutions of the Equation $f' = f$ with the Euler Approximation for Different Step Sizes

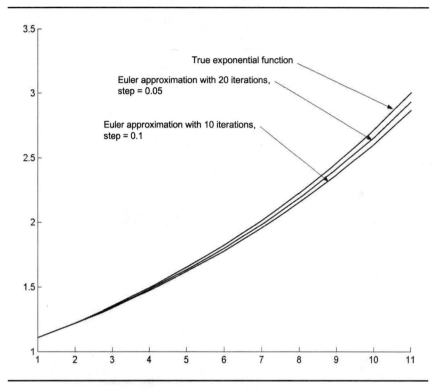

This equation describes oscillatory motion, such as the elongation of a pendulum or the displacement of a spring.

To approximate this equation we must approximate the second derivative. This could be done, for example, by combining difference quotients as follows:

$$f'(x) \approx \frac{f(x + \Delta x) - f(x)}{\Delta x}$$

$$f'(x + \Delta x) \approx \frac{f(x + 2\Delta x) - f(x + \Delta x)}{\Delta x}$$

$$f''(x) \approx \frac{f'(x + \Delta x) - f'(x)}{\Delta x}$$

$$= \frac{\dfrac{f(x + 2\Delta x) - f(x + \Delta x)}{\Delta x} - \dfrac{f(x + \Delta x) - f(x)}{\Delta x}}{\Delta x}$$

$$= \frac{f(x + 2\Delta x) - 2f(x + \Delta x) + f(x)}{(\Delta x)^2}$$

With this approximation, the original equation becomes

$$f''(x) + kf(x) \approx \frac{f(x + 2\Delta x) - 2f(x + \Delta x) + f(x)}{(\Delta x)^2} + kf(x) = 0$$

$$f(x + 2\Delta x) - 2f(x + \Delta x) + (1 + k(\Delta x)^2)f(x) = 0$$

We can thus write the approximation scheme:

$$f(x + \Delta x) = f(x) + \Delta x f'(x)$$

$$f(x + 2\Delta x) = 2f(x + \Delta x) - (1 + k(\Delta x)^2)f(x)$$

Given the increment Δx and the initial values $f(0), f'(0)$, using the above formulas we can recursively compute $f(0 + \Delta x)$, $f(0 + 2\Delta x)$, and so on. Exhibit 9.2 illustrates this computation.

In practice, the Euler approximation scheme is often not sufficiently precise and more sophisticated approximation schemes are used. For example, a widely used approximation scheme is the Runge-Kutta method. We give an example of the **Runge-Kutta method** in the case of the equation $f'' + f = 0$ which is equivalent to the linear system:

$$x' = y$$

$$y' = -x$$

In this case the Runge-Kutta approximation scheme is the following:

$$k_1 = hy(i)$$

$$h_1 = -hx(i)$$

EXHIBIT 9.2   Numerical Solution of the Equation $f'' + f = 0$ with the Euler Approximation

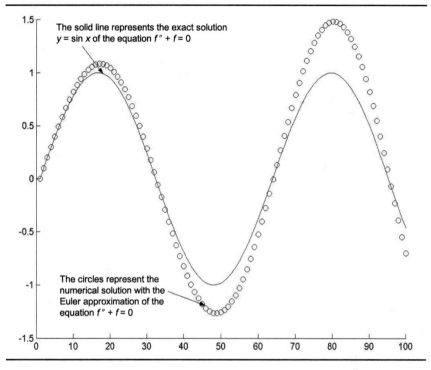

The solid line represents the exact solution $y = \sin x$ of the equation $f'' + f = 0$

The circles represent the numerical solution with the Euler approximation of the equation $f'' + f = 0$

$$k_2 = h\left[y(i) + \frac{1}{2}h_1\right]$$

$$h_2 = -h\left[x(i) + \frac{1}{2}k_1\right]$$

$$k_3 = h\left[y(i) + \frac{1}{2}h_2\right]$$

$$h_3 = -h\left[x(i) + \frac{1}{2}k_2\right]$$

$$k_4 = h[y(i) + h_3]$$

$$h_4 = -h[x(i) + k_3]$$

$$x(i + 1) = x(i) + \frac{1}{6}(k_1 + 2k_2 + 2k_3 + k_4)$$

$$y(i + 1) = y(i) + \frac{1}{6}(h_1 + 2h_2 + 2h_3 + h_4)$$

Exhibits 9.3 and 9.4 illustrate the results of this method in the two cases $f' = f$ and $f'' + f = 0$.

As mentioned above, this numerical method depends critically on our having as givens (1) the initial values of the solution and (2) its first derivative. Suppose that instead of initial values two boundary values were given, for instance the initial value of the solution and its value 1,000 steps ahead, that is, $f(0) = f_0$, $f(0 + 1{,}000\Delta x) = f_{1000}$. Conditions like these are rarely used in the study of dynamical systems as they imply foresight,

EXHIBIT 9.3   Numerical Solution of the Equation $f' = f$ with the Runge-Kutta Method After 10 Steps

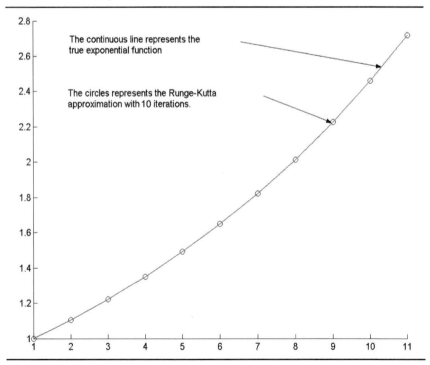

EXHIBIT 9.4 Numerical Solution of the Equation $f'' + f = 0$ with the Runge-Kutta Method

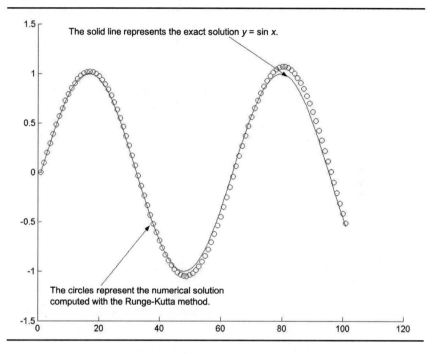

The solid line represents the exact solution $y = \sin x$.

The circles represent the numerical solution computed with the Runge-Kutta method.

that is, knowledge of the future position of a system. However, they often appear in static systems and when trying to determine what initial conditions should be imposed to reach a given goal at a given date.

In the case of boundary conditions, one cannot write a direct recursive scheme; it's necessary to solve a system of equations. For instance, we could introduce the derivative $f'(x) = \delta$ as an unknown quantity. The difference quotient that approximates the derivative becomes an unknown. We can now write a system of linear equations in the following way:

$$\begin{cases} f(\Delta x) = f_0 + \delta \Delta x \\ f(2\Delta x) = 2f(\Delta x) - (1 + k(\Delta x)^2)f_0 \\ f(3\Delta x) = 2f(2\Delta x) - (1 + k(\Delta x)^2)f(\Delta x) \\ \quad . \\ \quad . \\ \quad . \\ f_{1000} = 2f(999\Delta x) - (1 + k(\Delta x)^2)f(998\Delta x) \end{cases}$$

This is a system of 1,000 equations in 1,000 unknowns. Solving the system we compute the entire solution. In this system two equations, the first and the last, are linked to boundary values; all other equations are transfer equations that express the dynamics (or the law) of the system. This is a general feature of boundary value problems. We will encounter it again when discussing numerical solutions of partial differential equations.

In the above example, we chose a forward scheme where the derivative is approximated with the forward difference quotient. One might use a different approximation scheme, computing the derivative in intervals centered around the point x. When derivatives of higher orders are involved, the choice of the approximation scheme becomes critical. Recall that when we approximated first and second derivatives using forward differences, we were required to evaluate the function at two points $(i, i + 1)$ and three points $(i, i + 1, i + 2)$ ahead respectively. If purely forward schemes are employed, computing higher-order derivatives requires many steps ahead. This fact might affect the precision and stability of numerical computations.

We saw in the examples that the accuracy of a finite difference scheme depends on the discretization interval. In general, a finite difference scheme works, that is, it is consistent and stable, if the numerical solution converges uniformly to the exact solution when the length of the discretization interval tends to zero. Suppose that the precision of an approximation scheme depends on the length of the discretization interval Δx. Consider the difference $\delta f = \hat{f}(x) - f(x)$ between the approximate and the exact solutions. We say that $\delta f \to 0$ uniformly in the interval $[a, b]$ when $\Delta x \to 0$ if, given any ε arbitrarily small, it is possible to find a Δx such that $|\delta f| < \varepsilon$, $\forall x \in [a, b]$.

NONLINEAR DYNAMICS AND CHAOS

Systems of differential equations describe dynamical systems that evolve starting from initial conditions. A fundamental concept in the theory of dynamical system is that of the **stability of solutions**. This topic has become of paramount importance with the development of nonlinear dynamics and with the discovery of chaotic phenomena. We can only give a brief introductory account of this subject whose role in economics is still the subject of debate.

Intuitively, a dynamical system is considered stable if its solutions do not change much when the system is only slightly perturbed. There are different ways to perturb a system: changing parameters in its equations, changing the known functions of the system by a small amount, or changing the initial conditions.

Consider an equilibrium solution of a dynamical system, that is, a solution that is time invariant. If a stable system is perturbed when it is in a position of equilibrium, it tends to return to the equilibrium position or, in any case, not to diverge indefinitely from its equilibrium position. For example, a damped pendulum—if perturbed from a position of equilibrium—will tend to go back to an equilibrium position. If the pendulum is not damped it will continue to oscillate forever.

Consider a system of n equations of first order. (As noted above, systems of higher orders can always be reduced to first-order systems by enlarging the set of variables.) Suppose that we can write the system explicitly in the first derivatives as follows:

$$\begin{cases} \dfrac{dy_1}{dx} = f_1(x, y_1, ..., y_n) \\[2mm] \dfrac{dy_2}{dx} = f_2(x, y_1, ..., y_n) \\[2mm] \quad . \\ \quad . \\ \quad . \\ \dfrac{dy_n}{dx} = f_n(x, y_1, ..., y_n) \end{cases}$$

If the equations are all linear, a complete theory of stability has been developed. Essentially, linear dynamical systems are stable except possibly at singular points where solutions might diverge. In particular, a characteristic of linear systems is that they incur only small changes in the solution as a result of small changes in the initial conditions.

However, during the 1970s, it was discovered that nonlinear systems have a different behavior. Suppose that a nonlinear system has at least three degrees of freedom (that is, it has three independent nonlinear equations). The dynamics of such a system can then become chaotic in the sense that arbitrarily small changes in initial conditions might diverge. This sensitivity to initial conditions is one of the signatures of **chaos**. Note that while discrete systems such as discrete maps can exhibit chaos in one dimension, continuous systems require at least three degrees of freedom (that is, three equations).

Sensitive dependence from initial conditions was first observed in 1960 by the meteorologist Edward Lorenz of the Massachusetts Institute of Technology. Lorenz remarked that computer simulations of weather forecasts starting, apparently, from the same meteorological data could yield very different results. He argued that the numerical solutions of extremely sensitive differential equations such as those he was using produced diverging results due to rounding-off errors made by the computer system. His discovery was published in a meteorological journal where it remained unnoticed for many years.

Fractals

While in principle deterministic chaotic systems are unpredictable because of their sensitivity to initial conditions, the statistics of their behavior can be studied. Consider, for example, the chaos laws that describe the evolution of weather: while the weather is basically unpredictable over long periods of time, long-run simulations are used to predict the statistics of weather.

It was discovered that probability distributions originating from chaotic systems exhibit **fat tails** in the sense that very large, extreme events have nonnegligible probabilities.[5] It was also discovered that chaotic systems exhibit complex unexpected behavior. The motion of chaotic systems is often associated with **self-similarity** and fractal shapes.

Fractals were introduced in the 1960s by Benoit Mandelbrot, a mathematician working at the IBM research center in Yorktown Heights, New York. Starting from the empirical observation that cotton price time-series are similar at different time scales, Mandelbrot developed a powerful theory of fractal geometrical objects. Fractals are geometrical objects that are geometrically similar to part of themselves. Stock prices exhibit this property insofar as price time-series look the same at different time scales.

Chaotic systems are also sensitive to changes in their parameters. In a chaotic system, only some regions of the parameter space exhibit chaotic behavior. The change in behavior is abrupt and, in general, it cannot be predicted analytically. In addition, chaotic behavior appears in systems that are apparently very simple.

While the intuition that chaotic systems might exist is not new, the systematic exploration of chaotic systems started only in the 1970s. The discovery of the existence of nonlinear chaotic systems marked a conceptual crisis in the physical sciences: it challenges the very notion of the applicability of mathematics to the description of reality. Chaos laws are not testable on a large scale; their applicability cannot be predicted

---

[5] See W. Brock, D. Hsieh, and B. LeBaron, *Nonlinear Dynamics, Chaos, and Instability* (Cambridge, MA: MIT Press, 1991) and D. Hsieh, "Chaos and Nonlinear Dynamics: Application to Financial Markets," *Journal of Finance* 46 (1991), pp. 1839–1877.

analytically. Nevertheless, the statistics of chaos theory might still prove to be meaningful.

The economy being a complex system, the expectation was that its apparently random behavior could be explained as a deterministic chaotic system of low dimensionality. Despite the fact that tests to detect low-dimensional chaos in the economy have produced a substantially negative response, it is easy to make macroeconomic and financial econometric models exhibit chaos.[6] As a matter of fact, most macroeconomic models are nonlinear. Though chaos has not been detected in economic time-series, most economic dynamic models are nonlinear in more than three dimensions and thus potentially chaotic. At this stage of the research, we might conclude that if chaos exists in economics it is not of the low-dimensional type.

PARTIAL DIFFERENTIAL EQUATIONS

To illustrate the notion of a partial differential equation (PDE), let's start with equations in two dimensions. A n-order PDE in two dimensions x,y is an equation of the form

$$F\left(x, y, \frac{\partial f}{\partial x}, \frac{\partial f}{\partial y}, \ldots, \frac{\partial^{(i)} f}{\partial^{(k)} x \partial^{(i-k)} y}\right) = 0, 0 \leq k \leq i, 0 \leq i \leq n$$

A solution of the previous equation will be any function that satisfies the equation.

In the case of PDEs, the notion of initial conditions must be replaced with the notion of boundary conditions or initial plus boundary conditions. Solutions will be defined in a multidimensional domain. To identify a solution uniquely, the value of the solution on some subdomain must be specified. In general, this subdomain will coincide with the boundary (or some portion of the boundary) of the domain.

Diffusion Equation

Different equations will require and admit different types of boundary and initial conditions. The question of existence and uniqueness of solu-

---

[6] See W.A. Brock, W.D. Dechert, J.A. Scheinkman, and B. LeBaron, "A Test for Independence Based on the Correlation Dimension," *Econometric Reviews*, 15(3) (1996); and W. Brock and C. Hommes, "A Rational Route to Randomness," *Econometrica* 65 (1997), pp. 1059–1095.

tions of PDEs is a delicate mathematical problem. We can only give a brief account by way of an example.

Let's consider the **diffusion equation**. This equation describes the propagation of the probability density of stock prices under the random-walk hypothesis:

$$\frac{\partial f}{\partial t} = a^2 \frac{\partial^2 f}{\partial x^2}$$

The *Black-Scholes equation*, which describes the evolution of option prices (see Chapter 15), can be reduced to the diffusion equation.

The diffusion equation describes propagating phenomena. Call $f(t,x)$ the probability density that prices have value x at time t. In finance theory, the diffusion equation describes the time-evolution of the probability density function $f(t,x)$ of stock prices that follow a random walk. [7] It is therefore natural to impose initial and boundary conditions on the distribution of prices.

In general, we distinguish two different problems related to the diffusion equation: the **first boundary value problem** and the **Cauchy initial value problem**, named after the French mathematician Augustin Cauchy who first formulated it. The two problems refer to the same diffusion equation but consider different domains and different initial and boundary conditions. It can be demonstrated that both problems admit a unique solution.

The first boundary value problem seeks to find in the rectangle $0 \leq x \leq 1$, $0 \leq t \leq T$ a continuous function $f(t,x)$ that satisfies the diffusion equation in the interior Q of the rectangle plus the following initial condition,

$$f(0, x) = \phi(x), 0 \leq x \leq l$$

and boundary conditions,

$$f(t, 0) = f_1(t), \quad f(t, l) = f_2(t), \quad 0 \leq t \leq T$$

The functions f_1, f_2 are assumed to be continuous and $f_1(0) = \phi(0)$, $f_2(0) = \phi(l)$.

The Cauchy problem is related to an infinite half plane instead of a finite rectangle. It is formulated as follows. The objective is to find for

---

[7] In physics, the diffusion equation describes phenomena such as the diffusion of particles suspended in some fluid. In this case, the diffusion equation describes the density of particles at a given moment at a given point.

any x and for $t \geq 0$ a continuous and bounded function $f(t,x)$ that satisfies the diffusion equation and which, for $t = 0$, is equal to a continuous
and bounded function $f(0,x) = \phi(x)$, $\forall x$.

Solution of the Diffusion Equation

The first boundary value problem of the diffusion equation can be
solved exactly. We illustrate here a widely used method based on the
separation of variables which is applicable if the boundary conditions
on the vertical sides vanish (that is, if $f_1(t) = f_2(t) = 0$). The method
involves looking for a tentative solution in the form of a product of two
functions, one that depends only on t and the other that depends only
on x: $f(t,x) = h(t)g(x)$.

If we substitute the previous tentative solution in the diffusion equation

$$\frac{\partial f}{\partial t} = a^2 \frac{\partial^2 f}{\partial x^2}$$

we obtain an equation where the left side depends only on t while the
right side depends only on x:

$$\frac{dh(t)}{dt} g(x) = a^2 h(t) \frac{d^2 g(x)}{dx^2}$$

$$\frac{dh(t)}{dt} \frac{1}{h(t)} = a^2 \frac{d^2 g(x)}{dx^2} \frac{1}{g(x)}$$

This condition can be satisfied only if the two sides are equal to a constant. The original diffusion equation is therefore transformed into two
ordinary differential equations:

$$\frac{1}{a^2} \frac{dh(t)}{dt} = bh(t)$$

$$\frac{d^2 g(x)}{dx^2} = bg(x)$$

with boundary conditions $g(0) = g(l) = 0$. From the above equations and boundary conditions, it can be seen that b can assume only the negative values,

$$b = -\frac{k^2 \pi^2}{l^2}, k = 1, 2, ...$$

while the functions g can only be of the form

$$g(x) = B_k \sin \frac{k\pi}{l} x$$

Substituting for h, we obtain

$$h(t) = B'_k \exp\left(-\frac{a^2 k^2 \pi^2}{l^2} t\right)$$

Therefore, we can see that there are denumerably infinite solutions of the diffusion equation of the form

$$f_k(t, x) = C_k \exp\left(-\frac{a^2 k^2 \pi^2}{l^2} t\right) \sin \frac{k\pi}{l} x$$

All these solutions satisfy the boundary conditions $f(t,0) = f(t,l) = 0$. By linearity, we know that the infinite sum

$$f(t, x) = \sum_{k=1}^{\infty} f_k(t, x) = \sum_{k=1}^{\infty} C_k \exp\left(-\frac{a^2 k^2 \pi^2}{l^2} t\right) \sin \frac{k\pi}{l} x$$

will satisfy the diffusion equation. Clearly $f(t,x)$ satisfies the boundary conditions $f(t,0) = f(t,l) = 0$. In order to satisfy the initial condition, given that $\phi(x)$ is bounded and continuous and that $\phi(0) = \phi(l) = 0$, it can be demonstrated that the coefficients Cs can be uniquely determined through the following integrals, which are called the **Fourier integrals:**

$$C_k = \frac{2}{L}\int_0^L \phi(\xi)\sin\left(\frac{\pi k}{L}\xi\right)d\xi$$

The previous method applies to the first boundary value problem but cannot be applied to the Cauchy problem, which admits only an initial condition. It can be demonstrated that the solution of the Cauchy problem can be expressed in terms of a convolution with a **Green's function**. In particular, it can be demonstrated that the solution of the Cauchy problem can be written in closed form as follows:

$$f(t, x) = \frac{1}{2\sqrt{\pi}}\int_{-\infty}^{\infty}\frac{\phi(\xi)}{\sqrt{t}}\exp\left\{-\frac{(x-\xi)^2}{4t}\right\}d\xi$$

for $t > 0$ and $f(0,x) = \phi(x)$. It can be demonstrated that the Black-Scholes equation (see Chapter 15), which is an equation of the form

$$\frac{\partial f}{\partial t} + \frac{1}{2}\sigma^2 x^2\frac{\partial^2 f}{\partial x^2} + rx\frac{\partial f}{\partial x} - rf = 0$$

can be reduced through transformation of variables to the standard diffusion equation to be solved with the Green's function approach.

Numerical Solution of PDEs

There are different methods for the numerical solution of PDEs. We illustrate the finite difference methods which are based on approximating derivatives with finite differences. Other discretization schemes, such as finite elements and spectral methods are possible but, being more complex, they go beyond the scope of this book.

Finite difference methods result in a set of recursive equations when applied to initial conditions. When finite difference methods are applied to boundary problems, they require the solution of systems of simultaneous linear equations. PDEs might exhibit boundary conditions, initial conditions or a mix of the two.

The Cauchy problem of the diffusion equation is an example of initial conditions. The simplest discretization scheme for the diffusion equation replaces derivatives with their difference quotients. As for ordinary differential equations, the discretization scheme can be written as follows:

$$\frac{\partial f}{\partial t} \approx \frac{f(t + \Delta t, x) - f(t, x)}{\Delta t}$$

$$\frac{\partial^2 f}{\partial x^2} \approx \frac{f(t, x + \Delta x) - 2f(t, x) + f(t, x - \Delta x)}{(\Delta x)^2}$$

In the case of the Cauchy problem, this approximation scheme defines the forward recursive algorithm. It can be proved that the algorithm is stable only if the **Courant-Friedrichs-Lewy** (CFL) conditions

$$\Delta t < \frac{(\Delta x)^2}{2a^2}$$

are satisfied.

Different approximation schemes can be used. In particular, the forward approximation to the derivative used above could be replaced by centered approximations. Exhibit 9.5 illustrates the solution of a Cauchy problem for initial conditions that vanish outside of a finite interval. The simulation shows that solutions diffuse in the entire half space.

EXHIBIT 9.5 Solution of the Cauchy Problem by the Finite Difference Method

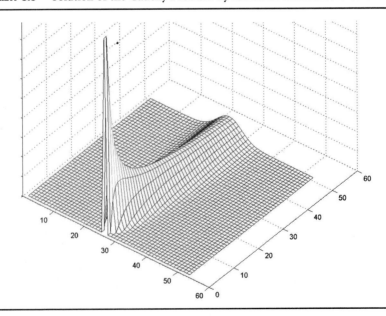

EXHIBIT 9.6 Solution of the First Boundary Problem by the Finite Difference Method

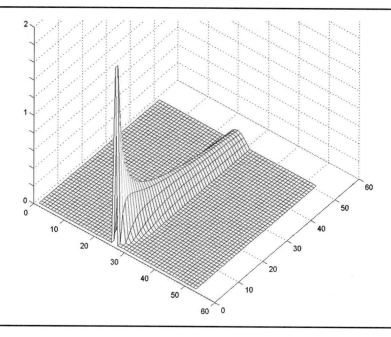

Applying the same discretization to a first boundary problem would require the solution of a system of linear equations at every step. Exhibit 9.6 illustrates this case.

SUMMARY

- Derivatives can be combined to form differential equations.
- Differential equations are conditions that must be satisfied by their solutions.
- Differential equations generally admit infinite solutions.
- Initial or boundary conditions are needed to identify solutions uniquely.
- Differential equations are the key mathematical tools for the development of modern science; in finance they are used in arbitrage pricing, to define stochastic processes, and to compute the time evolution of averages.
- Ordinary differential equations include only total derivatives; partial differential equations include partial derivatives.
- Differential equations can be solved in closed form or with numerical methods.

- Finite difference methods approximate derivatives with difference quotients.
- Initial conditions yield recursive algorithms.
- Boundary conditions require the solution of linear equations.

CHAPTER 10

Stochastic Differential Equations

Chapter 8 introduced stochastic integrals, a mathematical concept used for defining **stochastic differential equations,** the subject of this chapter. Stochastic differential equations solve the problem of giving meaning to a differential equation where one or more of its terms are subject to random fluctuations. For instance, consider the following deterministic equation:

$$\frac{dy}{dt} = f(t)y$$

We know from our discussion on differential equations (Chapter 9) that, by separating variables, the general solution of this equation can be written as follows:

$$y = A \exp[\int f(t)dt]$$

A stochastic version of this equation might be obtained, for instance, by perturbing the term f, thus resulting in the "stochastic differential equation"

$$\frac{dy}{y} = [f(t) + \varepsilon]dt$$

where ε is a random noise process.

As with stochastic integrals, in defining stochastic differential equations it is necessary to adopt an ensemble view: The solution of a stochastic differential equation is a stochastic process, not a single function. We will first provide the basic intuition behind stochastic differential equations and then proceed to formally define the concept and the properties.

THE INTUITION BEHIND STOCHASTIC DIFFERENTIAL EQUATIONS

Let's go back to the equation

$$\frac{dy}{dt} = [f(t) + \varepsilon]y$$

where ε is a continuous-time noise process. It would seem reasonable to define a continuous-time noise process informally as the continuous-time limit of a zero-mean, IID sequence, that is, a sequence of independent and identically distributed variables with zero mean (see Chapter 6). In a discrete time setting, a zero-mean, IID sequence is called a **white noise**. We could envisage defining a **continuous-time white noise** as the continuous-time limit of a discrete-time white noise. Each path of ε is a function of time $\varepsilon(\cdot, \omega)$. It would therefore seem reasonable to define the solution of the equation pathwise, as the family of functions that are solutions of the equations,

$$\frac{dy}{dt} = [f(t) + \varepsilon(t, \omega)]y$$

where each equation corresponds to a specific white noise path.

However this definition would be meaningless in the domain of ordinary functions. In other words, it would generally not be possible to find a family of functions $y(\cdot, \omega)$ that satisfy the above equations for each white-noise path and that form a reasonable stochastic process.

The key problem is that it is not possible to define a white noise process as a zero-mean stationary stochastic process with independent increments and continuous paths. Such a process does not exist in the domain of ordinary functions.[1] In discrete time the white noise process is obtained as the first-difference process of a random walk. Anticipating concepts that will be developed in Chapter 12 on time series analysis, the random walk is an **integrated nonstationary process**, while its first-difference process is a **stationary IID sequence**.

---

[1] It is possible to define a "generalized white noise process" in the domain of "tempered distributions." See Bernd Oksendal, *Stochastic Differential Equations: Third Edition* (Berlin: Springer, 1992).

The continuous-time limit of the random walk is the Brownian motion. However the paths of a Brownian motion are not differentiable. As a consequence, it is not possible to take the continuous-time limit of first differences and to define the white noise process as the derivative of a Brownian motion. In the domain of ordinary functions in continuous time, the white noise process can be defined only through its integral, which is the Brownian motion. The definition of stochastic differential equations must therefore be recast in integral form.

A sensible definition of a stochastic differential equation must respect a number of constraints. In particular, the solution of a stochastic differential equation should be a "perturbation" of the associated deterministic equation. In the above example, for instance, we want the solution of the stochastic equation

$$\frac{dy}{dy} = [f(t) + \varepsilon(t, \omega)]dt$$

to be a perturbation of the solution

$$y = A \, \exp\left(\int f(t)dt\right)$$

of the associated deterministic equation

$$\frac{dy}{y} = f(t)dt$$

In other words, the solution of a stochastic differential equation should tend to the solution of the associated deterministic equation in the limit of zero noise. In addition, the solutions of a stochastic differential equation should be the continuous-time limit of some discrete-time process obtained by discretization of the stochastic equation.

A formal solution of this problem was proposed by Kyosi Itô in the 1940s and, in a different setting, by Ruslan Stratonovich in the 1960s. Itô and Stratonovich proposed to give meaning to a stochastic differential equation through its integral equivalent. The Itô definition proceeds in two steps: in the first step, Itô processes are defined; in the second step, stochastic differential equations are defined.

■ *Step 1: Definition of Itô processes.* Given two functions $\varphi(t, \omega)$ and $\psi(t, \omega)$ that satisfy usual conditions to be defined later, an Itô process—also called a **stochastic integral**—is a stochastic process of the form:

$$Z(t, \omega) = \int_0^t \varphi(s, \omega)ds + \int_0^t \psi(s, \omega)dB_s(s, \omega)$$

An Itô process is a process that is the result of the sum of two summands: the first is an ordinary integral, the second an Itô integral. Itô processes are stable under smooth maps, that is, any smooth function of an Itô process is an Itô process that can be determined through the Itô formula (see Itô processes below).

■ *Step 2: Definition of stochastic differential equations.* As we have seen, it is not possible to write a differential equation plus a white-noise term which admits solutions in the domain of ordinary functions. However we can meaningfully write an **integral stochastic equation** of the form

$$X(t, \omega) = \int_0^t \varphi(s, X)ds + \int_0^t \psi(s, X)dB_s$$

It can be demonstrated that this equation admits solutions in the sense that, given two functions φ and ψ, there is a stochastic process X that satisfies the above equation. We stipulate that the above integral equation can be written in differential form as follows:

$$dX(t, \omega) = \varphi(t, X)dt + \psi(t, X)dB_t$$

Note that this is a definition; a stochastic differential equation acquires meaning only through its integral form. In particular, we *cannot* divide both terms by dt and rewrite the equation as follows:

$$\frac{dX(t, \omega)}{dt} = \varphi(t, X) + \psi(t, X)\frac{dB_t}{dt}$$

The above equation would be meaningless because the Brownian motion is not differentiable. This is the difficulty that precludes writing stochastic differential equations adding white noise pathwise. The differential notation of a stochastic differential equation is just a shorthand for the integral notation.

However we can consider a discrete approximation:

$$\Delta X(t, \omega) = \varphi^*(t, X)\Delta t + \psi^*(t, X)\Delta B_t$$

Note that in this approximation the functions $\varphi^*(t, X)$, $\psi^*(t, X)$ will not coincide with the functions $\varphi(t, X)$, $\psi(t, X)$. Using the latter would (in general) result in a poor approximation.

The following sections will define Itô processes and stochastic differential equations and study their properties.

ITÔ PROCESSES

Let's now formally define Itô processes and establish key properties, in particular the Itô formula. In the previous section we stated that an Itô process is a stochastic process of the form

$$Z(t, \omega) = \int_0^t a(s, \omega)ds + \int_0^t b(s, \omega)dB(s, \omega)$$

To make this definition rigorous, we have to state the conditions under which (1) the integrals exist and (2) there is no anticipation of information. Note that the two functions a and b might represent two stochastic processes and that the Riemann-Stieltjes integral might not exist for the paths of a stochastic process. We have therefore to demonstrate that both the Itô integral and the ordinary integral exist. To this end, we define **Itô processes** as follows.

Suppose that a 1-dimensional Brownian motion B_t is defined on a probability space $(\Omega, \mathfrak{I}, P)$ equipped with a filtration $\mathfrak{I}_t$. The filtration might be given or might be generated by the Brownian motion B_t. Suppose that both a and b are adapted to $\mathfrak{I}_t$ and jointly measurable in $\mathfrak{I} \times \mathfrak{R}$. Suppose, in addition, that the following two integrability conditions hold:

$$P\left[\int_0^t b^2(s, \omega)ds < \infty \text{ for all } t \geq 0\right] = 1$$

and

$$P\left[\int_0^t |a(s, \omega)|ds < \infty \text{ for all } t \geq 0\right] = 1$$

These conditions ensure that both integrals in the definition of Itô processes exist and that there is no anticipation of information. We can therefore define the Itô process as the following stochastic process:

$$Z(t, \omega) = \int_0^t a(s, \omega)ds + \int_0^t b(s, \omega)dB_s(s, \omega)$$

Itô processes can be written in the shorter differential form as

$$dZ_t = a\,dt + b\,dB_t$$

It should be clear that the latter formula is just a shorthand for the integral definition.

THE 1-DIMENSIONAL ITÔ FORMULA

One of the most important results concerning Itô processes is a formula established by Itô that allows one to explicitly write down an Itô process which is a function of another Itô process. **Itô's formula** is the stochastic equivalent of the change-of-variables formula of ordinary integration. We will proceed in two steps. First we will introduce Itô's formula for functions of Brownian motion and then for functions of general Itô processes. Suppose that the function $g(t,x)$ is twice continuously differentiable in $[0,\infty) \times R$ and that B_t is a one-dimensional Brownian motion. The function $Y_t = g(t,B_t)$ is a stochastic process. It can be demonstrated that the process $Y_t = g(t,B_t)$ is an Itô process of the following form

$$dY_t = \left(\frac{\partial g}{\partial t}(t, B_t) + \frac{1}{2}\frac{\partial^2 g}{\partial x^2}(t, B_t) \right)dt + \frac{\partial g}{\partial x}(t, B_t)dB_t$$

The above is Itô's formula in the case the underlying process is a Brownian motion. For example, let's suppose that $g(t,x) = x^2$. In this case we can write

$$\frac{\partial g}{\partial t} = 0,\ \frac{\partial g}{\partial x} = 2x,\ \frac{\partial^2 g}{\partial x^2} = 2$$

Inserting the above in Itô's formula we see that the process B_t^2 can be represented as the following Itô process

$$dY_t = dt + 2B_t dB_t$$

or, explicitly in integral form

$$Y_t = t + 2\int_0^t B_s dB_s$$

The nonlinear map $g(t,x) = x^2$ introduces a second term in dt. Note that we established the latter formula at the end of Chapter 8 in the form

$$\int_0^t B_s dB_s = \frac{1}{2}B_t^2 - \frac{1}{2}t$$

Let's now generalize Itô's formula.

Suppose that X_t is an Itô process given by $dX_t = adt + bdB_t$. As X_t is a stochastic process, that is, a function $X(t,\omega)$ of both time and the state, it makes sense to consider another stochastic process Y_t, which is a function of the former, $Y_t = g(t,X_t)$. Suppose that g is twice continuously differentiable on $[0,\infty) \times R$.

It can then be demonstrated (we omit the detailed proof) that Y_t is another Itô process that admits the representation

$$dY_t = \frac{\partial g}{\partial t}(t, X_t)dt + \frac{\partial g}{\partial x}(t, X_t)dX_t + \frac{1}{2}\frac{\partial^2 g}{\partial x^2}(t, X_t)(dX_t)^2$$

where differentials are computed formally according to the rules[2]

$$dt \cdot dt = dt \cdot dB_t = dB_t \cdot dt = 0, \, dB_t \cdot dB_t = dt$$

Itô's formula can be written (perhaps more) explicitly as

$$dY_t = \left(\frac{\partial g}{\partial t} + \frac{\partial g}{\partial x}a + \frac{1}{2}\frac{\partial^2 g}{\partial x^2}b^2\right)dt + \frac{\partial g}{\partial x}bdB_t$$

This formula reduces to the ordinary formula for the differential of a compound function in the case where $b = 0$ (that is, when there is no noise).

As a second example of application of Itô's formula, consider the geometric Brownian motion:

$$dX_t = \mu X_t dt + \sigma X_t dB_t$$

---

[2] These rules are known as the Box algebra.

where μ,σ are real constants, and consider the map $g(t,x) = \log x$. In this case, we can write

$$\frac{\partial g}{\partial t} = 0, \ \frac{\partial g}{\partial x} = \frac{1}{x}, \ \frac{\partial^2 g}{\partial x^2} = \frac{1}{x^2}$$

and Itô's formula yields

$$dY_t = d\log X_t = \left(\mu - \frac{1}{2}\sigma^2\right)dt + \sigma dB_t$$

STOCHASTIC DIFFERENTIAL EQUATIONS

An Itô process defines a process $Z(t,\omega)$ as the sum of the time integral of the process $a(t,\omega)$ plus the Itô integral of the process $b(t,\omega)$. Suppose that two functions $\varphi(t,x)$, $\psi(t,x)$ that satisfy conditions established below are given. Given an Itô process $X(t,\omega)$, the two processes $\varphi(t,X)$, $\psi(t,X)$ admit respectively a time integral and an Itô integral. It therefore makes sense to consider the following Itô process:

$$Z(t,\omega) = \int_0^t \varphi[s, X(s,\omega)]ds + \int_0^t \psi[s, X(s,\omega)]dB_s$$

The term on the right side transforms the process X into a new process Z. We can now ask if there are stochastic processes X that are mapped into themselves such that the following stochastic equation is satisfied:

$$X(t,\omega) = \int_0^t \varphi[s, X(s,\omega)]ds + \int_0^t \psi[s, X(s,\omega)]dB_s$$

The answer is positive under appropriate conditions. It is possible to prove the following **theorem of existence and uniqueness.** Suppose that a 1-dimensional Brownian motion B_t is defined on a probability space $(\Omega, \mathfrak{S}, P)$ equipped with a filtration $\mathfrak{S}_t$ and that B_t is adapted to the filtration $\mathfrak{S}_t$. Suppose also that the two measurable functions $\varphi(t,x)$, $\psi(t,x)$ map $[0,T] \times R \to R$ and that they satisfy the following conditions:

$$|\varphi(t, x)|^2 + |\psi(t, x)|^2 \le C(1 + |x|)^2, \ t \in [0, T], \ x \in R$$

and

$$|\varphi(t, x)| - \varphi(t, y) + |\psi(t, x)| - \psi(t, y) \leq D(|x - y|), \; t \in [0, T], \; x \in R$$

for appropriate constants C, D. The first condition is known as the linear growth condition, the last condition is the Lipschitz condition that we encountered in ordinary differential equation (see Chapter 9). Suppose that Z is a random variable independent of the σ-algebra $\mathfrak{I}_\infty$ generated by B_t for $t \geq 0$ such that $E(|Z|^2) < \infty$. Then there is a unique stochastic process X, defined for $0 \leq t \leq T$, with time-continuous paths such that $X_0 = Z$ and such that the following equation is satisfied:

$$X(t, \omega) = X_0 + \int_0^t \varphi[s, X(s, \omega)]ds + \int_0^t \psi[s, X(s, \omega)]dB_s$$

The process X is called a **strong solution** of the above equation.

The above equation can be written in differential form as follows:

$$dX(t, \omega) = \varphi[t, X(t, \omega)]dt + \psi[t, X(t, \omega)]dB_t$$

The differential form does not have an independent meaning; a differential stochastic equation is just a short albeit widely used way to write the integral equation.

The key requirement of a strong solution is that the filtration $\mathfrak{I}_t$ is given and that the functions φ, ψ are adapted to the filtration $\mathfrak{I}_t$. From the economic (or physics) point of view, this requirement translates the notion of causality. In simple terms, a strong solution is a functional of the driving Brownian motion and of the "inputs" φ, ψ. A strong solution at time t is determined only by the "history" up to time t of the inputs and of the random shocks embodied in the Brownian motion.

These conditions can be weakened. Suppose that we are given only the two functions $\varphi(t, x)$, $\psi(t, x)$ and that we must construct a process X_t, a Brownian motion B_t, and the relative filtration so that the above equation is satisfied. The equation still admits a unique solution with respect to the filtration generated by the Brownian motion B. It is however only a **weak solution** in the sense that, though there is no anticipation of information, it is not a functional of a given Brownian motion.[3] Weak and strong solutions do not necessarily coincide. However, any strong solution is also a weak solution with respect to the same filtration.

---

[3] See, for instance, Ioannis Karatzas and Steven E. Shreve, *Brownian Motion and Stochastic Calculus* (New York: Springer, 1991).

Note that the solution of a differential equation is a stochastic process. Initial conditions must therefore be specified as a random variable and not as a single value as for ordinary differential equations. In other words, there is an initial value for each state. It is possible to specify a single initial value as the initial condition of a stochastic differential equation. In this case the initial condition is a random variable where the probability mass is concentrated in a single point.

We omit the detailed proof of the theorem of uniqueness and existence. Uniqueness is proved using the Itô isometry and the Lipschitz condition. One assumes that there are two different solutions and then demonstrates that their difference must vanish. The proof of existence of a solution is similar to the proof of existence of solutions in the domain of ordinary equations. The solution is constructed inductively by a recursive relationship of the type

$$X^{(k+1)}(t, \omega) = \int_0^t \varphi[s, X^k(s, \omega)]ds + \int_0^t \psi[s, X^k(s, \omega)]dB_s$$

It can be shown that this recursive relationship produces a sequence of processes that converge to the unique solution.

GENERALIZATION TO SEVERAL DIMENSIONS

The concepts and formulas established so far for Itô (and Stratonovich) integrals and processes can be extended in a straightforward but often cumbersome way to multiple variables. The first step is to define a d-dimensional Brownian motion.

Given a probability space $(\Omega, \mathfrak{I}, P)$ equipped with a filtration $\{\mathfrak{I}_t\}$, a **d-dimensional standard Brownian motion** $B_t(\omega)$, is a stochastic process with the following properties:

- $B_t(\omega)$ is a d-dimensional process defined over the probability space $(\Omega, \mathfrak{I}, P)$ that takes values in R^d.
- $B_t(\omega)$ has continuous paths for $0 \leq t \leq \infty$.
- $B_0(\omega) = 0$.
- $B_t(\omega)$ is adapted to the filtration $\mathfrak{I}_t$.
- The increments $B_t(\omega) - B_s(\omega)$ are independent of the σ-algebra $\mathfrak{I}_s$ and have a normal distribution with mean zero and covariance matrix $(t - s)I_d$, where I_d is the identity matrix.

The above conditions state that the standard Brownian motion is a stochastic process that starts at zero, has continuous paths, and has normally distributed increments whose variances grow linearly with time.

The next step is to extend the definition of the Itô integral in a multi-dimensional environment. This is again a straightforward but cumbersome extension of the 1-dimensional case. Suppose that the following $r{\times}d$-dimensional matrix is given:

$$\mathbf{v} = \begin{bmatrix} v_{11} & \cdot & v_{1d} \\ \cdot & \cdot & \cdot \\ v_{r1} & \cdot & v_{rd} \end{bmatrix}$$

where each entry $v_{ij} = v_{ij}(t,\omega)$ satisfies the following conditions:

1. v_{ij} are $\mathcal{B}^d \times \mathfrak{I}$ measurable.
2. v_{ij} are $\mathfrak{I}_t$-adapted.
3. $P\left[\int_0^t (v_{ij})^2 ds < \infty \text{ for all } t \geq 0 \right] = 1$.

Then, we define the multidimensional Itô integral

$$\int_0^t v\, dB = \int_0^t \begin{bmatrix} v_{11} & \cdot & v_{1d} \\ \cdot & \cdot & \cdot \\ v_{r1} & \cdot & v_{rd} \end{bmatrix} \begin{bmatrix} dB_1 \\ \cdot \\ dB_d \end{bmatrix}$$

as the r-dimensional column vector whose components are the following sums of 1-dimensional Itô integrals:

$$\sum_{i=1}^{d} \int_0^t v_{ij}(s, \omega)\, dB_j(s, \omega)$$

Note that the entries of the matrix are functions of time and state: they form a vector of stochastic processes. Given the previous definition of Itô integrals, we can now extend the definition of Itô processes to the multidimensional case. Suppose that the functions u and v satisfy the conditions established for the one-dimensional case. We can then form a **multidimensional Itô process** as the following vector of Itô processes:

$$dX_1 = u_1 dt + v_{11} dB_1 + \ldots + v_{1d} dB_d$$

$$\ldots$$

$$dX_{1r} = u_r dt + v_{r1} dB_1 + \ldots + v_{rd} dB_d$$

or, in matrix notation

$$d\mathbf{X} = \mathbf{u} dt + \mathbf{v} dB$$

After defining the multidimensional Itô process, multidimensional stochastic equations are defined in differential form in matrix notation as follows:

$$d\mathbf{X}(t, \omega) = \mathbf{u}[t, X_1(t, \omega), \ldots, X_d(t, \omega)] dt$$
$$+ \mathbf{v}[t, X_1(t, \omega), \ldots, X_d(t, \omega)] dB$$

Consider now the multidimensional map: $g(t,x) \equiv [g_1(t,x), \ldots, g_d(t,x)]$, which maps the process X into another process $Y = g(t,X)$. It can be demonstrated that Y is a multidimensional Itô process whose components are defined according to the following rules:

$$dY_k = \frac{\partial g_k(t, X)}{\partial t} dt + \sum_i \frac{\partial g_k(t, X)}{\partial X_i} dX_i + \frac{1}{2} \sum_{i,j} \frac{\partial^2 g_k(t, X)}{\partial X_i \partial X_j} dX_i dX_j$$

$$dB_i dB_j = 1 \text{ if } i = j, 0 \text{ if } i \neq j, \; dB_i dt = dt dB_i = 0$$

SOLUTION OF STOCHASTIC DIFFERENTIAL EQUATIONS

It is possible to determine an explicit solution of stochastic differential equations in the linear case and in a number of other cases that can be reduced to linear equations through functional transformations. Let's first consider **linear stochastic equations** of the form:

$$dX_t = [A(t)X_t + a(t)] dt + \sigma(t) dB_t, \; 0 \leq t < \infty$$

$$X_0 = \xi$$

where B is an r-dimensional Brownian motion independent of the d-dimensional initial random vector ξ and the $(d \times d)$, $(d \times d)$, $(d \times r)$ matrices $A(t)$, $a(t)$, $\sigma(t)$ are nonrandom and time dependent.

The simplest example of a linear stochastic equation is the equation of an arithmetic Brownian motion with drift, written as follows:

$$dX_t = \mu dt + \sigma dB_t, \, 0 \le t < \infty$$

$$X_0 = \xi, \, \mu, \, \sigma \text{ constants}$$

In linear equations of this type, the stochastic part enters only in an additive way through the terms $\sigma_{ij}(t)dB_t$. The functions $\sigma(t)$ are sometimes called the instantaneous variances and covariances of the process. In the example of the arithmetic Brownian motion, μ is called the **drift of the process** and σ the **volatility of the process.**

It is intuitive that the solution of this equation is given by the solution of the associated deterministic equation, that is, the ordinary differential equation obtained by removing the stochastic part, plus the cumulated random disturbances. Let's first consider the associated deterministic differential equation

$$\frac{dx}{dt} = A(t)x + a(t), \, 0 \le t < \infty$$

where $x(t)$ is a d-dimensional vector with initial conditions $x(0) = \xi$.

It can be demonstrated that this equation has an absolutely continuous solution in the domain $0 \le t < \infty$. To find its solution, let's first consider the matrix differential equation

$$\frac{d\Phi}{dt} = A(t)\Phi, \, 0 \le t < \infty$$

This matrix differential equation has an absolutely continuous solution in the domain $0 \le t < \infty$. The matrix $\Phi(t)$ that solves this equation is called the **fundamental solution** of the equation. It can be demonstrated that $\Phi(t)$ is a nonsingular matrix for each t. Lastly, it can be demonstrated that the solution of the equation:

$$\frac{dx}{dt} = A(t)x + a(t), \, 0 \le t < \infty$$

with initial condition $x(0) = \xi$, can be written in terms of the fundamental solution as follows:

$$x(t) = \Phi(t)\left[x(0) + \int_0^t \Phi^{-1}(s)a(s)ds\right], 0 \leq t < \infty$$

Let's now go back to the stochastic equation

$$dX_t = [A(t)X_t + a(t)]dt + \sigma(t)dB_t, 0 \leq t < \infty$$

$$X_0 = \xi$$

Using Itô's formula, it can be demonstrated that the above linear stochastic equation admits the following unique solution:

$$X(t) = \Phi(t)\left[\xi + \int_0^t \Phi^{-1}(s)a(s)ds + \int_0^t \Phi^{-1}(s)\sigma(s)dB_s\right], 0 \leq t < \infty$$

This effectively demonstrates that the solution of the linear stochastic equation is the solution of the associated deterministic equation plus the cumulated stochastic term

$$\int_0^t \Phi^{-1}(s)\sigma(s)dB_s$$

To illustrate this, below we now specialize the above solutions in the case of arithmetic Brownian motion, Ornstein-Uhlenbeck processes, and geometric Brownian motion.

The Arithmetic Brownian Motion

The **arithmetic Brownian motion** in one dimension is defined by the following equation:

$$dX_t = \mu dt + \sigma dB_t$$

In this case, $A(t) = 0$, $a(t) = \mu$, $\sigma(t) = \sigma$ and the solution becomes

$$X = \mu t + \sigma B$$

The Ornstein-Uhlenbeck Process

The **Ornstein-Uhlenbeck process** in one dimension is a mean-reverting process defined by the following equation:

$$dX_t = -\alpha X_t dt + \sigma dB_t$$

It is a mean-reverting process because the drift is pulled back to zero by a term proportional to the process itself. In this case, $A(t) = -\alpha$, $a(t) = 0$, $\sigma(t) = \sigma$ and the solution becomes

$$X_t = X_0 + e^{-\alpha t} + \sigma \int_0^t e^{-\alpha(t-s)} dB_s$$

The Geometric Brownian Motion

The **geometric Brownian motion** in one dimension is defined by the following equation:

$$dX = \mu X dt + \sigma X dB$$

This equation can be easily reduced to the previous linear case by the transformation:

$$Y = \log X$$

Let's apply Itô's formula

$$dY_t = \left(\frac{\partial g}{\partial t} + \frac{\partial g}{\partial x} a + \frac{1}{2} \frac{\partial^2 g}{\partial x^2} b^2 \right) dt + \frac{\partial g}{\partial x} b \, dB_t$$

where

$$g(t, x) = \log x, \frac{\partial g}{\partial t} = 0, \frac{\partial g}{\partial t} = \frac{1}{x}, \frac{1}{x} \frac{\partial^2 g}{\partial x^2} = -\frac{1}{x^2}$$

We can then verify that the logarithm of the geometric Brownian motion becomes an arithmetic Brownian motion with drift

$$\mu' = \mu - \frac{1}{2}\sigma^2$$

The geometric Brownian motion evolves as a lognormal process:

$$X_t = x_0 \exp\left\{\left(\mu - \frac{1}{2}\sigma^2\right)t + \sigma B_t\right\}$$

SUMMARY

■ Stochastic differential equations give meaning to ordinary differential equations where some terms are subject to random perturbation.

■ Following Itô and Stratonovich, stochastic differential equations are defined through their integral equivalent: the differential notation is just a shorthand.

■ Itô processes are the sum of a time integral plus an Itô integral.

■ Itô processes are closed with respect to smooth maps: a smooth function of an Itô process is another Itô process defined through the Itô formula.

■ Stochastic differential equations are equations established in terms of Itô processes.

■ Linear equations can be solved explicitly as the sum of the solution of the associated deterministic equation plus a stochastic cumulative term.

CHAPTER 11

Financial Econometrics: Time Series Concepts, Representations, and Models

In this chapter and the next we introduce models of discrete-time stochastic processes (that is, time series) and address the general problem of estimating a model from a given set of empirical data. Recall from Chapter 6 that a stochastic process is a time-dependent random variable. Stochastic processes explored thus far, for instance Brownian motion and Itô processes, develop in continuous time. This means that time is a real variable that can assume any real value. In many applications, however, it is convenient to constrain time to assume only discrete values. A time series is a discrete-time stochastic process; that is, it is a collection of random variables X_i indexed with the integers $\ldots-n,\ldots,-2,-1,0,1,2,\ldots,n,\ldots$

In finance theory, as in the practice of quantitative finance, both continuous-time and discrete-time models are used. In many instances, continuous-time models allow simpler and more concise expressions as well as more general conclusions, though at the expense of conceptual complication. For instance, in the limit of continuous time, apparently simple processes such as white noise cannot be meaningfully defined. The mathematics of asset management tends to prefer discrete-time processes while the mathematics of derivatives tends to prefer continuous-time processes.

The first issue to address in financial econometrics is the spacing of discrete points of time. An obvious choice is regular, constant spacing. In this case, the time points are placed at multiples of a single time interval: $t = i\Delta t$. For instance, one might consider the closing prices at the end of each day. The use of fixed spacing is appropriate in many appli-

283

cations. Spacing of time points might also be irregular but deterministic. For instance, week-ends introduce irregular spacing in a sequence of daily closing prices. These questions can be easily handled within the context of discrete time series.

The diffusion of electronic transactions has made available high-frequency data related to individual transactions. These data are randomly spaced as the intervals between two transactions are random variables. If one wants to consider randomly spaced time intervals, discrete-time models will not suffice; one must use either marked point processes (discussed briefly in Chapter 13) or continuous-time processes through the use of master equations. In this chapter and the next we discuss only time series at discrete and fixed intervals of time. Here we introduce concepts, representations, and models of time series. In the next chapter we will discuss model selection and estimation.

CONCEPTS OF TIME SERIES

A **time series** is a collection of random variables X_t indexed with a discrete time index $t = \dots-2,-1,0,1,2,\dots$. The variables X_t are defined over a probability space $(\Omega,P,\Im)$, where Ω is the set of states, P is a probability measure, and $\Im$ is the σ-algebra of events, equipped with a discrete filtration $\{\Im_t\}$ that determines the propagation of information (see Chapter 6). A realization of a time series is a countable sequence of real numbers, one for each time point.

The variables X_t are characterized by **finite-dimensional distributions** (see the section on stochastic processes in Chapter 6) as well as by **conditional distributions**, $F_s(x_s/\Im_t)$, $s > t$. The latter are the distributions of the variable x at time s given the σ-algebra $\{\Im_t\}$ at time t. Note that conditioning is always conditioning with respect to a σ-algebra though (see Chapter 6) we will not always strictly use this notation and will condition with respect to the value of variables, for instance:

$$F_s(x_s/x_t),\ s > t$$

If the series starts from a given point, initial conditions must be fixed. Initial conditions might be a set of fixed values or a set of random variables. If the initial conditions are not fixed values but random variables, one has to consider the correlation between the initial values and the random shocks of the series. A usual assumption is that the initial conditions and the random shocks of the series are statistically independent.

How do we describe a time series? One way to describe a time series is to determine the mathematical form of the conditional distribution. This description is called an **autopredictive model** because the model predicts future values of the series from past values. However, we can also describe a time series as a function of another time series. This is called an **explanatory model** as one variable is explained by another. The simplest example is a regression model where a variable is proportional to another exogenously given variable plus a constant term. Time series can also be described as random fluctuations or adjustments around a deterministic path. These models are called **adjustment models**. Explanatory, autopredictive, and adjustment models can be mixed in a single model. The **data generation process** (DGP) of a series is a mathematical process that computes the future values of the variables given all information known at time t.

An important concept is that of a **stationary time series**. A series is stationary in the "strict sense" if all finite dimensional distributions are invariant with respect to a time shift. A series is stationary in a "weaker sense" if only the moments up to a given order are invariant with respect to a time shift. In this chapter, time series will be considered (weakly) stationary if the first two moments are time-independent. Note that a stationary series cannot have a starting point but must extend over the entire infinite time axis. Note also that a series can be strictly stationary (that is, have all distributions time-independent, but the moments might not exist). Thus a strictly stationary series is not necessarily weakly stationary.

A time series can be univariate or multivariate. A **multivariate time series** is a time-dependent random vector. The principles of modeling remain the same but the problem of estimation might become very difficult given the large numbers of parameters to be estimated.

Models of time series are essential building blocks for financial forecasting and, therefore, for financial decision-making. In particular asset allocation and portfolio optimization, when performed quantitatively, are based on some model of financial prices and returns. This chapter lays down the basic financial econometric theory for financial forecasting. We will introduce a number of specific models of time series and of multivariate time series, presenting the basic facts about the theory of these processes. The next chapter will tackle the problem of model estimation from empirical data. We will consider primarily models of financial assets, though most theoretical considerations apply to macroeconomic variables as well. These models include:

■ **Correlated random walks.** The simplest model of multiple financial assets is that of correlated random walks. This model is only a rough approximation of equity price processes and presents serious problems of estimation in the case of a large number of processes.

■ **Factor models.** Factor models address the problem of estimation in the case of a large number of processes. In a factor model there are correlations only among factors and between each factor and each time series. Factors might be exogenous or endogenously modeled.

■ **State-space models.** State-space models describe factors as autoregressive processes. They work in stationary and nonstationary environments. In the latter case, state-space models are equivalent to cointegrated models.

■ **Cointegrated models.** In a cointegrated model there are portfolios which are described by autocorrelated, stationary processes. All processes are linear combinations of common trends that are represented by the factors.

The above models are all linear. However, nonlinearities are at work in financial time series. One way to model nonlinearities is to break down models into two components, the first being a linear autoregressive model of the parameters, the second a regressive or autoregressive model of empirical quantities whose parameters are driven by the first. This is the case with most of today's nonlinear models (e.g., ARCH/GARCH models), Hamilton models, and Markov switching models.

There is a coherent modeling landscape, from correlated random walks and factor models to the modeling of factors, and, finally, the modeling of nonlinearities by making the model parameters vary. Before describing models in detail, however, let's present some key empirical facts about financial time series.

STYLIZED FACTS OF FINANCIAL TIME SERIES

Most sciences are stratified in the sense that theories are organized on different levels. The empirical evidence that supports a theory is generally formulated in a lower level theory. In physics, for instance, quantum mechanics cannot be formulated as a standalone theory but needs classical physics to give meaning to measurement. Economics is no exception. A basic level of knowledge in economics is represented by the so-called **stylized facts**. Stylized facts are statistical findings of a general nature on financial and economic time series; they cannot be considered raw data insofar as they are formulated as statistical hypotheses. On the other hand, they are not full-fledged theories.

Amongst the most important stylized facts from the point of view of finance theory, we can mention the following:

- Returns of individual stocks exhibit nearly zero autocorrelation at every lag.
- Returns of some equity portfolios exhibit significant autocorrelation.
- The volatility of returns exhibits hyperbolic decay with significant autocorrelation.
- The distribution of stock returns is not normal for time horizons from a few minutes to a few days. The exact shape is difficult to ascertain but power law decay cannot be rejected.
- The distribution of stock returns is close to a log-normal after a few days.
- There are large stock price drops (that is, market crashes) that seem to be outliers with respect to both normal distributions and power law distributions.
- Stock return time series exhibit significant cross-correlation.

These findings are, in a sense, model-dependent. For instance, the distribution of returns, a subject that has received a lot of attention, can be fitted by different distributions. There is no firm evidence on the exact value of the power exponent, with alternative proposals based on variable exponents. The autocorrelation is model-dependent while the exponential decay of return autocorrelation can be interpreted only as absence of linear dependence.

It is fair to say that these stylized facts set the stage for financial modeling but leave ample room for model selection. Financial time series seem to be nearly random processes that exhibit significant cross correlations and, in some instances, cross autocorrelations. The global structure of auto and cross correlations, if it exists at all, must be fairly complex and there is no immediate evidence that financial time series admit a simple DGP.

One more important feature of financial time series is the presence of trends. *Prima facie* trends of economic and financial variables are exponential trends. Trends are not quantities that can be independently measured. Trends characterize an entire stochastic model. Therefore there is no way to arrive at an assessment of trends independent from the model. We will see later in this chapter that a number of models reject the assumption of exponential trends. Exponential trends are, however, a reasonable first approximation.

Given the finite nature of world resources, exponential trends are not sustainable in the long run. However, they might still be a good approximation over limited time horizons. An additional insight into financial time series comes from the consideration of investors' behavior. If investors are risk averse, as required by the theory of investment (see Chapter 16) then price processes must exhibit a trade off between risk and returns. The combination of this insight with the assumption of exponential trends yields market models with possibly diverging exponential trends for prices and market capitalization.

Again, diverging exponential trends are difficult to justify in the long run as they would imply that after a while only one entity would dominate the entire market. Some form of reversion to the mean or more disruptive phenomena that prevent time series to diverge exponentially must be at work.

In the following sections we will proceed to describe the theory and the estimation procedures of a number of market models that have been proposed. After introducing general concepts of the measure of dependence between random variables, we will present the multivariate random walk model and will analyze in some detail the correlation structure of real markets. We will introduce dimensionality reduction techniques and multifactor models. We will then proceed to introduce cointegration, autoregressive models, state-space models, ARCH/GARCH models, Markov switching, and other nonlinear models.

INFINITE MOVING-AVERAGE AND AUTOREGRESSIVE REPRESENTATION OF TIME SERIES

There are several general representations (or models) of time series. This section introduces representations based on infinite moving averages or infinite autoregressions useful from a theoretical point of view. In the practice of econometrics, however, more parsimonious models such as the ARMA models (described in the next section) are used. Representations are different for stationary and nonstationary time series. Let's start with univariate stationary time series.

Univariate Stationary Series

The most fundamental model of a univariate stationary time series is the infinite moving average of a white noise process. In fact, it can be demonstrated that under mild regularity conditions, any univariate stationary causal time series admits the following **infinite moving average representation**:

$$x_t = \sum_{i=0}^{\infty} h_i \varepsilon_{t-i} + m$$

where the h_i are coefficients and ε_{t-i} is a one-dimensional zero-mean white-noise process. This is a **causal time series** as the present value of the series depends only on the present and past values of the noise process. A more general infinite moving-average representation would involve a summation which extends from $-\infty$ to $+\infty$. Because this representation would not make sense from an economic point of view, we will restrict ourselves only to causal time series.

A sufficient condition for the above series to be stationary is that the coefficients h_i are **absolutely summable:**

$$\sum_{i=0}^{\infty} |h_i|^2 < \infty$$

Also, in general it can be demonstrated that given any stationary process x_i, if the sequence of coefficients h_i is absolutely summable, then the process

$$y_i = \sum_{i=1}^{\infty} h_i x_i$$

is stationary.

The Lag Operator *L*

Let's now simplify the notation by introducing the lag operator L. The **lag operator** L is an operator that acts on an infinite series and produces another infinite series shifted one place to the left. In other words, the lag operator replaces every element of a series with the one delayed by one time lag:

$$L(x_t) = x_{t-1}$$

The n-th power of the lag operator shifts a series by n places:

$$L^n(x_t) = x_{t-n}$$

Negative powers of the lag operator yield the **forward operator** F, which shifts places to the right. The lag operator can be multiplied by a scalar and different powers can be added. In this way, linear functions of different powers of the lag operator can be formed as follows:

$$A(L) = \sum_{i=1}^{N} a_i L^i$$

Note that if the lag operator is applied to a series that starts from a given point, initial conditions must be specified.

Within the domain of stationary series, infinite power series of the lag operator can also be formed. In fact, as remarked above, given a stationary series, if the coefficients h_i are absolutely summable, the series

$$\sum_{i=1}^{\infty} h_i L^i x_t$$

is well defined in the sense that it converges and defines another stationary series. It therefore makes sense to define the operator:

$$A(L) = \sum_{i=1}^{\infty} h_i L^i$$

Now consider the operator $I - \lambda L$. If $|\lambda| < 1$, this operator can be **inverted** and its inverse is given by the infinite power series,

$$(I - \lambda L)^{-1} = \sum_{i=1}^{\infty} \lambda^i L^i$$

as can be seen by multiplying $I - \lambda L$ by the power series $\sum_{i=1}^{\infty} \lambda^i L^i$:

$$(I - \lambda L) \sum_{i=1}^{\infty} \lambda^i L^i = L^0 = I$$

On the basis of this relationship, it can be demonstrated that any operator of the type

$$A(L) = \sum_{i=1}^{N} a_i L^i$$

can be inverted provided that the solutions of the equation

$$\sum_{i=1}^{N} a_i z^i = 0$$

have absolute values strictly greater than 1. The inverse operator is an infinite power series

$$A^{-1}(L) = \sum_{i=1}^{\infty} \psi_i L^i$$

Given two linear functions of the operator L, it is possible to define their product

$$A(L) = \sum_{i=1}^{M} a_i L^i$$

$$B(L) = \sum_{j=1}^{N} b_i L^i$$

$$P(L) = A(L)B(L) = \sum_{i=1}^{M+N} p_i L^i$$

$$p_i = \sum_{r=1}^{i} a_r b_{i-r}$$

The convolution product of two infinite series in the lag operator is defined in a similar way

$$A(L) = \sum_{i=0}^{\infty} a_i L^i$$

$$B(L) = \sum_{j=0}^{\infty} b_i L^i$$

$$C(L) = A(L) \times B(L) = \sum_{k=0}^{\infty} c_k L^k$$

$$c_k = \sum_{s=0}^{k} a_s b_{k-s}$$

We can define the left-inverse (right-inverse) of an infinite series as the operator $A^{-1}(L)$, such that $A^{-1}(L) \times A(L) = I$. The inverse can always be computed solving an infinite set of recursive equations provided that $a_0 \neq 0$. However, the inverse series will not necessarily be stationary. A sufficient condition for stationarity is that the coefficients of the inverse series are absolutely summable.

In general, it is possible to perform on the symbolic series

$$H(L) = \sum_{i=1}^{\infty} h_i L^i$$

the same operations that can be performed on the series

$$H(z) = \sum_{i=1}^{\infty} h_i z^i$$

with z complex variable. However operations performed on a series of lag operators neither assume nor entail convergence properties. In fact, one can think of z simply as a symbol. In particular, the inverse does not necessarily exhibit absolutely summable coefficients.

Stationary Univariate Moving Average

Using the lag operator L notation, the infinite moving average representation can be written as follows:

$$x_t = \left(\sum_{i=0}^{\infty} h_i L^i \right) \varepsilon_t + m = H(L)\varepsilon_t + m$$

Consider now the inverse series:

$$\Pi(L) = \sum_{i=1}^{\infty} \lambda_i L^i, \ \Pi(L)H(L) = I$$

If the coefficients λ_i are absolutely summable, we can write

$$\varepsilon_t = \Pi(L)x_t = \sum_{i=1}^{\infty} \lambda_i L^i x_{t-i}$$

and the series is said to be **invertible**.

Multivariate Stationary Series

The concepts of infinite moving-average representation and of invertibility defined above for univariate series carry over immediately to the multivariate case. In fact, it can be demonstrated that under mild regularity conditions, any multivariate stationary causal time series admits the following **infinite moving-average representation**:

$$\mathbf{x}_t = \sum_{i=0}^{\infty} \mathbf{H}_i \varepsilon_{t-i} + \mathbf{m}$$

where the $\mathbf{H}_i$ are $n{\times}n$ matrices, ε_t is a n-dimensional, zero-mean, white noise process with nonsingular variance-covariance matrix Ω, and $\mathbf{m}$ is an n-vector of constants. The coefficients $\mathbf{H}_i$ are called **Markov coefficients**. This moving-average representation is called the **Wold representation**. Wold representation states that any series where only the past influences the present can be represented as an infinite moving average of white noise terms. Note that, as in the univariate case, the infinite moving-average representation can be written in more general terms as a sum which extends from $-\infty$ to $+\infty$. However a series of this type is not suitable for financial modeling as it is not causal (that is, the future influences the present). Therefore we consider only moving averages that extend to past terms.

Suppose that the Markov coefficients are an absolutely summable series:

$$\sum_{i=0}^{\infty} \|\mathbf{H}_i\| < +\infty$$

where $\|\mathbf{H}\|^2$ indicates the largest eigenvalue of the matrix $\mathbf{HH}'$. Under this assumption, it can be demonstrated that the series is stationary and that the (time-invariant) first two moments can be computed in the following way:

$$\text{cov}(\mathbf{x}_t \mathbf{x}_{t-h}) = \sum_{i=0}^{\infty} \mathbf{H}_i \mathbf{\Omega} \mathbf{H}'_{i-h}$$

$$E[\mathbf{x}_t] = \mathbf{m}$$

with the convention $\mathbf{H}_i = 0$ if $i < 0$. Note that the assumption that the Markov coefficients are an absolutely summable series is essential, otherwise the covariance matrix would not exist. For instance, if the $\mathbf{H}_i$ were identity matrices, the variances of the series would become infinite.

As the second moments are all constants, the series is weakly stationary. We can write the time-independent autocovariance function of the series, which is a $n \times n$ matrix whose entries are a function of the lag h, as

$$\mathbf{\Gamma}_{\mathbf{x}}(h) = \sum_{i=0}^{\infty} \mathbf{H}_i \mathbf{\Omega} \mathbf{H}'_{i-h}$$

Under the assumption that the Markov coefficients are an absolutely summable series, we can use the lag-operator L representation and write the operator

$$\mathbf{H}(L) = \sum_{i=0}^{\infty} \mathbf{H}_i L^i$$

so that the Wold representation of a series can be written as

$$\mathbf{x}_t = \mathbf{H}(L)\varepsilon + \mathbf{m}$$

The concept of invertibility carries over to the multivariate case. A multivariate stationary time series is said to be invertible if it can be represented in autoregressive form. Invertibility means that the white noise process can be recovered as a function of the series. In order to explain the notion of invertible processes, it is useful to introduce the **generating function** of the operator $\mathbf{H}$, defined as the following matrix power series:

$$H(z) = \sum_{i=0}^{\infty} H_i z^i$$

It can be demonstrated that, if $H_0 = I$, then $H(0) = H_0$ and the power series $H(z)$ is invertible in the sense that it is possible to formally derive the inverse series,

$$\Pi(z) = \sum_{i=0}^{\infty} \Pi_i z^i$$

such that

$$\Pi(z)H(z) = (\Pi \times H)(z) = I$$

where the product is intended as a convolution product. If the coefficients Π_i are absolutely summable, as the process x_t is assumed to be stationary, it can be represented in **infinite autoregressive form**:

$$\Pi(L)(x_t - m) = \varepsilon_t$$

In this case the process x_t is said to be invertible.

From the above, it is clear that the infinite moving average representation is a more general linear representation of a stationary time than the infinite autoregressive form. A process that admits both representations is called invertible.

Nonstationary Series

Let's now look at nonstationary series. As there is no very general model of nonstationary time series valid for all nonstationary series, we have to restrict somehow the family of admissible models. Let's consider a family of **linear, moving-average, nonstationary models** of the following type:

$$x_t = \sum_{i=0}^{t} H_i \varepsilon_{t-i} + h(t) z_{-1}$$

where the H_i are left unrestricted and do not necessarily form an absolutely summable series, $h(t)$ is deterministic, and z_{-1} is a random vector called the **initial conditions**, which is supposed to be uncorrelated with the white noise process. The essential differences of this linear model with respect to the Wold representation of stationary series are:

- The presence of a starting point and of initial conditions.
- The absence of restrictions on the coefficients.
- The index t which restricts the number of summands.

The first two moments of a linear process are not constant. They can be computed in a way similar to the infinite moving average case:

$$\text{cov}(\mathbf{x}_t \mathbf{x}_{t-h}) = \sum_{i=0}^{t} \mathbf{H}_i \mathbf{\Omega} \mathbf{H}'_{i-h} + \mathbf{h}(t)\text{var}(\mathbf{z})\mathbf{h}'$$

$$E[\mathbf{x}_t] = \mathbf{m}_t = \mathbf{h}(t)E[\mathbf{z}]$$

Let's now see how a linear process can be expressed in autoregressive form. To simplify notation let's introduce the processes $\tilde{\boldsymbol{\varepsilon}}_t$ and $\tilde{\mathbf{x}}_t$ and the deterministic series $\tilde{\mathbf{h}}(t)$ defined as follows:

$$\tilde{\boldsymbol{\varepsilon}}_t = \begin{cases} \boldsymbol{\varepsilon}_t \text{ if } t > 0 \\ 0 \text{ if } t < 0 \end{cases} \quad \tilde{\mathbf{x}}_t = \begin{cases} \mathbf{x}_t \text{ if } t > 0 \\ 0 \text{ if } t < 0 \end{cases} \quad \tilde{\mathbf{h}}(t) = \begin{cases} \mathbf{h}_t \text{ if } t > 0 \\ 0 \text{ if } t < 0 \end{cases}$$

It can be demonstrated that, due to the initial conditions, a linear process always satisfies the following autoregressive equation:

$$\Pi(L)\tilde{\mathbf{x}}_t = \boldsymbol{\varepsilon}_t + \Pi(L)\mathbf{h} \times (t)\mathbf{z}_{-1}$$

A random walk model

$$x_t = x_{t-1} + \varepsilon_t = \varepsilon_t + \sum_{i=1}^{t} \varepsilon_{t-i}$$

is an example of a linear nonstationary model.

The above linear model can also represent processes that are nearly stationary in the sense that they start from initial conditions but then converge to a stationary process. A process that converges to a stationary process is called **asymptotically stationary**.

We can summarize the previous discussion as follows. Under mild regularity conditions, any causal stationary series can be represented as an infinite moving average of a white noise process. If the series can also be represented in an autoregressive form, then the series is said to be invertible. Nonstationary series do not have corresponding general representations. Linear models are a broad class of nonstationary models and of asymptotically stationary models that provide the theoretical base for ARMA and state-space processes that will be discussed in the following sections.

ARMA REPRESENTATIONS

The infinite moving average or autoregressive representations of the previous section are useful theoretical tools but they cannot be applied to estimate processes. One needs a parsimonious representation with a finite number of coefficients. **Autoregressive moving average** (ARMA) models and state-space models provide such representation; though apparently conceptually different, they are statistically equivalent.

Stationary Univariate ARMA Models

Let's start with univariate stationary processes. An **autoregressive process of order** p – **AR**(p) is a process of the form:

$$x_t + a_1 x_{t-1} + \dots + a_p x_{t-p} = \varepsilon_t$$

which can be written using the lag operator as

$$A(L)x_t = (1 + a_1 L + \dots + a_p L^p)x_t = x_t + a_1 L x_t + \dots + a_p L^p x_{t-p} = \varepsilon_t$$

Not all processes that can be written in autoregressive form are stationary. In order to study the stationarity of an autoregressive process, consider the following polynomial:

$$A(z) = 1 + a_1 z + \dots + a_p z^p$$

where z is a complex variable.

The equation

$$A(z) = 1 + a_1 z + \dots + a_p z^p = 0$$

is called the **inverse characteristic equation**. It can be demonstrated that if the roots of this equation, that is, its solutions, are all different from 1

in modulus (that is, the roots do not lie on the unit circle), then the
operator $A(L)$ is invertible and admits the inverse representation:

$$x_t = A^{-1}(L)\varepsilon_t = \sum_{i=-\infty}^{+\infty} \lambda_i \varepsilon_{t-i}, \text{ with } \sum_{i=-\infty}^{+\infty} |\lambda_i| < +\infty$$

In addition, if the roots are all strictly greater than 1 in modulus, then
the representation only involves positive powers of L:

$$x_t = A^{-1}(L)\varepsilon_t = \sum_{i=-\infty}^{+\infty} \lambda_i \varepsilon_{t-i}, \text{ with } \sum_{i=0}^{+\infty} |\lambda_i| < +\infty$$

We can therefore say that, if the roots of the inverse characteristic equation of an autoregressive process are all strictly greater than 1 in modulus (that is, they lie outside the unit circle), then the process is invertible
as it admits a causal infinite moving average representation.

In order to avoid possible confusion, note that the solutions of the
inverse characteristic equation are the reciprocal of the solution of the
characteristic equation defined as

$$A(z) = z^p + a_1 z^{p-1} + \dots + a_p = 0$$

Therefore an autoregressive process is invertible with an infinite moving
average representation that only involves positive powers of the operator L if the solutions of the characteristic equation are all strictly
smaller than 1 in absolute value. This is the condition of invertibility
often stated in the literature.

Let's now consider finite moving-average representations. A process
is called a **moving average process of order** q – **MA(q)** if it admits the
following representation:

$$x_t = (1 + b_1 L + \dots + b_p L^q)\varepsilon_t = \varepsilon_t + b_1 \varepsilon_{t-1} + \dots + b_p \varepsilon_{t-q}$$

In a way similar to the autoregressive case, if the roots of the equation

$$B(z) = 1 + b_1 z + \dots + b_q z^q = 0$$

are all different from 1 in modulus, then the MA(q) process is invertible
and, therefore, admits the infinite autoregressive representation:

$$\varepsilon_t = B^{-1}(L)\varepsilon_t = \sum_{i=-\infty}^{+\infty} \pi_i \varepsilon_{t-i}, \text{ with } \sum_{i=0}^{+\infty} |\pi_i| < +\infty$$

In addition, if the roots of $B(z)$ are strictly greater than 1 in modulus, then the autoregressive representation only involves past values of the process:

$$\varepsilon_t = B^{-1}(L)\varepsilon_t = \sum_{i=0}^{+\infty} \pi_i \varepsilon_{t-i}, \text{ with } \sum_{i=0}^{+\infty} |\pi_i| < +\infty$$

As in the previous case, if one considers the characteristic equation,

$$B(z) = z^q + b_1 z^{q-1} + \ldots + b_q = 0$$

then the MA(q) process admits a causal autoregressive representation if the roots of the characteristic equation are strictly smaller than 1 in modulus.

Let's now consider, more in general, an ARMA process of order p,q. We say that a stationary process admits a minimal ARMA(p,q) representation if it can be written as

$$x_t + a_1 x_{t-1} + a_p x_{t-p} = b_1 \varepsilon_t + \ldots + b_q \varepsilon_{t-q}$$

or equivalently in terms of the lag operator

$$A(L)x_t = B(L)\varepsilon_t$$

where ε_t is a serially uncorrelated white noise with nonzero variance, $a_0 = b_0 = 1$, $a_p \neq 0$, $b_q \neq 0$, the polynomials A and B have roots strictly greater than 1 in modulus and do not have any root in common.

Generalizing the reasoning in the pure MA or AR case, it can be demonstrated that a generic process, which admits the ARMA(p,q) representation $A(L)x_t = B(L)\varepsilon_t$ is stationary if both polynomials A and B have roots strictly different from 1. In addition, if all the roots of the polynomial $A(z)$ are strictly greater than 1 in modulus, then the ARMA(p,q) process can be expressed as a moving average process:

$$x_t = \frac{B(L)}{A(L)} \varepsilon_t$$

Conversely, if all the roots of the polynomial $B(z)$ are strictly greater than 1, then the ARMA(p,q) process can be expressed as an autoregressive process:

$$\varepsilon_t = \frac{A(L)}{B(L)} x_t$$

Note that in the above discussions every process was centered—that is, it had zero constant mean. As we were considering stationary processes, this condition is not restrictive as the eventual nonzero mean can be subtracted.

Note also that ARMA stationary processes extend through the entire time axis. An ARMA process, which begins from some initial conditions at starting time $t = 0$, is not stationary even if its roots are strictly outside the unit circle. It can be demonstrated, however, that such a process is asymptotically stationary.

Nonstationary Univariate ARMA Models

So far we have considered only stationary processes. However, ARMA equations can also represent nonstationary processes if some of the roots of the polynomial $A(z)$ are equal to 1 in modulus. A process defined by the equation

$$A(L)x_t = B(L)\varepsilon_t$$

is called an **Autoregressive Integrated Moving Average** (ARIMA) process if at least one of the roots of the polynomial A is equal to 1 in modulus. Suppose that λ be a root with multiplicity d. In this case the ARMA representation can be written as

$$A'(L)(I - \lambda L)^d x_t = B(L)\varepsilon_t$$

$$A(L) = A'(L)(I - \lambda L)^d$$

However this formulation is not satisfactory as the process A is not invertible if initial conditions are not provided; it is therefore preferable to offer a more rigorous definition, which includes initial conditions. Therefore, we give the following definition of nonstationary integrated ARMA processes.

A process x_t defined for $t \geq 0$ is called an **Autoregressive Integrated Moving Average process**—ARIMA(p,d,q)—if it satisfies a relationship of the type

$$A(L)(I - \lambda L)^d x_t = B(L)\varepsilon_t$$

where:

- The polynomials $A(L)$ and $B(L)$ have roots strictly greater than 1.
- ε_t is a white noise process defined for $t \geq 0$.
- A set of initial conditions $(x_{-1}, ..., x_{-p-d}, \varepsilon_t, ..., \varepsilon_{-q})$ independent from the white noise is given.

Later in this chapter we discuss the interpretation and further properties of the ARIMA condition.

Stationary Multivariate ARMA Models

Let's now move on to consider stationary multivariate processes. A stationary process which admits an infinite moving-average representation of the type

$$\mathbf{x}_t = \sum_{i=0}^{\infty} \mathbf{H}_i \boldsymbol{\varepsilon}_{t-i}$$

where ε_{t-i} is an n-dimensional, zero-mean, white-noise process with nonsingular variance-covariance matrix $\boldsymbol{\Omega}$ is called an **autoregressive moving average**—ARMA(p,q)—**model**, if it satisfies a difference equation of the type

$$A(L)x_t = B(L)\varepsilon_t$$

where **A** and **B** are matrix polynomials in the lag operator L of order p and q respectively:

$$A(L) = \sum_{i=1}^{p} \mathbf{A}_i L^i, \ \mathbf{A}_0 = \mathbf{I}, \ \mathbf{A}_p \neq 0$$

$$\mathbf{B}(L) = \sum_{j=1}^{p} \mathbf{B}_j L^j, \, \mathbf{B}_0 = \mathbf{I}, \, \mathbf{B}_q \neq 0$$

If $q = 0$, the process is purely autoregressive of order p; if $q = 0$, the process is purely a moving average of order q. Rearranging the terms of the difference equation, it is clear that an ARMA process is a process where the i-th component of the process at time t, $x_{i,t}$, is a linear function of all the components at different lags plus a finite moving average of white noise terms.

It can be demonstrated that the ARMA representation is not unique. The nonuniqueness of the ARMA representation is due to different reasons, such as the existence of a common polynomial factor in the autoregressive and the moving-average part. It entails that the same process can be represented by models with different pairs p,q. For this reason, one would need to determine at least a minimal representation—that is, an ARMA(p,q) representation such that any other ARMA(p',q') representation would have $p' > p$, $q' > q$. With the exception of the univariate case, these problems are very difficult from a mathematical point of view and we will not examine them in detail.

Let's now explore what restrictions on the polynomials $\mathbf{A}(L)$ and $\mathbf{B}(L)$ ensure that the relative ARMA process is stationary. Generalizing the univariate case, the mathematical analysis of stationarity is based on the analysis of the polynomial $\det[\mathbf{A}(z)]$ obtained by formally replacing the lag operator L with a complex variable z in the matrix $\mathbf{A}(L)$ whose entries are finite polynomials in L.

It can be demonstrated that if the complex roots of the polynomial $\det[\mathbf{A}(z)]$, that is, the solutions of the algebraic equation $\det[\mathbf{A}(z)] = 0$, which are in general complex numbers, all lie outside the unit circle, that is, their modulus is strictly greater than one, then the process that satisfies the ARMA conditions,

$$\mathbf{A}(L)\mathbf{x}_t = \mathbf{B}(L)\boldsymbol{\varepsilon}_t$$

is stationary. The demonstration is based on formally solving the ARMA equation, writing (see Chapter 5 on matrix algebra)

$$\mathbf{x}_t = \mathbf{A}^{-1}(L)\mathbf{B}(L)\boldsymbol{\varepsilon}_t = \frac{adj[\mathbf{A}(L)]}{\det[\mathbf{A}(L)]}\mathbf{B}(L)\boldsymbol{\varepsilon}_t$$

If the roots of the polynomial $\det[\mathbf{A}(z)]$ lie outside the unit circle, then it can be shown that

$$\frac{adj[\mathbf{A}(L)]}{\det[\mathbf{A}(L)]}\mathbf{B}(L)\boldsymbol{\varepsilon}_t = \sum_{i=1}^{\infty} \mathbf{H}_i L^i \boldsymbol{\varepsilon}_t, \text{ with } \sum_{i=1}^{\infty} \mathbf{H}_i \text{ absolutely summable}$$

which demonstrates that the process $\mathbf{x}_t$ is stationary.[1] As in the univariate case, if one would consider the equations in $1/z$, the same reasoning applies but with roots strictly inside the unit circle.

A stationary ARMA(p,q) process is an autocorrelated process. Its time-independent autocorrelation function satisfies a set of linear difference equations. Consider an ARMA(p,q) process which satisfies the following equation:

$$\mathbf{A}_0 \mathbf{x}_t + \mathbf{A}_1 \mathbf{x}_{t-1} + \ldots + \mathbf{A}_P \mathbf{x}_{t-P} = \mathbf{B}_0 \boldsymbol{\varepsilon}_t + \mathbf{B}_1 \boldsymbol{\varepsilon}_{t-1} + \ldots + \mathbf{B}_q \boldsymbol{\varepsilon}_{t-q}$$

where $\mathbf{A}_0 = \mathbf{I}$. By expanding the expression for the autocovariance function, it can be demonstrated that the autocovariance function satisfies the following set of linear difference equations:

$$\mathbf{A}_0 \boldsymbol{\Gamma}_h + \mathbf{A}_1 \boldsymbol{\Gamma}_{h-1} + \ldots + \mathbf{A}_P \boldsymbol{\Gamma}_{h-p} = \begin{cases} 0 \text{ if } h > q \\ \sum_{j=0}^{q-h} \mathbf{B}_{j+h} \boldsymbol{\Omega} \mathbf{H}'_j \end{cases}$$

where $\boldsymbol{\Omega}$ and $\mathbf{H}_i$ are, respectively, the covariance matrix and the Markov coefficients of the process in its infinite moving-average representation:

$$\mathbf{x}_t = \sum_{i=0}^{\infty} \mathbf{H}_i \boldsymbol{\varepsilon}_{t-i}$$

From the above representation, it is clear that if the process is purely MA, that is, if $p = 0$, then the autocovariance function vanishes for lag $h > q$.

It is also possible to demonstrate the converse of this theorem. If a linear stationary process admits an autocovariance function that satisfies the following equations,

$$\mathbf{A}_0 \boldsymbol{\Gamma}_h + \mathbf{A}_1 \boldsymbol{\Gamma}_{h-1} + \ldots + \mathbf{A}_P \boldsymbol{\Gamma}_{h-p} = 0 \text{ if } h > q$$

[1] Christian Gourieroux and Alain Monfort, *Time Series and Dynamic Models* (Cambridge: Cambridge University Press, 1997).

then the process admits an ARMA(p,q) representation. In particular, a stationary process is a purely finite moving-average process MA(q), if and only if its autocovariance functions vanish for $h > q$, where q is an integer.

Nonstationary Multivariate ARMA Models

Let's now consider nonstationary series. Consider a series defined for $t \geq 0$ that satisfies the following set of difference equations:

$$\mathbf{A}_0 \mathbf{x}_t + \mathbf{A}_1 \mathbf{x}_{t-1} + \dots + \mathbf{A}_P \mathbf{x}_{t-P} = \mathbf{B}_0 \boldsymbol{\varepsilon}_t + \mathbf{B}_1 \boldsymbol{\varepsilon}_{t-1} + \dots + \mathbf{B}_q \boldsymbol{\varepsilon}_{t-q}$$

where, as in the stationary case, $\boldsymbol{\varepsilon}_{t-i}$ is an n-dimensional zero-mean, white noise process with nonsingular variance-covariance matrix $\boldsymbol{\Omega}$, $\mathbf{A}_0 = \mathbf{I}$, $\mathbf{B}_0 = \mathbf{I}$, $\mathbf{A}_p \neq 0$, $\mathbf{B}_q \neq 0$. Suppose, in addition, that initial conditions $(\mathbf{x}_{-1},\dots,\mathbf{x}_{-p},\boldsymbol{\varepsilon}_t,\dots,\boldsymbol{\varepsilon}_{-q})$ are given. Under these conditions, we say that the process $\mathbf{x}_t$, which is well defined, admits an ARMA representation.

A process $\mathbf{x}_t$ is said to admit an ARIMA representation if, in addition to the above, it satisfies the following two conditions: (1) $\det[\mathbf{B}(z)]$ has all its roots strictly outside of the unit circle, and (2) $\det[\mathbf{A}(z)]$ has all its roots outside the unit circle but with at least one root equal to 1. In other words, an ARIMA process is an ARMA process that satisfies some additional conditions. Later in this chapter we will clarify the meaning of integrated processes.

Markov Coefficients and ARMA Models

For the theoretical analysis of ARMA processes, it is useful to state what conditions on the Markov coefficients ensure that the process admits an ARMA representation. Consider a process $\mathbf{x}_t$, stationary or not, which admits a moving-average representation either as

$$\mathbf{x}_t = \sum_{i=0}^{\infty} \mathbf{H}_i \boldsymbol{\varepsilon}_{t-i}$$

or as a linear model:

$$\mathbf{x}_t = \sum_{i=0}^{t} \mathbf{H}_i \boldsymbol{\varepsilon}_{t-i} + \mathbf{h}(t)\mathbf{z}$$

The process $\mathbf{x}_i$ admits an ARMA representation if and only if there is an integer q and a set of p matrices $\mathbf{A}_i$, $i = 0, \dots, p$ such that the

Markov coefficients H_i satisfy the following linear difference equation starting from q:

$$\sum_{j=0}^{p} A_j H_{l-j} = 0 \, , \, l > q$$

Therefore, any ARMA process admits an infinite moving-average representation whose Markov coefficients satisfy a linear difference equation starting from a certain point. Conversely, any such linear infinite moving-average representation can be expressed parsimoniously in terms of an ARMA process.

Hankel Matrices and ARMA Models

For the theoretical analysis of ARMA processes it is also useful to restate the above conditions in terms of the Hankel infinite matrices.[2] It can be demonstrated that a process, stationary or not, which admits either the infinite moving average representation

$$\mathbf{x}_t = \sum_{i=0}^{\infty} H_i \boldsymbol{\varepsilon}_{t-i}$$

or a linear moving average model

$$\mathbf{x}_t = \sum_{i=0}^{t} H_i \boldsymbol{\varepsilon}_{t-i} + h(t)\mathbf{z}$$

also admits an ARMA representation if and only if the Hankel matrix formed with the sequence of its Markov coefficients has finite rank or, equivalently, a finite column rank or row rank.

STATE-SPACE REPRESENTATION

There is another representation of time series called **state-space models**. As we will see in this section, state-space models are equivalent to ARMA models. While the latter are typical of econometrics, state-space models originated in the domain of engineering and system analysis. Consider a

---

[2] Hankel matrices are explained in Chapter 5.

system defined for $t \geq 0$ and described by the following set of linear difference equations:

$$\begin{cases} \mathbf{z}_{t+1} = \mathbf{A}\mathbf{z}_t + \mathbf{B}\mathbf{u}_t \\ \mathbf{x}_t = \mathbf{C}\mathbf{z}_t + \mathbf{D}\mathbf{u}_t + \mathbf{E}\mathbf{s}_t \end{cases}$$

where

$\mathbf{x}_t$ = an n-dimensional vector
$\mathbf{z}_t$ = a k-dimensional vector
$\mathbf{u}_t$ = an m-dimensional vector
$\mathbf{s}_t$ = a k-dimensional vector
$\mathbf{A}$ = a $k{\times}k$ matrix
$\mathbf{B}$ = a $k{\times}m$ matrix
$\mathbf{C}$ = an $n{\times}k$ matrix
$\mathbf{D}$ = an $n{\times}m$ matrix
$\mathbf{E}$ = an $n{\times}k$ matrix

In the language of system theory, the variables $\mathbf{u}_t$ are called the **inputs** of the system, the variables $\mathbf{z}_t$ are called the **state variables** of the system, and the variables $\mathbf{x}_t$ are called the **observations** or **outputs** of the system, and $\mathbf{s}_t$ are deterministic terms that describe the deterministic components if they exist.

The system is formed by two equations. The first equation is a purely autoregressive AR(1) process that describes the dynamics of the state variables. The second equation is a static regression of the observations over the state variables, with inputs as innovations. Note that in this state-space representation the inputs $\mathbf{u}_t$ are the same in both equations. It is possible to reformulate state space models with different, independent inputs for the states, and the observables. The two representations are equivalent.

The fact that the first equation is a first order equation is not restrictive as any AR(p) system can be transformed into a first-order AR(1) system by adding variables. The new variables are defined as the lagged values of the old variables. This can be illustrated in the case of a single second-order autoregressive equation:

$$X_{t+1} = \alpha_0 X_t + \alpha_1 X_{t-1} + \varepsilon_{t+1}$$

Define $Y_t = X_{t-1}$. The previous equation is then equivalent to the first-order system:

$$X_{t+1} = \alpha_0 X_t + \alpha_1 Y_t + \varepsilon_{t+1}$$

$$Y_{t+1} = X_t$$

This transformation can be applied to systems of any order and with any number of equations. Recall from Chapter 9 that a similar procedures is applied to systems of differential equations.

Note that this state-space representation is not restricted to white noise inputs. A state-space representation is a mapping of inputs into outputs. Given a realization of the inputs u_t and an initial state z_0, the realization of the outputs x_t is fixed. The state-space representation can be seen as a **black-box**, characterized by A, B, C, D, and z_0 that maps any m-dimensional input sequence into an n-dimensional output sequence. The mapping $S = S(A,B,C,D,z_0)$ of $u \rightarrow x$ is called a **black-box representation** in system theory.

State-space representations are not unique. Given a state-space representation, there are infinite other state-space representations that implement the same mapping $u \rightarrow x$. In fact, given any nonsingular (invertible) matrix Q, it can be easily verified that

$$S(A, B, C, D, z_0) = S(QAQ^{-1}, QB, CQ^{-1}, D, Qz_0)$$

Any two representations that satisfy the above condition are called **equivalent**.

The **minimal size** of a system that admits a state-space representation is the minimum possible size k of the state vector. A representation is called **minimal** if its state vector has size k.

We can now establish the connection between state-space and infinite moving-average representations and the equivalence of ARMA and state-space representations. Consider a n-dimensional process x_t, which admits an infinite moving-average representation

$$x_t = \sum_{i=0}^{\infty} H_i \varepsilon_{t-i}$$

where ε_t is an n-dimensional, zero-mean, white noise process with non-singular variance-covariance matrix Ω and $H_0 = I$, or a linear moving average model

$$\mathbf{x}_t = \sum_{i=0}^{t} \mathbf{H}_i \boldsymbol{\varepsilon}_{t-i} + \mathbf{h}(t)\mathbf{z}$$

It can be demonstrated that this system admits the state-space representation:

$$\begin{cases} \mathbf{z}_{t+1} = \mathbf{A}\mathbf{z}_t + \mathbf{B}\boldsymbol{\varepsilon}_t \\ \mathbf{x}_t \quad = \mathbf{C}\mathbf{z}_t + \mathbf{D}\boldsymbol{\varepsilon}_t \end{cases}$$

if and only if its Hankel matrix is of finite rank. In other words, a time series which admits an infinite moving-average representation and has a Hankel matrix of finite rank can be generated by a state-space system where the inputs are the noise. Conversely, a state-space system with white-noise as inputs generates a series that can be represented as an infinite moving-average with a Hankel matrix of finite rank. This conclusion is valid for both stationary and nonstationary processes.

Equivalence of State-Space and ARMA Representations

We have seen in the previous section that a time series which admits an infinite moving-average representation can also be represented as an ARMA process if and only if its Hankel matrix is of finite rank. Therefore we can conclude that a time series admits an ARMA representation if and only if it admits a state-space representation. ARMA and state-space representations are equivalent.

To see the equivalence between ARMA and state-space models, consider a univariate ARMA(p,q) model

$$x_t = \sum_{i=1}^{p} \varphi_t x_{t-i} + \sum_{j=0}^{q} \psi_j \varepsilon_{t-j}, \ \psi_0 = 1$$

This ARMA model is equivalent to the following state-space model

$$x_t = \mathbf{C}z_t$$

$$z_t = \mathbf{A}z_{t-1} + \varepsilon_t$$

where

$$\mathbf{C} = [\varphi_1 \ \dots \ \varphi_p \ 1 \ \psi_1 \ \dots \ \psi_q]$$

$$z_t = \begin{bmatrix} x_{t-1} \\ \vdots \\ x_{t-p} \\ \varepsilon_t \\ \varepsilon_{t-1} \\ \vdots \\ \varepsilon_{t-q} \end{bmatrix} \quad \text{and } \mathbf{A} = \begin{bmatrix} -\varphi_1 & \cdots & -\varphi_p & 1 & \psi_1 & \cdots & \psi_{q-1} & \psi_q \\ 1 & \cdots & 0 & 0 & 0 & \cdots & 0 & 0 \\ \vdots & \vdots & \vdots & \vdots & \vdots & \vdots & \vdots & \vdots \\ 0 & \cdots & 1 & 0 & 0 & \cdots & 0 & 0 \\ 0 & \cdots & 0 & 0 & 0 & \cdots & 0 & 0 \\ \vdots & \vdots & \vdots & \vdots & \vdots & \vdots & \vdots & \vdots \\ 0 & \cdots & 0 & 0 & 0 & \cdots & 1 & 0 \end{bmatrix}$$

In general, the number of states will be larger than the number of observations. However, the number of states can be reduced model reduction techniques.[3]

The connection between ARMA and state-space models has a deep meaning that will be elucidated after introducing the concept of cointegration and after generalizing the concept of state-space modeling. As we will see, both cointegration and state-space modeling implement a fundamental **dimensionality reduction** which plays a key role in the econometrics of financial time series.

INTEGRATED SERIES AND TRENDS

This section introduces the fundamental notions of trend stationary series, difference stationary series, and integrated series. Consider a one-dimensional time series. A **trend stationary series** is a series formed by a deterministic trend plus a stationary process. It can be written as

$$X_t = f(t) + \varepsilon(t)$$

A trend stationary process can be transformed into a stationary process by subtracting the trend. Removing the deterministic trend entails that the deterministic trend is known. A trend stationary series is an example of an adjustment model.

Consider now a time series X_t. The operation of differencing a series consists of forming a new series $Y_t = \Delta X_t = X_t - X_{t-1}$. The operation of differencing can be repeated an arbitrary number of times. For instance, differencing twice the series X_t yields the following series:

---

[3] The idea of applying model reduction techniques to state-space models was advocated by, among others, Masanao Aoki. See M. Aoki and A. Havenner, "State Space Modeling of Multiple Time Series," *Econometric Reviews* (1991), pp. 10:1–59.

$$Z_t = \Delta Y_t = \Delta(\Delta X_t) = (X_t - X_{t-1}) - (X_{t-2} - X_{t-3})$$
$$= X_t - X_{t-1} - X_{t-2} + X_{t-3}$$

Differencing can be written in terms of the lag operator as

$$\Delta X_t^d = (1 - L)^d X_t$$

A **difference stationary series** is a series that is transformed into a stationary series by differencing. A difference stationary series can be written as

$$\Delta X_t = \mu + \varepsilon(t)$$

$$X_t = X_{t-1} + \mu + \varepsilon(t)$$

where $\varepsilon(t)$ is a zero-mean stationary process and μ is a constant. A trend stationary series with a linear trend is also difference stationary, if spacings are regular. The opposite is not generally true. A time series is said to be **integrated of order n** if it can be transformed into a stationary series by differencing n times.

Note that the concept of integrated series as defined above entails that a series extends on the entire time axis. If a series starts from a set of initial conditions, the difference sequence can only be asymptotically stationary.

There are a number of obvious differences between trend stationary and difference stationary series. A trend stationary series experiences stationary fluctuation, with constant variance, around an arbitrary trend. A difference stationary series meanders arbitrarily far from a linear trend, producing fluctuations of growing variance. The simplest example of difference stationary series is the random walk.

An integrated series is characterized by a **stochastic trend**. In fact, a difference stationary series can be written as

$$X_t = \mu t + \left[\sum_{s+0}^{t-1} \varepsilon(s)\right] + \varepsilon(t)$$

The difference $X_t - X_t^*$ between the value of a process at time t and the best affine prediction at time $t-1$ is called the **innovation** of the process. In the above linear equation, the stationary process $\varepsilon(t)$ is the innovation process. A key aspect of integrated processes is that innovations

$\varepsilon(t)$ never decay but keep on accumulating. In a trend stationary process, on the other hand, past innovations disappear at every new step.

These considerations carry over immediately in a multidimensional environment. Multidimensional trend stationary series will exhibit multiple trends, in principle one for each component. Multidimensional difference-stationary series will yield a stationary process after differencing.

Let's now see how these concepts fit into the ARMA framework, starting with univariate ARMA model. Recall that an ARIMA process is defined as an ARMA process in which the polynomial B has all roots outside the unit circle while the polynomial A has one or more roots equal to 1. In the latter case the process can be written as

$$A'(L)\Delta^d x_t = B(L)\varepsilon_t$$

$$A(L) = (1 - L)^d A'(L)$$

and we say that the process is integrated of order n. If initial conditions are supplied, the process can be inverted and the difference sequence is asymptotically stationary.

The notion of integrated processes carries over naturally in the multivariate case but with a subtle difference. Recall from earlier discussion in this chapter that an ARIMA model is an ARMA model:

$$\mathbf{A}(L)\mathbf{x}_t = \mathbf{B}(L)\boldsymbol{\varepsilon}_t$$

which satisfies two additional conditions: (1) $\det[\mathbf{B}(z)]$ has all its roots strictly outside of the unit circle, and (2) $\det[\mathbf{A}(z)]$ has all its roots outside the unit circle but with at least one root equal to 1.

Now suppose that, after differencing d times, the multivariate series $\Delta^d \mathbf{x}_t$ can be represented as follows:

$$\mathbf{A}'(L)\mathbf{x}_t = \mathbf{B}'(L)\boldsymbol{\varepsilon}_t, 1 \text{ with } \mathbf{A}'(L) = \mathbf{A}(L)\Delta^d$$

In this case, if (1) $\mathbf{B}'(z)$ is of order q and $\det[\mathbf{B}'(z)]$ has all its roots strictly outside of the unit circle and (2) $\mathbf{A}'(z)$ is of order p and $\det[\mathbf{A}'(z)]$ has all its roots outside the unit circle, then the process is called ARIMA(p,d,q). Not all ARIMA models can be put in this framework as different components might have a different order of integration.

Note that in an ARIMA(p,d,q) model each component series of the multivariate model is individually integrated. A multivariate series is integrated of order d if every component series is integrated of order d.

Note also that ARIMA processes are not invertible as infinite moving averages, but as discussed, they can be inverted in terms of a generic linear moving average model with stochastic initial conditions. In addition, the process in the d-differences is asymptotically stationary.

In both trend stationary and difference stationary processes, innovations can be serially autocorrelated. In the ARMA representations discussed in the previous section, innovations are serially uncorrelated white noise as all the autocorrelations are assumed to be modeled in the ARMA model. If there is residual autocorrelation, the ARMA or ARIMA model is somehow misspecified.

The notion of an integrated process is essentially linear. A process is integrated if stationary innovations keep on adding indefinitely. Note that innovations could, however, cumulate in ways other than addition, producing essentially nonlinear processes. In ARCH and GARCH processes for instance, innovations do not simply add to past innovations.

The behavior of integrated and nonintegrated time series is quite different and the estimation procedures are different as well. It is therefore important to ascertain if a series is integrated or not. Often a preliminary analysis to ascertain integratedness suggests what type of model should be used.

A number of statistical tests to ascertain if a univariate series is integrated are available. Perhaps the most widely used and known are the Dickey-Fuller (DF) and the Augmented Dickey-Fuller (ADF) tests. The DF test assumes as a null hypothesis that the series is integrated of order 1 with uncorrelated innovations. Under this assumption, the series can be written as a random walk in the following form:

$$X_{t+1} = \rho X_t + b + \varepsilon_t$$

$$\rho = 1$$

$$\varepsilon_t \text{ IID}$$

where IID is an independent and identical sequence (see Chapter 6).

In a sample generated by a model of this type, the value of ρ estimated on the sample is stochastic. Estimation can be performed with the **ordinary least square** (OLS) method. Dickey and Fuller[4] determined the theoretical distribution of ρ and computed the critical values of ρ that

---

[4] See William H. Greene, *Econometric Analysis: Fifth Edition* (Upper Sadle River, NJ: Prentice-Hall, 2003).

correspond to different confidence intervals. The theoretical distribution of ρ is determined computing a functional of the Brownian motion.

Given a sample of a series, for instance a series of log prices, application of the DF test entails computing the autoregressive parameter ρ on the given sample and comparing it with the known critical values for different confidence intervals. The strict hypothesis of random walk is too strong for most econometric applications. The DF test was extended to cover the case of correlated residuals that are modeled as a linear model. In the latter case, the DF test is called the **Augmented Dickey Fuller** or **ADF test**. The Phillips and Perron test is the DF test in the general case of autocorrelated residuals.

SUMMARY

- A time series is a discrete-time stochastic process, that is, a denumerable collection of random variables indexed by integer numbers.
- Any stationary time series admits an infinite moving average representation, that is to say, it can be represented as an infinite sum of white noise terms with appropriate coefficients.
- A time series is said to be invertible if it can also be represented as an infinite autoregression, that is, an infinite sum of all past terms with appropriate coefficients.
- ARMA models are parsimonious representations that involve only a finite number of moving average and autoregressive terms.
- An ARMA model is stationary if all the roots of the inverse characteristic equation of the AR or the MA part have roots with modulus strictly greater than one.
- A process is said to be integrated of order p if it becomes stationary after differencing p times.
- A state-space model is a regression of observable variables over an ARMA model of lower dimensionality.
- Every ARMA process admits a state-space representation.

CHAPTER 12

Financial Econometrics: Model Selection, Estimation, and Testing

In economics and finance theory models are rarely determined by strong theoretical considerations. Often, one or more families of models compete as plausible explanations of empirical data. Therefore, a specific family of models has to be selected and, within a given family, parameters have to be estimated. In this chapter we discuss criteria for model selection and parameter estimation.

MODEL SELECTION

Science works by making hypotheses and testing them. In the physical sciences, in particular, hypotheses are mathematical models typically tested with a very high level of precision under a variety of experimental settings. In the usual process of scientific inquiry, models can be understood as the product of human creativity. How the general concepts of science are formed and modified to account for new empirical evidence has been the subject of intense study.[1]

With the advent of fast computers, an automatic approach to science—and to the creative process in general—has been made possible. The Nobel laureate Herbert Simon was a strong advocate of the idea that the creative discovery process can be automated as an algorithmic (that is, step-by-step) search in a space of different possibilities.

---

[1] See for instance Thomas Kuhn, *The Structure of Scientific Revolutions: Third Edition* (Chicago: University of Chicago Press, 1996).

315

Since the pioneering work of Simon, many different search strategies have been proposed by statisticians and researchers in artificial intelligence. Most approaches to searching strategies are based on minimizing a "distance" from an objective. In the case of econometrics, the objective of searching is to find the best model that describes data. Searches are implemented by optimization of some functional.

The problem with the search approach is that the search space is infinite. Even if the search space can be made finite by applying some sort of discretization, its size for real-life problems is enormous. Any practical application of the idea of automatic searches requires that the search space is constrained. Econometrics, as well as statistics and data mining, constrains the search space by searching within given families of models.

In econometrics, the selection of the model family is typically performed on the basis of theoretical considerations as in the physical sciences. There is no way that an *unconstrained* search for models might yield positive results. Various tools might help to decide what family of models to adopt but, ultimately, model selection is a creative decision based on theoretical grounds. Once a family of models is selected, there are still choices to be made as regards the constraints to apply.

A typical top-down approach to constraining searches consists of starting with a broad family of unrestricted models, for instance, as explained later in this chapter, Vector Autoregressive Models (VAR), and then proceeding by constraining them, for instance by applying error correction constraints as discussed later. A typical bottom-up approach starts with a family of highly constrained models suggested by theory and then progressively relaxes constraints.

As there is a large amount of uncertainty in econometrics, model selection is never definitive and many different models may coexist as competing or synergic explanations of the same empirical facts, leading to model uncertainty. One can deal with this by giving weights to various models, e.g., predict with the weighted average of the prediction from several models. This process can be performed under a classical statistical framework or under a Bayesian statistical framework if prior probabilities can be assigned to models.[2] In this sense, econometrics is quite different from the physical sciences where the coexistence of competing theories is a rare event.

Econometric models generally entail the selection of parameters or even the selection of a specific model within a family. This is the realm of algorithmic searches, generally in the form of optimization procedures.

---

[2] A classical reference to Bayesian statistics with emphasis on statistical inference as decision theory is: Josè M. Bernardo and Adrian F.M. Smith, *Bayesian Theory* (Chichester, U.K.: John Wiley & Sons., 2000).

For instance, an econometrician might decide, on theoretical grounds, to adopt an ARMA family of models. Searches will then help determine parameters such as the order of the model and the estimation of the model parameter. We will return to the problem of determining the model complexity and estimating parameters in the following sections.

The above considerations apply to parametric models, that is, models that include parameters to be estimated. There are statistical models that appear to be nonparametric. Nonparametric models are typically based on the empirical estimation of probability distribution functions. Nonparametric models are typically simple models as there is no practical way to estimate empirically complex models.

In summary, econometrics follows a general scientific principle of formulation and testing of theoretical hypotheses. However, econometric hypotheses are generally formulated as a family of models with parameters to be optimized. Econometrics is thus an instance of a general process of learning.[3]

LEARNING AND MODEL COMPLEXITY

If one had an infinite amount of empirical data and an infinite amount of computational resources, econometric models could in principle be selected with arbitrary accuracy. However as empirical data are finite and, generally, scarce, many different models fit empirical data. The key problem of statistical learning is that most families of models can be parameterized so that they can fit a finite sample of data with arbitrary accuracy. For instance, if an arbitrary number of lags is allowed, an ARMA model can be made to fit any sample of data with arbitrary accuracy. A model of this type, however, would have very poor forecasting ability. The phenomenon of fitting sample data with excessive accuracy is called **overfitting**.

In the classical formulation of the physical sciences, overfitting is a nonissue as models are determined with theoretical considerations and are not adaptively fit to data. The problem of overfitting arises in connection with broad families of models that are able to fit any set of data with arbitrary accuracy. Avoiding overfitting is essentially a problem of

---

[3] Christian Gourieroux and Alain Monfort, *Statistics and Econometric Models* (Cambridge: Cambridge University Press, 1995); D.F. Hendry, "Econometrics: Alchemy or Science?" *Economica* 47 (1980), pp. 387–406, reprinted in D.F. Hendry, *Econometrics: Alchemy or Science?* (Oxford: Blackwell Publishers, 1993, and Oxford University Press, 2000); D.F. Hendry, *Dynamic Econometrics* (Oxford: Oxford University Press, 1995); and Vladimir N. Vapnik, *Statistical Learning Theory* (New York: John Wiley and Sons, 1998).

selecting the right model complexity. The complexity of a model is sometimes identified with its dimensionality, that is, with the number of free parameters of the model.

The problem of model complexity is intimately connected with the concept of algorithmic compressibility introduced in the 1960s independently by Andrei Kolmogorov[4] and Gregory Chaitin.[5] In intuitive terms, algorithmic complexity is defined as the minimum length of a program able to reproduce a given stream of data. If the minimum length of a program able to generate the given sequence is the same as the length of the data stream, then there is no algorithmic compressibility and data can be considered purely random. If, on the other hand, a short program is able to describe a long stream of data, then the level of algorithmic compressibility is high and scientific explanation is possible.

Models can only describe algorithmically compressible data. In a nutshell, the problem of learning is to find the right match between the algorithmic compressibility of the data and the dimensionality of the model. In practice, it is a question of implementing a trade-off between the accuracy of the estimate and the size of the sample.

Various methodologies have been proposed. Some early proposals are empirical rules of thumb, based on increasing the model complexity until there is no more gain in the forecasting accuracy of the model. These procedures require partitioning the data in training and test sets, so that models can be estimated on the **training data** and tested on the test data.

Procedures such as the **Box-Jenkins methodology** for the determination of the right ARMA model can be considered ad hoc methods based on specific characteristics of the model, for instance, the decay of the autocorrelation function in the case of ARMA models.

More general criteria for model complexity are based on results from information theory. The **Akaike Information Criteria** (AIC) proposed by Akaike[6] is a model selection criterion based on the information content of the model. The **Bayesian Information Criteria** (BIC) proposed by Schwartz[7] is another model selection criterion based on information theory in a Bayesian context.

---

[4] Andrei N. Kolmogorov, "Three Approaches to the Quantitative Definition of Information," *Problems of Information Transmission* 1 (1965), pp. 1–7.

[5] Gregory J. Chaitin, "On the Length of Programs for Computing Finite Binary Sequences," *Journal of Association Computational Mathematics* 13 (1965), pp. 547–569.

[6] H. Akaike, "Information Theory and an Extension of the Maximum Likelihood Principle," in B.N. Petrov and F. Csake (eds.), *Second International Symposium on Information Theory* (Budapest: Akademiai Kiado, 1973), pp. 267–281.

[7] Gideon Schwarz, "Estimating the Dimension of a Model," *Annals of Statistics* 6 (1978), pp. 461–464.

Recently, the theory of learning has been given a firm theoretical basis by Vladimir Vapnik and Alexey Chervonenkis.[8] The Vapnik-Chervonenkis (VC) theory of learning is a complex theoretical framework for learning that, when applicable, is able to give precise theoretical bounds to the learning abilities of models. The VC theory has been applied in the context of nonlinear models thus originating the so-called Support Vector Machines. Though its theoretical foundation is solid, the practical applicability of the VC theory is complex. It has not found yet a broad following in the world of econometrics.

MAXIMUM LIKELIHOOD ESTIMATE

Once the dimensionality of the model has been chosen, parameters need to be estimated. This is the somewhat firmer ground of statistical estimation. An **estimator** of a parameter is a statistic, that is, a function computed on the sample data. For instance, the empirical average

$$\bar{x} = \sum_{i=1}^{n} x_i$$

of an n-sample is an estimator of the population mean. An estimator is called **unbiased** if its expected value coincides with the theoretical parameter. An estimator is called **consistent** if a sequence of estimators computed on a sequence of samples whose size tends to infinity converges to the true theoretical value of the parameter.

An estimator is a stochastic quantity when computed on a sample. Given a model, the distribution of the estimator on samples of a given size is determined and can be computed. Different estimators of the same parameters will be characterized by different distributions when computed on samples of the same size. The variance of the estimator's distribution is an indication of the quality of the approximation offered by the estimator. An **efficient estimator** has the lowest possible variance. A lower bound of an estimator variance is given by the **Cramer-Rao bound**.

The Cramer-Rao bound is a theoretical lower bound to the accuracy of estimates. It can be formulated as follows. Suppose that a population sample $\mathbf{X}$ has a joint density $f(\mathbf{x}|\vartheta)$ that depends on a parameter ϑ and that $Y = g(\mathbf{X})$ is an unbiased estimator of ϑ. Y is a random variable that depends on the sample. The Cramer-Rao bound prescribes a lower

---

[8] Vapnik, *Statistical Learning Theory*.

bound for the variance σ_Y^2 of Y. In fact, under mild regularity conditions, it can be demonstrated that

$$\sigma_Y^2 = \text{var } Y \geq \frac{1}{I_n}$$

$$I_n = nE\left\{\left[\frac{\partial}{\partial\theta}\log f(\mathbf{X}|\theta)\right]^2\right\}$$

The Cramer-Rao bound can be generalized to the estimates of a k-vector of parameters $\boldsymbol{\theta}$. In this case, one must consider the Fisher information matrix $I(\boldsymbol{\theta})$ (see below) which is defined as the variance-covariance matrix of the vector

$$\frac{\partial}{\partial\theta}\log f(\mathbf{X}|\theta)$$

It can be demonstrated that the difference between the variance-covariance matrix of the vector $\boldsymbol{\theta}$ and the inverse of the Fisher information matrix is a nonnegative definite matrix.

This does not mean that the entries of the variance-covariance matrix of the vector $\boldsymbol{\theta}$ are systematically bigger than the elements of the inverse of the Fisher information matrix. However, we can determine a lower bound for the variance of each parameter θ_i. In fact, as all the diagonal elements a nonnegative definite matrix are nonnegative, the following relationship holds:

$$\sigma_{\theta_i}^2 = \text{var } \theta_i \geq \{\mathbf{I}^{-1}\}_{i,i}$$

In other words, the lower bound of the variance of the i-th parameter θ_i is the i-th diagonal entry of the inverse of the Fisher information matrix. Estimators that attain the Cramer-Rao bound are called **efficient estimators**. In the following section we will show that the **maximum likelihood (ML)** estimators attain the Cramer-Rao lower bound and are therefore efficient estimators.

There are various methodologies for determining estimators. An important methodology is based on the **maximum likelihood estimation (MLE)**. MLE is a principle of statistical estimation which, given a parametric model, prescribes choosing those parameters that maximize the likelihood of the sample under the model. This idea is highly intuitive: If one throws a coin and obtains 75 heads out of 100 trials, one believes that the probabilities of head and tail are ¾ and ¼ respectively and not that one is experiencing a very unlikely run of heads.

Suppose that an n-sample $\mathbf{x} = (x_1,...,x_n)$ with a joint density function $f(\mathbf{x}/\vartheta)$ is given. Suppose also that the density depends on a set of parameters ϑ. The **likelihood function** is any function $L(\vartheta)$ proportional to $f(\mathbf{x}/\vartheta)$:

$$L(\vartheta) \propto f(\mathbf{x}|\vartheta)$$

computed on the given sample. The MLE prescribes to choose those parameters ϑ that maximize the likelihood. If the sample is formed by independent draws from a density, then the likelihood is the product of individual likelihoods:

$$f(\mathbf{x}/\vartheta) = \prod_{i=1}^{n} f(x_i|\vartheta)$$

$$L(\vartheta) \propto \prod_{i=1}^{n} f(x_i|\vartheta)$$

In this case, in order to simplify calculations, one normally computes the **log-likelihood** defined as the logarithm of the likelihood, so that the product is transformed into a sum. As the logarithm is an increasing function, maximizing the likelihood or the log likelihood gives the same results.

The MLE is an estimation method which conforms to general scientific principles. From a statistical point of view, it has interesting properties. In fact, it can be demonstrated that a ML estimator is an efficient estimator (that is, an estimator which attains the minimum possible variance).

In the case of independent samples, the classical theory of ML estimators can be resumed as follows. Let Y_i, $i = 1,2,...,n$ be n independent variables with probability density functions $f_i(y_i|\theta)$, where θ is a k-vector of parameters to be estimated. Let the joint density of n independent observations $\mathbf{y} = (y_i)$ of the variables Y_i be

$$f(\mathbf{y}|\theta) = \prod_{i=1}^{n} f_i(y_i|\theta) = L(\mathbf{y}|\theta)$$

The log-likelihood function of the sample is

$$\log L(\mathbf{y}|\boldsymbol{\theta}) = \sum_{i=1}^{n} \log f_i(y_i|\boldsymbol{\theta})$$

The **Fisher score function** *u* is defined as the *k*-vector of the first derivatives of the log-likelihood:

$$\mathbf{u}(\boldsymbol{\theta}) = [u_j(\boldsymbol{\theta})]$$

$$u_j(\boldsymbol{\theta}) = \frac{\partial}{\partial \theta_j} \log L(\mathbf{y}|\boldsymbol{\theta}), j = 1,2,...,k$$

The ML estimator $\hat{\boldsymbol{\theta}}$ of the true parameter $\boldsymbol{\theta}$ is obtained equating the score to zero: $\mathbf{u}(\hat{\boldsymbol{\theta}}) = 0$. It can be demonstrated that the mean of the score evaluated at the true parameter value vanishes: $E[\mathbf{u}(\boldsymbol{\theta})] = 0$. The variance-covariance matrix of the score is called the **Fisher information matrix**:

$$\text{var/cov}[\mathbf{u}(\boldsymbol{\theta})] = E[\mathbf{u}(\boldsymbol{\theta})\mathbf{u}^T(\boldsymbol{\theta})] = \mathbf{I}(\boldsymbol{\theta})$$

Under mild regularity conditions it can be demonstrated that the following relationship holds:

$$\mathbf{I}(\boldsymbol{\theta}) = -E\left[\frac{\partial^2 \log L(\boldsymbol{\theta})}{\partial \theta_i \partial \theta_j}\right]$$

The matrix of the second derivatives on the right side is called the **observed information matrix**. The classical theory of ML estimators states that, in large samples, the distribution of the ML estimator $\hat{\boldsymbol{\theta}}$ of $\boldsymbol{\theta}$ is approximately normal with parameters $[\boldsymbol{\theta}, \mathbf{I}^{-1}(\boldsymbol{\theta})]$, that is, the following relationship holds:

$$\hat{\boldsymbol{\theta}} \sim N[\boldsymbol{\theta}, \mathbf{I}^{-1}(\boldsymbol{\theta})]$$

This relationship tells us that ML estimators are efficient estimators as their variance attains the Cramer-Rao bound. The asymptotic joint normality of the ML estimators can be used to construct a number of tests and confidence intervals.

Suppose that one wants to estimate a regressive model $Y = aX + b + \varepsilon$ from a sample of n pairs (y_i, x_i). The linear regressive model is characterized by the two parameters a and b, which can be estimated with the **Ordinary Least Square** (OLS) method. The OLS computes the straight line that minimizes the sum of the squares of the distances of the samples from that straight line.

In a probabilistic setting, the estimates $\hat{a}, \hat{b}$ of the two parameters a and b depend on the sample. They obey a distribution that depends on the distribution of the errors ε. It can be demonstrated that, if the errors are normally distributed IID sequences than the OLS estimators $\hat{a}, \hat{b}$ are unbiased ML estimators. They are therefore efficient estimators. If the errors are IID variables with finite variance but are not normally distributed, then the OLS estimators $\hat{a}, \hat{b}$ of the two parameters a and b are unbiased estimators but not necessarily ML estimators.

The OLS estimation procedure is very general. It can be demonstrated that any linear unconstrained autoregressive model with normal innovations can be estimated with OLS estimators and that the ensuing estimators are unbiased ML estimators and thus efficient estimators.

One can also estimate directly the moments of a distribution. In particular, in a multivariate environment we have to estimate the variance-covariance matrix Ω. It can be demonstrated that the variance-covariance matrix can be estimated through empirical variances and covariances. Consider two random variables X, Y.

The **empirical covariance** between the two variables is defined as follows:

$$\hat{\sigma}_{X,Y} = \frac{1}{n} \sum_{i=1}^{n} (X_i - \overline{X})(Y_i - \overline{Y})$$

where the empirical means of the variables are:

$$\overline{X} = \frac{1}{n} \sum_{i=1}^{n} X_i$$

$$\overline{Y} = \frac{1}{n} \sum_{i=1}^{n} Y_i$$

The **correlation coefficient** is the covariance normalized with the product of the respective empirical standard deviations:

$$\hat{\rho}_{X,\,Y} = \frac{\hat{\sigma}_{X,\,Y}}{\hat{\sigma}_X \hat{\sigma}_Y}$$

Empirical standard deviations are defined as follows:

$$\hat{\sigma}_X = \sqrt{\sum_{i=1}^{n} (X_i - \bar{X})^2}$$

$$\hat{\sigma}_Y = \sqrt{\sum_{i=1}^{n} (Y_i - \bar{Y})^2}$$

It can be demonstrated that the empirical covariance matrix is an unbiased estimator of the variance-covariance matrix. If innovations are jointly normally distributed, it is also an ML estimator.

LINEAR MODELS OF FINANCIAL TIME SERIES

Let's now apply previous general theoretical considerations and those of the previous chapter to modeling financial time series. This section describes linear models of financial time series using the concepts introduced in the previous sections. Linear financial models are regressive and/or autoregressive models where a series is regressed over exogenous variables and/or its own past under a number of constraints.

In the practice of asset and portfolio management, models of prices, returns, and rates are used as inputs to asset selection methodologies such as semiautomated investment processes, heuristic computational procedures, or full-fledged optimization procedures. The following chapters on methods for asset management will explain how the computational models described in this and the following chapter translate into asset and portfolio management strategies. We will start with random walk models and progressively introduce more complex factor-based models.

RANDOM WALK MODELS

Consider a time series of prices P_t of a financial asset. Assume there are no cash payouts. The **simple net return** of the asset between periods $t - 1$ and t is defined as

$$R_t = \frac{P_t - P_{t-1}}{P_{t-1}} = \frac{P_t}{P_{t-1}} - 1$$

From this definition it is clear that the **compound return** $R_t(k)$ over k periods is:

$$R_t(k) = \frac{P_t}{P_{t-k}} - 1 = \prod_{i=0}^{k-1} \frac{P_{t-i}}{P_{t-i+1}} - 1 = \prod_{i=0}^{k-1} (R_{t-i}+1) - 1$$

Consider now the logarithms of prices and returns:

$$p_t = \log P_t$$

$$r_t = \log (1 + R_t)$$

$$r_t(k) = \log [1 + R_t(k)]$$

Following standard usage, we denote prices and returns with upper case letters and their logarithms with lower case letters. As the logarithms of a product is the sum of the logarithms, we can write:

$$r_t = \log (1 + R_t) = \log \frac{P_t}{P_{t-1}} = p_t - p_{t-1}$$

$$r_t(k) = \log [1 + R_t(k)] = r_t + r_{t-1} + \dots + r_{t-k+1}$$

Note that for real-world price time series, if the time interval is small, the numerical value of returns will also be small. Therefore, as a first approximation, we can write

$$r_t = \log (1 + R_t) \approx R_t$$

The simplest model of equity prices consists in assuming that logarithmic returns are an IID sequence. Under this assumption we can write: $r_t = \mu + \varepsilon_t$, where μ is a constant and ε_t is a white noise, that is, a zero-mean, finite-variance IID sequence. Under this model we can write

$$p_t = p_{t-1} + \mu + \varepsilon_t$$

A time series of this form is called an **arithmetic random walk**. It is a generalization of the simple random walk that was introduced in Chapter 6. The arithmetic random walk is the simplest example of an integrated process.

Let's go back to simple net returns. From the above definition, it is clear that we can write

$$1 + R_t = e^{\mu + \varepsilon_t}$$

If the white noise is normally distributed, then the returns R_t are lognormally distributed. Recall that we found a simple correspondence between a geometric Brownian motion with drift and an arithmetic Brownian motion with drift. In fact, using Itô's Lemma, we found that, if the process S_t follows a geometric Brownian motion with drift

$$\frac{dS}{S} = \mu dt + \sigma dB$$

its logarithm $s_t = \log S_t$ then follows the arithmetic Brownian motion with drift:

$$ds = \left(\mu - \frac{1}{2}\sigma^2\right)dt + \sigma dB$$

In discrete time, there is no equivalent simple formula as we have to integrate over a finite time step. If the logarithms of prices follow a discrete-time arithmetic random walk with normal increments, the prices themselves follow a time series with lognormal multiplicative increments written as

$$P_t = (1 + R_t)P_{t-1} = e^{\mu + \varepsilon_t}P_{t-1}$$

The arithmetic random walk model of log price processes is suggested by theoretical considerations of market efficiency. As we have seen in Chapter 3, it was Bachelier who first suggested Brownian motion as a model of stock prices. Recall that the Brownian motion is the continuous-time version of the random walk. Fama and Samuelson formally introduced the notion of efficient markets which makes it reasonable to assume that log price processes evolve as random walks.

The question of the empirical adequacy of the random walk model is very important from the practical point of view. Whatever notion or tools for financial optimization one adopts, a stock price model is a basic ingredient. Therefore substantial efforts have been devoted to proving or disproving the random walk hypothesis.[9]

There are many statistical tests aimed at testing the random walk hypothesis. A typical test takes the random walk as a null hypothesis. The number of runs (that is, consecutive sequences of positive or negative returns) and the linear growth of the variance are parameters used in classical random walk tests. More recent tests are based on the work of Aldous and Diaconis[10] on the distribution of sequences of positive and negative returns.

There is no definite response. Typical tests fail to reject the null hypothesis of random walk behavior with a high level of confidence on a large percentage of equity price processes. This does not mean that the random walk hypothesis is confirmed, but only that it is a reasonable first approximation. As we will see in the following sections, other models have been proposed.

CORRELATION

Before moving on to more sophisticated models, let's consider random walk models of portfolios of equities as opposed to single price processes. Let's therefore consider a multivariate random walk model of an equity portfolio assuming that each log price process evolves as an arithmetic random walk. We will consider a set of n time series $p_{i,t}$, $i = 1, ..., n$ that represent log price processes. Suppose that each time series is a random walk written as

$$p_{i,t} = p_{i,t-1} + \mu_i + \varepsilon_{i,t}$$

A multivariate random walk can be represented in vector form as follows:

---

[9] See John Y. Campbell, Andrew W. Lo, and A. Craig MacKinley, *The Econometrics of Financial Markets* (Princeton, NJ: Princeton University Press, 1997).

[10] David Aldous and Persi Diaconis, "Shuffling Cards and Stopping Times," *American Mathematical Monthly* 8 (1986), pp. 333–348.

$$p_t = p_{t-1} + \mu + \varepsilon_t$$

The key difference with respect to univariate random walks is that one needs to consider cross correlations as the random disturbances ε_t will be characterized by a covariance matrix Ω whose entries $\sigma_{i,j}$ are the covariances between asset i and asset j. Covariance and correlation are one way of expressing the notion of functional dependence between random variables. Consider two random variables X, Y.

The **covariance** between the two variables is defined as

$$\sigma_{X,Y} = \text{Cov}(X, Y) = E\{[X - E(X)][Y - E(Y)]\} = E(XY) - E(X)E(Y)$$

The **correlation coefficient** is the covariance normalized with the product of the respective standard deviations:

$$\rho_{X,Y} = \text{Corr}(X, Y) = \frac{\text{Cov}(X, Y)}{\sqrt{\text{Var}(X)\text{Var}(Y)}}$$

$$= \frac{\sigma_{X,Y}}{\sigma_X \sigma_Y}$$

The correlation coefficient expresses a measure of linear dependence. Suppose that the variables X, Y have finite mean and variance and that are linearly dependent so that

$$Y = aX + b + \varepsilon$$

The above relationship is called a **linear regression** (see Chapter 6). It can be demonstrated that the correlation coefficient between X and Y is related to the parameter a in the following way:

$$a = \rho_{X,Y} \frac{\sigma_X}{\sigma_Y}$$

The correlation coefficient can assume values between -1 and $+1$ inclusive. It can be demonstrated that the variables X, Y are proportional without any noise term if and only if the correlation coefficient is $+/-1$. If the regression has a noise term, then the correlation coefficient assumes a value intermediate between -1 and $+1$. If variables are independent, then the correlation coefficient is zero. The converse is not true. In fact, it is possible that two variables exhibit nonlinear dependence though the correlation coefficient is zero. Uncorrelated variables are not necessarily independent. If the variables X, Y have a nonlinear dependence relationship, then the correlation coefficient might become meaningless.[11]

RANDOM MATRICES

Modeling log prices of equity portfolios as a set of correlated arithmetic random walks is only a rough approximation in the sense that this model, when estimated, has poor forecasting ability. A key reason is that the full variance-covariance matrix is unstable. This fact can be ascertained in different ways. A simple test is the computation of the variance-covariance matrix over a moving window. If one performs this computation on a broad set of equity price processes such as the S&P 500, the result is a matrix that fluctuates in a nearly random way although the average correlation level is high, in the range of 15 to 17%. Exhibit 12.1 illustrates the amount of fluctuations in a correlation matrix estimated over a moving window. The plot represents the average when the sampling window moves.

An evaluation of the random nature of the variance-covariance matrix was proposed by Laloux, Cizeau, Bouchaud, and Potters[12] using the **Random Matrices Theory** (RMT). This theory was developed in the 1950s in the domain of quantum physics.[13] A random matrix is the variance covariance matrix of a set of independent random walks. As such, its entries are a set of zero-mean independent and identically distributed variables. The mean of the random correlation coefficients is zero as these coefficients have a symmetrical distribution in the range $[-1, +1]$.

Interesting results can be demonstrated in the case that both the number of sample points M and the number N of time series tend to infinity. Suppose that both T and N tend to infinity with a fixed ratio

$$Q = M/N \geq 1$$

[11] See Paul Embrechts, Filip Lindskog, and Alexander McNeil, "Modelling Dependence with Copulas and Applications to Risk Management," Chapter 8 in S. Rachev (ed.), *Handbook of Heavy Tailed Distributions in Finance* (Amsterdam: Elsevier/North Holland, 2003).

[12] L. Laloux, P. Cizeau, J.-P. Bouchaud, and M. Potters, "Noise Dressing of Financial Correlation Matrices," *Physics Review Letter* 83 (1999), pp. 1467–1470.

[13] M.L. Mehta, *Random Matrix Theory* (New York: Academic Press, 1995).

EXHIBIT 12.1   Fluctuations of the Variance-Covariance Matrix

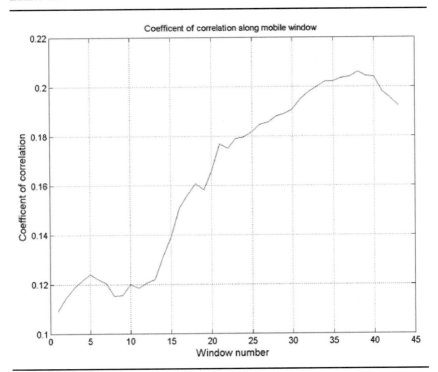

It can then be demonstrated that the density of eigenvalues of the random matrix tends to the following distribution:

$$\rho(\lambda) = \frac{Q}{2\pi\sigma^2} \cdot \frac{\sqrt{(\lambda_{max} - \lambda)(\lambda_{min} - \lambda)}}{\lambda}$$

$$M, N \to \infty, Q = M/N \geq 1$$

$$\lambda_{max, min} = \sigma^2 \left[1 + \frac{1}{Q} \pm 2\sqrt{\frac{1}{Q}}\right]$$

where σ^2 is the average eigenvalue of the matrix. Exhibit 12.2 illustrates the theoretical function and a sample computed on 500 simulated independent random walks. The shape of the distribution of the eigenvalues is the signature of randomness.

EXHIBIT 12.2 Theoretical Distribution of the Eigenvalues in a Random Matrix and Distribution of the Eigenvalues in a Sample of 500 Simulated Independent Random Walks

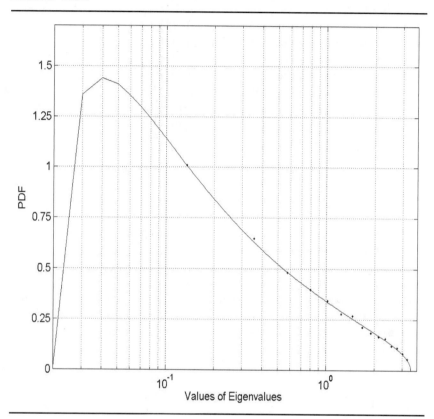

If the variance-covariance matrix entries do not have a zero mean, then the spectrum of the eigenvalues is considerably different. Malevergne and Sornette[14] demonstrate that if the entries of the variance-covariance matrix are all equal—with the obvious exception of the elements on the diagonal—then a very large eigenvalue appears while all the others are equal to a single degenerate eigenvalue. The eigenvector corresponding to the large eigenvalue has all components proportional to 1, that is, its components have equal weights.

---

[14] Y. Malevergne and D. Sornette, "Collective Origin of the Coexistence of Apparent RMT Noise and Factors in Large Sample Correlation Matrices," Cond-Mat 02/0115, 1, no. 4 (October 2002).

If the entries of the variance-covariance matrix are random but with nonzero average, it can be demonstrated that a large eigenvalue still appears. However, a small number of large eigenvalues also appear while the bulk of the distribution resembles that of a random matrix. The eigenvector corresponding to the largest eigenvalue includes all components with all equal weights proportional to 1.

If we compute the distribution of the eigenvalues of the variance-covariance matrix of the S&P 500 over a window of two years, we obtain a distribution of eigenvalues which is close to the distribution of a random matrix with some exception. In particular, the empirical distribution of eigenvalues fits well the theoretical distribution with the exception of a small number of eigenvalues that have much larger values. Following the reasoning of Malevergne and Sornette, the existence of a large eigenvalue with a corresponding eigenvector of 1s in a large variance-covariance matrix arises naturally in cases where correlations have a random distribution with a nonzero mean.

This analysis shows that there is little information in the variance-covariance matrix of a large portfolio. Only a few eigenvalues carry information while the others are simply the result of statistical fluctuations in the sample correlation. Note that it is the entire matrix which is responsible for the structure of eigenvalues, not just a few highly correlated assets. This can be clearly seen in the case of a variance-covariance matrix whose entries are all equal. Clearly there is no privileged correlation between any couple of assets but a very large eigenvalue nevertheless appears.

MULTIFACTOR MODELS

The analysis of the previous section demonstrates that modeling an equity portfolio as a set of correlated random walks is only a rough approximation. Though the random walk test cannot be rejected at the level of individual securities and though there are significant empirical correlations between securities, the global structure of large portfolios is more intricate than a set of correlated random walks.

Failure in modeling log price processes as correlated random walks might happen for several reasons: There might be nonlinearities in the DGPs of price processes; dependence between log price processes might not be linear. There might be structural changes (which are a discrete form of nonlinearity). What is empirically ascertained is that the variance-covariance matrix of a large set of price processes is not stable and that its eigenvalues have a distribution that resembles the distribution of the eigenvalues of a random matrix with the exception of a few large eigenvalues.

These considerations lead to adopting models where the correlation structure is concentrated in a number of factors. A model for asset log prices which is compatible with the findings on the correlation matrices is the generic multifactor model that we can write as follows:

$$\mathbf{x} = \mathbf{a} + \mathbf{Bf} + \boldsymbol{\varepsilon}$$

where $\mathbf{x}$ is the n-vector of the process to be modeled, $\mathbf{f}$ is a k-vector of common factors with $k \ll n$, $\mathbf{a}$ is an n-vector of constants, $\mathbf{B}$ is an $n \times k$ matrix and $\boldsymbol{\varepsilon}$ is an n-vector of random disturbances such that:

$$E[\boldsymbol{\varepsilon}|\mathbf{f}] = 0$$

$$E[\boldsymbol{\varepsilon}\boldsymbol{\varepsilon}'|\mathbf{f}] = \Sigma$$

The key advantage of multifactor models, that we discuss in Chapter 18, is that the number of factors is generally much smaller than the number of variables, thus implementing a substantial dimensionality reduction. Note that in the above form, a multifactor model is a static regression model, not a dynamic econometric model; it describes the static regression relationship of the process variables on factors.

As explained in the previous chapter, state-space models combine a multifactor regression model with an autoregressive model for the factors. This combination of autoregressive models for the factors and of multifactor regressive models for the process variables result in important families of dynamic models including models of cointegrating relationships.

The latter point raises an important issue in modern econometrics. In principle, the variables $\mathbf{x}$ can be any sort of economic or financial quantities. However, multifactor models were developed and are used mainly in the context of financial econometrics. In that context, the variables $\mathbf{x}$ generally represent returns. This is by no means the only possible or useful interpretation of factor models. In fact, cointegration models are effectively multifactor models whose main variables are log prices and whose factors are the common trends.

There are therefore two different interpretations for and uses of factor models in financial econometrics. The most widely used factor models are models of returns such that factorization implements a dimensionality reduction. However, more recently factor models—either as cointegrated models of returns and prices or, equivalently, as state-space models of prices—have been introduced to capture additional economic information contained in asset prices, especially equity prices.[15]

CAPM

Let's begin by discussing multifactor models of returns. There are many different ways of writing such models depending on the nature of the factors. The first, and most famous, factor model is the **Capital Asset Pricing Model** (CAPM) developed by Sharpe-Lintner-Mossin. In the CAPM there is only one factor given by the portfolio of all investable assets. Each log price process can be written as follows:

$$x_i = \beta_i + \alpha_i f + \sigma$$

In its original formulation, the CAPM was derived as a general equilibrium theory; the actual asset price process is the fixed point where the collective action of all agents trying to maximize their utility does not produce any change in the price process, thus the situation of equilibrium.

CAPM assumes the joint normality of returns and the independence of returns from one period to another; the single factor evolves as an arithmetic random walk. This version of the CAPM is conceptually restrictive and difficult to test given that the market portfolio, which is the portfolio of all investable assets, is difficult to define and measure.

A later version of CAPM called Conditional CAPM or C(CAPM) was proposed. Essentially, the Conditional CAPM assumes that there is only one factor driving all prices, but does not impose the restriction that such a factor is the market portfolio or that it evolves as a random walk.

---

[15] The literature on dynamic factor models is ample. Here is a selection of widely quoted papers: M. Forni, M. Hallin, M. Lippi, and L. Reichlin, "The Generalized Dynamic Factor Model: Identification and Estimation," *Review of Economics and Statistics* 82, no. 4 (2000), pp. 540–554; J.F. Geweke, "The Dynamic Factor Analysis of Economic Time-Series Models" in D.J. Aigner and A.S. Goldberger (eds.) *Latent Variables in Socioeconomic Models* (Amsterdam: North Holland, 1981); J.F. Geweke and K.J. Singleton, "Maximum Likelihood 'Confirmatory' Factor Analysis of Economic Time Series," *International Economic Review* 22, no. 1, pp. 37–54; D. Quah and T.J. Sargent, "A Dynamic Index Model for Large Cross Sections," in J.H. Stock and M.W. Watson (eds.), *Business Cycles, Indicators and Forecasting* (Chicago, IL: The University of Chicago Press, 1993), pp. 285–309; J.H. Stock and M.W. Watson, "Diffusion Indexes," NBER Working Paper W6702, 1998; J.H. Stock and M.W. Watson, "New Indexes of Coincident and Leading Economic Indications," in O.J. Blanchard and S. Fischer (eds.), NBER Macroeconomics Annual 1989 (Cambridge, MA: M.I.T. Press, 1989); M.W. Watson and R.F. Engle, "Alternative Algorithms for Estimation of Dynamic MIMIC, Factor, and Time Varying Coefficient Regression Models," *Journal of Econometrics* 23 (1983), pp. 385–400.

Asset Pricing Theory (APT) Models

Asset pricing models based on a single factor have been criticized as unduly restrictive and truly multifactor models have been proposed. In a multifactor model of asset prices, the restriction of absence of arbitrage must be imposed. The Arbitrage Pricing Theory (APT) of Roll and Ross allows multiple factors and fixes all other price processes on the basis of absence of arbitrage (see Chapter 14).

APT models can be divided into two different categories in function of how factors are treated. In the one, factors are portfolios or exogenous variables such as macroeconomic factors; in the other, factors are either modeled or not.

First consider the case of given exogenous factors. In this case, the APT model must be estimated as a constrained regressive model. Constraints typically forbid the possibility of using simple ordinary least square (OLS) estimates. Thus the estimation procedures are generally based on the direct application of Maximum Likelihood principles.

PCA and Factor Models

If factors are not given, they must be determined with statistical learning techniques. Given the variance-covariance matrix, if factors are portfolios, one can determine factors using the technique of Principal Components Analysis (PCA).

Principal Components Analysis (PCA) implements a dimensionality reduction of a set of observations. The concept of PCA is the following. Consider a set of n time series X_i, for example the 500 series of returns of the S&P 500. Consider next a linear combination of these series, that is, a portfolio of securities. Each portfolio P is identified by an n-vector of weights ω_P and is characterized by a variance σ_P^2. In general, the variance σ_P^2 will depend on the portfolio's weights ω_P. Lastly consider a normalized portfolio which has the largest possible variance. In this context, a normalized portfolio is a portfolio such that the squares of the weights sum to one.

If we assume that returns are IID sequences, jointly normally distributed with variance-covariance matrix Ω, a lengthy direct calculation demonstrates that each portfolio's return will be normally distributed with variance

$$\sigma_P^2 = \omega_P^T \Omega \omega_P$$

Therefore the normalized portfolio of maximum variance can be determined in the following way:

$$\text{Maximize } \boldsymbol{\omega}_P^T \boldsymbol{\Omega} \boldsymbol{\omega}_P$$

subject to the normalization condition

$$\boldsymbol{\omega}_P^T \boldsymbol{\omega}_P = 1$$

where the product is a scalar product. It can be demonstrated that the solution of this problem is the eigenvector $\boldsymbol{\omega}_1$ corresponding to the largest eigenvalue λ_1 of the variance-covariance matrix $\boldsymbol{\Omega}$. As $\boldsymbol{\Omega}$ is a variance-covariance matrix, the eigenvalues are all real.

Consider next the set of all normalized portfolios orthogonal to $\boldsymbol{\omega}_1$, that is, portfolios completely uncorrelated with $\boldsymbol{\omega}_1$. These portfolios are identified by the following relationship:

$$\boldsymbol{\omega}_1^T \boldsymbol{\omega}_P = \boldsymbol{\omega}_P^T \boldsymbol{\omega}_1 = 0$$

We can repeat the previous reasoning. Among this set, the portfolio of maximum variance is given by the eigenvector $\boldsymbol{\omega}_2$ corresponding to the second largest eigenvalue λ_2 of the variance-covariance matrix $\boldsymbol{\Omega}$. If there are n distinct eigenvalues, we can repeat this process n times. In this way, we determine the n portfolios P_i of maximum variance. The weights of these portfolios are the ortho-normal eigenvectors of the variance-covariance matrix $\boldsymbol{\Omega}$. Note that each portfolio is a time series which is a linear combination of the original time series X_i. The coefficients are the portfolios' weights.

These portfolios of maximum variance are all mutually uncorrelated. It can be demonstrated that we can recover all the original return time series as linear combinations of these portfolios:

$$X_i = \sum_{i=1}^{n} \alpha_i P_i$$

Thus far we have succeeded in replacing the original n correlated time series X_i with n uncorrelated time series P_i with the additional insight that each X_i is a linear combination of the P_i. Suppose now that only p of the portfolios P_i have a significant variance, while the remaining $n-p$ have very small variances. We can then implement a dimensionality reduction by choosing only those portfolios whose variance is significantly different from zero. Let's call these portfolios **factors** *F*.

It is clear that we can approximately represent each series X_i as a linear combination of the factors plus a small uncorrelated noise. In fact we can write

$$X_i = \sum_{i=1}^{p} \alpha_i F_i + \sum_{i=p+1}^{n} \alpha_i P_i = \sum_{i=1}^{p} \alpha_i F_i + \varepsilon$$

where the last term is a noise term. Therefore to implement PCA one computes the eigenvalues and the eigenvectors of the variance-covariance matrix and chooses the eigenvalues significantly different from zero. The corresponding eigenvectors are the weights of portfolios that form the factors. Criteria of choice are somewhat arbitrary.

Note that PCA works either on the variance-covariance matrix or on the correlation matrix. The technique is the same but results are generally different. PCA applied to the variance-covariance matrix is sensitive to the units of measurement, which determine variances and covariances. This observation does not apply to returns, which are dimensionless quantities. However, if PCA is applied to prices and not to returns, the currency in which prices are expressed matters; one obtains different results in different currencies. In these cases, it might be preferable to work with the correlation matrix.

We have described PCA in the case of time series, which is the relevant case in econometrics. However PCA is a generalized dimensionality reduction technique applicable to any set of multidimensional observations. It admits a simple geometrical interpretation which can be easily visualized in the three-dimensional case. Suppose a cloud of points in the three-dimensional Euclidean space is given. PCA finds the planes that cut the cloud of points in such a way as to obtain the maximum variance.

Suppose that there is a **strict factor structure**, which means that returns exactly follow the model

$$r = a + Bf + \varepsilon$$

with

$$E[\varepsilon|f] = 0$$

$$E[\varepsilon\varepsilon'|f] = \Sigma$$

The matrix **B** can be obtained diagonalizing the variance-covariance matrix. In general, the structure of factors will not be strict and one will try to find an approximation by choosing only the largest eigenvalues.

Factors can also be obtained through another statistical procedure called **factor analysis**. Factor analysis estimates factors using a maximum likelihood procedure. Suppose that factors are not portfolios but exogenous variables, such as macroeconomic variables. In this case, the factor structure is given and the estimation problem becomes one of estimating a regression relationship. This problem can be solved through maximum likelihood estimates.

Let's now summarize the previous discussion on multifactor models. From the point of view of econometrics, the key justification of factor models is dimensionality reduction. It can be empirically ascertained that the empirical variance-covariance matrices computed over reasonable time windows are unstable and noisy. This might be due to various reasons, in particular to the fact that functional dependence between variables is more complex than a simple structure of linear correlation. The key problem is to extract maximum information from noise. Multifactor models attempt to provide a solution to this problem within the domain of simple regressive models. There are different families of multifactor models: regression over given exogenous variables, factor analysis under the assumption of multivariate random walks, state-space models. In addition, multifactor models might be applied to both returns and prices.

VECTOR AUTOREGRESSIVE MODELS

The next step is to model factors. This requires introducing a broad family of ARMA models called **Vector Autoregressive (VAR) Models**. A VAR model is a multivariate AR(n) model. In a VAR model the current value of each variable is a linear function of the past values of all variables plus random disturbances. In full generality, a VAR model can be written as follows:

$$\mathbf{x}_t = \mathbf{A}_1 \mathbf{x}_{t-1} + \mathbf{A}_2 \mathbf{x}_{t-2} + \dots + \mathbf{A}_p \mathbf{x}_{t-p} + \mathbf{D}\mathbf{s}_t + \boldsymbol{\varepsilon}_t$$

where $\mathbf{x}_t = (x_{1,t}, \dots, x_{n,t})$ is a multivariate stochastic time series in vector notation, $\mathbf{A}_i, i = 1,2,\dots,p$, and $\mathbf{D}$ are deterministic $n \times n$ matrices, $\boldsymbol{\varepsilon}_t = \varepsilon_{1,t}, \dots, \varepsilon_{n,t}$ is a multivariate white noise with variance-covariance matrix $\boldsymbol{\Omega} = \{\sigma_{ij}\}$ and $\mathbf{s}_t = s_{1,t}, \dots, s_{n,t}$ is a vector of deterministic terms. Using the lag-operator L notation, a VAR model can be written in the following form:

$$\mathbf{x}_t = (\mathbf{A}_1 L + \mathbf{A}_2 L^2 + \dots + \mathbf{A}_n L^N)\mathbf{x}_t + \mathbf{D}\mathbf{s}_t + \boldsymbol{\varepsilon}_t$$

VAR models can be written in equivalent forms that will be useful in the next section. In particular, a VAR model can be written in terms of the differences $\Delta \mathbf{x}_t$ in the following error-correction form:

$$\Delta \mathbf{x}_t = (\mathbf{\Phi}_1 L + \mathbf{\Phi}_2 L^2 + \ldots + \mathbf{\Phi}_{n-1} L^{n-1})\Delta \mathbf{x}_t + \mathbf{\Pi} L^{n-1} \mathbf{x}_t + \mathbf{D}\mathbf{s}_t + \boldsymbol{\varepsilon}_t$$

where the first $n - 1$ terms are in first differences and the last term is in levels.

The multivariate random walk model of log prices is the simplest VAR model:

$$\mathbf{x}_t = \mathbf{x}_t + \mathbf{m} + \boldsymbol{\varepsilon}_t$$

$$\Delta \mathbf{x}_t = \mathbf{m} + \boldsymbol{\varepsilon}_t$$

Note that in this model log prices are autoregressive while returns (that is, the first differences) are simply correlated multivariate white noise plus a constant term.

As we know from our discussion on ARMA models (see Chapter 11), the stationarity and stability properties of a VAR model depend on the roots of the polynomial matrix

$$\mathbf{A}_1 z + \mathbf{A}_2 z^2 + \ldots + \mathbf{A}_n z^N$$

In particular, if all the roots of the above polynomial are strictly outside the unit circle, then the VAR process is stationary. In this case, the VAR process can be inverted and rewritten as an infinite moving average of a white-noise process. If all the roots are outside the unit circle with the exception of some root which is on the unit circle, then the VAR process is integrated. In this case it cannot be inverted as an infinite moving average. If some of the roots are inside the unit circle, then the process is explosive. If the VAR process starts at some initial point characterized by initial values or distributions, then the process cannot be stationary. However, if all the roots are outside the unit circle, the process is asymptotically stationary. If some root is equal to 1, then the process can be differentiated to obtain an asymptotically stationary process.

COINTEGRATION

Let's now look at the problem of representation of multivariate time series from a different angle. Recall that a variable is integrated of order

n if it can be transformed into a stationary series differencing n times. In particular, a univariate time series X is integrated of order 1 if it can be represented as follows:

$$X_{t+1} = \rho X_t + b + \varepsilon_t$$
$$\rho = 1$$

ε_t stationary possibly autocorrelated

The key feature of an integrated time series is that random innovations never decay. Most economic variables are integrated variables. In particular, testing for integration in log price processes one finds that the null of integration cannot be rejected in most cases. For instance, testing the log price processes in the S&P 500 using a standard test such as the ADF test, the null of integration cannot be rejected in about 90% of time series as shown in Exhibit 12.3. Nor can the null hypothesis of integration be rejected for economic time series such as the monetary mass (M3) or the Gross Disposable Product.

Suppose that a set of time series integrated of order 1 is given. Though each series is integrated of order 1, for instance they are arithmetic random walks, there might be linear combinations of the series which are stationary. If this happens, the series are said to be **cointegrated**. The financial meaning of cointegration is the following. Individual log price processes can be arithmetic random walks but there are portfolios, in general long-short portfolios, which are stationary, and thus mean reverting around a constant mean. In other words, individual securities might be totally unpredictable random walks but portfolios might be more predictable. We will come back to the question of the empirical findings of cointegration in real-world economic time series and price processes. First, we need to define cointegration mathematically.

EXHIBIT 12.3   Integratedness of the S&P 500

Period	Number of Series	Type of Test	Integratedness	Percentage
From Jan. 1, 2001 to Dec. 31, 2003	487 series in the S&P 500	Augmented Dickey-Fuller test with two lags, 95% confidence level.	422 series I(1) 65 series I(0)	87% integrated

The concept of **cointegration,** introduced by Granger in 1981,[16] can be expressed in the following way. Suppose that a set of n time series, integrated of order 1, is given. If there is a linear combination of the series

$$\delta_t = \sum_{i=1}^{n} \beta_i x_{i,t}$$

which is stationary, then the series $x_{i,t}$ are said to be cointegrated. Any linear combination as the one above is called a **cointegrating relationship.** Given n time series, there can be from none to at most $n-1$ cointegrating relationships.

Though a definition of cointegration of this type is often given in the literature, it should be clear that it is strictly applicable only to processes that extend in time from $-\infty$ to $+\infty$. Series that start from some initial instant cannot be stationary but can be, at most, asymptotically stationary. To make the definition of cointegration more general, one should allow asymptotic stationarity instead of strict stationarity.

Cointegrating relationships express long-run equilibrium between time series. As noted above, in financial terms, cointegrating relationships represent stationary portfolios. Suppose there are n time series $x_{i,t}$, $i = 1,...,n$ and $k < n$ cointegrating relationships. It can be demonstrated that there are $n-k$ integrated time series $u_{j,t}$, $j = 1,...,n-k$, called **common trends,** such that every time series $x_{i,t}$ can expressed as a linear combination of the common trends plus a stationary disturbance:

$$x_{it} = \sum_{j=1}^{n-k} \gamma_j u_{j,t} + \eta_{i,t}$$

This is clearly a multifactor representation of integrated processes.

Is there a general representation of cointegrated processes? The answer is affirmative. Granger was able to demonstrate the fundamental theorem according to which a multivariate integrated process is cointegrated if and only if it can be represented in the **Error Correction Model** (ECM) form. The ECM representation is a representation of a multivariate process in first differences with corrections in levels as follows:

---

[16] C.W.J. Granger, "Some Properties of Time Series Data and Their Use in Econometric Model Specification," *Journal of Econometrics* 16 (1981), pp. 121–130.

$$\Delta \mathbf{x}_{t+1} = \left(\sum_{i=1}^{n-1} \mathbf{A} L^i \right) \Delta \mathbf{x}_t + \boldsymbol{\alpha}\boldsymbol{\beta}' \mathbf{x}_t + \boldsymbol{\eta}_t$$

where $\boldsymbol{\alpha}$ is a $p{\times}r$ matrix, $\boldsymbol{\beta}$ is a a $p{\times}r$ matrix with $\boldsymbol{\alpha}\boldsymbol{\beta}' = \boldsymbol{\Pi}$ and $\boldsymbol{\eta}_t$ is a vector of stationary disturbances.

Within the basic framework of ECM, different cointegration models have been proposed. Two major models need mention:

- The **Autoregressive Distributed Lag** (ARDL) model which explicitly takes into account exogenous variables that are not cointegrated among themselves.[17]
- The **Dynamic Cointegration Approach** which models the long-run cointegration relationships not as a static regression but as a dynamic model with a small number of lags.

Cointegration of log price processes makes sense from an economic point of view. Prices must somehow follow a common trend otherwise they will, in the long run, diverge indefinitely. This is not a real economic justification of cointegration. Even if in the long run all processes end up as fluctuations around some common trend, it does not mean that they are cointegrated. Many other possible mechanisms might be at work, such as discrete adjustment.

State-Space Modeling and Cointegration

The notion of state-space modeling is that empirically measurable economic variables are a linear regression over a set of hidden variables modeled as an autoregressive process. State-space models represent dynamical factor models as the states are the hidden factors of the model. The **state-space representation** introduced above can be generalized in many different ways, in particular by letting the noise terms be different in the state equations and in the regressions.

As we have seen earlier in this chapter, there is equivalence between state-space models and ARMA models. In particular, there is equivalence between cointegrated models represented by ECM models, and state-space models. The factors are the common trends.

---

[17] See M.H. Pesaran and Y. Shin, "An Autoregressive Distributed Lag Modeling Approach to Cointegration Analysis," Chapter 11 in S. Strom (ed.), *Econometrics and Economic Theory in the 20th Century: The Ragnar Fresh Centennial Symposium* (Cambridge: Cambridge University Press, 1999).

Empirical Evidence of Cointegration in Equity Prices

It is now time to discuss the empirical evidence that support various types of models. The usual tests do not reject the random walk hypothesis for more than 90% of stocks investigated. The average correlation of the S&P 500 computed in the 2001–2003 period is roughly 17% as shown in Exhibit 12.1. The distribution of the eigenvalues of the correlation matrix has the distribution shown in Exhibit 12.4. The distribution of the eigenvalues is quite close to the theoretical shape for large portfolios of a random matrix with the exception of a number of eigenvalues.

Cointegration is more difficult to ascertain. A number of academic studies have found contradicting evidence about mean reversion around exponential trends. Poterba and Summers[18] found positive evidence of mean reversion of stock prices around exponential trends. This early

EXHIBIT 12.4   Distribution of the Eigenvalues of the S&P 500

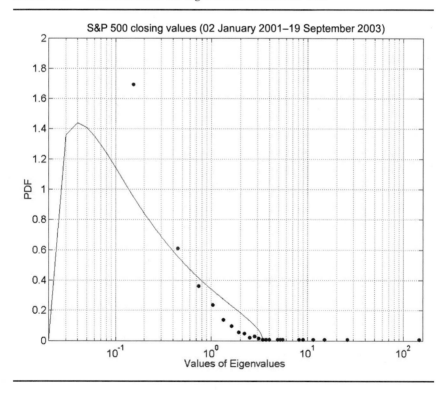

[18] J. Poterba and L. Summers, "Mean Reversion in Stock Prices: Evidence and Implications," *Journal of Financial Economics* 79 (1988), pp. 22–25.

evidence has not been confirmed by later studies.[19] Kim, Nelson and Startz have argued that mean-reversion is a pre-World War II phenomenon.[20] However, more recent papers give new support to the hypothesis of mean reversion.[21]

Common trends in exchange rates have documented by Baillie and Bollerslev[22] and by Kasa[23] in equity prices. Cross-correlations at different lags between equities have been reported in the literature. For instance, Campbell, Lo, and MacKinley[24] report significant autocorrelations of portfolio returns for selected portfolios, a fact that is attributed to the existence of autocross-correlations. An interpretation of the same phenomena on the same data set based on cointegration has been proposed by Kanas and Kouretas.[25]

Evidence on asset price cointegration and the use of cointegration in asset allocation and portfolio management is discussed in a number of papers. See, for instance, Lucas,[26] Alexander,[27] and Alexander and Dimitriu.[28] In most cases cointegrating relationships are found in small portfolios. How to select the cointegrated portfolios in large sets of price

---

[19] See: Eugene F. Fama and Kenneth.R. French, "Permanent and Temporary Components of Stock Prices," *Journal of Political Economy* 96, no. 2 (1988), pp. 246–273 and Campbell, Lo, and MacKinley, *The Econometrics of Financial Markets*.

[20] M.J. Kim, C.R. Nelson and R. Startz, "Mean Reversion in Stock Prices? A Reappraisal of the Empirical Evidence," *Review of Economic Studies* 58 (1991), pp. 515–528.

[21] See: Kent Daniel (2001) "Power and Size of Mean Reversion Tests," *Journal of Empirical Finance* 8, no. 5 (December 2001), pp. 493–535; Steen Nielsen and Jan Overgaard Olesen, "Regime-Switching Stock Returns and Mean Reversion," Working paper 11–2000, Department of Economics and EPRU, Copenhagen Business School; and Ole Risager, "Random Walk or Mean Reversion: the Danish Stock Market since World War I," Working paper 7–98, Department of Economics and EPRU, Copenhagen Business School.

[22] R. Baillie and T. Bollerslev, "Common Stochastic Trends in a System of Exchange Rates," *Journal of Finance* 44 (1989), pp. 167–182.

[23] K. Kasa, "Common Stochastic Trends in International Stock Markets," *Journal of Monetary Economics* 29 (1992), pp. 95–124.

[24] See Campbell, Lo, and MacKinley, *The Econometrics of Financial Markets*.

[25] A. Kanas and G.P. Kouretas, "A Cointegration Approach to the Lead-Lag Effect Among Size-Sorted Equity Portfolios," 2001.

[26] A. Lucas, "Strategic and Tactical Asset Allocation and the Effect of Long-Run Equilibrium Relations," Research Memorandum, Vrije Universiteit Amsterdam, 1997-42 (1997).

[27] C.O. Alexander, "Optimal Hedging Using Cointegration," *Philosophical Transactions of the Royal Society* A 357 (1999), pp. 2039–2058.

[28] C.O. Alexander and A. Dimitriu, "The Cointegration Alpha: Enhanced Index Tracking and Long-Short Equity Market Neutral Strategies," Discussion Paper 2002-08, ISMA Centre Discussion Papers in Finance Series, 2002.

processes is a critical issue. Usual tests for cointegration cannot be applied to large portfolios such as the S&P 500 given the computational cost: The space of possible cointegrating relationships is simply too large to be searched effectively.

Effective methods to reduce the search space are needed. The discovery of cointegrating relationships is a tremendous advantage from a trading point of view. As discussed by Alexander, it allows, for instance, to engineer parsimonious portfolios for index tracking and to create profitable trading strategies for hedge funds. Possible solutions to this problem remain proprietary. The consideration of the equivalence of cointegration and state-space modeling might be a step in this direction. Effective algorithms for determining state space models are described in the engineering and, more recently, in the econometric literature.[29]

NONSTATIONARY MODELS OF FINANCIAL TIME SERIES

Let's now proceed to explore a number of nonlinear models. The existence of nonlinearities in financial time series has been documented in many works.[30] However identifying and estimating a reasonable nonlinear model remains a highly challenging task. The key problem is the explosion of the search space, the so called "curse of dimensionality" entailed by nonlinear models.

Models based on neural networks and many other families of universal function approximators have been explored both in the literature and in the practice of financial trading. These models try to estimate a nonlinear DGP. We will not deal with these models which are highly specialized and often used as proprietary trading models.

However, a number of relatively simple nonlinear models have demonstrated their ability to capture important nonlinear phenomena. The first (and perhaps the best known) of such models, is the ARCH/GARCH family of models. Another class of nonlinear models are the Markov switching models, where a Markov chain drives discrete changes in the model parameters. Perhaps the best known of these models is the Hamilton model, though a variety of Markov switching VAR models have been proposed. These models are appealing because they implement, in a coherent statistical framework, the idea of structural change which is reasonable from an economic standpoint.

---

[29] D. Bauer and M. Wagner, "Estimating Cointegrated Systems Using Subspace Algorithms," *Journal of Econometrics* 111 (2002), pp. 47–84.
[30] Campbell, Lo, and MacKinley, *The Econometrics of Financial Markets*.

The ARCH/GARCH Family of Models

The ARCH models were proposed by Engle[31] as a model of inflation. The empirical fact behind ARCH models is the clustering of volatility observed in many economic and financial series. If instantaneous volatility is defined as a hidden variable in a price model and estimated as the variance of returns over relatively long periods, one finds periods of high volatility followed by periods of low volatility and vice versa.

Note that a new strain of econometric literature deals with instantaneous volatility as an observed variable. The observability of volatility is made possible by the availability of high frequency data. In this case, there is a variety of models for the volatility process, in particular **long-memory fractional models**.[32] We maintain the classical definition of volatility as a hidden variable.

Engle proposed a model in the spirit of state-space modeling where volatility is modeled by an autoregressive process and then injected multiplicatively in the price process. More precisely, the simplest ARCH model is defined as follows:

$$x_t = \sqrt{\beta + \lambda x_{t-1}^2}\, z_t$$

In the above equation, x is the process variable and the terms z form an IID sequence. The ARCH model was extended by Bollerslev,[33] who proposed the GARCH family of models. In the GARCH models, volatility is modeled as a more general ARMA process and then treated as before:

$$x_t = \sigma_t z_t$$

$$\sigma_t = \beta + \sum_{i=1}^{p} \lambda_i x_{t-i}^2 + \sum_{j=1}^{q} \delta_j \sigma_{t-j}^2$$

The key ingredients of ARCH modeling are an ARMA process for volatility and a regressive process where volatility multiplies a white-noise

---

[31] R.F. Engle, "Autoregressive Conditional Heteroscedasticity with Estimates of the Variance of United Kingdom Inflation," *Econometrica* 50 (July 1982), pp. 987–1007.

[32] T.G. Andersen, T. Bollerslev, F.X. Diebold, and P. Labys, "Modeling and Forecasting Realized Volatility," *Econometrica* 71, 2003, pp. 529–626.

[33] T. Bollerslev, "Generalized Autoregressive Conditional Heteroscedasticity," *Journal of Econometrics* 31 (1986), pp. 307–327.

process. If the ARMA process for volatility is integrated (that is, it has unit roots) then the GARCH process is called Integrated GARCH or IGARCH.

The ARCH technology is not restricted to univariate processes but can be extended to multivariate processes. Multivariate GARCH processes model the entire variance-covariance matrix as an autoregressive process.

Multivariate models of the ARCH-GARCH type become rapidly unmanageable as the number of parameters to estimate grows with the fourth power of the number of assets. Dimensionality reduction is called for. Different proposals have been made, in particular factor models for the volatility process.

The random terms z might have arbitrary distributions. In practice, normality is often assumed. However, though the conditional distribution is normal, the unconditional distribution of a GARCH process is not normal but exhibits fat tails (see Chapter 13). This feature of GARCH processes, in addition to the modeling of volatility clustering, has made them attractive as models of returns. Returns at short time horizons are, in fact, not normally distributed but exhibit fat tails. However, fitting different families of GARCH processes to empirical return data has shown that GARCH models cannot fit simultaneously the volatility clustering and the fat-tailedness of returns. Distributions of the shock z other than normal have been tried, for instance T-Student distributions, but no good fit of volatility and returns has been reported in the literature. GARCH models can be considered a useful econometric tool, but not a firm theory of price processes.

Markov Switching Models

Markov switching models belong to a vast family of models that have found applications in many fields other than econometrics, such as genomics and speech recognition. The economic idea behind Markov switching models is that the economy undergoes discrete switches between economic states at random times. To each state corresponds a set of model parameters.

One of the first Markov switching models proposed is the Hamilton[34] model. The **Hamilton model** is based on two states, a state of "expansion" and a state of "recession." Periods of recession are followed by periods of expansion and vice versa. The time of transition between states is governed by a two-state Markov chain. In each state, price processes follow a random walk model.

---

[34] J.D. Hamilton, "A New Approach to the Economic Analysis of Nonstationary Time Series and the Business Cycle," *Econometrica* 57 (1989), pp. 357–384.

The Hamilton model can be extended to an arbitrary number of states and to more general VAR models. In a Markov switching context, a VAR model

$$\mathbf{x}_t = [\mathbf{A}_1(s_t)L + \mathbf{A}_2(s_t)L^2 + \ldots + \mathbf{A}_n(s_t)L^N]\mathbf{x}_t + \mathbf{m}(s_t) + \boldsymbol{\varepsilon}_t$$

has parameters that depend on a set of hidden states that are governed by a discrete-state, discrete-time Markov chain with transition probability matrix:

$$p_{i,j} = \Pr(s_{t+1} = i \mid s_t = i)$$

$$\sum_{j=1}^{M} p_{i,j} = 1$$

Estimation of Markov switching VAR models can be done within a general maximum likelihood framework. The estimation procedure is rather complex as approximate iteration techniques are used. Hamilton[35] made use of the **Expectation Maximization** (EM) **algorithm** which had been proposed earlier in a broader context.[36] Other numerical techniques are available and are now implemented in commercial software packages.

Markov switching VAR models have been applied to macroeconomic problems, in particular to the explanation of business cycles. Applications to the modeling of large portfolios present significant problems of estimation given the large number of data necessary.

Markov switching models are, in fact, typically estimated over long periods of time, say 20 or 30 years. If one wants to construct coherent data sets for broad aggregates such as the S&P 500, one rapidly runs into problems as many firms, over periods of that length, undergo significant change such as mergers and acquisitions or stock splits. As one cannot simply exclude these firms as doing so would introduce biases in the estimation process, ad hoc adjustment procedures are needed to handle change. Despite these difficulties, however, Markov switching models can be considered a promising technique for financial econometrics.

---

[35] J.D. Hamilton, "Analysis of Time Series Subject to Changes in Regime," *Journal of Econometrics* 45 (1990), pp. 39–70.
[36] A.P. Dempster, N.M. Laird, and D.B. Rubin, "Maximum Likelihood Estimation From Incomplete Data Via the EM Algorithm," *Journal of the Royal Statistical Society* 39 (1977), Series B, 1–38.

SUMMARY

- Model selection cannot be completely automated because the search space is too large.
- Econometrics constrains the search for an optimal model within model classes.
- If a family of models can fit data with arbitrary accuracy, then criteria for choosing the optimal model complexity are needed.
- Overfitting occurs when a model is too complex and thus fits unpredictable noise.
- Akaike Information Criteria and Bayesian Information Criteria are complexity selection criteria based on information theory.
- The Vapnik-Chervonenkis theory of learning has given a rigorous theoretical basis to the principles of statistical learning.
- An estimator is a random variable function of the sample data that approximates a given parameter of a distribution.
- The Cramer-Rao bound prescribes lower bounds for the variance of estimators.
- Maximum Likelihood Estimate (MLE) chooses those parameters that maximize likelihood on samples.
- For unconstrained regressions, MLE coincides with Ordinary Least Square estimation.
- MLE estimators are efficient estimators, that is, they attain the Cramer-Rao variance lower bound.
- The simplest asset price model is the random walk.
- A multivariate correlated random walk is a model for the joint price process of a set of asset prices.
- A large set of price processes exhibits nearly random variance-covariance matrix of the return process.
- Factor models reduce the dimensionality of the variance-covariance matrix of the return process.
- Principal component analysis identifies a generally small number of stable factors.
- Vector Autoregressive (VAR) models capture the dynamics of time series.
- It is impossible to describe large sets of asset price processes with unrestricted VAR models because the number of parameters is too high and therefore not stable.
- Cointegration captures common stable trends thus implementing a dimensionality reduction.
- Cointegrated time series can be represented with a constrained Error Correction VAR model.
- State-space models are equivalent to Error Correction models.

- State-of–the-art nonlinear econometric models use an autoregressive process to drive the parameters of another model.
- ARCH/GARCH models use an ARMA model to drive the volatility parameter.
- Markov switching models use a Markov chain to drive the parameters of an autoregressive model.

CHAPTER 13

Fat Tails, Scaling, and Stable Laws

Most models of stochastic processes and time series examined thus far assume that distributions have finite mean and finite variance. In this chapter we describe fat tailed distributions with infinite variance. Fat-tailed distributions have been found in many financial economic variables ranging from forecasting returns on financial assets to modeling recovery distributions in bankruptcies. They have also been found in numerous insurance applications such as catastrophic insurance claims and in value-at-risk measures employed by risk managers.

In this chapter, we review the related concepts of fat-tailed, power-law and Levy-stable distributions, scaling and self-similarity, as well as explore the mechanisms that generate these distributions. We discuss the key intuition relative to the applicability of fat-tailed or scaling processes to finance: In a fat-tailed or scaling world (as opposed to an ergodic world), the past does not offer an exhaustive set of possible configurations. Adopting, as an approximation, a scaling description of financial phenomena implies the belief that only a small space of possible configurations has been explored; vast regions remain unexplored.

We begin with the mathematics of fat-tailed processes, followed by a discussion of classical Extreme Value Theory for independent and identically distributed sequences. We then explore the consequences of eliminating the assumption of independence and discuss different concepts of scaling and self similarity. Finally, we present evidence of fat tails in financial phenomena and discuss applications of Extreme Value Theory.

SCALING, STABLE LAWS, AND FAT TAILS

Let's begin with a review of the different but related concepts and properties of fat tails, power laws, and stable laws. These concepts appear
frequently in the financial and economic literature, applied to both random variables and stochastic processes.

Fat Tails

Consider a random variable X. By definition, X is a real-valued function
from the set Ω of the possible outcomes to the set R of real numbers,
such that the set $(X \leq x)$ is an event. Recall from Chapter 6 that if $P(X \leq
x)$ is the probability of the event $(X \leq x)$, the function $F(x) = P(X \leq x)$ is a
well-defined function for every real number x. The function $F(x)$ is called
the **cumulative distribution function**, or simply the distribution function,
of the random variable X. Note that X denotes a function $\Omega \to R$, x is a
real variable, and $F(x)$ is an ordinary real-valued function that assumes
values in the interval $[0,1]$. If the function $F(x)$ admits a derivative

$$f(x) = \frac{dF(x)}{dx}$$

The function $f(x)$ is called the **probability density of the random variable** X. The function $\bar{F}(x) = 1 - F(x)$ is the tail of the distribution $F(x)$.
The function $\bar{F}(x)$ is called the **survival function**.

Fat tails are somewhat arbitrarily defined. Intuitively, a fat-tailed distribution is a distribution that has more weight in the tails than some reference distribution. The exponential decay of the tail is generally assumed as
the borderline separating fat-tailed from light-tailed distributions. In the literature, distributions with a power-law decay of the tails are referred to as
heavy-tailed distributions. It is sometimes assumed that the reference distribution is Gaussian (i.e., normal), but this is unsatisfactory; it implies, for
instance, that exponential distributions are fat-tailed because Gaussian tails
decay as the *square* of an exponential and thus faster than an exponential.

These characterizations of fat-tailedness (or heavy-tailedness) are not
convenient from a mathematical and statistical point of view. It would be
preferable to define fat-tailedness in terms of a function of some essential
property that can be associated to it. Several proposals have been
advanced. Widely used definitions focus on the moments of the distribution. Definitions of fat-tailedness based on a single moment focus either on
the second moment, the variance, or the kurtosis, defined as the fourth
moment divided by the square of the variance. In fact, a distribution is
often considered fat-tailed if its variance is infinite or if it is leptokurtic

(i.e., its kurtosis is greater than 3). However, as remarked by Bryson[1] definitions of this type are too crude and should be replaced by more complete descriptions of tail behavior.

Others consider a distribution fat-tailed if all its exponential moments are infinite, $E[e^{sX}] = \infty$ for every $s \geq 0$. This condition implies that the moment-generating function does not exist. Some suggest weakening this condition, defining fat-tailed distributions as those distributions that do not have a finite exponential moment of first order. Exponential moments are particularly important in finance and economics when the logarithm of variables, for instance logprices, are the primary quantity to be modeled.[2]

Fat-tailedness has a consequence of practical importance: the probability of **extremal events** (i.e., the probability that the random variable assumes large values) is much higher than in the case of normal distributions. A fat-tailed distribution assigns higher probabilities to extremal events than would a normal distribution. For instance, a six-sigma event (i.e., a realized value of a random variable whose difference from the mean is six times the size of the standard deviation) has a near zero probability in a Gaussian distribution but might have a nonnegligible probability in fat-tailed distributions.

The notion of fat-tailedness can be made quantitative as different distributions have different degrees of fat-tailedness. The degree of fat-tailedness dictates the weight of the tails and thus the probability of extremal events. Extreme Value Theory attempts to estimate the entire tail region, and therefore the degree of fat-tailedness, from a finite sample. A number of indicators for evaluating the size of extremal events have been proposed; among these are the extremal claim index proposed in Embrechts, Kluppelberg, and Mikosch,[3] which plays an important role in risk management.

The Class $\mathfrak{L}$ of Fat-Tailed Distributions

Many important classes of fat-tailed distributions have been defined; each is characterized by special statistical properties that are important in given application domains. We will introduce a number of such classes in order of inclusion, starting from the class with the broadest membership: the class $\mathfrak{L}$, which is defined as follows. Suppose that F is a

---

[1] M.C. Bryson, "Heavy-Tailed Distributions," in N.L. Kotz and S. Read (eds.), *Encyclopedia of Statistical Sciences*, Vol. 3 (New York: John Wiley & Sons, 1982), pp. 598–601.

[2] See G. Bamberg and D. Dorfleitner, "Fat Tails and Traditional Capital Market Theory," Working Paper, University of Augsburg, August 2001.

[3] P. Embrechts, C. Kluppelberg, and T. Mikosch, *Modelling Extremal Events for Insurance and Finance* (Berlin: Springer, 1999).

distribution function defined in the domain $(0,\infty)$ with $F < 1$ in the entire domain (i.e., F is the distribution function of a positive random variable with a tail that never decays to zero). It is said that $F \in \mathcal{L}$ if, for any $y > 0$, the following property holds:

$$\lim_{x \to \infty} \frac{\bar{F}(x-y)}{\bar{F}(x)} = 1, \; \forall y > 0$$

We can rewrite the above property in an equivalent (and perhaps more intuitive from the probabilistic point of view) way. Under the same assumptions as above, it is said that, given a positive random variable X, its distribution function $F \in \mathcal{L}$ if the following property holds for any $y > 0$:

$$\lim_{x \to \infty} P(X > x + y | X > x) = \lim_{x \to \infty} \frac{\bar{F}(x+y)}{\bar{F}(x)} = 1, \; \forall y > 0$$

Intuitively, this second property means that if it is known that a random variable exceeds a given value, then it will exceed any bigger value. Some authors define a distribution as being heavy-tailed if it satisfies this property. [4]

It can be demonstrated that if a distribution $F(x) \in \mathcal{L}$, then it has the following properties:

- Infinite exponential moments of every order: $E[e^{sX}] = \infty$ for every $s \geq 0$
- $\lim_{x \to \infty} \bar{F}(x)e^{\lambda x} = \infty, \; \forall \lambda > 0$

As distributions in class $\mathcal{L}$ have infinite exponential moments of every order, they satisfy one of the previous definitions of fat-tailedness. However they might have finite or infinite mean and variance.

The class $\mathcal{L}$ is in fact quite broad. It includes, in particular, the two classes of subexponential distributions and distributions with regularly varying tails that are discussed in the following sections.

Subexponential Distributions

A class of fat-tailed distributions, widely used in insurance and telecommunications, is the class S of **subexponential distributions**. Introduced

---

[4] See, for example, K. Sigman, "A Primer on Heavy-Tailed Distributions," *Queueing Systems*, 1999.

by Chistyakov in 1964, subexponential distributions can be characterized by two equivalent properties: (1) the convolution closure property
of the tails and (2) the property of the sums.[5]

The **convolution closure property** of the tails prescribes that the
shape of the tail is preserved after the summation of identical and independent copies of a variable. This property asserts that, for $x \to \infty$, the
tail of a sum of independent and identical variables has the same shape
as the tail of the variable itself. As the distribution of a sum of n independent variables is the n-convolution of their distributions, the convolution closure property can be written as

$$\lim_{x \to \infty} \frac{\bar{F}^{n^*}(x)}{\bar{F}(x)} = n$$

Note that Gaussian distributions do not have this property although
the sum of independent Gaussian distributions is again a Gaussian distribution. Subexponential distributions can be characterized by another
important (and perhaps more intuitive) property, which is equivalent to
the convolution closure property: In a sum of n variables, the largest value
will be of the same order of magnitude as the sum itself. For any n, define

$$S_n(x) = \sum_{i=1}^{n} X_i$$

as a sum of independent and identical copies of a variable X and call M_n
their maxima. In the limit of large x, the probability that the tail of the
sum exceeds x equals the probability that the largest summand exceeds x:

$$\lim_{x \to \infty} \frac{P(S_n > x)}{P(M_n > x)} = 1$$

The class S of subexponential distributions is a proper subset of the
class $\mathfrak{L}$. Every subexponential distribution belongs to the class $\mathfrak{L}$ while it
can be demonstrated (but this is not trivial) that there are distributions

---

[5] See, for example, C. M. Goldie and C. Kluppelberg, "Subexponential Distributions," in R.J. Adler, R.E. Feldman, and M.S. Taqqu (eds.), *A Practical Guide to
Heavy Tails: Statistical Techniques and Applications* (Boston: Birkhauser, 1998), pp.
435–459 and Embrechts, Kluppelberg, and Mikosch, *Modelling Extremal Events for
Insurance and Finance.*

that belong to the class $\mathfrak{L}$ but not to the class S. Distributions that have both properties are called subexponential as it can be demonstrated that, as all distributions in $\mathfrak{L}$, they satisfy the property:

$$\lim_{x \to \infty} \bar{F}(x)e^{\lambda x} = \infty \, , \, \forall \lambda > 0$$

Note, however, that the class of distributions that satisfies the latter property is broader than the class of subexponential distributions; this is because the former includes, for instance, the class $\mathfrak{L}$.[6]

Subexponential distributions do not have finite exponential moments of any order, that is, $E[e^{sX}] = \infty$ for every $s \geq 0$. They may or may not have a finite mean and/or a finite variance. Consider, in fact, that the class of subexponential distributions includes both Pareto and Weibull distributions. The former have infinite variance but might have finite or infinite mean depending on the index; the latter have finite moments of every order (see below).

The key indicators of subexponentiality are (1) the equivalence in the distribution of the tail between a variable and a sum of independent copies of the same variable and (2) the fact that a sum is dominated by its largest term. The importance of the largest terms in a sum can be made more quantitative using measures such as the *large claims index* introduced in Embrechts, Kluppelberg, and Mikosch that quantifies the ratio between the largest p terms in a sum and the entire sum.

The class of subexponential distributions is quite large. It includes not only Pareto and stable distributions but also log-gamma, lognormal, Benkander, Burr, and Weibull distributions. Pareto distributions and stable distributions are a particularly important subclass of subexponential distributions; these will be described in some detail below.

Power-Law Distributions

Power-law distributions are a particularly important subset of subexponential distributions. Their tails follow approximately an inverse power law, decaying as $x^{-\alpha}$. The exponent α is called the **tail index** of the distribution. To express formally the notion of approximate power-law decay, we need to introduce the class $\mathfrak{R}(\alpha)$, equivalently written as $\mathfrak{R}_\alpha$ of regularly varying functions.

A positive function f is said to be regularly varying with index α or $f \in \mathfrak{R}(\alpha)$ if the following condition holds:

---

[6] See Sigman, "A Primer on Heavy-Tailed Distributions."

$$\lim_{x \to \infty} \frac{f(tx)}{f(x)} = t^{\alpha}$$

A function $f \in \Re(0)$ is called **slowly varying**. It can be demonstrated that a regularly varying function $f(x)$ of index α admits the representation $f(x) = x^{\alpha}l(x)$ where $l(x)$ is a slowly varying function.

A distribution F is said to have a **regularly varying tail** if the following property holds:

$$\bar{F} = x^{-\alpha}l(x)$$

where l is a slowly varying function. An example of a distribution with a regularly varying tail is Pareto's law. The latter can be written in various ways, including the following:

$$\bar{F}(x) = P(X > x) = \frac{c}{c + x^{\alpha}} \text{ for } x \geq 0$$

Power-law distributions are thus distributions with regularly varying tails. It can be demonstrated that they satisfy the convolution closure property of the tail. The distribution of the sum of n independent variables of tail index α is a power-law distribution of the same index α. Note that this property holds in the limit for $x \to \infty$. Distributions with regularly varying tails are therefore a proper subset of subexponential distributions.

Being subexponential, power laws have all the general properties of fat-tailed distributions and some additional ones. One particularly important property of distributions with regularly varying tails, valid for every tail index, is the **rank-size order property**. Suppose that samples from a power law of tail index α are ordered by size, and call S_r the size of the rth sample. One then finds that the law

$$S_r = ar^{-\frac{1}{\alpha}}$$

is approximately verified. The well-known **Zipf's law** is an example of this rank-size ordering. Zipf's law states that the size of an observation is inversely proportional to its rank. For example, the frequency of words in an English text is inversely proportional to their rank. The same is approximately valid for the size of U.S. cities.

Many properties of power-law distributions are distinctly different in the three following ranges of α: $0 < \alpha \leq 1$, $1 < \alpha \leq 2$, $\alpha > 2$. The threshold $\alpha = 2$ for the tail index is important as it marks the separation between the applicability of the standard Central Limit Theorem; the threshold $\alpha = 1$ is important as it separates variables with a finite mean from those with infinite mean. Let's take a closer look at the Law of Large Numbers and the Central Limit Theorem.

The Law of Large Numbers and the Central Limit Theorem

There are four basic versions of the Law of the Large Numbers (LLN), two Weak Laws of Large Numbers (WLLN), and two Strong Laws of Large Numbers (SLLN).

The two versions of the WLLN are formulated as follows.

1. Suppose that the variables X_i are IID with finite mean $E[X_i] = E[X] = \mu$. Under this condition it can be demonstrated that the empirical average tends to the mean in probability:

$$\overline{X}_n = \frac{\sum\limits_{i=1}^{n} X_i}{n} \xrightarrow[n \to \infty]{P} E[X] = \mu$$

2. If the variables are only independently distributed (ID) but have finite means and variances (μ_i, σ_i), then the following relationship holds:

$$\overline{X}_n = \frac{\sum\limits_{i=1}^{n} X_i}{n} \xrightarrow[n \to \infty]{P} \frac{\sum\limits_{i=1}^{n} \overline{X}_i}{n} = \frac{\sum\limits_{i=1}^{n} \mu_i}{n}$$

In other words, the empirical average of a sequence of finite-mean finite-variance variables tends to the average of the means.

The two versions of the SLLN are formulated as follows.

1. The empirical average of a sequence of IID variables X_i tends almost surely to a constant a if and only if the expected value of the variables is finite. In addition, the constant a is equal to μ. Therefore, if and only if $|E[X_i]| = |E[X]| = |\mu| < \infty$ the following relationship holds:

$$\overline{X}_n = \frac{\sum\limits_{i=1}^{n} X_i}{n} \xrightarrow[n \to \infty]{A.S.} E[X] = \mu$$

where convergence is in the sense of almost sure convergence.

2. If the variables X_i are only independently distributed (ID) but have finite means and variances (μ_i, σ_i) and

$$\lim_{n \to \infty} \frac{1}{n^2} \sum_{i=1}^{n} \sigma_i^2 < \infty$$

then the following relationship holds:

$$\overline{X}_n = \frac{\sum\limits_{i=1}^{n} X_i}{n} \xrightarrow[n \to \infty]{A.S.} \frac{\sum\limits_{i=1}^{n} \overline{X}_i}{n} = \frac{\sum\limits_{i=1}^{n} \mu_i}{n}$$

Suppose the variables are IID. If the scaling factor n is replaced with $\sqrt{n}$, then the limit relation no longer holds as the normalized sum

$$\frac{\sum\limits_{i=1}^{n} X_i}{\sqrt{n}}$$

diverges. However, if the variables have finite second-order moments, the classical version of the Central Limit Theorem (CLT) can be demonstrated. In fact, under the assumption that both first- and second-order moments are finite, it can be shown that

$$\frac{S_n - n\mu}{\sigma\sqrt{n}} \xrightarrow{D} \Phi$$

$$S_n = \sum_{i=1}^{n} X_i$$

where μ, σ are respectively the expected value and standard deviation of X, and Φ the standard normal distribution.

If the tail index $\alpha > 1$, variables have finite expected value and the SLNN holds. If the tail index $\alpha > 2$, variables have finite variance and the CLT in the previous form holds. If the tail index $\alpha \leq 2$, then variables have infinite variance: The CLT in the previous form does not hold. In fact, variables with $\alpha \leq 2$ belong to the domain of attraction of a stable law of index α. This means that a sequence of properly normalized and centered sums tends to a stable distribution with infinite variance. In this case, the CLT takes the form

$$\frac{S_n - n\mu}{n^{\frac{1}{\alpha}}} \xrightarrow{D} G_\alpha, \text{ if } 1 < \alpha \leq 2$$

$$\frac{S_n}{n^{\frac{1}{\alpha}}} \xrightarrow{D} G_\alpha, \text{ if } 0 < \alpha \leq 1$$

where G are stable distributions as defined below. Note that the case $\alpha = 2$ is somewhat special: variables with this tail index have infinite variance but fall nevertheless in the domain of attraction of a normal variable, that is, G_2. Below the threshold 1, distributions have neither finite variance nor finite mean. There is a sharp change in the normalization behavior at this tail-index threshold.

Stable Distributions

Stable distributions are *not*, in their generality, a subset of fat-tailed distributions as they include the normal distribution. There are different, equivalent ways to define stable distributions. Let's begin with a key property: the equality in distribution between a random variable and the (normalized) independent sum of any number of identical replicas of the same variable. This is a different property than the closure property of the tail insofar as (1) it involves not only the tail but the entire distribution and (2) equality in distribution means that distributions have the same functional form but, possibly, with different parameters. Normal distributions have this property: The sum of two or more normally distributed variables is again a normally distributed variable. But this property holds for a more general class of distributions called **stable dis-**

tributions or **Levy-stable distributions**. Normal distributions are thus a special type of stable distributions.

The above can be formalized as follows: Stable distributions can be defined as those distributions for which the following identity in distribution holds for any number $n \geq 2$:

$$\sum_{i=1}^{n} X_i \overset{D}{=} C_n X + D_n$$

where X_i are identical independent copies of X and the C_n, D_n are constants. Alternatively, the same property can be expressed stating that stable distributions are distributions for which the following identity in distribution holds:

$$AX_1 + BX_2 \overset{D}{=} CX + D$$

Stable distributions are also characterized by another property that might be used in defining them: a stable distribution has a **domain of attraction** (i.e., it is the limit in distribution of a normalized and centered sum of identical and independent variables). Stable distributions coincide with all variables that have a domain of attraction.

Except in the special cases of Gaussian ($\alpha = 2$), symmetric Cauchy ($\alpha = 1$, $\beta = 0$) and stable inverse Gaussian ($\alpha = \frac{1}{2}$, $\beta = 0$) distributions, stable distributions cannot be written as simple formulas; formulas have been discovered but are not simple. However, stable distributions can be characterized in a simple way through their characteristic function, the Fourier transform of the distribution function. In fact, this function can be written as

$$\Phi_X(t) = \exp\{i\gamma t - c|t|^{\alpha}[1 - i\beta \operatorname{sign}(t)z(t, \alpha)]\}$$

where $t \in R$, $\gamma \in R$, $c > 0$, $\alpha \in (0,2)$, $\beta \in [-1,1]$, and

$$z(t, \alpha) = \tan\frac{\pi\alpha}{2} \text{ if } \alpha \neq 1$$

$$z(t, \alpha) = -2\log|t| \text{ if } \alpha = 1$$

It can be shown that only distributions with this characteristic function are stable distributions (i.e., they are the only distributions closed under summation). A stable law is characterized by four parameters: α, β, c, and γ. Normal distributions correspond to the parameters: $\alpha = 2$, $\beta = 0$, $\gamma = 0$.

Even if stable distributions cannot be written as simple formulas, the asymptotic shape of their tails can be written in a simple way. In fact, with the exception of Gaussian distributions, the tails of stable laws obey an inverse power law with exponent α (between 0 and 2). Normal distributions are stable but are an exception as their tails decay exponentially.

For stable distributions, the CLT holds in the same form as for inverse power-law distributions. In addition, the functions in the domain of attraction of a stable law of index $\alpha < 2$ are characterized by the same tail index. This means that a distribution G belongs to the domain of attraction of a stable law of parameter $\alpha < 2$ if and only if its tail decays as α. In particular, Pareto's law belongs to the domain of attraction of stable laws of the same tail index.

EXTREME VALUE THEORY FOR IID PROCESSES

In this section we introduce a number of important probabilistic concepts that form the conceptual basis of **Extreme Value Theory** (EVT). The objective of EVT is to estimate the entire tail of a distribution from a finite sample by fitting to an appropriate distribution those values of the sample that fall in the tail. Two concepts play a crucial role in EVT: (1) the behavior of the upper order statistics (i.e., the largest k values in a sample) and, in particular, of the sample maxima; and (2) the behavior of the points where samples exceed a given threshold. We will explore the limit distributions of maxima and the distribution of the points of exceedances of a high threshold. Based on these concepts a number of estimators of the tail index in sequences of independent and identically distributed (IID) variables are presented.

Maxima

In the previous sections we explored the behavior of sums. The key result of the theory of sums is that the behavior of sums simplifies in the limit of properly scaled and centered infinite sums regardless of the shape of individual summands. If sums converge, their limit distributions can only be stable distributions. In addition, the normalized sums of finite-mean, finite-variance variables always converge to a normal variable.

A parallel theory can be developed for maxima, informally defined as the largest value in a sample. The limit distribution of maxima, if it exists, belongs to one of three possible distributions: Frechet, Weibull, or Gumbel. This result forms the basis of classical EVT. Each limit distribution of maxima has its own Maximum Domain of Attraction. In addition, limit laws are max-stable (i.e., they are closed with respect to maxima). However, the behavior of maxima is less robust than the behavior of sums. Maxima do not converge to limit distributions for important classes of distributions, such as Poisson or geometric distributions.

Consider a sequence of independent variables X_i with common, nondegenerate distribution F and the maxima of samples extracted from this sequence:

$$M_1 = X_1, M_n = \max(X_1,...,X_n)$$

The maxima M_n form a new sequence of random variables which are not, however, independent.

As the variables of the sequence X_i are assumed to be independent, the distribution F_n of the maxima M_n can be immediately written down:

$$F(x)_n = P(X_1 \le x \vee ... \vee X_n \le x) = F^n(x)$$

where $\vee$ is the logical symbol for *and*.

If the distribution F, which is a non-decreasing function, reaches 1 at a finite point x_F—that is, if $x_F = \sup\{x: F(x) < 1\} < \infty$, then

$$\lim_{n \to \infty} P(M_n < x) = \lim_{n \to \infty} F_n(x) = 0 \text{ , for } x < x_F$$

If x_F is finite,

$$P(M_n < x) = F_n(x) = 1 \text{ , for } x > x_F$$

The point x_F is called the **right endpoint** of the distribution F.

Exhibit 13.1 illustrates the behavior of maxima in the case of a normal distribution. Given a normal distribution with mean zero and variance one, 100,000 samples of 20 elements each are selected. For each sample, the maximum is chosen. The distribution of the maxima and the empirical distribution of independent draws from the same normal are illustrated in the exhibit.

A deeper understanding of the behavior of maxima can be obtained considering sequences of normalized and centered maxima. Consider the following sequence: $c_n^{-1}(M_n - d_n)$ where $c_n > 0$, $d_n \in R$ are constants.

EXHIBIT 13.1   The Distribution of the Maxima of a Normal Variable

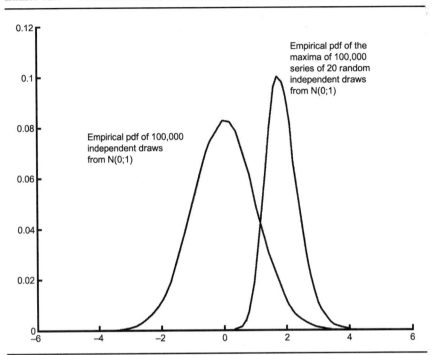

A fundamental result on the behavior of maxima is the Fisher-Tippett theorem which can be stated as follows. Consider a sequence of IID variables X_i and the relative sequence of maxima M_n. If there exist two sequences of constants $c_n > 0$, $d_n \in R$ and a nondegenerate distribution function H such that

$$c_n^{-1}(M_n - d_n) \xrightarrow{D} H$$

then H is one of the following distributions:

$$\text{Frechet: } \Phi_\alpha(x) = \begin{cases} 0 & x \le 0 \\ \exp(-x^{-\alpha}) & x > 0 \end{cases} \qquad \alpha > 0$$

$$\text{Weibull: } \Psi_\alpha(x) = \begin{cases} \exp[-(-x)^{-\alpha}] & x < 0 \\ 1 & x \ge 0 \end{cases} \qquad \alpha > 0$$

$$\text{Gumbel: } \Lambda(x) = \exp\{-e^{-x}\}, x \in R$$

The limit distribution H is unique, in the sense that different sequences of normalizing constants determine the same distribution.

The three above distributions—Frechet, Weibull, and Gumbel—are called **standard extreme value distributions**. They are continuous functions for every real x. Random variables distributed according to one of the extreme value distributions are called **extremal random variables**.

As an example, consider a standard exponential variable X. As $F(x) = P(X \le x) = 1 - e^{-x}$, $x \ge 0$ the distribution of the maxima is $P(M_n \le x) = F^n(x) = (1 - e^{-x})^n$, $x \ge 0$. If we choose $d_n = \ln n$, we can write: $P(M_n - d_n \le x) = P(M_n \le \ln n + x) = (1 - n^{-1}e^{-x})^n$, $x \ge 0$. For any given x, $(1 - n^{-1}e^{-x})^n \to \exp(-e^{-x})$, which shows that the maxima of standard exponential variables centered with $d_n = \ln n$ tend to a Gumbel distribution. Exhibit 13.2 illustrates the three distributions: Frechet, Gumbel, and Weibull.

We can now ask if there are conditions on the distribution F that ensure the existence of centering and scaling constants and the convergence to an extreme value distribution. To this end, let's first introduce

EXHIBIT 13.2   The Distribution of Frechet, Gumbel, and Weibull

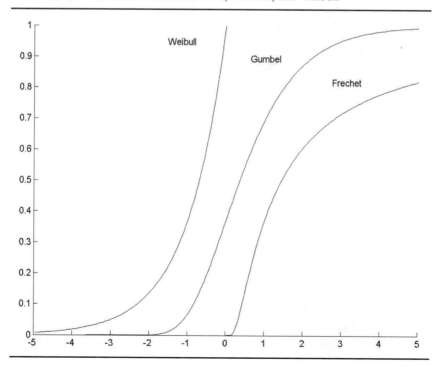

the concept of the **Maximum Domain of Attraction** (MDA) of an extreme value distribution H or MDA(H).

A random variable X is said to belong to the MDA(H) of the extreme value distribution H if there exist constants $c_n > 0$, $d_n \in R$ such that

$$c_n^{-1}(M_n - d_n) \overset{D}{\to} H$$

Two distribution functions F, G are said to be **tail equivalent** if they have the same right endpoints and the following condition holds:

$$\lim_{x \to \infty} \frac{\bar{F}(x)}{\bar{G}(x)} = c, \, 0 < c < \infty$$

Tail equivalence is an important concept for characterizing MDAs. In fact, it can be demonstrated that every MDA(H) is closed with respect to tail equivalence (i.e., if two distribution functions F and G are tail equivalent $F \in$ MDA(H) if and only if $G \in$ MDA(H)). Tail equivalence allows for a powerful characterization of the three MDAs.

Let's first define the **quantile function**. Given a distribution function F, the quantile function of F, written $F^{\leftarrow}(x)$, is defined as follows:

$$F^{\leftarrow}(x) = \inf[s \in R: F(s) \geq x], \, 0 < x < 1$$

The MDA of the Frechet Distribution

The Frechet distribution is written as $\Phi_\alpha(x) = \exp(-x^{-\alpha})$. Let's start by observing that the tail of the Frechet distribution decays as an inverse power law. In fact, we can write $1 - \Phi_\alpha(x) = 1 - \exp(-x^{-\alpha}) \approx x^{-\alpha}$ for $x \to \infty$.

It can be demonstrated that a distribution function F belongs to the MDA of a Frechet distribution $\Phi_\alpha(x)$, $\alpha > 0$ if and only if there is a slowly varying function L such that $\bar{F}(x) = x^{-\alpha}L(x)$. In this case, the constants assume the values

$$c_n = (1/F^{\leftarrow})(n), \, d_n = 0$$

We can rewrite this condition more compactly as follows:

$$F \in \text{MDA}(\Phi_\alpha) \Leftrightarrow \bar{F} \in R_{-\alpha}$$

From the above definitions it can be demonstrated that the following five distributions belong to the MDA of the Frechet distribution: (1) Pareto; (2) Cauchy; (3) Burr; (4) Stable laws with exponent $\alpha < 2$; or (5) log-gamma distribution.

The MDA of the Weibull Distribution

The Weibull distribution is written as follows:

$$\Psi_\alpha = \exp[-(-x^{-\alpha})]$$

The Weibull and the Frechet distributions are closely related to each other. In fact, it is clear from the definition that the following relationship holds:

$$\Psi_\alpha(x) = \Phi_\alpha(-x^{-1}), x > 0$$

One can therefore expect that the MDA of the two distributions are closely related. In fact, it can be demonstrated that a distribution function F belongs to the MDA of a Weibull distribution $\alpha > 0$ if and only if

$$x_F < \infty$$

and

$$\bar{F}(x_F - x^{-1}) = x^{-\alpha}L(x)$$

where L is a slowly varying function.
  If

$$F \in \text{MDA}(\Psi_\alpha)$$

then

$$c_n^{-1}(M_n - x_F) \xrightarrow{D} \Psi_\alpha$$

The MDA of the Weibull distribution includes important distributions such as the distribution uniform in $(0,1)$, power laws truncated to the right, and Beta distributions.

The MDA of the Gumbel Distribution

The Gumbel distribution is written as $\Lambda(x) = \exp[-\exp(-x)]$. Observe that the Gumbel distribution has exponential tails. This fact can be easily ascertained through Taylor expansion. There is no simple characterization of the MDA of the Gumbel Distribution.

The MDA of a Gumbel distribution encompasses a large class of distributions that includes the exponential distribution, the normal distribution, and the lognormal distribution. Though the Gumbel distribution has exponential tails, its MDA includes subexponential distributions such as the Berktander distribution, as explained in Goldie and Resnick.[7]

Max-Stable Distributions

Stable distributions remain unchanged after summation; **max-stable distributions** remain unchanged after taking maxima. A non-degenerate random variable X and the relative distribution is called max-stable if there are constants $c_n > 0$, $d_n \in R$ such that the following conditions are satisfied

$$\max(X_1, ..., X_n) \overset{D}{=} c_n X + d_n$$

where $X, X_1, ..., X_n$ are IID variables.

It can be demonstrated that the class of max-stable distributions coincides with the class of possible limit laws for normalized and centered maxima. In view of the previous discussions, the max-stable laws are the three possible limit laws: Frechet, Weibull, and Gumbel.

Generalized Extreme Value Distributions

The three extreme value distributions, Frechet, Weibull, and Gumbel, can be represented as a one-parameter family of distributions through the **Standard Generalized Extreme Value Distribution** (GEV) of Jenkinson and Von Mises. Define the distribution function H_ξ as follows:

$$H_\xi = \begin{cases} \exp[-(1 + \xi x)^{-1/\xi}] & \text{for } \xi \neq 0 \\ \exp(-\exp(-x)) & \text{for } \xi = 0 \end{cases}$$

where $1 + \xi x > 0$. One can see from the definition that $\xi = \alpha^{-1} > 0$ corresponds to the Frechet distribution, $\xi = 0$ corresponds to the Gumbel distribution, and $\xi = -\alpha^{-1} < 0$ corresponds to the Weibull distribution. We can now introduce the related location-scale dependent family $H_{\xi;\mu,\psi}$ by replacing the argument x with $(x - \mu)/\psi$.

---

[7] C.M. Goldie and S. Resnick, "Distributions that are Both Subexponential and in the Domain of Attraction of an Extreme-Value Distribution," *Advanced Applied Probability*, 20 (1988), pp. 706–718.

Order Statistics

The behavior of **order statistics** is a useful tool for characterizing fat-tailed distributions. For instance, the famous Zipf's law is an example of the behavior of order statistics. Consider a sample $X_1, ..., X_n$ made of n independent draws from the same distribution F. Let's arrange the sample in decreasing order:

$$X_{n,n} \leq ... \leq X_{1,n}$$

The random variable $X_{k,n}$ is called the **kth upper order statistic.** It can be demonstrated that the distribution of the *kth* upper order statistic is

$$F_{k,n} = P(X_{k,n} < x) = \sum_{r=0}^{k-1} \bar{F}^r(x)F^{n-r}(x)$$

In addition, if F is continuous, it has a density with respect to F such that

$$F_{k,n} = \int_{-\infty}^{x} f_{k,n}(z)dF(z)$$

where

$$f_{k,n} = \frac{n!}{(k-1)!(n-k)!}\bar{F}^{k-1}(x)F^{n-k}(x)$$

The differences between two consecutive variables in a sample $X_{k,n} - X_{k+1,n}$ are random variables called **spacings**. In the case of variables with finite right endpoint x_F the zero-th spacing is defined as: $X_{0,n} - X_{1,n} = x_F - X_{1,n}$. The distribution of spacings depends on the distribution F. For instance, it can be demonstrated that the spacings of an exponential random variable are independent, exponential random variables with mean $1/n$ for a n-sample. Spacings are a key concept for the definition of the Hill estimator, as explained later in this section.

Another key concept, which is related to spacings, is that of **quantile transformation**. Let $X_1, ..., X_n$ be IID variables with distribution function F and let $U_1, ..., U_n$ be IID variables uniformly distributed on the interval (0,1). Recall that, given a distribution function F, the quantile function of F, written $F^{\leftarrow}(x)$, is defined as follows:

$$F^{\leftarrow}(x) \ = \ \inf\{s \in R \colon F(s) \geq x\}, \, 0 < x < 1$$

It can be demonstrated that the following results hold:

- $F^{\leftarrow}(U_1) \stackrel{D}{=} X_1$
- $(X_{1,n}, ..., X_{n,n}) \stackrel{D}{=} [F^{\leftarrow}(U_{1,n}), ..., F^{\leftarrow}(U_{n,n})]$
- The random variable $F(X_1)$ has a uniform distribution on (0,1) if and only if F is a continuous function.

To appreciate the importance of the quantile transformation, let's introduce first the notion of **empirical distribution function** and second the Glivenko-Cantelli theorem. The empirical distribution function F_n of a sample $X_1, ..., X_n$ is defined as follows:

$$F_n(x) \ = \ \frac{1}{n} \sum_{i=1}^{n} I(X_i \leq x)$$

where I is the indicator function. In other words, for each x, the empirical distribution function counts the number of samples that are less than or equal to x.

The **Glivenko-Cantelli theorem** provides the theoretical underpinning of nonparametric statistics. It states that, if the samples $X_1, ..., X_n$ are independent draws from the distribution F, the empirical distribution function F_n tends to F for large n in the sense that

$$\Delta_n \ = \ \sup_{x \in R} |F_n(x) - F(x)| \stackrel{a.s.}{\to} 0 \, , \text{ for } n \to \infty$$

The quantile transformation tells us that in cases where F is a Pareto distribution, if we approximate n random draws from a uniformly distributed variable as the sequence $1, 2, ..., n$, then the corresponding values of the sample $X_1, ..., X_n$ will be

$$\frac{1}{1}, \frac{1}{2}, ..., \frac{1}{n}$$

which is a statement of the Zipf's law.

From the quantile transformation, the limit law of the ratio between two successive order statistics can also be inferred. Suppose that an (infinite) population is distributed according to a distribution $F \in \mathfrak{R}(\alpha)$ with regularly varying tails. Suppose that n samples are randomly and independently drawn from this distribution and ordered in function of size: $X_{n,n} \geq X_{n-1,n} \geq \ldots \geq X_{1,n}$. It can be demonstrated that the following property holds:

$$\frac{X_{k,n}}{X_{k+1,n}} = 1, \frac{k}{n} \to 0$$

Point Process of Exceedances or Peaks over Threshold

We have now reviewed the behavior of sums, maxima, and upper order statistics of continuous random variables. Yet another approach to EVT is based on point processes; herein we will use point processes only to define the point process of exceedances.

Point processes can be defined in many different ways. To illustrate the mathematics of point processes, let's first introduce the homogeneous Poisson process. A **homogeneous Poisson process** is defined as a process $N(t)$ that starts at zero, i.e., $N(0) = 0$, and has independent stationary increments. In addition, the random variable $N(t)$ is distributed as a Poisson variable with parameter λt. $N(t)$ is therefore a time-dependent discrete variable that can assume nonnegative integer values. Exhibit 13.3 illustrates the distribution of a Poisson variable.

A homogeneous Poisson process can also be defined as a random sequence of points on the real line. Consider all discrete sequences of points on the real line separated by random intervals. Intervals are independent random variables with exponential distribution. This is the usual definition of a Poisson process. Call $N(t)$ the number of points that fall in the interval $[0,t]$. It can be demonstrated that $N(t)$ is a homogeneous Poisson process according to the previous definition.

This latter definition can be generalized to define point processes. Intuitively, a generic point process is a random collection of discrete points in some space. From a mathematical point of view, it is convenient to describe a point process through the distribution of the number of points that fall in an arbitrary set.[8] In the case of homogeneous Poisson processes, we consider the number of points that fall in a given interval; for a generic point process, it is convenient to consider a wider class of sets.

Consider a subspace E of a finite dimensional Euclidean space of dimension n. Consider also the σ-algebra $\mathfrak{B}$ of the Borel sets generated by open sets in E. The space E is called the state space. For each point x in E and for each set $A \in \mathfrak{B}$, define the **Dirac measure** ε_x as

---

[8] D.R. Cox and V. Isham, *Point Processes* (London: Chapman and Hall, 1980).

EXHIBIT 13.3   Distribution of a Poisson Variable

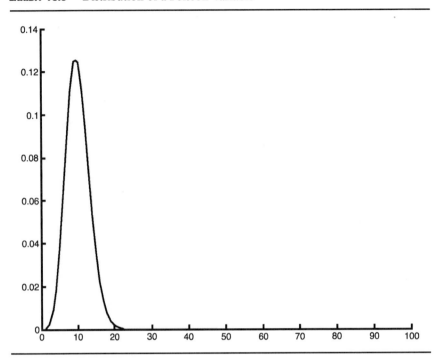

$$\varepsilon_x = \begin{cases} 1 \text{ if } x \in A \\ 0 \text{ if } x \notin A \end{cases}$$

For any given sequence x_i, $i \geq 1$ of points in E, define the following set function:

$$m(A) = \sum_{i=1}^{\infty} \varepsilon_{x_i}(A) = \text{card}\{i : X_i \in A\}, A \in \mathfrak{B}$$

It can be verified that $m(A)$ is a measure $\mathfrak{B}$, called a **counting measure**. If a counting measure is finite on each compact set, then it is called a **point measure**. In other words, any given countable sequence in E generates a counting measure on $\mathfrak{B}$.

A point process is obtained associating to each family of sets $A_i \in \mathfrak{B}$ the joint probability distributions:

$$\Pr\{m(A_i) = n_i; \ i = 1, 2, \ldots, k; \ k = 1, 2, \ldots\}$$

To make this definition mathematically rigorous, a point process can be defined as a measurable map from some probability space to the set of all point measures equipped with an appropriate σ-algebra. Besides the mathematical details, it should be clear that point processes are defined by the probability distribution of the number of points that fall in each set A of some σ-algebra. The key ingredients of point processes are (1) counting measures that associate to each set A the number of points of each discrete sequence that falls in A with the additivity restrictions of measures and (2) probability distributions defined over the space of counting measures.

Equipped with the general concept of point processes, we can now define the **point process of exceedances**. Consider a threshold formed by any real number u and a sequence of random variables X_i, $i = 1, 2, \ldots$. The point process of exceedances with state space $E = (0,1)$ counts the number of instances where the random variables X_i exceed the threshold u:

$$N_n(A) = \sum_{i=1}^{\infty} \varepsilon_{i/n}(A) = \operatorname{card}\{i \le n \text{ and } X_i > u\}$$

Note that in this case the state space specifies the size of the sample.

Estimation

In the previous sections we presented some key topics related to the probability structure of the tails of distributions, be they light- or fat-tailed. Let's now turn to the problem of estimation which is the key practical task. The problem of estimation for EVT is essentially the problem of estimating the tail of a distribution from a finite sample. The key statistical idea of EVT from the point of view of estimation is to use only those sample data that belong to the tail and not the entire sample. This notion has to be made precise by finding criteria that allow one to separate the tail from the bulk of the distribution. Therefore, the estimation problem of EVT distribution can be broken down into three separate subproblems:

- Identify the beginning of the tail.
- Identify the shape of the tail, in particular discriminate if it is a power-law tail.
- Estimate the tail parameters, in particular the tail index in the case of a power-law tail.

It turns out that these three problems cannot be easily separated. In fact, there is no reliable constructive theory for solving all these problems automatically. In particular, the choice of the statistical model (i.e., the distribution that best describes data) is a classical problem of formulating and validating a scientific hypothesis in a probabilistic context. However, there are many tools and tests to help the modeler in this endeavor.

The first fundamental tool is the graphical representation of data, in particular the **quantile plot** or **QQ-plot** defined as the following set:

$$\left\{ X_{k,n}, F^{\leftarrow}\left(\frac{n-k+1}{n+1}\right) : k = 1, 2, ..., n \right\}$$

The quantile transformation and the Glivenko-Cantelli theorem allow concluding that this plot must be approximately linear. Should F be a Pareto distribution, the linearity of the QQ-plot is another statement of Zipf's law. The quantile plot allows a quick verification of a statistical hypotheses by checking the approximate linearity of the plot. It also allows the modeler to form a preliminary opinion on where the tail begins and whether the model fails at the far end of the tail.

Though invaluable as an exploratory tool, graphics rely on human judgment and intuition. Rigorous tests are needed. A starting point is parameter estimation for the Generalized Extreme Value (GEV) Distribution that we write as

$$H_{\xi;\mu,\psi}(x) = \exp\left\{ -\left(1 + \xi\frac{x-\mu}{\psi}\right)^{-1/\xi} \right\}, \; 1 + \xi\frac{x-\mu}{\psi} > 0$$

with the convention that the case $\xi = 0$ corresponds to the Gumbel distribution:

$$H_{0;\mu,\psi}(x) = \exp\left\{ -e^{-\frac{x-\mu}{\psi}} \right\}, \; x \in R$$

We saw above that these distributions are the limit distributions, if they exist, of the normalized maxima of IID sequences. Suppose that the data to be estimated are independent draws from some EGV. This is a rather strong assumption that we will progressively relax. This assumption might be justified in domains where long series of data are available so that the sample data are the maxima of blocks of consecutive data. Though this assumption is probably too strong in the domain of finance, it is useful to elaborate its consequences.

Standard methodologies exist for parameter estimation in this case. In particular, the usual maximum likelihood (ML) methodology can be used for fitting the best GEV to data. Note that if the above distributions fit maxima we have to divide data into blocks and consider the maxima of each block. To apply ML, we have to compute the likelihood function on the data and choose the parameters that maximize it. This can be done with numerical integration methods.

An estimation method alternative to ML is the method of moments which consists in equating empirical moments with theoretical moments. An ample literature on various versions of the method of moments exists.[9]

Let's now release the assumption that the sequence of empirical data are independent draws from an exact GEV and replace this with the weaker assumption that empirical data are independent draws from $F \in$ MDA(H_ξ). If we assume that the limit distribution is a Frechet distribution, then data must be independent draws from some distribution F whose tail has the form:

$$\bar{F} = x^{-\alpha} L(x)$$

where L is a slowly varying function as described earlier in this chapter. For this reason, estimation under this weaker assumption is semiparametric in nature. We will now introduce a number of estimators of the shape parameter ξ.

The Pickand Estimator

The Pickand estimator $\hat{\xi}_{k,n}^{(P)}$ for an n-sample of independent draws from a distribution $F \in$ MDA(H_ξ) is defined as

$$\hat{\xi}_{k,n}^{(P)} = \frac{1}{\ln 2} \ln \frac{X_{k,n} - X_{2k,n}}{X_{2k,n} - X_{4k,n}}$$

where the $X_{k,n}$ are upper order statistics.

---

[9] For a discussion of the different methods, see R. L. Smith, "Extreme Value Theory," in W. Ledermann (ed.), *Handbook of Applicable Mathematics, Supplement*, (Chichester, U.K.: John Wiley & Sons, 1990), pp. 437–472. For a discussion of the method of probability-weighted moments, see J.R.M. Hosking, J.R. Wallis, and E.F. Wood, "Estimation of the Generalized Extreme-Value Distribution by the Method of Probability-Weighted Moments," *Technometrics* 27 (1985), pp. 251–261.

It can be demonstrated that the Pickand estimator has the following properties:

■ *Weak consistency*:

$$\hat{\xi}^{(P)}_{k,n} \xrightarrow{P} \xi, \; n \to \infty, \; k \to \infty, \; \frac{k}{n} \to 0$$

■ *Strong consistency*:

$$\hat{\xi}^{(P)}_{k,n} \xrightarrow{a.s.} \xi, \; n \to \infty, \; \frac{k}{\ln(\ln n)} \to \infty, \; \frac{k}{n} \to 0$$

■ Asymptotic normality under technical conditions.

The Pickand estimator is an estimator of the parameter ξ that does not require any assumption on the type of limit distribution. Let's now examine the Hill estimator, which requires the prior knowledge that sample data are independent draws from a Frechet distribution. Later in this chapter we will see that the assumption of independence can be weakened.

The Hill Estimator

Suppose that $X_1, ..., X_n$ are independent draws from a distribution $F \in \text{MDA}(\Phi_\alpha)$, $\alpha > 0$ so that $\bar{F} = x^{-\alpha}L(x)$ where L is a slowly varying function. The Hill estimator can be obtained as a MLE based on the k upper order statistics. The Hill estimator takes the following form:

$$\hat{\alpha}^{(H)} = \hat{\alpha}^{(H)}_{k,n} = \left(\frac{1}{k} \sum_{j=1}^{k} \ln X_{j,n} - \ln X_{k,n} \right)^{-1}$$

The Hill estimator has the same weak and strong consistency property as well as asymptotic normality as the Pickand estimator. The Hill estimator is by far the most popular estimator of the tail index. It has the advantage of being robust to some dependency in the data but can perform very poorly in case of deviations from strict Pareto behavior. In addition, it is subject to a bias-variance trade-off in the following sense: The variance of the Hill estimator depends on the ratio k/n: it decreases for increasing k. However, using a large fraction of the data will introduce bias in the estimator.

As stated above, a critical tenet of EVT is the idea of fitting the tail rather than the entire distribution. A number of articles on the automatic determination of the optimal subset of samples to be included in the tail have appeared. One approach to the automatic determination of the tail sample using the variance-bias trade-off was proposed by Drees and Kaufmann,[10] while Dacorogna, Muller, Pictet, and de Vries[11] and Danielsson and de Vries[12] proposed methods based on a bootstrap approach.

The **moment ratio estimator** is a generalization of the Hill estimator. Consider the following estimator of the second order moments of the k upper order statistic:

$$\hat{M}_{k,n} = \frac{1}{k}\left(\sum_{j=1}^{k} \ln X_{j,n} - \ln X_{k+1,n}\right)^2$$

The moment ratio estimator is defined as follows:

$$\hat{\alpha}_{k,n}^{(m)} = \frac{1}{2}\left(\frac{\hat{M}_{k,n}}{\hat{\alpha}_{k,n}^{(H)}}\right)$$

Niklas Wagner and Terry Marsh[13] did extensive simulation analysis of various estimators. Their finding is that the moment ratio estimator outperforms the Hill estimator in sequences with a dependence structure (this is discussed further in the next section).

The Hill estimator was extended by Dekkers, Einmal, and de Haan[14] to cover the entire range of shape parameters ξ. A number of other estimators have been proposed. In particular, under the assumption that financial data follow a stable process, estimation procedures based on regression analysis has been suggested. In fact, the assumption of stable

---

[10] H. Drees and E. Kaufmann, "Selecting the Optimal Sample Fraction in Univariate Extreme Value Estimation," *Stochastic Processes and their Application* 75 (2000), pp. 254–274.

[11] M.M. Dacorogna, U.A. Muller, O.V. Pictet, and C.G. de Vries, "The Distribution of Extremal Foreign Exchange Rate Returns in Extremely Large Data Sets," Olsen & Associates preprint, Zurich, 1995.

[12] J. Danielsson and C.G. de Vries, "Tail Index and Quantile Estimation with Very High Frequency Data," *Journal of Empirical Finance* 4 (1977), pp. 241–257.

[13] N. Wagner and T. Marsh, "On Adaptive Tail Index Estimation for Financial Return Models," Research Program in Finance, Working Paper RPF-295, Hans School of Management, University of California, Berkeley, November 2000.

[14] See A.L.M. Dekkers and L. de Haan, "On the Estimation of the Extreme-Value Index and Large Quantile Estimation," *Annals of Statistics* 17 (1989), pp. 1795–1832.

behavior, or at least of exact Pareto tail, naturally leads to fitting a linear model in a logarithmic scale. There is an ample literature on this topic with a number of useful discussions, though empirical studies based on Monte Carlo simulations are still limited.[15]

The estimation methods reviewed above are based on the behavior of maxima and upper order statistics; another methodology uses the points of exceedances of high thresholds. Estimation methodologies based on the points of exceedances require an appropriate model for the point process of exceedances that was defined in general terms previously in this chapter.

ELIMINATING THE ASSUMPTION OF IID SEQUENCES

In the previous sections we reviewed a number of mathematical tools that are used to describe fat-tailed processes under the key assumption of IID sequences. In this section we discuss the implications of eliminating this assumption. However, in finance theory the assumption of stationary sequences of independent variables is only a first approximation; it has been challenged in several instances. Consider individual price time series. The autocorrelation function of returns decays exponentially and goes to near zero at very short-time horizons while the autocorrelation function of volatility decays only hyperbolically and remains different from zero for long periods. In addition, if we consider portfolios made of many securities, price processes exhibit patterns of cross correlations at different time-lags and, possibly, cointegrating relationships. These findings offer additional reasons to consider the assumption of serial independence as only a first approximation.

If we now consider the question of stationarity, empirical findings are more delicate. The non-stationarity that can be removed by differencing is easy to handle and does not present a problem. The critical issue is whether financial time series can be modeled with a single Data Generation Process (DGP) that remains the same for the entire period under consideration or if the model must be modified. Consider, for instance, the question of structural breaks. At a basic level, structural breaks entail nonstationarity as the model parameters change with time and thus the finite-dimension distributions change with time. However, at a higher level one might try to model structural changes, for instance through state-space models or Markov switching models. In this way, stationarity is recovered but at the price of a more complex, serially autocorrelated model.

EVT for multivariate models with complex patterns of serial correlations loses its generality and becomes model-dependent. One has to evaluate each model in terms of its behavior as regards extremes. In this section we will explore a number of models that have been proposed for modeling financial time series: ARCH and GARCH models and, more in general, state-space models. First, however, a number of methodological considerations are in order.

In the context of IID sequences, EVT tries to answer the question of how to estimate a distribution with heavy tails given only a limited amount of data. The model is the simplest (i.e., a sequence of IID variables) and the question is how to extrapolate from finite samples to the entire tail. In the context of IID distributions, conditional and unconditional distributions coincide. However, if we release the IID assumption, we have to specify the model and to estimate the entire model—not just the tail of one variable. Conditional and unconditional distributions no longer coincide. For instance, there are families of models that are conditionally normal and unconditionally fat-tailed.

Here difficulties begin as model estimation might be complex. In addition, estimation of some specific tail might not be the primary concern in model estimation. In the context of variables with a dependence structure, EVT can be thought of as a methodology to estimate the tails of the unconditional distribution, leaving aside the question of full model estimation.

An important methodological question is whether fat-tailedness is generated by the transformation of a sequence of zero-mean, finite variance IID variables (i.e., white noise) or whether innovations themselves have fat tails (i.e., so-called **colored noise**). For instance, as we will see, GARCH models entail fat-tailed return distributions as the result of the transformation of white noise. On the other hand, one might want to estimate an Autoregressive Moving Average (ARMA) model under the assumption of innovations with infinite variance.

Understanding how power laws and, more in general, fat tails are generated from normal variables has been a primary concern of econometrics and econophysics. Given the universality of power laws in economics, it is clearly important to understand how they are generated. These questions go well beyond the statistical analysis of heavy-tailed processes and involve questions of economic theories. Essentially, one wants to understand how the decisions of a large number of economic agents do not average out but produce cascading and amplification phenomena.

The Law of Large Numbers tells that if individual processes are independent and have finite variance, then phenomena average out in aggregate and tend to an average limit. However, if individual processes have fat tails, phenomena do not average out even in the infinite limit. The weight of individual tails prevails and drives the aggregate process. Philip W. Anderson, the corecipient of the 1997 Nobel Prize in Physics, remarked:

> Much of the real world is controlled as much by the "tails" of distributions as by means or averages: by the exceptional, not the mean; by the catastrophe, not the steady drip; by the very rich, not the "middle class." We need to free ourselves from "average" thinking.[16]

When and if fat-tailed drivers exist, they control the ensemble to which they belong. But what generates these powerful drivers? Models that generate fat tails from standard normal innovations attempt to answer this question. Different types of models have been proposed. One such category of models is purely geometric and exploits mathematical theories such as percolation and random graph. Others exploit phenomena of dynamic nonlinear self-reinforcing cascades of events.

Percolation models are based on the well known mathematical fact that in regular spatial structures of nodes connected by links, a uniform density of links produces connected subsets of nodes whose size is distributed according to power laws. Percolation models are time-transversal models: They model aggregation at any given time. They might be used to explain how fat-tailed IID sequences are generated.

Dynamic financial econometric models exploit cascading phenomena due to nonlinearities, in particular multiplicative noise. In a deterministic setting, it is well known that nonlinear chaotic models generate sequences that, when analyzed statistically, exhibit fat-tailed distributions. The same happens when noise is subject to nonlinear transformation. In the next sections, we explore simple ARMA models, ARCH-GARCH models, subordinated models, and state-space models, all examples of dynamic financial econometric models.

Before doing this, however, let's go back to the question of estimation. As observed above, if variables are not IID but can be considered generated by a DGP, the question of estimation is no longer the estimation of a variable but that of estimating a model or a theory. The estima-

---

[16] Philip W. Anderson, "Some Thoughts About Distribution in Economics," in W. B. Arthur, S. N. Durlaf, and D.A. Lane (eds.), *The Economy as an Evolving Complex System II* (Reading, MA: Addison-Wesley, 1997).

tion of the eventual tail index is part of a larger effort. However, empirical data are a sequence of samples characterized by an unconditional distribution. One might want to understand if estimation procedures used for IID sequences can be applied in this more general setting. For instance, one might want to understand if tail-index estimators such as the Hill estimator can be used in the case of serially correlated sequences generated by a generic DGP.

From a practical standpoint, this question is quite important as one wants to estimate the tails even if one does not know exactly what model generated the sequence. Clearly, there is no general answer to this problem. However, the behavior of a number of estimators under different DGPs has been explored through simulation as explained in the following section.

Heavy-Tailed ARMA Processes

Let's first consider the infinite moving average representation of a univariate stationary series:

$$x_t = \sum_{i=0}^{\infty} h_i \varepsilon_{t-i} + m$$

under the assumption that innovations are IID α-stable laws of tail index α. By the properties of stable distributions it can be demonstrated that the finite-dimensional distributions of the process x are α-stable. However, restrictions on the coefficients need to be imposed. It can be demonstrated that a sufficient condition to ensure that the process x exists and is stationary is the following:

$$\sum_{i=0}^{\infty} |h_i|^{\alpha} < \infty$$

As we have seen in the previous section, a general univariate ARMA(p,q) model is written as follows:

$$X_t = \sum_{i=1}^{p} \alpha_i X_{t-i} + \sum_{j=1}^{q} \alpha_j Z_{t-j}$$

where the Z are IID variables.

Using the Lag Operator—L—notation, L^i represents the variable at i lags, the ARMA(p,q) model is written as follows:

$$X_t = \sum_{i=1}^{p} L^i X_t + \sum_{j=1}^{q} L^j Z_t$$

The theory of ARMA processes developed in Chapters 11 and 12 can be carried over at least partially to cover the case of fat-tailed innovations. In particular, an ARMA(p,q) process with IID α-stable innovations admits a stationary, infinite moving average representation under the same conditions as in the classical finite-variance case. The coefficients of the moving average satisfy the condition

$$\sum_{i=0}^{\infty} |b_i|^{\alpha} < \infty$$

In the case of fat-tailed innovations, covariances, and autocovariances looses their meaning. It can also be demonstrated, however, that the empirical autocorrelation function is meaningful and is asymptotically normal. It can be demonstrated that maximum likelihood estimates can be extended to the infinite variance case, though through a number of ad hoc processes.

ARCH/GARCH Processes

As we saw in Chapter 12, The simplest ARCH model can be written as follows. Suppose that X is the random variable to be modeled, Z is a sequence of independent standard normal variables, and σ is a hidden variable. The ARCH(1) model is written as

$$X_t = \sigma_t Z_t$$

$$\sigma_t^2 = \beta + \delta X_{t-1}^2$$

This basic model was extended by Bollerslev[17] who proposed the GARCH(p,q) model written as

$$X_t = \sigma_t Z_t$$

---

[17] Tim Bollerslev, "Generalized Autoregressive Conditional Heteroscedasticity," *Journal of Econometrics* 31 (1989), pp. 307–327.

$$\sigma_t^2 = \beta + \sum_{i=1}^{p} \gamma_i \sigma_{t-i}^2 + \sum_{i=1}^{q} \delta_i X_{t-i}^2$$

The IID variables Z can be standard normal variables or other symmetrical, eventually fat-tailed, variables.

Let's first observe that model parameters must be constrained in order to guarantee the stationarity of the model. Stationarity conditions depend on each model. No general simple expression for the stationarity conditions is available.

Due to the multiplicative nature of noise, GARCH models are able to generate fat-tailed distributions even if innovations have finite variance. This fact was established by Kesten[18] in 1973. The tail index can be theoretically computed at least in the case GARCH(1,1). Suppose a GARCH(1,1) stationary process with Gaussian innovation is given. It can be demonstrated that

$$P(X > x) \approx \frac{c}{2} x^{-2\kappa}$$

where κ is the solution of an integral equation. In the generic p, q case, the return process is still fat-tailed but no practical way to compute the index from model parameter is known.

Subordinated Processes

Subordinated processes allow the time scale to vary. Subordinated models are, in a sense, the counterpart of stochastic volatility models insofar as they model the change in volatility by contracting and expanding the time scale. The first model was proposed in 1973 by Clark.[19] Subordinated models have been extensively studied by Ghysels, Gourieroux, and Josiak.[20]

Subordinated models can be applied quite naturally in the context of trading. Individual trades are randomly spaced. In modern electronic exchanges, the time and size of trades are individually recorded thus allowing for accurate estimates of the distributional properties of inter-trades intervals. Consideration of random spacings between trades natu-

---

[18] H. Kesten, "Random Difference Equations and Renewal Theory for Products of Random Matrices" *Acta Mathematica* 131 (1973), pp. 207–248.

[19] P.K. Clark, "A Subordinated Stochastic Process Model with Finite Variance for Speculative Prices," *Econometrica* 41 (January 1973), pp. 735–755.

[20] E. Ghysels, C. Gourieroux, and J. Josiak, "Market Time and Asset Price Movement Theory and Estimation," Working Paper 95-32 Cyrano, Montreal, 1995.

rally leads to the consideration of subordinated models. Subordinated models generate unconditional fat-tailed distributions.

Markov Switching Models

The GARCH family of models is not the only family of serially correlated models able to produce fat tails starting from normally distributed innovations. State-space models and Markov-switching models present the same feature. The basic ideas of state-space models and Markov switching models is to split the model into two parts: (1) a regressive model that regresses the model variable over a hidden variable and (2) an autoregressive model that describes the hidden variables.

In its simplest linear form, a state-space model is written as follows:

$$X_t = \alpha Z_t + \varepsilon_t$$

$$Z_t = \beta Z_{t-1} + \delta_t$$

where ε_t, δ_t are normally distributed independent white noises. State-space models can also be written in a multiplicative form:

$$X_t = \alpha Z_{t-1} + \varepsilon_t$$

$$\alpha_t = \beta \alpha_{t-1} + \delta_t$$

If the second equation is a Markov chain, the model is called a **Markov-switching model**. A well-known example of Markov-switching models is the Hamilton model in which a two-state Markov chain drives the switch between two different regressions.

Purely linear state-space models exhibit fat tails only if innovations are fat-tailed. However, multiplicative state-space models and Markov-switching models can exhibit fat tails even if innovations are normally distributed. There is a growing literature on Markov-switching and multiplicative state-space models and a relatively large number of different models, univariate as well as multivariate, have been proposed. Stochastic volatility models are the continuous-time version of multiplicative state-space models.

Estimation

Let's now go back to the question of model estimation in a non-IID framework. Suppose that we want to estimate the tail index of the unconditional distribution of a set of empirical observations in the general setting of non-

IID variables. Note that if variables are fat-tailed, we cannot say that they are serially autocorrelated as moments of second order generally do not exist. Therefore we have to make some hypothesis on the DGP.

There is no general theory of estimation under arbitrary DGP. Both theoretical and simulation work are limited to specific DGPs. ARMA models have been extensively studied. EVT holds for ARMA models under general non-clustering conditions.[21]

Often only simulation results are available. A fairly ample set of results are available for GARCH(1,1) models. For these models Resnick and Starica[22] showed that the Hill estimator is a consistent estimator of the tail index. Wagner and Marsh compared the performance of the Hill estimator and of the moment ratio estimator for three model classes: IID α-stable returns, IID symmetric student, and GARCH(1,1) with student-t innovation. They found that, in an adoptive framework, the moment ratio estimator generally yields results superior to the Hill estimator.

Scaling and Self-Similarity

The concept of scaling is now quite frequently evoked in economics and finance. Let's begin by making a distinction between scaling and self-similarity and some of the properties associated with inverse power laws within or outside the Levy-stable scaling regime. These concepts have different, and not equivalent, definitions.

The concepts of scaling and self-similarity apply to distributions, processes or structures. Self-similarity was introduced as a property that applies to geometrical self-similar objects (i.e., fractal structures). In this context, self-similarity means that a structure can be put into a one-to-one correspondence with a part of itself. Note that no finite structure can have this property; self-similarity is the mark of infinite structures. Self-similarity entails **scaling**: If a fractal structure is expanded by a given factor, its measure expands by a power of the same factor.[23] The notion of scaling is often expressed as **absence of scale**, meaning that a scaling object looks the same at any scale, large or small: It is impossible to ascertain the size of a portion of a scaling object by looking at its shape. The classical illustration is a Norwegian coastline with its fjords and fjords within fjords that look the same regardless of the scale.

---

[21] See Embrechts, Kluppelberg, and Mikosch, *Modelling Extremal Events for Insurance and Finance.*

[22] S. Resnick and C. Starica, "Tail Index Estimation for Dependent Data," *Annals of Applied Probability* 8 (1998), pp. 1156–1183.

[23] For an introduction to fractals, see J. Falconer, *Fractal Geometry* (Chichester, U.K.: John Wiley & Sons, 1990).

However, scaling can be defined without making reference to fractals. In its simplest form, the notion of scaling entails a variable x and an observable A which is a function of $A = A(x)$. If the observable obeys a scaling relationship, there is a constant factor between x and A in the sense that $A(\lambda x) = \lambda^s A(x)$, where s is the scaling exponent that does not depend on x. The only function $A(x)$ that satisfies this relationship is a power law. In the three-dimensional Euclidean space, volume scales as the third power of linear length and surface as the second power, while fractals scale according to their fractal dimension.

The same ideas can be applied in a random context, but require careful reasoning. A power-law distribution has a scaling property as multiplying the variable by a factor multiplies probabilities by a constant factor, regardless of the level of the variable. This means that the ratio between the probability of the events $X > x$ and $X > ax$ depends only on a power of a, not on x. As an inverse power law is not defined at zero, scaling in this sense is a property of the tails. The probabilistic interpretation of this property is the following: the probability that an observation exceeds ax conditional on the knowledge that the observation exceeds x does not depend on x but only on a.

There are, however, other meanings attached to scaling and these might be a source of confusion. In the context of physical phenomena, scaling is often intended as *identity of distribution after aggregation*. The same idea is also behind the theory of groups of renormalization and the notion of self-similarity applied to structures such as coastlines. In the latter case, the intuitive meaning of self-similarity is that if one *aggregates* portions of the coastline, approximating their shape with a straight line, and then rescales; the resulting picture is qualitatively similar to the original. The same idea applies to percolation structures: By aggregating "sites" (i.e., points in a percolation lattice) into supersites and carefully redefining links, one obtains the same distribution of connected clusters.

Applying the idea of aggregation in a random context, self-similarity seems to mean that, after rescaling, the distribution of the sum of independent copies of a random variable maintains the same shape of the distribution of the variable itself. Note that this property holds *only* for the tails of subexponential distributions—and it holds strictly only for stable laws that have tails in the (0,2) range but whose shape is not a power law except, approximately, in the tails. It also holds for Gaussian distributions that do not have power-law tails.

Scaling acquires yet another meaning when applied to stochastic processes that are functions of time. The most common among the different meanings is the following: A stochastic process is said to have a **scaling property** if there is no natural scale for looking at its paths and distributions. Intuitively, this means that it is not possible to gauge the scale of a sample by looking at its distribution; there is absence of scale. An example from finance comes from price patterns. If a price pattern is generated by a process with the scaling property, the plots of average daily and monthly prices will appear to be perfectly similar in distribution; looking at the plot, it's impossible to tell if it refers to daily or monthly prices.

Self-similarity is another way of expressing the same concept. A process is self-similar if a portion of the process is similar to the entire process. As we are considering a random environment, self-similarity applies to distributions, not to the actual realization of a process. Let's now make these concepts more precise.

A stochastic process $X(t)$ is said to be **self-similar** (ss) of index H (H-ss) if all its finite-dimensional distributions obey the scaling relationship:

$$(X_{kt_1}, X_{kt_2}, ..., X_{kt_m}) \overset{D}{=} k^{-H}(X_{t_1}, X_{t_2}, ..., X_{t_m}) \forall k > 0$$

$$0 < H < 1 , \ t_1, t_2, ..., t_m > 0$$

The above expression means that the scaling of time by the factor k scales the variables X by the factor k^H. It gives precise meaning to the notion of self-similarity applied to stochastic processes.

There is a wide variety of self-similar processes that cannot be characterized in a simple way as scaling laws: The scaling property of stochastic processes might depend upon the shape of distributions as well as the shape of correlations. Let's restrict our attention to processes that are self-similar with stationary increments (sssi) and with index H (H-sssi). These processes can be either Gaussian or non-Gaussian. Note that a Gaussian process is a process whose finite-dimensional distributions are all Gaussian.

Gaussian H-sssi processes might have independent increments or exhibit long-range correlations. The only Gaussian H-sssi process with independent increment is the Brownian motion, but there are an infinite number of **fractional** Brownian motions, which are Gaussian H-sssi processes with long-range correlations. Thus there are an infinite variety of Gaussian self-similar processes. Among the many non-Gaussian H-sssi processes with independent increments are the stable Levy processes, which are random walks whose increments follow a stable distribution.[24]

There is another definition of self-similarity for stochastic processes which makes use of the concept of aggregation; it is closer, at least in spirit, to the theory of renormalization groups. Consider a stationary

---

[24] See G. Samorodnitsky and M.S. Taqqu, *Stable Non-Gaussian Random Processes* (New York: Chapman & Hall, 1994).

infinite sequence of independent and identically distributed variables X_i, $i \geq 1$. Create consecutive nonoverlapping blocks of m variables and define the corresponding aggregated sequence of level m averaging over each block as follows:

$$X_k^{(m)} = \frac{1}{m} \sum_{i=(k-1)m+1}^{km} X_i$$

A sequence is called **exactly self-similar** if, for any integer m the following relationship holds:

$$X \overset{D}{=} m^{1-H} X^{(m)}$$

A stationary sequence is called **asymptotically self-similar** if the above relationship holds only for $m \to \infty$.

When we apply the notion of scaling to stochastic processes—the natural setting for economics and finance—we have to abandon the simple characterization of scaling as inverse power laws. Though the scaling property is in itself characterized through simple power laws, the scaling processes are complex and rich mathematical structures entailing a variety of distributions and correlation functions. In particular, the long-range correlation structure of the process plays a role as important as the distribution of its variables.

EVIDENCE OF FAT TAILS IN FINANCIAL VARIABLES

To appreciate the applicability of scaling laws, let's first look at the range of variation of the economic and financial variables with which they are generally associated. Variables such as income, personal wealth, corporate size, and market capitalization span many orders of magnitude. Large insurance claims cover at least three orders of magnitude, with the largest claims reaching billions of dollars.[25] Bankruptcies cover a similarly broad range of orders of magnitude.[26] Daily stock returns span some two orders of magnitude. However, economic variables such as interest rates or GNP rates span a smaller set of values. Obviously the range of variables is not in itself a

---

[25] See Embrechts, Kluppelberg, and Mikosch, *Modelling Extremal Events for Insurance and Finance.*

[26] For empirical evidence on the Japanese experience, see H. Aoyama, Y. Nagahara, M. P. Okazaki, W. Souma, H. Takayasu, and M. Takayasu, "Pareto's Law for Income of Individuals and Debt of Bankrupt Companies," *Cond-Mat* 0006038, 2000.

sign of scaling or inverse power laws, but these variables cover a broad enough range of values to make the scaling approximation meaningful.

The first example of scaling laws in economics is due to the economist Pareto in the nineteenth century. Pareto observed that, above some threshold, the proportion of individuals with an income in excess of x is inversely proportional to x. Generalizing, a distribution of the type

$$F(x) = P(X > x) = \frac{1}{x^\alpha} \text{ for } x \geq 1$$

is called a Pareto law.

The presence of scaling laws has also been researched in price behavior. In 1963 Mandelbrot[27] observed self-similarity in economic time series when he discovered that cotton price time series had approximately the same shape at different time scales. Based on this empirical discovery, Mandelbrot later proposed stable laws and fractional Brownian motions as a model for price behavior.

Since Mandelbrot's observations, researchers have been trying to prove or disprove the existence of inverse power laws in the area of asset returns. The jury is still out. A first remark is that scaling laws of returns apply only to short-term (from one minute to a few days) returns. Beyond this time horizon, returns exhibit complex behavior that depends on the length and positioning of the observation periods.

One of the first systematic studies of the distribution of high-frequency data was conducted by Zurich-based Olsen & Associates on exchange rates.[28] Olsen researchers found that many exchange rates follow scaling laws with exponents < 2. More recently, several as yet unpublished studies have look at fat-tailed returns in less traded currencies: Payaslioglu[29] used tail index estimation for the Turkish lira and Chobanov, Mateev, Mittnik and Rachev[30] looked at the Bulgarian lev.

---

[27] Benoit Mandelbrot, "The Variation of Certain Speculative Prices," *Journal of Business* 36 (1963), pp. 394–419.

[28] U.A. Muller, M.M. Dacorogna, and O.V. Pictet, "Heavy Tails in High Frequency Financial Data," in R. Adler, R. Feldman, and M.S. Taqqu (eds.) *A Practical Guide to Heavy Tails: Statistical Techniques for Analysing Heavy-Tailed Distributions* (Boston: Birkhauser, 1997).

[29] Cem Payaslioglu, "Tail Behavior of Return Distributions of Exchange Rates under Different Regimes: A Case Study for Turkey."

[30] G. Chobanov, P. Mateev, S. Mittnik, and S. Rachev, "Modeling the Distribution of Highly Volatile Exchange-rate Time Series" in P.M. Robinson and M. Rosenblatt (eds.), *Athens Conference on Applied Probability and Time Series, Volume II: Time Series Analysis* (New York: Springer, 1996).

In the area of stock price returns at short time horizons, initial findings by Mantegna and Stanley[31] seemed to indicate truncated inverse power laws with exponents in the range 1.4–1.6, well within the scaling regime. More recent findings by Plerou et al[32] point to an exponent 3 without truncation, well outside the Levy stable regime. Johanson and Sornette[33] suggest that market crashes are not the fat tails of return distributions, but outliers. Still other studies, for instance Laherre and Sornette,[34] found that returns are better described by a function rather than by a single exponent, thus creating multifractal distributions.

Applying the notion of stable laws to stock price returns raises additional questions. The infinite variance property of stable laws is somewhat in contrast with empirical findings about stock returns, most of which seem to indicate finite variance, though higher order moments might become infinite. This is in agreement with the use of volatility as a key parameter in financial risk management. Stable laws, on the other hand, would require abandoning the notion of volatility. It seems fair to conclude that stable laws are not a good approximation to stock returns, though inverse power laws with exponent >2 might still hold.

As noted above, the fundamental practical importance of the presence of stable laws in economic and financial phenomena is that they would render risk management and financial decision-making difficult: If variables are governed by stable laws, there is no possibility of diversifying risk. Modeling with fat-tailed distributions has the status of a theoretical hypothesis as it implies extrapolating that the future will bring unbounded innovation. In the insurance industry, for example, the assumption of scaling is appropriate in domains such as catastrophe insurance, where there is no natural bound to the size of catastrophes and where experience has shown that very large catastrophic events do indeed occur.

---

[31] R. N. Mantegna and H.E. Stanley, "Scaling Behavior in the Dynamics of an Economic Index," *Nature* 46 (1995), p. 376.

[32] V. Plerou, P. Gopikrishnan, L.A.N. Amaral, M. Meyer, and H.E. Stanley, "Scaling of the Distribution of Price Fluctuations of Individual Companies," *Physical Review E* 60, no. 6, Part A (December 1999), pp. 6519–6529

[33] A. Johansen and D. Sornette, "Stock Market Crashes Are Outliers," *European Physical Journal* B 9, no. 1 (February 1998), pp. 141–143.

[34] J. Laherre and D. Sornette, "Stretched Exponential Distributions in Nature and Economy: 'Fat Tails' with Characteristic Scales," *European Physical Journal* B 2 (1998), p. 525.

ON THE APPLICABILITY OF EXTREME VALUE THEORY IN FINANCE

In financial applications, EVT for fat-tailed processes has been applied to questions of risk management and portfolio optimization, especially portfolios with exposure to credit risk.

We can illustrate the importance of fat-tailed processes in credit risk management using an example prepared by Srichander Ramaswamy[35] Exhibit 13.4 shows the credit risk of a 23-corporate bond portfolio under different modeling assumptions. Risk values in the first column are computed considering default losses under the assumption that joint asset return distribution is normal. Values in the second column are computed under the same distributional assumptions but consider not only default losses but also the losses incurred due to rating migration. The values in the third column are computed under the assumption that the joint distribution of asset returns is a multivariate t with 8 degrees of freedom.

The risk measures considered are Unexpected Loss (UL) measured by the standard deviation in the second row, credit risk Value-at-Risk (CrVaR) in the third row, and Expected Shortfall Risk (ESR) in the fourth row. (We will discuss these measures in Chapter 22, where we cover risk management.) The Expected Loss tabulated in the first row is a measure of credit cost and not of risk.

As explained in Chapter 22, under the assumption of multivariate normality, the three risk measures UL, VaR, and ES are equivalent; however, if we drop this assumption, the three risk measures are no longer equivalent. Observe, in particular, that moving from a multivariate nor-

EXHIBIT 13.4 Portfolio Credit Risk Measures Under Different Modeling Assumptions

Description	Default Mode and Multivariate Normal	Migration Mode and Multivariate Normal	Migration Mode and Multivariate t-Distributed
Expected loss	13.9 bp	34.1 bp	34.0 bp
Unexpected loss	65.9 bp	88.9 bp	105.1 bp
CrVaR at 90% confidence	0.0 bp	102.9 bp	96.6 bp
ESR at 90% confidence	139.0 bp	240.3 bp	256.2 bp

---

[35] This illustration is adapted from his book, *Managing Credit Risk in Corporate Bond Portfolios: A Practitioner's Guide* (Hoboken, NJ: John Wiley & Sons, 2004).

mal to a multivariate t CrVaR drops from 102.9 basis points to 96.6 basis points but ES grows from 240.3 basis points to 256.2 basis points. This happens because the t-distribution is more fat-tailed than the normal distribution. As a consequence, VaR underestimates the risk of large losses.

Though there are still questions as to whether asset prices have a finite variance, there is little doubt that financial time series are not Gaussian. Large events happen at a rate incompatible with Gaussian behavior. This problem must be addressed from the point of view of both risk management and financial optimization.

Many issues regarding risk management have been discussed in the literature. A number of key issues are summarized by Mulvey who points out the need to correctly address problems stemming from contagion phenomena and from the possibility of joint actions such as those occurring in market crashes.[36] A better understanding of the dynamics of these events could lead to effective measures to protect market participants from unnecessary risk.

SUMMARY

- Fat-tailed laws have been found in many economic variables
- Fully approximating a finite economic system with fat-tailed laws depends on an accurate statistical analysis of the phenomena, but also on a number of the theoretical implications of subexponentiality and scaling.
- Modeling financial variables with stable laws implies the assumption of infinite variance, which seems to contradict empirical observations.
- Scaling laws might still be an appropriate modeling paradigm given the complex interaction of distributional shape and correlations in price processes.
- Scaling laws might help in understanding not only the sheer size of economic fluctuations but also the complexity of economic cycles.

[36] John M. Mulvey, "Risk Management Systems for Long-term Investors: Addressing/Managing Extreme Events," Working Paper, May 2001, Operations Research and Financial Engineering Department, Bendheim Center for Finance, Princeton University.

CHAPTER 14

Arbitrage Pricing: Finite-State Models

The *Principle of Absence of Arbitrage* is perhaps the most fundamental principle of finance theory. In the presence of arbitrage opportunities, there is no trade-off between risk and returns because it is possible to make unbounded risk-free gains. The principle of absence of arbitrage is fundamental for understanding asset valuation in a competitive market. This chapter discusses arbitrage pricing in a finite-state, discrete-time setting. In the following chapter we extend the discussion to a continuous-time, continuous-state setting.

THE ARBITRAGE PRINCIPLE

Let's begin by defining what is meant by arbitrage. In its simple form, *arbitrage* is the simultaneous buying and selling of an asset at two different prices in two different markets. The arbitrageur profits without risk by buying cheap in one market and simultaneously selling at the higher price in the other market. Such opportunities for arbitrage are rare. In fact, a single arbitrageur with unlimited ability to sell short could correct a mispricing condition by financing purchases in the underpriced market with proceeds of short sales in the overpriced market. (*Short-selling* means selling an asset that is not owned in anticipation of a price decline. The mechanism for doing this is described in Chapter 2.) This means that riskless arbitrage opportunities are short-lived.

Less obvious arbitrage opportunities exist in situations where a *package of assets* can produce a payoff (expected return) identical to an asset that is priced differently. This arbitrage relies on a fundamental

393

principle of finance called the *law of one price,* which states that a given asset must have the same price regardless of the location where the asset is traded and the means by which one goes about creating that asset. The law of one price implies that if the payoff of an asset can be synthetically created by a package of assets, the price of the package and the price of the asset whose payoff it replicates must be equal.

When a situation is discovered whereby the price of the package of assets differs from that of an asset with the same payoff, rational investors will trade these assets in such a way so as to restore price equilibrium. This market-mechanism is founded on the fact that an arbitrage transaction does not expose the investor to any adverse movement in the market price of the assets in the transaction.

For example, consider how we can produce an arbitrage opportunity involving three assets A, B, and C. These assets can be purchased today at the prices shown below, and can each produce only one of two payoffs (referred to as State 1 and State 2) a year from now:

Asset	Price	Payoff in State 1	Payoff in State 2
A	$70	$50	$100
B	60	30	120
C	80	38	112

While it is not obvious from the data presented above, an investor can construct a portfolio of assets A and B that will have the identical return as asset C in both State 1 and State 2. Let w_A and w_B be the proportion of assets A and B, respectively, in the portfolio. Then the payoff (i.e., the terminal value of the portfolio) under the two states can be expressed mathematically as follows:

- ■ If State 1 occurs: $\$50\,w_A + \$30\,w_B$
- ■ If State 2 occurs: $\$100\,w_A + \$120\,w_B$

We create a portfolio consisting of A and B that will reproduce the payoff of C regardless of the state that occurs one year from now. Here is how: for either condition (State 1 and State 2) we set the payoff of the portfolio equal to the payoff for C as follows:

- ■ State 1: $\$50\,w_A + \$30\,w_B = \$38$
- ■ State 2: $\$100\,w_A + \$120\,w_B = \$112$

We also know that $w_A + w_B = 1$. If we solved for the weights for w_A and w_B that would simultaneously satisfy the above equations, we would find that the portfolio should have 40% in asset A (i.e., $w_A = 0.4$) and 60% in asset B (i.e., $w_B = 0.6$). The cost of that portfolio will be equal to

$$(0.4)(\$70) + (0.6)(\$60) = \$64$$

Our portfolio (i.e., package of assets) comprised of assets A and B has the same payoff in State 1 and State 2 as the payoff of asset C. The cost of asset C is $80 while the cost of the portfolio is only $64. This is an arbitrage opportunity that can be exploited by buying assets A and B in the proportions given above and shorting (selling) asset C.

For example, suppose that $1 million is invested to create the portfolio with assets A and B. The $1 million is obtained by selling short asset C. The proceeds from the short sale of asset C provide the funds to purchase assets A and B. Thus, there would be no cash outlay by the investor. The payoffs for States 1 and 2 are shown below:

Asset	Investment	State 1	State 2
A	$400,000	$285,715	$571,429
B	600,000	300,000	1,200,000
C	–1,000,000	–475,000	–1,400,000
Total	0	110,715	371,429

ARBITRAGE PRICING IN A ONE-PERIOD SETTING

We can describe the concepts of arbitrage pricing in a more formal mathematical context. It is useful to start in a simple one-period, finite-state setting as in the example of the previous section. This means that we consider only one period and that there is only a finite number M of states of the world. In this setting, asset prices can assume only a finite number of values.

The assumption of finite states is not as restrictive as it might appear. In practice, security prices can only assume a finite number of values. Stock prices, for example, are not real numbers but integer fractions of a dollar. In addition, stock prices are nonnegative numbers and it is conceivable that there is some very high upper level that they cannot exceed. In addition, whatever simulation we might perform is a finite-state simulation given that the precision of computers is finite.

The finite number of states represents uncertainty. There is uncertainty because the world can be in any of the M states. At time 0 it is not known in what state the world will be at time 1. Uncertainty is quantified by probabilities but a lot of arbitrage pricing theory can be developed without any reference to probabilities. Suppose there are N securities. Each security i pays d_{ij} number of dollars (or of any other unit of account) in each state of the world j. The payoff of each security need not be a positive number. For instance, a derivative instrument might have negative payoffs in some states of the world. Therefore, in a one-period setting, the securities are formally represented by an $N \times M$ matrix $D = \{d_{ij}\}$ where the d_{ij} entry is the payoff of security i in state j. Recall from Chapter 5 that the matrix D can also be written as a set of N row vectors:

$$D = \begin{bmatrix} \mathbf{d}_1 \\ \cdot \\ \mathbf{d}_N \end{bmatrix}, \quad \mathbf{d}_i = \begin{bmatrix} d_{i1} \cdot d_{iM} \end{bmatrix}$$

where the M-vector $\mathbf{d}_i$ represents the payoffs of security i in each of the M states.

Each security is characterized by a price S. Therefore, the set of N securities is characterized by an N-vector S and an $N \times M$ matrix D. Suppose, for instance, there are two states and three securities. Then the three securities are represented by

$$S = \begin{bmatrix} S_1 \\ S_2 \\ S_3 \end{bmatrix}, \quad D = \begin{bmatrix} d_{11} & d_{12} \\ d_{21} & d_{22} \\ d_{31} & d_{32} \end{bmatrix}$$

Every row of the D matrix represents one security, every column one state. Note that in a one-period setting, prices are defined at time 0 while payoffs are defined at time 1. There is no payoff at time 0 and there is no price at time 1. A portfolio is represented by a N-vector of weights θ. In our example of a market with two states and three securities, a portfolio is a 3-vector:

$$\theta = \begin{bmatrix} \theta_1 \\ \theta_2 \\ \theta_3 \end{bmatrix}$$

The market value S_θ of a portfolio θ at time 0 is a scalar given by the scalar product:

$$S_\theta = \mathbf{S}\theta = \sum_{i=1}^{N} S_i \theta_i$$

Its payoff $\mathbf{d_\theta}$ at time 1 is the M-vector:

$$\mathbf{d_\theta} = \mathbf{D'}\theta$$

The price of a security and the market value of a portfolio can be negative numbers. In the previous example of a two-state, three-security market we obtain

$$S_\theta = \mathbf{S}\theta = S_1\theta_1 + S_2\theta_2 + S_3\theta_3$$

$$\mathbf{d_\theta} = \mathbf{D'}\theta = \begin{bmatrix} d_{11} & d_{21} & d_{31} \\ d_{12} & d_{22} & d_{32} \end{bmatrix} \begin{bmatrix} \theta_1 \\ \theta_2 \\ \theta_3 \end{bmatrix} = \begin{bmatrix} d_{11}\theta_1 + d_{21}\theta_2 + d_{31}\theta_3 \\ d_{12}\theta_1 + d_{22}\theta_2 + d_{32}\theta_3 \end{bmatrix}$$

Let's introduce the concept of arbitrage in this simple setting. As we have seen, arbitrage is essentially the possibility of making money by trading without any risk. Therefore, we define an arbitrage as any portfolio θ which has a negative market value $S_\theta = \mathbf{S}\theta < 0$ and a nonnegative payoff $D_\theta = \mathbf{D'}\theta \geq 0$ or, alternatively, a nonpositive market value $S_\theta = \mathbf{S}\theta \leq 0$ and a positive payoff $D_\theta = \mathbf{D'}\theta > 0$.

State Prices

Next we define state prices. A *state-price vector* is a strictly positive M-vector ψ such that security prices can be written as $\mathbf{S} = \mathbf{D}\psi$. In other words, given a state-price vector, if it exists, security prices can be recovered as a weighted average of the securities' payoffs, where the state-price vector gives the weights. In the previous two-state, three-security example we can write:

$$\psi = \begin{bmatrix} \psi_1 \\ \psi_2 \end{bmatrix}$$

$$\mathbf{S} = \mathbf{D}\psi$$

$$
\begin{bmatrix} S_1 \\ S_2 \\ S_3 \end{bmatrix} = \begin{bmatrix} d_{11} & d_{12} \\ d_{21} & d_{22} \\ d_{31} & d_{32} \end{bmatrix} \begin{bmatrix} \psi_1 \\ \psi_2 \end{bmatrix} = \begin{bmatrix} d_{11}\psi_1 + d_{12}\psi_2 \\ d_{21}\psi_1 + d_{22}\psi_2 \\ d_{31}\psi_1 + d_{32}\psi_2 \end{bmatrix}
$$

Given security prices and payoffs, state prices can be determined solving the system:

$$
d_{11}\psi_1 + d_{12}\psi_2 = S_1
$$
$$
d_{21}\psi_1 + d_{22}\psi_2 = S_2
$$
$$
d_{31}\psi_1 + d_{32}\psi_2 = S_3
$$

This system admits solutions if and only if there are two linearly independent equations and the third equation is a linear combination of the other two. Note that this condition is necessary but not sufficient to ensure that there are state prices as state prices must be strictly positive numbers.

A portfolio θ is characterized by payoffs $\mathbf{d_\theta} = \mathbf{D'\theta}$. Its price is given, in terms of state prices, by: $S_\theta = \mathbf{S\theta} = \mathbf{D\psi\theta} = d_\theta\psi$.

It can be demonstrated that there is no arbitrage if and only if there is a state-price vector. The formal demonstration is quite complicated given the inequalities that define an arbitrage portfolio. It hinges on the **Separating Hyperplane Theorem**, which says that, given any two convex disjoint sets in R^M, it is possible to find a hyperplane separating them. A hyperplane is the locus of points x_i that satisfy a linear equation of the type:

$$
a_0 + \sum_{i=1}^{M} a_i x_i = 0
$$

Intuitively, however, it is clear that the existence of state prices ensures that the law of one price introduced in the previous section is automatically satisfied. In fact, if there are state prices, two identical payoffs have the same price, regardless of how they are constructed. This is because the price of a security or of any portfolio is univocally determined as a weighted average of the payoffs, with the state prices as weights.

Risk-Neutral Probabilities

Let's now introduce the concept of risk-neutral probabilities. Given a state-price vector, consider the sum of its components $\psi_0 = \psi_1 + \psi_2 + \ldots + \psi_M$. Normalize the state-price vector by dividing each component by the sum ψ_0. The normalized state-price vector

$$\Psi = \{\psi_j\} = \left\{ \frac{\psi_j}{\psi_0} \right\}$$

is a set of positive numbers whose sum is one. These numbers can be interpreted as probabilities. They are not, in general, the real probabilities associated with states. They are called *risk-neutral probabilities*. We can then write

$$S \frac{1}{\psi_0} = D\Psi$$

We can interpret the above relationship as follows: The normalized security prices are their expected payoffs under these special probabilities. In fact, we can rewrite the above equation as

$$\bar{S}_i = \frac{S_i}{\psi_0} = E[d_i]$$

where expectation is taken with respect to risk-neutral probabilities. In this case, security prices are the discounted expected payoffs under these special risk-neutral probabilities.

Suppose that there is a portfolio $\bar{\theta}$ such that $d_{\bar{\theta}} = D'\bar{\theta} = \{1,1,...,1\}$. This portfolio can be one individual risk-free security. As we have seen above $S\theta = d_\theta \psi$, which implies that $\psi_0 = \bar{\theta}S$ is the discount on riskless borrowing.

Complete Markets

Let's now define the concept of *complete markets*, a concept that plays a fundamental role in finance theory. In the simple setting of the one-period finite-state market, a complete market is one in which the set of possible portfolios is able to replicate an arbitrary payoff. Call span(D) the set of possible portfolio payoffs which is given by the following expression:

$$\text{span}(D) \equiv \{D'\theta : \theta \in R^M\}$$

A market is complete if span(D) = R^M.

A one-period finite-state complete market is one where the equation

$$\mathbf{D}'\boldsymbol{\theta} = \xi: \xi \in R^M$$

always admits a solution. Recall from Chapter 5 on matrix algebra that this is the case if and only if the rank of D is M. This means that there are at least M linearly independent payoffs—that is, there are as many linearly independent payoffs as there are states. Let's write down explicitly the system in the two-state three-security market.

$$\mathbf{D}'\boldsymbol{\theta} = \xi$$

$$\begin{bmatrix} d_{11} & d_{21} & d_{31} \\ d_{12} & d_{22} & d_{32} \end{bmatrix} \begin{bmatrix} \theta_1 \\ \theta_2 \\ \theta_3 \end{bmatrix} = \begin{bmatrix} \xi_1 \\ \xi_2 \end{bmatrix}$$

$$d_{11}\theta_1 + d_{21}\theta_2 + d_{31}\theta_3 = \xi_1$$
$$d_{12}\theta_1 + d_{22}\theta_2 + d_{32}\theta_3 = \xi_2$$

Recall from Chapter 5 that this system of linear equations admits solutions if and only if the rank of the coefficient matrix is 2. This condition is not verified, for example, if the securities have the same payoff in each state. In this case, the relationship $\xi_1 = \xi_2$ must always be verified. In other words, the three securities can only replicate portfolios that have the same payoff in each state.

In this simple setting it is easy to associate risk-neutral probabilities with real probabilities. In fact, suppose that the vector of real probabilities $\mathbf{p}$ is associated to states so that p_i is the probability of the i-th state. For any given M-dimensional vector $\mathbf{x}$, we write its expected value under the real probabilities as

$$E[\mathbf{x}] = \mathbf{p}\mathbf{x} = \sum_{i=1}^{M} p_i x_i$$

It can be demonstrated that there is no arbitrage if and only if there is a strictly positive M-vector $\boldsymbol{\pi}$ such that: $S = E[\mathbf{D}\boldsymbol{\pi}]$. Any such vector $\boldsymbol{\pi}$ is called a *state-price deflator*. To see this point, define

$$\pi_i = \frac{\psi_i}{p_i}$$

Prices can then be expressed as

$$S_i = \sum_{j=1}^{M} d_{ij} \psi_j = \sum_{j=1}^{M} p_j d_{ij} \frac{\psi_j}{p_j} = \sum_{j=1}^{M} p_j d_{ij} \pi_j$$

which demonstrates that $S = E[D\pi]$.

We can now specialize the above calculations in the numerical case of the previous section. Recall that in the previous section we gave the example of three securities with the following prices and payoffs expressed in dollars:

$$S = \begin{bmatrix} 70 \\ 60 \\ 80 \end{bmatrix}$$

$$D = \begin{bmatrix} 50 & 100 \\ 30 & 120 \\ 38 & 112 \end{bmatrix}$$

We first compute the relative state prices:

$$50\psi_1 + 100\psi_2 = 70$$
$$30\psi_1 + 120\psi_2 = 60$$
$$38\psi_1 + 112\psi_2 = 80$$

Solving the first two equations, we obtain

$$\begin{bmatrix} \psi_1 \\ \psi_2 \end{bmatrix} = \begin{bmatrix} \frac{4}{5} \\ \frac{3}{10} \end{bmatrix}$$

However, the third equation is not satisfied by these values for the state prices. As a consequence, there does not exist a state-price vector which confirms that there are arbitrage opportunities as observed in the first section.

Now suppose that the price of security C is $64 and not $80. In this case, the third equation is satisfied and the state-price vector is the one shown above. Risk-neutral probabilities can now be easily computed. Here is how. First sum the two state prices: $\frac{4}{5} + \frac{3}{10} = \frac{11}{10}$ to obtain

$$\psi_0 = \psi_1 + \psi_2 = {}^{11}\!/\!_{10}$$

and consequently the risk-neutral probabilities:

$$\psi = \begin{bmatrix} \psi_1 \\ \psi_2 \end{bmatrix} = \begin{bmatrix} \psi_1/\psi_0 \\ \psi_2/\psi_0 \end{bmatrix} = \begin{bmatrix} {}^8\!/\!_{11} \\ {}^3\!/\!_{11} \end{bmatrix}$$

Risk-neutral probabilities sum to one while state prices do not. We can now check if our market is complete. Write the following equations:

$$50\theta_1 + 30\theta_2 + 38\theta_3 = \xi_1$$

$$100\theta_1 + 120\theta_2 + 112\theta_3 = \xi_2$$

The rank of the coefficient matrix is clearly 2 as the determinant of the first minor is different from zero:

$$\begin{bmatrix} 50 & 30 \\ 100 & 120 \end{bmatrix} = 50 \times 120 - 100 \times 30 = 300 \neq 0$$

Our sample market is therefore complete and arbitrage-free. A portfolio made with the first two securities can replicate any payoff and the third security can be replicated as a portfolio of the first two.

ARBITRAGE PRICING IN A MULTIPERIOD FINITE-STATE SETTING

The above basic results can be extended to a multiperiod finite-state setting using the probabilistic concepts developed in Chapter 6. The economy is represented by a probability space $(\Omega, \Im, P)$ where Ω is the set of possible states, $\Im$ is the algebra of events (recall that we are in a finite-state setting and therefore there are only a finite number of events), and P is a probability function. As the number of states is finite, finite probabilities $P(\{\omega\}) \equiv P(\omega) \equiv p_\omega$ are defined for each state. There is only a finite number of dates from 0 to T.

Propagation of Information

Recall from Chapter 6 that the propagation of information is represented by a filtration $\Im_t$ that, in the finite case, is equivalent to an information structure I_t. The latter is a discrete, hierarchical organization of partitions I_t with the following properties:

$$I_k \equiv (\{A_{ik}\}); \quad k = 0, \dots, T; \quad i = 1, \dots, M_k; \quad 1 = M_1 \leq \cdot \leq M_k \leq \cdot \leq M_T = M$$

$$A_{ik} \cap A_{jk} = \varnothing \text{ if } i \neq j \text{ and } \bigcup_{i=1}^{M_k} A_{ik} = \Omega$$

and, in addition, given any two sets A_{ik}, A_{jh}, with $h > k$, either their intersection is empty $A_{ik} \cap A_{jh} = \varnothing$ or $A_{ik} \supseteq A_{jh}$. In other words, the partitions become more refined with time.

Each security i is characterized by a payoff process d_t^i and by a price process S_t^i. In this finite-state setting, d_t^i and S_t^i are discrete variables that, given that there are M states, can be represented by M-vectors $\mathbf{d}_t^i = [d_t^i(\omega)]$ and $\mathbf{S}_t^i = [S_t^i(\omega)]$ where $d_t^i(\omega)$ and $S_t^i(\omega)$ are, respectively, the payoff and the price of the i-th asset at time t, $0 \leq t \leq T$ and in state $\omega \in \Omega$. Following Chapter 6, all payoffs and prices are stochastic processes adapted to the filtration $\Im_t$. Recall from Chapter 6 that, given that d_t^i and S_t^i are adapted processes in a finite probability space, they have to assume a constant value on each partition of the information structure I_t. It is convenient to introduce the following notation:

$$d_{A_{jt}}^i = d_t^i(\omega), \; \omega \in A_{jt}$$

$$S_{A_{jt}}^i = S_t^i(\omega), \; \omega \in A_{jt}$$

where $d_{A_{jt}}^i$ and $S_{A_{jt}}^i$ represent the constant values that the processes d_t^i and S_t^i assume on the states that belong to the sets A_{jt} of each partition I_t. There is $M_0 = 1$ value for $d_{A_{j0}}^i$ and $S_{A_{j0}}^i$, M_t values for $d_{A_{jt}}^i$ and $S_{A_{jt}}^i$ and $M_T = M$ values for $d_{A_{jT}}^i$ and $S_{A_{jT}}^i$. The same notation and the same consideration can be applied to any process adapted to the filtration $\Im_t$.

Trading Strategies

We have to define the meaning of trading strategies in this multiperiod setting. A trading strategy is a sequence of portfolios θ such that θ_t is the portfolio held at time t after trading. To ensure that there is no anticipation of information, each trading strategy θ must be an adapted process. The payoff d^θ generated by a trading strategy is an adapted process d_t^θ with the following time dynamics:

$$d_t^\theta = \theta_{t-1}(S_t + d_t) - \theta_t S_t$$

An arbitrage is a trading strategy whose payoff process is nonnegative and not always zero. In other words, an arbitrage is a trading strategy which is never negative and which is strictly positive for some instants and some states. Note that imposing the condition that payoffs are always nonnegative forbids any initial positive investment that is a negative payoff.

A *consumption process* is any nonnegative adapted process. Markets are said to be complete if any consumption process can be obtained as the payoff process of a trading strategy with some initial investment. *Market completeness* means that any nonnegative payoff process can be replicated with a trading strategy.

State-Price Deflator

We will now extend the concept of state-price deflator to a multiperiod setting. A state-price deflator is a strictly positive adapted process π_t such that the following set of M equations hold:

$$S_t^i = \frac{1}{\pi_t} E_t \left[\sum_{j=t+1}^{T} \pi_j d_j^i \right]$$

In other words, a state-price deflator is a strictly positive process such that prices S_t^i are random variables equal to the conditional expectation of discounted payoffs with respect to the filtration $\Im$. As noted above, in this finite-state setting a filtration is equivalent to an information structure I_t. Note that in the above stochastic equation—which is a set of M equations, one for each state, the term on the left, the prices S_t^i, is an adapted process that, as mentioned, assumes constant values on each set of the partition I_t. The term on the right is a conditional expectation multiplied by a factor $1/\pi_t$. The process π_t is adapted by definition and, therefore, assumes constant values $\pi_{A_{it}}$ on each set of the partition I_t.

In this finite setting, conditional expectations are expectations computed with conditional probabilities. Recall from Chapter 6 that conditional expectations are adapted processes. Therefore they assume one value at $t = 0$, M_j values for $t = j$, and M values at the last date.

To illustrate the above, let's write down explicitly the above equation in terms of the notation $d_{A_{jt}}^i$ and $S_{A_{jt}}^i$. Note first that

$$P(\{\omega\}|A_{kt}) = \frac{P(\{\omega\}\cap A_{kt})}{P(A_{kt})} = \frac{P(\{\omega\})}{P(A_{kt})}, \text{ if } \omega \in A_{kt}, 0 \text{ if } \omega \notin A_{kt}$$

Given that the probability space is finite,

$$P(A_{jt}) = \sum_{\omega \in A_{jt}} p_\omega$$

As we defined $P(\{\omega\}) \equiv p_\omega$ the previous equation becomes

$$P(\{\omega\}|A_{kt}) = \frac{P(\{\omega\}\cap A_{kt})}{P(A_{kt})} = \frac{P(\{\omega\})}{P(A_{kt})} = \frac{p_\omega}{\left(\sum_{\omega \in A_{kt}} p_\omega\right)}$$

if $\omega \in A_{kt}$, 0 if $\omega \notin A_{kt}$.

Pricing Relationships
We can now write the pricing relationship as follows:

$$S^i_{A_{kt}} = \frac{1}{\pi_{A_{kt}}}\left[\sum_{\omega \in A_{kt}}\left(P(\{\omega\}|A_{kt})\left(\sum_{j=t+1}^{T}\pi_j(\omega)d^i_j(\omega)\right)\right)\right]$$

$$= \frac{1}{\pi_{A_{kt}}}\left[\sum_{\omega \in A_{kt}}\left(\frac{p_\omega}{\left(\sum_{\omega \in A_{kt}} p_\omega\right)}\left(\sum_{j=t+1}^{T}\pi_j(\omega)d^i_j(\omega)\right)\right)\right]$$

$$A_{kt}\in I_t, 1 \le k \le M_t$$

The above formulas generalize to any trading strategy. In particular, if there is a state-price deflator, the market value of any trading strategy is given by

$$\theta_t \times S_t = \frac{1}{\pi_t}E\left[\sum_{j=t+1}^{T}\pi_j d^\theta_j\right]$$

$$(\theta_t S_t)_{A_{kt}} = \frac{1}{\pi_{A_{kt}}} \left[\sum_{\omega \in A_{kt}} \left(P(\{\omega\} | A_{kt}) \left(\sum_{j=t+1}^{T} \pi_j(\omega) d_j^{\theta}(\omega) \right) \right) \right]$$

$$= \frac{1}{\pi_{A_{kt}}} \left[\sum_{\omega \in A_{kt}} \left(\frac{p_{\omega}}{\left(\sum_{\omega \in A_{kt}} p_{\omega} \right)} \left(\sum_{j=t+1}^{T} \pi_j(\omega) d_j^{\theta}(\omega) \right) \right) \right]$$

It is possible to demonstrate that the payoff-price pair (d_t^i, S_t^i) admits no arbitrage if and only if there is a state-price deflator. These concepts and formulas generalize those of a one-period setting to a multiperiod setting.

Given a payoff-price pair (d_t^i, S_t^i) it is possible to compute the state-price deflator, if it exists, from the previous equations. In fact, it is possible to write a set of linear equations in the π_t, π_{t-1} for each period. One can proceed backward from the period T to period 1 writing a homogeneous system of linear equations. As the system is homogeneous, one of the variables can be arbitrarily fixed; for example, the initial value π_0 can be assumed equal to 1. If the system admits nontrivial solutions and if all solutions are strictly positive, then there are state-price deflators.

Examples

To illustrate the above, let's write down explicitly the previous formulas for prices, extending the example of the previous section to a two-period setting. We assume there are three securities and two periods, that is, three dates $(0,1,2)$ and four states, indicated with the integers 1,2,3,4, so that $\Omega = \{1,2,3,4\}$. Assume that the information structure is given by the following partitions of events:

$$I_i \equiv (I_0 \equiv \{A_{1,0}\}, I_1 \equiv \{A_{1,1}, A_{2,1}\}, I_2 \equiv \{A_{1,2}, A_{2,2}, A_{3,2}, A_{4,2}\})$$

$$A_{1,0} = \{1+2+3+4\}, A_{1,1} = \{1+2\}, A_{2,1} = \{3+4\}$$

$$A_{1,2} = \{1\}, A_{2,2} = \{2\}, A_{3,2} = \{3\}, A_{4,2} = \{4\}$$

where we use + to indicate logical union, so that, for example, $\{1 + 2\}$ is the event formed by states 1 and 2. The interpretation of the above notation is the following. At time zero the world can be in any possible state, that is, the securities can take any possible path. Therefore the partition at time zero is formed by the event {1 + 2 + 3 + 4}. At time 1, the set of states is partitioned into two mutually exclusive events, {1 + 2} or {3 + 4}. At time 2 the partition is formed by all individual states. Note that this is a particular example; different partitions would be logically admissible.

Exhibit 14.1 represents the above structure. Each security is characterized by a price process and a payoff process adapted to the information structure. Each process is a collection of three discrete random variables indexed with the time indexes 0,1,2. Each discrete random variable is a 4-vector as it assumes as many values as states. However, as processes are adapted, they must assume the same value on each partition of the information structure. Note also that payoffs are zero at date zero and prices are zero at date 2. Therefore, in this example, we can put together these vectors in two 3×4 matrices for each security as follows

$$
\{S_t^i(\omega)\} \equiv
\begin{bmatrix}
S_0^i(1) & S_1^i(1) & 0 \\
S_0^i(2) & S_1^i(2) & 0 \\
S_0^i(3) & S_1^i(3) & 0 \\
S_0^i(4) & S_1^i(4) & 0
\end{bmatrix}
; \{d_t^i(\omega)\} \equiv
\begin{bmatrix}
0 & d_1^i(1) & d_2^i(1) \\
0 & d_1^i(2) & d_2^i(2) \\
0 & d_1^i(3) & d_2^i(3) \\
0 & d_1^i(4) & d_2^i(4)
\end{bmatrix}
$$

The following relationships hold:

$$
S_0^i(1) = S_0^i(2) = S_0^i(3) = S_0^i(4) = S_{A_{1,0}}^i; S_1^i(1) = S_1^i(2) = S_{A_{1,1}}^i;
$$

EXHIBIT 14.1   An Information Structure with Four States and Three Dates

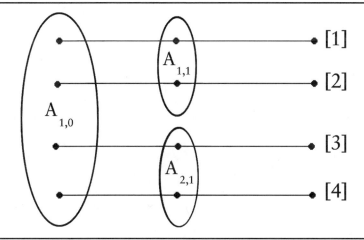

$$S_1^i(3) = S_1^i(4) = S_{A_{2,1}}^i$$

$$d_1^i(1) = d_1^i(2) = d_{A_{1,1}}^i; \; d_1^i(3) = d_1^i(4) = d_{A_{2,1}}^i$$

where, as above, $S_t^i(\omega)$ is the price of security i in state ω at moment t and $d_t^i(\omega)$ is the payoff of security i in state ω at time t with the restriction that processes must assume the same value on partitions. This is because processes are adapted to the information structure so that there is no anticipation of information. One must not be able to discriminate at time 0 events that will be revealed at time 1 and so on.

Observe that there is no payoff at time 0 and no price at time 2 and that the payoffs at time 2 have to be intended as the final liquidation of the security as in the one-period case. Payoffs at time 1, on the other hand, are intermediate payments. Note that the number of states is chosen arbitrarily for illustration purposes. Each state of the world represents a path of prices and payoffs for the set of three securities. To keep the example simple, we assume that of all the possible paths of prices and payoffs only four are possible.

The state-price deflator can be represented as follows:

$$\{\pi_t(\omega)\} \equiv \begin{bmatrix} \pi_0(1) & \pi_1(1) & \pi_2(1) \\ \pi_0(2) & \pi_1(2) & \pi_2(2) \\ \pi_0(3) & \pi_1(3) & \pi_2(3) \\ \pi_0(4) & \pi_1(4) & \pi_2(4) \end{bmatrix}$$

$$\pi_0(1) = \pi_0(2) = \pi_0(3) = \pi_0(4)$$

$$\pi_1(1) = \pi_1(2) \quad \pi_1(3) = \pi_1(4)$$

A probability p_ω is assigned to each of the four states of the world. The probability of each event is simply the sum of the probabilities of its states. We can write down the formula for security prices in this way:

$$S_{A_{1,2}}^i = S_2^i(1) = S_{A_{2,2}}^i = S_2^i(2) = S_{A_{3,2}}^i = S_2^i(3) = S_{A_{4,2}}^i = S_2^i(4) = 0$$

$$S^i_{A_{1,1}} = S^i_1(1) = S^i_1(2)$$

$$= \frac{1}{\pi_{A_{1,1}}}[P(A_{1,2}|A_{1,1})\pi_2(1)d^i_2(1) + P(A_{2,2}|A_{1,1})\pi_2(2)d^i_2(2)]$$

$$= \frac{1}{\pi_{A_{1,1}}}\left[\frac{p_1}{p_1+p_2}\pi_2(1)d^i_2(1) + \frac{p_2}{p_1+p_2}\pi_2(2)d^i_2(2)\right]$$

$$S^i_{A_{2,1}} = S^i_1(3) = S^i_1(4)$$

$$= \frac{1}{\pi_{A_{2,1}}}[P(A_{3,2}|A_{2,1})\pi_2(3)d^i_2(3) + P(A_{4,2}|A_{2,1})\pi_2(4)d^i_2(4)]$$

$$= \frac{1}{\pi_{A_{2,1}}}\left[\frac{p_3}{p_3+p_4}\pi_2(3)d^i_2(3) + \frac{p_4}{p_3+p_4}\pi_2(4)d^i_2(4)\right]$$

$$S^i_{A_{1,0}} = \left\{p_1[\pi_{A_{1,1}}d^i_{A_{1,1}} + \pi_2(1)d^i_2(1)] + p_2[\pi_{A_{1,1}}d^i_{A_{1,1}} + \pi_2(2)d^i_2(2)]\right.$$

$$\left. + p_3[\pi_{A_{1,2}}d^i_{A_{1,2}} + \pi_2(3)d^i_2(3)] + p_4[\pi_{A_{1,2}}d^i_{A_{1,2}} + \pi_2(4)d^i_2(4)]\right\}$$

These equations illustrate how to compute the state-price deflator knowing prices, payoffs, and probabilities. They form a homogeneous system of linear equations in $\pi_2(1)$, $\pi_2(2)$, $\pi_2(3)$, $\pi_2(4)$, $\pi_{A_{1,1}}$, $\pi_{A_{2,1}}$, $\pi_{A_{1,0}}$.

$$p_1d^i_2(1)\pi_2(1) + p_2d^i_2(2)\pi_2(2) - S^i_{A_{1,1}}(p_1+p_2)\pi_{A_{1,1}} = 0$$

$$p_3d^i_2(3)\pi_2(3) + p_4d^i_4(4)\pi_2(4) - S^i_{A_{2,1}}(p_3+p_4)\pi_{A_{2,1}} = 0$$

$$p_1d^i_2(1)\pi_2(1) + p_2d^i_2(2)\pi_2(2) + p_3d^i_2(3)\pi_2(3) + p_4d^i_4(4)\pi_2(4)$$
$$+ (p_1+p_2)d^i_{A_{1,1}}\pi_{A_{1,1}} + (p_3+p_4)d^i_{A_{2,3}}\pi_{A_{2,3}} - S^i_{A_{1,0}}\pi_{A_{1,0}} = 0$$

Substituting, we obtain

$$p_1d^i_2(1)\pi_2(1) + p_2d^i_2(2)\pi_2(2) - S^i_{A_{1,1}}(p_1+p_2)\pi_{A_{1,1}} = 0$$

$$p_3 d_2^i(3)\pi_2(3) + p_4 d_4^i(4)\pi_2(4) - S_{A_{2,1}}^i(p_3 + p_4)\pi_{A_{2,1}} = 0$$

$$[(p_1 + p_2)S_{A_{1,1}}^i + (p_1 + p_2)d_{A_{1,1}}^i]\pi_{A_{1,1}}$$
$$+ [(p_3 + p_4)S_{A_{2,1}}^i + (p_3 + p_4)d_{A_{2,1}}^i]\pi_{A_{2,1}} - S_{A_{1,0}}^i\pi_{A_{1,0}} = 0$$

This homogeneous system must admit a strictly positive solution to yield a state-price deflator. There are seven unknowns. However, as the system is homogeneous, if nontrivial solutions exist, one of the unknowns can be arbitrarily fixed, for example $\pi_{A_{1,0}}$. Therefore, six independent equations are needed. Each asset provides two conditions, so a minimum of three assets are needed.

To illustrate the point, we assume that all states (which are also events in this discrete example) have the same probability 0.25. Thus the events of the information structure have the following probabilities: the single event at time zero has probability 1, the two events at time 1 have probability 0.5, and the four events at time 2 coincide with individual states and have probability 0.25. Conditional probabilities are shown in Exhibit 14.2.

For illustration purposes, let's write the following matrices for payoffs for each security at each date in each state:

$$\{d_1^i(\omega)\} \equiv \begin{bmatrix} 0 & 15 & 50 \\ 0 & 15 & 100 \\ 0 & 20 & 70 \\ 0 & 20 & 110 \end{bmatrix}; \{d_2^i(\omega)\} \equiv \begin{bmatrix} 0 & 8 & 30 \\ 0 & 8 & 120 \\ 0 & 15 & 40 \\ 0 & 15 & 140 \end{bmatrix}; \{d_3^i(\omega)\} \equiv \begin{bmatrix} 0 & 5 & 38 \\ 0 & 5 & 112 \\ 0 & 8 & 42 \\ 0 & 8 & 130 \end{bmatrix}$$

We will assume that the state-price deflator is the following given process:

$$\{\pi_t(\omega)\} \equiv \begin{bmatrix} 1 & 0.8 & 0.7 \\ 1 & 0.8 & 0.75 \\ 1 & 0.9 & 0.75 \\ 1 & 0.9 & 0.8 \end{bmatrix}$$

Each price is computed according to the previous equations. For example, calculations related to asset 1 are as follows:

$$S_2^1(1) = S_2^1(2) = S_2^1(3) = S_2^1(4) = 0$$

EXHIBIT 14.2 Conditional Probabilities

$$P(A_{1,1}|A_{1,0}) = \frac{P(A_{1,1} \cap A_{1,0})}{P(A_{1,0})} = \frac{P\{1+2\}}{P\{1+2+3+4\}} = 0.5$$

$$P(A_{1,2}|A_{1,0}) = \frac{P(A_{1,2} \cap A_{1,0})}{P(A_{1,0})} = \frac{P\{1\}}{P\{1+2+3+4\}} = 0.25$$

$$P(A_{3,2}|A_{1,0}) = \frac{P(A_{3,2} \cap A_{1,0})}{P(A_{1,0})} = \frac{P\{3\}}{P\{1+2+3+4\}} = 0.25$$

$$P(A_{1,2}|A_{1,1}) = \frac{P(A_{1,2} \cap A_{1,1})}{P(A_{1,1})} = \frac{P\{1\}}{P\{1+2\}} = \frac{0.25}{0.5} = 0.5$$

$$P(A_{2,2}|A_{1,1}) = \frac{P(A_{2,2} \cap A_{1,1})}{P(A_{1,1})} = \frac{P\{2\}}{P\{1+2\}} = \frac{0.25}{0.5} = 0.5$$

$$P(A_{3,2}|A_{1,1}) = \frac{P(A_{3,2} \cap A_{1,1})}{P(A_{1,1})} = \frac{P\{\emptyset\}}{P\{1+2\}} = 0$$

$$P(A_{4,2}|A_{1,1}) = \frac{P(A_{4,2} \cap A_{1,1})}{P(A_{1,1})} = \frac{P\{\emptyset\}}{P\{1+2\}} = 0$$

$$P(A_{2,1}|A_{1,0}) = \frac{P(A_{2,1} \cap A_{1,0})}{P(A_{1,0})} = \frac{P\{3+4\}}{P\{1+2+3+4\}} = 0.5$$

$$P(A_{2,2}|A_{1,0}) = \frac{P(A_{2,2} \cap A_{1,0})}{P(A_{1,0})} = \frac{P\{2\}}{P\{1+2+3+4\}} = 0.25$$

$$P(A_{4,2}|A_{1,0}) = \frac{P(A_{4,2} \cap A_{1,0})}{P(A_{1,0})} = \frac{P\{4\}}{P\{1+2+3+4\}} = 0.25$$

$$P(A_{1,2}|A_{2,1}) = \frac{P(A_{1,2} \cap A_{2,1})}{P(A_{2,1})} = \frac{P\{\emptyset\}}{P\{1+2\}} = 0$$

$$P(A_{2,2}|A_{2,1}) = \frac{P(A_{2,2} \cap A_{2,1})}{P(A_{2,1})} = \frac{P\{\emptyset\}}{P\{1+2\}} = 0$$

$$P(A_{3,2}|A_{2,1}) = \frac{P(A_{3,2} \cap A_{2,1})}{P(A_{2,1})} = \frac{P\{3\}}{P\{3+4\}} = 0.5$$

$$P(A_{4,2}|A_{2,1}) = \frac{P(A_{4,2} \cap A_{2,1})}{P(A_{2,1})} = \frac{P\{4\}}{P\{3+4\}} = 0.5$$

$$S^1_{A_{1,1}} = \frac{1}{0.8}(0.5 \times 0.7 \times 50 + 0.5 \times 075 \times 100) = 68.75$$

$$S^1_{A_{2,1}} = \frac{1}{0.9}(0.5 \times 0.75 \times 70 + 0.5 \times 0.8 \times 110) = 78.05$$

$$S^1_{A_{1,0}} = \frac{1}{1}[0.25(0.8 \times 15 + 0.7 \times 50) + 0.25(0.8 \times 15 + 0.75 \times 100)$$

$$+ 0.25(0.9 \times 20 + 0.75 \times 70) + 0.25(0.9 \times 20 + 0.8 \times 110)]$$
$$= 68.75$$

$$S^2_2(1) = S^2_2(2) = S^2_2(3) = S^2_2(4) = 0$$

$$S^2_{A_{1,1}} = \frac{1}{0.8}(0.5 \times 0.7 \times 30 + 0.5 \times 0.75 \times 120) = 69.37$$

$$S^2_{A_{2,1}} = \frac{1}{0.9}(0.5 \times 0.75 \times 40 + 0.5 \times 0.8 \times 140) = 78.88$$

$$S^2_{A_{1,0}} = \frac{1}{1}[0.25(0.8 \times 8 + 0.7 \times 30) + 0.25(0.8 \times 8 + 0.75 \times 120)$$

$$+ 0.25(0.9 \times 15 + 0.75 \times 40) + 0.25(0.9 \times 15 + 0.8 \times 140)]$$
$$= 73.2$$

$$S^3_2(1) = S^3_2(2) = S^3_2(3) = S^3_2(4) = 0$$

$$S^3_{A_{1,1}} = \frac{1}{0.8}(0.5 \times 0.7 \times 38 + 0.5 \times 0.75 \times 112) = 69.12$$

$$S^3_{A_{2,1}} = \frac{1}{0.9}(0.5 \times 0.75 \times 42 + 0.5 \times 0.8 \times 130) = 75.27$$

$$S^3_{A_{1,0}} = \frac{1}{1}[0.25(0.8 \times 5 + 0.7 \times 38) + 0.25(0.8 \times 5 + 0.75 \times 112)$$

$$+ 0.25(0.9 \times 8 + 0.75 \times 42) + 0.25(0.9 \times 8 + 0.8 \times 130)]$$
$$= 67.125$$

With the above equations we computed prices from payoffs and state-price deflators. If prices and payoffs were given, we could compute state-price deflators from the homogeneous system for state prices established above. Suppose that the following price processes were given:

$$\{S_t^1(\omega)\} = \begin{bmatrix} 68.75 & 68.75 & 0 \\ 68.75 & 68.75 & 0 \\ 68.75 & 78.05 & 0 \\ 68.75 & 78.05 & 0 \end{bmatrix}$$

$$\{S_t^2(\omega)\} = \begin{bmatrix} 73.2 & 69.37 & 0 \\ 73.2 & 69.37 & 0 \\ 73.2 & 78.88 & 0 \\ 73.2 & 78.88 & 0 \end{bmatrix}$$

$$\{S_t^3(\omega)\} = \begin{bmatrix} 67.125 & 69.12 & 0 \\ 67.125 & 69.12 & 0 \\ 67.125 & 75.27 & 0 \\ 67.125 & 75.27 & 0 \end{bmatrix}$$

We could then write the following system of equations to compute state-price deflators:

$$0.25 \times 50 \times \pi_2(1) + 0.25 \times 100 \times \pi_2(2) - 68.75 \times 0.5 \times \pi_{A_{1,1}} = 0$$

$$0.25 \times 70 \times \pi_2(1) + 0.25 \times 110 \times \pi_2(2) - 78.05 \times 0.5 \times \pi_{A_{1,1}} = 0$$

$$(55 \times 0.5 + 0.5 \times 15) \times \pi_{A_{1,1}} + (70.25 \times 0.5 + 0.5 \times 20) \times \pi_{A_{2,1}}$$
$$- 68.75 \times \pi_{A_{1,0}} = 0$$

$$0.25 \times 30 \times \pi_2(1) + 0.25 \times 120 \times \pi_2(2) - 69.37 \times 0.5 \times \pi_{A_{1,1}} = 0$$

$$0.25 \times 40 \times \pi_2(1) + 0.25 \times 140 \times \pi_2(2) - 78.88 \times 0.5 \times \pi_{A_{1,1}} = 0$$

$$(55.5 \times 0.5 + 0.5 \times 8) \times \pi_{A_{1,1}} + (71 \times 0.5 + 0.5 \times 15) \times \pi_{A_{2,1}}$$
$$- 73.2 \times \pi_{A_{1,0}} = 0$$

$$0.25 \times 38 \times \pi_2(1) + 0.25 \times 115 \times \pi_2(2) - 69.12 \times 0.5 \times \pi_{A_{1,1}} = 0$$

$$0.25 \times 42 \times \pi_2(1) + 0.25 \times 130 \times \pi_2(2) - 75.27 \times 0.5 \times \pi_{A_{1,1}} = 0$$

$$(55 \times 0.5 + 0.5 \times 15) \times \pi_{A_{1,1}} + (70.25 \times 0.5 + 0.5 \times 20) \times \pi_{A_{2,1}}$$
$$- 67.125 \times \pi_{A_{1,0}} = 0$$

It can be verified that this system, obviously, is solvable and returns the same state-price deflators as in the previous example.

Equivalent Martingale Measures

We now introduce the concept and properties of **equivalent martingale measures**. This concept has become fundamental for the technology of derivative pricing. The idea of equivalent martingale measures is the following. Recall from Chapter 6 that a martingale is a process X_t such that at any time t its conditional expectation at time s, $s > t$ coincides with its present value: $X_t = E_t[X_s]$. In discrete time, a martingale is a process such that its value at any time is equal to its conditional expectation one step ahead. In our case, this principle can be expressed in a different but equivalent way by stating that prices are the discounted expected values of future payoffs. The law of iterated expectation then implies that price plus payoff processes are martingales.

In fact, assume that we can write

$$S_t = E_t \left[\sum_{j=t+1}^{T} d_j \right]$$

then the following relationship holds:

$$S_t = E_t \left[\sum_{j=t+1}^{T} d_j \right] = E_t \left[d_{t+1} + E_{t+1} \left[\sum_{j=t+1+1}^{T} d_j \right] \right] = E_t[d_{t+1} + S_{t+1}]$$

Given a probability space, price processes are not, in general, martingales. However it can be demonstrated that, in the absence of arbitrage, there is an artificial probability measure in which all price processes, appropriately discounted, become martingales. More precisely, we will see that in the absence of arbitrage there is an artificial probability measure Q in which the following discounted present value relationship holds:

$$S_t^i = E_t^Q \left[\sum_{j=t+1}^{T} \frac{d_j^i}{R_{t,j}} \right]$$

We can rewrite this equation explicitly as follows:

$$S_t^i = E_t^Q \left[\sum_{j=t+1}^{T} \frac{d_j^i}{R_{t,j}} \right] = E_t^Q \left[\frac{d_{t+1}^i}{R_{t,t+1}} + \frac{1}{R_{t,t+1}} \sum_{j=t+2}^{T} \frac{d_j^i}{R_{t+1,j}} \right]$$

$$= E_t^Q \left[\frac{d_{t+1}^i}{R_{t,t+1}} + \frac{E_{t+1}^Q}{R_{t,t+1}} \left[\sum_{j=t+2}^{T} \frac{d_j^i}{R_{t,j}} \right] \right] = E_t^Q \left[\frac{d_{t+1}^i + S_{t+1}^i}{R_{t,t+1}} \right]$$

which shows that the discounted price plus payoff process is a martingale. The terms on the left are the price processes, the terms on the right are the conditional expectations under the probability measure Q of the payoffs discounted with the risk-free payoff.

The measure Q is a mathematical construct. The important point is that this new probability measure can be computed either from the real probabilities if the state-price deflators are known or directly from the price and payoff processes. This last observation illustrates that the concept of arbitrage depends only on the structure of the price and payoff processes and not on the actual probabilities. As we will see later in this chapter, equivalent martingale measures greatly simplify the computation of the pricing of derivatives.

Let's assume that there is short-term risk-free borrowing in the sense that there is a trading strategy able to pay for any given interval (t,s) one sure dollar at time s given that $(d_t d_{t+1} ... d_{s-1})^{-1}$ has been invested at time t. Equivalently, we can define for any time interval (t,s) the payoff of a dollar invested risk-free at time t as $R_{t,s} = (d_t d_{t+1} ... d_{s-1})$.

We now define the concept of **equivalent probability measures**. Given a probability measure P the probability measure Q is said to be equivalent to P if both assign probability zero to the same events. An equivalent probability measure Q is an equivalent martingale measure if all price processes discounted with $R_{i,j}$ become martingales. More precisely, Q is an equivalent martingale measure if and only if the market value of any trading strategy is a martingale:

$$\theta_t \times S_t = E_t^Q \left[\sum_{j=t+1}^{T} \frac{d_j^\theta}{R_{t,j}} \right]$$

Risk-Neutral Probabilities

Probabilities computed according to the equivalent martingale measure Q are the risk-neutral probabilities. Risk-neutral probabilities can be explicitly computed. Here is how. Call q_ω the risk-neutral probability of state ω. Let's write explicitly the relationship

$$S_t^i = E_t^Q\left[\frac{d_j^i}{R_{t,j}}\right]$$

as follows:

$$S_{A_{kt}}^i = \sum_{\omega \in A_{kt}} \frac{q_\omega}{Q(A_{kt})}\left[\sum_{j=t+1}^{T} \frac{d_j^i(\omega)}{R_{t,j}}\right] = \sum_{\omega \in A_{kt}} \frac{q_\omega}{\left(\sum\limits_{\omega \in A_{kt}} q_\omega\right)}\left[\sum_{j=t+1}^{T} \frac{d_j^i(\omega)}{R_{t,j}}\right]$$

The above system of equations determines the risk-neutral probabilities. In fact, we can write, for each risky asset, M_t linear equations, where M_t is the number of sets in the partition I_t plus the normalization equation for probabilities. From the above equation, one can see that the system can be written as

$$\sum_{\omega \in A_{k,t}} q_\omega\left[\sum_{j=t+1}^{T} \frac{d_j^i(\omega)}{R_{t,j}} - S_{A_{kt}}^i\right] = 0$$

$$\sum_{\omega=1}^{S} q_\omega = 1$$

This system might be determined, indetermined, or impossible. The system will be impossible if there are arbitrage opportunities. This system will be indetermined if there is an insufficient number of securities. In this case, there will be an infinite number of equivalent martingale measures and the market will not be complete.

Now consider the relationship between risk-neutral probabilities and state-price deflators. Consider a probability measure P and a nonnegative random variable Y with expected value on the entire space equal to 1. Define a new probability measure as $Q(B) = E[1_B Y]$ for any event B and where 1_B is the indicator function of the event B. The random variable Y is called the **Radon-Nikodym derivative** of Q and it is written

$$Y = \frac{dQ}{dP}$$

It is clear from the definition that P and Q are equivalent probability measures as they assign probability zero to the same events. Note that in the case of a finite-state probability space the new probability measure is defined on each state and is equal to

$$q_\omega = Y(\omega)p_\omega$$

Suppose π_t is a state-price deflator. Let Q be the probability measure defined by the Radon-Nikodym derivative:

$$\xi_T = \frac{\pi_T R_{0,T}}{\pi_0}$$

The new state probabilities under Q are the following:

$$q_\omega = \frac{\pi_T(\omega)R_{0,T}}{\pi_0(\omega)}p_\omega$$

Define the density process ξ_t for Q as $\xi_t = E_t[\xi_T]$. As $\xi_t = E_t[\xi_T]$ is an adapted process, we can write:

$$(E_t[\xi_T])_{A_{kt}} = \xi_{A_{kt}} = \sum_{\omega \in A_{kt}} \frac{p_\omega}{P(A_{kt})}\xi_T(\omega) = \sum_{\omega \in A_{kt}} \frac{p_\omega}{P(A_{kt})}\frac{\pi_T(\omega)R_{0,T}}{\pi_0(\omega)}$$

$$= \frac{\pi_{A_{kt}}R_{0,t}}{\pi_0(\omega)}\frac{1}{\pi_{A_{kt}}}\sum_{\omega \in A_{kt}}\frac{p_\omega}{P(A_{kt})}\pi_T[\pi_0(\omega)]R_{t,T} = \frac{\pi_{A_{kt}}R_{0,t}}{\pi_0}$$

As $R_{t,s} = (d_t d_{t+1}...d_{s-1})$ is the payoff at time s of one dollar invested in a risk-free asset at time t, $s > t$, we can then write the following equations:

$$1 = \frac{1}{\pi_t}E_t[\pi_s R_{t,s}]$$

Therefore,

$$1 = \frac{1}{\pi_{A_{kt}}}\left[\sum_{\omega \in A_{kt}} P(\{\omega\}|A_{kt})\pi_s(\omega)R_{t,s}\right] = \frac{1}{\pi_{A_{kt}}}\left[\sum_{\omega \in A_{kt}} \frac{p_\omega}{P(A_{kt})}\pi_s(\omega)R_{t,s}\right]$$

$$1 \le k \le M_t$$

Substituting in the previous equation, we obtain, for each interval (t, T),

$$\xi_{A_{kt}} = (E_t[\xi_T])_{A_{kt}} = \frac{\pi_{A_{kt}}R_{0,t}}{\pi_{A_{10}}}$$

which we can rewrite in the usual notation as

$$\xi_t = E_t[\xi_T] = \frac{\pi_t R_{0,t}}{\pi_{10}}$$

We can now state the following result. Consider any $\mathfrak{I}_j$-measurable variable x_j. This condition can be expressed equivalently stating that x_j assumes constant values on each set of the partition I_j. Then the following relationship holds:

$$E_t^Q[x_j] = E_t^P \frac{1}{\xi_t}[\xi_j x_j]$$

To see this, consider the following demonstration, which hinges on the fact that x_j assumes a constant value on each A_{hj} and, therefore, can be taken out of sums. In addition, as demonstrated above, from

$$1 = \frac{1}{\pi_t}E_t[\pi_s R_{t,s}]$$

the following relationship holds:

$$P(A_{kt})\pi_{A_{kt}} = \sum_{\omega \in A_{kt}} p_\omega \pi_s(\omega)R_{t,s}$$

$$1 \le k \le M_t$$

$$(E_t^Q[x_j])_{A_{kt}} = \sum_{\omega \in A_{kt}} \frac{q_\omega}{Q(A_{kt})} x_j(\omega) = \sum_{\omega \in A_{kt}} \frac{p_\omega}{Q(A_{kt})} \frac{\pi_T(\omega) R_{0,T}}{\pi_0(\omega)} x_j(\omega)$$

$$= \frac{1}{Q(A_{kt})} \sum_{A_{hj} \subset A_{kt}} \left[\sum_{\omega \in A_{hj}} \frac{R_{0,j} R_{j,T} p_\omega \pi_T(\omega) x_j(\omega)}{\pi_0(\omega)} \right]$$

$$= \frac{1}{Q(A_{kt})} \sum_{A_{hj} \subset A_{kt}} \left[\frac{x_{A_{hj}} R_{0,j}}{\pi_0(\omega)} \sum_{\omega \in A_{hj}} R_{j,T} p_\omega \pi_T(\omega) \right]$$

$$= \frac{1}{Q(A_{kt})} \sum_{A_{hj} \subset A_{kt}} \left[\frac{x_{A_{hj}} R_{0,j} \pi_{A_{hj}} P(A_{hj})}{\pi_0(\omega)} \right]$$

$$= \frac{1}{Q(A_{kt})} \sum_{A_{hj} \subset A_{kt}} [x_{A_{hj}} \xi_{A_{hj}} P(A_{hj})]$$

$$= \frac{1}{\xi_{A_{kt}}} \sum_{A_{hj} \subset A_{kt}} \frac{x_{A_{hj}} \xi_{A_{hj}} P(A_{hj})}{P(A_{kt})} = \frac{1}{\xi_{A_{kt}}} [E_t^P(\xi_j x_j)_{A_{kt}}]$$

Let's now apply the above result to the relationship:

$$S_t^i = \frac{1}{\pi_t} E_t \left[\sum_{j=t+1}^{T} \pi_j d_j^i \right] = \frac{\pi_0}{\pi_t} E_t \left[\sum_{j=t+1}^{T} \frac{\pi_j R_{t,j}}{\pi_0} \frac{d_j^i}{R_{t,j}} \right]$$

$$= \frac{\pi_0}{\pi_t R_{0,j}} E_t \left[\sum_{j=t+1}^{T} \frac{\pi_j R_{0,j}}{\pi_0} \frac{d_j^i}{R_{t,j}} \right] = E_t^Q \left(\frac{d_j^i}{R_{t,j}} \right)$$

We have thus demonstrated the following results: There is no arbitrage if and only if there is an equivalent martingale measure. In addition, π_t is a state-price deflator if and only if an equivalent martingale measure Q has the density process defined by

$$\xi_t = \frac{\pi_t R_{0,t}}{\pi_0}$$

In addition, it can be demonstrated that, if there is no arbitrage, markets are complete if and only if there is a unique equivalent martingale measure.

Examples

To illustrate the above we now proceed to detail the calculations for the previous example of three assets, three dates, and four states. Let's first write the equations for the risk-free asset:

$$1 = \frac{1}{\pi_{A_{kt}}}\left[\sum_{\omega \in A_{kt}} \frac{p_\omega}{P(A_{kt})}\pi_s(\omega)R_{t,s}\right]$$

$$1 = \frac{1}{\pi_{A_{11}}}\left(\frac{p_1}{p_1+p_2}\pi_2(1)R_{1,2} + \frac{p_2}{p_1+p_2}\pi_2(2)R_{1,2}\right)$$

$$1 = \frac{1}{\pi_{A_{21}}}\left(\frac{p_3}{p_3+p_4}\pi_2(3)R_{1,2} + \frac{p_4}{p_3+p_4}\pi_2(4)R_{1,2}\right)$$

$$1 = \frac{1}{\pi_{A_{10}}}[p_1\pi_2(1)R_{0,2} + p_2\pi_2(2)R_{0,2} + p_3\pi_2(3)R_{0,2} + p_4\pi_2(4)R_{0,2}]$$

$$\pi_{A_{11}} = \pi_1(1) = \pi_1(2)$$

$$\pi_{A_{21}} = \pi_1(3) = \pi_1(4)$$

$$\pi_{A_{10}} = \pi_0(1) = \pi_0(2) = \pi_0(3) = \pi_0(4)$$

We can now rewrite the pricing relationships for the other risky assets as follows:

At date 2, prices are zero: $S_2^i = 0$.
At date 1, the relationship

$$S_1^i = E_1\left[\frac{d_2^i}{R_{1,2}}\right]$$

holds. In fact, we can write the following:

$$
\begin{aligned}
S^i_{A_{1,1}} &= S^i_1(1) = S^i_1(2) \\[4pt]
&= \frac{1}{\pi_1(2)}[P(A_{1,2}|A_{1,1})\pi_2(1)d^i_2(1) + P(A_{2,2}|A_{1,1})\pi_2(2)d^i_2(2)] \\[4pt]
&= \frac{1}{\pi_{11}}\left(\frac{p_1}{p_1+p_2}\pi_2(1)R_{1,2}\frac{d^i_2(1)}{R_{1,2}} + \frac{p_2}{p_1+p_2}\pi_2(2)R_{1,2}\frac{d^i_2(2)}{R_{1,2}}\right) \\[4pt]
&= \left[Q(A_{1,2}|A_{1,1})\frac{d^i_2(1)}{R_{1,2}} + Q(A_{2,2}|A_{1,1})\frac{d^i_2(2)}{R_{1,2}}\right] \\[4pt]
&= \left[\frac{q_1}{q_1+q_2}\frac{d^i_2(1)}{R_{1,2}} + \frac{q_2}{q_1+q_2}\frac{d^i_2(2)}{R_{1,2}}\right]
\end{aligned}
$$

$$
\begin{aligned}
S^i_{A_{2,1}} &= S^i_1(3) = S^i_1(4) \\[4pt]
&= \left[Q(A_{3,2}|A_{1,1})\frac{d^i_2(3)}{R_{1,2}} + Q(A_{4,2}|A_{1,1})\frac{d^i_2(4)}{R_{1,2}}\right] \\[4pt]
&= \left[\frac{q_3}{q_3+q_4}\frac{d^i_2(3)}{R_{1,2}} + \frac{q_4}{q_3+q_4}\frac{d^i_2(4)}{R_{1,2}}\right]
\end{aligned}
$$

At date 0, the relationship

$$
S^i_0 = E_0\left[\frac{d^i_1}{R_{0,1}} + \frac{d^i_2}{R_{0,2}}\right]
$$

holds. In fact we can write the following:

$$
\begin{aligned}
S^i_{A_{1,0}} &= S^i_0(1) = S^i_0(2) = S^i_0(3) = S^i_0(4) \\[6pt]
&= \frac{1}{\pi_{A_{10}}}\left\{
\begin{aligned}
&p_1[\pi_1(1)d^i_1(1) + \pi_2(1)d^i_2(1)] \\
&+ p_2[\pi_1(2)d^i_1(2) + \pi_2(2)d^i_2(2)] \\
&+ p_3[\pi_1(3)d^i_1(3) + \pi_2(3)d^i_2(3)] \\
&+ p_4[\pi_1(4)d^i_1(4) + \pi_2(4)d^i_2(4)]
\end{aligned}
\right\}
\end{aligned}
$$

$$= p_1 \left[\frac{\pi_1(1)R_{0,1}}{\pi_{A_{1,0}}} \frac{d_1^i(1)}{R_{0,1}} + \frac{\pi_2(1)R_{0,2}}{\pi_{A_{1,0}}} \frac{d_2^i(1)}{R_{0,2}} \right]$$

$$+ p_2 \left[\frac{\pi_1(2)R_{0,1}}{\pi_{A_{1,0}}} \frac{d_1^i(2)}{R_{0,1}} + \frac{\pi_2(2)R_{0,2}}{\pi_{A_{1,0}}} \frac{d_2^i(2)}{R_{0,2}} \right]$$

$$+ p_3 \left[\frac{\pi_1(3)R_{0,1}}{\pi_{A_{1,0}}} \frac{d_1^i(3)}{R_{0,1}} + \frac{\pi_2(3)R_{0,2}}{\pi_{A_{1,0}}} \frac{d_2^i(3)}{R_{0,2}} \right]$$

$$+ p_4 \left[\frac{\pi_1(4)R_{0,1}}{\pi_{A_{1,0}}} \frac{d_1^i(4)}{R_{0,1}} + \frac{\pi_2(4)R_{0,2}}{\pi_{A_{1,0}}} \frac{d_2^i(4)}{R_{0,2}} \right]$$

$$= p_1 \left\{ \frac{\pi_1(1)R_{0,1}}{\pi_{A_{1,0}}} \frac{d_1^i(1)}{R_{0,1}} \frac{1}{\pi_{11}} \left[\frac{p_1}{p_1+p_2} \pi_2(1)R_{1,2} + \frac{p_2}{p_1+p_2} \pi_2(2)R_{1,2} \right] \right\}$$

$$+ p_2 \left\{ \frac{\pi_1(2)R_{0,1}}{\pi_{A_{1,0}}} \frac{d_1^i(2)}{R_{0,1}} \frac{1}{\pi_{21}} \left[\frac{p_1}{p_1+p_2} \pi_2(1)R_{1,2} + \frac{p_2}{p_1+p_2} \pi_2(2)R_{1,2} \right] \right\}$$

$$+ p_3 \left\{ \frac{\pi_1(3)R_{0,1}}{\pi_{A_{1,0}}} \frac{d_1^i(3)}{R_{0,1}} \frac{1}{\pi_{31}} \left[\frac{p_3}{p_3+p_4} \pi_2(3)R_{1,2} + \frac{p_4}{p_3+p_4} \pi_2(4)R_{1,2} \right] \right\}$$

$$+ p_4 \left\{ \frac{\pi_1(4)R_{0,1}}{\pi_{A_{1,0}}} \frac{d_1^i(4)}{R_{0,1}} \frac{1}{\pi_{41}} \left[\frac{p_3}{p_3+p_4} \pi_2(3)R_{1,2} + \frac{p_3}{p_3+p_4} \pi_2(4)R_{1,2} \right] \right\}$$

$$+ q_1 \frac{d_2^i(1)}{R_{0,2}} + q_2 \frac{d_2^i(2)}{R_{0,2}} + q_3 \frac{d_2^i(3)}{R_{0,2}} + q_4 \frac{d_2^i(4)}{R_{0,2}}$$

$$= \frac{d_1^i(1)}{R_{0,1}} \left[\frac{p_1 \pi_2(1)}{\pi_{A_{1,0}}} R_{0,2} + \frac{p_2 \pi_2(2)}{\pi_{A_{1,0}}} R_{0,2} \right] + \frac{d_2^i(3)}{R_{0,1}} \left[\frac{p_3 \pi_2(3)}{\pi_{A_{1,0}}} R_{0,2} + \frac{p_4 \pi_2(4)}{\pi_{A_{1,0}}} R_{0,2} \right]$$

$$+ q_1 \frac{d_2^i(1)}{R_{0,2}} + q_2 \frac{d_2^i(2)}{R_{0,2}} + q_3 \frac{d_2^i(3)}{R_{0,2}} + q_4 \frac{d_2^i(4)}{R_{0,2}}$$

$$= q_1 \frac{d_1^i(1)}{R_{0,1}} + q_2 \frac{d_1^i(2)}{R_{0,1}} + q_3 \frac{d_1^i(3)}{R_{0,1}} + q_4 \frac{d_1^i(4)}{R_{0,1}}$$

$$+ q_1 \frac{d_2^i(1)}{R_{0,2}} + q_2 \frac{d_2^i(2)}{R_{0,2}} + q_3 \frac{d_2^i(3)}{R_{0,2}} + q_4 \frac{d_2^i(4)}{R_{0,2}}$$

PATH DEPENDENCE AND MARKOV MODELS

The value of a derivative instrument might depend on the path of its past values. Consider a lookback option on a stock—that is, a derivative instrument on a stock whose payoff at time t is the maximum difference between the price of the stock and a given value K at any moment prior to t. Call V_t the payoff of the lookback option at time t. We can then write:

$$V_t = \max_{0 \le k < t} (S_k - K)^+$$

The notation $(S_k - K)^+$ means $S_k - K$ if the difference is positive, 0 otherwise, that is, $(S_k - K)^+ = \max(S_k - K, 0)$. Because its value depends on the entire path taken by the underlying stock, a lookback option is a path-dependent security.

An adapted process X_t is said to be a Markov process if its conditional distribution at time t depends only on the value of the process at time $t - 1$ and not on the value of the process at dates $t - 2, t - 3, \dots$. The Markov property can be formally stated as follows:

$$P(X_t | X_{t-1}) = P(X_t | X_{t-1}, X_{t-2}, \dots, X_0)$$

THE BINOMIAL MODEL

Let's now introduce the simple but important multiperiod finite-state model known as the **binomial model**. The binomial model is important because it gives a simple and mathematically tractable model of stock price behavior that tends, in the limit of a zero time step, to a Brownian motion. We introduce a market populated by one risk-free asset and by one or more risky assets whose price(s) follow(s) a binomial or trinomial model. In the next section we will see how to compute the price of derivative instruments in this market.

In the binomial model of stock prices, we assume that at each time step the stock price will assume one of two possible values. This is a restriction of the general multiperiod finite-state model described in the previous sections and in Chapter 6 on probability. The latter is, as we have seen in the previous section, a hierarchical structure of partitions of the set of states. The number of sets in any partition is arbitrary, provided that partitions grow more refined with time.

The binomial model assumes that there are two positive numbers, d and u, such that $0 < d < u$ and such that at each time step the price S_t of the risky asset changes to dS_t or to uS_t. In general one assumes that $0 < d < 1 < u$ so that d represents a price decrease (a movement down) while u represents a price increase (a movement up). It is often required that

$$d = \frac{1}{u}$$

In this case an equal number of movements up and down leave prices unchanged. The binomial model is a Markov model as the distribution of S_t clearly depends only on the value of S_{t-1}.

A binomial model can be graphically represented by a tree. For example, Exhibit 14.3 shows a binomial model for three periods. A binomial model over T time steps, from 0 to T, produces a total of 2^T paths. Therefore, the corresponding space of states has 2^T states. However, the number of different final prices $S_T = u^k d^{T-k} S_0$, $k = 0,1,...,T$ is determined solely by the number of u and d in each path and increases by 1 at each time step; there are as many final prices as dates. For example, the model in Exhibit 14.3 shows three final prices and four states.

Note that there is a simple relationship between the numbers d and u and returns. In fact, we can write,

$$R_t(\text{up}) = \frac{S_{t+1} - S_t}{S_t} = \frac{uS_t - S_t}{S_t} = u - 1$$

$$R_t(\text{down}) = d - 1$$

EXHIBIT 14.3   Binomial Model: The Figure Illustrates a Binomial Tree with Three Dates, Three Final Prices, and Four States: *uu,ud,du,dd*

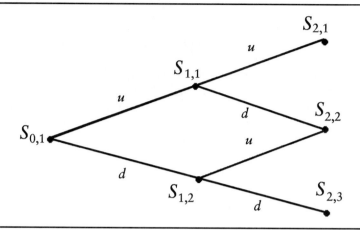

Real probabilities of states are typically constructed from the probabilities of a movement up or down. Call p the probability of a movement up; $1 - p$ is thus the probability of a movement down. Suppose that the state s, which is identified by a price path, has k movements *up* and $T - k$ movements *down*. The probability of the state s is

$$p_s = p^k(1-p)^{T-k}$$

Consider the final date T. Each of the possible final prices $S_T = u^k d^{T-k} S_0$, $k = 0,1,...,T$ can be obtained through

$$\binom{T}{k} = \frac{T!}{k!(T-k)!}$$

paths with k movements up and $T - k$ movements down. The probability distribution of final prices is therefore a binomial distribution:

$$P(S_T = u^k d^{T-k} S_0) = \binom{T}{k} p^k(1-p)^{T-k}$$

Following the same reasoning, one can demonstrate that at any intermediate date the probability distribution of prices is a binomial distribution as follows:

$$P(S_t = u^k d^{t-k} S_0) = \binom{y}{k} p^k (1-p)^{t-k}$$

Next introduce a risk-free security. In the setting of a binomial model, a risk-free security is simply a security such that $d = u = 1 + r$ where $r > 0$ is the positive risk-free rate. To avoid arbitrage it is clearly necessary that $d < 1 + r < u$. In fact, if the interest rate is inferior to both the up and down returns, one can make a sure profit by buying the risky asset and shorting the risk-free asset. If the interest rate is superior to both the up and down returns, one can make a sure profit by shorting the risky asset and buying the risk-free asset. Denote by b_t the price of the risk-free asset at time t. From the definition of price movement in the binomial model we can write: $b_t = (1 + r)^t b_0$.

Risk-Neutral Probabilities for the Binomial Model

Let's now compute the risk-neutral probabilities. In the setting of binomial models, the computation of risk-neutral probabilities is simple. In fact we have to impose the condition:

$$q_t = E_t^Q[q_{t+1}]$$

which we can explicitly write as follows:

$$S_t = \frac{qu S_t + (1-q)d S_t}{1+r}$$

$$1 + r = qu + d - qd$$

$$q = \frac{1+r-d}{u-d}$$

$$1 - q = \frac{u-1-r}{u-d}$$

As we have assumed $0 < d < 1 + r < u$, the condition $0 < q < 1$ holds. Therefore we can state that the unique risk-neutral probabilities are

$$q = \frac{1+r-d}{u-d}$$

$$1 - q = \frac{u - 1 - r}{u - d}$$

The binomial model is complete and arbitrage free.

Suppose that there is more than one risky asset, for example two risky assets, in addition to the risk-free asset. At each time step each risky asset can go either up or down. Therefore there are four possible joint movements at each time step: uu, ud, du, dd that we identify with the states 1,2,3,4. Four probabilities must be determined at each time step; four equations are therefore needed. Two equations are provided by the martingale conditions:

$$S_t^1 = \frac{q_1 u S_t^1 + q_2 u S_t^1 + q_3 u S_t^1 + q_4 u S_t^1}{1 + r}$$

$$S_t^2 = \frac{q_1 u S_t^2 + q_3 u S_t^2 + q_2 u S_t^2 + q_4 u S_t^2}{1 + r}$$

A third equation is provided by the fact that probabilities must sum to 1. The fourth condition, however, is missing. The model is incomplete.

The problem of approximating price processes when there are two stocks and one bond and where the stock prices follow two correlated lognormal processes has long been of interest to financial economists. As seen above, with two stocks and one bond available for trading, markets cannot be completed by dynamic trading. This is not the case in the continuous-time model, in which markets can be completed by continuous trading in the two stocks and the bond. Different solutions to this problem have been proposed in the literature.[1]

VALUATION OF EUROPEAN SIMPLE DERIVATIVES

Consider a market formed by a risky asset (a stock) that follows the binomial model plus a risk-free asset. As we have seen in the previous section, this market is complete and its risk-neutral probabilities are

---

[1] Hua He, "Convergence from Discrete- to Continuous-Time Contingent Claims Prices," *Review of Financial Studies* 3, no. 4 (1990), pp. 523–546.

$$q = \frac{1+r-d}{u-d}$$

$$1-q = \frac{u-1-r}{u-d}$$

Let's introduce in this market a derivative instrument. The condition of absence of arbitrage univocally determines the price of this third security. Consider first a European call option on the stock with expiration date $\tau < T$ and with exercise price $K > 0$. Recall from Chapter 2 that a European call option is a security that gives its holder the right but not the obligation to purchase the stock at time τ at price K. Therefore, the payoff process of the option is zero before time τ and, at time τ, is

$$C_\tau^\tau = \max(S_\tau - K, 0)$$

Let's compute the value of the option C_t^τ at any time $0 < t < \tau$. Given that the binomial model is complete, the value C_t^τ can be computed as the discounted payoff at time t using the risk-neutral probabilities. Using the formulas of the previous sections, we can therefore write

$$C_t^\tau = E_t^Q\left[\frac{C_\tau^\tau}{(1+r)^{\tau-t}}\right]$$

This formula can be explicitly computed as follows. The distribution of the payoff of the option at time τ under the risk-neutral probabilities is the following:

$$P[C_\tau^\tau = (u^k d^{\tau-t-k} S_0 - K)^+] = \binom{\tau-t}{k} q^k (1-q)^{\tau-t-k}$$

Therefore the conditional expectation under the risk-neutral probabilities becomes

$$C_t^\tau = \frac{1}{(1+r)^{\tau-t}} \sum_{k=0}^{\tau-t} (u^k d^{\tau-t-k} S_0 - K)^+ \binom{\tau-t}{k} q^k (1-q)^{\tau-t-k}$$

More generally, we give the following definition: A simple European derivative instrument with expiration time τ is a financial instrument whose payoff is zero for $0 \le t < \tau$ and is an $\mathfrak{I}_\tau$-measurable random variable V_τ at time τ. Recall from Chapter 6 that in this finite-state context, a variable is $\mathfrak{I}_t$-measurable if it assumes a constant value on each of the sets of the partition I_t.

Given the risk-neutral probability measure Q, the value at time t of the simple European derivative instrument can be computed as follows:

$$V_t = E_t^Q \left[\frac{V_\tau}{(1+r)^{\tau-t}} \right]$$

If the underlying stock is represented by a binomial model, the value of the European derivative instrument can be explicitly computed as:

$$V_t = \frac{1}{(1+r)^{\tau-t}} \sum_{k=0}^{\tau-t} V_\tau \binom{\tau-t}{k} q^k (1-q)^{\tau-t-k}$$

VALUATION OF AMERICAN OPTIONS

In order to define American options we have first to define the concept of a *stopping time*. In fact, American options can be exercised at any moment prior to expiration date in function of some exercising policy. These policies define a stopping time. A stopping time is a random time s, i.e., a random variable s such that

$$\{ \omega \in \Omega; \, s(\omega) = k \} \in \mathfrak{I}_k$$

Consider now an adapted process X_t and a stopping time s. Define a payoff process d^s as $d_t^s = 0$ if $t \ne s$ and $d_\tau^s = X_s$. Under the risk-neutral probabilities we can write a valuation formula:

$$V_t^s = E_t^Q \frac{X_s}{(1+r)^{s-t}}$$

These formulas allow the valuation of American securities in complete markets.

ARBITRAGE PRICING IN A DISCRETE-TIME, CONTINUOUS-STATE SETTING

Let's now discuss the discrete-time, continuous-state setting. This is an important setting as it is, for example, the setting of the Arbitrage Pricing Theory (APT) Model that we will discuss later in this chapter.

As in the previous discrete-time, discrete-state setting, we use the probabilistic concepts developed in Chapter 6. The economy is represented by a probability space $(\Omega, \Im, P)$ where Ω is the set of possible states, $\Im$ is the σ-algebra of events (formed, in this continuous-state setting, by a nondenumerable number of events), and P is a probability function. As the number of states is infinite, the probability of each state is zero and only events, in general, formed by nondenumerable states, have a finite probability. There are only a finite number of dates from 0 to T. Recall from Chapter 6 that the propagation of information is represented by a finite filtration $\Im_t$, $t = 0,1,...,T$. In this case, the filtration $\Im_t$ is not equivalent to an information structure I_t.

Each security i is characterized by a payoff process d_t^i and by a price process S_t^i. In this continuous-state setting, d_t^i and S_t^i are formed by a finite number of continuous variables. As before, $d_t^i(\omega)$ and $S_t^i(\omega)$ are, respectively, the payoff and the price of the i-th asset at time t, $0 \le t \le T$ and in state $\omega \in \Omega$. Following Chapter 6, all payoffs and prices are stochastic processes adapted to the filtration $\Im$.

To develop an intuition for continuous-state arbitrage pricing, consider the previous multiperiod, finite-state case with a very large number M of states, $M >> N$ where N is the number of securities. Recall from our earlier discussion in this chapter that risk-neutral probabilities can be computed solving the following system of linear equations:

$$\sum_{\omega \in A_{k,t}} q_\omega \left[\sum_{j=t+1}^{T} \frac{d_j^i(\omega)}{R_{t,j}} - S_{A_{kt}}^i \right] = 0$$

$$\sum_{\omega = 1}^{M} q_\omega = 1$$

Recall also that at each date t the information structure I_t partitions the set of states into M_t subsets. Each partition therefore yields $N \times M_t$ equations and the system is formed by a total of

$$N \times \sum_{t=0}^{T-1} M_t$$

equation plus the probability normalizing equation. Consider that the previous system can be broken down, at each date t, into separate blocks formed by N equations (one for each asset) of the following type:

$$\sum_{\omega \in A_{kt}} q_\omega^* \sum_{j=t+1}^{T} \frac{d_j^i}{R_{t,j}} = S_{A_{kt}}$$

$$q_\omega^* = \frac{q_\omega}{\sum_{\omega \in A_{kt}} q_\omega}$$

Each of these systems can be solved individually for the conditional probabilities q_ω^*. Recall that a system of this type admits a solution if and only if the coefficient matrix and the augmented coefficient matrix have the same rank. If the system is solvable, its solution will be unique if and only if the number of unknowns is equal to the rank of the coefficient matrix.

If the above system is not solvable then there are arbitrage opportunities. This occurs if the payoffs of an asset are a linear combination of those of other assets, but its price is not the same linear combination of the prices of the other assets. This happens, in particular, if two assets have the same payoff in each state but different prices. In these cases, in fact, the rank of the coefficient matrix is inferior to the rank of the augmented matrix.

Under the assumption

$$M \gg N \times \sum_{t=0}^{T-1} M_t$$

this system, if it is solvable, will be undetermined. Therefore, there will be infinite equivalent risk-neutral probabilities and the market will not be complete. Going to the limit of an infinite number of states, the above reasoning proves, heuristically, that a discrete-time continuous-state market with a finite number of securities is inherently incomplete. In addition, there will be arbitrage opportunities only if the random variable that represents the payoff of an asset is a linear combination of the random variables that represent the payoffs of other assets, but the random variables that represent prices are not in the same relationship.

The above discussion can be illustrated in the case of multiple assets, each following a binomial model. If there are N linearly independent assets, the price paths in the interval $(0,T)$ will form a total of 2^{NT} states. In a binomial model, we can limit our considerations to one time step as the other steps are identical. In one step, each price S_t^i at time t can go up to $S_t^i u^i$ or down to $S_t^i d^i$ at time $t + 1$. Given the prices $\{S_t^i\} \equiv \{S_t^1, S_t^2, ..., S_t^N\}$ at time t, there will be, at the next time step, $2N$ possible combinations $\{S_t^1 w^1, S_t^2 w^2, ..., S_t^N w^N\}$, $w^i = u^i$ or d^i.

Suppose that there are 2^{NT} states and that each combination of prices identifies a state. This means that at each date t the information structure I_t partitions the set of states into 2^{Nt} subsets. Each set of the partition is partitioned into 2^N subsets at the next time step. This yields $2^{N(t+1)}$ subsets at time $t + 1$.

Note that this partitioning is compatible with any correlation structure between the random variables that represent prices. In fact, correlations depend on the value of the probability assigned to each state while the partitioning we assume depends on how different prices are assigned to different states.

Risk-neutral probabilities q_i, $i = 1,2,...,2^N$ can be determined solving the following system of martingale conditions:

$$\sum_{j=1}^{2^N} q_j S_t^i w^i(j) = S_t^i$$

$$\sum_{j=1}^{2^N} q_j = 1$$

$$j = 1,2,...,2^N, i = 1,2,...,N$$

which becomes, after dividing each equation by S_t^i, the following:

$$\sum_{j=1}^{2^N} q_j w^i(j) = 1$$

$$\sum_{j=1}^{2^N} q_j = 1$$

where $w^i(j) = u^i$ or d^i for asset i in state j.

It can be verified that, under the previous assumptions and provided prices are positive, the above system admits infinite solutions. In fact, as $N + 1 < 2^N$, the number of equations is larger than the number of unknowns. Therefore, if the system is solvable it admits infinite solutions. To verify that the system is indeed solvable, let's choose the first asset and partition the set of states into two events corresponding to the movement up or down of the same asset. Assign to these events probabilities as in the binomial model

$$q_t^1 = \frac{1 - r + d_t^1}{u_t^1 - d_t^1} \text{ and } 1 - q_t^1$$

Choose a second asset and partition each of the previous events into two events corresponding to the movements up or down of the second asset. We can now assign the following probabilities to each of the following four events:

$$q_t^1 q_t^2, \, q_t^1(1 - q_t^2), \, (1 - q_t^1)q_t^2, \, (1 - q_t^2)(1 - q_t^1)$$

It can be verified that these numbers sum to one. The same process can be repeated for each additional asset. We obtain a set of positive numbers that sum to one and that satisfy the system by construction. There are infinite other possible constructions. In fact, at each step, we could multiply probabilities by "correlation factors" (i.e., numbers that form a 2×2 correlation matrix) and still obtain solutions to the system.

We can therefore conclude that a system of positive binomial prices such as the one above plus a risk-free asset is arbitrage-free and forms an incomplete market. Recall from Chapter 8 that if we let the number of states tend to infinity, the binomial distribution converges to a normal distribution. We have therefore demonstrated heuristically that a multivariate normal distribution plus a risk-free asset forms an incomplete and arbitrage-free market. Note that the presence of correlations does not change this conclusion.

Let's now see under what conditions this conclusion can be changed. Go back to the multiple binomial model, assuming, as before, that there are N assets and T time steps. There is no logical reason to impose that the number of states be 2^{NT}. As we can consider each time step separately, suppose that there is only one time step and that there are a number of states less than or equal to the number of assets plus 1: $M \leq N + 1$. In this case, the martingale condition that determines risk-neutral probabilities becomes:

$$\sum_{j=1}^{M} q_j w^i(j) = 1$$

$$\sum_{j=1}^{N} q_j = 1$$

There are M equations and $N + 1$ unknowns with $M \leq N + 1$. This system will either determine unique risk-neutral probabilities or will be unsolvable. Therefore, the market will be either complete and arbitrage-free or will exhibit arbitrage opportunities. Note that in this case we cannot use the constructive procedure used in the previous case.

What is the economic meaning of the condition that the number of states be less than or equal to the number of assets? To illustrate this point, assume that the number of states is $M = 2^K \leq N + 1$. This means that we can choose K assets whose independent price processes identify all the states as in the previous case. Now add one more asset. This asset will go up or down not in specific states but in events formed by a number of states. Suppose it goes up in the event A and goes down in the event B. These events are determined by the value of the first K assets. In other words, the new asset will be a function of the first K assets. An interesting case is when the new asset can be expressed as a linear function of the first K assets. We can then say that the first K assets are factors and that any other asset is expressed as a linear combination of the factors.

Consider that, given the first K assets, it is possible to determine state-price deflators. These state-price deflators will not be uniquely determined. Any other price process must be expressed as a linear combination of state-price deflators to avoid arbitrage. If all price processes are arbitrage-free, the market will be complete if it is possible to determine uniquely the risk-neutral probabilities.

If we let the number of states become very large, the number of assets must become large as well. Therefore it is not easy to develop simple heuristic arguments in the limit of a large economy. What we can say is that in a large discrete economy where the number of states is less than or equal to the number of assets, if there are no arbitrage opportunities the market might be complete. If the market is complete and arbitrage-free, there will be a number of factors while all other processes will be linear combinations of these factors. These considerations will be further developed in Chapter 18.

APT MODELS

In the previous sections we presented the general theory of arbitrage pricing. The most fundamental principle of finance theory, absence of arbitrage, applies to all price processes. In this section we present a special case of the theory which applies to equity prices. In 1976 Stephen Ross published a seminal paper[2] where he argued that equity returns can be represented as a linear regression over a small set of factors and that expected returns are determined by principle of absence of arbitrage. This pricing theory is called the Arbitrage Pricing Theory (APT).

APT is formulated in a one period setting. Suppose that equity returns can be written as follows:

$$\mathbf{r} = \mathbf{a} + \mathbf{B}\mathbf{f} + \boldsymbol{\varepsilon}$$

where $\mathbf{r}$ is the n-vector of returns to be modeled, $\mathbf{f}$ is a k-vector of common factors with $k << n$, $\mathbf{a}$ is an n-vector of constants, $\mathbf{B}$ is a $n{\times}k$ matrix and $\boldsymbol{\varepsilon}$ is an n-vector of random disturbances such that:

$$E[\boldsymbol{\varepsilon}|\mathbf{f}] = 0$$

$$E[\boldsymbol{\varepsilon}\boldsymbol{\varepsilon}'|\mathbf{f}] = \Sigma$$

In the above relationships, the factors are stochastic variables. APT states that, if there is no arbitrage, the constants $\mathbf{a}$ in the above relationship must all be equal to the risk-free rate.

In a one period setting, if there are only a finite number of securities traded at discrete dates and if the price of each security can take any value regardless of the prices of other securities, clearly no arbitrage opportunity is possible. In fact, given any portfolio, infinite price paths can assume negative values. In a probabilistic context it might happen that the probability of making a loss starting from zero investment might be small but not zero.

APT holds in the limit of a large economy. Ross assumed that well-diversified portfolios exist; this implies that stochastic fluctuations go to zero in the limit of very large portfolios. This is not to say that portfolio behavior becomes deterministic in the limit of large portfolios as factors are assumed to be stochastic; it does however mean that uncertainty is completely captured by the dynamics of factors. Under this assumption, Ross demonstrated that the following relationship holds for large economies:

---

[2] Stephen Ross, "The Arbitrage Theory of Capital Asset Pricing," *Journal of Economic Theory* 13, no. 3 (December 1976), pp. 341–360.

$$E[\mathbf{r}] = \lambda_0 \mathbf{1} + \mathbf{B}\lambda$$

where λ are risk premia. This relationship says that each asset's return is equal to the risk-free rate λ_0 plus a linear combination of factors.

In the original formulation, the above linear relationship holds only approximately in the limit of an infinite economy. Any finite number of assets can be mispriced, that is, violate the above relationship. The APT relationship can be made rigorous with additional restrictions on agent behavior.

Testing APT

The original formulation of APT does not identify factors. Subsequently a number of researchers tried to tackle the problem. As we will see in Chapter 18, factors can be either exogenously given factors or abstract factors formed by particular portfolios. A number of studies have tried to identify macroeconomic factors responsible for stock returns.[3] Statistical techniques such as factor analysis or principal components analysis have also been used.

The approximate nature of APT makes it difficult to test it. In fact, the APT holds only in the limit of an infinite economy while any finite number of securities can be arbitrarily priced without affecting the arbitrage principle. For this reason it has been suggested that APT cannot be tested at all.[4] Based on a given selection of factors APT has been tested with the techniques that we will explain in the following sections.

Testing APT when Factors are Portfolios

Suppose that factors are given portfolios and that there is a risk-free asset. This means that it is known (or at least assumed) that the model in excess returns takes the form

$$\mathbf{z}_t = \mathbf{a} + \mathbf{B}\mathbf{f}_t + \boldsymbol{\varepsilon}_t$$

---

[3] See, for example, Chen, Nai-Fu, Richard R. Roll, and Stephen A. Ross, "Economic Forces and the Stock Market," *Journal of Business* 59, no. 3 (1986), pp. 383–404 and Michael A. Berry, Edwin Burmeister, and Marjorie B. McElroy, "Sorting out Risk Using Known APT Factors," *Financial Analysts Journal* 44, no. 2 (1988), pp. 29–42.
[4] Phoebus J. Dhrymes, Irwin Friend, and N. Bulent Gultekin, "A Critical Re-Examination of the Empirical Evidence on the Arbitrage Pricing Theory," *Journal of Finance* 39, no. 2 (1988), pp. 323–346.

$$\mathbf{f} = (f_1, ..., f_k)\,, K << N$$

$$f_i = \sum_{s=1}^{s_i} \alpha_s r_{i_s}$$

where $r_{i_s} = z_{i_s} - a_{i_s}$ and α_s are the weights of those portfolios that identify factors.

APT requires that the constants **a**, when the model is formulated in excess returns, are zero. To test APT the model parameters have first to be estimated. Suppose that returns are normal IID variables and that the multifactor model is unconstrained. Model estimation can be done by Maximum Likelihood methods which are, in this case, identical to Ordinary Least Square (OLS) estimates. The model parameters are then obtained as the empirical moments, as follows:

$$\hat{a} = \hat{\mu} - \hat{\mathbf{B}}\hat{\mu}_K$$

$$\hat{\mathbf{B}} = \frac{\displaystyle\sum_{t=1}^{T} (\mathbf{z}_t - \hat{\mu})(\mathbf{z}_{Kt} - \hat{\mu}_K)}{\displaystyle\sum_{t=1}^{T} (\mathbf{z}_{Kt} - \hat{\mu}_K)(\mathbf{z}_{Kt} - \hat{\mu}_K)}$$

$$\hat{\mu} = \frac{1}{T}\sum_{t=1}^{T} \mathbf{z}_t$$

$$\hat{\mu}_K = \frac{1}{T}\sum_{t=1}^{T} \mathbf{z}_{Kt}$$

Now suppose that there is a risk-free asset and that the model is constrained by the APT constraints. In this case, we can still use MLE estimation which yields a zero intercept and the following sensitivities:

$$\hat{\mathbf{B}} = \frac{\displaystyle\sum_{t=1}^{T} \mathbf{z}_t \mathbf{z'}_{Kt}}{\displaystyle\sum_{t=1}^{T} \mathbf{z}_{Kt}\mathbf{z'}_{Kt}}$$

The APT restriction can be tested with Likelihood Ratio methods which compare the likelihood of the constrained and unconstrained model.

Testing and Estimating APT When Factors are not Portfolios

If factors are not portfolios and if they are given exogenous processes, multifactor models are multivariate regressions on the factors. If the regression innovations are assumed to be jointly normally distributed and no restriction is imposed, models can be estimated with MLE methods that are, in this case, equivalent to OLS estimates. Writing the multifactor model in real returns, OLS estimation yields the following results:

$$\hat{\mathbf{a}} = \hat{\mu} - \hat{\mathbf{B}}\hat{\mu}_K$$

$$\hat{\mathbf{B}} = \frac{\displaystyle\sum_{t=1}^{T}(r_t - \hat{\mu})(f_{Kt} - \hat{\mu}_K)}{\displaystyle\sum_{t=1}^{T}(f_{Kt} - \hat{\mu}_K)(f_{Kt} - \hat{\mu}_K)}$$

$$\hat{\mu} = \frac{1}{T}\sum_{t=1}^{T} r_t$$

$$\hat{\mu}_K = \frac{1}{T}\sum_{t=1}^{T} f_{Kt}$$

Testing the zero intercept restriction from the above estimates can be performed using MLE methods. Note that in this case only one model is estimated because factors are given. Should factors be portfolios, the constrained and unconstrained models yield different factors.

SUMMARY

- The law of one price states that a given asset must have the same price regardless of the means by which one goes about creating that asset.
- Arbitrage is the simultaneous buying and selling of an asset at two different prices in two different markets.
- A finite-state one-period market is represented by a vector of prices and a matrix of payoffs.
- A state-price vector is a strictly positive vector such that prices are the product of the state-price vector and the payoff matrix.
- There is no arbitrage if and only if there is a state-price vector.
- A market is complete if an arbitrary payoff can be replicated by a portfolio.
- A finite-state one-period market is complete if there are as many linearly independent assets as states.
- A multiperiod finite-state economy is represented by a probability space plus an information structure.
- In a multiperiod finite-state market each security is represented by a payoff process and a price process.
- An arbitrage is a trading strategy whose payoff process is nonnegative and not always zero.
- A market is complete if any nonnegative payoff process can be replicated with a trading strategy.
- A state-price deflator is a strictly positive process such that prices are random variables equal to the conditional expectation of discounted payoffs.
- A martingale is a process such that at any time t its conditional expectation at time s, $s > t$ coincides with its present value.
- In absence of arbitrage there is an artificial probability measure in which all price processes, appropriately discounted, become martingales.
- Given a probability measure P, the probability measure Q is said to be equivalent to P if both assign probability zero to the same events.
- The binomial model assumes that there are two positive numbers, d, and u, such that $0 < d < u$ and such that at each time step the price S of the risky asset changes to dS or to uS.
- The distribution of prices of a binomial model is a binomial distribution.
- The binomial model is complete.
- The Arbitrage Pricing Theory (APT) asserts that each asset's return is equal to the risk-free rate plus a linear combination of factors.
- The APT can be tested with maximum likelihood methods.

CHAPTER 15

Arbitrage Pricing: Continuous-State, Continuous-Time Models

In the previous chapter we described arbitrage pricing using finite-state models. In this chapter we describe arbitrage pricing in the continuous-state, continuous-time setting. There are a number of important conceptual changes in going from a discrete-state, discrete-time setting to a continuous-state, continuous-time setting. First, each state of the world has probability zero. As described in Chapter 6, this precludes the use of standard conditional probabilities for the definition of conditional expectation and requires the use of filtrations (rather than of information structures) to describe the propagation of information. Second, the tools of matrix algebra are inadequate; the more complex tools of calculus and stochastic calculus described in Chapters 4, 8, 9, and 10, respectively, are required. Third, simple generalizations are rarely possible as many pathological cases appear in connection with infinite sets.

THE ARBITRAGE PRINCIPLE IN CONTINUOUS TIME

Let's start with the definition of basic concepts. The economy is represented by a probability space $(\Omega, \mathfrak{I}, P)$ where Ω is the set of possible states, $\mathfrak{I}$ is the σ-algebra of events, and P is a probability measure. Time is a continuous variable in the interval $[0,T]$. Recall from Chapter 6 that the propagation of information is represented by a filtration $\mathfrak{I}_t$. The latter is a family of σ-algebras such that $\mathfrak{I}_t \subseteq \mathfrak{I}_s$, $t < s$.

Each security i is characterized by a payoff-rate process δ_t^i and by a price process S_t^i. In this continuous-state setting, δ_t^i and S_t^i are real variables with a continuous range such that $\delta_t^i(\omega)$ and $S_t^i(\omega)$ are, respectively, the payoff-rate and the price of the i-th asset at time t, $0 \leq t \leq T$ and in state $\omega \in \Omega$. Note that δ_t^i represents a rate of payoff and not a payoff as was the case in the discrete-time setting. The payoff-rate process must be interpreted in the sense that the cumulative payoff of each individual asset is

$$D_t^i = \int_0^t \delta_s^i ds$$

We assume that the number of assets is finite. We can therefore use the vector notation to indicate a set of processes. For example, we write δ_t and S_t to indicate the vector process of payoff rates and prices respectively. Following Chapter 6, all payoff-rates and prices are stochastic processes adapted to the filtration $\Im$. One can make assumptions about the price and the payoff-rate processes. For example, it can be assumed that price and payoff-rate processes satisfy a set of stochastic differential equations or that they exhibit finite jumps. Later in this chapter we will explore a number of these processes.

As explained in Chapter 6, conditional expectations are defined as partial averaging. In fact, given a variable X_s, $s > t$, its conditional expectation $E_t[X_s]$ is defined as a variable that is $\Im_t$-measurable and whose average on each set $A \in \Im_t$ is the same as that of X:

$$Y_t = E_t[X_s] \Leftrightarrow E[Y_t(\omega)] = E[X_s(\omega)]$$

for $\omega \in A$, $\forall A \in \Im_t$ and Y is $\Im_t$-measurable.

The law of iterated expectations applies as in the finite-state case:

$$E_t[E_u(X_s)] = E_t[X_s]$$

In a continuous-state setting, conditional expectations are variables that assume constant values on the sets of infinite partitions. Imagine the evolution of a variable X. At the initial date, X_0 identifies the entire space Ω. At each subsequent date t, the space Ω is partitioned into an infinite number of sets, each determined by one of the infinite values of X_t.[1] However, these sets have measure zero. In fact, they are sets of the

---

[1] One can visualize this process as a tree structure with an infinite number of branches and an infinite number of branching points. However, as the number of branches and of branching points is a continuum, intuition might be misleading.

type: $\{A: \omega \in A \Leftrightarrow X_t(\omega) = x\}$ determined by specific values of the variable X_t. These sets have probability zero as there is an infinite number of values X_t. As a consequence, we cannot define conditional expectation as expectation under the usual definition of conditional probabilities the same way we did in the case of finite-state setting.

Trading Strategies and Trading Gains

We have to define the meaning of trading strategies in the continuous-state, continuous-time setting; this requires the notion of *continuous trading*. Mathematically, continuous trading means that the composition of portfolios changes continuously at every instant and that these changes are associated with trading gains or losses. A trading strategy is a (vector-valued) process $\theta = \{\theta^i\}$ such that $\boldsymbol{\theta}_t = \{\theta^i_t\}$ is the portfolio held at time t. To ensure that there is no anticipation of information, each trading strategy θ must be an adapted process.

Given a trading strategy, we have to define the gains or losses associated with it. In discrete time, the trading gains equal the sum of payoffs plus the change of a portfolio's value

$$\sum_{t=0}^{T} \left(\sum_i d^i_t \theta^i_t \right) + \sum_i S^i_T \theta^i_T - \sum_i S^i_0 \theta^i_0$$

over a finite interval $[0,T]$.

We must define trading gains when time is a continuous variable. Recall from Chapter 8 that it is not possible to replace finite sums of stochastic increments with pathwise Riemann-Stieltjes integrals after letting the time interval go to zero. The reason is that, though we can assume that paths are continuous, we cannot assume that they have bounded variation. As a consequence, pathwise Riemann-Stieltjes integrals generally do not exist. However, we can assume that paths are of bounded quadratic variation. Under this latter assumption, using Itô isometry, we can define pathwise Itô integrals and stochastic integrals.

Let's first assume that the payoff-rate process is zero, so that there are only price processes. Under this assumption, the trading gain T_t of a trading strategy can be represented by a stochastic integral:

$$T_t = \int_0^t \boldsymbol{\theta}_s d\mathbf{S}_s = \sum_i \int_0^t \theta^i_s dS^i_s$$

In the rest of this section, we will not strictly adhere to the vector notation when there is no risk of confusion. For example, we will write

$\theta \cdot S$ to represent the scalar product $\theta \cdot \mathbf{S}$. If a payoff-rate process is associated with each asset, we have to add the gains consequent to the payoff-rate process. We therefore define the gain process

$$G_t^i = S_t^i + D_t^i$$

as the sum of the price processes plus the cumulative payoff-rate processes and we define the trading gains as the stochastic integral

$$T_t = \int_0^t \theta_s d\mathbf{G}_s = \sum_i \int_0^t \theta_s^i dG_s^i$$

How can we match the abstract notion of a stochastic integral with the buying and selling of assets? In discrete time, trading gains have a meaning that is in agreement with the practical notion of buying a portfolio of assets, holding it for a period, and then selling it at market prices, thus realizing either a gain or a loss. One might object that in continuous time this meaning is lost. How can a process where prices change so that their total variation is unbounded be a reasonable representation of financial reality? This is a question of methodology that is relevant to every field of science. In classical physics, the use of continuous models was assumed to reflect reality; time and space, for example, were considered continuous. Quantum physics upset the conceptual cart of classical physics and the reality of continuous processes has since been questioned at every level. In quantum physics, a theory is considered to be nothing but a model useful as a mathematical device to predict measurements. This is, in essence, the theory set forth in the 1930s by Niels Bohr and the School of Copenhaghen; it has now become mainstream methodology in physics. It is also, ultimately, the point of view of positive economics. In a famous and widely quoted essay, Milton Friedman, recipient of the 1976 Nobel Prize in Economic Science, wrote:

> The relevant question to ask about the "assumptions" of a theory is not whether they are descriptively "realistic," for they never are, but whether they are sufficiently good approximations for the purpose in hand. And this question can be answered only by seeing whether the theory works, which means if it yields sufficiently accurate predictions.[2]

---

[2] Milton Friedman, *Essays in the Theory of Positive Economics* (Chicago: University of Chicago Press, 1953).

In the spirit of positive economics, continuous-time financial models are mathematical devices used to predict, albeit in a probabilistic sense, financial observations made at discrete intervals of time. Stochastic gains predict trading gains only at discrete intervals of time—the only intervals that can be observed. Continuous-time finance should be seen as a logical construction that meets observations only at a finite number of dates, not as a realistic description of financial trading.

Let's consider processes without any intermediate payoff. A self-financing trading strategy is a trading strategy such that the following relationships hold:

$$\theta_t S_t = \sum_i \theta_t^i S_t^i = \sum_i \left(\theta_0^i S_0^i + \int_0^t \theta_t^i dS_t^i \right), \, t \in [0, T]$$

We first define arbitrage in the absence of a payoff-rate process. An arbitrage is a self-financing trading strategy such that: $\theta_0 S_0 < 0$ and $\theta_T S_T \geq 0$, or $\theta_0 S_0 \leq 0$ and $\theta_T S_T > 0$. If there is a payoff-rate process, a self-financing trading strategy is a trading strategy such that the following relationships hold:

$$\theta_t S_t = \sum_i \theta_t^i S_t^i = \sum_i \left(\theta_0^i S_0^i + \int_0^t \theta_t^i dG_t^i \right), \, t \in [0, T]$$

where $G_t^i = S_t^i + D_t^i$ is the gain process as previously defined. An arbitrage is a self-financing trading strategy such that: $\theta_0 S_0 < 0$ and $\theta_T S_T \geq 0$, or $\theta_0 S_0 \leq 0$ and $\theta_T S_T > 0$.

ARBITRAGE PRICING IN CONTINUOUS-STATE, CONTINUOUS-TIME

The abstract principles of arbitrage pricing are the same in a discrete-state, discrete-time setting as in a continuous-state, continuous-time setting. Arbitrage pricing is relative pricing. In the absence of arbitrage, the price and payoff-rate processes of a set of basic assets fix the prices of other assets given the payoff-rate process of the latter. If markets are complete, every price process can be computed in this way. In a discrete-state, discrete-time setting, the computation of arbitrage pricing is done with matrix algebra. In fact, in the absence of arbitrage, every price process can be expressed in two alternative ways:

1. Prices S_t^i are equal to the normalized conditional expectation of payoffs deflated with state prices under the real probabilities:

$$S_t^i = \frac{1}{\pi_t} E_t \left[\sum_{j=t+1}^{T} \pi_j d_j^i \right]$$

2. Prices S_t^i are equal to the conditional expectation of discounted payoffs under the risk-neutral probabilities

$$S_t^i = E_t^Q \left[\sum_{j=t+1}^{T} \frac{d_j^i}{R_{t,j}} \right]$$

State-price deflators and risk-neutral probabilities can be computed solving systems of linear equations for a kernel of basic assets. The above relationships are algebraic linear equations that fix all price processes.

In a continuous-state, continuous-time setting, the principle of arbitrage pricing is the same. In the absence of arbitrage, given a number of basic price and payoff stochastic processes, other processes are fixed. The latter are called *redundant securities* as they are not necessary to fix prices. If markets are complete, every price process can be fixed in this way. In order to make computations feasible, some additional assumptions are made, in particular all payoff-rate and price processes are assumed to be Itô processes.

The theory of arbitrage pricing in a continuous-state, continuous-time setting uses the same tools as in a discrete-state, discrete-time setting. Under an equivalent martingale measure, all price processes become martingales. Therefore prices can be determined as discounted present value relationships. Equivalent martingale measures are the same concept as state-price deflators: After appropriate deflation, all processes become martingales. The key point of arbitrage pricing theory is that both equivalent martingale measures and state-price deflators can be determined from a subset of the market. All other processes are redundant.

In the following sections we will develop the theory of arbitrage pricing in steps. First, we will illustrate the principles of arbitrage pricing in the case of options, arriving at the Black-Scholes option pricing formula. We will then extend this theory to more general derivative securities. Subsequently, we will state arbitrage pricing theory in the context of equivalent martingale measures and of state-price deflators.

OPTION PRICING

We will now apply the concepts of arbitrage pricing to option pricing in a continuous-state, continuous-time setting. Suppose that a market consists of three assets: a risk-free asset (which allows risk-free borrowing and lending at the risk-free rate of interest), a stock, and a European option. We will show that the price processes of a stock and of a risk-free asset fix the price process of an option on that stock.

Suppose the risk-free rate is a constant r. Recall from Chapter 4 that the value V_t of a risk-free asset with constant rate r evolves according to the deterministic differential equation of continually compounding interest rates:

$$dV_t = rV_t dt$$

The above is a differential equation with separable variables. After separating the variables, the equation can be written as

$$\frac{dV_t}{V_t} = rdt$$

which admits the solution $V_t = V_0 e^{rt}$ where V_0 is the initial value of the bank account. This formula can also be interpreted as the price process of a risk-free bond with deterministic rate r.

Stock Price Processes

Let's now examine the price process of the stock. Consider the process $y = \alpha t + \sigma B_t$ where B_t is a standard Brownian motion. From the definition of Itô integrals, it can be seen that this process, which is called an **arithmetic Brownian motion**, is the solution of the following diffusion equation:

$$dy_t = \alpha dt + \sigma dB_t$$

where α is a constant called the **drift of the diffusion** and σ is a constant called the **volatility of the diffusion**.

Consider now the process $S_t = S_0 e^{(\alpha t + \sigma B_t)}$, $t \geq 0$. Applying Itô's lemma it is easy to see that this process, which is called a **geometric Brownian motion**, is an Itô process that satisfies the following stochastic differential equation:

$$dS_t = \mu S_t dt + \sigma S_t dB_t; S_0 = x$$

where x is an initial value, $\mu = \alpha + \frac{1}{2}\sigma^2$ and B_t is a standard Brownian motion. We assume that the stock price process follows a geometric Brownian motion and that there is no payoff-rate process.

Now consider a European call option which gives the owner the right but not the obligation to buy the underlying stock at the exercise price K at the expiry date T. Call Y_t the price of the option at time t. The price of the option as a function of the stock price is known at the final expiry date. If the option is rationally exercised, the final value of the option is

$$Y_T = \max(S_T - K, 0)$$

In fact, the option can be rationally exercised only if the price of the stock exceeds K. In that case, the owner of the option can buy the underlying stock at the price K, sell it immediately at the current price S_t and make a profit equal to $(S_T - K)$. If the stock price is below K, the option is clearly worthless. After T, the option ceases to exist.

How can we compute the option price at every other date? We can arrive at the solution in two different but equivalent ways: (1) through hedging arguments and (2) the equivalent martingale measures. In the following sections we will introduce hedging arguments and equivalent martingale measures.

Hedging

To hedge means to protect against an adverse movement. The seller of an option is subject to a liability as, from his point of view, the option has a negative payoff in some states. In our context, hedging this option means to form a self-financing trading strategy formed with the stock plus the risk-free asset in appropriate proportions such that the option plus this hedging portfolio is risk free. Hedging the option implies that the hedging portfolio perfectly replicates the option payoff in every possible state.

A European call option has only one payoff at the expiry date. It therefore suffices that the hedging portfolio replicates the option payoff at that date. Suppose that there is a self-financing trading strategy (θ_t^1, θ_t^2) in the bond and the stock such that

$$\theta_t^1 V_T + \theta_t^2 S_T = Y_T$$

To avoid arbitrage, the price of the option at any moment must be equal to the value of the hedging self-financing trading strategy. In fact, suppose that at any time $t < T$ the self-financing strategy (θ_t^1, θ_t^2) has a value lower than the option:

$$\theta_t^1 V_t + \theta_t^2 S_t < Y_t$$

An investor could then sell the option for Y_t, make an investment $\theta_t^1 V_t + \theta_t^2 S_t$ in the trading strategy, and at time T liquidate both the option and the trading strategy. As $\theta_T^1 V_T + \theta_t^2 S_T = Y_T$ the final liquidation has value zero in every state of the world, so that the initial profit $Y_t - \theta_t^1 V_T + \theta_t^2 S_T$ is a risk-free profit. A similar reasoning could be applied if, at any time $t < T$, the strategy (θ_t^1, θ_t^2) had a value higher than the option. Therefore, we can conclude that if there is a self-financing trading strategy that replicates the option's payoff, the value of the strategy must coincide with the option's price at every instant prior to the expiry date.

Observe that the above reasoning is an instance of the law of one price that we discussed in the previous chapter. If two portfolios have the same payoffs at every moment and in every state of the world, their price must be the same. In particular, if a trading strategy has the same payoffs of an asset, its value must coincide with the price of that asset.

The Black-Scholes Option Pricing Formula

Let's now see how the price of the option can be computed. Assume that the price of the option is a function of time and of the price of the underlying stock: $Y_t = C(S_t, t)$. This assumption is reasonable but needs to be justified; for the moment it is only a hint as to how to proceed with the calculations. It will be justified later by verifying that the pricing formula produces the correct final payoff.

As S_t is assumed to be an Itô process, in particular a geometric Brownian motion, $Y_t = C(S_t, t)$—which is a function of S_t—is an Itô process as well. Therefore, using Itô's formula, we can write down the stochastic equation that Y_t must satisfy. Recall from Chapter 8 that Itô's formula prescribes that:

$$dY_t = \left[\frac{\partial C(S_t, t)}{\partial t} + \frac{\partial C(S_t, t)}{\partial S_t} S_t \mu + \frac{1}{2} \frac{\partial^2 C(S_t, t)}{\partial S_t^2} S_t^2 \sigma^2 \right] dt + \frac{\partial C(S_t, t)}{\partial S_t} \sigma S_t dB$$

Suppose now that there is a self-financing trading strategy $Y_t = \theta_t^1 V_t + \theta_t^2 S_t$. We can write this equation as

$$\int_0^t dY_t = \theta_t^1 \int_0^t dV_t + \theta_t^2 \int_0^t dS_t$$

or, in differential form, as

$$dY_t = \theta_t^1 dV_t + \theta_t^2 dS_t = (\theta_t^1 r V_t + \theta_t^2 \mu S_t) dt + \theta_t^2 \sigma S_t dB_t$$

If the trading strategy replicates the option price process, the two expressions for dY_t—the one obtained through Itô's lemma and the other obtained through the assumption that there is a replicating self-financing trading strategy—must be equal:

$$(\theta_t^1 r V_t + \theta_t^2 \mu S_t) dt + \theta_t^2 \sigma S_t dB_t$$

$$= \left[\frac{\partial C(S_t, t)}{\partial t} + \frac{\partial C(S_t, t)}{\partial S_t} S_t \mu + \frac{1}{2} \frac{\partial^2 C(S_t, t)}{\partial S_t^2} S_t^2 \sigma^2 \right] dt + \frac{\partial C(S_t, t)}{\partial S_t} \sigma S_t dB_t$$

The equality of these two expressions implies the equality of the coefficients in dt and dB respectively. Equating the coefficients in dB yields,

$$\theta_t^2 = \frac{\partial C(S_t, t)}{\partial S_t}$$

As $Y_t = C(S_t, t) = \theta_t^1 V_t + \theta_t^2 S_t$, substituting, we obtain

$$\theta_t^1 = \frac{1}{V_t} \left[C(S_t, t) - \frac{\partial C(S_t, t)}{\partial S_t} S_t \right]$$

We have now obtained the self-financing trading strategy in function of the stock and option prices. Substituting and equating the coefficients of dt yields,

$$\frac{1}{V_t} \left[C(S_t, t) - \frac{\partial C(S_t, t)}{\partial S_t} S_t \right] r V_t + \frac{\partial C(S_t, t)}{\partial S_t} \mu S_t$$

$$= \frac{\partial C(S_t, t)}{\partial t} + \frac{\partial C(S_t, t)}{\partial S_t} S_t \mu + \frac{1}{2} \frac{\partial^2 C(S_t, t)}{\partial S_t^2} S_t^2 \sigma^2$$

Simplifying and eliminating common terms, we obtain

$$-rC(S_t, t) + r\frac{\partial C(S_t, t)}{\partial S_t}S_t + \frac{\partial C(S_t, t)}{\partial t} + \frac{1}{2}\frac{\partial^2 C(S_t, t)}{\partial S_t^2}S_t^2\sigma^2 = 0$$

If the function $C(S_t, t)$ satisfies this relationship, then the coefficients in dt match. The above relationship is a partial differential equation (PDE). In Chapter 9 we discussed how to solve this equation with suitable boundary conditions. Boundary conditions are provided by the payoff of the option at the expiry date:

$$Y_T = C(S_T, T) = \max(S_T - K, 0)$$

The closed-form solution of the above PDE with the above boundary conditions was derived by Fischer Black and Myron Scholes[3] and referred to as the *Black-Scholes option pricing formula*:

$$C(S_t, t) = x\Phi(z) - e^{-r(T-t)}K\Phi(z - \sigma\sqrt{T-t})$$

with

$$z = \frac{\log(S_t/K) + \left(r + \frac{1}{2}\sigma^2\right)(T-t)}{\sigma\sqrt{T-t}}$$

and where Φ is the cumulative normal distribution.

Let's stop for a moment and review the logical steps we have followed thus far. First, we defined a market made by a stock whose price process follows a geometric Brownian motion and a bond whose price process is a deterministic exponential. We introduced into this market a European call option. We then made two assumptions: (1) The option's price process is a deterministic function of the stock price process; and (2) the option's price process can be replicated by a self-financing trading strategy.

If the above assumptions are true, we can write a stochastic differential equation for the option's price process in two different ways: (1) Using Itô's lemma, we can write the option price stochastic process as a function of the stock stochastic process; and (2) using the assumption that there is a replicating trading strategy, we can write the option price

---

[3] Fischer Black and Myron Scholes, "The Pricing of Options and Corporate Liabilities," *Journal of Political Economy* 81 (1973), pp. 637–654.

stochastic process as the stochastic process of the trading strategy. As the two equations describe the same process, they must coincide. Equating the coefficients in the deterministic and stochastic terms, we can determine the trading strategy and write a deterministic partial differential equation (PDE) that the pricing function of the option must satisfy. The latter PDE together with the boundary conditions provided by the known value of the option at the expiry date uniquely determine the option pricing function.

Note that the above is neither a demonstration that there is an option pricing function, nor a demonstration that there is a replicating trading strategy. However, if both a pricing function and a replicating trading strategy exist, the above process allows one to determine both by solving a partial differential equation. After determining a solution to the PDE, one can verify if it provides a pricing function and if it allows the creation of a self-financing trading strategy. Ultimately, the justification of the existence of an option's pricing function and of a replicating self-financing trading strategy resides in the possibility of actually determining both. Absence of arbitrage assures that this solution is unique.

Generalizing the Pricing of European Options

We can now generalize the above pricing methodology to a generic European option and to more general price processes for the bond and for the underlying stock. In the most general case, the process underlying a derivative need not be a stock price process. However, we suppose that the underlying is a stock price process so that replicating portfolios can be formed. We generalize in three ways:

- The option's payoff is an arbitrary finite-variance random variable.
- The stock price process is an Itô process.
- The short-rate process is stochastic.

Following the definition given in the finite-state setting, we define a European option on some underlying process S_t as an asset whose payoff at time T is given by the random variable $Y_T = g(S_T)$ where $g(x)$, $x \in R$ is a continuous real-valued function. In other words, a European option is defined as a security whose payoff is determined at a given expiry date T as a function of some underlying random variable. The option has a zero payoff at every other date $t \in [0,T]$. This definition clearly distinguishes European options from American options which yield payoffs at random stopping times.

Let's now generalize the price process of the underlying stock. We represent the underlying stock price process as a generic Itô process. Recall from Chapter 8 that a generic univariate Itô process can be represented through the differential stochastic equation:

$$dS_t = \mu(S_t, t)dt + \sigma(S_t, t)dB_t; S_0 = x$$

where x is the initial condition, B is a standard Brownian motion, and $\mu(S_t, t)$ and (S_t, t) are given functions $R \times [0, \infty) \to R$. The geometric Brownian motion is a particular example of an Itô process.

Let's now define the bond price process. We retain the risk-free nature of the bond but let the interest rate be stochastic. Recall that in a discrete-state, discrete-time setting, a bond was defined as a process that, at each time step, exhibits the same return for each state though the return can be different in different time steps. Consequently, in continuous-time we define a bond price process as the following integral:

$$V_t = V_0 e^{\int_0^t r(S_u, u)du}$$

where r is a given function that represents the stochastic rate. In fact, the rate r depends on the time t and on the stock price process S_t. Application of Itô's lemma shows that the bond price process satisfies the following equation:

$$dV_t = V_t r(S_t, t)dt$$

We can now use the same reasoning that led to the Black-Scholes formula. Suppose that there are both an option pricing function $Y_t = C(S_t, t)$ and a replicating self-financing trading strategy

$$Y_t = \theta_t^1 V_t + \theta_t^2 S_t$$

We can now write a stochastic differential equation for the process Y_t in two ways:

1. Applying Itô's lemma to $Y_t = C(S_t, t)$
2. Directly to $Y_t = \theta_t^1 V_t + \theta_t^2 S_t$

The first approach yields

$$dY_t = \left[\frac{\partial C(S_t, t)}{\partial t} + \frac{\partial C(S_t, t)}{\partial S_t} \mu(S_t, t) + \frac{1}{2} \frac{\partial^2 C(S_t, t)}{\partial S_t^2} \sigma^2(S_t, t) \right] dt$$
$$+ \frac{\partial C(S_t, t)}{\partial S_t} \sigma(S_t, t) dB_t$$

The second approach yields

$$dY_t = [\theta_t^1 r(S_t, t) V_t + \theta_t^2 \mu(S_t, t)] dt + \theta_t^2 \sigma(S_t, t) dB_t$$

Equating coefficients in dt, Db we obtain the trading strategy

$$\theta_t^1 = \frac{1}{V_t} \left[C(S_t, t) - \frac{\partial C(S_t, t)}{\partial S_t} S_t \right]$$

$$\theta_t^2 = \frac{\partial C(S_t, t)}{\partial S_t}$$

and the PDE

$$-r(x, t)C(x, t) + r(x, t)\frac{\partial C(x, t)}{\partial x} x + \frac{\partial C(x, t)}{\partial t} + \frac{1}{2}\frac{\partial^2 C(x, t)}{\partial x^2}\sigma^2(x, t) = 0$$

with the boundary conditions $C(S_T, T) = g(S_T)$. Solving this equation we obtain a candidate option pricing function. In each specific case, one can then verify that the option pricing function effectively solves the option pricing problem.

STATE-PRICE DEFLATORS

We now extend the concepts of state prices and equivalent martingale measures to a continuous-state, continuous-time setting. As in the previous sections, the economy is represented by a probability space $(\Omega, \Im, P)$ where Ω is the set of possible states, $\Im$ is the σ-algebra of events, and P is a probability measure. Time is a continuous variable in the interval $[0, T]$. The propagation of information is represented by a filtration $\Im_t$.

A multivariate standard Brownian motion $B = (B_1,...,B_D)$ in R^D adapted to the filtration $\Im_t$ is defined over this probability space. From Chapter 10 we know that there are mathematical subtleties that we will not take into consideration, as regards whether (1) the filtration is given and the Brownian motion is adapted to the filtration or (2) the filtration is generated by the Brownian motion.

Suppose that there are N price processes $\mathbf{X} = (X^1,...,X^N)$ that form a multivariate Itô process in R^N. Trading strategies are adapted processes $\theta = (\theta^1,...,\theta^N)$ that represent the quantity of each asset held at each instant. In order to ensure the existence of stochastic integrals, we require the processes $(X^1,...,X^N)$ and any trading strategy to be of bounded variation. Let's first suppose that there is no payoff-rate process. This assumption will be relaxed in a later section. Suppose also that one of these processes, say X_t^1, is defined by a short-rate process r, so that

$$X_t^1 = e^{\int_0^t r_u du}$$

or

$$dX_t^1 = r_t X_t^1 dt$$

where r_t is a deterministic function of t called the *short-rate process*. Note that X_t^1 could be replaced by a trading strategy. We can think of r_t as the risk-free short-term continuously compounding interest rate and of X_t^1 as a risk-free continuously compounding bank account.

The concept of arbitrage and of trading strategy was defined in the previous section. We now introduce the concept of deflators in a continuous-time continuous-state setting. Any strictly positive Itô process is called a **deflator**. Given a deflator Y we can deflate any process X, obtaining a new deflated process

$$X_t^Y = X_t Y_t$$

For example, any stock price process of a nondefaulting firm or the risk-free bank account is a deflator. For technical reasons it is necessary to introduce the concept of regular deflators. A **regular deflator** is a deflator that, after deflation, leaves unchanged the set of admissible bounded-variation trading strategies.

We can make the first step towards defining a theory of pricing based on equivalent martingale measures. It can be demonstrated that if

Y is a regular deflator, a trading strategy θ is self-financing with respect to the price process $\mathbf{X} = (X^1,...,X^N)$ if and only if it is self-financing with respect to the deflated price process

$$\mathbf{X}^Y = (Y_t X_t^1, ..., Y_t X_t^N)$$

In addition, it can be demonstrated that the price process $\mathbf{X} = (X^1,...,X^N)$ admits no arbitrage if and only if the deflated price process

$$\mathbf{X}^Y = (Y_t X_t^1, ..., Y_t X_t^N)$$

admits no arbitrage.

A *state-price deflator* is a deflator π with the property that the deflated price process $\mathbf{X}^\pi$ is a martingale. As explained in Chapter 6, a martingale is a stochastic process M_t such that its current value equals the conditional expectation of the process at any future time: $M_t = E_t[M_s]$, $s > t$. For each price process X_t^i, the following relationship therefore holds:

$$\pi_t X_t^i = E_t[\pi_s X_s^i], s > t$$

This definition is the equivalent in continuous time of the definition of a state-price deflator that was given in discrete time in the previous chapter. In fact, recall that we defined a state-price deflator as a process π such that

$$S_t^i = \frac{1}{\pi_t} E_t\left[\sum_{j=t+1}^{T} \pi_j d_j^i \right]$$

If there is no intermediate payoff, as in our present case, the previous relationship can be written as

$$\pi_t S_t^i = E_t[\pi_T S_T^i] = E_t[E_{t+1}[\pi_T S_T^i]] = E_t[\pi_{t+1} S_{t+1}^i]$$

The next proposition states that if there is a regular state-price deflator then there is no arbitrage. The demonstration of this proposition hinges on the fact that, as the deflated price process is a martingale, the following relationship holds:

$$E\left[\int_0^T \theta_u dS_u^\pi\right] = 0$$

and therefore any self-financing trading strategy is a martingale. We can thus write

$$\theta_0 S_0^\pi = E[\theta_T S_T^\pi]$$

If

$$\theta_T S_T^\pi \geq 0 \text{ then } \theta_0 S_0^\pi \geq 0 \text{ and if } \theta_T S_T^\pi > 0 \text{ then } \theta_0 S_0^\pi > 0$$

which shows that there cannot be any arbitrage.

We have now stated that the existence of state-price deflators ensures the absence of arbitrage. The converse of this statement in a continuous-state, continuous-time setting is more delicate and will be dealt with later. We will now move on to equivalent martingale measures.

EQUIVALENT MARTINGALE MEASURES

In the previous section we saw that if there is a regular state-price deflator then there is no arbitrage. A state-price deflator transforms every price process and every self-financing trading strategy into a martingale. We will now see that, after discounting by an appropriate process, price processes become martingales through a transformation of the real probability measure into an equivalent martingale measure.[4] This theory parallels the theory of equivalent martingale measures developed in the discrete-state, discrete-time setting. First some definitions must be discussed.

Given a probability measure P, the probability measure Q is said to be equivalent to P if both assign probability zero to the same events, that is, if $P(A) = 0$ if and only if $Q(A) = 0$ for every event A. The equivalent probability measure Q is said to be an equivalent martingale mea-

---

[4] The theory of equivalent martingale measures was developed in the following articles: J.M. Harrison and S.R. Pliska, "A Stochastic Calculus Model of Continuous Trading: Complete Markets," *Stochastic Process Application* 15 (1985), pp. 313–316; J.M. Harrison and S.R. Pliska, "Martingales and Stochastic Integrals in the Theory of Continuous Trading," *Stochastic Process Application* 11 (1981), pp. 215–260 and, J.M. Harrison and D.M. Kreps, "Martingales and Arbitrage in Multiperiod Securities Markets," *Journal of Economic Theory* 20 (June 1979), pp. 381–408.

sure for the process X if X is a martingale with respect to Q and if the Radon-Nikodym derivative

$$\xi = \frac{dQ}{dP}$$

has finite variance. The definition of the Radon-Nikodym derivative is the same here as it is in the finite-state context. The Radon-Nikodym derivative is a random variable ξ such that $Q(A) = E^P[\xi I_A]$ for every event A where I_A is the indicator function of the event A.

To develop an intuition for this definition, consider that any stochastic process X is a time-dependent random variable X_t. The latter is a family of functions $\Omega \rightarrow R$ from the set of states to the real numbers indexed with time such that the sets $\{X_t(\omega) \leq x\}$ are events for any real x. Given the probability measure P, the finite-dimension distributions of the process X are determined. The equivalent measure Q determines another set of finite-dimension distributions. However, the correspondence between the process paths and the states remains unchanged.

The requirement that P and Q are equivalent is necessary to ensure that the process is effectively the same under the two measures. There is no assurance that given an arbitrary process an equivalent martingale measure exists. Let's assume that an equivalent martingale measure does exist for the N-dimensional price process $\mathbf{X} = (X^1,...,X^N)$. It can be demonstrated that if the price process $\mathbf{X} = (X^1,...,X^N)$ admits an equivalent martingale measure then there is no arbitrage.

The proof is similar to that for state-price deflators as discussed above. Under the equivalent martingale measure Q, which we assume exists, every price process and every self-financing trading strategy becomes a martingale. Using the same reasoning as above it is easy to see that there is no arbitrage.

This result can be generalized; here is how. If there is a regular deflator Y such that the deflated price process $\mathbf{X}^Y = (Y_t X_t^1, ..., Y_t X_t^N)$ admits an equivalent martingale measure, then there is no arbitrage. The proof hinges on the result established in the previous section that, if there is a regular deflator Y, the price process $\mathbf{X}$ admits no arbitrage if and only if the deflated price process $\mathbf{X}^Y$ admits no arbitrage.

Note that none of these results is constructive. They only state that the existence of an equivalent martingale measure with respect to a price process ensures the absence of arbitrage. Conditions to ensure the existence of an equivalent martingale measure with respect to a price process are given in the next section.

EQUIVALENT MARTINGALE MEASURES AND GIRSANOV'S THEOREM

We first need to establish an important mathematical result known as **Girsanov's Theorem**. This theorem applies to Itô processes. Let's first state Girsanov's theorem in simple cases. Let X be a single-valued Itô process where B is a single-valued standard Brownian motion:

$$X_t = x + \int_0^t \mu_s ds + \int_0^t \sigma_s dB_s$$

Suppose that a process v and a process θ such that $\sigma_t \theta_t = \mu_t - v_t$ are given. Suppose, in addition, that the process θ satisfies the Novikov condition which requires

$$E\left[e^{\left(\frac{1}{2}\int_0^t \theta_s^2 ds\right)} \right] < \infty$$

Then, there is a probability measure Q equivalent to P such that the following integral

$$\hat{B}_t = B_t + \int_0^t \theta_s ds$$

defines a standard Brownian motion $\hat{B}_t$ in R on $(\Omega, \Im, Q)$ with the same standard filtration of the original Brownian motion B_t. In addition, under Q the process X becomes

$$X_t = x + \int_0^t v_s ds + \int_0^t \sigma_s d\hat{B}_s$$

Girsanov's Theorem states that we can add drift to a standard Brownian motion and still obtain a standard Brownian motion under another probability measure. In addition, by changing the probability measure we can arbitrarily change the drift of an Itô process.

The same theorem can be stated in multiple dimensions. Let X be an N-valued Itô process:

$$X_t = x + \int_0^t \mu_s ds + \int_0^t \sigma_s dB_s$$

In this process, μ_s is an N-vector process and σ_s is an $N \times D$ matrix. Suppose that there are both a vector process $v = (v^1,...,v^N)$ and a vector process $\theta = (\theta^1,...,\theta^N)$ such that $\sigma_t \theta_t = \mu_t - v_t$ where the product $\sigma_t \theta_t$ is not a scalar product but is performed component by component. Suppose, in addition, that the process θ satisfies the Novikov condition:

$$E\left[e^{\left(\frac{1}{2} \int_0^t \theta \cdot \theta ds \right)} \right] < \infty$$

Then there is a probability measure Q equivalent to P such that the following integral

$$\hat{B}_t = B_t + \int_0^t \theta_s ds$$

defines a standard Brownian motion $\hat{B}_t$ in R^D on $(\Omega, \Im, Q)$ with the same standard filtration of the original Brownian motion B_t. In addition, under Q the process X becomes

$$X_t = x + \int_0^t v_s ds + \int_0^t \sigma_s d\hat{B}_s$$

Girsanov's Theorem essentially states that under technical conditions (the Novikov condition) by changing the probability measure, it is possible to transform an Itô process into another Itô process with arbitrary drift. Prima facie, this result might seem unreasonable. In the end the drift of a process seems to be a fundamental feature of the process as it defines, for example, the average of the process. Consider, however, that a stochastic process can be thought as the set of all its possible paths. In the case of an Itô process, we can identify the process with the set of all continuous and square integrable functions. As observed above, the drift is an average and it is determined by the probability measure on which the process is defined. Therefore, it should not be surprising that by changing the probability measure it is possible to change the drift.

The Diffusion Invariance Principle

Note that Girsanov's Theorem requires neither that the process X be a martingale nor that Q be an equivalent martingale measure. If X is indeed a martingale under Q, an implication of Girsanov's Theorem is the diffusion invariance principle which can be stated as follows. Let X be an Itô process:

$$dX_t = \mu_t dt + \sigma_t dB_t$$

If X is a martingale with respect to an equivalent probability measure Q, then there is a standard Brownian motion $\hat{B}_T$ in R^D under Q such that

$$dX_t = \sigma_t d\hat{B}_t$$

Let's now apply the previous results to a price process $X = (V, S^1, ..., S^{N-1})$ where

$$dS_t = \mu_t dt + \sigma_t dB_t$$

and

$$dV_t = r_t V_t dt$$

If the short-term rate r is bounded, V_t^{-1} is a regular deflator. Consider the deflated processes:

$$Z_t = S_t V_t^{-1}$$

By Itô's lemma, this process satisfies the following stochastic equation:

$$dZ_t = \left(-r_t Z_t + \frac{\mu_t}{V_t} \right) dt + \frac{\sigma_t}{V_t} dB_t$$

Suppose there is an equivalent martingale measure Q. Under the equivalent martingale measure Q, the discounted price process

$$Z_t = S_t V_t^{-1}$$

is a martingale. In addition, by the diffusion invariance principle there is a standard Brownian motion $\hat{B}_t$ in R^D under Q such that:

$$dZ_t = \frac{\sigma_t}{V_t} d\hat{B}_t$$

Applying Itô's lemma, given that $Z_t V_t = S_t$, we obtain the fundamental result:

$$dS_t = r_t dt + \sigma_t d\hat{B}_t$$

This result states that, under the equivalent martingale measure, all price processes become Itô processes with the same drift.

Application of Girsanov's Theorem to Black-Scholes Option Pricing Formula

To illustrate Girsanov's Theorem, let's see how the Black-Scholes option pricing formula can be obtained from an equivalent martingale measure. In the previous setting, let's assume that $N = 3$, $d = 1$, r_t is a constant and

$$\sigma_t = \sigma S_t$$

with σ constant. Let S be the stock price process and C be the option price process. The option's price at time T is

$$C = \max(S_T^1 - K)$$

In this setting, therefore, the following three equations hold:

$$dS_t = \mu_t^S dt + \sigma S_t^S dB_t$$

$$dC_t^2 = \mu_t^c dt + \sigma_t^c dB_t$$

$$dV_t = r V_t dt$$

Given that $C_t V_t^{-1}$ is a martingale, we can write

$$C_t = V_t E_t^Q \left[\frac{C_T^2}{V_t} \right] = E_t^Q [e^{-r(T-t)} \max(S_T - K)]$$

It can be demonstrated by direct computation that the above formula is equal to the Black-Scholes option pricing formula presented earlier in this chapter.

EQUIVALENT MARTINGALE MEASURES AND COMPLETE MARKETS

In the continuous-state, continuous-time setting, a market is said to be complete if any finite-variance random variable Y can be obtained as the terminal value at time T of a self-financing trading strategy θ: $Y = \theta_T X_T$. A fundamental theorem of arbitrage pricing states that, in the absence of arbitrage, a market is complete if and only if there is a unique equivalent martingale measure. This is condition can be made more specific given that the market is populated with assets that follow Itô processes. Suppose that the price process is $X = (V, S^1, \ldots, S^{N-1})$ where, as in the previous section:

$$dS_t = \mu_t dt + \sigma_t dB_t$$

$$dV_t = rV_t dt$$

and **B** is a standard Brownian motion $B = (B^1, \ldots, B^D)$ in R^D.

It can be demonstrated that markets are complete if and only if rank$(\sigma) = d$ almost everywhere. This condition should be compared with the conditions for completeness we established in the discrete-state setting in the previous chapter. In that setting, we demonstrated that markets are complete if and only if the number of linearly independent price processes is equal to the maximum number of branches leaving a node. In fact, market completeness is equivalent to the possibility of solving a linear system with as many equations as branches leaving each node.

In the present continuous-state setting, there are infinite states and so we need different types of considerations. Roughly speaking, each price process (which is an Itô process) depends on D independent sources of uncertainty as we assume that the standard Brownian motion is D-dimensional. In a finite-state setting this means that, if processes are Markovian, at each time step any process can jump to D different values. The market is complete if there are D independent price processes. Note that the number D is arbitrary.

EQUIVALENT MARTINGALE MEASURES AND STATE PRICES

We will now show that equivalent martingale measures and state prices are the same concept. We use the same setting as in the previous sections. Suppose that Q is an equivalent martingale measure after deflation by the process

$$\frac{1}{V_t^1} = e^{\int_0^t -r_u du}$$

where r is a bounded short-rate process. The density process ξ_t for Q is defined as

$$\xi_t = E_r\left[\frac{dQ}{dP}\right], t \in [0,T]$$

where

$$\left[\frac{dQ}{dP}\right]$$

is the Radon-Nikodym derivative of Q with respect to P. As in the discrete-state setting, the Radon-Nikodym derivative of Q with respect to P is a random variable

$$\xi = \left[\frac{dQ}{dP}\right]$$

with average value on the entire space equal to 1 and such that, for every event A, the probability of A under Q is the average of ξ:

$$P^Q(A) = E_A[\xi]$$

It can be demonstrated that, given any $\mathfrak{I}_t$-measurable random variable W, the density process ξ_t for Q has the following property:

$$E_t^Q[W] = \frac{E_t[W\xi_t]}{\xi_t}$$

To gain an intuition for the Radon-Nikodym derivative in a continuous-state setting, let's assume that the probability space is the real line equipped with the Borel σ-algebra and with a probability measure P. In this case, $\xi = \xi(x)$, $R \rightarrow R$ and we can write

$$Q(A) = \int_A \xi dP$$

or, $dQ = \xi dP$. Given any random variable X with density f under P and density q under Q, we can then write

$$E^Q[X] = \int_R x q(x) dx = \int_R x \xi(x) f(x) dx$$

In other words, the random variable ξ is a function that multiplies the density f to yield the density q.

We can now show the following key result. Given an equivalent martingale measure with density process ξ_t a state-price deflator is given by the process

$$\pi_t = \xi_t e^{\int_0^t -r_u du}$$

Conversely, given a state-price deflator π_t, the density process

$$\xi_t = e^{\int_0^t r_u du} \frac{\pi_t}{\pi_0}$$

defines an equivalent martingale measure. In fact, suppose that Q is an equivalent martingale measure for X^Y with $\pi_t = \xi_t Y_t$ where

$$Y_t = e^{\int_0^t -r_u du}$$

Then, using the above relationship we can write:

$$E_t[\pi_t X_t] = E_t[\xi_t X_t^Y] = \xi_t E_t^Q[\xi_t X_t^Y] = \xi_t X_t^Y = \pi_t X_t$$

which shows that π_t is a state-price deflator. The same reasoning in reverse order demonstrates that if π_t is a state-price deflator then:

$$\xi_t = e^{\int_0^t r_u du} \frac{\pi_t}{\pi_0}$$

is a density process for Q.

ARBITRAGE PRICING WITH A PAYOFF RATE

In the analysis thus far, we assumed that there is no intermediate payoff. The owner of an asset makes a profit or a loss due only to the changes in value of the asset. Let's now introduce a payoff-rate process δ_t^i for each asset i. The payoff-rate process must be interpreted in the sense that the cumulative payoff of each individual asset is

$$D_t^i = \int_0^t \delta_s^i ds$$

We define a gain process

$$G_t^i = S_t^i + D_t^i$$

By the linearity of the Itô integrals, we can write any trading strategy as

$$\int_0^t \theta_t dG_t = \int_0^t \theta_t dX_t + \int_0^t \theta_t dD_t$$

If there is a payoff-rate process, a self-financing trading strategy is a trading strategy such that the following relationships hold:

$$\theta_t S_t = \sum_i \theta_t^i S_t^i = \sum_i \left(\theta_t^i S_t^i + \int_0^t \theta_t^i dG_t^i \right), t \in [0,T]$$

An arbitrage is, as before, a self-financing trading strategy such that

$$\theta_0 S_0 < 0 \text{ and } \theta_T S_T \geq 0, \text{ or } \theta_0 S_0 \leq 0 \text{ and } \theta_T S_T > 0$$

The previous arguments extend to this case. An equivalent martingale measure for the pair (D,S) is defined as an equivalent probability measure Q such that the Radon-Nikodym derivative

$$\xi = \left[\frac{dQ}{dP}\right]$$

has finite variance and the process $G = S + D$ is a martingale. Under these conditions, the following relationship holds:

$$S_t = E_t^Q\left[e^{\int_t^T -r_u du} + \int_t^T e^{\int_t^s -r_u du} dD_s\right]$$

IMPLICATIONS OF THE ABSENCE OF ARBITRAGE

We saw that the existence of an equivalent martingale measure or of state-price deflators implies absence of arbitrage. We have also seen that, in the absence of arbitrage, markets are complete if and only if there is a unique equivalent martingale measure.

In a discrete-state, discrete-time context we could establish the complete equivalence between the existence of state-price deflators, equivalent martingale measures and absence of arbitrage, in the sense that any of these conditions implies the other two. In addition, the existence of a unique equivalent martingale measure implies absence of arbitrage and market completeness.

In the present continuous-state context, however, absence of arbitrage implies the existence of an equivalent martingale measure and of state price deflators only under rather restrictive and complex technical conditions. If we want to relax these conditions, the condition of absence of arbitrage has to be slightly modified. These discussions are quite technical and will not be presented in this chapter.[5]

---

[5] See F. Delbaen and W. Schachermayer, "The Fundamental Theorem of Asset Pricing for Unbounded Stochastic Processes," *Mathematische Annalen* 312, no. 2 (October 1999), pp. 215–250 and F. Delbaen and W. Schachermayer, "A General Version of the Fundamental Theorem of Asset Pricing," *Mathematische Annalen* 300, no. 3 (November 1994), pp. 463–520.

WORKING WITH EQUIVALENT MARTINGALE MEASURES

The concepts established in the preceding sections of this chapter might seem very complex, abstract, and scarcely useful. On the contrary, they entail important simplifications in the computation of derivative prices. We will see examples of these computations when we cover bond pricing and credit derivatives in later chapters. Here we want to make a few general comments on how these tools are used.

The key result of the arbitrage pricing theory is that, under the equivalent martingale measure, all discounted price processes become martingales and all price processes have the same drift. Therefore, all calculations can be performed under the assumption that the change to an equivalent martingale measure has been made. This environment allows important simplifications. For example, as we have seen, the option pricing problem becomes a problem of computing the present value of simpler processes.

Obviously one has to go back to a real environment at the end of the pricing exercise. This is essentially a calibration problem, as risk-neutral probabilities have to be estimated from real probabilities. Despite this complication, the equivalent martingale methodology has proved to be an important tool in derivative pricing.

SUMMARY

- A trading strategy is a vector-valued process that represents portfolio weights at each moment.
- Trading gains are defined as stochastic integrals.
- A self-financing trading strategy is one whose value at every moment is the initial value plus the trading gains at that moment.
- An arbitrage is a self-financing trading strategy whose initial value is either negative and the final value nonnegative or the initial value nonnegative and the final value positive.
- The Black-Scholes option pricing formula can be established by replicating self-financing trading strategies.
- The Black-Scholes pricing argument is based on constructing a self-financing trading strategy that replicates the option price in each state and for each time.
- Absence of arbitrage implies that a replicating self-financing trading strategy must have the same price as the option.

- The Black-Scholes option pricing formula is obtained solving the partial differential equation implied by the equality of the replicating self-financing trading strategy and the option price process.
- A deflator is any strictly positive Itô process; a state-price deflator is a deflator with the property that the deflated price process is a martingale.
- If there is a (regular) state-price deflator then there is no arbitrage; the converse is true only under a number of technical conditions.
- Two probability measures are said to be equivalent if they assign probability zero to the same event.
- Given a process X on a probability space with probability measure P, the probability measure Q is said to be an equivalent martingale measure if it is equivalent to P and X is a martingale with respect to Q (plus other conditions).
- If there is a regular deflator such that the deflated price process admits an equivalent martingale measure, then there is no arbitrage.
- Under the equivalent martingale measure, all Itô price processes have the same drift.
- In the absence of arbitrage, a market is complete if and only if there is a unique equivalent martingale measure.

CHAPTER 16

Portfolio Selection Using Mean-Variance Analysis

As explained in Chapter 3, a major step in the direction of the quantitative management of portfolios was made in the 1950s by Harry Markowitz in his paper "Portfolio Selection" published in 1952 in the *Journal of Finance*.[1] The ideas introduced in this article have come to form the foundations of what is now popularly referred to as *mean-variance analysis* (M-V analysis) for reasons explained in this chapter, and *Modern Portfolio Theory* (MPT). Initially, M-V analysis generated relatively little interest, but with time, the financial community adopted the thesis, and now 50 years later, financial models based on those very same principles are constantly being reinvented to incorporate new findings that result from that seminal work.

Though widely applicable, M-V analysis has had the most influence in the practice of portfolio management. In its simplest form, M-V analysis provides a framework to construct and select portfolios based on the expected performance of the investments and the risk appetite of the investor. M-V analysis also introduced a whole new terminology, which now has become the norm in the area of investment management.

It may be useful to mention here that the theory of portfolio selection is a normative theory. A *normative theory* is one that describes a standard or norm of behavior that investors should pursue in constructing a portfolio, in contrast to a theory that is actually followed. Asset

---

[1] Harry M. Markowitz, "Portfolio Selection," *Journal of Finance* (March 1952), pp. 77–91. In 1959 Markowitz expanded his ideas in book form: Harry M. Markowitz, *Portfolio Selection: Efficient Diversification of Investments* (New York: John Wiley, 1959).

pricing theory such as the capital asset pricing model, which we discuss in the next chapter, goes on to formalize the relationship that should exist between asset returns and risk if investors constructed and selected portfolios according to mean-variance analysis. In contrast to a normative theory, asset pricing theory is a *positive theory*—a theory that hypothesizes how investors behave rather than how investors should behave. Based on that hypothesized behavior of investors, we derive an asset pricing model that provides the expected return is derived.

Our objective in this chapter is to explain the principles of mean-variance analysis and present a formal mathematical treatment for determining "efficient portfolios." The extensions of Markowitz's formulation includes the case where a risk-free asset is available in the capital market. This leads to efficient portfolio's that dominate efficient portfolios that can be constructed in a capital market in which there is no risk-free asset. We then provide an application of how M-V analysis is used in portfolio selection. While there have been many applications of M-V analysis in the areas of finance and insurance, we present an application to the asset allocation problem. This decision involves deciding how to allocate funds across major asset classes.

DIVERSIFICATION AS A CENTRAL THEME IN FINANCE

Conventional wisdom has always dictated "not putting all your eggs in one basket." In more technical terms, this old adage is addressing the benefits of diversification. Markowitz quantified the concept of diversification, or "undiversification" through the statistical notion of covariance, or correlation. In essence, the old adage is saying that putting all your money in investments that may all perform poorly at the same time—that is, whose returns are highly correlated—is not a very prudent investment strategy—no matter how small the chance is that any one single investment will perform poorly. This is because if any one single investment performs poorly, it is very likely, due to its high correlation with the other investments, that the other investments are also going to perform poorly, leading to the poor performance of the portfolio.

The concept of diversification is so intuitive and so strong that it has been continuously applied to different areas within finance. Indeed, a vast number of the innovations surrounding finance have either been an application of the concept of diversification, or the introduction of new methods of obtaining improved estimates of the variances and covariances, thereby, allowing for a more precise measure of diversification, and consequently, for a more precise measure of risk.

Markowitz considered an investor who, at time t, decides what portfolio of investments to choose; the time horizon of the investor is Δt. The investor makes decisions on the gains and losses he or she will make at time $t + \Delta t$, without considering eventual gains and losses either during or after the period Δt. At time $t + \Delta t$, the investor will reconsider the situation and decide anew; this last condition is called *myopic*.

Nonmyopic investment strategies must be adopted when it is necessary to make trade-offs at future dates between consumption and investment or when significant trading costs related to specific subsets of investments are incurred. We will handle these issues later in this chapter and when we discuss bond portfolio management in Chapter 21 where we apply the multistage optimization technology discussed in Chapter 7.[2]

Markowitz reasoned that investors should decide on the basis of a trade-off between risk and return. He made the assumption that returns are normally distributed and that risk is measured by the variance of the return distribution. In the 1950s when asset pricing theories were not yet developed, the assumption of joint normality of returns was a reasonable statistical assumption. It was based on the fact that asset returns are influenced by many different independent facts. Recall from Chapter 6 on probability theory that the sum of many small random disturbances tends to a normal distribution.

Markowitz argued that for any given level of expected returns investors should choose the portfolios with minimum variance from amongst the set of all possible portfolios that can be constructed. The set of all possible portfolios that can be constructed is called the *feasible set*. In this simple one-period model, variance of returns is a measure of uncertainty and thus of risk. *Minimum variance portfolios* are called *mean-variance-efficient portfolios*. The set of all mean-variance efficient portfolios is called the *efficient frontier*.

Exhibit 16.1 presents the MPT investment process (mean-variance optimization or the theory of portfolio selection). Notice in the exhibit that the result of the analysis is the selection of the optimal portfolio. We describe what is meant by an optimal portfolio later in this chapter.

Though its implementation can get quite complicated, the theory is relatively straightforward. Here we want to give an intuitive and practical view of MPT. The theory dictates that given estimates of the returns, volatilities, and correlations of a set of investments, and constraints on investment choices (for example, maximum exposures and turnover

---

[2] There are applications of multistage optimization in equity portfolio management though these are not as common in the bond portfolio management area. See, for example, John M. Mulvey and Hercules Vladimirou, "Stochastic Network Optimization Models for Investment Planning," *Management Science* 38, no. 11, pp. 1642–1664.

EXHIBIT 16.1   The MPT Investment Process

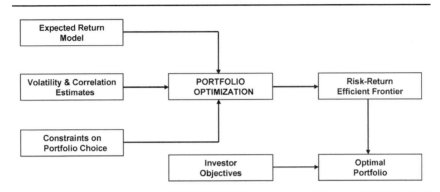

Source: Exhibit 2 in Frank J. Fabozzi, Francis Gupta, and Harry M. Markowitz, "The Legacy of Modern Portfolio Theory," *Journal of Investing* (Fall 2002), p. 8.

constraints) it is possible to perform an optimization that results in the risk-return or mean-variance efficient frontier.[3] This frontier is efficient because underlying every point on this frontier is a portfolio that results in the greatest possible return for that level of risk, or results in the smallest possible risk for that level of return. The portfolios that lie on the frontier make up the *set of efficient portfolios*.

When the efficient frontier is constructed using the M-V formulation developed by Markowitz, they are referred to as *Markowitz efficient portfolios* and the set or frontier of these portfolios is called the *Markowitz efficient frontier*. Exhibit 16.2 provides a graphical depiction of the Markowitz efficient frontier based on the feasible portfolios that can be constructed. The Markowitz efficient frontier is the upper portion of the curve from II to III.

MARKOWITZ'S MEAN-VARIANCE ANALYSIS

Let's now place the above in a formal mathematical context developing the analysis of mean-variance optimization. Suppose first that an investor has to choose a portfolio formed of N risky assets. The investor's choice is embodied in an N-vector $\mathbf{w} = \{w_i\}$ of weights where each weight i represents the percentage of the i-th asset held in the portfolio. Suppose assets' returns are jointly normally distributed with an N-vec-

---

[3] In practice this optimization is performed using an off-the-shelf asset allocation package.

EXHIBIT 16.2   Feasible and Markowitz Efficient Portfolios[a]

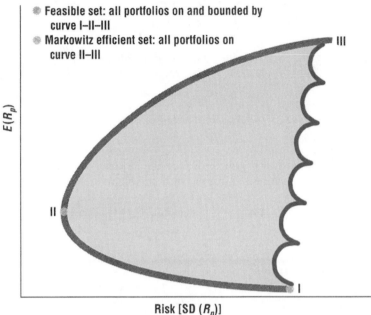

- Feasible set: all portfolios on and bounded by curve I–II–III
- Markowitz efficient set: all portfolios on curve II–III

[a] The picture is for illustrative purposes only. The actual shape of the feasible region depends on the returns and risks of the assets chosen and the correlation among them.

tor of expected returns $\mu = \{\mu_i\}$ and an $N \times N$ variance-covariance matrix $\Sigma = \{\sigma_{ij}\}$. Under these assumptions, the return of a portfolio a with weights $\mathbf{w}_a = \{w_i\}_a$ is a random variable, which is the sum of normally distributed random variables. Therefore, it is a normally distributed random variable with the following mean and variance:

$$\mu_a = \mathbf{w}_a{}'\mu$$

$$\sigma_a^2 = \mathbf{w}_a{}'\Sigma\mathbf{w}_a$$

For instance, if there are only two assets with weights $\mathbf{w}_a{}' = \{w_{a1}w_{a2}\}$, then the portfolios expected return is

$$\mu_a = w_{a1}\mu_1 + w_{a2}\mu_2$$

and its variance is

$$
\begin{aligned}
\sigma_a^2 &= \begin{bmatrix} w_{a1} & w_{a2} \end{bmatrix} \begin{bmatrix} \sigma_{11} & \sigma_{12} \\ \sigma_{21} & \sigma_{22} \end{bmatrix} \begin{bmatrix} w_1 \\ w_2 \end{bmatrix} \\
&= \{ w_{a1}\sigma_{11} + w_{a1}\sigma_{21} \quad w_{a2}\sigma_{12} + w_{a2}\sigma_{22} \} \begin{bmatrix} w_1 \\ w_2 \end{bmatrix} \\
&= w_{a1}^2\sigma_{11} + w_{a2}^2\sigma_{22} + 2w_{a1}w_{a2}\sigma_{12} \\
&= w_{a1}^2\sigma_1^2 + w_{a2}^2\sigma_2^2 + 2w_{a1}w_{a2}\sigma_{12}
\end{aligned}
$$

By choosing the portfolio's weights, an investor chooses among the available mean-variance pairs. Following Markowitz, the investor's problem is a constrained minimization problem in the sense that the investor must seek

$$
\min(\sigma_a^2) = \min(\mathbf{w}_a' \Sigma \mathbf{w}_a)
$$

subject to the constraints

$$
\mu_a = \mathbf{w}_a' \mathbf{\mu}
$$

$$
\mathbf{w}_a' \mathbf{\iota} = 1, \mathbf{\iota}' = [1, 1, ..., 1]
$$

This is a constrained optimization problem which can be solved with the method of Lagrange multipliers. Recall from Chapter 7 that this method transforms a constrained optimization problem into an unconstrained optimization problem by forming the Lagrangian, that is, the sum of the function to be optimized and a linear combination of the constraints. In this case, the Lagrangian is

$$
L = \mathbf{w}_a' \Sigma \mathbf{w}_a + \delta_1(\mu_a - \mathbf{w}_a' \mathbf{\mu}) + \delta_2(1 - \mathbf{w}_a' \mathbf{\iota})
$$

The original optimization problem becomes the problem of unconstrained maximization of the Lagrangian. To solve this problem, it is sufficient to set to zero the partial derivatives of the Lagrangian. Solving yields

$$
\mathbf{w}_a = \mathbf{g} + \mathbf{h}\mu_a
$$

where $\mathbf{g}$ and $\mathbf{h}$ are two vectors which are functions of $\mathbf{\mu}$ and Σ.

Consider the mean-variance plane, that is, a two-dimensional Cartesian plane whose coordinates are mean and variance. In this plane, each portfolio is represented by a point. Consider now the set of all efficient portfolios with all possible efficient mean-variance pairs. This set is what we referred to earlier as the efficient frontier. Later in this chapter we show actual efficient frontiers.

CAPITAL MARKET LINE

As demonstrated by William Sharpe,[4] James Tobin,[5] and John Lintner [6] the efficient set of portfolios available to investors who employ M-V analysis in the absence of a risk-free asset is inferior to that available when there is a risk-free asset.[7] We present this formulation in this section.[8]

Assume a risk-free asset with a risk-free return denoted by R_f. The investor has to choose a combination of the N risky assets plus the risk-free asset. The weights $\mathbf{w}_R = \{w_i\}_R$ do not have to sum to 1 as the remaining part $(1 - \mathbf{w}_R'\iota)$ can be invested in the risk-free asset. Note that this portion of investment can be positive or negative if we allow risk-free borrowing and lending. The portfolio's expected return and variance are:

$$\mu_a = \mathbf{w}_R'\mathbf{\mu} + (1 - \mathbf{w}_R'\iota)R_f$$

$$\sigma_a^2 = \mathbf{w}_R'\mathbf{\Sigma}\mathbf{w}_R$$

The portfolio variance is the same expression as before because the risk-free asset has zero variance and zero covariances with the risky assets.

---

[4] William F. Sharpe, "Capital Asset Prices: A Theory of Market Equilibrium Under Conditions of Risk," *Journal of Finance* (September 1964), pp. 425–442.

[5] James Tobin, "Liquidity Preference as a Behavior Towards Risk," *Review of Economic Studies* (February 1958), pp. 65–86.

[6] John Lintner, "The Valuation of Risk Assets and the Selection of Risky Investments in Stock Portfolios and Capital Budgets," *Review of Economics and Statistics* (February 1965), pp. 13–37.

[7] The portfolio selection model was further extended by Fischer Black in the case of a restriction on short selling. See "Capital Market Equilibrium with Restricted Borrowings," *Journal of Business* (July 1972), pp. 444–455.

[8] For a comprehensive discussion of these models and computational issues, see Harry M. Markowitz (with a chapter and program by Peter Todd), *Mean-Variance Analysis in Portfolio Choice and Capital Markets* (New Hope, PA: Frank J. Fabozzi Associates, 2000, originally published in 1987).

The investor's problem is again a constrained optimization problem that can be stated as

$$\min(\sigma_a^2) = \min(\mathbf{w}_R' \mathbf{\Sigma} \mathbf{w}_R)$$

subject to the constraints

$$\mu_a = \mathbf{w}_R' \mathbf{\mu} + (1 - \mathbf{w}_R' \iota) R_f$$

This problem can be solved again with the method of Lagrange multipliers. The Lagrangian is

$$L = \mathbf{w}_R' \mathbf{\Sigma} \mathbf{w}_R + d[\mu_a - \mathbf{w}_R' \mathbf{\mu} - (1 - \mathbf{w}_R' \iota) R_f]$$

Equating to zero the derivatives of the Lagrangian with respect to the weights and to the Lagrange multiplier d, we obtained the solution of the constrained minimization problem. The solution of this problem has an interesting feature that leads to the CAPM as we will see in the next chapter. In fact, developing the lengthy computations, the optimal portfolio weights can be written as

$$\mathbf{w}_R = C \mathbf{\Sigma}^{-1} (\mathbf{\mu} - R_f \iota)$$

$$C = \frac{\mu_a - R_f}{(\mathbf{\mu} - R_f \iota)' \mathbf{\Sigma}^{-1} (\mathbf{\mu} - R_f \iota)}$$

The above formula shows that the weights of the risky assets of any minimum-variance portfolio are proportional to the same vector. The proportionality constant is C. Therefore, with a risk-free asset, all minimum variance portfolios are a combination of the risk-free asset and of a given risky portfolio. This risky portfolio is called the *tangency portfolio*.

With the exception of the tangency portfolio, the minimum variance portfolios that are a combination of the tangency portfolio and the risk-free asset are superior to the portfolio on the Markowitz efficient frontier that has the same level of risk.

Deriving the Capital Market Line

To derive the Capital Market Line (CML), we begin with the efficient frontier. In the absence of a risk-free asset, Markowitz efficient portfolios can be constructed as a constrained minimum problem based on expected return and variance, with the optimal portfolio being the one portfolio selected based on the investor's preference (which later we will see is quantified by the investor's utility function). The efficient frontier changes, however, once a risk-free asset is introduced and assuming that investors can borrow and lend at the risk-free rate. This is illustrated in Exhibit 16.3.

Every combination of the risk-free asset and the efficient portfolio *M*, which we referred to as the tangency portfolio in the previous section, is shown on the line drawn from the vertical axis at the risk-free rate tangent to the Markowitz efficient frontier. All the portfolios on the line are feasible for the investor to construct. Portfolios to the left of portfolio *M* represent combinations of risky assets and the risk-free asset. Portfolios to the right of portfolio *M* include purchases of risky assets made with funds borrowed at the risk-free rate. Such a portfolio is called a *leveraged portfolio* because it involves the use of borrowed funds. The line from the risk-free rate that is tangent to the efficient frontier of risky assets is called the *capital market line* (CML).

Let's compare a portfolio on the CML to a portfolio on the Markowitz efficient frontier with the same risk in Exhibit 16.3. For

EXHIBIT 16.3   Capital Market Line and the Markowitz Efficient Frontier

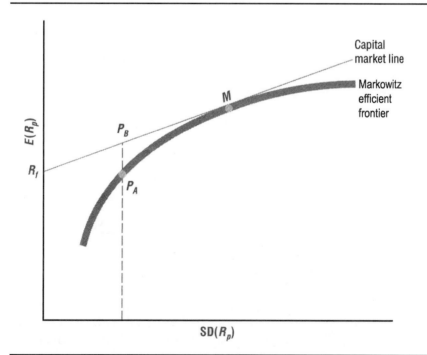

example, compare portfolio P_A, which is on the Markowitz efficient frontier, with portfolio P_B, which is on the CML and therefore some combination of the risk-free asset and the efficient portfolio M. Notice that for the same risk the expected return is greater for P_B than for P_A. By Assumption 2, a risk-averse investor will prefer P_B to P_A. That is, P_B will dominate P_A. In fact, this is true for all but one portfolio on the CML, portfolio M, which is on the Markowitz efficient frontier. With the introduction of the risk-free asset, we can now say that an investor will select a portfolio on the CML that represents a combination of borrowing or lending at the risk-free rate and the efficient portfolio M.

We can derive a formula for the CML algebraically. Based on the assumption of homogeneous expectations regarding the inputs in the portfolio construction process, all investors can create an efficient portfolio consisting of w_f placed in the risk-free asset and w_M in the tangency portfolio, portfolio M, where w represents the corresponding percentage (weight) of the portfolio allocated to each asset.

Thus, $w_f + w_M = 1$ or $w_f = 1 - w_m$. The expected return is equal to the weighted average of the expected returns of the two assets. Therefore, the expected portfolio return, $E(R_p)$, is equal to

$$E(R_p) = w_f R_f + w_M E(R_M)$$

Since we know that $w_f = 1 - w_M$, we can rewrite $E(R_p)$ as follows:

$$E(R_p) = (1 - w_M) R_f + w_M E(R_M)$$

This can be simplified as follows:

$$E(R_p) = R_f + w_M [E(R_M) - R_f]$$

Earlier in this chapter we derived the variance of a portfolio containing only two assets. The variance of the portfolio consisting of the risk-free asset and portfolio M is

$$\text{var}(R_p) = w_f^2 \, \text{var}(R_f) + w_M^2 \, \text{var}(R_M) + 2w_f w_M \, \text{cov}(R_f, R_M)$$

We know that the variance of the risk-free asset, $\text{var}(R_f)$, is equal to zero. This is because there is no possible variation in the return since the future return is known. The covariance between the risk-free asset and portfolio M, $\text{cov}(R_f, R_M)$, is zero. This is because the risk-free asset has no variability and therefore does not move at all with the return on portfolio M which is a risky portfolio. Substituting these two values into the formula for the portfolio's variance, we get

$$\text{var}(R_p) = w_M^2 \ \text{var}(R_M)$$

In other words, the variance of the portfolio is represented by the weighted variance of portfolio M. We can solve for the weight of portfolio M by substituting standard deviations for variances. Since the standard deviation is the square root of the variance, we can write

$$\text{SD}(R_p) = w_M\text{SD}(R_M)$$

and therefore

$$w_M = \frac{\text{SD}(R_p)}{\text{SD}(R_M)}$$

If we substitute the above result and rearrange terms we get the CML:

$$E(R_p) = R_f + \left[\frac{E(R_M) - R_f}{\text{SD}(R_M)}\right]\text{SD}(R_p)$$

What is Portfolio M?

Now we know that portfolio M is pivotal to the CML; we now need to know what portfolio M is. That is, how does an investor construct portfolio M? Eugene Fama demonstrated that portfolio M must consist of all assets available to investors, and each asset must be held in proportion to its market value relative to the total market value of all assets.[9] That is, tangency portfolio M is the "market portfolio." So, rather than referring to the market portfolio, we can simply refer to the "market."

Recall that using Lagrange multipliers we formally demonstrated in a previous section that in the presence of risk-free lending and borrowing the optimal portfolio held by investors is made up of the risk-free asset and of one special portfolio called the tangency portfolio. This important property is called separation. We can now complete the previous demonstration: if risk-free lending and borrowing is allowed the market is M-V efficient and each investor holds the risk-free asset plus a portfolio proportional to the market.

---

[9] Eugene F. Fama, "Efficient Capital Markets: A Review of Theory and Empirical Work," *Journal of Finance* (May 1970), pp. 383–417.

Risk Premium in the CML

With homogeneous expectations, $SD(R_M)$ and $SD(R_p)$ are the market's consensus for the expected return distributions for portfolio M and portfolio p. The risk premium for the CML is

$$\left[\frac{E(R_M) - R_f}{SD(R_M)}\right] SD(R_p)$$

Let's examine the economic meaning of the risk premium.

The numerator of the first term is the expected return from investing in the market beyond the risk-free return. It is a measure of the reward for holding the risky market portfolio rather than the risk-free asset. The denominator is the market risk of the market portfolio. Thus, the first term measures the *reward per unit of market risk*. Since the CML represents the return offered to compensate for a perceived level of risk, each point on the CML is a balanced market condition, or equilibrium. The slope of the CML (i.e., the first term) determines the additional return needed to compensate for a unit change in risk. That is why the slope of the CML is also referred to as the *equilibrium market price of risk*.

The CML says that the expected return on a portfolio is equal to the risk-free rate plus a risk premium equal to the market price of risk (as measured by the reward per unit of market risk) times the quantity of risk for the portfolio (as measured by the standard deviation of the portfolio). That is,

$$ER_p = R_f + \text{market price of risk} \times \text{quantity of risk}$$

THE CML AND THE OPTIMAL PORTFOLIO

Given that the new efficient frontier is the CML, how does one select the optimal portfolio? That is, how does one determine the optimal combination of the market portfolio and the risk-free asset in which to invest? This depends on the preferences of the investors. To understand this, we must introduce the notion of utility functions and indifference curves.

Utility Functions and Indifference Curves

In life there are many situations where entities (i.e., individuals and firms) face two or more choices. The economic "theory of choice" uses the concept of a utility function to describe the way entities make decisions when faced with a set of choices. A *utility function* assigns a (numeric) value to all possible choices faced by the entity. The utility index has the property that pair *a* is preferred to pair *b* if and only if the utility of *a* is higher than that of *b*. The higher the value of a particular choice, the greater the utility derived from that choice. The choice that is selected is the one that results in the maximum utility given a set of constraints faced by the entity.

The assumption that an investor's decision-making process can be represented as optimization of a utility function goes back to Pareto (see Chapter 3). Utility functions can represent a broad set of preference ordering. The precise conditions under which a preference ordering can be expressed through a utility function have been widely explored in the literature.[10]

In portfolio theory too, entities are faced with a set of choices. Different portfolios have different levels of expected return and risk. Also, the higher the level of expected return, the larger the risk. Entities are faced with the decision of choosing a portfolio from the set of all possible risk/return combinations. Whereas they like return, they dislike risk. Therefore, entities obtain different levels of utility from different risk/return combinations. The utility obtained from any possible risk/return combination is expressed by the utility function. Put simply, the utility function expresses the preferences of entities over perceived risk and expected return combinations.

A utility function can be expressed in graphical form by a set of indifference curves. Exhibit 16.4 shows indifference curves labeled u_1, u_2, and u_3. By convention, the horizontal axis measures risk and the vertical axis measures expected return. Each curve represents a set of portfolios with different combinations of risk and return. All the points on a given indifference curve indicate combinations of risk and expected return that will give the same level of utility to a given investor. For example, on utility curve u_1 there are two points u and u', with u having a higher expected return than u', but also having a higher risk.

Because the two points lie on the same indifference curve, the investor has an equal preference for (or is indifferent between) the two points, or, for that matter, any point on the curve. The (positive) slope of an indifference curve reflects the fact that, to obtain the same level of utility, the investor requires a higher expected return in order to accept higher risk. For the three indifference curves shown in Exhibit 16.4, the utility the investor receives is greater the further the indifference curve is from the horizontal axis because that curve represents a higher level of return at every level of risk. Thus, for the three indifference curves shown in the exhibit, u_3 has the highest utility and u_1 the lowest.

---

[10] See, for example, Akira Takayama, *Mathematical Economics* (Cambridge, U.K.: Cambridge University Press, 1985).

EXHIBIT 16.4   Indifference Curves

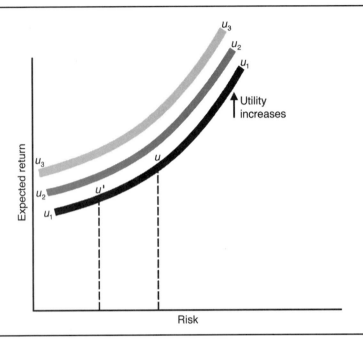

Selection of the Optimal Portfolio

A reasonable assumption is that investors are *risk averse*. A risk-averse investor is an investor who, when faced with choosing between two investments with the same expected return but two different risks, prefers the one with the lower risk.

In selecting portfolios, an investor seeks to maximize the expected portfolio return given his tolerance for risk. Given a choice from the set of efficient portfolios, the *optimal portfolio* is the one that is preferred by the investor. In terms of utility functions, the optimal portfolio is the efficient portfolio which has the maximum utility.

The particular efficient portfolio on the CML that the investor will select will depend on the investor's risk preference. This can be seen in Exhibit 16.5, which is the same as Exhibit 16.2 but has the investor's indifference curves included. The investor will select the portfolio on the CML that is tangent to the highest indifference curve, u_3 in the exhibit.

Notice that without the risk-free asset, an investor could only get to u_2, which is the indifference curve that is tangent to the Markowitz efficient frontier. Thus, the opportunity to borrow or lend at the risk-free rate results in a capital market where risk-averse investors will prefer to

EXHIBIT 16.5   Optimal Portfolio and the Capital Market Line

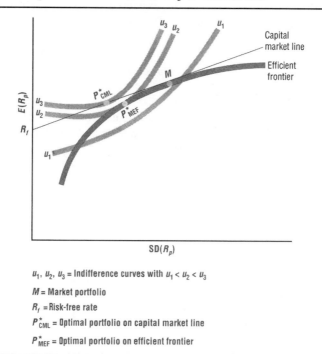

u_1, u_2, u_3 = Indifference curves with $u_1 < u_2 < u_3$

M = Market portfolio

R_f = Risk-free rate

P^*_{CML} = Optimal portfolio on capital market line

P^*_{MEF} = Optimal portfolio on efficient frontier

hold portfolios consisting of combinations of the risk-free asset and the tangency portfolio M on the Markowitz efficient frontier.

EXTENSION OF THE MARKOWITZ MEAN-VARIANCE MODEL TO INEQUALITY CONSTRAINTS

The earlier optimization model introduced by Markowitz is useful from a theoretical point of view, but it is insufficient from the point of view of a portfolio manager who wants to optimize a real portfolio. In fact, the above model has a number of serious shortcomings. In the next chapter we will introduce the notion of systematic risk and nonsystematic risk. A limitation of the Markowitz model presented above is that it only minimizes systematic risk given a target expected return, but it does not set any objectives for systematic risk. The latter can be set by constraining the portfolio exposure to selected risk factors. We will discuss these risk factors in the next chapter.

Suppose asset returns are determined by a multifactor model (as described in Chapter 18) so that the expected return of the i-th security is a linear combination of p factors. We can then write

$$\mu_i = \alpha_i + \sum_{j=1}^{p} \beta_{ij} f_j, \, j = 1,2,...,p$$

where μ_i are expected returns and f_j are the expectations of factors.

Exposure to the j-th factor can be controlled by constraining the beta β_{aj} of portfolio a relative to that factor:

$$\sum_{i=1}^{N} w_{ai} \beta_{ij} = \beta_{aj}$$

where w_{ai} are the weights of portfolio a.

A portfolio manager might want to maximize a portfolio's return given a target level of risk. This problem would lead to maximizing a linear function subject to quadratic constraints of the form

$$\mathbf{w}_a' \Sigma \mathbf{w}_a = w_a$$

In practice, however, a portfolio manager prefers to minimize a function of the type:

$$\mathbf{w}_a' \Sigma \mathbf{w}_a - \lambda \mathbf{w}_a' \mu$$

where μ is the vector of securities' expected returns and λ is a risk-aversion parameter. A function of this type implements a compromise between risk and returns.

Finally, a portfolio manager needs to impose lower thresholds on portfolio weights to avoid portfolios being made up of a large number of small holdings. This implies the constraints $w_{ai} \geq b_i$. In practice, therefore, mean-variance portfolio selection leads to a quadratic optimization problem of the following type:

Minimize

$$\mathbf{w}_a' \Sigma \mathbf{w}_a - \lambda \mathbf{w}_a' \mu$$

subject to

$$\mathbf{Aw}_a = \mathbf{c}$$

and

$$w_{ai} \geq b_i$$

where the equation $\mathbf{Aw}_a = \mathbf{c}$ constrains sector exposure. This is a quadratic programming problem of the type described in Chapter 7.

In addition to the above, managers might want to impose turnover or tradability constraints in the sense that assets can only be traded in given lots. As observed in Chapter 7, these constraints result in a mixed-integer programming problem, which is generally more difficult to solve than quadratic programming problems.

The technology of optimization is presently available on desktop computers. Mathematical software such as Matlab routinely solves quadratic portfolio optimization problems of the type described above. However special care is still needed in applying optimization technology. In fact, optimization is sensitive to expected return forecasts that are themselves typically unreliable.[11]

A SECOND LOOK AT PORTFOLIO CHOICE

The mean-variance framework suggested by Markowitz is based on utility functions defined on expected returns and variance. We now have to generalize the optimization framework proposed by Markowitz in a fully probabilistic setting. This generalization allows the consideration of nonnormal distributions and paves the way for multiperiod portfolio choice. The three key ingredients in a portfolio optimization methodology are (1) a return forecast, (2) a utility function, and (3) an optimizer.

The Return Forecast

The return forecast has to be intended as a probabilistic forecast. This means that models supply a joint pdf of all the assets that might contribute to forming the optimal portfolio. A return forecast implies a process dynamics.

The first, and simplest, dynamics is the assumption that returns are independent and identical normal (IIN) variables and, therefore, price

---

[11] See, for example, Peter Muller, "Empirical Tests of Biases in Equity Portfolio Optimization," in Stavros Zenios (ed.), *Financial Optimization* (Cambridge, MA, Cambridge University Press, 1993).

processes are random walks. This assumption entails that the expected returns of each asset are known constants. Later in this chapter we will consider autoregressive linear models and nonlinear models that follow a more complex dynamics than the assumption of IID variables.

The Utility Function

In the mean-variance framework, utility functions are defined on expected returns and variances. The probability structure of returns is summarized by returns and variances. Utility functions express the trade-off between risk and return preferred by the investor or by the asset manager. By choosing a utility function, an investor decides how much return he or she wants to be compensated for taking more risk. The choice of utility functions is dictated by (1) a question of mathematical and computational tractability and (2) the risk-return preferences of the investor.

In the one-period framework of Markowitz, utility is a function of two variables: mean and variance. In this way, the problem of portfolio choice becomes a problem of finding the return-variance pair with the maximum utility:

$$\arg \max U(\mathbf{w}/\boldsymbol{\mu}, \boldsymbol{\Sigma})$$

where "arg" is shorthand to denote "argument" and with the constraints

$$\mu_a = \mathbf{w}_a{}'\boldsymbol{\mu}$$

$$\mathbf{w}'\iota = 1 , \iota' = [1, 1, ..., 1]$$

This is a problem of constrained maximum. Additional constraints might be imposed, for instance, that weights are all positive and/or that weights are within given intervals. The first condition precludes short selling; the second condition ensures that no asset has a weight either too big or too small.

In a more general probabilistic setting, utility functions are defined on the variables of interest, be they returns or consumption. The investor's risk preference is represented by the shape of the utility function. A linear function corresponds to risk neutrality. A concave function, that is, a function with negative second derivative, expresses risk aversion in so far as utility grows less rapidly than the variable.

A formal measure of absolute risk aversion is defined as

$$r_A(x) = -U''(x)/U'(x)$$

This measure expresses the intuitive fact that the more the utility function is curved, the more the investor is risk-averse. Listed below are some examples of utility functions:

- *Linear utility function:*

$$U(x) = a + bx, \ U'(x) = b, \ U''(x) = 0$$

The linear function is not concave; it represents a risk-neutral investor.

- *Power utility function:*

$$U(x) = \frac{x^{1-a} - 1}{1-a}, \ U'(x) = x^{-a}, \ U''(x) = -ax^{-a-1} < 0$$

The power utility function is concave; it represents a risk-averse investor.

- *Logarithmic utility function:*

$$U(x) = \ln(x), \ U'(x) = 1/x, \ U''(x) = -1/x^2 < 0$$

The logarithmic utility function is concave; it represents a risk-averse investor.

- *Quadratic utility function:*

$$U(x) = a + bx - \frac{c}{2}x^2, \ U'(x) = b - cx, \ U''(x) = -c < 0$$

The quadratic utility function is concave; it represents a risk-averse investor.

In a probabilistic setting, the utility function is a monotone function of a random variable and is, therefore, a random variable itself. To optimize, one single utility number must be defined for each portfolio choice. Utility is therefore defined as the expected value of stochastic utility:

$$U = E[U(x)] = \int_{-\infty}^{+\infty} p(x)U(x)dx$$

From this definition, it is clear why concavity represents risk aversion. To see this point, it is useful to imagine a discrete world where only a discrete set of states is possible. In a discrete setting, utility is defined as a discrete, finite or infinite sum:

$$U = E[U(x)] = \sum p(x_i)U(x_i)$$

To each state corresponds a discrete finite probability. A risk-neutral investor does not require any compensation for risk-taking: the investor is indifferent to choices where the increment in the variable is inversely proportional to the decrease in probability. For instance, a risk-neutral investor will be indifferent to choices where the halving of probability is compensated with the doubling of consumption. However, a risk-averse investor will require more than a simple proportionality: a halving of probability must be compensated with more than a doubling of consumption.

Optimizers

An optimizer is a software program that searches the maximum of a (multivariate) function. If we know both the analytical expression of the function to be optimized and the constraints to be applied, the method of Lagrange multiplier yields closed-form solutions. However, if no analytical expression is available or if the function is too complex, numerical optimization techniques must be used. Numerical optimizers work by searching a space of likely maxima or minima.

Mathematical optimization is a well-established technology and, outside of finance, is also used in many areas of science and technology. Different optimization technologies are employed, depending on the functions to be optimized and the constraints to be imposed. Statistical optimization technologies such as simulated annealing and genetic algorithms have been employed to allow the optimization of generic functions with multiple local minima and/or maxima. Chapter 7 provides a brief introduction to optimization technology.

A Global Probabilistic Framework for Portfolio Selection

We are now ready to state the global principles of portfolio selection. Portfolio selection works by finding those portfolio weights that maximize expected portfolio utility. Formally, we will have a joint probability distribution of returns $p(\mathbf{x})$ defined over the vector of returns $\mathbf{r}$. For each vector of portfolio weights $\mathbf{w}_a$ the portfolio return will be $\mathbf{w}_a'\mathbf{r}$. The portfolio's utility will be a stochastic variable U with a pdf that can be computed from the joint pdf of returns. For instance, if returns are jointly normal, the portfolio pdf will be normal. The portfolio selection problem is to maximize the expected value of this stochastic utility in function of portfolio weights:

$$\arg \max E[U(\mathbf{r}, \mathbf{w}_a)]$$

Portfolio optimization is a relatively mature technology, though its formal implementation is not yet widespread in the industry. The problem is one of sensitivity to forecasts. Practitioners who have implemented the optimization technology typically report a great sensitivity of the optimization to forecast errors. Because the optimizer looks for the best opportunities within the pdf that has been fed to it, any mistake in the estimation of the pdf is magnified by the optimizer. This has led some in the industry to refer to optimization as "error maximization."[12]

RELAXING THE ASSUMPTION OF NORMALITY

We can relax the assumption that returns are jointly normally distributed. It is a well known fact that returns are not normally distributed at short-time horizons of the order of days. As we saw in Chapter 13, fat-tailed distributions were proposed to represent returns at such short time horizons. At the longer time horizons typical of portfolio management, the assumption of normality is more plausible empirically speaking. However, deviations from normality exist, either because of rare large price movements or because of the importance of moments of order higher than variance.

The general utility maximization framework discussed above is very general and can be applied, in principle, to arbitrary distribution functions provided that the maxima exist. Henrik Dahl, Alexander Meeraus, and Stavros Zenios[13] argue that most financial engineering problems can be cast into an optimization framework. However practical statistical and computational problems arise when there is the need to estimate moments of high order in a multivariate environment. Extreme Value

---

[12] Muller, "Empirical Tests of Biases in Equity Portfolio Optimization."
[13] Henrik Dahl, Alexander Meeraus, and Stavros Zenios, "Some Financial Optimization Models: I and II," in *Financial Optimization*.

Theory (EVT) might help to determine the tails of some distributions. In this way, as we have seen in Chapter 13, it becomes possible to manage the risk associated with large movements. As observed by Jobst and Zenios[14] the tails of the return distribution significantly affect portfolio performance.

A new framework for portfolio selection with arbitrary distributions was proposed by Malevergne and Sornette.[15] Their framework is based on transforming arbitrary variables into normal variables. The distribution of the transformed variables is then determined via the principle of entropy maximization.[16] They showed that the new transformed variables conserve the structure of correlation of the original variables as measured by copula functions. In this way they recovered the multivariate distribution of the original variables.

MULTIPERIOD STOCHASTIC OPTIMIZATION

The factor market models explored thus far are static linear regressions with an underlying dynamic that is either exogenously given or consists of the assumption of IID returns; these optimization models are myopic one-period optimization models. From the point of view of investor behavior, one-period models are based on the assumption that wealth is consumed at the end of the period.

An investor must solve the problem of optimal portfolio selection. This means that at every trading moment the investor has to revise the selected portfolio and to decide what fraction of wealth is consumed and what fraction is reinvested. Suppose that an investor is characterized by a time-separable utility function defined over the consumption process. A time-separable utility function is such that the total utility is the sum of utility in different periods, each discounted by an appropriate time-discount factor. It is implicitly assumed that the utility derived by the consumption of one unit at some future date is less than the utility derived from the same consumption at the present date.

Call C_t consumption at time t. The investor's consumption of period t is a fraction of his or her wealth at the beginning of period t. The remaining

---

[14] Norbert J. Jobst and Stavros A. Zenios, "The Tail That Wags the Dog: Integrating Credit Risk in Asset Portfolios," *The Journal of Risk Finance* (Fall 2001), pp. 31–44.
[15] Y. Malevergne and D. Sornette, "Higher-Moment Portfolio Theory with Multivariate Weibull Distributions," unpublished paper.
[16] The Principle of Entropy Maximization chooses the distribution that has the maximum entropy among those compatible with a set of constraints. In general, constraints are given by the values of empirically determined moments.

wealth is invested at a rate R_t. An infinite stream of consumption is possible if the return rate is positive. We will write utility in the following form:

$$U_t(C) = \sum_{i=0}^{\infty} d^i U(C_{t+i})$$

where C is a shorthand for a realization of the consumption process and $d < 1$ is the time discount factor of utility. In the following formulation we will consider an infinite horizon, i.e., consumption extends over an infinite stream at all future dates. It is also possible to consider only a finite number of steps ahead; in this case, one needs to write a utility function for final wealth in order to establish a trade-off between consumption and final wealth. As in the previous single-period case, utility is a random variable as consumption is a stochastic process. We will therefore define utility as the expected value of stochastic utility as follows:

$$U_t = E_t \left[\sum_{i=0}^{\infty} d^i U(C_{t+i}) \right]$$

The process dynamics are given by the following equation:

$$W_{t+1} = (1 + R_t)[W_t - C_t]$$

where R_t is the portfolio stochastic return. The investor's portfolio selection consists of maximizing his expected utility given a return rate process for the portfolio and an initial endowment. The solution of this problem can be obtained through the methods of stochastic multistage optimization. The solution of the infinite horizon problem implies that first-order conditions, called **Euler conditions**, are satisfied for each asset. Euler conditions are the following:

$$U'(C_t) = dE_t[(1 + R_{i,t+1})U'(C_{t+1})]$$

where $R_{i,t}$ is the period t return of the i-th asset. The left hand side of the equation is the utility the investor derives from consuming one unit less at time t while the right hand side is the additional expected utility that derives from consuming at time $t + 1$ the unit saved at time t and invested at rate R_t. Optimality implies that the two coincide.

If we take the unconditional expectation and divide by $U'(C_t)$ we can write the above equations in the following form:

$$1 = E[(1 + R_{i,t})M_t]$$

where

$$M_{t+1} = d\frac{U'(C_{t+1})}{U'(C_t)}$$

is a random variable known as the *stochastic discount factor.*

APPLICATION TO THE ASSET ALLOCATION DECISION[17]

One of the most direct and widely used applications of MPT is asset allocation. Because the asset allocation decision is so important, almost all financial advisors determine an optimal portfolio for their clients—be they institutional or individual—by performing an asset allocation analysis using a set of asset classes.[18] They begin by selecting a set of asset classes (e.g., domestic large cap and small cap stocks, long-term bonds, international stocks, etc.). To obtain estimates of the returns and volatilities and correlations they generally start with the historical performance of the indexes representing these asset classes.[19] Exhibit 16.6 shows the major asset classes and an index commonly used to represent the performance characteristics of that asset class (i.e., mean and standard deviation of return). These estimates are used as inputs in the mean-variance optimization which results in an efficient frontier. Then using some criteria (for instance, using Monte Carlo simulations to compute the wealth distributions of the candidate portfolios), they pick an optimal portfolio allocation. Finally, this portfolio is implemented using either index or actively managed funds.

---

[17] This illustration draws from Frank J. Fabozzi, Francis Gupta, and Harry M. Markowitz, "Applying Mean-Variance," Chapter 3 in Frank J. Fabozzi and Harry M. Markowitz (eds.), *The Theory and Practice of Investment Management* (Hoboken, NJ: John Wiley & Sons, 2002).

[18] The following two studies conclude that asset allocation is a major determinant of portfolio performance: Gary L. Brinson, Randolph Hood, and Gilbert Beebower, "Determinants of Portfolio Performance," *Financial Analysts Journal* (July/August 1986), pp. 39–44 and Gary L. Brinson, Randolph Hood, and Gilbert Beebower, "Determinants of Portfolio Performance II: An Update," *Financial Analysts Journal* (May/June 1991), pp. 40–48.

[19] Not all institutional asset managers use this method to obtain estimates of expected returns.

EXHIBIT 16.6 Asset Classes and Commonly Used Indexes

Index	Asset Class	Inception Date
U.S. 30 day T-bill	U.S. Cash	1/26
Lehman Brothers aggregate bond	U.S. Bonds	1/76
S&P 500	U.S. Large Cap Equity	1/26
Russell 2000	U.S. Small Cap Equity	1/79
MSCI EAFE	Europe/Japan Equity	1/70
MSCI EM Free	Emerging Markets Equity	1/88

Source: Exhibit 3.6 in Frank J. Fabozzi, Francis Gupta, and Harry M. Markowitz, "Applying Mean-Variance," Chapter 3 in Frank J. Fabozzi and Harry M. Markowitz (eds.), *The Theory and Practice of Investment Management* (Hoboken, NJ: John Wiley & Sons, 2002), p. 49.

Once the funds are allocated to portfolio managers who specialize in the asset class, each portfolio manager selects the specific securities to be included in the portfolio. The portfolio can be actively managed or indexed. In fact, M-V analysis can be employed to construct the specific securities from within an asset class.

The Inputs

There are a number of approaches that can be used to obtain estimates of the inputs that are used in a mean-variance optimization, and all approaches have their pros and cons. Since the use of historical returns is the approach that is most commonly used, it may be useful to present a discussion on this method.

As explained in Chapters 11 and 12, in the language of econometrics the above means that historical returns (i.e., the empirical average of past returns), are an estimate of the expected values of returns. This entails a model of returns, in particular a stationary model of returns. The assumption that returns are independent and identically distributed (IID) sequences[20] is the simplest model where historical returns are an estimate of expected returns.

Exhibit 16.7 uses monthly returns over different and varying time periods to present the annualized historical returns for four market indexes.

One drawback of using the historical performance to obtain estimates is clearly evident from this exhibit. Historical returns are not stable, the future does not repeat the past. This is one of the reasons

---

[20] See Chapter 6 for the definition of an IID sequence.

EXHIBIT 16.7   Annualized Returns Using Historical Performance Depend on the Time Period

Period	Lehman Aggregate	S&P 500	MSCI EAFE	MSCI EM Free
Five year				
1990–1995	9.2%	15.9%	10.5%	16.3%
1996–2000	6.3	18.3	8.2	0.1
Ten year				
1990–2000	7.7	17.1	9.3	8.2

Note: Based on monthly returns of Ibbotson Associates.
Source: Exhibit 3.3 in Frank J. Fabozzi, Francis Gupta, and Harry M. Markowitz, "Applying Mean-Variance," Chapter 3 in Frank J. Fabozzi and Harry M. Markowitz (eds.), *The Theory and Practice of Investment Management* (Hoboken, NJ: John Wiley & Sons, 2002), p. 46.

econometricians have pushed to study dynamic return models, for instance Markov switching Hamilton models, that might capture fluctuations such as those that appear in the exhibit.[21] Note that, even using more complex models, fluctuations of the estimates will still exist. They are an ineliminable consequence of the global uncertainty in financial markets. The point is that the fluctuation of the estimates should not be too large to invalidate the model that is assumed.

Based on historical performance, a portfolio manager looking for estimates of the expected returns for these four asset classes to use as inputs for obtaining the set of efficient portfolios at the end of 1995 might have used the estimates from the five-year period, 1990–1995. Then according to the portfolio manager's expectations, over the next five years, only the U.S. equity market (as represented by the S&P 500) outperformed, while U.S. bonds, Europe and Japan and Emerging Markets all underperformed. In particular, the performance of Emerging Markets was dramatically different from its expected performance (actual performance of 0.1% versus an expected performance of 16.3%). This finding is disturbing, because if portfolio managers cannot have faith in the inputs that are used to solve for the efficient portfolios, then it is not possible for them to have much faith in the outputs (i.e., the makeup and expected performance of the efficient and optimal portfolios).

Portfolio managers who were performing the exercise at the beginning of 2001 faced a similar dilemma. Should they use the historical returns for the 1996–2000 period? That would generally imply that the

---

[21] For a discussion of these techniques, see Chapter 18.

optimal allocation has a large holding of U.S. equity (since that was the asset class that performed well), and an underweighting to U.S. bonds and emerging markets equity. But then what if the actual performance over the next five years is more like the 1990–1995 period? In that case the optimal portfolio is not going to perform as well as a portfolio that had a good exposure to bonds and emerging markets equity. (Note that emerging markets equity outperformed U.S. equity under that scenario.) Or, should the portfolio managers use the estimates computed by using 10 years of monthly performance?

This is also true when trying to obtain estimates for the variances and correlations. Exhibit 16.8 presents the standard deviations for the same indexes over the same time periods. Though the risk estimates for the Lehman Aggregate and EAFE indexes are quite stable, the estimates for the S&P 500 and EM Free are significantly different over different time periods. However, the volatility of the indexes does shed some light on the problem of estimating expected returns as presented in Exhibit 16.8. MSCI EM Free, the index with the largest volatility, also has the largest difference in the estimate of the expected return. Intuitively, this makes sense—the greater the volatility of an asset, the harder it is to predict its future performance.

Exhibit 16.9 shows the five-year rolling correlation between the S&P 500 and MSCI EAFE. In January 1996, the correlation between the returns of the S&P 500 and EAFE was about 0.45 over the prior five years (1991–1995). Consequently, a portfolio manager would have expected the correlation over the next five years to be around that estimate. However, for the five-year period ending December 2000, the cor-

EXHIBIT 16.8   Annualized Standard Deviations Using Historical Performance Depend on the Time Period

Period	Lehman Aggregate	S&P 500	MSCI EAFE	MSCI EME Free
Five year				
1990–1995	4.0%	10.1%	15.5%	18.0%
1996–2000	4.8	17.7	15.6	27.4
Ten year				
1990–2000	3.7	13.4	15.0	22.3

Note: Source of monthly returns is Ibbotson Associates.
Source: Exhibit 3.4 in Frank J. Fabozzi, Francis Gupta, and Harry M. Markowitz, "Applying Mean-Variance," Chapter 3 in Frank J. Fabozzi and Harry M. Markowitz (eds.), *The Theory and Practice of Investment Management* (Hoboken, NJ: John Wiley & Sons, 2002), p. 47.

EXHIBIT 16.9   Correlation Between Returns of the S&P 500 and MSCI EAFE Indexes

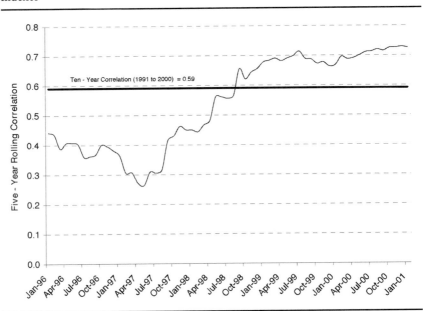

Source: Exhibit 3.5 in Frank J. Fabozzi, Francis Gupta, and Harry M. Markowitz, "Applying Mean-Variance," Chapter 3 in Frank J. Fabozzi and Harry M. Markowitz (eds.), *The Theory and Practice of Investment Management* (Hoboken, NJ: John Wiley & Sons, 2002), p. 48.

relation between the assets slowly increased to 0.73. Historically, this was an all-time high. In January 2001, should the portfolio manager assume a correlation 0.45 or 0.73 between the S&P 500 and EAFE over the next five years? Or does 0.59, the correlation over the entire ten-year period (1991–2000) sound more reasonable?

In reality, if portfolio managers believe that the inputs based on the historical performance of an asset class are not a good reflection of the future expected performance of that asset class, they may objectively or subjectively alter the inputs. Different portfolio managers may have different beliefs, in which case the alterations will be different.[22] The important thing here is that all alterations have theoretical justifications, which, in turn, ultimately leads to an optimal portfolio that closely aligns to the future expectations of the portfolio manager.

---

[22] It is quite common that the optimal strategic bond/equity mix within a portfolio differs significantly across portfolio managers.

There are some purely objective arguments as to why we can place more faith in the estimates obtained from historical data for some assets over others. Exhibit 16.6 shows the inception dates for commonly used asset class indexes. Since there are varying lengths of histories available for different asset classes (for instance, U.S. and European markets not only have longer histories, but their data are also more accurate), inputs of some asset classes can generally be estimated more precisely than the estimates of others.[23]

When solving for the efficient portfolios, the differences in precision of the estimates should be explicitly incorporated into the analysis. But MPT assumes that all estimates are as precise or imprecise, and therefore, treats all asset classes equally. Most commonly, practitioners of mean-variance optimization incorporate their beliefs on the precision of the estimates by imposing constraints on the maximum exposure of some asset classes in a portfolio. The asset classes on whom these constraints are imposed are generally those whose expected performances are either harder to estimate, or those whose performances are estimated less precisely.[24]

The extent to which we can use personal judgment to subjectively alter estimates obtained from historical data depends on our understanding what factors influence the returns on assets, and what is their impact. The political environment within and across countries, monetary and fiscal policies, consumer confidence, and the business cycles of sectors and regions are some of the key factors that can assist in forming future expectations of the performance of asset classes.

To summarize, it would be fair to say that using historical returns to estimate parameters that can be used as inputs to obtain the set of efficient portfolios depends on whether the underlying economies giving rise to the observed outcomes of returns are strong and stable. Strength and stability of economies comes from political stability and consistency in economic policies. It is only after an economy has a lengthy and proven record of a healthy and consistent performance under varying (political and economic) forces that impact free markets, can historical performance of its markets be seen as a fair indicator of their future performance.

---

[23] Statistically, the precision of an estimate is proportional to the amount of information that is used to estimate it. That is, the more data used to obtain an estimate, the greater the precision of the estimate.

[24] An alternate method for incorporating beliefs into M-V analysis is presented in Fisher Black and Robert Litterman, "Asset Allocation: Combining Investor Views With Market Equilibrium," *Journal of Fixed Income* 1(1991), pp. 7–18.

Portfolio Selection: An Example

Using an explicit example we now illustrate how asset managers and financial advisors use M-V analysis to build optimal portfolios for their clients and shed some light into the selection of an optimal portfolio. In this example we will construct an efficient frontier made up of U.S. bonds and U.S. and international equity. Exhibit 16.10 presents the forward-looking assumptions for the four asset classes.

These inputs are an example of estimates that are *not* totally based on historical performance of these asset classes. The expected return estimates are created using a risk premium approach (i.e., obtaining the historical risk premiums attached to bonds, large-cap, mid-cap, small-cap, and international equity) and then have been subjectively altered to include the asset manager's expectations regarding the future long-run (5 to 10 years) performance of these asset classes. The risk and correlation figures are mainly historical.

The next step is to use a software package to perform the optimization that results in the efficient frontier. For purposes of exposition, Exhibit 16.11 presents the efficient frontier using only two of the four asset classes from Exhibit 16.10—U.S. bonds and large cap equity. We highlight two efficient portfolios on the frontier: A and B corresponding to standard deviations of 9% and 12%, respectively. Portfolio B has the higher risk, but it also has the higher expected return. We suppose that one of these two portfolios is the optimal portfolio for a hypothetical client.

Exhibit 16.12 presents the compositions of portfolios A and B, and some important characteristics that may assist in the selection of the optimal portfolio for the client. As one would expect, the more conser-

EXHIBIT 16.10   Forward Looking Inputs (Expected Returns, Standard Deviations, and Correlations)

Expected Return	Std. Dev. of Return	Asset Class Return Correlations		1	2	3	4
6.4%	4.7%	U.S. bonds	1	1.00			
10.8	14.9	U.S. large cap equity	2	0.32	1.00		
11.9	19.6	U.S. small cap equity	3	0.06	0.76	1.00	
11.5	17.2	EAFE international equity	4	0.17	0.44	0.38	1.00

Source: Exhibit 3.7 in Frank J. Fabozzi, Francis Gupta, and Harry M. Markowitz, "Applying Mean-Variance," Chapter 3 in Frank J. Fabozzi and Harry M. Markowitz (eds.), *The Theory and Practice of Investment Management* (Hoboken, NJ: John Wiley & Sons, 2002), p. 51.

EXHIBIT 16.11 The Efficient Frontier Using Only U.S. Bonds and U.S. Large Cap Equity from Exhibit A

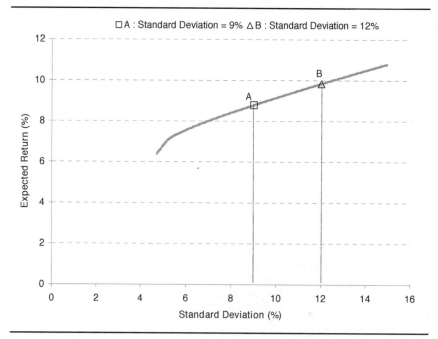

Source: Exhibit 3.8 in Frank J. Fabozzi, Francis Gupta, and Harry M. Markowitz, "Applying Mean-Variance," Chapter 3 in Frank J. Fabozzi and Harry M. Markowitz (eds.), *The Theory and Practice of Investment Management* (Hoboken, NJ: John Wiley & Sons, 2002), p. 51.

vative portfolio (A), allocates more to the conservative asset class, bonds. Portfolio A allocated a little more than 45% of the portfolio to bonds, while portfolio B only allocates 22% to that asset class. This results in significantly higher standard deviation for Portfolio B (12% versus 9%). In exchange for the 3% (or 300 basis points) of higher risk, portfolio B results in 104 basis points of higher expected return (9.83% versus 8.79%). This is the risk/return trade-off that the client faces. Does the increase in the expected return compensate the client for the increased risk?

As mentioned earlier, another approach to selecting between the two efficient portfolios is to translate the differences in risk in terms of differences in the wealth distribution over time. The higher the risk, the wider the spread of the distribution. A wider spread implies a greater upside and a greater downside. Exhibit 16.12 also presents the 95th percentile, expected, and 5th percentiles for $100 invested in portfolios A and B over

EXHIBIT 16.12 Monte Carlo Wealth Distributions to the Risk/Return Trade-Off of Portfolios A and B: Growth of $100

Characteristic	Portfolio A	Portfolio B
U.S. bonds	45.8%	22.0%
U.S. large cap equity	54.2	78.0
Expected return	8.79%	9.83%
Standard deviation	9.00%	12.00%
Return per unit of risk	98 bps	82 bps

Growth of $100	1 Year	5 Years	10 Years	1 Year	5 Years	10 Years
95th percentile (upside)	$124	$203	$345	$131	$232	$424
Average (expected)	109	152	232	110	160	255
5th percentile (downside)	95	111	146	91	104	137

Note: Assumes annual rebalancing.
Source: Exhibit 3.9 in Frank J. Fabozzi, Francis Gupta, and Harry M. Markowitz, "Applying Mean-Variance," Chapter 3 in Frank J. Fabozzi and Harry M. Markowitz (eds.), *The Theory and Practice of Investment Management* (Hoboken, NJ: John Wiley & Sons, 2002), p. 52.

1, 5, and 10 years, respectively.[25] Over a one-year period, there is a 1 in 20 chance that the $100 invested in portfolio A will grow to $124, but there is also a 1 in 20 chance that the portfolio will lose $5 (i.e., it will it shrink to $95). In comparison, for portfolio B there is a 1 in 20 chance that $100 will grow to $130 (the upside is $6 more than if invested in portfolio A). But there is also a 1 in 20 chance that the portfolio will shrink to $91 (the downside is $4 more than if invested in portfolio A). If the investment horizon is one year, is this investor willing to accept a 1 in 20 chance of losing $9 instead of $4 for a 1 in 20 chance of gaining $31 instead of $24?[26] The answer depends on the investor's risk aversion.

As the investment horizon becomes longer, the chances that a portfolio will lose its principal keep declining. Over 10 years, there is a 1 in

---

[25] The 95th percentile captures the upside associated with a 1 in 20 chance, while the 5th percentile represents the downside associated with a 1 in 20 chance.

[26] It may be useful to mention here that more recently researchers in behavioral finance have found some evidence to suggest that investors view the upside and downside differently. In particular, they equate each downside dollar to more than one upside dollar. For a good review of the behavioral finance literature, see Hersh Shefrin (ed.), *Behavioral Finance* (Northampton, MA: Edward Elgar Publishing, Ltd., 2001).

20 chance that portfolio A will grow to $345, but there is also a 1 in 20 chance that the portfolio will only grow to $146 (the chances that the portfolio results in a balance less than $100 are much smaller). In comparison, over 10 years, there is a 1 in 20 chance that portfolio B will grow to $424 (the upside is $79 more than if invested in portfolio A)! And there is a 1 in 20 chance that the portfolio will only grow to $137—that is only $7 less than if invested in portfolio A! Also portfolio B's average (expected) balance over 10 years is $23 more than portfolio A's ($255 versus $232). Somehow, compounding makes the more risky portfolio seem more attractive over the longer run. In other words, a portfolio that may not be acceptable to the investor over a short run may be acceptable over a longer investment horizon. In summary, it is sufficient to say that the optimal portfolio depends not only on risk aversion, but also on the investment horizon.

Inclusion of More Asset Classes

Exhibit 16.13 compares the efficient frontier using two asset classes, namely, U.S. bonds and large cap equity with one obtained from using

EXHIBIT 16.13   Expanding the Efficient Frontier Using All Asset Classes

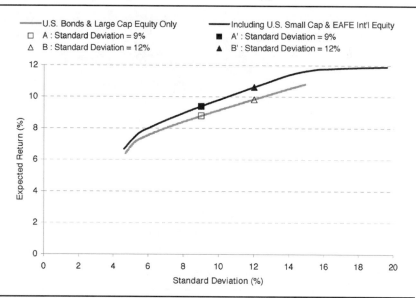

Source: Exhibit 3.10 in Frank J. Fabozzi, Francis Gupta, and Harry M. Markowitz, "Applying Mean-Variance," Chapter 3 in Frank J. Fabozzi and Harry M. Markowitz (eds.), *The Theory and Practice of Investment Management* (Hoboken, NJ: John Wiley & Sons, 2002), p. 54.

all four asset classes in the optimization. The inclusion of U.S. small cap and EAFE international equity into the mix makes the opportunity set bigger (i.e., the frontier covers a larger risk/return spectrum). It also moves the efficient frontier outwards (i.e., the frontier results in a larger expected return at any given level of risk, or conversely, results in a lower risk for any given level of expected return). The frontier also highlights portfolios A′ and B′—the portfolios with the same standard deviation as portfolios A and B, respectively.

Exhibit 16.14 shows the composition of the underlying portfolios that make up the frontier. Interestingly, U.S. small cap and EAFE international equity—the more aggressive asset classes—are included in all the portfolios. Even, the least risky portfolio has a small allocation to these two asset classes. On the other hand, U.S. large cap equity—an asset class that is thought of as the backbone of a domestic portfolio—gets excluded from the more aggressive portfolios.

Exhibit 16.15 compares the composition of portfolios A and B to A′ and B′, respectively. Both the new portfolios, A′ and B′, find U.S. small

EXHIBIT 16.14   Composition of the Efficient Frontier

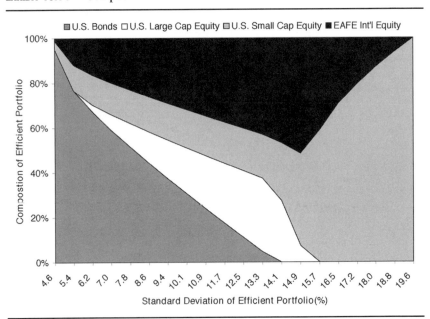

Source: Exhibit 3.11 in Frank J. Fabozzi, Francis Gupta, and Harry M. Markowitz, "Applying Mean-Variance," Chapter 3 in Frank J. Fabozzi and Harry M. Markowitz (eds.), *The Theory and Practice of Investment Management* (Hoboken, NJ: John Wiley & Sons, 2002), p. 55.

EXHIBIT 16.15 Composition of Equally Risky Efficient Portfolios in the Expanded Frontier

Asset Class	Standard Deviation = 9.0%		Standard Deviation = 12.0%	
	A	A′	B	B′
U.S. bonds	34.3%	40.4%	22.0%	15.1%
U.S. large cap equity	18.7	15.8	78.0	27.8
U.S. small cap equity	—	16.1	—	18.6
EAFE international equity	—	27.7	—	38.5
Expected return	8.79%	9.39%	9.83%	10.61%
Standard deviation	9.00%	9.00%	12.00%	12.00%
Return per unit of risk	98 bps	104 bps	82 bps	88 bps

Source: Exhibit 3.12 in Frank J. Fabozzi, Francis Gupta, and Harry M. Markowitz, "Applying Mean-Variance," Chapter 3 in Frank J. Fabozzi and Harry M. Markowitz (eds.), *The Theory and Practice of Investment Management* (Hoboken, NJ: John Wiley & Sons, 2002), p. 55.

cap and EAFE international equity very attractive and replace a significant proportion of U.S. large cap equity with those asset classes. In portfolio B′ the more aggressive mix, the allocation to U.S. bonds also declines (15.1% versus 22%).

Inclusion of U.S. small cap and EAFE international equity results in the sizable increases in the expected return and return per unit of risk. In particular, the conservative portfolio A′ has an expected return of 9.39% (60 basis points over portfolio A) and the aggressive portfolio B′ has an expected return of 10.61% (78 basis points over portfolio B). Note also that there is an increase in the returns per unit of risk.

The huge allocations to U.S. small cap and EAFE international equity in portfolios A′ and B′ may be uncomfortable for some investors. U.S. small cap equity is the most risky asset class and EAFE international equity is the second most aggressive asset class. The conservative portfolio allocates more than 40% of the portfolio to these two asset classes, while the aggressive allocates more than 50%. As discussed in the section on using inputs based on historical returns, these two would also be the asset classes whose expected returns would be harder to estimate. Consequently, investors may not want to allocate more than a certain amount to these two asset classes.

On a separate note, investors in the U.S. may also want to limit their exposure to EAFE international equity. This may be simply because of psychological reasons. Familiarity leads them to believe that domestic asset classes are "less" risky.[27] Exhibit 16.16 presents the composition of the efficient frontier when the maximum allocation to EAFE is constrained at 10% of the portfolio. As a result of this constraint, all the portfolios now receive an allocation of U.S. large cap equity.

Exhibit 16.17 compares the composition portfolios A' and B' to portfolios A" and B" the respective equally risky portfolios that lie on the constrained efficient frontier. In the conservative portfolio A", the combined allocation to U.S. small cap and EAFE international equity has declined to 30% (from 43.8%) and in B" it has fallen to 34.8% (from 57.1%). Also now the bond allocation increases for both the portfolios.

The decline in the expected return can be used to quantify the cost of this constraint. The conservative portfolio's expected return fell from 9.39% to 9.20%—a decline of 19 basis points. This cost may be well

EXHIBIT 16.16   Composition of the Constrained Efficient Frontier
Maximum Allocation to EAFE International Equity = 10%

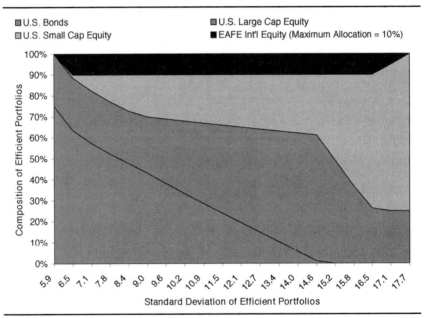

Source: Exhibit 3.13 in Frank J. Fabozzi, Francis Gupta, and Harry M. Markowitz, "Applying Mean-Variance," Chapter 3 in Frank J. Fabozzi and Harry M. Markowitz (eds.), *The Theory and Practice of Investment Management* (Hoboken, NJ: John Wiley & Sons, 2002), p. 57.

---

[27] Similarly, investors in Europe may believe that EAFE equity is "less" risky than U.S. equity and may want to limit their exposure to U.S. asset classes.

EXHIBIT 16.17   The Benefits and Costs of Constraining an Efficient Frontier

Asset Class	Unconstrained		Maximum Allocation to EAFE International Equity = 10.0%	
	A′	B′	A″	B″
U.S. bonds	40.4%	15.1%	43.1%	20.1%
U.S. large cap equity	15.8	27.8	26.9	45.1
U.S. small cap equity	16.1	18.6	20.0	24.8
EAFE international equity	27.7	38.5	10.0	10.0
Expected return	9.39%	10.61%	9.20%	10.26%
Standard deviation	9.00%	12.00%	9.00%	12.00%
Cost of constraint	—	—	19 bps	35 bps

Note: Assumes annual rebalancing.
Source: Exhibit 3.14 in Frank J. Fabozzi, Francis Gupta, and Harry M. Markowitz, "Applying Mean-Variance," Chapter 3 in Frank J. Fabozzi and Harry M. Markowitz (eds.), *The Theory and Practice of Investment Management* (Hoboken, NJ: John Wiley & Sons, 2002), p. 57.

worth it for an investor whose optimal appetite for risk is 9%. The more aggressive portfolio pays more for the constraint (10.61% – 10.26% = 35 basis points).[28]

EXTENSIONS OF THE BASIC ASSET ALLOCATION MODEL

In mean-variance analysis, the variance (standard deviation) of returns is the proxy measure for portfolio risk. As a supplement, the probability of not achieving a portfolio expected return can be calculated. This type of analysis, referred to as *risk-of-loss analysis,* would be useful in determining the most appropriate mix from the set of optimal portfolio allocations.[29] In the context of setting investment strategy for a pension fund that has a long-term normal asset allocation policy established, the

---

[28] For a discussion on the benefits and costs of constraints, see Francis Gupta and David Eichhorn, "Mean-Variance Optimization for Practitioners of Asset Allocation," in Frank J. Fabozzi (ed.), *Handbook of Portfolio Management* (New York: John Wiley & Sons, 1998), pp. 57–74.
[29] Risk of loss analysis as well as the multiple scenario analysis and short-term/long-term analysis described next, were developed by Gifford Fong Associates in the early 1980s. See Chapter 4 and Appendix B in H. Gifford Fong and Frank J. Fabozzi, *Fixed Income Portfolio Management* (Homewood, IL: Dow-Jones-Irwin, 1985).

value of the probability of loss for the desired return benchmark over the long-term horizon can be used as the maximum value for the short term. For example, if the long-term policy has a 15% probability of loss for 0% return, the mix may be changed over the short run, as long as the probability of loss of the new mix has a maximum of 15%. Therefore, by taking advantage of short-term expectations to maximize return, the integrity of the long-term policy is retained. A floor or base probability of loss is therefore established that can provide boundaries within which strategic return/risk decisions may be made. As long as the alteration of the asset allocation mix does not violate the probability of loss, increased return through strategies such as tactical asset allocation can be pursued.

Mean-variance analysis has been extended to multiple possible scenarios. Each assumed scenario is believed to be an assessment of the asset performance in the long run, over the investment horizon. A probability can be assigned to each scenario so that an efficient set can be constructed for the composite scenario. It is often the case, however, that an investor expects a very different set of input values in mean-variance analysis that are applicable in the short run, say, the next 12 months. For example, the long-term expected return on equities may be estimated at 15% but over the next year the expected return on equities may be only 5%. The investment objectives are still stated in terms of the portfolio performance over the entire investment horizon. However, the return characteristics of each asset class are described by one set of values over a short period and another set of values over the balance of the investment horizon. A mean-variance analysis can be formulated that simultaneously optimizes over the two periods.[30]

Finally, mean-variance analysis has been extended to explicitly incorporate the liabilities of pension funds.[31] This extension requires not only the return distribution of asset classes that must be considered in an optimization model, but also the liabilities.

---

[30] See Harry M. Markowitz and André F. Perold, "Portfolio Analysis with Factors and Scenarios," *Journal of Finance* (September 1981), pp. 871–877.

[31] See Martin L. Leibowitz, Stanley Kogelman, and Lawrence N. Bader, "Asset Performance and Surplus Control—A Dual-Shortfall Approach," in Robert D. Arnott and Frank J. Fabozzi (eds.), *Active Asset Allocation* (Chicago: Probus Publishing, 1992). The mean-variance model they present strikes a balance between asset performance and the maintenance of acceptable levels of its downside risk, and surplus performance and the maintenance of acceptable levels of its downside risk.

SUMMARY

- The principles of financial optimization were established by Markowitz in 1952.
- The key idea of Markowitz is that financial decision-making should be based on an optimal trade-off between risk and returns.
- Markowitz's seminal work proposed optimizing a trade-off between variance and the expected returns of a portfolio under the assumption of joint normality of returns.
- The key principle behind mean-variance optimization is diversification.
- Markowitz's work had a lasting influence on the investment management community; investment management principles are still deeply influenced by these ideas.
- Portfolios that achieve the minimum variance for a given expected return are called minimum-variance portfolios.
- Minimum-variance portfolios are called mean-variance efficient portfolios; the set of mean-variance efficient portfolios form the efficient frontier.
- The theoretical problem of finding mean-variance efficient portfolios leads to an optimization problem solvable in closed form with the technique of Lagrange multipliers.
- Sharpe, Tobin, and Lintner extended the portfolio selection model in the presence of a risk-free asset; the mean-variance portfolios are those that are a combination of the tangency portfolio and the risk-free asset.
- In the presence of a risk-free asset the efficient frontier becomes the Capital Market Line which is the straight line tangent to the Market Portfolio.
- If realistic constraints are added, namely sector exposure and tradability constraints, the problem becomes one of quadratic programming or a mixed-integer programming to be solved with numerical techniques.
- Markowitz's mean-variance formulation can be used for portfolio selection as well as asset allocation.
- Risk-of-loss-analysis is an extension of the basic model. It considers the risk of not achieving a portfolio's expected return.
- The basic mean-variance analysis can also be extended to cover the liabilities of pension funds.
- The theory of Markowitz can be extended in a one-period setting as maximization of expected utility.
- In a multiperiod setting agents maximize utility defined on consumption.
- In a multiperiod setting agents determine at each step the optimal trade-off between investment and consumption.

CHAPTER 17

Capital Asset Pricing Model

The mean-variance approach to portfolio selection and its generalizations require a model for variance and expected returns to feed to the optimizer. Asset price and/or return models belong to three different families:

- *General Equilibrium Theories.* These determine price processes as the equilibrium between demand and supply of markets populated by economic agents whose behavior is known. General equilibrium theories are therefore truly economic theories based on specific assumptions on the behavior of agents. The following models are general equilibrium models: CAPM, Conditional CAPM, multifactor CAPM, and Consumption CAPM.
- *Arbitrage Pricing Models.* Arbitrage pricing is relative pricing insofar as the prices and therefore the returns of a set of assets depend on another set of processes. Arbitrage pricing was discussed in Chapters 14 and 15.
- *Econometric Models.* These are statistical models of prices or returns. They model prices or returns as endogenous phenomena and/or establish links between prices and returns and exogenous variables. The justification of econometric models is empirical, that is, they are valid insofar as they fit empirical data. They are not derived from economic theory although economic theory might suggest econometric models. For example, Markov switching models are rooted in the theory of economic cycles.

The subject of this chapter is the *Capital Asset Pricing Model* (CAPM) formulated by William Sharpe, John Lintner, and Jan Mossin.[1] As explained in the previous chapter, portfolio selection based on mean-variance analysis is a normative theory that describes the investment behavior of market agents in constructing a portfolio. Given this investment behavior, the capital asset pricing model formalizes the relationship that should exist between asset returns and risk.

CAPM ASSUMPTIONS

The CAPM is an equilibrium asset pricing model derived from a set of assumptions. Here we demonstrate how the CAPM is derived.

The CAPM is an abstraction of the real world capital markets and, as such, is based upon some assumptions. These assumptions simplify matters a great deal, and some of them may even seem unrealistic. However, these assumptions make the CAPM more tractable from a mathematical standpoint. The CAPM assumptions are as follows:

- *Assumption 1.* Investors make investment decisions based on the expected return and variance of returns.
- *Assumption 2.* Investors are rational and risk averse.
- *Assumption 3.* Investors subscribe to the Markowitz method of portfolio diversification.
- *Assumption 4.* Investors all invest for the same period of time.
- *Assumption 5.* Investors have the same expectations about the expected return and variance of all assets.
- *Assumption 6.* There is a risk-free asset and investors can borrow and lend any amount at the risk-free rate.
- *Assumption 7.* Capital markets are completely competitive and frictionless.

The first five assumptions deal with the way investors make decisions. The last two assumptions relate to characteristics of the capital market. Some of these assumptions require further explanation. As explained in Chapter 16, in mean-variance analysis, it is assumed that

---

[1] William F. Sharpe, "Capital Asset Prices," *Journal of Finance* (September 1964), pp. 425–442. Others who reached a similar conclusion regarding the pricing of risk assets include: John Lintner, "The Valuation of Risk Assets and the Selection of Risky Investments in Stock Portfolio and Capital Budgets," *Review of Economics and Statistics* (February 1965), pp. 13–37 and Jan Mossin, "Equilibrium in a Capital Asset Market," *Econometrica* (October 1966), pp. 768–783.

investors make investment decisions based on two parameters, the expected return and the variance of returns. Assumption 1 indicates that in the CAPM the same two parameters are used by investors. Assumption 2 indicates that in order to accept greater risk, investors must be compensated by the opportunity of realizing a higher return.

The CAPM assumes (Assumption 3) that the risk-averse investor will ascribe to Markowitz's methodology of reducing portfolio risk by combining assets with counterbalancing covariances or correlations. By Assumption 4, all investors are assumed to make investment decisions over some single-period investment horizon. How long that period is (i.e., six months, one year, two years, etc.) is not specified. In reality, the investment decision process is more complex than that, with many investors having more than one investment horizon. Nonetheless, the assumption of a one-period investment horizon is necessary to simplify the mathematics of the theory.

To obtain the Markowitz efficient frontier which we will be used in developing the CAPM, it will be assumed that investors have the same expectations with respect to the inputs that are used to derive the efficient portfolios: asset returns, variances, and covariances. This is Assumption 5 and is referred to as the "homogeneous expectations assumption."

It is assumed that there is a risk-free asset. An investor in this asset earns a risk-free rate. Moreover, it is assumed that investors cannot only earn a risk-free rate, but if they want to borrow, they can do so at the risk-free rate (Assumption 6).

Finally, it is assumed that the capital market is perfectly competitive (Assumption 7). In general, this means the number of buyers and sellers is sufficiently large, and all investors are small enough relative to the market so that no individual investor can influence an asset's price. Consequently, all investors are price takers, and the market price is determined where there is equality of supply and demand. In addition, according to Assumption 7, there are no transaction costs or impediments that interfere with the supply of and demand for an asset.

SYSTEMATIC AND NONSYSTEMATIC RISK

A risk-averse investor who makes decisions based on expected return and variance should construct an efficient portfolio using a combination of the market portfolio and the risk-free rate. The combinations are identified by the CML. Based on this result, Sharpe derived an asset pricing model that shows how a risky asset should be priced. In the process of doing so, we can fine-tune our thinking about the risk associated with an asset. Specifically, we can show that the appropriate risk that investors should be compensated for accepting is not the variance of an asset's return but some other quantity. In order to do this, let's take a closer look at risk.

We can do this by looking at the variance of the portfolio.

The proof is as follows. The variance of a portfolio consisting of N assets is equal to

$$\text{var}(R_p) = \sum_{i=1}^{N} \sum_{j=1}^{N} w_i w_j \text{cov}(R_i, R_j)$$

If we substitute M (market portfolio) for p and denote by w_{iM} and w_{jM}, the proportion invested in asset i and j in the market portfolio, then the above equation can be rewritten as

$$\text{var}(R_M) = \sum_{i=1}^{N} \sum_{j=1}^{N} w_{iM} w_{jM} \text{cov}(R_i, R_j)$$

It can be demonstrated that the above equation can be expressed as follows:

$$\text{var}(R_M)$$
$$= w_{1M} \sum_{j=1}^{N} w_{jM} \text{cov}(R_1, R_j) + w_{2M} \sum_{j=1}^{N} w_{jM} \text{cov}(R_2, R_j)$$
$$+ \ldots + w_{NM} \sum_{j=1}^{N} w_{NM} \text{cov}(R_N, R_j)$$

The covariance of asset i with the market portfolio, $\text{cov}(R_i, R_M)$, is expressed as follows:

$$\text{cov}(R_i, R_M) = \sum_{j=1}^{N} w_{jM} \text{cov}(R_j, R_j)$$

Substituting the right-hand side of the left-hand side of the equation into the prior equation, gives

$$\text{var}(R_M)$$
$$= w_{1M} \text{cov}(R_1, R_M) + w_{2M} \text{cov}(R_2, R_M) + \ldots + w_{NM} \text{cov}(R_N, R_M)$$

Notice that the portfolio variance does not depend on the variance of the assets comprising the market portfolio but on their covariance with the market portfolio. Sharpe defines the degree to which an asset covaries with the market portfolio as the asset's *systematic risk*. More specifically, he defined systematic risk as the portion of an asset's variability that can be attributed to a common factor. Systematic risk is the minimum level of risk that can be obtained for a portfolio by means of diversification across a large number of randomly chosen assets.

As such, systematic risk is that which results from general market and economic conditions that cannot be diversified away. Sharpe defined the portion of an asset's variability that can be diversified away as *nonsystematic risk*. It is also sometimes called *unsystematic risk*, *diversifiable risk*, *unique risk*, *residual risk*, and *company-specific risk*. This is the risk that is unique to an asset.

Consequently, total risk (as measured by the variance) can be partitioned into systematic risk as measured by the covariance of asset i's return with the market portfolio's return and nonsystematic risk. The relevant risk is the systematic risk. We will see how to measure the systematic risk later. How diversification reduces nonsystematic risk for portfolios is illustrated in Exhibit 17.1. The vertical axis shows the variance of the portfolio return. The variance of the portfolio return represents the *total risk* for the portfolio (systematic plus nonsystematic).

EXHIBIT 17.1   Systematic and Unsystematic Portfolio Risk

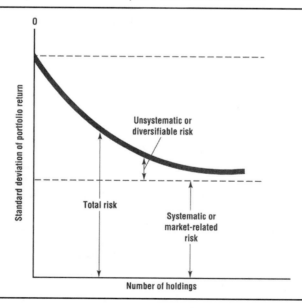

The horizontal axis shows the number of holdings of different assets (e.g., the number of common stock held of different issuers).

As can be seen, as the number of asset holdings increases, the level of nonsystematic risk is almost completely eliminated (i.e., diversified away). Studies of different asset classes support this. For example, for common stock, several studies suggest that a portfolio size of about 20 randomly selected companies will completely eliminate nonsystematic risk leaving only systematic risk.[2]

SECURITY MARKET LINE

The CML represents an equilibrium condition in which the expected return on a portfolio of assets is a linear function of the expected return on the market portfolio. Individual assets do not fall on the CML. Instead, it can be demonstrated that the following relationship holds for individual assets:[3]

$$E(R_i) = R_f + \left[\frac{E(R_i) - R_f}{\text{var}(R_M)} \right] \text{cov}(R_i, R_M)$$

The above equation is called the *security market line* (SML).

In equilibrium, the expected return of individual securities will lie on the SML and *not* on the CML. This is true because of the high degree of nonsystematic risk that remains in individual assets that can be diversified out of portfolios. In equilibrium, only efficient portfolios will lie on both the CML and the SML.

The SML also can be expressed as

$$E(R_i) = R_f + [E(R_i) - R_f] \frac{\text{cov}(R_i, R_M)}{\text{var}(R_M)}$$

The ratio $\text{cov}(R_i, R_M)/\text{var}(R_M)$ can be estimated empirically using return data for the market portfolio and the return on the asset. The

---

[2] The first empirical study of this type was by Wayne H. Wagner and Sheila Lau, "The Effect of Diversification on Risks," *Financial Analysts Journal* (November–December 1971), p. 50.
[3] For the proof, see William F. Sharpe, *Portfolio Theory and Capital Markets* (New York, NY: McGraw Hill, 1970), pp. 86–91.

empirical analogue for the above equation is the following linear regression, called the *characteristic line*:

$$r_{it} - r_{ft} = \alpha_i + \beta_i \, [r_{Mt} - r_{ft}] + e_{it}$$

where e_{it} is the error term.

The beta term β_i in the above regression is the estimate of the ratio in the SML equation that is

$$\beta_i = \frac{\text{cov}(R_i, R_M)}{\text{var}(R_M)}$$

Substituting β_i into the SML equation gives the beta-version of the SML:

$$E(R_i) = R_f + \beta_i \, [E(R_M) - R_f]$$

This is the CAPM. It states that, given the assumptions of the CAPM, the expected return on an individual asset is a positive linear function of its index of systematic risk as measured by beta. The higher the beta is, the higher the expected return.

An investor pursuing an active strategy will search for underpriced securities to purchase and overpriced securities to avoid (sell if held in the current portfolio, or sold short if permitted). If an investor believes that the CAPM is the correct asset pricing model, then the SML can be used to identify mispriced securities. A security where the market prices it such that the expected return is less than the expected return as predicted by the SML is an undervalued security. In contrast, an overvalued security is one where the market prices the security such that its expected return is greater than that predicted by the SML.

In equilibrium, the expected return of individual securities will lie on the SML and not on the CML. This is true because of the high degree of unsystematic risk that remains in individual securities that can be diversified out of portfolios of securities. It follows that the only risk investors will pay a premium to avoid is market risk. Hence, two assets with the same amount of systematic risk will have the same expected return. In equilibrium, only efficient portfolios will lie on both the CML and the SML. This underscores the fact that the systematic risk measure, beta, is most correctly considered as an index of the contribution of an individual security to the systematic risk of a well-diversified portfolio of securities.

Estimating the Characteristic Line

The characteristic line is estimated using regression analysis. In fact, all the data required are the same except for the risk-free rate each period. The coefficient of determination, denoted by R-squared, indicates the strength of the relationship. Specifically, it measures the percentage of the variation in the return on a stock explained by the return by the market portfolio (proxied by the S&P 500 in our illustration). The value ranges from 0 to 1. The higher the R-squared, the greater the proportion of systematic risk relative to total risk. For individual stocks, the R-squared is typically in the 0.3 area. That is, for individual stocks systematic risk is small relative to nonsystematic risk. For well-diversified portfolio, the R-squared is typically greater than 0.9.

TESTING THE CAPM

Testing the CAPM has been a major endeavor of financial econometrics. The number of articles found under the general heading "tests of the CAPM" is impressive. One bibliographic compilation lists almost 1,000 papers on the topic. Consequently, only the basic results are given here.

In general, a methodology referred to as "two-pass regression" is used to test the CAPM. The first pass involves the estimation of beta for each security by means of a time series regression described by characteristic line. The betas from the first-pass regression are then used to form portfolios of securities ranked by portfolio beta. The portfolio returns, the return on the risk-free asset, and the portfolio betas are then used to estimate the second-pass, cross-sectional regression:

$$R_p - R_F = b_o + b_1\beta_p + e_p$$

where the parameters to be estimated are b_o and b_1, and e_p is the error term for the regression. The return data are frequently aggregated into five-year periods for this regression.

Deriving the Empirical Analogue of the CML

The above equation is the empirical analogue of a beta version of the CML. To see this, subtract R_F from both sides of the CML equation

$$E[R_i] = R_f + \frac{[E(R_M) - R_f]}{\text{var}(R_M)}\text{cov}(R_iR_m)$$

which can then can be rewritten as

$$E[R_i] - R_f = \frac{[E(R_M) - R_f]}{\text{var}(R_M)} \text{cov}(R_i R_m)$$

The above is the CML in "risk-premium form" because the value on the left-hand side of the equation is the portfolio's expected return over the risk-free rate. By adding an error term and a constant term, b_0, the above equation becomes

$$E(R_p) - R_F = b_0 + \beta_p [E(R_M) - R_F] + e_p$$

The actual process of testing the CAPM using the two-pass regression methodology involves the consideration of some econometric problems (e.g., measurement error, correlated error terms, and beta instability).[4]

Emprical Implications

Assuming that the capital market can be described as one in which there is no opportunity for investors to use information from previous periods to earn abnormal returns, several testable hypotheses for the empirical analogue of the CML implied by the CAPM can be listed:

1. The relationship between beta and return should be linear.
2. The intercept term, b_0, should not differ significantly from zero.
3. The coefficient for beta, b_1, should equal the risk premium $(R_M - R_F)$.
4. Beta should be the only factor that is priced by the market. That is, other factors such as the variance or standard deviation of the returns, and variables that we will discuss in later chapters such as the price/earnings ratio, ratio, dividend yield, and firm size should not add any significant explanatory power to the equation.
5. Over long periods of time, the rate of return on the market portfolio should be greater than the return on the risk-free asset. This is because the market portfolio has more risk than the risk-free asset. Hence, risk-averse investors would price it so as to generate a greater return.

---

[4] The interested reader should consult Merton H. Miller and Myron S. Scholes, "Rates of Return in Relation to Risk," Chapter 2 in Michael C. Jensen (ed.), *Studies in the Theory of Capital Markets* (New York: Praeger, 1972), pp. 79–121; Eugene F. Fama, *Foundations of Finance* (New York: Basic Books, 1976); Richard Roll, "Performance Evaluation and Benchmark Errors II," *Journal of Portfolio Management* (Winter 1981), pp. 17–22; and Richard Roll, "A Critique of the Asset Pricing Theory's Tests," *Journal of Financial Economics* (March 1977), pp. 129–176 for a discussion of these issues.

General Findings of Empirical Tests of the CAPM

The general results of the empirical tests of the CAPM are as follows:

1. The relationship between beta and return appears to be linear, hence the functional form of the CAPM seems to be correct.
2. The estimated intercept term, b_0, is significantly different from zero and consequently different from what is hypothesized for this value.
3. The estimated coefficient for beta, b_1, is less than $R_M - R_F$. The combination of results 2 and 3 suggests that low beta stocks have higher returns than the CAPM predicts and high beta stocks have lower returns than CAPM predicts.
4. Beta is not the only factor priced by the market. Several studies have discovered other factors that explain stock returns. These include a price/earnings factor,[5] a dividend factor,[6] a firm size factor,[7] and both a firm size factor and a book/market factor.[8]
5. Over long periods of time (usually 20–30 years), the return on the market portfolio is greater than the risk-free rate.

A Critique of Tests of the CAPM

One of the most controversial papers written on the CAPM is Richard Roll's "A Critique of the Asset Pricing Theory's Tests."[9] We will discuss the major points of Roll's argument here. Following Roll's argument, the CAPM is a general equilibrium model based upon the existence of a market portfolio that is defined as the value-weighted portfolio of all investment assets. Furthermore, the market portfolio is defined to be ex ante mean-variance efficient. This means that the market portfolio lies on the ex ante Markowitz efficient frontier for all investors.

Roll demonstrates that the only true test of the CAPM is whether the market portfolio is in fact ex ante mean-variance efficient. However, the

---

[5] See Sanjoy Basu, "Investment Performance of Common Stocks in Relation to Their Price-Earnings Ratios," *Journal of Finance* (June 1977), pp. 663–682 and "The Relationship Between Earnings' Yield, Market Value and Return for NYSE Common Stocks," *Journal of Financial Economics* (June 1983), pp. 129–156.

[6] Robert Litzenberger and Krishna Ramaswamy, "The Effect of Personal Taxes and Dividends on Capital Asset Prices," *Journal of Financial Economics* (June 1979), pp. 163–195.

[7] Rolf Banz, "The Relationship Between Return and Market Value of Common Stocks," *Journal of Financial Economics* (March 1981). pp. 3–18.

[8] Eugene Fama and Kenneth French, "The Cross-Section of Expected Returns," *Journal of Finance* (June 1992), pp. 427–465.

[9] Richard Roll, "A Critique of the Asset Pricing Theory's Tests."

true market portfolio is, in fact, ex ante since it includes all investment assets (e.g., stocks, bonds, real estate, art objects, and human capital).

The consequences of this "nonobservability" of the true market portfolio are:

1. Tests of the CAPM are extremely sensitive to which market proxy is used, even though returns on most market proxies (e.g., the S&P 500 and the NYSE index) are highly correlated.
2. A researcher cannot unambiguously discern whether the CAPM failed a test because the true market portfolio was ex ante mean-variance inefficient, or because the market proxy was inefficient. Alternatively, the researcher cannot unambiguously discern whether a test supported the CAPM because the true market portfolio was ex ante mean-variance efficient or because the market proxy was efficient.
3. The effectiveness of variables such as dividend yield in explaining risk-adjusted asset returns is evidence that the market proxies used to test the CAPM are not ex ante mean-variance efficient.

Hence, Roll submits that the CAPM is not testable until the exact composition of the true market portfolio is known, and the only valid test of the CAPM is to observe whether the ex ante true market portfolio is mean-variance efficient. As a result of his findings, Roll states that he does not believe there ever will be an unambiguous test of the CAPM. He does not say that the CAPM is invalid. Rather, Roll says that there is likely to be no unambiguous way to test the CAPM and its implications due to the nonobservability of the true market portfolio and its characteristics.

Does this mean that the CAPM is useless to the financial practitioner? The answer is no, it does not. What it means is that the implications of the CAPM should be viewed with caution.

Merton and Black Modifications of the CAPM

Several researchers have modified the CAPM. Here we will briefly describe two modifications.

Suppose that there is no risk-free rate and that investors cannot borrow and lend at the risk-free rate (Assumption 6). How does that affect the CAPM? Fischer Black examined how the original CAPM would change if there is no risk-free asset in which the investor can borrow and lend.[10] He demonstrated that neither the existence of a risk-free asset nor the requirement that investors can borrow and lend at the risk-

---

[10] Fischer Black, "Capital Market Equilibrium with Restricted Borrowing," *Journal of Business* (July 1972), pp. 444–455.

free rate is necessary for the theory to hold. Black's argument was as follows. The beta of a risk-free asset is zero. Suppose that a portfolio can be created such that it is uncorrelated with the market. That portfolio would then have a beta of zero, and Black labeled that portfolio a "zero-beta portfolio." He set forth the conditions for constructing a zero-beta portfolio and then showed how the CAPM can be modified accordingly. Specifically, the return on the zero-beta portfolio is substituted for the risk-free rate.

Now let's look at the assumption that the only relevant risk is the variance of asset returns (Assumption 1). That is, it is assumed that the only risk factor that an investor is concerned with is the uncertainty about the future price of a security. Investors, however, usually are concerned with other risks that will affect their ability to consume goods and services in the future. Three examples would be the risks associated with future labor income, the future relative prices of consumer goods, and future investment opportunities. Consequently, using the variance of expected returns as the sole measure of risk would be inappropriate in the presence of these other risk factors. Recognizing these other risks that investors face, Robert Merton modified the CAPM based on consumers deriving their optimal lifetime consumption when they face such non-market risk factors.[11]

CAPM and Random Matrices

Let's take a look at CAPM from a different angle. Under the assumption of IID returns, the CAPM is the statement that the entire market is driven by only one factor represented by the market portfolio. Plerou et al[12] analyzed the distribution and stability of the eigenvalues of the variance-covariance matrix of large portfolios. Their conclusion can be summarized as follows:

- *The majority of the eigenvalues fall within the bounds of Random Matrix Theory (RMT).* This means that the majority of eigenvalues do not carry genuine correlation information. This confirms results already described in the literature.[13]
- *A number of eigenvalues are definitely outside the RMT bounds.* The eigenvector corresponding to the largest eigenvalue includes all assets,

[11] Robert C. Merton, "An Intertemporal Capital Asset Pricing Model," *Econometrica* (September 1973), pp. 867–888.
[12] Vasiliki Plerou, Parameswaran Gopikrishnan, Bernd Rosenow, Luis A. Nunes Amaral, Thomas Guhr, and H. Eugene Stanley, "Random matrix approach to cross correlations in financial data," Physical *Review* 65 (June 2002).
[13] Random matrices are covered in Chapter 12.

though not necessarily in equal proportion. This eigenvector approximately corresponds to the entire market. The other largest eigenvalues correspond to eigenvectors that identify market sectors. The eigenvectors corresponding to the largest eigenvalues exhibit some degree of stability in time, the most stable being those corresponding to the largest eigenvalues. Stability is measured by computing eigenvalues and eigenvectors on a moving window and counting the percentage of assets forming each eigenvector that remain unchanged.

Based on a remarkably large data set, work by Plerou et al. identifies a number of different meaningful eigenvectors. The multiplicity of eigenvectors corresponding to large eigenvalues suggests a structure of multiple factors as portfolios. Note that the largest eigenvector is not the market portfolio. In fact, the market portfolio includes all investable assets. Therefore, it includes assets that are not in the largest eigenvector. This fact leaves open the door to a possible coexistence of CAPM and multifactor models. In order to explore this point, we need first to discuss the Conditional CAPM, Asset Pricing Theory, and multifactor models. We discuss the Conditional CAPM in this chapter and the last two models in the next chapter.

THE CONDITIONAL CAPM

As we have seen, the CAPM is embodied in a static linear regression of asset returns over the market portfolio whose explanatory power has been questioned by, among others, Fama and French.[14] Ravi Jagannathan and Zheniu Wang[15] suggested a solution: They made the CAPM regression coefficients conditional on some global information set, thereby generalizing the model. Called the **Conditional CAPM** or C(CAPM), this model represents each expected return r_{it} given the information set at time t by the conditional linear regression:

$$E[\mathbf{r}_t/I_{t-1}] = \alpha + \beta E[\mathbf{f}_t/I_{t-1}]$$

$$\beta_{is} = \frac{\text{cov}(r_{it}f_{st}/I_{t-1})}{\text{var}(f_{st}/I_{t-1})}$$

---

[14] Fama and French, "The Cross-Section of Expected Stock Returns."

[15] Ravi Jagannathan and Zhenyu Wang, "The Conditional CAPM and the Cross-Section of Expected Returns," *Journal of Finance* 51, no. 1, pp. 3–53.

A difficulty with C(CAPM) is to identify the conditioning relationships as well as the market portfolio. Jagannathan and Wang show that the unconditional returns generated by a C(CAPM) can be thought of as being generated by a two-factor model where one factor is the unconditional beta and the other represents the fluctuations of beta. This conclusion can be generalized. A C(CAPM) model is equivalent to a nonlinear factor model.[16]

Jagannathan and Wang show that the C(CAPM) is able to represent the cross section of stock returns with a greater accuracy than the conventional unconditional CAPM. They also show that the empirical accuracy of the unconditional CAPM is greatly improved by adding human capital to the market portfolio. Human capital is not a tradable asset, at least not in the same sense as financial assets.

BETA, BETA EVERYWHERE

In the development of both modern portfolio theory and CAPM, the Greek letter beta appears. Certainly to the mathematically trained, this presents no problem. However, it caused confusion in the investment management community. The use of the term "beta" in the two theories was as follows. First, because of the difficulty of working with the covariance matrix at the time, Markowitz suggested using as a proxy measure of the full covariance matrix a covariance of a security's return with some index.[17] Sharpe picked up on this suggestion and proposed the following model for doing so which he referred to as the *market model*:[18]

$$r_{it} = \alpha_i + \beta_i\, r_{mt} + u_{it}$$

Note that the index need not be a market portfolio—hence the use of m rather than M in the above equation. When Sharpe estimated the market model, he used a stock market index.

Then beta appeared in the CAPM where it is estimated from the characteristic line which we discussed earlier. The market model and the characteristic line look almost identical. The difference is simply that

---

[16] For more on this subject see, for instance, Adrian Pagan, "The Econometrics of Financial Markets," *Journal of Empirical Finance* 3 (1996), pp. 15–102.

[17] Harry M. Markowitz, *Portfolio Selection: Second Edition* (Cambridge, MA: Basil Blackwell Ltd., 1991), p. 100.

[18] William F. Sharpe, "A Simplified Model for Portfolio Analysis," *Management Science* (January 1963), pp. 277–293.

the characteristic line measures the return relative to the risk-free rate in each period. In the case of the characteristic line, a proxy for the market portfolio is used. This is in contrast to the market model where the index need not be the market portfolio.

This distinction between the beta in the market model and the beta in the characteristic line is important. As we will see in the next section, critics of portfolio selection and the CAPM have incorrectly made statements about the drawbacks of these theories because they fail to understand the distinction between these two betas. Adding to the confusion was that Sharpe introduced both of these beta concepts around the same time (1963 and 1964).

THE ROLE OF THE CAPM IN INVESTMENT MANAGEMENT APPLICATIONS

In 1980, a highly regarded magazine published an article with the title "Is Beta Dead?"[19] In response to this article, in its Winter 1981 issue *The Journal of Portfolio Management* published a series of articles. The article by Barr Rosenberg in particular provides an excellent discussion of the CAPM and its role.[20]

The key to the CAPM's contribution to investment management theory is clearly stated by Rosenberg:

> The CAPM is theory, but, paradoxically, the role of the CAPM as "theory" leading to application has been less important than its role in mobilizing attention and defining constructs. We should keep in mind that the CAPM is not "true," since many of its assumptions are not exactly satisfied in the real world. Indeed, the CAPM rules out active management and investment research, and thus abolishes most applications at the stroke of a pen, by virtue of the unrealistic assumptions that it makes. (p. 5)

That is, even though the CAPM is not true it does not mean that the constructs introduced by the theory are not important. Constructs introduced in the development of the theory include the notion of a market portfolio, systematic risk, diversifiable risk, and beta. As Rosenberg

---

[19] Anise Wallace, "Is Beta Dead?" *Institutional Investor* (July 1980), pp. 23–30.
[20] Barr Rosenberg, "The Capital Asset Pricing Model and the Market Model," *The Journal of Portfolio Management* (Winter 1981), pp. 5–16.

notes: "These ideas play an important role in the methods of 'modern portfolio theory.'"

In the next chapter we will discuss another asset pricing model that introduces risk factors other than market risk. Earlier in this chapter we also discussed other models that consider nonmarket risk factors. However, these do not invalidate the important constructs developed by the CAPM. Rosenberg concludes his article with the following statement:

> The question of rewards for factors other than equity market risk has been the subject of active study and controversy for a decade—and no doubt will continue to be so in the decades to come. Nevertheless, no one has refuted the existence of equilibrium reward for equity market risk; indeed, it has rarely been questioned, although the magnitude has been in doubt. The concept of reward to equity market risk (or beta) is a theoretical insight, that, in my view, is likely to endure. (p. 16).

Fast forward a little more than two decades since the publication of the Rosenberg article and his conclusions still hold.[21]

Moreover, Markowitz has explained that the major reason for the debate is the confusion between the beta that is associated with the market model (estimated to avoid having to compute all covariances for assets in a portfolio) and the beta in the CAPM, a point we emphasized in the previous section.[22]

SUMMARY

- The Capital Asset Pricing Model (CAPM) is a general equilibrium theory based on the assumption that investors are rational and subscribe to the Markowitz mean-variance framework.
- A key finding of the CAPM is that, in a situation of equilibrium between demand and supply, if agents optimize in the sense of mean-

---

[21] These sentiments were echoed in a presentation by Peter Bernstein in a keynote address on the occasion of the fifth anniversary of the establishment of the International Center for Financial Management & Engineering (FAME) in Geneva on February 7, 2002. (See "How Modern is Modern Portfolio Theory?" *Economics and Portfolio Strategy*, Peter L. Bernstein, Inc., March 15, 2002.)

[22] Harry M. Markowitz, "The 'Two Beta' Trap," *The Journal of Portfolio Management* (Fall 1984), pp. 12–20.

variance optimization, then the total investable portfolio, called the market portfolio, is mean-variance efficient.

■ From the mean-variance efficiency of the market portfolio, Sharpe, Lintner, Treynor, and Mossin were able to derive the fundamental linear relationship between the expected value of each security and that of the market portfolio.

■ In the CAPM, risk is decomposed into diversifiable risk and systematic or market risk; it is only systematic risk for which an investor should be compensated.

■ CAPM has been extensively tested using regression-based procedures.

■ The fundamental linearity of risk-return relationship seems to be confirmed; however, it seems likely that more than one factor is needed to explain returns.

■ The empirical testability of CAPM has been questioned given that the market portfolio cannot be empirically identified.

■ CAPM has had a lasting influence on finance theory and on the practice of asset management.

CHAPTER 18

Multifactor Models and Common Trends for Common Stocks

In this chapter we discuss how multifactor models are used in the management of equity portfolios; in Chapter 20 we will discuss how they are applied to bond portfolio management. Multifactor models are a broad family of econometric models. Essentially, a multivariate process admits a multifactor representation if it can be approximately (or exactly) expressed as a function of another multivariate process of a smaller dimensionality. The general multifactor formulation of a model has to be clearly distinguished from the economic theory that might be behind it. In fact, multifactor models might be the expression of an economic theory as well as the result of an explicit econometric dimensionality reduction process.

For example, the Capital Asset Pricing Model (CAPM) is a general equilibrium theory which is embodied in a single-factor linear model. In this case, the factorization is the expression of a theoretical formulation. The same considerations apply to the Arbitrage Pricing Theory (APT): a multifactor model embodies a pricing theory based on the absence of arbitrage. However, given a multivariate process, econometric factor analysis techniques yield a dimensionality reduction which is also embodied in a multifactor model. In the latter case the process is purely statistic, not supported by theory. In this sense, the statement, often found in the literature, that CAPM and APT are factor models might be slightly misleading. It should be clear that both are economic theories, general equilibrium and arbitrage pricing respectively, which happen to be expressed as multifactor models.

It is likely that in the long run all price processes follow one single common trend with the exception of disruptive events such as bankruptcies or mergers and acquisitions. This trend-following behavior, however, might exhibit a complex dynamical structure. Within the time horizons that are empirically available, multiple trends, mean reversion, and structural breaks are at work. We will first analyze classical multifactor models of returns and how they are constructed and used in investment management. Subsequently, we will discuss dynamic factor models.

MULTIFACTOR MODELS

Let's introduce multifactor models of returns. The general form of a linear multifactor market model of returns can be written in one of the following ways:

$$E[r] = \alpha + \beta'E[f]$$

$$E[r_{it}|f_t] = \alpha_i + \beta_i f_t$$

$$r_{it} = \alpha_i + \sum_{s=1}^{p} \beta_{is} f_{st} + \varepsilon_t$$

where:

r_{it} = the return of the i-th security at time t
a_i = constants specific for the i-th security
β_{is} = the sensitivity of the i-th security to the s-th factor
f_t = the s-th factor at time t and ε_t is a noise process

In this linear regression model, assuming that factors are orthogonal (that is, uncorrelated), the sensitivities β_{is}, referred to as *betas*, can be written as:

$$\beta_{is} = \frac{\text{cov}(r_{it}f_{st})}{\text{var}(f_{st})}$$

As both returns and factors are assumed to be stationary stochastic processes, unconditional means and covariances are time-independent constants. The first formulation expresses a linear relationship between the unconditional means of the returns and of the factors. The second formulation is the linear regression function which expresses a linear relationship between the mean of returns at time t conditional on the realization of the factors at the same time; the third is the standard formulation of the linear regression of returns on factors.

Obviously returns and factors are all defined on the same probability space and have a joint pdf.[1] Recall from Chapter 6 on probability theory that joint multivariate normal distributions factorize in a linear regression. In the case of joint normality, returns, factors and noise all have normal joint distributions. However other distributions, for instance the Student-t, factorize in a linear regression while distributions such as lognormal and Pareto distributions do not factorize in a linear regression.

Factors range from innovations to exogenous variables, such as macroeconomic variables, to abstract factors formed as linear combinations of the processes. The multifactor model is a regression between variables at the same time and does not specify a dynamics for these variables. In other words, a multifactor model is not, per se, a predictive model. To perform forecasts and parameter estimates, a process dynamics of factors must be specified. The simplest dynamic assumption is that factors are independent and identically distributed (IID) variables. In this case, the noise is a white noise. Other specifications of factors dynamics have been proposed; these will be discussed later.

Factor market models can be generalized to include linear conditional factor models where factors and returns are conditional on some information set I known at time $t - 1$. The information set will contain the history of returns and factors up to time $t - 1$ and, possibly, other variables. Linear conditional factor models are written as follows:

$$E[\mathbf{r}_t|I_{t-1}] = \alpha + \beta E[\mathbf{f}_t|I_{t-1}]$$

where the constants are now time-dependent and conditional on the information set:

$$\beta_{is} = \frac{\text{cov}(r_{it}f_{st}|I_{t-1})}{\text{var}(f_{st}|I_{t-1})}$$

---

[1] For a discussion of what families of joint pdfs admit a linear regression function, see, amongst other, A. Spanos, *Statistical Foundations of Econometric Modeling* (Cambridge, U.K.: Cambridge University Press, 1986).

Determination of Factors

Let's now see how factors can be determined. Exogenous factors are determined through considerations of macroeconomic theory and fundamentals of each firm. Abstract factors are determined through a process of statistical analysis. We begin by describing the determination of exogenous factors and then of abstract factors.

Exogenous Factors[2]

There are several commercially available fundamental multifactor risk models. Investment management companies often develop their own proprietary models. Brokerage firms have developed models that they make available to institutional clients. In this section, we will focus on a commercially available model from Barra. The basic relationship to be estimated in a multifactor risk model is

$$R_i - R_f = \beta_{i,F1} R_{F1} + \beta_{i,F2} R_{F2} + \dots + \beta_{i,FH} R_{FH} + e_i$$

where:

R_i = rate of return on stock i
R_f = risk-free rate of return
$\beta_{i,Fj}$ = sensitivity of stock i to risk factor j
R_{Fj} = rate of return on risk factor j
e_i = nonfactor (specific) return on security i

The above function is referred to as a *return generating function.*

Fundamental factor models use company and industry attributes and market data as "descriptors." Examples are price/earnings ratios, book/price ratios, estimated earnings growth, and trading activity. The estimation of a fundamental factor model begins with an analysis of historical stock returns and descriptors about a company. In the Barra model, for example, the process of identifying the risk factors begins with monthly returns for 1,900 companies that the descriptors must explain. Descriptors are not the "risk factors" but instead they are the candidates for risk factors. The descriptors are selected in terms of their ability to explain stock returns. That is, all of the descriptors are potential risk factors but only those that appear to be important in explaining stock returns are used in constructing risk factors.

---

[2] The discussion in this section draws from Frank J. Fabozzi, Frank J. Jones, and Raman Vardharaj, "Multi-Factor Equity Risk Models," Chapter 13 in Frank J. Fabozzi and Harry M. Markowitz (eds.), *The Theory and Practice of Investment Management* (Hoboken, NJ: John Wiley & Sons, 2002).

Once the descriptors that are statistically significant in explaining stock returns are identified, they are grouped into "risk indices" to capture related company attributes. For example, descriptors such as market leverage, book leverage, debt-to-equity ratio, and company's debt rating are combined to obtain a risk index referred to as "leverage." Thus, a risk index is a combination of descriptors that captures a particular attribute of a company. The Barra fundamental multifactor risk model, the "E3 model" being the latest version, has 13 risk indices and 55 industry groups. Exhibit 18.1 lists the 13 risk indices in the Barra model.[3]

Also shown in the exhibit are the descriptors used to construct each risk index. The 55 industry classifications are further classified into sectors. For example, the following three industries comprise the energy sector: energy reserves and production, oil refining, and oil services. The consumer noncyclicals sector consists of the following five industries: food and beverages, alcohol, tobacco, home products, and grocery stores. The 13 sectors in the Barra model are basic materials, energy, consumer noncyclicals, consumer cyclicals, consumer services, industrials, utility, transport, health care, technology, telecommunications, commercial services, and financial.

Given the risk factors, information about the exposure of every stock to each risk factor $(\beta_{i,Fj})$ is estimated using statistical analysis. For a given time period, the rate of return for each risk factor (R_{Fj}) also can be estimated using statistical analysis. The prediction for the expected return can be obtained from the above equation for any stock. The nonfactor return (e_i) is found by subtracting the actual return for the period for a stock from the return as predicted by the risk factors.

Moving from individual stocks to portfolios, the predicted return for a portfolio can be computed. The exposure to a given risk factor of a portfolio is simply the weighted average of the exposure of each stock in the portfolio to that risk factor. For example, suppose a portfolio has 42 stocks. Suppose further that stocks 1 through 40 are equally weighted in the portfolio at 2.2%, stock 41 is 5% of the portfolio, and stock 42 is 7% of the portfolio. Then the exposure of the portfolio to risk factor j is

$$0.022\ \beta_{1,Fj} + 0.022\ \beta_{2,Fj} + \ldots + 0.022\ \beta_{40,Fj} + 0.050\ \beta_{41,Fj} + 0.007\ \beta_{42,Fj}$$

The nonfactor error term is measured in the same way as in the case of an individual stock. However, in a well diversified portfolio, the nonfactor error term will be considerably less for the portfolio than for the individ-

---

[3] For a more detailed description of each descriptor, see Appendix A in *Barra, Risk Model Handbook United States Equity: Version 3* (Berkeley, CA: Barra, 1998). A listing of the 55 industry groups is provided in Exhibit 13.9.

ual stocks in the portfolio. The same analysis can be applied to a stock market index because an index is nothing more than a portfolio of stocks.

Abstract Factors

Suppose now that factors are abstract static factors under the assumption that returns are normally distributed IID variables. Under this assumption, two basic techniques can be used: factor analysis and principal components analysis. We'll begin with factor analysis.

Suppose that there is a strict factor structure with a known number of undetermined factors of the form:

$$\mathbf{r} = \boldsymbol{\alpha} + \mathbf{Bf} + \boldsymbol{\varepsilon}$$

$$f_i = \sum_{s=1}^{N} \alpha_s r_s$$

where factors are linear combinations of returns. A strict factor structure means that factors explain all the covariance between the process components. Under this assumption, factors are processes with a variance-covariance matrix $\boldsymbol{\Omega}_F$ while the innovations $\boldsymbol{\varepsilon}$ are assumed to be uncorrelated and have a diagonal variance-covariance matrix $\mathbf{D}$. Under these assumptions, the variance-covariance matrix $\boldsymbol{\Omega}$ of the multivariate process $\mathbf{r}$ of returns can be written as the sum of two contributions:

$$\boldsymbol{\Omega} = \mathbf{B}\boldsymbol{\Omega}_F\mathbf{B}' + \mathbf{D}$$

This representation is not unique as factors are not uniquely determined. In fact, given any set of factors, one obtains another set of factors by multiplying the former by an orthonormal matrix $\mathbf{G}, \mathbf{GG}' = \mathbf{I}$. This indeterminacy allows one to choose orthogonal factors with unit variance so that their variance-covariance matrix is a unitary matrix and the return process variance-covariance matrix can be written as:

$$\boldsymbol{\Omega} = \mathbf{BB}' + \mathbf{D}$$

This relationship is a constraint on the return variance-covariance matrix. The latter can be estimated with MLE techniques. The resulting computations are numerically complex. However, many software packages efficiently perform factor analysis. After estimating the matrix of factor sensitivities, the factors themselves can be estimated with MLE

EXHIBIT 18.1   Barra E3 Model Risk Definitions

Descriptors in Risk Index	Risk Index
Beta times sigma	Volatility
Daily standard deviation	
High-low price	
Log of stock price	
Cumulative range	
Volume beta	
Serial dependence	
Option-implied standard deviation	
Relative strength	Momentum
Historical alpha	
Log of market capitalization	Size
Cube of log of market capitalization	Size nonlinearity
Share turnover rate (annual)	Trading activity
Share turnover rate (quarterly)	
Share turnover rate (monthly)	
Share turnover rate (five years)	
Indicator for forward split	
Volume to variance	
Payout ratio over five years	Growth
Variability in capital structure	
Growth rate in total assets	
Earnings growth rate over the last five years	
Analyst-predicted earnings growth	
Recent earnings change	
Analyst-predicted earnings-to-price	Earnings yield
Trailing annual earnings-to-price	
Historical earnings-to-price	
Book-to-price ratio	Value
Variability in earnings	Earnings variability
Variability in cash flows	
Extraordinary items in earnings	
Standard deviation of analyst-predicted earnings-to-price	
Market leverage	Leverage
Book leverage	
Debt to total assets	
Senior debt rating	
Exposure to foreign currencies	Currency sensitivity
Predicted dividend yield	Dividend yield
Indicator for firms outside US-E3 estimation universe	Nonestimation Universe indicator

Source: Adapted from Table 8-1 in Barra, *Risk Model Handbook United States Equity: Version 3* (Berkeley, CA: Barra, 1998), pp. 71–73. Adapted with permission.

techniques. In general one finds the entire set of N returns as one factor plus a number of additional factors as we have seen in Chapter 12.

Another statistical technique for determining factors is **principal components analysis** (PCA). As explained in Chapter 12, PCA is implemented by computing the eigenvalues of the estimated variance-covariance matrix. As shown in the study by Plerou et al., the distribution of eigenvalues typically follows that of a random matrix with the exception of a number of outliers. These outliers are the eigenvalues and the corresponding eigenvectors that form the factors.

PCA (as well as factor analysis) is a powerful statistical technique with a deep economic interpretation. To see this point, let's analyze the largest eigenvalues and the corresponding eigenvectors. The largest eigenvalue corresponds to an eigenvector whose components are all approximately equal to $1/N$. Therefore, the largest eigenvalue corresponds to the entire market.

The other large eigenvalues correspond to eigenvectors that have only a subset of components different from zero. The important finding is that these eigenvectors correspond to specific market sectors. In fact, the assets corresponding to the nonzero components of the largest eigenvectors correspond with good approximation to the Standard & Poor's market sector classification. Exhibit 18.2 shows the results obtained by performing PCA on the correlation matrix of the S&P 500 stocks in the period January 2, 2001–September 19, 2003. The ten largest eigenvalues correspond with good approximation to ten sectors of the Standard & Poor's classification.[4]

That the ten largest eigenvalues correspond to ten sectors of the Standard and Poor's classification is a powerful and somewhat surprising result in empirical financial econometrics. Performing PCA on a large aggregate of stock prices, we find that the information-carrying eigenvalues identify stable subsets of the market that correspond to meaningful sectors. It is an important theoretical-empirical finding that lends support to the use of factor analysis in financial econometrics.

The eigenvector corresponding to the largest eigenvalue identifies the entire market. Note that this eigenvector is a totally different concept than the "market portfolio" of the CAPM. In fact, the market portfolio of the CAPM, which is obtained as a General Equilibrium Theory and not as a factor model, includes all investable assets and not only stocks. Performing PCA on a large aggregate of stock prices one obtains a multiplicity of factors. In principle, on a very large sample, the two methods—factor analysis and PCA—yield the same result. On a finite sample, however, results might differ significantly. Note that both factor analysis and PCA tend to solve the problems of the sample limitations.

---

[4] The details of the methodology to arrive at these results can be found in Plerou, et al., "Random Matrix Approach to Cross Correlations in Financial Data."

EXHIBIT 18.2 PCA Performed on Correlations Matrix of S&P 500 Stocks, January 2, 2001–September 19, 2003

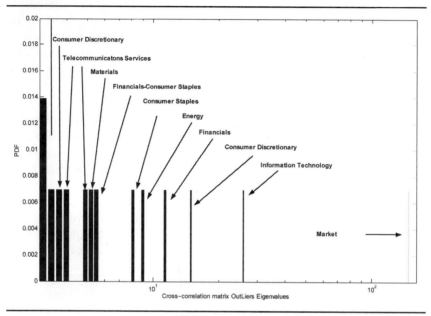

DYNAMIC MARKET MODELS OF RETURNS

Now let's consider stationary return processes with a dynamics more complex than that of an IID sequence of variables. A reasonable generalization of factor market models are state-space models of the form that was described in Chapter 12:

$$r_t = \alpha + Az_t + B\varepsilon_t$$

$$z_{t+1} = Cz_t + D\varepsilon_t$$

Note that z is non-observable. Therefore, the noise term can be placed either at t or $t - 1$. The first equation is the usual regression of a factor market model while the second equation is a **one-lag stationary Vector Auto Regressive**—denoted by VAR(1)—model that describes the autoregressive dynamics of the factors. Note that we assume that the above equations describe the dynamics of returns; the following section discusses how similar equations might describe prices.

Dynamic market models of this type can be used to create meaningful scenarios for multistage stochastic optimization. The VAR part of the model might describe the evolution of macroeconomic variables. If the objective is to apply multistage optimization and stay within the domain of linear models of returns, state-space models are the models of choice. As we have seen in Chapter 11, any stationary or asymptotically stationary linear model can be represented in this form.

Estimation of State-Space Models

Methods for the estimation of state-space models were originally developed for engineering applications. State-space systems can be estimated using MLE methods.[5] In 1990 Masanao Aoki[6] introduced a methodology called the **subspace algorithm** to estimate state-space models; Dietmar Bauer and Martin Wagner[7] subsequently showed how to apply subspace algorithms to cointegrated systems.

It was R. E. Kalman[8] who, in 1960, introduced a recursive methodology for making forecasts based on state-space models. Known as the **Kalman filter**, the methodology proved very successful in engineering before being applied more recently in economics and finance. Given a state-space model, a Kalman filter computes recursively the best estimate of state:

$$\hat{z}_t = E[z_t | r_0, ..., r_t]$$

Kalman filters are now implemented in many software packages.

DYNAMIC MODELS FOR PRICES

The models discussed above are single factor or multifactor linear models of returns; the risk-return trade-off entailed by these models leads to price processes that diverge exponentially. To see this point, consider that, given log prices, returns are approximately differences of log-prices. Therefore, log-prices are obtained by adding returns (i.e., they are a random-walk) and the real prices are then obtained taking the

---

[5] See, for instance, Helmut Luetkepohl, *Introduction to Multiple Time Series Analysis* (New York: Springer, 1991).

[6] Masanao Aoki, *State Space Modelling of Time Series* (New York: Springer, 1990).

[7] D. Bauer and M. Wagner, "Estimating Cointegrated Systems Using Subspace Algorithms," *Journal of Econometrics* 11 (2002), pp. 47–84.

[8] R.E. Kalman, "A New Approach to Linear Filtering and Prediction Problems," *Transactions of the ASME-Journal of Basic Engineering* (March 1960), pp. 35–45.

exponentials. If returns are jointly normally distributed, then log prices are jointly normally distributed while the real prices are lognormally distributed. Suppose that a variable X is normally distributed with expected value and variance μ, σ^2. The variable e^x is lognornomally distributed with the following expected value and variance:

$$e^{\mu + \frac{1}{2}\sigma^2}, \; \sigma^2(e^{\sigma^2} - 1)$$

If returns are Independent and Identical Normal (IIN) variables, linear factor models imply that prices with different factor sensitivities will have different average returns, an expression of the risk-return trade-off required by investors. In addition, the variance of log prices will grow linearly with time at different rates for each process. The means that different price processes will therefore evolve exponentially at different rates and diverge exponentially. Under the assumption that factors behave as a stationary Vector Auto Regressive (VAR) Model as in the state space-models, the dependence is more complex but there is still an exponential divergence of prices.

An exponential divergence of prices is not sustainable in the long run. Clearly corrective phenomena are at work in financial markets, though exactly how corrections are made is the subject of different hypotheses. It has been hypothesized that stock price processes are subject to discrete regime-changes; this assumption, widely studied in the literature, leads to nonlinear models. It has also been hypothesized that disruptive phenomena are at work, so that the price of a firm's stock might grow rapidly but then the firm is subject to phenomena such as bankruptcy, merger, acquisition or corporate restructuring; this links financial theory to macroeconomics and is beyond the scope of this book. A third hypothesis is that correction phenomena—and perhaps discrete changes—are always at work in markets; these phenomena can be modeled within the domain of linear models with the techniques of cointegration. The fact that portfolio separation in a fixed and closed economy implies collinearity lends additional theoretical support to the cointegration of asset prices. Bossaert showed how cointegration naturally arises if one slightly relaxes the assumption of separation.[9]

Cointegration (see Chapter 12 can be modeled in two different but equivalent ways, using either state-space models or Error Correction Models (ECMs). ECMs are VAR models with restrictions. Consider that it is always possible to write a VAR model in ECM form:

---

[9] Peter Bossaerts, "Common Nonstationary Components of Asset Prices," *Journal of Economic Dynamics and Control* 12 (1988), pp. 347–364.

$$\Delta x_t = (\Phi_1 L + \Phi_2 L^2 + \ldots + \Phi_{n-1} L^{n-1}) \Delta x_t + \Pi x_t + m + \varepsilon_t$$

The error correction restrictions apply to the matrix Π. An ECM is a VAR model with $\Pi = \alpha\beta'$ where α, β are $n \times r$ matrices. The term in level provides the error correction. The Granger Representation Theorem demonstrated by Granger in 1987[10] states that if a process is cointegrated with r cointegrating relationships then the above ECM holds.

James Stock and Mark Watson[11] first observed in 1988 that a cointegrated model with r cointegrating relationships admits $n-r$ common trends. The implication is that all time series can be written in the form

$$x_t = a + A z_t + \eta_t$$

where the z_t are the common stochastic trends, which are $I(1)$ integrated processes, and the η_t are stationary processes.

Models for cointegration can be extended in various ways. In the context of cointegration, Hashem Pesaran and Yongcheol Shin[12] introduced the **Autoregressive Distributed Lag** (ARDL) models. An ARDL model contains exogenous variables that are not cointegrated among themselves. It has the following form:

$$x_t = \alpha_0 + \alpha_1 t + (\Phi_1 L + \Phi_2 L^2 + \ldots + \Phi_p L^p) x_t + \beta z_t$$
$$+ (\beta_1 L + \beta_2 L^2 + \ldots + \beta_q L^q) \Delta z_t + u_t$$
$$0 = (P_1 L + P_2 L^2 + \ldots + P_s L^s) \Delta z_t + \varepsilon_t$$

where the z are $I(1)$ noncointegrated variables and the y exhibit r cointegrating relationships. Pesaran and Shin demonstrated that the classical approach to ARDL systems that are valid for stationary processes can be extended to integrated processes.

Cointegration models can also be extended in the sense of **dynamic cointegration** (or **polynomial cointegration**). Cointegrating relationships are static relationships between variables taken at the same time;

[10] R.F. Engle and C.W.J. Granger, "Cointegration and Error Correction: Representations, Estimation and Testing," *Econometrica* 55 (1987), pp. 252–276.

[11] James Stock and Mark Watson, "Testing for Common Trends," *Journal of the American Statistical Association* 83 (December 1988), pp. 1097–1107.

[12] Hashem M. Pesaran and Yongcheol Shin, "An Autoregressive Distributed Lag Modelling Approach to Cointegration Analysis," Chapter 11 in S. Strom (ed.), *Econometrics and Economic Theory in the 20th Century* (Cambridge, U.K.: Cambridge University Press, 1999).

dynamic cointegration introduces a small number of lags in the cointegrating relationship. In other words, cointegration reduces the order of integration by applying linear regressions between variables; dynamic cointegration reduces the order of integration by applying autoregressive modeling. A VAR model with n lags

$$\mathbf{x}_t = \mathbf{A}_1\mathbf{x}_{t-1} + \mathbf{A}_2\mathbf{x}_{t-2} + \dots + \mathbf{A}_n\mathbf{x}_{t-n} + \boldsymbol{\varepsilon}_t$$

exhibits dynamic cointegration if there exists a *stationary* autoregressive combination of the variables of the type

$$\boldsymbol{\alpha}'\mathbf{x}_t + \boldsymbol{\beta}'\Delta\mathbf{x}_t$$

Cointegration and dynamic cointegration can coexist in the same model in the sense that variables can be cointegrated and dynamically cointegrated. Note that, if the log price process is integrated of order 1, then the return process is stationary so that factor models for returns and cointegrated models for prices can coexist. In addition, linear combinations of prices and returns can also be stationary.

Cointegration is equivalent to the existence of common stochastic trends. This property is also expressed by the equivalence between an ECM and a state-space model. Recall that a state-space model is written as

$$\mathbf{x}_t = \mathbf{a} + \mathbf{A}\mathbf{z}_t + \mathbf{B}\boldsymbol{\mu}_t$$

$$\mathbf{z}_{t+1} = \mathbf{C}\mathbf{z}_t + \mathbf{D}\boldsymbol{\varepsilon}_t$$

where state-space variables are either stationary or integrated variables. Although a cointegrated price system of price processes can always be expressed as a state-space model, the variables in the state-space representation might include lagged prices. This fact was shown in Chapter 12 when addressing the question of the equivalence between ARMA models and state-space models. In general, prices might be expressed in the following factor form:

$$\mathbf{p}_t = \mathbf{s}_t + \sum_{i=1}^{p} \mathbf{A}_i\mathbf{p}_{t-i} + \sum_{j=0}^{q} \mathbf{B}_j\mathbf{f}_{t-j} + \mathbf{u}_t$$

$$\mathbf{f}_t = \sum_{k=1}^{s} \mathbf{C}_k \mathbf{f}_{t-k} + \mathbf{\eta}_t$$

where the price processes $\mathbf{p}_t$ have an autoregressive distributed-lag dynamics, the factors $\mathbf{f}_t$ follow a VAR or VARMA model, the terms $\mathbf{u}_t$ are idiosyncratic (i.e., they are mutually uncorrelated), and $\mathbf{s}_t$ are deterministic terms. The terms $\mathbf{u}_t$ and $\mathbf{\eta}_t$ might be white noise or might be autocorrelated (i.e., they are a stationary process that obeys ARMA equations).

Factor models can be cast in the state-space representation. Consider, for example, the following model:

$$\mathbf{p}_t = \mathbf{Bf}_t + \mathbf{u}_t$$

$$\mathbf{f}_t = \sum_{k=1}^{s} \mathbf{C}_k \mathbf{f}_{t-k} + \mathbf{\eta}_t$$

and

$$\mathbf{u}_t = \sum_{k=1}^{q} \mathbf{H}_k \mathbf{u}_{t-k} + \mathbf{\varepsilon}_t$$

An equivalent state-space model can be obtained by defining the following state vector:

$$\mathbf{z}_t' = [\mathbf{f}_t \ldots \mathbf{f}_{t-p} \mathbf{u}_t \ldots \mathbf{u}_{t-q}]$$

and the following transition matrix:

$$\mathbf{z}_t = \begin{bmatrix} \mathbf{C}_1 & \cdots & \mathbf{C}_{s-1} & \mathbf{C}_s & . & 0 & & & 0 \\ \mathbf{I} & & 0 & 0 & . & & & & \\ & \ddots & \vdots & \vdots & . & & & & \\ 0 & \cdots & \mathbf{I} & 0 & . & 0 & & & 0 \\ . & . & . & . & . & . & . & & . \\ 0 & & & 0 & . & \mathbf{H}_1 & \cdots & \mathbf{H}_{q-1} & \mathbf{H}_q \\ & & & . & \mathbf{I} & & 0 & 0 \\ & & & . & & \ddots & \vdots & \vdots \\ 0 & & & 0 & . & 0 & \cdots & \mathbf{I} & 0 \end{bmatrix} \mathbf{z}_{t-1} + \begin{bmatrix} \mathbf{\eta}_t \\ 0 \\ \vdots \\ 0 \\ \mathbf{\varepsilon}_t \\ 0 \\ \vdots \\ 0 \end{bmatrix}$$

The static-factor model and the common-trend cointegrated model are special cases of the above general dynamic factor model. The ARDL model is a dynamic factor model with additional restrictions.

A conceptual parallel can be made between state-space models and factor models. Recall that factor models essentially address the problem of a nearly random cross-correlation matrix. The correlation coefficients of a large correlation matrix are essentially random. To recover a meaningful correlation structure, every process is represented as a linear regression on a set of factors and only correlations between factors are considered.

Were we to attempt an estimate of a global VAR model of a large portfolio of equity prices or return processes, we would run into the same problem of finding meaningless random autocross correlation coefficients. This is because the matrices that represent all the correlations at different time lags are nearly random. State-space models extract the useful auto-correlation information from a large set of auto-cross-correlation data.

Estimation and Testing of Cointegrated Systems

The estimation and testing of cointegrated systems is a complex issue on which there is vast literature. The two major methods for estimation of cointegrated systems are due to Engle and Granger[13] and Johansen.[14] The Engle-Granger method is based on writing down explicitly the long-run regression equation and subsequently estimating the short term corrections. The Johansen methodology applies directly MLE methods. Stock and Watson[15] proposed PCA to determine the common trends.[16]

When dealing with large sets of asset prices, in particular equity prices, the techniques of Engle-Granger and Johansen are not applicable. The PCA-based approach of Stock and Watson, on the other hand, can be applied to hundreds of price processes. The Stock and Watson methodology is based on the observation that if there are r cointegration relationships the resulting n-r common trends are integrated $I(1)$ while the r cointegrating portfolios are stationary $I(0)$. Consequently, it is reasonable to assume that the integrated portfolios have maximum variance. Therefore, performing PCA on the variance-covariance matrix of the price process should lead to identification of the number and the

---

[13] Engle and Granger, "Cointegration and Error Correction: Representations, Estimation and Testing."

[14] S. Johansen, *Likelihood-based Inference in Cointegrated Vector Autoregressive Models* (Oxford: Oxford University Press, 1995).

[15] Stock and Watson, "Testing for Common Trends."

[16] The interested reader should consult the original works quoted or, G.S. Maddala and In-Moo Kim, *Unit Roots, Cointegration, and Structural Changes* (Cambridge, U.K.: Cambridge University Press, 1988).

weights of cointegrating vectors. The PCA-based approach can also be applied in the frequency domain. The analysis in the frequency domain is an alternative way of analyzing time series. It is based on constructing a transform of the time series which is the discrete equivalent of a Fourier transform discussed in Chapter 4.[17]

An alternative estimation methodology which is suitable for large sets is the subspace-space algorithm introduced by Aoki (ref. cited) in the context of stationary systems and extended by Bauer and Wagner (ref. cited) to integrated systems and to polynomial cointegration.[18]

Cointegration and Financial Time Series

Cointegration is an important technique for portfolio management: It allows an investor to detect mispricings and thus sources of profit. In fact, if a set of price processes exhibit cointegration, relative returns are autocorrelated and therefore predictable. In other words, as we will see in Chapter 19, although individual price processes might be unpredictable random walks, there are portfolios which exhibit a stationary, mean-reverting behavior. For this reason cointegration has attracted the attention of both academics and practitioners, especially in the areas of index tracking and hedge fund management.

However, cointegration technology was initially developed in the area of macroeconomics where only a small number of variables, generally less than 10, are used. Extending the concepts of cointegration to a large number of equity prices or return processes is difficult both from the numerical and theoretical standpoints. Assume, for example, that one is working on a large set of equity log-price processes such as those in the S&P 500. Standard cointegration estimation and testing methods such as the Johansen procedures do not work for sets of processes of this size.

Consider also that in finite samples of sets of processes such as those found in the S&P 500, spurious cointegrating relationships will be detected. This happens because in a large set of independent processes a cointegration test run on a relatively small sample of points will randomly test positive for many cointegrating relationship. For example, one finds a significant number, in the range of a few percentage points, of cointegrated pairs of processes in computer-generated independent arithmetic random walks.

---

[17] P.C.B. Phillips and S. Ouliaris, "Testing for Cointegration Using Principal Components Methods," *Journal of Economic Dynamics and Control* 12 (1988), pp. 205–230.

[18] The subspace algorithm is quite complex and technical. The interested reader should consult the papers by Bauer and Wagner.

When testing for cointegration on a large set, one has therefore to take an ensemble view. In analyzing macroeconomic series, the question is whether they are cointegrated or not; in analyzing a large number of financial time series, the problem is not if there are cointegrating relationships but if the number of cointegrating relationships found in the sample is high enough to warrant the belief that the system has a cointegration structure.

Another important issue—strictly related to the above—is the structure of cointegration. Cointegration can be found within highly cointegrated market segments (i.e., subsets of processes) that exhibit a high number of cointegrating relationships. Alternatively, cointegration can be found between market segments—perhaps on a different time scale. This cointegration structure will be reflected in the structure of common trends.

These issues are presently inadequately addressed in the literature, although much proprietary empirical and analytical work has been done by some asset management firms. Studies of cointegration in financial processes has been performed at the level of indexes or broad aggregates. Evidence of cointegration have been found between stock indexes in different countries and between different indexes in the same country. One of the most quoted studies on cointegration in equity prices is the 1992 study by Kenneth Kasa.[19] who found evidence of cointegration between stock indexes in five different countries. Using models with from 1 to 14 lags, Kasa found that the number of lags plays an important role: Cointegration is revealed more clearly with many lags. In a critical review of this and other studies on cointegration on various assets, Godbout and van Norden[20] concluded that the size of the sample might be responsible for significant distortions.

Carol Alexander[21] and coworkers at the ISMA Center in Reading, United Kingdom, found cointegration within small-size high-capitalization liquid indexes such as the Dow Jones Industrial Average (DJIA). Their empirical findings corroborate the intuition that equity prices are in some way mean-reverting around one or more common stochastic trends. Alexander has developed trading strategies used for both index tracking and long-short equity portfolios based on replicating the first common factor of the market.

---

[19] Kenneth Kasa, "Common Stochastic Trends in International Stock Markets," *Journal of Monetary Economics* 29 (1992), pp. 95–124.
[20] Marie-Josee Gobbout and Simon van Norden, "Reconsidering Cointegration in International Finance: Three Case Studies of Size Distortion in Finite Samples," Working Paper 97-1, Bank of Canada, 1997.
[21] Carol Alexander and Anca Dimitriu, "The Cointegration Alpha: Enhanced Index Tracking and Long - Short Equity Market Neutral Strategies," Working Paper, April 2002.

Special cointegration models have been described in the literature. In particular, the well-documented lead-lag effect described by Andrew Lo and Craig MacKinlay[22] leads to a cointegration model. The lead-lag effect is the strong correlation which exists between the returns at time t of portfolios of small firms, the laggards, and the return at time $t - 1$ of portfolios of large firms, the leaders. This effect can be tested either as direct correlation between returns or as autocorrelation of portfolios that include firms of different sizes.

In the original formulation of Lo and MacKinlay, the model is simple as there is only one exogenous factor. Consider the returns of the two portfolios of large firms and small firms; the Lo and MacKinlay model is written as follows, with the return of small firms a regression on the lagged factor:

$$r_{Lt} = \mu_L + \beta_{1L}f_t + \varepsilon_{Lt}$$

$$r_{St} = \mu_S + \beta_{1S}f_t + \beta_{2S}f_{t-1} + \varepsilon_{St}$$

Angelos Kanas and Georgios Kouretas[23] have cast the lead-lag effect of size-sorted portfolios into a cointegration framework using state-space modeling in the form of ARDL models for prices. Summing up returns to get prices and solving, they arrive at the following ARDL equation:

$$p_{St} = a + bt + \beta p_{Lt-1} + e_t$$

where e is an autocorrelated process that includes the single common factor.

In summary, cointegration and/or state-space modeling are powerful modeling techniques whose applicability to real price processes has been empirically tested. However, the practical implementation of state-space models of large portfolios presents significant challenges given that cointegration is largely unstable.

NONLINEAR DYNAMIC MODELS FOR PRICES AND RETURNS

While the models for portfolio management discussed above are linear models, the linearity of equity price processes has been challenged by

---

[22] Andrew Lo and Craig MacKinlay, "When Are Contrarian Profits Due to Stock Market Overreaction?" *Review of Financial Studies* 3 (1990), pp. 175–206.

[23] Angelos Kanas and Georgios Kouretas, "A Cointegration Approach to the Lead-Lag Effect Among Size-Sorted Equity Portfolios," Working Paper, 2001

studies that appear to demonstrate that equity price processes are not linear in the sense that their DGP is a nonlinear function. Volatility clustering and structural breaks are the most widely cited nonlinear effects. This lead to the development of nonlinear models for portfolio management; nonlinear dynamics and universal approximation schemes for DGPs such as neural networks have been widely described. However, tests for low-dimensional nonlinear dynamics have not given consistently positive results. Despite a period of intense experimentation during the 1990s, the techniques of nonlinear dynamics have not been successful in describing price processes.

Nevertheless, approximation schemes remain a subject of study and experimentation. Vector support machines based on the Vapnik-Chervonenkis theory of learning (see Chapter 12) are one of the latest additions to a long series of adaptive methods. By their nature, adaptive methods produce nonlinear DGPs that change continuously. While general conclusions are difficult, many experiments have confirmed that nonlinear approximation schemes have some predictive power—some trading strategies based on them have been profitable. However, most efforts are now confined to proprietary trading systems.

Two classes of nonlinear methods that have received a lot of attention, at both the theoretical and practical levels, are (1) ARCH-GARCH methods and (2) Markov switching and multiplicative state-space methods. Both are based on splitting the model into two parts: one part is a linear regressive or autoregressive model, the other an autoregressive model that drives the first.

The ARCH model (described in Chapter 12) was initially proposed to model the clustering of volatility. Its generalization, the GARCH family of models, applies to processes such as financial time series that exhibit volatility clustering. The GARCH(m,q) model represents the observed process, for example equity returns, as a sequence of IID variables multiplied by a coefficient which obeys an ARMA(m,q) model as follows:

$$r_t = \sigma_t \varepsilon_t$$

$$\sigma_t^2 = \sum_{i=1}^{m} \alpha_i \sigma_{t-i}^2 + \sum_{j=1}^{q} \beta_j r_{t-j}$$

The GARCH(m,q) model can be further generalized to multivariate processes by modeling not only the process's volatility but the entire variance-covariance matrix. In this form the model is known as **multi-**

variate **GARCH**. Because multivariate GARCH becomes rapidly unmanageable with the number of assets, simplified forms have been proposed.

GARCH models are not necessarily stationary insofar as their stationarity depends on the coefficients of the ARMA process. If the ARMA process is not stationary, then the process is called IGARCH.

While ARCH and GARCH models model volatility, asset pricing models require that returns depend on volatility as higher volatility commands a higher return. To capture the dependence of returns on volatility, Engle, Lilien, and Robins[24] suggested adding an expected return term to the GARCH equations. Equations then become

$$r_t = \mu_t + \sigma_t \varepsilon_t$$

$$\mu_t = \gamma_0 + \gamma_1 \sigma_t^2$$

$$\sigma_t^2 = \sum_{i=1}^{m} \alpha_i \sigma_{t-i}^2 + \sum_{j=1}^{q} \beta_j r_{t-j}$$

This model is called **M-ARCH** or **ARCH in mean**. Recall that M-ARCH is also a way to represent the conditional CAPM.

While ARCH and GARCH models are based on empirical findings of volatility clustering, Markov-switching models are based on a generalization of the idea that a model's parameters cannot be considered stable for long periods of time. If our objective is to retain linear models as the basic DGP, then we have to accept that parameters will change in time. Markov switching models use a Markov chain to drive the parameters of a basic linear model. The Hamilton model, for example, uses a Markov chain to drive the parameters of a random walk. In a more general Markov-switching VAR, a Markov chain drives the parameters of a VAR model. Continuous-state autoregressive models might replace Markov chains, thus originating multiplicative state-space models. ARCH and GARCH models follow this modeling strategy.

If the objective is to model a large collection of price processes, for example the price processes in some broad index, then dimensionality reduction techniques must be applied. Envisage an outer driver, be it a Markov chain or an autoregressive model, that drives the parameters of

[24] R. Engle, D. Lilien, and R. Robins, "Estimating Time-Varying Risk Premia in the Term Structure: the ARCH-M Model," *Econometrica* 55 (1987), pp. 391–407.

a state-space model. One thereby creates a dynamic model of the factors that drive a regressive model. As of this writing, however, the statistical properties of these models have not been thoroughly investigated.

SUMMARY

- Multifactor models are linear regressions over a number of variables called factors.
- Factors can be exogenous variables or abstract variables formed by portfolios.
- The Arbitrage Pricing Theory (APT) asserts that each asset's return is equal to the risk-free rate plus a linear combination of factors.
- The APT can be tested with maximum likelihood methods.
- Exogenous factors can be determined with fundamental analysis.
- Abstract factors can be determined with factor analysis or principal component analysis.
- Principal component analysis identifies the largest eigenvalues of the variance-covariance matrix or the correlation matrix.
- The largest eigenvalues correspond to eigenvectors that identify the entire market and sectors that correspond to industry classification.
- Multifactor models allow the decomposition of risk into systematic risk and residual risk.
- The most general formulation of the portfolio selection problem is utility maximization in a multiperiod setting.
- In a multiperiod setting, agents make a decision between consumption and investment at each date; the Consumption CAPM is obtained by aggregating all agents in a single representative agent and imposing consumption optimality conditions.
- Factor models can be extended in a dynamic environment as state-space models.
- Error correction models and state-space models are equivalent.
- Through cointegration and state space-models it is possible to represent large portfolios through dynamic factor models.
- There is empirical evidence of cointegration in stock prices.
- Nonlinear models of stock prices have been proposed, ARCH/GARCH and Markov switching models being two examples.

CHAPTER 19

Equity Portfolio Management

In this chapter we review strategies for equity portfolios, taking a close look at active and passive management, the decision as to whether or not to pursue an active or passive management, style investing, and the different types of active strategies that can be employed. We stress the role of multifactor risk models in the portfolio construction process. We begin the chapter with a discussion of the equity portfolio management process.

INTEGRATING THE EQUITY PORTFOLIO MANAGEMENT PROCESS

In Chapter 1, the investment management process was described as a series of five distinct steps. In practice, portfolio management requires an integrated approach. There must be recognition that superior investment performance results when valuable ideas are implemented in a cost-efficient manner. The process of investing—as opposed to the process of investment—includes innovative stock selection and portfolio strategies as well as efficient cost structures for the implementation of any portfolio strategy.[1] The integrated approach to managing equity portfolios recognizes that the value added by the manager is the result of information value less the implementation cost of trading. This difference in value is referred to as "captured value," a term coined by Wayne Wagner and Mark Edwards.[2]

---

[1] Wayne H. Wagner and Mark Edwards, "Implementing Investment Strategies: The Art and Science of Investing," Chapter 11 in Frank J. Fabozzi (ed.), *Active Equity Portfolio Management* (New Hope, PA: Frank J. Fabozzi Associates, 1998).

[2] Wagner and Edwards, "Implementing Investment Strategies: The Art and Science of Investing."

This view that an investing process requires an integrated approach to portfolio management is reinforced by Barra, a vendor of analytical systems used by portfolio managers. Barra emphasizes that superior investment performance is the product of careful attention paid by equity managers to the following four elements:

■ Forming reasonable return expectations
■ Controlling portfolio risk to demonstrate investment prudence
■ Controlling trading costs
■ Monitoring total investment performance

Accordingly, the investing process that includes these four elements are all equally important in realizing superior investment performance. In Chapter 4, several quantitative models for general expected returns were described. As for the second element, we will discuss the process of controlling risk in this chapter and in more detail in Chapter 23. Trading costs were explained in Chapter 2.

ACTIVE VERSUS PASSIVE PORTFOLIO MANAGEMENT

In practice there are investors who pursue different degrees of active management and different degrees of passive management. It would be helpful to have some way of quantifying the degree of active or passive management. John Loftus of Pacific Investment Management Company (PIMCO) has suggested that one way of classifying the various types of equity strategies is in terms of two measures—alpha and tracking error.[3] These measures begin with the calculation of the *active return* for a period. The active return is the difference between the actual portfolio return for a given period (say, a month) and the benchmark index return for the same period. *Alpha* is defined as the average active return over some time period. So, if there are 12 monthly active returns observed, then the average of the 12 monthly active returns is the alpha. *Tracking error* is the standard deviation of the active return. In the next section, we discuss tracking error in more detail. Tracking error occurs because the risk profile of a portfolio differs from that of the risk profile of the benchmark index.

Based on these measures, Loftus proposes the classification scheme shown in Exhibit 19.1. While there may be disagreements as to the values

---

[3] John S. Loftus, "Enhanced Equity Indexing," Chapter 4 in Frank J. Fabozzi (ed.), *Perspectives on Equity Indexing* (New Hope, PA: Frank J. Fabozzi Associates, 2000).

EXHIBIT 19.1 Measures of Management Categories

	Indexing	Active Management	Enhanced Indexing
Expected alpha	0%	2.0% or higher	0.5% to 2.0%
Tracking error	0% to 0.2%	4.0% or higher	0.5% to 2.0%

Source: Exhibit 2 in John S. Loftus, "Enhanced Equity Indexing," Chapter 4 in Frank J. Fabozzi (ed.), *Perspectives on Equity Indexing* (New Hope, PA: Frank J. Fabozzi Associates, 2000), p. 84.

proposed by Loftus, the exhibit does provide some guidance. In an indexing strategy, the portfolio manager seeks to construct a portfolio that matches the risk profile of the benchmark index, the expected alpha is zero and, except for transaction costs and other technical issues discussed later when we cover the topic of indexing, the tracking error should be, in theory, zero. Due to these other issues, tracking error will be a small positive value. At the other extreme, a manager who pursues an active strategy by constructing a portfolio that significantly differs from the risk profile of the benchmark portfolio has an expected alpha of more than 2% and a large tracking error—a tracking error of 4% or higher.

Using tracking error as our guide and the fact that a manager can construct a portfolio whose risk profile can differ to any degree from the risk profile of the benchmark index, we have a conceptual framework for understanding common stock portfolio management strategies. For example, there are managers that will construct a portfolio with a risk profile close to that of the benchmark index but intentionally not identical to it. Such a strategy is called *enhanced indexing*. This strategy will result in the construction of a portfolio that has greater tracking error relative to an indexing strategy. In the classification scheme proposed by Loftus, for an enhanced indexer the expected alpha does not exceed 2% and the tracking error is 0.5% to 2%.

TRACKING ERROR

When a portfolio manager's benchmark is a market index, risk is measured by the standard deviation of the return of the portfolio relative to the return of the benchmark. This risk measure is called *tracking error* and is computed as follows:

■ *Step 1.* Compute the total return for a portfolio for each period.
■ *Step 2.* Obtain the total return for the benchmark for each period.

■ *Step* 3. Obtain the difference between the values found in Step 1 and Step 2. The difference is referred to as the *active return.*
■ *Step* 4. Compute the standard deviation of the active returns. The resulting value is the tracking error.

The tracking error measurement is in terms of the observation period. So, if monthly returns are used, the tracking error is a monthly tracking error. Typically, tracking error is computed using either weekly or monthly data. Tracking error is annualized as follows:

$$\text{Annual tracking error} = \text{Monthly tracking error} \times \sqrt{f}$$

where f is 12 for monthly observations or 52 for weekly observations.

A portfolio created to match the benchmark index (i.e., an index fund) that regularly has zero active returns (that is, always matches its benchmark's actual return) would have a tracking error of zero. But a portfolio that is actively managed that takes positions substantially different from the benchmark would likely have large active returns, both positive and negative, and thus would have an annual tracking error of, say, 5% to 10%. A hybrid portfolio (e.g., enhanced index fund) that combines an index portfolio with an active portfolio would typically have a tracking error below 2%.

An enhanced index portfolio's is simply a combination of an indexed portfolio and an active portfolio. That is, the tracking error of the enhanced index portfolio is simply the tracking error of the active portion times its weight in the overall portfolio. For example, if the active portion constitutes 10% of the enhanced index fund (the other 90% being indexed), and the tracking error of the active portion is 5%, then the tracking error of the enhanced index fund is 0.5% (= 10% × 5%). To see this, let r = return, w = weight, σ^2 (.) = variance, and $\rho(.,.)$ = correlation. Using the following notation for subscripts, b = benchmark, I = indexed portfolio, a = active portfolio, p = enhanced index portfolio (a combination of the indexed portfolio and the active portfolio), then

$$r_p = w_i r_i + w_a r_a$$

since $w_i + w_a = 1$,

$$r_p - r_b = w_i (r_i - r_b) + w_a (r_a - r_b)$$

So, the tracking error variance of the enhanced index portfolio equals

$$\sigma^2(r_p - r_b) = \sigma^2\{w_i(r_i - r_b)\} + \sigma^2\{w_a(r_a - r_b)\}$$
$$+ 2w_i w_a \rho(r_i - r_b, r_a - r_b)\sigma(r_i - r_b)\sigma(r_a - r_b)$$

But, the variance and the standard deviation of the indexed portfolio relative to the benchmark would be zero. So, the first and the last terms in the above equation vanish, leaving.

$$\sigma^2(r_p - r_b) = \sigma^2\{w_a (r_a - r_b)\}$$

Taking the square root on both sides, we have

$$\sigma(r_p - r_b) = \sigma(w_a(r_a - r_b))$$

Since, $\sigma(w_a(r_a - r_b))$ is the tracking error of the active portion, the tracking error of the enhanced index portfolio is the product of weight of the active portfolio and the tracking error of the active portfolio.

Backward-Looking versus Forward-Looking Tracking Error

We have just described how to calculate tracking error based on the actual active returns observed for a portfolio. Calculations computed for a portfolio based on a portfolio's actual active returns reflect the portfolio manager's decisions during the observation period with respect to the factors that affect tracking error. We call tracking error calculated from observed active returns for a portfolio *backward-looking tracking error*, *ex post tracking error*, or *actual tracking error*.

A problem with using backward-looking tracking error in portfolio management is that it does not reflect the effect of current decisions by the portfolio manager on the future active returns and hence the future tracking error that may be realized. If, for example, the manager significantly changes the portfolio's exposure to risk factors during the observation period, then the backward-looking tracking error, which is calculated using data from prior periods would not accurately reflect the current portfolio risks going forward. That is, the backward-looking tracking error will have little predictive value and can be misleading regarding portfolio risks going forward.

The portfolio manager needs a forward-looking estimate of tracking error to reflect the portfolio risk going forward. The way this is done in practice is by constructing a multifactor risk model using as the market index the portfolio manager's benchmark. Given a manager's current portfolio holdings, the portfolio's current exposure to the various risk factors can be calculated and compared to the benchmark's exposures to the factors. Using the differential factor exposures and the risks of the factors, a *forward-looking tracking error* for the portfolio can be computed. This tracking error is also referred to as *predicted tracking error* and *ex ante tracking error*. Given a forward-looking tracking error, a range for the future possible portfolio active return can be calculated assuming that the active returns are normally distributed.

It should be noted that there is no guarantee that the forward-looking tracking error at the start of, say, a year would exactly match the backward-looking tracking error calculated at the end of the year. There are two reasons for this. The first is that as the year progresses and changes are made to the composition of the portfolio, the forward-looking tracking error estimate would change to reflect the new exposure to risk factors. The second is that the accuracy of the forward-looking tracking error at the beginning of the year depends on the extent of the stability in the variances and correlations used in the statistical model to estimate forward-looking tracking error. These problems notwithstanding, the average of forward looking tracking error estimates obtained at different times during the year will be reasonably close to the backward-looking tracking error estimate obtained at the end of the year.

The forward-looking tracking error is a useful in risk control and portfolio construction. The manager can immediately see the likely effect on tracking error of any intended change in the portfolio. Thus, scenario analysis can be performed by a portfolio manager to assess proposed portfolio strategies and eliminate those that would result in tracking error beyond a specified tolerance for risk. We will illustrate the use of multifactor risk models and tracking error later in this chapter and in bond portfolio management in Chapter 21.

The Impact of Portfolio Size, Benchmark Volatility, and Portfolio Beta on Tracking Error[4]

There are have been several empirical studies that have investigated the relationship between a portfolio's variance and number of stocks. These studies have found that between 15–20 names are needed to eliminate most of the unsystematic risk in a portfolio. These studies focus on the standard deviation of returns of a portfolio relative to a benchmark, not on tracking error.

Tracking error decreases as the portfolio progressively includes more of the stocks that are in the benchmark index. This effect is illustrated in Exhibit 19.2 which shows the effect of portfolio size for a large

---

[4] This discussion draws from Raman Vardharaj, Frank J. Fabozzi, and Frank J. Jones, "Determinants of Tracking Errors for Equity Portfolios," unpublished manuscript, October 2003.

EXHIBIT 19.2 Tracking Error versus the Number of Benchmark Stocks in the Portfolio

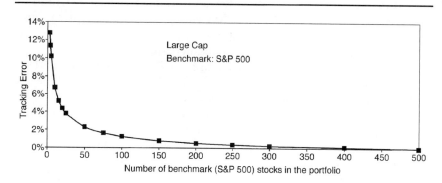

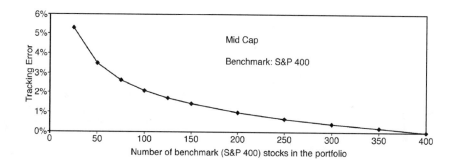

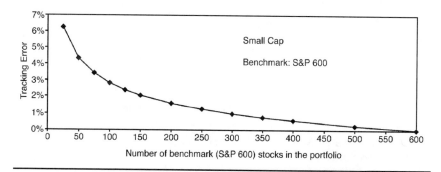

Source: Exhibit 7.2 in Raman Vardharaj, Frank J. Jones, and Frank J. Fabozzi, "Tracking Error and Common Stock Portfolio Management," Chapter 7 in Frank J. Fabozzi and Harry M. Markowitz (eds.), *The Theory and Practice of Investment Management* (New York: John Wiley & Sons, Inc., 2002), p. 171.

capitalization portfolio benchmarked to the S&P 500, a mid-cap portfolio benchmarked to the S&P 400, and a small cap portfolio benchmarked to the S&P 600.[5] Notice that an optimally chosen portfolio of just 50 stocks can track the S&P 500 within 2.3%. For mid cap and small cap stocks, the corresponding tracking errors are 3.5% and 4.3%, respectively. In contrast, tracking error increases as the portfolio progressively includes more stocks that are not in the benchmark. This effect is illustrated in Exhibit 19.3. In this case, the benchmark index is the S&P 100 and the portfolio progressively includes more and more stocks from the S&P 500 that are not in S&P 100. The result is that the tracking error with respect to the S&P 100 rises.

The impact of benchmark volatility is as follows. Managed portfolios generally hold only a fraction of the assets in their benchmark. Given this, a highly volatile benchmark index (as measured in terms of standard deviation) would be harder to track closely than a generally less volatile benchmark index.

This can be seen by using the market model:

$$r_p = \beta r_m + e$$

EXHIBIT 19.3   Tracking Error versus the Number of Nonbenchmark Stocks in the Portfolio

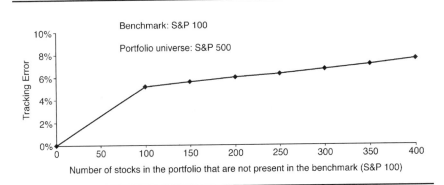

Source: Exhibit 7.3 in Raman Vardharaj, Frank J. Jones, and Frank J. Fabozzi, "Tracking Error and Common Stock Portfolio Management," Chapter 7 in Frank J. Fabozzi and Harry M. Markowitz (eds.), *The Theory and Practice of Investment Management* (New York: John Wiley & Sons, Inc., 2002), p. 171.

---

[5] The tracking errors for the various portfolios were obtained from Barra Aegis software. These are forward-looking tracking errors rather than backward-looking tracking errors. Also, the portfolios were optimally constructed to minimize tracking error.

where

r_p = return of the portfolio in excess of the constant risk-free rate
r_m = return of the market index in excess of the constant risk-free rate
e = residual error term
β = beta of the portfolio

Subtracting market excess return (i.e., r_m) from both sides, we get

$$r_a = r_p - r_m = (\beta - 1)r_m + e$$

where r_a is the active return. Therefore,

$$\sigma^2(r_p - r_m) = (\beta - 1)^2\sigma^2(r_m) + \sigma^2(e)$$

There would be no correlation between r_m and the error term due to the regression. The left hand side of the above equation is the portfolio tracking error variance. So, we have

$$\sigma(r_p - r_m) = (\beta - 1)\sigma(r_m)$$

As can be seen from the above equation, holding other things equal, tracking error increases with market volatility.

To quantify the relationship between portfolio beta and tracking error, look again at the formula for the tracking error from the market model given above. Let w = weight of the portfolio invested in the benchmark index; $(1 - w)$ = weight of the portfolio invested in cash; r_p = portfolio return in excess of the risk-free return on cash, and; r_b = benchmark index return in excess of the risk-free return on cash. Because the excess return on cash is zero, we know that

$$r_p = wr_b + (1 - w)\,0 = wr_b$$

If β is the portfolio beta versus the benchmark index, then letting $\sigma(.,.)$ denote the covariance,

$$\beta = \sigma(r_p, r_b)/\sigma^2(r_b) = w\sigma^2(r_b)/\sigma^2(r_b) = w$$

Next we know that, $r_p - r_b = (w - 1)r_b = (\beta - 1)r_b$

$$\sigma^2(r_p - r_b) = (w - 1)^2\sigma^2(r_b) = (\beta - 1)^2\sigma^2(r_b)$$

Taking square root on both sides and denoting |.| as absolute value, we see the following relationship between tracking error and portfolio beta:

$$\sigma(r_p - r_b) = |w - 1|\sigma(r_b) = |\beta - 1|\sigma(r_b)$$

Portfolio tracking error with respect to the benchmark index increases when both the beta falls below 1 and when the beta rises above 1. The same is true of the weight of the portfolio in the benchmark index. So, as portfolio increases the proportion of cash held, even though its absolute risk falls, its tracking error (i.e., relative risk) rises.

In the above example, we make the simplistic assumption that the manager only chooses between holding the market portfolio and cash when making changes to its beta. In the more general case, where the manager can hold any number of stocks in any proportion, its beta can differ from 1 due to other reasons. But, even in this general case, the tracking error increases when the portfolio beta deviates from the market beta.

EQUITY STYLE MANAGEMENT

Before we discuss the various types of active and passive strategies, let's discuss an important topic regarding what has come to be known as *equity investment styles*. Several academic studies found that there were categories of stocks that had similar characteristics and performance patterns. Moreover, the returns of these stock categories performed differently than other categories of stocks. That is, the returns of stocks within a category were highly correlated and the returns between categories of stocks were relatively uncorrelated. As a result of these studies, practitioners began to view these categories of stocks with similar performance as a "style" of investing. Using size as a basis for categorizing style, some managers became "large cap" investors while others "small cap" investors. ("Cap" means market capitalization.) Moreover, there was a commonly held belief that a manager could shift "styles" to enhance performance return.

Today, the notion of an equity investment style is widely accepted in the investment community. Next we look at the popular equity style types and the difficulties of classifying stocks according to style.

Types of Equity Styles

Stocks can be classified by style in many ways. The most common is in terms of one or more measures of "growth" and "value." Within a growth and value style there is often a substyle based on some measure of size. The motivation for the value/growth style categories can be explained in terms of the most common measure for classifying stocks as growth or value—the price-to-book value per share (P/B) ratio. Earnings growth will increase the book value per share. Assuming no change in the P/B ratio, a stock's price will increase if earnings grow—as higher book value times a constant P/B ratio leads to higher stock price. A manager who is growth oriented is concerned with earnings growth and seeks those stocks from a universe of stocks that have higher relative earnings growth. The growth manager's risks are that growth in earnings will not materialize and/or that the P/B ratio will decline.

For a value manager, concern is with the price component rather than with the future earnings growth. Stocks would be classified as value stocks within a universe of stocks if they are viewed as cheap in terms of their P/B ratio. By cheap it is meant that the P/B ratio is low relative to the universe of stocks. The expectation of the manager who follows a value style is that the P/B ratio will return to some normal level and thus even with book value per share constant, the price will rise. The risk is that the P/B ratio will not increase.

Within the value and growth categories there are substyles. With the notion of style investing came stock market indexes that could be used to represent different styles. There are three major services that provide popular style indexes based on capitalization. Standard & Poor's together with Barra publishes cap-based growth and value indexes based on three S&P indexes: the S&P 500 Index (also called the S&P Composite Index), the Mid Cap 400 Index, and the Small Cap 600 indexes. Based on its Russell 1000, Russell 3000, and Russell Top 200, Frank Russell publishes three large cap style indexes. It also produces a mid-cap index and a small cap based on both the Russell 2000 and Russell 2500 indexes. A large, mid-, and small cap set of indexes is also produced by Wilshire Associates.

From the statistical point of view identifying styles means classifying stocks. Classification is a broad topic in statistics. Classification used for style analysis is typically unsupervised insofar as no given example is needed. The simplest unsupervised technique is linear discriminant analysis. If stocks are characterized by a number of attributes, linear discriminant analysis tries to find a hyperplane that discriminates between two groups. Consider, for instance "value" and "growth." Each stock is characterized by a pair of value and growth numbers. Therefore, all stocks can be visualized as a set of points in the value-growth plane. Discriminant analysis tries to find the straight line that cuts that set in two subsets in some optimal way. Criteria for optimal cutting are needed. Nonlinear discriminant analysis might use nonlinear functions as discriminant.

Discriminant analysis divides a set into two parts. However, one might want to classify stocks in several groups. In this case, the problem is one of clustering. Clustering means forming groups so that objects in each group are similar while objects in different groups are dissimilar. For instance, classification in several different styles is an example of clustering. To perform clustering one needs a distance function that gives the distance between any two objects. Clustering will find groups, i.e., clusters, that have the minimum possible distance. A popular way of classifying stocks is through hierarchical clustering based on correlation distance.[6]

Style Classification Systems

Now that we have a general idea of the two main style categories, growth and value, and the further refinement by size, let's see how a portfolio manager goes about classifying stocks that fall into the categories. We call the methodology for classifying stocks into style categories as a *style classification system*. Vendors of style indices have provided direction for developing a style classification system. However, managers will develop their own system.

Developing such a system is not a simple task. To see why, let's take a simple style classification system where we just categorize stocks into value and growth using one measure, the price-to-book value ratio. The lower the P/B ratio the more the stock looks like a value stock. The style classification system would then be as follows:

■ Step 1. Select a universe of stocks.
■ Step 2. Calculate the total market capitalization of all the stocks in the universe.
■ Step 3. Calculate the P/B ratio for each stock in the universe.
■ Step 4. Sort the stocks from the lowest P/B ratio to the highest P/B ratio.
■ Step 5. Calculate the accumulated market capitalization starting from the lowest P/B ratio stock to the highest P/B ratio stock.
■ Step 6. Select the lowest P/B stocks up to the point where one-half the total market capitalization computed in Step 2 is found.
■ Step 7. Classify the stocks found in Step 6 as value stocks.
■ Step 8. Classify the remaining stocks from the universe as growth stocks.

While this style classification system is simple, it has both theoretical and practical problems. First, from a theoretical point of view, in

---

[6] Clustering is broad topic. An excellent reference is Richard O. Duda, Peter E. Heart, and David G. Stork, *Pattern Classification* (New York: John Wiley & Sons, 2001).

terms of the P/B ratio there is very little distinguishing the last stock on the list that is classified as value and the first stock on the list classified as growth. From a practical point of view, the transaction costs are higher for implementing a style using this classification system. The reason is that the classification is at a given point in time based on the prevailing P/B ratio and market capitalizations. At a future date, P/B ratios and market capitalizations will change, resulting in a different classification of some of the stocks. This is often the case for those stocks on the border between value and growth that could jump over to the other category. This is sometimes called "style jitter." As a result, the manager will have to rebalance the portfolio to sell off stocks that are not within the style classification sought.

There are two refinements that have been made to style classification systems in an attempt to overcome these two problems. First, more than one categorization variable has been used in a style classification system. Categorization variables that have been used based on historical and/or expectational data include dividend/price ratio (i.e., dividend yield), cash flow/price ratio (i.e., cash flow yield), return on equity, and earnings variability, and earnings growth. As an example of this refinement, consider the style classification system developed by one firm, Frank Russell, for the Frank Russell style indices. The universe of stocks included (either 1,000 for the Russell 1000 index or 2,000 for the Russell 2000 index) were classified as part of their value index or growth index using two categorization variables. The two variables are the B/P ratio and a long-term growth forecast of earnings.[7]

The second refinement has been to develop better procedures for making the cut between growth and value. This involves not classifying every stock into one category or the other. Instead, stocks may be classified into three groups: "pure value," "pure growth," and "middle-of-the-road" stocks. The three groups would be such that they each had one third of the total market capitalization. The two extreme groups, pure value and pure growth, are not likely to face any significant style jitter. The middle-of-the road stocks are assigned a probability of being value or growth.

Thus far our focus has been on style classification in terms of value and growth. As we noted earlier, substyle classifications are possible in terms of size. Within a value and growth classification, there can be a model determining large value and small value stocks, and large growth and small growth stocks. The variable most used for classification of size is a company's market capitalization. To determine large and small, the total market capitalization of all the stocks in the universe consid-

---

[7] "Russell Equity Indices: Index Construction and Methodology," Frank Russell Company, July 8, 1994 and September 6, 1995.

ered is first calculated. The cutoff between large and small is the stock that will give an equal market capitalization. Even here though, one might worry about "size jitter."

PASSIVE STRATEGIES

There are two types of passive strategies: a buy-and-hold strategy and an indexing strategy. In a *buy-and-hold strategy,* a portfolio of stocks based on some criterion is purchased and held to the end of some investment horizon. There is no active buying and selling of stocks once the portfolio is created. While referred to as a passive strategy, there are elements of active management. Specifically, the investor who pursues this strategy must determine which stock issues to buy.

An indexing strategy is the more commonly followed passive strategy. With this strategy, the manager does not attempt to identify undervalued or overvalued stock issues based on fundamental security analysis. Nor does the manager attempt to forecast general movements in the stock market and then structure the portfolio so as to take advantage of those movements. Instead, an indexing strategy involves designing a portfolio to track the total return performance of a benchmark index. Next we explain how that is done.

Constructing an Indexed Portfolio

In constructing a portfolio to replicate the performance of the benchmark index, sometimes referred to as the *indexed portfolio* or the *tracking portfolio*, there are several approaches that can be used. One approach is to purchase all stock issues included in the benchmark index in proportion to their weightings. A second approach, referred to as the *capitalization approach*, is one in which the manager purchases a number of the largest capitalized names in the benchmark index and equally distributes the residual stock weighting across the other issues in the benchmark index. For example, if the top 150 highest-capitalization stock issues are selected for the replicating portfolio and these issues account for 70% of the total capitalization of the benchmark index, the remaining 30% is evenly proportioned among the other stock issues.

Another approach is to construct an indexed portfolio with fewer stock issues than the benchmark index. Two methods used to implement this approach are the cellular (or stratified sampling) method and the multifactor risk model method.

In the *cellular method*, the manager begins by defining risk factors by which the stocks that make up a benchmark index can be categorized. A typical risk factor is the industry in which a company operates. Other factors might include risk characteristics such as beta or capitalization. The use of two characteristics would add a second dimension to the stratification. In the case of the industry categorization, each company in the benchmark index is assigned to an industry. This means that the companies in the benchmark have been stratified by industry. The objective of this method is then to reduce residual risk by diversifying across all industries in the same proportion as the benchmark index. Stock issues within each cell or stratum, or in this case industry, can then be selected randomly or by some other criterion such as capitalization ranking.

The second method is using a multifactor risk model to construct a portfolio that matches the risk profile of the benchmark index. By doing so, a predicted tracking error close to zero can be obtained. In the case of smaller portfolios, this approach is ideal since the manager can assess the tradeoff of including more stock issues versus the higher transaction costs for constructing the indexed portfolio. This can be measured in terms of the effect on predicted tracking error.

Index Tracking and Cointegration

As seen earlier in this chapter, using tools such as multifactor models, index trackers try to replicate the returns of the index. This methodology has the advantage of being in line with classical methods of portfolio management. In fact, it can be easily cast in the mean-variance framework. However, it has the disadvantage that errors grow in time. In fact, tracking error is assumed to grow with the square root of time. However, if the tracking portfolio is cointegrated with the index, errors are stationary. In this case, a time dependent tracking error is suboptimal.

The techniques of cointegration are clearly important for index tracking. Its use in index tracking was pioneered by Carol Alexander at the ISMA Centre in Reading, United Kingdom. In fact, because cointegration allows a manager to specify a stationary tracking error and, therefore, an optimal global index tracking methodology, the techniques of cointegration can be applied to any portfolio that is strongly cointegrated with an index.

The key challenge of cointegration methods is to find the right cointegrating portfolio. This is a difficult task when working with large portfolios. As mentioned above, standard cointegration tests do not work for large portfolios. One possible solution is the use economic considerations that might suggest the choice of particular market segments which can be tested for cointegration in aggregate. A more abstract approach is to use state-space models to find meaningful common factors.

ACTIVE INVESTING

In contrast with passive investing, active investing makes sense when a moderate to low degree of capital market efficiency is present in the financial markets (or areas thereof). This happens when the active investor has (1) better information than most other investors (namely, the "consensus" investors); and/or (2) the investor has a more productive way of looking at a given information set to generate active rewards.

In general, active strategies can be classified as either a top-down approach or a bottom-up approach. We discuss each approach below.

Top-Down Approaches to Active Investing

Before delving into the "top-down" active approach to investing, we must first reflect on the different connotations of top-down investing. In principle, one can distinguish between three types of top-down investing—one of which is passive, while two are active. We'll first explain the top-down passive connotation. Specifically, we know that modern portfolio theory emphasizes that investors should hold efficient portfolios. As we explained in Chapter 16, an efficient portfolio is one that maximizes expected return for any given level of expected risk. The MPT framework can in turn be viewed as a top-down passive approach to investing because an investor is only concerned with *portfolio choices*—albeit efficient ones at that—rather than stock selection choices by company, industry, and even market sector.

Indeed, the top-down maximization of expected portfolio return for a given risk level occurs without any direct interest by the investor in the specific names of companies that comprise the efficient portfolio—other than to say that an individual company, industry, or sector has the potential to enhance portfolio return and reduce risk through efficient diversification. Since an efficient portfolio—such as the market portfolio—is a passively constructed portfolio, one must therefore be careful to distinguish between top-down passive investing and top-down active investing.

Given the amount of the portfolio's funds to be allocated to the equity market, the manager must then decide how much to allocate among the sectors and industries of the equity market. In making the active asset allocation decision, a manager who follows a macroeconomic approach to top-down investing often relies on an analysis of the equity market to identify those sectors and industries that will benefit the most on a relative basis from the anticipated economic forecast. Once the amount to be allocated to each sector and industry is made, the manager then looks for the individual stocks to include in the portfolio. The top-down approach looks at changes in several macroeconomic factors to assess the expected active return on securities and portfolios. As noted before, prominent economic variables include changes in commodity prices, interest rates, inflation, and economic productivity.

Additionally, the macroeconomic outlook approach to top-down investing can be both quantitative and qualitative in nature. From the former perspective, equity managers employ factor models in their top-down attempt at generating abnormal returns (i.e., positive alpha). The power of top-down factor models is that given the macroeconomic risk measures and factor sensitivities, a portfolio's risk exposure profile can be quantified and controlled. In this way, it is possible to see why a portfolio is likely to generate abnormally high or low returns in the marketplace.

Bottom-Up Approaches to Active Investing

The "bottom-up" approach to active investing makes sense when numerous pricing inefficiencies exist in the capital markets (or components thereof). An investor who follows a bottom-up approach to investing focuses either on (1) technical aspects of the market or (2) the economic and financial analysis of individual companies, giving relatively less weight to the significance of economic and market cycles.

The investor who pursues a bottom-up strategy based on certain technical aspects of the market is said to be basing stock selection on *technical analysis*. The primary research tool used for investing based on economic and financial analysis of companies is called *security analysis* and falls into two categories, traditional fundamental analysis and quantitative fundamental analysis.

Traditional fundamental analysis often begins with the financial statements of a company in order to investigate its revenue, earnings, and cash flow prospects, as well as its overall corporate debt burden.[8] Growth in revenue, earnings, and cash flow on the income statement side and the relative magnitude of corporate leverage from current and anticipated balance sheets are frequently used by fundamental equity analysts in forming an opinion of the investment merits of a particular company's stock.

Specifically, the fundamental analyst attempts to determine the fair market value (or the "intrinsic value") of the stock, using, for example, a price-to-earnings or price-to-book value multiplier. The estimated "fair value" of the firm is then compared to the actual market price to see if the stock is correctly priced in the capital market. "Cheap stocks," or potential buy opportunities, have a current market price below the

---

[8] Benjamin Graham and David Dodd developed the classical approach to equity securities analysis. Their approach is explained in *Security Analysis* (New York: McGraw-Hill, 1934). Notable investors who have successfully employed the traditional approach to equity security analysis include Warren Buffet of Berkshire Hathaway, Inc. and Peter Lynch of Fidelity Management & Research Co.

estimated intrinsic value, while "expensive" or overvalued stocks have a market price that exceeds the calculated present worth of the stock.

Quantitative fundamental analysis seeks to assess the value of securities using a statistical model derived from historical information about security returns. The most commonly used model is the *fundamental multifactor risk model* that we will explain later in this chapter. In addition to identifying the expected return for a security, a fundamental factor model can be used to construct a portfolio or rebalance a portfolio as demonstrated later in this chapter.

Bruce Jacobs and Kenneth Levy refer to strategies that employ quantitative methods to select stocks and to construct portfolios that have the same risk profile as a benchmark index but provide the opportunity to enhance returns relative to that benchmark index at appropriate incremental level as an "engineered approach" to portfolio management.

Fundamental Law of Active Management

The information ratio is the ratio of alpha to the tracking error. It is a reward (as measured by alpha) to risk (as measured by tracking error) ratio. The higher the information ratio, the better the performance of the manager. Two portfolio managers, Richard Grinold and Ronald Kahn, have developed a framework—which they refer to as the "fundamental law of active management"—for explaining how the information ratio changes as a function of:[9]

1. The *depth* of an active manager's skill
2. The *breadth* or number of independent insights or investment opportunities.

In formal terms, the information ratio can be expressed as

$$IR = IC \times BR^{0.5}$$

where:

IR = the information ratio
IC = the information coefficient
BR = the number of independent insights or opportunities available to the active manager

In the above expression, the information ratio (IR) is the reward-to-risk ratio for an active portfolio manager. In turn, the information coef-

---

[9] For a practical discussion of this active management "law," see Ronald N. Kahn, "The Fundamental Law of Active Management," *BARRA Newsletter* (Winter 1997).

ficient (IC) is a measure of the depth of an active manager's skill. On a more formal basis, IC measures the "correlation" between actual returns and those predicted by the portfolio manager. According to the fundamental law of active management, the information ratio also depends on breadth (BR), which reflects the number of creative insights or active investment opportunities available to the investment manager.

There are several interesting implications of the fundamental law of active management. First, we see that the information ratio goes up when manager skill level rises for a given number of independent insights or active opportunities. This fact should be obvious, as a more skillful manager should produce higher risk-adjusted returns, compared with a less skilled manager whose performance is evaluated over the *same* set of investment opportunities (possibly securities). Second, a prolific manager with a large number of independent insights for a given skill level can, in principle, produce a higher information ratio than a manager with the same skill but a limited number of investment opportunities.

Equally important, the fundamental law of active management suggests that a manager with a high skill level, but a limited set of opportunities, may end up producing the *same* information ratio as a manager having a relatively lower level of skill but more active opportunities. According to Ronald Kahn,[10] a market timer with an uncanny ability to predict the market may end up earning the same information ratio on the average as a somewhat less skillful stock picker. This might happen because the stock picker has numerous potentially mispriced securities to evaluate, while the otherwise successful market timer may be constrained by the number of realistic market forecasts per year (due, perhaps, to quarterly forecasting or macroeconomic data limitations). Thus, the ability to profitably evaluate an investment opportunity (skill) and the number of independent insights (breadth) is key to successful active management.

With an understanding of the fundamental law of active management, we can now look at the risk of failing to produce a given level of active portfolio return. In this context, Bruce Jacobs and Kenneth Levy suggest that even traditional equity managers face a portfolio management dilemma involving a trade-off between the depth, or "goodness," of their equity management insights and the breadth or scope of their equity management ideas.[11] According to Jacobs and Levy, the breadth of active research conducted by equity managers is constrained in practical terms by the number of investment ideas (or securities) that can be

[10] See Kahn, "The Fundamental Law of Active Management."
[11] Jacobs and Levy, "Investment Management: An Architecture for the Equity Market."

implemented (researched) in a timely and cost-efficient manner. This trade-off is shown in Exhibit 19.4.

The exhibit displays the relationship between the depth of equity manager insights (vertical axis) and the breadth of those insights (horizontal axis). The depth of equity manager insights is measured in formal terms by the information coefficient (IC, on the vertical axis), while the breadth (BR) of manager insights can be measured by the potential number of investment ideas or the number of securities in the manager's acceptable universe. When the breadth of equity manager insights is low—as in the case of traditional equity management, according to Jacobs and Levy—then the depth, or "goodness" of each insight needs to be high in order to produce a constant level of active reward-to-active risk (information ratio, IR). Exhibit 19.4 shows that this low breadth/high depth combination produces the same level of active reward that would be associated with a pair-wise high number of investable ideas (or securities) and a relatively low level of equity manager "goodness" or depth per insight.

In a risk management context, one can say that the probability of failure to achieve a given level of active reward is quite high when the breadth of investment ideas or securities to be analyzed is very low. If the market is price efficient, that scenario is likely in the traditional fundamental analysis approach to active equity management discussed earlier. On the other hand, the risk of not achieving a given level of active reward is low when

EXHIBIT 19.4   Combination of Breadth (Number) of Insights and Depth, or "Goodness," of Insights Needed to Produce a Given Investment Return/Risk Ratio

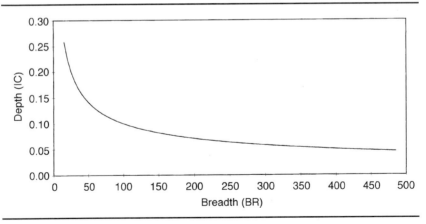

Source: See Bruce I. Jacobs and Kenneth N. Levy, "Investment Management: An Architecture for the Equity Market," Chapter 1 in Frank J. Fabozzi (ed.), *Active Equity Portfolio Management* (New Hope, PA: Frank J. Fabozzi Associates, 1998), p. 6.

the breadth of implementable manager ideas is high. This can happen in a world where active managers employ an engineered approach to active portfolio management. However, if the capital market is largely price efficient, then the probability of failing to produce any level of active reward is high (near one). With market efficiency, investable ideas are transparent, and their active implications are already fully impounded in security prices.

Strategies Based on Technical Analysis

Given the preceding developments, we would be remiss for not shedding some insight on active strategies based on technical analysis. In this context, various common stock strategies that involve only historical price movement, trading volume, and other technical indicators have been suggested since the beginning of stock trading. Many of these strategies involve investigating patterns based on historical trading data (past price data and trading volume) to forecast the future movement of individual stocks or the market as a whole. Based on observed patterns, mechanical trading rules indicating when a stock should be bought, sold, or sold short are developed. Thus, no consideration is given to any factor other than the specified technical indicators. This approach to active management is called *technical analysis*. Because some of these strategies involve the analysis of charts that plot price and/or volume movements, investors who follow a technical analysis approach are sometimes called *chartists*. The overlying principle of these strategies is to detect changes in the supply of and demand for a stock and capitalize on the expected changes.

Simple Filter Rules

The simplest type of technical strategy is to buy and sell on the basis of a predetermined movement in the price of a stock; the rule is basically if the stock increases by a certain percentage, the stock is purchased and held until the price declines by a certain percentage, at which time the stock is sold. The percentage by which the price must change is called the "filter." Each investor pursuing this technical strategy decides his or her own filter.

Moving Averages

Some technical analysts make decisions to buy or sell a stock based on the movement of a stock over an extended period of time (for example, 200 days). An average of the price over the time period is computed, and a rule is specified that if the price is greater than some percentage of the average, the stock should be purchased; if the price is less than some percentage of the average, the stock should be sold. The simplest way to calculate the average is to calculate a simple moving average. Assuming that the time period selected by the technical analyst is 200 days, then the average price over the 200 days is determined. A more complex moving average can be calculated by giving greater weight to more recent prices.

Advance/Decline Line

On each trading day, some stocks will increase in price or "advance" from the closing price on the previous trading day, while other stocks will decrease in price or decline from the closing price on the previous trading day. It has been suggested by some market observers that the cumulative number of advances over a certain number of days minus the cumulative number of declines over the same number of days can be used as an indicator of short-term movements in the stock market.

Relative Strength

The *relative strength* of a stock is measured by the ratio of the stock price to some price index. The ratio indicates the relative movement of the stock to the index. The price index can be the index of the price of stocks in a given industry or a broad-based index of all stocks. If the ratio rises, it is presumed that the stock is in an uptrend relative to the index; if the ratio falls, it is presumed that the stock is in a downtrend relative to the index. Similarly, a relative strength measure can be calculated for an industry group relative to a broad-based index. Relative strength is also referred to as *price momentum* or *price persistence*.

Short Interest Ratio

Some technical analysts believe that the ratio of the number of shares sold short relative to the average daily trading volume is a technical signal that is valuable in forecasting the market. This ratio is called the *short interest ratio*. However, the economic link between this ratio and stock price movements can be interpreted in two ways. On one hand, some market observers believe that if this ratio is high, this is a signal that the market will advance. The argument is that short sellers will have to eventually cover their short position by buying the stocks they have shorted and, as a result, market prices will increase. On the other hand, there are some market observers who believe this a bearish signal being sent by market participants who have shorted stocks in anticipation of a declining market.

Market Overreaction

To benefit from favorable news or to reduce the adverse effect of unfavorable news, investors must react quickly to new information.[12]

---

[12] Werner DeBondt and Richard Thaler, "Does the Market Overreact?" *Journal of Finance* (July 1985), pp. 793–805.

According to cognitive psychologists, people tend to overreact to extreme events. People tend to react more strongly to recent information and they tend to heavily discount older information.

The question is, do investors follow the same pattern? That is, do investors overreact to extreme events? The *overreaction hypothesis* suggests that when investors react to unanticipated news that will benefit a company's stock, the price rise will be greater than it should be given that information, resulting in a subsequent decline in the price of the stock. In contrast, the overreaction to unanticipated news that is expected to adversely affect the economic well-being of a company will force the price down too much, followed by a subsequent correction that will increase the price.

If, in fact, the market does overreact, investors may be able to exploit this to realize positive abnormal returns if they can (1) identify an extreme event, and (2) determine when the effect of the overreaction has been impounded in the market price and is ready to reverse. Investors who are capable of doing this will pursue the following strategies. When positive news is identified, investors will buy the stock and sell it before the correction to the overreaction. In the case of negative news, investors will short the stock and then buy it back to cover the short position before the correction to the overreaction.

Nonlinear Dynamic Models and Chaos

Technical analysis has taken a more scientific twist with the development of nonlinear dynamics and chaos theory. Patterns generated by nonlinear dynamic models can be very complex and appear nearly random. A number of studies have tried to ascertain whether the apparent randomness of price processes could be generated by deterministic nonlinear processes. A chaotic process rapidly becomes unpredictable. There are, however, chaotic processes that are relatively simple and that maintain a certain level of predictability. Models of weather, for instance, are chaotic but still allow to make reasonable weather forecast.

A number of chaos scientists hoped to discover that economic laws could be expressed as simple chaotic processes. In particular, it was hoped to discover that price processes could be described as simple chaotic laws with some level of predictability. Should this be the case, chaos theory offers a reasonable toolbox to recover the chaotic model from past data. In fact, if the chaotic dynamic is simple, a fundamental theorem of chaos theory, the theorem of Takens, offers a way to fully reconstruct chaotic dynamics from a sufficient number of past data. In addition, functional approximation schemes such as neural networks could be used to approximate the chaotic dynamics.

The key point is that **Takens theorem** and all approximation schemes work only if the dynamic is simple.[13] A number of tests have been devised to check if economic and financial quantities can be effectively be represented as a simple chaotic laws. Among the tests, in particular the BDS test (see Chapter 9) is popular amongst economists. The results of tests are generally negative. There is no compelling evidence that reasonably simple chaotic dynamics can explain financial processes.

Despite these negative theoretical results, technical rules based on neural networks or directly on the Takens theorem have been proposed and continue to be proposed.

These rules have shown some result. This is not necessarily in contrast with the negative theoretical finding. One might find some profitability in trading rules even if the dynamics is theoretically not simple.

Technical Analysis and Statistical Nonlinear Pattern Recognition

Technical analysis can also be cast in terms of statistical pattern recognition. A number of models that fundamentally differ from a random walk or a martingale model have been proposed. *Pair trading* and *cointegration-based strategies* are perhaps the best known examples of statistical models that exploit statistical patterns.

The empirical literature offers contradicting evidence. There is agreement that asset price processes offer some level of forecastability.[14] There are also theoretical reasons to believe that price processes in a finite economy must exhibit cointegration[15] and therefore recognizable patterns. ARCH and GARCH behavior is another source of nonlinear statistical patterns. What is not clear, however, is the profitability that can be associated to these statistical findings once the trading costs are taken into account.

---

[13] Simple dynamics means that there is a low-dimensionality attractor. Chaos theory is a complex subject. The interested reader should consult Robert C. Hilborn, *Chaos and Nonlinear Dynamics* (New York: Oxford University Press, 2000).

[14] See W. Brock, J. Lakonishok, and B. LeBaron, "Simple Technical Trading Rules and the Stochastic Properties of Stock Returns," Working paper 90–22, Wisconsin Madison Social Systems; and John Campbell, Andrew Lo, and Craig MacKinlay, *The Econometrics of Financial Markets* (Princeton, NJ: Princeton University Press, 1997).

[15] See Marlene Cerchi and Arthur Havenner, "Cointegration and Stock Prices: The Random Walk on Wall Street Revisited," Journal *of Economic Dynamics and Control* 12 (1988), pp. 333–346; Peter Bossaerts, "Common Nonstationary Components of Asset Prices," *Journal of Economic Dynamics and Control* 12 (1988), pp. 347–364; and, Barr Rosenberg and J.A. Ohlson, "The Stationary Distribution of Returns and Portfolio Separation in Capital Markets: A Fundamental Contradiction," *Journal of Financial and Quantitative Analysis* 11 (1976), pp. 393–401.

Market-Neutral Strategies and Statistical Arbitrage

Market-neutral strategies are portfolio management strategies aimed at obtaining a positive return regardless of market conditions; a typical way to achieve this result is long-short equity portfolio management. In general, a market-neutral strategy will specify four elements:

- Market neutrality is normally defined as lack of correlation with some broad index such as the S&P 500.
- The return objective varies in function of market conditions. In a bear market, a market-neutral strategy might be happy with a modest 5% return while double-digit return rates might be required in normal conditions.
- In general, return volatility bounds are set low, significantly lower than the market volatility. Often this requirement is imposed by central banks.
- A maximum draw-down.

The above requirements might seem contrary to finance theory as they appear to violate the risk-return trade-offs of efficient markets. They might also seem contrary to common sense as conservative prescriptions for volatility and draw-dawns are coupled with aggressive return objectives. The only possible response to these criticisms is that market neutral-strategies represent only a small fraction of the market—those pockets of inefficiency inevitable in (and perhaps instrumental to) a large efficient market.

Let's now describe *statistical arbitrage*, a method used to obtain market neutral strategies. Statistical arbitrage exploits the existence of small probabilistic profit opportunities that become nearly deterministic on a large scale. It was made possible by the diffusion of electronic transactions that have greatly reduced transaction costs. Obviously transaction costs and bid-ask spreads might reduce profit opportunities to nearly zero or even cause losses.

To understand the working of statistical arbitrage, recall that in the limit of a large economy and under the assumption that it is possible to completely diversify portfolios, the APT conditions are valid. Recall also that the APT conditions are represented by zero intercept. The same condition is valid in the case of single-factor CAPM. As a consequence, if a large number of non-zero intercepts exist, then large profits can be made with zero initial investment and little risk.

To demonstrate the above, we start with a single-factor market model with nonzero intercepts:

$$r_i = \alpha_i + \beta_i r_M + \varepsilon$$

where the noise term exhibits only local correlation and tends to zero over large portfolios. Market return is stochastic and therefore uncertain. Suppose, however, that there are many returns with similar betas but with different alphas. The no-arbitrage condition forbids this situation for an infinite economy but leaves open the possibility that a finite number of such situations exist.

For each beta, or more likely for each beta band as betas will not be strictly equal, invest in a long portfolio with the positive alphas and a short portfolio with the negative alphas. Repeat the operation for each band of beta. The resulting portfolio will implement a simple statistical arbitrage strategy. It will be nearly market-neutral, with profit depending only on the spreads between alphas and not on the direction of the market.

There are several caveats. First, the appropriate distribution of betas and alphas must exist. This is an empirical question that cannot be solved a priori. Second, there are residual risks, as the noise term will be reduced but not completely eliminated and betas will not be strictly equal. Third, the factor model might be misspecified and therefore unstable.

Contrarian strategies where managers go short on overpriced stocks and long on underpriced stocks are also possible. Long-short strategies of this type started in the 1980s with so-called *pair trading* reportedly initiated by a trading group working at Morgan Stanley. Under the direction of Nunzio Tartaglia, this group's strategy consisted in forming pairs of stocks that had a small distance measured by the relative variance. Setting appropriate thresholds, underpriced stocks are bought and overpriced stocks sold.

The ideas underlying contrarian strategies are ultimately formalized by the concepts of cointegration and error correction. When applied to price, processes error correction represents changes in returns when prices diverge from some common trend. Many efforts at building true statistical arbitrage techniques therefore make use of cointegration techniques. In terms of cointegration, one implements statistical arbitrage by searching for cointegrating relationships. Each cointegrating relationship represents a stationary, mean-reverting portfolio. Being autocorrelated, these portfolios are more predictable than other portfolios or individual stocks.

As most implementations are proprietary, the different approaches are only partially described. The key problem is to find true cointegrated portfolios. In practice, there are several approaches; these include:

- *Searching for cointegrated pairs of stocks.* This can be performed with standard cointegration tests and techniques. However results are very noisy as a large fraction of the cointegrated pairs will be spurious. In practice, the number of cointegrated pairs has to be reduced.

■ *Searching for cointegrated indexes.* This is performed testing cointegration on existing, commercially available indexes. These indices typically reflect economic sectors or geographies. After determining that cointegration among the indexes exists, one has to select stocks within the index to reduce transaction costs.

■ *Searching for common trends.* This is a recent development in statistical arbitrage. It is based on approximate robust techniques for finding factors using state space models. Factors, in this sense, are linear combinations of price processes not of returns.

In summary, statistical arbitrage is a new methodology for managing long-short equity portfolios based on finding stable trends that signal profit opportunities. Trends might be determined with classical factor models of returns. More recently, cointegration techniques are being used.

APPLICATION OF MULTIFACTOR RISK MODELS

In the previous chapter, we explained how factors are determined. In this section we will see how multifactor risk models are used. In our illustration with use the Barra model described in the previous chapter.

Risk Decomposition

The real usefulness of a linear multifactor model lies in the ease with which the risk of a portfolio with several assets can be estimated. Consider a portfolio with 100 assets. Risk is commonly defined as the variance of the portfolio's returns. So, in this case, we need to find the variance-covariance matrix of the 100 assets. That would require us to estimate 100 variances (one for each of the 100 assets) and 4,950 covariances among the 100 assets. That is, in all we need to estimate 5,050 values, a very difficult undertaking. Suppose, instead, that we use a 3 factor model to estimate risk. Then, we need to estimate (1) the three factor loadings for each of the 100 assets (i.e., 300 values); (2) the six values of the factor variance-covariance matrix; and (3) the 100 residual variances (one for each asset). That is, in all, we need to estimate only 406 values. This represents a nearly 90% reduction from having to estimate 5,050 values, a huge improvement. Thus, with well-chosen factors, we can substantially reduce the work involved in estimating a portfolio's risk. Note that the ease of estimation of correlation parameters is another facet of the fact that factor models capture the stable correlation information.

Multifactor risk models allow a manager and a client to decompose risk in order to assess the *potential* performance of a portfolio to the risk factors and to assess the *potential* performance of a portfolio relative to a benchmark. This is the portfolio construction and risk control application of the model. Also, the *actual* performance of a portfolio relative to a benchmark can be assessed. This is the performance attribution analysis application of the model.

Barra suggests that there are various ways that a portfolio's total risk can be decomposed when employing a multifactor risk model.[16] Each decomposition approach can be useful to managers depending on the equity portfolio management that they pursue. The four approaches are (1) total risk decomposition; (2) systematic-residual risk decomposition; (3) active risk decomposition; and (4) active systematic-active residual risk decomposition. We describe each below and explain how managers pursuing different management strategies (i.e., active versus passive) will find the decomposition helpful in portfolio construction and evaluation.

In all of these approaches to risk decomposition, the total return is first divided into the risk-free return and the total excess return. The *total excess return* is the difference between the *actual* return realized by the portfolio and the risk-free return. The risk associated with the total excess return, called *total excess risk*, is what is further partitioned in the four approaches.

Total Risk Decomposition

There are managers who seek to minimize total risk. For example, a manager pursuing a long-short or market neutral strategy, as discussed later in this chapter, seek to construct a portfolio that minimizes total risk. For such managers, total risk decomposition which breaks down the total excess risk into two components—*common factor risks* (e.g., capitalization and industry exposures) and *specific risk*—is useful. This decomposition is shown in Exhibit 19.5. There is no provision for market risk, only risk attributed to the common factor risks and company-specific influences (i.e., risk unique to a particular company and therefore uncorrelated with the specific risk of other companies). Thus, the market portfolio is not a risk factor considered in this decomposition.

Systematic-Residual Risk Decomposition

There are managers who seek to time the market or who intentionally make bets to create a different exposure than that of a market portfolio. Such managers would find it useful to decompose total excess risk into systematic risk and residual risk as shown in Exhibit 19.6. Unlike in the

---

[16] See Chapter 4 in Barra, *Risk Model Handbook United States Equity: Version 3*. The discussion to follow in this section follows that in the Barra publication.

EXHIBIT 19.5 Total Risk Decomposition

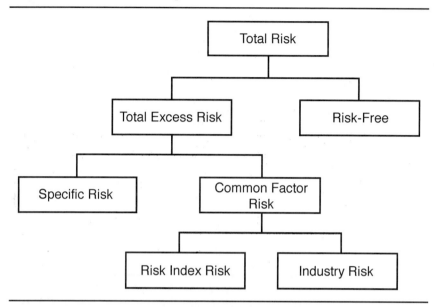

Source: Figure 4.2 in Barra, *Risk Model Handbook United States Equity: Version 3* (Berkeley, CA: Barra, 1998), p. 34. Reprinted with permission.

total risk decomposition approach just described, this view brings market risk into the analysis.

Residual risk in the systematic-residual risk decomposition is defined in a different way than residual risk is in the total risk decomposition. In the systematic-residual risk decomposition, residual risk is risk that is uncorrelated with the market portfolio. In turn, residual risk is partitioned into specific risk and common factor risk. Notice that the partitioning of risk described here is different from that in the APT model described earlier in this chapter. In that section, all risk factors that could not be diversified away were referred to as "systematic risks." In our discussion here, risk factors that cannot be diversified away are classified as market risk and common factor risk. Residual risk can be diversified to a negligible level.

Active Risk Decomposition

The active risk decomposition approach is useful for assessing a portfolio's risk exposure and actual performance relative to a benchmark index is explained. that purpose. In this type of decomposition, shown in Exhibit 19.7, the total excess return is divided into *benchmark risk* and *active risk*.

EXHIBIT 19.6   Systematic-Residual Risk Decomposition

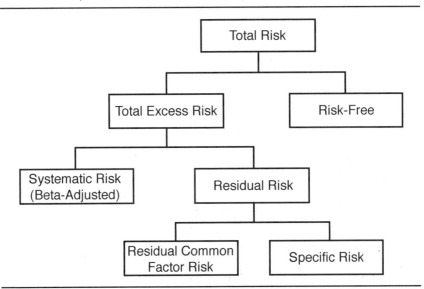

Source: Figure 4.3 in Barra, *Risk Model Handbook United States Equity: Version 3* (Berkeley, CA: Barra, 1998), p. 34. Reprinted with permission.

Benchmark risk is defined as the risk associated with the benchmark portfolio. Active risk or tracking error is the risk that results from the manager's attempt to generate a return that will outperform the benchmark. The active risk is further partitioned into common factor risk and specific risk.

Active Systematic-Active Residual Risk Decomposition

There are managers who overlay a market-timing strategy on their stock selection. That is, they not only try to select stocks they believe will outperform but also try to time the purchase of the acquisition. For a manager who pursues such a strategy, it will be important in evaluating performance to separate market risk from common factor risks. In the active risk decomposition approach just discussed, there is no market risk identified as one of the risk factors. Since market risk (i.e., systematic risk) is an element of active risk, its inclusion as a source of risk is preferred by managers. When market risk is included, we have the active systematic-active residual risk decomposition approach shown in Exhibit 19.8. Total excess risk is again divided into benchmark risk and active risk. However, active risk is further divided into active systematic risk (i.e., active market risk) and active residual risk. Then active residual risk is divided into common factor risks and specific risk.

EXHIBIT 19.7   Active Risk Decomposition

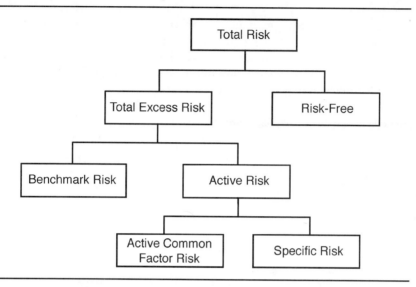

Source: Figure 4.4 in Barra, *Risk Model Handbook United States Equity: Version 3* (Berkeley, CA: Barra, 1998), p. 34. Reprinted with permission.

EXHIBIT 19.8   Active Systematic-Active Residual Risk Decomposition

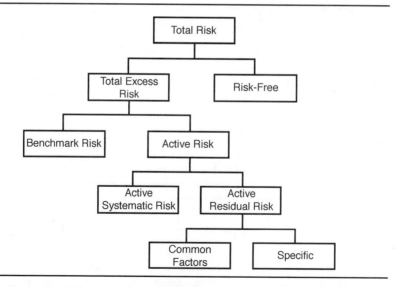

Source: Figure 4.5 in Barra, *Risk Model Handbook United States Equity: Version 3* (Berkeley, CA: Barra, 1998), p. 37. Reprinted with permission.

Summary of Risk Decomposition

The four approaches to risk decomposition are just different ways of slicing up risk to help a manager in constructing and controlling the risk of a portfolio and for a client to understand how the manager performed. Exhibit 19.9 provides an overview of the four approaches to carving up risk into specific/common risks, systematic/residual risks, and benchmark/active risks.

Portfolio Construction and Risk Control

The power of a multifactor risk model is that given the risk factors and the risk factor sensitivities, a portfolio's risk exposure profile can be quantified and controlled. The three examples below show how this can be done so that the a manager can avoid making unintended bets. In the examples, we use the Barra E3 factor model.[17]

EXHIBIT 19.9   Risk Decomposition Overview

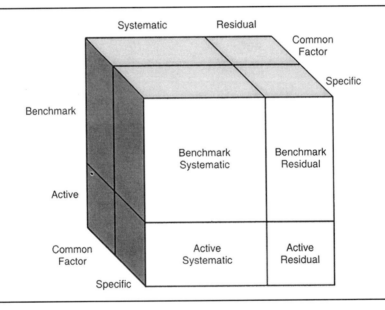

Source: Figure 4.6 in Barra, *Risk Model Handbook United States Equity: Version 3* (Berkeley, CA: Barra, 1998), p. 38. Reprinted with permission.

---

[17] The illustrations are taken from Frank J. Fabozzi, Frank J. Jones, and Raman Vardharaj, "Multi-Factor Risk Models," Chapter 13 in Frank J. Fabozzi and Harry M. Markowitz (eds.), *The Theory and Practice of Investment Management* (Hoboken, NJ: John Wiley & Sons, 2002).

Assessing the Exposure of a Portfolio

A fundamental multifactor risk model can be used to assess whether the current portfolio is consistent with a manager's strengths. Exhibit 19.10 is a list of the top 15 holdings of Portfolio ABC as of September 30, 2000. Exhibit 19.11 is a risk-return report for the same portfolio. The portfolio had a total market value of over $3.7 billion, 202 holdings, and a predicted beta of 1.20. The risk report also shows that the portfolio had an active risk of 9.83%. This is its tracking error with respect to the benchmark, the S&P 500. Notice that over 80% of the active risk variance (which is 96.67) comes from the common factor risk variance (which is 81.34), and only a small proportion comes from the stock-specific risk variance (which is 15.33). Clearly, the manager of this portfolio has placed fairly large factor bets.

Exhibit 19.12a assesses the factor risk exposures of Portfolio ABC relative to those of the S&P 500, its benchmark. The first column shows the exposures of the portfolio, and the second column shows the exposures for the benchmark. The last column shows the active exposure, which is

EXHIBIT 19.10   Portfolio ABC's Holdings (Only the Top 15 Holdings Shown)

Portfolio:	ABC Fund	Benchmark:	S&P 500	Model Date:	2000-10-02
Report Date:	2000-10-15	Price Date:	2000-09-29	Model:	U.S. Equity 3

Name	Shares	Price ($)	Weight (%)	Beta	Main Industry Name	Sector
General Elec. Co.	2,751,200	57.81	4.28	0.89	Financial Services	Financial
Citigroup, Inc.	2,554,666	54.06	3.72	0.98	Banks	Financial
Cisco Sys., Inc.	2,164,000	55.25	3.22	1.45	Computer Hardware	Technology
EMC Corp., Mass.	1,053,600	99.50	2.82	1.19	Computer Hardware	Technology
Intel Corp.	2,285,600	41.56	2.56	1.65	Semiconductors	Technology
Nortel Networks Corp. N	1,548,600	60.38	2.52	1.40	Electronic Equipment	Technology
Corning, Inc.	293,200	297.50	2.35	1.31	Electronic Equipment	Technology
International Business	739,000	112.50	2.24	1.05	Computer Software	Technology
Oracle Corp.	955,600	78.75	2.03	1.40	Computer Software	Technology
Sun Microsystems, Inc.	624,700	116.75	1.96	1.30	Computer Hardware	Technology
Lehman Bros. Hldgs. Inc.	394,700	148.63	1.58	1.51	Sec. & Asset Management	Financial
Morgan Stanley Dean Wi.	615,400	91.44	1.52	1.29	Sec. & Asset Management	Financial
Walt Disney Co.	1,276,700	38.25	1.32	0.85	Entertainment	Cnsmr. Services
Coca-Cola Co.	873,900	55.13	1.30	0.68	Food & Beverage	Cnsmr. (non-cyc.)
Microsoft Corp.	762,245	60.31	1.24	1.35	Computer Software	Technology

Source: Exhibit 13.7 in Frank J. Fabozzi, Frank J. Jones, and Raman Vardharaj, "Multi-Factor Risk Models," Chapter 13 in Frank J. Fabozzi and Harry M. Markowitz (eds.), *The Theory and Practice of Investment Management* (Hoboken, NJ: John Wiley & Sons, 2002).

EXHIBIT 19.11   Portfolio ABC's Risk-Return Decomposition

Number of Assets	202	Total Shares	62,648,570
		Average Share Price	$59.27
Portfolio Beta	1.20	Portfolio Value	$3,713,372,229.96

Risk Decomposition	Variance	Standard Deviation (%)
Active Specific Risk	15.33	3.92
Active Common Factor		
Risk Indices	44.25	6.65
Industries	17.82	4.22
Covariance	19.27	
Total Active Common Factor Risk[a]	81.34	9.02
Total Active[b]	96.67	9.83
Benchmark	247.65	15.74
Total Risk	441.63	21.02

[a] Equal to Risk Indices + Industries + Covariances
[b] Equal to Active Specific Risk + Total Active Common Factor Risk
Source: Exhibit 13.8 in Frank J. Fabozzi, Frank J. Jones, and Raman Vardharaj, "Multi-Factor Risk Models," Chapter 13 in Frank J. Fabozzi and Harry M. Markowitz (eds.), *The Theory and Practice of Investment Management* (Hoboken, NJ: John Wiley & Sons, 2002).

the difference between the portfolio exposure and the benchmark exposure. The exposures to the risk index factors are measured in units of standard deviation, while the exposures to the industry factors are measured in percentages. The portfolio has a high active exposure to the momentum risk index factor. That is, the stocks held in the portfolio have significant momentum. The portfolio's stocks were smaller than the benchmark average in terms of market cap. The industry factor exposures reveal that the portfolio had an exceptionally high active exposure to the semiconductor industry and electronic equipment industry. Exhibit 19.12b combines the industry exposures to obtain sector exposures. It shows that Portfolio ABC had a very high active exposure to the Technology sector. Such large bets can expose the portfolio to large swings in returns.

An important use of such risk reports is the identification of portfolio bets, both explicit and implicit. If, for example, the manager of Portfolio ABC did not want to place such a large Technology sector bet or momentum risk index bet, then she (or he) can rebalance the portfolio to minimize any such bets.

EXHIBIT 19.12   Analysis of Portfolio ABC's Exposures
a. Analysis of Risk Exposures to S&P 500

Factor Exposures

Risk Index Exposures (Std. Dev.)

	Mgd.	Bmk.	Act.		Mgd.	Bmk.	Act.
Volatility	0.220	−0.171	0.391	Value	−0.169	−0.034	−0.136
Momentum	0.665	−0.163	0.828	Earnings variation	0.058	−0.146	0.204
Size	−0.086	0.399	−0.485	Leverage	0.178	−0.149	0.327
Size nonlinearity	0.031	0.097	−0.067	Currency sensitivity	0.028	−0.049	0.077
Trading Activity	0.552	−0.083	0.635	Yield	−0.279	0.059	−0.338
Growth	0.227	−0.167	0.395	Non-EST universe	0.032	0.000	0.032
Earnings yield	−0.051	0.081	−0.132				

Industry Weights (Percent)

	Mgd.	Bmk.	Act.		Mgd.	Bmk.	Act.
Mining and Metals	0.013	0.375	−0.362	Heavy Machinery	0.000	0.062	−0.062
Gold	0.000	0.119	−0.119	Industrial Parts	0.234	1.086	−0.852
Forestry and Paper	0.198	0.647	−0.449	Electric Utility	1.852	1.967	−0.115
Chemicals	0.439	2.386	−1.947	Gas Utilities	0.370	0.272	0.098
Energy Reserves	2.212	4.589	−2.377	Railroads	0.000	0.211	−0.211
Oil Refining	0.582	0.808	−0.226	Airlines	0.143	0.194	−0.051
Oil Services	2.996	0.592	2.404	Truck/Sea/Air Freight	0.000	0.130	−0.130
Food & Beverages	2.475	3.073	−0.597	Medical Services	1.294	0.354	0.940
Alcohol	0.000	0.467	−0.467	Medical Products	0.469	2.840	−2.370
Tobacco	0.000	0.403	−0.403	Drugs	6.547	8.039	−1.492
Home Products	0.000	1.821	−1.821	Electronic Equipment	11.052	5.192	5.860
Grocery Stores	0.000	0.407	−0.407	Semiconductors	17.622	6.058	11.564
Consumer Durables	0.165	0.125	0.039	Computer Hardware	12.057	9.417	2.640
Motor Vehicles and Parts	0.000	0.714	−0.714	Computer Software	9.374	6.766	2.608
Apparel and Textiles	0.000	0.191	−0.191	Defense and Aerospace	0.014	0.923	−0.909
Clothing Stores	0.177	0.308	−0.131	Telephone	0.907	4.635	−3.728
Specialty Retail	0.445	2.127	−1.681	Wireless Telecom.	0.000	1.277	−1.277
Department Stores	0.000	2.346	−2.346	Information Services	0.372	1.970	−1.598
Constructn. and Real Prop.	0.569	0.204	0.364	Industrial Services	0.000	0.511	−0.511
Publishing	0.014	0.508	−0.494	Life/Health Insurance	0.062	1.105	−1.044
Media	1.460	2.077	−0.617	Property/Casualty Ins.	1.069	2.187	−1.118
Hotels	0.090	0.112	−0.022	Banks	5.633	6.262	−0.630
Restaurants	0.146	0.465	−0.319	Thrifts	1.804	0.237	1.567
Entertainment	1.179	1.277	−0.098	Securities and Asst. Mgmt.	6.132	2.243	3.888
Leisure	0.000	0.247	−0.247	Financial Services	5.050	5.907	−0.857
Environmental Services	0.000	0.117	−0.117	Internet	3.348	1.729	1.618
Heavy Electrical Eqp.	1.438	1.922	−0.483	Equity REIT	0.000	0.000	0.000

Note: Mgd. = Managed; Bmk. = S&P 500 (the benchmark); Act. = Active = Managed − Benchmark

EXHIBIT 19.12 (Continued)
b. Analysis of Sector Exposures Relative to S&P 500

Sector Weights (Percent)

	Mgd.	Bmk.	Act.		Mgd.	Bmk.	Act.
Basic Materials	0.65	3.53	−2.88	Utility	2.22	2.24	−0.02
Mining	0.01	0.38	−0.36	Electric Utility	1.85	1.97	−0.12
Gold	0.00	0.12	−0.12	Gas Utility	0.37	0.27	0.10
Forest	0.20	0.65	−0.45	Transport	0.14	0.54	−0.39
Chemical	0.44	2.39	−1.95	Railroad	0.00	0.21	−0.21
Energy	5.79	5.99	−0.20	Airlines	0.14	0.19	−0.05
Energy Reserves	2.21	4.59	−2.38	Truck Freight	0.00	0.13	−0.13
Oil Refining	0.58	0.81	−0.23	Health Care	8.31	11.23	−2.92
Oil Services	3.00	0.59	2.40	Medical Provider	1.29	0.35	0.94
Cnsmr (non-cyc.)	2.48	6.17	−3.70	Medical Products	0.47	2.84	−2.37
Food/Beverage	2.48	3.07	−0.60	Drugs	6.55	8.04	−1.49
Alcohol	0.00	0.47	−0.47	Technology	53.47	30.09	23.38
Tobacco	0.00	0.40	−0.40	Electronic Equipment	11.05	5.19	5.86
Home Prod.	0.00	1.82	−1.82	Semiconductors	17.62	6.06	11.56
Grocery	0.00	0.41	−0.41	Computer Hardware	12.06	9.42	2.64
Cnsmr. (cyclical)	1.36	6.01	−4.66	Computer Software	9.37	6.77	2.61
Cons. Durables	0.17	0.13	0.04	Defense and Aerospace	0.01	0.92	−0.91
Motor Vehicles	0.00	0.71	−0.71	Internet	3.35	1.73	1.62
Apparel	0.00	0.19	−0.19	Telecommunications	0.91	5.91	−5.00
Clothing	0.18	0.31	−0.13	Telephone	0.91	4.63	−3.73
Specialty Retail	0.45	2.13	−1.68	Wireless	0.00	1.28	−1.28
Dept. Store	0.00	2.35	−2.35	Commercial Services	0.37	2.48	−2.11
Construction	0.57	0.20	0.36	Information Services	0.37	1.97	−1.60
Cnsmr Services	2.89	4.69	−1.80	Industrial Services	0.00	0.51	−0.51
Publishing	0.01	0.51	−0.49	Financial	19.75	17.94	1.81
Media	1.46	2.08	−0.62	Life Insurance	0.06	1.11	−1.04
Hotels	0.09	0.11	−0.02	Property Insurance	1.07	2.19	−1.12
Restaurants	0.15	0.47	−0.32	Banks	5.63	6.26	−0.63
Entertainment	1.18	1.28	−0.10	Thrifts	1.80	0.24	1.57
Leisure	0.00	0.25	−0.25	Securities/Asst. Mgmt.	6.13	2.24	3.89
Industrials	1.67	3.19	−1.51	Financial Services	5.05	5.91	−0.86
Env. Services	0.00	0.12	−0.12	Equity REIT	0.00	0.00	0.00
Heavy Electrical	1.44	1.92	−0.48				
Heavy Mach.	0.00	0.06	−0.06				
Industrial Parts	0.23	1.09	−0.85				

Note: Mgd = Managed; Bmk = Benchmark; Act = Active = Managed − Benchmark
Source: Exhibit 13.9 in Frank J. Fabozzi, Frank J. Jones, and Raman Vardharaj, "Multi-Factor Risk Models," Chapter 13 in Frank J. Fabozzi and Harry M. Markowitz (eds.), *The Theory and Practice of Investment Management* (Hoboken, NJ: John Wiley & Sons, 2002).

Risk Control Against a Stock Market Index

The objective in equity indexing is to match the performance of some specified stock market index with little tracking error. To do this, the risk profile of the indexed portfolio must match the risk profile of the designated stock market index. Put in other terms, the factor risk exposure of the indexed portfolio must match as closely as possible the exposure of the designated stock market index to the same factors. Any differences in the factor risk exposures result in tracking error. Identification of any differences allows the indexer to rebalance the portfolio to reduce tracking error.

To illustrate this, suppose that an index manager has constructed a portfolio of 50 stocks to match the S&P 500. Exhibit 19.13 shows output of the exposure to the Barra risk indices and industry groups of the 50-stock portfolio and the S&P 500. The last column in the exhibit shows the difference in the exposure. The differences are very small except for the exposures to the size factor and one industry (equity REIT). That is, the 50-stock portfolio has more exposure to the size risk index and equity REIT industry.

The illustration in Exhibit 19.13 uses price data as of December 31, 2001. It demonstrates how a multifactor risk model can be combined with an optimization model to construct an indexed portfolio when a given number of holdings is sought. Specifically, the portfolio analyzed in Exhibit 19.13 is the result of an application in which the manager wants a portfolio constructed that matches the S&P 500 with only 50 stocks and that minimizes tracking error. Not only is the 50-stock portfolio constructed, but the optimization model combined with the factor model indicates that the tracking error is only 2.19%. Since this is the optimal 50-stock portfolio to replicate the S&P 500 that minimizes tracking error risk, this tells the index manager that if he or she seeks a lower tracking error, more stocks must be held. Note, however, that the optimal portfolio changes as time passes and prices move.

Tilting a Portfolio

Now let's look at how an active manager can construct a portfolio to make intentional bets. Suppose that a portfolio manager seeks to construct a portfolio that generates superior returns relative to the S&P 500 by tilting it toward low P/E stocks. At the same time, the manager does not want to increase tracking error significantly. An obvious approach may seem to be to identify all the stocks in the universe that have a lower than average P/E. The problem with this approach is that it introduces unintentional bets with respect to the other risk indices.

EXHIBIT 19.13   Factor Exposures of a 50-Stock Portfolio that Optimally Matches the S&P 500

Risk Index Exposures (Std. Dev.)

	Mgd.	Bmk.	Act.		Mgd.	Bmk.	Act.
Volatility	−0.141	−0.084	−0.057	Value	−0.072	−0.070	−0.003
Momentum	−0.057	−0.064	0.007	Earnings variation	−0.058	−0.088	0.029
Size	0.588	0.370	0.217	Leverage	−0.206	−0.106	−0.100
Size nonlinearity	0.118	0.106	0.013	Currency sensitivity	−0.001	−0.012	0.012
Trading activity	−0.101	−0.005	−0.097	Yield	0.114	0.034	0.080
Growth	−0.008	−0.045	0.037	Non-EST universe	0.000	0.000	0.000
Earnings yield	0.103	0.034	0.069				

Industry Weights (Percent)

	Mgd.	Bmk.	Act.		Mgd.	Bmk.	Act.
Mining and Metals	0.000	0.606	−0.606	Heavy Machinery	0.000	0.141	−0.141
Gold	0.000	0.161	−0.161	Industrial Parts	1.124	1.469	−0.345
Forestry and Paper	1.818	0.871	0.947	Electric Utility	0.000	1.956	−1.956
Chemicals	2.360	2.046	0.314	Gas Utilities	0.000	0.456	−0.456
Energy Reserves	5.068	4.297	0.771	Railroads	0.000	0.373	−0.373
Oil Refining	1.985	1.417	0.568	Airlines	0.000	0.206	−0.206
Oil Services	1.164	0.620	0.544	Truck/Sea/Air Freight	0.061	0.162	−0.102
Food and Beverages	2.518	3.780	−1.261	Medical Services	1.280	0.789	0.491
Alcohol	0.193	0.515	−0.322	Medical Products	3.540	3.599	−0.059
Tobacco	1.372	0.732	0.641	Drugs	9.861	10.000	−0.140
Home Products	0.899	2.435	−1.536	Electronic Equipment	0.581	1.985	−1.404
Grocery Stores	0.000	0.511	−0.511	Semiconductors	4.981	4.509	0.472
Consumer Durables	0.000	0.166	−0.166	Computer Hardware	4.635	4.129	0.506
Motor Vehicles & Parts	0.000	0.621	−0.621	Computer Software	6.893	6.256	0.637
Apparel and Textiles	0.000	0.373	−0.373	Defense and Aerospace	1.634	1.336	0.297
Clothing Stores	0.149	0.341	−0.191	Telephone	3.859	3.680	0.180
Specialty Retail	1.965	2.721	−0.756	Wireless Telecom.	1.976	1.565	0.411
Department Stores	4.684	3.606	1.078	Information Services	0.802	2.698	−1.896
Constructn. and Real Prop.	0.542	0.288	0.254	Industrial Services	0.806	0.670	0.136
Publishing	2.492	0.778	1.713	Life/Health Insurance	0.403	0.938	−0.535
Media	1.822	1.498	0.323	Property/Casualty Ins.	2.134	2.541	−0.407
Hotels	1.244	0.209	1.035	Banks	8.369	7.580	0.788
Restaurants	0.371	0.542	−0.171	Thrifts	0.000	0.362	−0.362
Entertainment	2.540	1.630	0.910	Securities and Asst. Mgmt.	2.595	2.017	0.577
Leisure	0.000	0.409	−0.409	Financial Services	6.380	6.321	0.059
Environmental Services	0.000	0.220	−0.220	Internet	0.736	0.725	0.011
Heavy Electrical Eqp.	1.966	1.949	0.017	Equity REIT	2.199	0.193	2.006

Note: Mgd = Managed; Bmk = S&P 500 (the benchmark); Act = Active = Managed − Benchmark

Source: Exhibit 13.10 in Frank J. Fabozzi, Frank J. Jones, and Raman Vardharaj, "Multi-Factor Risk Models," Chapter 13 in Frank J. Fabozzi and Harry M. Markowitz (eds.), *The Theory and Practice of Investment Management* (Hoboken, NJ: John Wiley & Sons, 2002).

Instead, an optimization method combined with a multifactor risk model can be used to construct the desired portfolio. The necessary inputs to this process are the tilt exposure sought and the benchmark stock market index. Additional constraints can be placed, for example, on the number of stocks to be included in the portfolio. The Barra optimization model can also handle additional specifications such as forecasts of expected returns or alphas on the individual stocks.

In our illustration, the tilt exposure sought is towards low P/E stocks, that is, towards high earnings yield stocks (since earnings yield is the inverse of P/E). The benchmark is the S&P 500. We seek a portfolio that has an average earnings yield that is at least 0.5 standard deviations more than that of the earnings yield of the benchmark. We do not place any limit on the number of stocks to be included in the portfolio. We also do not want the active exposure to any other risk index factor (other than earnings yield) to be more than 0.1 standard deviations in magnitude. This way we avoid placing unintended bets. While we do not report the holdings of the optimal portfolio here, Exhibit 19.14 provides an analysis of that portfolio by comparing the risk exposure of the 50-stock optimal portfolio to that of the S&P 500.

SUMMARY

- The investing process involves forming reasonable return expectations, controlling portfolio risk to demonstrate investment prudence, controlling trading costs, and monitoring total investment performance.
- The different degrees of active management and different degrees of passive management can be measured in terms of tracking error.
- The active return is the difference between the actual portfolio return for a given period and the benchmark index return for the same period.
- Alpha is defined as the average active return over some time period.
- The information ratio is the ratio of alpha to the tracking error.
- Tracking error is the standard deviation of the active return and occurs because the risk profile of a portfolio differs from that of the risk profile of the benchmark index.
- Backward-looking tracking error measures the tracking error based on active returns; forward-looking tracking error measures the potential tracking error of a portfolio.
- Portfolio size, benchmark volatility, and portfolio beta have an impact on tracking error.

EXHIBIT 19.14   Factor Exposures of a Portfolio Tilted Towards Earnings Yield

Risk Index Exposures (Std. Dev.)

	Mgd.	Bmk.	Act.		Mgd.	Bmk.	Act.
Volatility	−0.126	−0.084	−0.042	Value	0.030	−0.070	0.100
Momentum	0.013	−0.064	0.077	Earnings variation	−0.028	−0.088	0.060
Size	0.270	0.370	−0.100	Leverage	−0.006	−0.106	0.100
Size nonlinearity	0.067	0.106	−0.038	Currency sensitivity	−0.105	−0.012	−0.093
Trading activity	0.095	−0.005	0.100	Yield	0.134	0.034	0.100
Growth	−0.023	−0.045	0.022	Non-EST universe	0.000	0.000	0.000
Earnings Yield	0.534	0.034	0.500				

Industry Weights (Percent)

	Mgd.	Bmk.	Act.		Mgd.	Bmk.	Act.
Mining and Metals	0.022	0.606	−0.585	Heavy Machinery	0.000	0.141	−0.141
Gold	0.000	0.161	−0.161	Industrial Parts	1.366	1.469	−0.103
Forestry and Paper	0.000	0.871	−0.871	Electric Utility	4.221	1.956	2.265
Chemicals	1.717	2.046	−0.329	Gas Utilities	0.204	0.456	−0.252
Energy Reserves	4.490	4.297	0.193	Railroads	0.185	0.373	−0.189
Oil Refining	3.770	1.417	2.353	Airlines	0.000	0.206	−0.206
Oil Services	0.977	0.620	0.357	Truck/Sea/Air Freight	0.000	0.162	−0.162
Food and Beverages	0.823	3.780	−2.956	Medical Services	0.000	0.789	−0.789
Alcohol	0.365	0.515	−0.151	Medical Products	1.522	3.599	−2.077
Tobacco	3.197	0.732	2.465	Drugs	7.301	10.000	−2.699
Home Products	0.648	2.435	−1.787	Electronic Equipment	0.525	1.985	−1.460
Grocery Stores	0.636	0.511	0.125	Semiconductors	3.227	4.509	−1.282
Consumer Durables	0.000	0.166	−0.166	Computer Hardware	2.904	4.129	−1.224
Motor Vehicles and Parts	0.454	0.621	−0.167	Computer Software	7.304	6.256	1.048
Apparel and Textiles	0.141	0.373	−0.232	Defense and Aerospace	1.836	1.336	0.499
Clothing Stores	0.374	0.341	0.033	Telephone	6.290	3.680	2.610
Specialty Retail	0.025	2.721	−2.696	Wireless Telecom.	2.144	1.565	0.580
Department Stores	3.375	3.606	−0.231	Information Services	0.921	2.698	−1.777
Constructn. and Real Prop.	9.813	0.288	9.526	Industrial Services	0.230	0.670	−0.440
Publishing	0.326	0.778	−0.452	Life/health Insurance	1.987	0.938	1.048
Media	0.358	1.498	−1.140	Property/Casualty Ins.	4.844	2.541	2.304
Hotels	0.067	0.209	−0.141	Banks	8.724	7.580	1.144
Restaurants	0.000	0.542	−0.542	Thrifts	0.775	0.362	0.413
Entertainment	0.675	1.630	−0.955	Securities and Asst. Mgmt.	3.988	2.017	1.971
Leisure	0.000	0.409	−0.409	Financial Services	5.510	6.321	−0.811
Environmental Services	0.000	0.220	−0.220	Internet	0.434	0.725	−0.291
Heavy Electrical Eqp.	1.303	1.949	−0.647	Equity REIT	0.000	0.193	−0.193

Note: Mgd = Managed; Bmk = S&P 500 (the benchmark); Act = Active = Managed – Benchmark

Source: Exhibit 13.11 in Frank J. Fabozzi, Frank J. Jones, and Raman Vardharaj, "Multi-Factor Risk Models," Chapter 13 in Frank J. Fabozzi and Harry M. Markowitz (eds.), *The Theory and Practice of Investment Management* (Hoboken, NJ: John Wiley & Sons, 2002).

■ Practitioners view categories of stocks with similar historical performance as a "style" of investing with the two main style categories being growth and value.

■ There are methodologies for classifying stocks into style categories.

■ There are two types of passive strategies: a buy-and-hold strategy and an indexing strategy with the latter being the more common strategy pursued by institutional investors.

■ In constructing the tracking or indexed portfolio a manager can use the capitalization approach which involves either purchasing all stock issues included in the benchmark index in proportion to their weightings or purchasing a number of the largest capitalized names in the benchmark index and equally distributes the residual stock weighting across the other issues in the benchmark index.

■ Two approaches to construct an indexed portfolio with fewer stock issues than the benchmark index are the cellular (or stratified sampling) method and the multifactor risk model method.

■ The "fundamental law of active management" explains how the information ratio changes as a function of the depth of an active manager's skill and the breadth or number of independent insights or investment opportunities.

■ Technical analysis strategies are active management strategies whose overlying principle is to detect changes in the supply of and demand for a stock and capitalize on the expected changes.

■ Technical analysis has taken a more scientific twist with the development of nonlinear dynamics and chaos theory.

■ Market-neutral strategies seek a positive return regardless of market conditions. A typical way to achieve this result is by constructing an appropriate portfolio consisting of long and short equity positions.

■ Statistical arbitrage is a new methodology for managing long-short equity portfolios based on finding stable trends that signal profit opportunities.

■ Multifactor risk models permit the decomposition of risk in order to assess the potential performance of a portfolio to the risk factors, the potential performance of a portfolio relative to a benchmark, and the actual performance of a portfolio relative to a benchmark

■ In risk decomposition, the total return is first divided into the risk-free return and the total excess return (the difference between the actual return realized by the portfolio and the risk-free return); the total excess risk is further partitioned into specific/common risks, systematic/residual risks, and benchmark/active risks.

CHAPTER 20

Term Structure Modeling and Valuation of Bonds and Bond Options

In this chapter we introduce the concepts and mathematical technology of bond and bond option valuation. We will begin by analyzing the behavior of bond prices in a deterministic interest rate environment (i.e., assuming that interest rates are known at every future date). We will then move on to a full stochastic description of interest rates and of the term structure of interest rates and will tackle bond and bond option valuation problems in this environment.

The term structure of interest rates plays a key role in financial decision-making and investment management. Richard McEnally and James Jordan[1] provide the following list of uses for the term structure of interest rates:

■ Analyzing the potential returns for investments with different maturities.
■ Assessing market consensus expectations of future interest rates.
■ Pricing bonds and other fixed-income contractual obligations.
■ Pricing contingent claims in which the underlying is a fixed-income security.
■ Arbitraging between bonds with different maturities.
■ Forming expectations about the economy (e.g., economic activity and inflation).

---

[1] Richard W. McEnally and James V. Jordan, "The Term Structure of Interest Rates," Chapter 43 in Frank J. Fabozzi (ed.), *The Handbook of Fixed Income Securities: Fifth Edition* (Chicago: Irwin Professional Publishing, 1997), pp. 818–822.

The estimation of the term structure of interest rates is referred to as *term structure modeling*. We will explain how this is done in this chapter.

BASIC PRINCIPLES OF VALUATION OF DEBT INSTRUMENTS

A useful way of understanding the valuation of debt instruments and how this relates to interest rates is to use the principle that, in perfect markets, all riskless instruments have the same short-term return which must coincide with the riskless short-term rate for that period. This condition may be expected to be enforced through arbitrage. The 1-period rate of return from, say, an instrument with maturity n and a cash flow denoted by $(a_1, ..., a_n)$, consists of the cash payment, a_1, plus the capital gain, or the difference between the next-period price and the current price of the security, expressed as a percentage of initial value.

Let us denote by $_nP_j$ the price j periods $(j < n)$ from the present of an instrument maturing n periods later; the capital gain for the current period is: $_{n-1}P_1 - {_n}P_0$. Hence the condition that the 1-period return from holding the instrument must be equal to the short-term rate for the forthcoming period, denoted by r_1, can be written as

$$\frac{a_1 + ({_{n-1}}P_1 - {_n}P_0)}{{_n}P_0} = r_1 \tag{20.1}$$

Solving for $_nP_0$,

$$_nP_0 = \frac{a_1 + {_{n-1}}P_1}{1 + r_1} \tag{20.2}$$

The reason why the right-hand side of equation (20.2) must be the equilibrium price of the n-period asset is that, as can be verified, if the current price, $_nP_0$, were larger than the right-hand side of equation (20.2), then the 1-period return of the debt instrument, given by equation (20.1), would be smaller than the return r_1 obtainable by investing in the 1-period debt instrument. As a result, no one would want to hold it, causing its price to drop. Similarly, if $_nP_0$ is smaller than the right-hand side of equation (20.2), this yield for the debt instrument would be larger than r_1, and everyone would want to hold it.

Next we observe that $_{n-1}P_1$ must satisfy an equation like equation (20.2), or

$$_{n-1}P_1 = \frac{a_2 + {}_{n-2}P_2}{1 + r_2}$$

Substituting this equation into equation (20.2), we get

$$_nP_0 = \frac{a_1}{(1 + r_1)} + \frac{a_2 + {}_{n-2}P_2}{(1 + r_1)(1 + r_2)}$$

Repeating the same substitution recursively, up to the maturity of the debt instrument, we find

$$_nP_0 = \frac{a_1}{(1 + r_1)} + \frac{a_2}{(1 + r_1)(1 + r_2)} + \ldots + \frac{a_n}{(1 + r_1)(1 + r_2)\ldots(1 + r_n)} \quad (20.3)$$

In other words, the debt instrument must equal the sum of the present value of the payments that the debtor is required to make until maturity.

Let's illustrate the principles to this point. Assume that the length of a period is one year. Suppose that an investor purchases a 4-year debt instrument with the following payments promised by the borrower:

Year	Interest Payment	Principal Repayment	Cash Flow
1	$100	$0	$100
2	120	0	120
3	140	0	140
4	150	1,000	1,150

In terms of our notation: $a_1 = \$100$; $a_2 = \$120$; $a_3 = \$140$; $a_4 = \$1,150$. Assume that the 1-year rates for the next four years are: $r_1 = 0.07$; $r_2 = 0.08$; $r_3 = 0.09$; $r_4 = 0.10$. The current value or price of this debt instrument today, denoted $_4P_0$, using equation (20.3) is then

$$_4P_0 = \frac{100}{(1.07)} + \frac{120}{(1.07)(1.08)} + \frac{140}{(1.07)(1.08)(1.09)}$$
$$+ \frac{1,150}{(1.07)(1.08)(1.09)(1.10)} = \$1,138.43$$

YIELD-TO-MATURITY MEASURE

Next we must consider how to construct a measure that will permit us to compare the rate of return of debt instruments having different cash flows and different maturities. For 1-period debt instruments, the measure is clear; it is provided by the left-hand side of equation (20.1). But that approach cannot be generalized readily to long-term debt instruments. For instance, for an instrument with a cash flow (a_1, a_2), the measure $(a_1 + a_2)/P_0$ would not be a useful measure of yield. In the first place, if we seek a measure that can be used to compare instruments of different maturities, it must measure return per unit of time. And second, the proposed measure ignores the timing of receipts, thus failing to reflect the time value of money.

The widely accepted solution to this problem is provided by a measure known as the *yield to maturity*. It is defined as the interest rate that makes the present value of the cash flow equal to the market value (price) of the instrument. Thus for the debt instrument in equation (20.3), the yield to maturity is the interest rate y that satisfies the following equation:

$$_nP_0 = \frac{a_1}{(1+y)} + \frac{a_2}{(1+y)^2} + \dots + \frac{a_n}{(1+y)^n} \tag{20.4}$$

In general, the yield to maturity must be found by trial and error or by using an iterative technique like Newton-Raphson. If the debt instrument is a bond, the cash flow $(a_1 \dots a_n)$ can be written as $(C, C, \dots, C + M)$, where C is the coupon payment and M the maturity value. Equation (20.4) can be rewritten as

$$P = \frac{C}{(1+y)} + \frac{C}{(1+y)^2} + \dots + \frac{C+M}{(1+y)^n} \tag{20.5}$$

After dividing both sides of equation (20.5) by M, to obtain the price per dollar of maturity value, and factoring C, we obtain

$$\frac{P}{M} = \frac{C}{M}\sum_{t=1}^{n}\frac{1}{(1+y)^t} + \frac{1}{(1+y)^n} \tag{20.6}$$

Recognizing that the summation on the right-hand side of equation (20.6) is the sum of a geometric progression, we can rewrite the equation as

$$\frac{P}{M} = \frac{C}{M}\left[\frac{1-(1+y)^{-n}}{y}\right] + \frac{1}{(1+y)^{n}} \tag{20.7}$$

The yield to maturity is the solution to equation (20.7) for y, the yield of an n-period bond. In equation (20.7) P/M is the so-called *par value relation*, usually expressed as a percentage. If it is equal to one, the bond sells "at par"; if it is larger than one, it sells at a "premium"; and if it is less than one, it sells at a "discount." C/M is the coupon rate expressed as a ratio.

So far we have not specified the unit of time for measuring the frequencies with which interest is computed and the coupons are paid. Interest rates (and maturity) customarily are quoted per year (e.g., 7% per year), and we shall follow this convention; this means that in equation (20.7) it is implicitly assumed that the coupon rate is C per year and paid once a year. In fact, in the United States almost all bonds pay interest twice a year. Each coupon payment therefore amounts to $C/2$, which must be discounted twice a year at half the annual yield or $y/2$. As a result, equation (20.7) is changed to

$$\frac{P}{M} = \frac{C}{2M}\left[\frac{1-(1+y/2)^{-2n}}{y/2}\right] + \frac{1}{(1+y/2)^{2n}} \tag{20.8}$$

To illustrate calculation of the yield to maturity of a bond with semiannual coupon payments, consider a 7%, 20-year bond with a maturity or par value of $100, and selling for 74.26%, or 74.26 cents per $1 of par value. The cash flow for this bond per dollar of par value is: 40 six-month payments of $0.035, and $1 received in 40 six-month periods from now. The present value at various semiannual interest rates $(y/2)$ is:

Interest rate $(y/2)$:	3.5%	4.0%	4.5%	5.0%	5.5%	6.0%	6.5%
Present value (P/M):	1.0000	0.9010	0.8160	0.7426	0.6791	0.6238	0.5756

When a 5.0% semiannual interest rate is used, the present value of the cash flows is equal to 0.7426 per $1 of par value, which is the price of the bond. Hence, 5.0% is the semiannual yield to maturity.

The annual yield to maturity should, strictly speaking, be found by compounding 5.0% for one year. That is, it should be 10.25. But the convention adopted by the bond market is to double $y/2$, the semiannual yield to maturity. Thus, the yield to maturity for the bond above is 10% (two times 5.0%). The yield to maturity computed using this convention of doubling the semiannual yield is called the *bond equivalent yield*.

Premium Par Yield

In general, equation (20.7) and equation (20.8) cannot be solved explicitly for y (for $n > 2$); these equations must be solved by trial and error or by using an iterative technique—with one important exception. It is apparent from equation (20.7) that the par value, P/M, increases as the coupon rate, C/M, increases. Now consider a bond whose coupon rate is such that the corresponding value of P/M is one—that is, the bond sells at par. Then equation (20.7) becomes:

$$1 = \frac{C}{M}\left[\frac{1-(1+y)^{-n}}{y}\right] + \frac{1}{(1+y)^n} \tag{20.9}$$

Equation (20.9) can be solved explicitly for y; the solution is $y = C/M$. In other words, if a bond sells at par, its yield to maturity is the same as its coupon rate; for example, if a 7.75%, 20-year bond sells at par, its yield to maturity is 7.75%. This means that, for a bond to be issued at par, the coupon rate offered must be the same as the market-required yield for that maturity. The coupon rate of an n-period bond selling at par may be labeled the *n-period par yield*.

It can also be verified from equation (20.9) that if the coupon rate on a bond is less than the required yield to maturity, or par yield, the bond will sell at a discount; the converse is true for a bond with a coupon above par yield. The explanation for this relation is self-evident: if the cash payment per period—namely, the coupon is below the required yield per period, the difference must be made up by an increase in price, or capital gain, over the life of the bond. This requires that the price of the bond be lower than its maturity value. In the United States, bonds (other than zero-coupon bonds) customarily are issued with a yield to maturity as to insure that the issue sells at close to par.

Reinvestment of Cash Flow and Yield

The yield to maturity takes into account the coupon income and any capital gain or loss that the investor will realize by holding the bond to maturity. The measure has its shortcomings, however. We might think that if we acquire for P a bond of maturity n and yield y, then at maturity we can count on obtaining a terminal value equal to $P(1 + y)^n$. This inference is not justified. By multiplying both sides of equation (20.5) by $(1 + y)^n$, we obtain

$$P(1 + y)^n = C(1 + y)^{n-1} + C(1 + y)^{n-2} + C + M$$

For the terminal value to be $P(1 + y)^n$, each of the coupon payments must be reinvested until maturity at an interest rate equal to the yield to maturity. If the coupon payment is semiannual, then each semiannual payment must be reinvested at the yield y.

Clearly, as the equation indicates, the investor will realize the yield to maturity that is calculated at the time of purchase only if (1) all the coupon payments can be reinvested at the yield to maturity, and (2) the bond is held to maturity. With respect to the first assumption, the risk that an investor faces is that future interest rates at which the coupon can be reinvested will be less than the yield to maturity at the time the bond is purchased. This risk is referred to as *reinvestment risk*. And if the bond is not held to maturity, it may have to be sold for less than its purchase price, resulting in a return that is less than the yield to maturity. The risk that a bond will have to be sold at a loss is referred to as *interest rate risk*.

Our focus in this section has been on coupon-bearing bonds. In the special case of a bond that produces only one cash flow, the maturity value, the yield to maturity does measure the rate at which the initial investment rises. We can see this if we substitute zero for the coupon payments in the last equation. As explained in Chapter 3, bonds that do not make coupon payments are called zero-coupon bonds. The advantage of these bonds is that they do not expose the investor to reinvestment risk. Zero-coupon bonds play a key role in the valuation process as explained later.

THE TERM STRUCTURE OF THE INTEREST RATES AND THE YIELD CURVE

The relationship between the yield on bonds of the same credit quality but different maturities is generically referred to as the *term structure of interest rates*. The graphical depiction of the term structure of interest rates is called the *yield curve*.

There are different yield measures that can be used to construct the yield curve. As we will see in this chapter, the alternative yield measures that can be used are (1) the yield to maturity on a country's benchmark government bonds; (2) the spot rate; (3) the forward rates; and (4) and the swap rate. We will explain the last three yield measures later in this chapter. Market participants typically construct yield curves from the market prices and yields in the government bond market of a country or from swap rates. As we will see, the other two rates—spot rates and forward rates—are derived from market information.

In the United States it is the U.S. Treasury securities market and the resulting yield curve is referred to as the *Treasury yield curve*. Two reasons account for this tendency. First, Treasury securities are free of default risk, and differences in creditworthiness do not affect yield estimates. Second, the Treasury market offers the fewest problems of illiquidity or infrequent trading.

Typically in constructing a yield curve using Treasury yields the on-the-run Treasury issues are used. These are the most recently auctioned Treasury issues. In the United States, the U.S. Department of the Treasury currently issues 3-month and 6-month Treasury bills and 2-year, 5-year, and 10-year Treasury notes. Treasury bills are zero-coupon instruments and Treasury notes are coupon-paying instruments. Hence, there are not many data points from which to construct a Treasury yield curve, particularly after two years. At one time, the U.S. Treasury issued 30-year securities (referred to as Treasury bonds). However, the Treasury stopped this practice. In constructing a Treasury yield curve, market participants use the last issued Treasury bond (which has a maturity less than 30 years) to estimate the 30-year yield. The 2-year, 5-year, and 10-year Treasury notes and an estimate of the 30-year Treasury bond is used to construct the Treasury yield curve. On September 5, 2003, Lehman Brothers reported the following values for these four yields:

2 year	1.71%
5 year	3.25%
10 year	4.35%
30 year	5.21%

To fill in the yield for the 25 missing whole year maturities (3 year, 4 year, 6 year, 7 year, 8 year, 9 year, 11 year, and so on to the 29-year maturity), the yield for the 25 whole-year maturities are interpolated from the yield on the surrounding maturities. The simplest interpolation, and the one most commonly used in practice, is simple linear interpolation.

For example, suppose that we want to fill in the gap for each one year of maturity. To determine the amount to add to the on-the-run Treasury yield as we go from the lower maturity to the higher maturity, the following formula is used:

$$(y_H - y_L)/N$$

where:

y_H = yield at higher maturity
y_L = yield at lower maturity
N = number of years between two observed maturity points

The estimated on-the-run yield for all intermediate whole-year maturities is found by adding to the yield at the lower maturity the amount computed from the above formula.

For example, using the September 5, 2003 yields, the 5-year yield is 3.25% and the 10-year yield is the 4.35%% are used to obtain the interpolated 6-year, 7-year, 8-year, and 9-year yields by first calculating:

$$(4.35\% - 3.25\%)/5 = 0.22\%$$

Then,

$$
\begin{aligned}
\text{interpolated 6-year yield} &= 3.25\% + 0.22\% = 3.47\% \\
\text{interpolated 7-year yield} &= 3.47\% + 0.22\% = 3.69\% \\
\text{interpolated 8-year yield} &= 3.69\% + 0.22\% = 3.91\% \\
\text{interpolated 9-year yield} &= 3.91\% + 0.22\% = 4.13\%
\end{aligned}
$$

Thus, when market participants talk about a yield on the Treasury yield curve that is not one of the on-the-run maturities—for example, the 8-year yield—it is only an approximation. Notice that there is a large gap between the maturity points. This may result in misleading yields for the interim maturity points when estimated using the linear interpolation method.

Another factor complicates the relationship between maturity and Treasury yield in constructing the Treasury yield curve. The yield for on-the-run Treasury issues may be distorted by the fact that these securities can be financed at cheaper rates and as a result can offer a lower yield than in the absence of this financing advantage. There are investors who purchase securities with borrowed funds and use the securities purchased as collateral for the loan. This type of collateralized borrowing is called a *repurchase agreement*. Since dealers, for whatever reason, want to obtain use of these securities for their own trading activities, they are willing to loan funds to investors at a lower interest rate than is otherwise available for borrowing in the market. Consequently, impounded into the price of an on-the-run Treasury security is the cheaper financing available, resulting in a lower yield for an on-the-run than would prevail in the absence of attractive financeability.

From a practical viewpoint, the key function of the Treasury yield curve is to serve as a benchmark for pricing bonds and setting yields in all other sectors of the debt market—bank loans, mortgages, corporate debt, and international bonds. However, the Treasury yield curve is an unsatisfactory measure of the relation between required yield and maturity. The key reason is that securities with the same maturity may actually carry different yields. This phenomenon reflects the role and impact of differences in the bonds' coupon rates. Hence, it is necessary to develop more accurate and reliable estimates of the term structure of interest rates. We will show how this is done later. Basically, the approach consists of identifying yields that apply to zero-coupon bonds and, therefore, eliminates the problem of nonuniqueness in the yield-maturity relationship.

Limitations of Using the Yield to Value a Bond

The price of a bond is the present value of its cash flow. However, in our illustrations and our discussion of the pricing of a bond above, we assume that one interest rate should be used to discount all the bond's cash flows. The appropriate interest rate is the yield on a Treasury security, with the same maturity as the bond, plus an appropriate risk premium or spread.

To illustrate the problem with using the Treasury yield curve to determine the appropriate yield at which to discount the cash flow of a bond, consider the following two hypothetical 5-year Treasury bonds, A and B. The difference between these two Treasury bonds is the coupon rate, which is 12% for A and 3% for B. The cash flow for these two bonds per $100 of par value for the 10 six-month periods to maturity would be:

Period	Cash Flow for A	Cash Flow for B
1–9	$6.00	$1.50
10	106.00	101.50

Because of the different cash flow patterns, it is not appropriate to use the same interest rate to discount all cash flows. Instead, each cash flow should be discounted at a unique interest rate that is appropriate for the time period in which the cash flow will be received. But what should be the interest rate for each period?

The correct way to think about bonds A and B in order to avoid arbitrage opportunities is not as bonds but as packages of cash flows. More specifically, they are packages of zero-coupon instruments. Thus, the interest earned is the difference between the maturity value and the price paid. For example, bond A can be viewed as 10 zero-coupon instruments: one with a maturity value of $6 maturing six months from now; a second with a maturity value of $6 maturing one year from now; a third with a maturity value of $6 maturing 1.5 years from now, and so on. The final zero-coupon instrument matures 10 six-month periods from now and has a maturity value of $106. Likewise, bond B can be viewed as 10 zero-coupon instruments: one with a maturity value of $1.50 maturing six months from now; one with a maturity value of $1.50 maturing one year from now; one with a maturity value of $1.50 maturing 1.5 years from now, and so on. The final zero-coupon instrument matures 10 six-month periods from now and has a maturity value of $101.50. Obviously, in the case of each coupon bond, the value or price of the bond is equal to the total value of its component zero-coupon instruments.

Valuing a Bond as a Package of Cash Flows

In general, any bond can be viewed as a package of zero-coupon instruments. That is, each zero-coupon instrument in the package has a maturity equal to its coupon payment date or, in the case of the principal, the maturity date. The value of the bond should equal the value of all the component zero-coupon instruments. If this does not hold, it is possible for a market participant to generate riskless profits by stripping the security and creating stripped securities. We will demonstrate this later in this chapter.

To determine the value of each zero-coupon instrument, it is necessary to know the yield on a zero-coupon Treasury with that same maturity that we referred to as the spot rate earlier. The spot rate curve is the graphical depiction of the relationship between the spot rate and its maturity. Because there are no zero-coupon Treasury debt issues with a maturity greater than one year issued by the U.S. Department of the Treasury, it is not possible to construct such a curve solely from observations of market activity. Rather, it is necessary to derive this curve from theoretical considerations as applied to the yields of actual Treasury securities. Such a curve is called a *theoretical spot rate curve*.

Obtaining Spot Rates from the Treasury Yield Curve

We will now explain the process of creating a theoretical spot rate curve from the yield curve that is based on the observed yields of Treasury securities. The process involves the following:

1. Select the universe of Treasury securities to be used to construct the theoretical spot rates.
2. Obtain the theoretical spot rates using bootstrapping.
3. Create a smooth continuous curve.

We will return to the first and the third tasks later in this chapter. For now, we want to show how the theoretical spot rates can be obtained from the interpolated yields on Treasury securities (i.e., the Treasury yield curve). To simplify the illustration, we will assume that an estimated Treasury yield curve is as shown in Exhibit 20.1. The 6-month and 1-year Treasury securities are assumed to be zero-coupon Treasury securities.

The process of extracting the theoretical spot rates from the Treasury yield curve is called *bootstrapping*. To explain this process, we use the data for the price, annualized yield (yield to maturity), and maturity

EXHIBIT 20.1   Hypothetical Treasury Yields (Interpolated)

Period	Years	Annual Par Yield to Maturity (BEY) (%)[a]	Price	Spot Rate (BEY) (%)[a]
1	0.5	3.00	—	3.0000
2	1.0	3.30	—	3.3000
3	1.5	3.50	100.00	3.5053
4	2.0	3.90	100.00	3.9164
5	2.5	4.40	100.00	4.4376
6	3.0	4.70	100.00	4.7520
7	3.5	4.90	100.00	4.9622
8	4.0	5.00	100.00	5.0650
9	4.5	5.10	100.00	5.1701
10	5.0	5.20	100.00	5.2772
11	5.5	5.30	100.00	5.3864
12	6.0	5.40	100.00	5.4976
13	6.5	5.50	100.00	5.6108
14	7.0	5.55	100.00	5.6643
15	7.5	5.60	100.00	5.7193
16	8.0	5.65	100.00	5.7755
17	8.5	5.70	100.00	5.8331
18	9.0	5.80	100.00	5.9584
19	9.5	5.90	100.00	6.0863
20	10.0	6.00	100.00	6.2169

[a] The yield to maturity and the spot rate are annual rates. They are reported as bond-equivalent yields. To obtain the semiannual yield or rate, one half the annual yield or annual rate is used.

of the 20 hypothetical Treasury securities shown in Exhibit 20.1. The basic principle of bootstrapping is that the value of the Treasury security should be equal to the value of the package of zero-coupon Treasury securities that duplicates the coupon bond's cash flow.

Consider the 6-month and 1-year Treasury securities in Exhibit 20.1. These securities are assumed to be zero-coupon instruments. Therefore, their annualized yield of 3% and 3.3% are respectively the 6-month spot and the rate 1-year spot rate. Given these two spot rates, we can compute the spot rate for a theoretical 1.5-year zero-coupon Treasury. The price of a theoretical 1.5-year Treasury should equal the present value of three cash flows from an actual 1.5-year coupon Treasury, where the yield used for discounting is the spot rate corresponding to the cash flow. Using \$100 as par, the cash flow for the 1.5-year coupon Treasury is \$1.75 for the first two 6-month periods and \$101.75 in 1.5 years when the bond matures. Letting z_t represent one-half the annualized spot rate for period t, then the absence of arbitrage requires that the present value of the three cash flows when discounted at the spot rates equal the market price, \$100 in our illustration. That is,

$$\frac{1.75}{(1+z_1)^1} + \frac{1.75}{(1+z_2)^2} + \frac{101.75}{(1+z_3)^3} = 100$$

Since the 6-month spot rate and 1-year spot rate are 3.0% and 3.3%, respectively, we know that: $z_1 = 0.015$ and $z_2 = 0.0165$. Substituting these spot rates into the above equation and solving for z_3, we obtain 1.7527%. Doubling this yield, we obtain the bond-equivalent yield of 3.5053%, which is the theoretical 1.5-year spot rate. That rate is the spot rate that the market would apply to a 1.5-year zero-coupon Treasury security if, in fact, such a security existed.

Given the theoretical 1.5-year spot rate, we can obtain the theoretical 2-year spot rate. The cash flows for the 2-year coupon Treasury security follows from Exhibit 20.1. Since the annual coupon rate is 3.9%, the cash flow for the first three periods is \$1.95 and the cash flow for the fourth period is \$101.95. Given the spot rate for the first three periods ($z_1 = 0.015$, $z_2 = 0.0165$, and $z_3 = 0.017527$), the 4-period spot rate is then found by solving the following equation:

$$\frac{1.95}{(1.015)^1} + \frac{1.95}{(1.0165)^2} + \frac{1.95}{(1.017527)^3} + \frac{101.95}{(1+z_4)^4} = 100$$

The value for z_4 is 0.019582 or 1.9582%. Doubling this yield, we obtain the theoretical 2-year spot rate bond-equivalent yield of 3.9164%.

One can follow this approach sequentially to derive the theoretical 2.5-year spot rate from the calculated values of z_1, z_2, z_3, and z_4, and the price and coupon of the 2.5-year bond in Exhibit 20.1. Further, one could derive theoretical spot rates for the remaining 15 half-yearly rates.

The spot rates thus obtained are shown in the last column of Exhibit 20.1. They represent the term structure of Treasury spot rates for maturities up to 10 years.

In practice, yields for interim maturities are not readily available for government bond markets. Hence, to construct a continuous spot rate curve requires the use of a methodology described later in this chapter.

Using Spot Rates to the Arbitrage-Free Value of a Bond

Finance theory tells us that the theoretical price of a Treasury security should be equal to the present value of the cash flow where each cash flow is discounted at the appropriate theoretical spot rate For example, if the Treasury spot rates shown in the last column of Exhibit 20.1 are used to compute the arbitrage-free value of an 8% 10-year Treasury security, the present value of the cash flow would be found to be $115.2619. If a 4.8% coupon 10-year Treasury bond is being valued based on the Treasury spot rates shown in Exhibit 20.1, the arbitrage-free value is $90.8428.

Suppose that the 8% coupon, 10-year Treasury issue is valued using the traditional approach based on 6% (i.e., the yield on a 10-year Treasury coupon bond shown in Exhibit 20.1). Discounting all cash flows at 6% would produce a value for the 8% coupon bond of $114.8775. Consider what would happen if the market priced the security at $114.8775. The value based on the Treasury spot rates is $115.2619. Faced with this situation, a securities dealer can buy the 8% 10-year issue for $114.8775, strip off each coupon payment and the maturity value, and sell each cash flow in the market at the spot rates shown in Exhibit 20.1. By doing so, the proceeds that will be received by the dealer are $115.2619. This results in an arbitrage profit of $0.3844 (= $115.2619 − $114.8775). Securities dealers recognizing this arbitrage opportunity will bid up the price of the 8% 10-year Treasury issue in order to acquire it and strip it. Once the price is up to around $115.2619 (the arbitrage-free value), the arbitrage opportunity is eliminated.

We have just demonstrated how stripping of a Treasury issue will force the market value to be close to its arbitrage-free value when the market price is less than the arbitrage-free value. When a Treasury issue's market price is greater than the arbitrage-free value, a securities dealer can capture the arbitrage value by a process referred to as *reconstitution*. Basically, the securities dealer can purchase a package of stripped Treasury securities traded in the market so as to create a synthetic Treasury coupon security that is worth more than the same maturity and the same coupon Treasury issue. The sale of the resulting synthetic coupon security that is created will force the price down to its arbitrage-free value.

The Discount Function

A more convenient way of characterizing the term structure of interest rates is by means of the discount function. The discount function specifies the present value of a cash flow in the future. It can therefore be interpreted as the price of a pure risk-free discount bond of a given maturity with a $1 face value. The discount function (D_n) is related to spot rates as follows:

$$D_n = \frac{1}{(1 + z_n)^n}$$

The reason for describing the term structure in terms of the discount function is that bond prices can be expressed in an easy way in terms of it. The price of a bond is simply the sum of the products of the cash flow expected from the bond at time t and the discount function for time t. That is, for a bond with a maturity n and a cash flow of C for periods $1,...,n-1$ and maturity value of M, the price is

$$\sum_{t-1}^{n-1} D_t C + D_n (C + M)$$

Forward Rates

In addition to spot rates and discount functions to describe the term structure, there is another important analytical concept that can be used to describe the term structure: *forward* rates. Forward rates can be derived from the Treasury yield curve by using arbitrage arguments, just as we did for spot rates.

To illustrate the process of obtaining 6-month forward rates, we will use the yield curve and corresponding spot rate curve from Exhibit 20.1. For this construction, we will use a very simple arbitrage: If two investments have the same cash flows and have the same risk, they should have the same value.

Consider an investor who has a 1-year investment horizon and is faced with the following two alternatives:

- *Alternative* 1. Buy a 1-year Treasury security
- *Alternative* 2. Buy a 6-month Treasury security and, when it matures in six months, buy another 6-month Treasury security

The investor will be indifferent toward the two alternatives if they produce the same return over the 1-year investment horizon. The investor knows the spot rate on the 6-month Treasury security and the 1-year Treasury security. However, he does not know what yield will be available on a 6-month Treasury security that will be purchased six months from now. That is, he does not know the 6-month forward rate six months from now. Given the spot rates for the 6-month Treasury security and the 1-year Treasury security, the forward rate on a 6-month Treasury security is the rate that equalizes the dollar return between the two alternatives.

Letting $X denote the face amount of the 6-month Treasury security, z_1 is one-half the bond-equivalent yield (BEY) of the theoretical 6-month spot rate, and z_2 represents one-half the BEY of the theoretical 1-year spot rate, then the investor will be indifferent toward the two alternatives if

$$X(1 + z_1)(1 + f) = X(1 + z_2)^2$$

where f is the 6-month forward rate six months from now. Solving, we get

$$f = \frac{(1 + z_2)^2}{(1 + z_1)} - 1$$

Doubling f gives the BEY for the 6-month forward rate six months from now. In our illustration, f is 1.8% and therefore the 6-month forward rate on a BEY basis is 3.6%.

We can generalize the 1-period forward rates as follows.[2] Let f_n denote the 1-period forward rate contract that will begin at time n. Then f_0 is simply the current 1-period spot rate.

Exhibit 20.2 shows all of the 6-month (i.e., 1-period) forward rates for the Treasury yield curve and corresponding spot rate curve shown in Exhibit 20.1. The forward rates reported in Exhibit 20.2 are the annualized rates on a bond-equivalent basis. The set of these forward rates is called the *short-term forward-rate curve*.

The relationship between the n-period spot rate, the current 6-month spot rate, and the 6-month forward rates is as follows:

$$z_n = [(1 + z_1)(1 + f_1)(1 + f_2) ... (1 + f_{n-1})]^{1/n} - 1$$

The discount function can be expressed in terms of forward rates as follows:

$$D_n = \frac{1}{[(1 + z_1)(1 + f_1)(1 + f_2)...(1 + {}_1f_{n-1})]^{1/n} - 1}$$

Swap Curve

Instead of using a government spot rate curve, market participants are more often using the swap curve or London Interbank Offered Rate (LIBOR) curve for reasons described below. A swap curve is derived

---

[2] We will generalize the notation later in this chapter when continuous time is used.

EXHIBIT 20.2   Short-Term Forward Rates

Notation	Forward Rate
$_1f_0$	3.00
$_1f_1$	3.60
$_1f_2$	3.92
$_1f_3$	5.15
$_1f_4$	6.54
$_1f_5$	6.33
$_1f_6$	6.23
$_1f_7$	5.79
$_1f_8$	6.01
$_1f_9$	6.24
$_1f_{10}$	6.48
$_1f_{11}$	6.72
$_1f_{12}$	6.97
$_1f_{13}$	6.36
$_1f_{14}$	6.49
$_1f_{15}$	6.62
$_1f_{16}$	6.76
$_1f_{17}$	8.10
$_1f_{18}$	8.40
$_1f_{19}$	8.72

from observed swap rates in the interest rate swap market. In a generic interest rate swap two parties agree to exchange cash flows based on a notional amount where (1) one party pays a fixed rate and receives a floating rate and (2) the other party agrees to pay a floating rate and receives a fixed rate. The fixed rate is called the *swap rate*. A swap curve can be constructed that is unique to a country where there is a swap market for converting fixed cash flows to floating cash flows in that country's currency.

Typically, the reference rate for the floating rate is 3-month LIBOR. Effectively, the swap curve indicates the fixed rate (i.e., swap rate) that a party must pay to lock in 3-month LIBOR for a specified future period. By locking in 3-month LIBOR it is meant that a party that pays the floating rate (i.e., agrees to pay 3-month LIBOR) is locking in a borrowing rate; the party receiving the floating rate is locking in an amount to be received. Because 3-month LIBOR is being exchanged, the swap curve is also called the LIBOR curve.

The convention in the swap market is to quote the reference rate flat (i.e., no spread) and quote the fixed-rate side as a spread over a benchmark (typically the yield on a government bond) with the same maturity as the swap.

Effectively the swap rate reflects the risk of the counterparty to the swap failing to satisfy its obligation. Consequently, the swap curve does not reflect rates for a default-free obligation. Instead, the swap curve reflects credit risk. Since the counterparty in swaps are typically bank-related entities, the swap curve reflects the credit risk of the banking sector—effectively, it is an interbank or AA rated curve.

Investors and issuers use the swap market for hedging and arbitrage purposes, and the swap curve as a benchmark for evaluating performance of fixed-income securities and the pricing of fixed-income securities. Since the swap curve is effectively the LIBOR curve and investors borrow based on LIBOR, the swap curve is more useful to funded investors than a government yield curve.

The increased application of the swap curve for these activities is due to its advantages over using the government bond yield curve as a benchmark. Before identifying these advantages, it is important to understand that the drawback of the swap curve relative to the government bond yield curve could be poorer liquidity. In such instances, the swap rates would reflect a liquidity premium. Fortunately, liquidity is not an issue in many countries as the swap market has become highly liquid, with narrow bid-ask spreads for a wide range of swap maturities. In some countries swaps may offer better liquidity than that country's government bond market. The advantages of the swap curve over a government bond yield curve are:[3]

1. There is almost no government regulation of the swap market. The lack of government regulation makes swap rates across different markets more comparable. In some countries, there are some sovereign issues that offer various tax benefits to investors and, as a result, for global investors it makes comparative analysis of government rates across countries difficult because some market yields do not reflect their true yield.
2. The supply of swaps depends only on the number of counterparties that are seeking or are willing to enter into a swap transaction at any given time. Since there is no underlying government bond, there

[3] See Uri Ron, "A Practical Guide to Swap Curve Construction," Chapter 6 in Frank J. Fabozzi (ed.), *Interest Rate, Term Structure, and Valuation Modeling* (New York: John Wiley & Sons, 2002).

can be no effect of market technical factors that may result in the yield for a government bond issue being less than its true yield.[4]

3. Comparisons across countries of government yield curves is difficult because of the differences in sovereign credit risk. In contrast, the credit risk as reflected in the swaps curve are similar and make comparisons across countries more meaningful than government yield curves. Sovereign risk is not present in the swap curve because, as noted earlier, the swap curve is viewed as an interbank yield curve or AA yield curve.

4. There are more maturity points available to construct a swap curve than a government bond yield curve. More specifically, what is quoted daily in the swap market are swap rates for 2-, 3-, 4-, 5-, 6-, 7-, 8-, 9-, 10-, 15-, and 30-year maturities. Thus, in the swap market there are 10 market interest rates with a maturity of two years and greater. In contrast, in the U.S. Treasury market, for example, there are only three market interest rates for on-the-run Treasuries with a maturity of two years or greater (2, 5, and 10 years) and one of the rates, the 10-year rate, may not be a good benchmark because it is often on special in the repo market. Moreover, because the U.S. Treasury has ceased the issuance of 30-year bonds, there is no 30-year yield available.

In the valuation of fixed-income securities, it is not the Treasury yield curve that is used as the basis for determining the appropriate discount rate for computing the present value of cash flows but the Treasury spot rates. The Treasury spot rates are derived from the Treasury yield curve using the bootstrapping process. Similarly, it is not the swap curve that is used to for discounting cash flows when the swap curve is the benchmark but the corresponding spot rates. The spot rates are derived from the swap curve in exactly the same way—using the bootstrapping methodology. The resulting spot rate curve is called the *LIBOR spot rate curve*. Moreover, a forward rate curve can be derived from the spot rate curve. The same thing is done in the swap market. The forward rate curve that is derived is called the *LIBOR forward rate curve*.

Consequently, if we understand the mechanics of moving from the yield curve to the spot rate curve to the forward rate curve in the Treasury market, there is no reason to repeat an explanation of that process here for the swap market; that is, it is the same methodology, just different yields are used.

---

[4] For example, a government bond issue being on "special" in the repurchase agreement market.

CLASSICAL ECONOMIC THEORIES ABOUT THE DETERMINANTS OF THE SHAPE OF THE TERM STRUCTURE

As mentioned earlier, the Treasury yield curve shows the relationship between the yield to maturity on Treasury securities and maturity. Historically, three shapes have been observed: an upward sloping yield curve (the most typical and therefore referred to as a "normal" yield curve), an downward sloping yield curve (also referred to as an "inverted" yield curve), and a flat yield curve. Exhibit 20.3 shows the yield curve for four countries on September 5, 2003 and September 12, 2003: United States, Germany, United Kingdom, and Japan. Notice that all four yield curves are upward sloping.

While we know that the yield curve is not the same as the term structure of interest rates, what will the shape of the spot rate curve and short-term forward rate curve look like? If the yield curve is upward sloping, the spot rate curve will lie above the yield curve, and the forward rate curve

EXHIBIT 20.3   Global Bellwether Yield Curves, September 5, 2003 and September 12, 2003

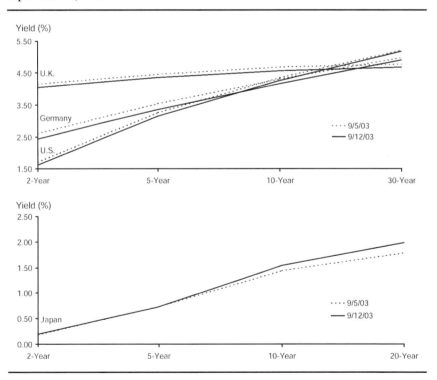

EXHIBIT 20.3   (*Continued*)

		Yields (%)			
		2-Yr	5-Yr	10-Yr	30-Yr
United	9/5/03	1.71	3.25	4.35	5.21
States	9/12/03	1.62	3.15	4.26	5.17
	W-o-W Chg (bp)	−9	−10	−9	−4
Germany	9/5/03	2.60	3.54	4.30	4.98
	9/12/03	2.44	3.36	4.17	4.90
	W-o-w Chg (bp)	−16	−18	−13	−8
United	9/5/03	4.16	4.46	4.69	4.77
Kingdom	9/12/03	4.05	4.36	4.57	4.69
	W-o-w Chg (bp)	−11	−10	−12	−8
Japan	9/5/03	0.19	0.74	1.44	1.79
	9/12/03	0.20	0.73	1.54	1.98
	W-o-w Chg (bp)	1	−1	10	19

Source: Lehman Brothers, "Global Relative Value," *Fixed Income Research*, September 8, 2003, p. 13.

will lie above the spot rate curve. The reverse is true if the yield curve is downward sloping. If the yield curve is flat, all three curves are flat.

Two major economic theories have evolved to account for these observed shapes of the yield curve: *expectations theories* and *market segmentation theory*. We describe these theories below. However, these are qualitative theories that tend to explain general features of market behavior. The quantitative determination of interest rates is a major problem of macroeconomics; it is made particularly challenging by the fact that interest rates are influenced by both market forces and by the decisions of central banks. In principle, General Equilibrium Theories (GET) can determine interest rates endogenously. However, GET remain an abstract tool; it is virtually impossible to apply them to practical forecasting. In practice, the forecast of interest rates for bond and bond option valuation is made using econometric models. Later in this chapter we will take a look at the structure and form of econometric models used to forecast interest rates, or represent their stochastic evolution.

Expectations Theories

There are several forms of the expectations theory: *pure expectations theory*, *liquidity theory*, and *preferred habitat theory*. Expectations theories share a hypothesis about the behavior of short-term forward rates and also assume that the forward rates in current long-term bonds are closely related to the market's expectations about future short-term rates. These three expectations theories differ, however, as to whether other factors also affect forward rates, and how. The pure expectations theory postulates that no systematic factors other than expected future short-term rates affect forward rates; the liquidity theory and the preferred habitat theory assert that there are other factors. Accordingly, the last two forms of the expectations theory are sometimes referred to as *biased expectations theories*.

Pure Expectations Theory

According to the pure expectations theory, the forward rates exclusively represent the expected future spot rates. Thus the entire term structure at a given time reflects the market's current expectations of the family of future short-term rates. Under this view, a rising term structure must indicate that the market expects short-term rates to rise throughout the relevant future. Similarly, a flat term structure reflects an expectation that future short-term rates will be mostly constant, and a falling term structure must reflect an expectation that future short rates will decline steadily.

We can illustrate this theory by considering how the expectation of a rising short-term future rate would affect the behavior of various market participants so as to result in a rising yield curve. Assume an initially flat term structure, and suppose that subsequent economic news leads market participants to expect interest rates to rise.

1. Those market participants interested in long-term bonds would not want to buy long-term bonds because they would expect the yield structure to rise sooner or later, resulting in a price decline for the bonds and a capital loss on the long-term bonds purchased. Instead, they would want to invest in short-term debt obligations until the rise in yield had occurred, permitting them to reinvest their funds at the higher yield.
2. Speculators expecting rising rates would anticipate a decline in the price of long-term bonds and therefore would want to sell any long-term bonds they own and possibly to "short sell" some they do not own. (Should interest rates rise as expected, the price of longer-term bonds will fall. Because the speculator sold these bonds short and can then purchase them at a lower price to cover the short sale, a profit will be earned.) Speculators will reinvest in short-term bonds.
3. Borrowers wishing to acquire long-term funds would be pulled toward borrowing now in the long end of the market by the expectation that borrowing at a later time would be more expensive.

All these responses would tend either to lower the net demand for, or to increase the supply of, long-maturity bonds, and all three responses would increase demand for short-term bonds. This would require a rise in long-term yields in relation to short-term yields; that is, these actions by investors, speculators, and borrowers would tilt the term structure upward until it is consistent with expectations of higher future interest rates. By analogous reasoning, an unexpected event leading to the expectation of lower future rates will result in the yield curve sloping downward.

Unfortunately, the pure expectations theory suffers from one shortcoming, which, qualitatively, is quite serious. It neglects the risks inherent in investing in bonds. If forward rates were perfect predictors of future interest rates, the future prices of bonds would be known with certainty. The return over any investment period would be certain and independent of the maturity of the instrument initially acquired and of the time at which the investor needed to liquidate the instrument. However, with uncertainty about future interest rates and hence about future prices of bonds, these instruments become risky investments in the sense that the return over some investment horizon is unknown.

There are two risks that cause uncertainty about the return over some investment horizon: interest rate risk and reinvestment risk. *Interest rate risk* is the uncertainty about the price of the bond at the end of the investment horizon. For example, an investor who plans to invest for five years might consider the following three investment alternatives: (1) invest in a 5-year bond and hold it for five years; (2) invest in a 12-year bond and sell it at the end of five years; and (3) invest in a 30-year bond and sell it at the end of five years. The return that will be realized for the second and third alternatives is not known because the price of each long-term bond at the end of five years is not known. In the case of the 12-year bond, the price will depend on the yield on 7-year debt securities five years from now; and the price of the 30-year bond will depend on the yield on 25-year bonds five years from now. Because forward rates implied in the current term structure for a future 12-year bond and a future 25-year bond are not perfect predictors of the actual future rates, there is uncertainty about the price for both bonds five years from now. Thus there is interest rate risk; that is, the risk that the price of the bond will be lower than currently expected at the end of the investment horizon. An important feature of interest rate risk is that it is greater the longer the maturity of the bond.

The second risk has to do with the uncertainty about the rate at which the proceeds from a bond can be reinvested until the expected maturity date. This risk is referred to as *reinvestment risk*. For example, an investor who plans to invest for five years might consider the following three alternative investments: (1) invest in a 5-year bond and hold it for five years; (2) invest in a 6-month instrument and when it matures, reinvest the proceeds in six-month instruments over the entire 5-year investment horizon; and (3) invest in a 2-year bond and when it matures, reinvest the proceeds in a 3-year bond. The risk in the second and third alternatives is that the return over the 5-year investment horizon is unknown because rates at which the proceeds can be reinvested until maturity are unknown.

As noted by John Cox, Jonathan Ingersoll, and Stephen Ross, in practice, there are at least five variants of the pure expectations theory that have been put forth in the financial literature.[5]

1. Globally equal expected-holding-period return theory
2. Local expectations theory
3. Unbiased expectations theory
4. Return-to-maturity expectations theory
5. Yield-to-maturity theory[6]

The *globally expected-holding-period return theory* asserts that the expected return for a given holding period is the same regardless of the maturity of the bonds held. So, for example, an investor who has a holding period of three years is expected to have the same 5-year return whether the investor (1) purchased a 1-year bond today and when it matures reinvests the proceeds in a 4-year bond; (2) purchased a 2-year bond today and when it matures reinvest the proceeds in a 3-year bond; or (3) purchased a 10-year bond and sold it at the end of three years. The globally expected-holding-period return theory is the broadest interpretation of the pure expectations theory.

The second variant of the pure expectations theory, the *local expectations theory*, is more restrictive about the relevant holding period for which the returns are expected to be equal. It is restricted to short-term holding periods that begin today. An investor with a 6-month holding period, for example, would have the same expected return if (1) a 6-month bond is purchased today; (2) a 3-year bond is purchased today; or (3) a 20-year bond is purchased today.

The *unbiased expectations theory* asserts that the spot rates that the market expects in the future are equal to today's the forward rates.

---

[5] John Cox, Jonathan Ingersoll, and Stephen Ross, "A Re-examination of Traditional Hypotheses about the Term Structure of Interest Rates," *Journal of Finance* (September 1981), pp. 769–799.

[6] The labels for the last four variants of the pure expectations theory are those given by Cox, Ingersoll, and Ross. The first label is given by McEnally and Jordan, "The Term Structure of Interest Rates," p. 829.

Thus, the forward rates are viewed as the market's consensus of future interest rates. The *return-to-maturity theory* asserts that the return that can be realized if a zero-coupon bond is held to maturity is the same return expected by following a strategy of buying shorter term maturity bonds and reinvesting them until the maturity of the zero-coupon bond. For example, if an investor purchases a 5-year zero-coupon bond, then the known return from holding that bond to maturity is the same as the expected return from buying a 6-month bond today and reinvesting the proceeds when it matures in another six-month bond and then continuing to reinvest in six-month instruments until the end of the fifth year. The *yield-to-maturity theory* asserts the same as in the return-to-maturity theory except that this variant of the pure expectations theory is in terms of periodic returns.

As Cox, Ingersoll, and Ross have demonstrated, these interpretations are not exact equivalents nor are they consistent with each other, in large part because they offer different treatments of the two risks associated with realizing a return (i.e., interest rate risk and reinvestment risk). Furthermore, Cox, Ingersoll, and Ross showed that only one of the five variants of the pure expectations theory is consistent with equilibrium: the local expectations theory.

Liquidity Theory

We have explained that the drawback of the pure expectations theory is that it does not consider the risks associated with investing in bonds. Nonetheless, there is indeed risk in holding a long-term bond for one period, and that risk increases with the bond's maturity because maturity and price volatility are directly related. Given this uncertainty, and the reasonable consideration that investors typically do not like uncertainty, some economists and financial analysts have suggested a different theory. This theory states that investors will hold longer-term maturities if they are offered a long-term rate higher than the average of expected future rates by a risk premium that is positively related to the term to maturity. Put differently, the forward rates should reflect both interest rate expectations and a "liquidity" premium (really a risk premium), and the premium should be higher for longer maturities.

According to this theory, which is called the *liquidity theory of the term structure*, the implied forward rates will not be an unbiased estimate of the market's expectations of future interest rates because they embody a liquidity premium. Thus, an upward-sloping yield curve may reflect expectations that future interest rates either (1) will rise, or (2) will be flat or even fall, but with a liquidity premium increasing fast enough with maturity so as to produce an upward-sloping yield curve.

Preferred Habitat Theory

Another theory, known as *the preferred habitat theory*, also adopts the view that the term structure reflects the expectation of the future path of interest rates as well as a risk premium. However, the preferred habitat theory rejects the assertion that the risk premium must rise uniformly with maturity. Proponents of the preferred habitat theory say that the latter conclusion could be accepted if all investors intend to liquidate their investment at the shortest possible date while all borrowers are anxious to borrow long. This assumption can be rejected since institutions have holding periods dictated by the nature of their liabilities.

The preferred habitat theory asserts that, to the extent that the demand and supply of funds in a given maturity range do not match, some lenders and borrowers will be induced to shift to maturities showing the opposite imbalances. However, they will need to be compensated by an appropriate risk premium whose magnitude will reflect the extent of aversion to either price or reinvestment risk. Thus, this theory proposes that the shape of the yield curve is determined by both expectations of future interest rates and a risk premium, positive or negative, to induce market participants to shift out of their preferred habitat. Clearly, according to this theory, yield curves sloping up, down, flat, or humped are all possible.

Market Segmentation Theory

The *market segmentation theory* also recognizes that investors have preferred habitats dictated by the nature of their liabilities. This theory also proposes that the major reason for the shape of the yield curve lies in asset/liability management constraints (either regulatory or self-imposed) and/or creditors (borrowers) restricting their lending (financing) to specific maturity sectors. However, the market segmentation theory differs from the preferred habitat theory in that it assumes that neither investors nor borrowers are willing to shift from one maturity sector to another to take advantage of opportunities arising from differences between expectations and forward rates. Thus, for the segmentation theory, the shape of the yield curve is determined by supply of and demand for securities within each maturity sector.

BOND VALUATION FORMULAS IN CONTINUOUS TIME

Recall that the price of a coupon-paying bond can be expressed as the price of a package of cash flows as follows:

$$P = \frac{C}{(1 + z_1)^1} + \frac{C}{(1 + z_2)^2} + \ldots + \frac{C + M}{(1 + z_N)^N}$$

where z_i is the spot rate relative to the i-th period. The coefficients

$$D_i = \frac{1}{(1 + z_i)^i}$$

are called the discount function or discount factors.

In continuous time, as it will be demonstrated in the below, if short-term interest rates are constant, the bond valuation formula is

$$P = \frac{C}{e^{1 \times i}} + \frac{C}{e^{2 \times i}} + \ldots + \frac{C + M}{e^{N \times i}}$$

If short-term rates are variable, the formula is:

$$P = Ce^{-\int_0^1 i(s)\,ds} + Ce^{-\int_0^2 i(s)\,ds} + \ldots + (C + M)e^{-\int_0^N i(s)\,ds}$$

To consider bond valuation in continuous time, we will use many relationships related to yield and interest rates in a stochastic environment. We begin by explicitly computing a number of these relationships in a deterministic environment (that is, assuming that interest rates are a known function of time) then extending these relationships to a stochastic environment.

In the case of a zero-coupon bond, the financial principles of valuation are those illustrated earlier when we considered very small time intervals, in the limit infinitesimal time interval. We denote by T the time of maturity of a bond. At a point in time $s < T$ the time to maturity is $t = T - s$. In the infinitesimal interval dt, the bond value $P(t)$ changes by an amount dP according to the following equation:

$$dP = -iP\,dt$$

where i is the deterministic short-term interest rate.

If M is the principal to be repaid at maturity, we have the initial condition $M = P(0)$. The solution of this an ordinary differential equation with separable variables whose solution is

$$P = Me^{-it} = Me^{-i(T-s)}$$

If the interest rate is a known function of time, the above equation becomes

$$dP = -i(t)Pdt$$

This too is an equation with separable variables whose solution is

$$P = Me^{-\int_s^T i(u)du}$$

where M is the principal to be repaid. The equivalence pathwise between capital appreciation and present value is valid only if interest rates are known.

In the above expression, the interest rate i is the instantaneous rate of interest, also called the *short-term rate*. In continuous time, the short-term rate is the limit of the interest rate over a short time interval when the interval goes to zero. As observations can only be performed at discrete dates, the short-term rate is a function $i(t)$ such that

$$e^{\int_{t_1}^{t_2} i(s)ds}$$

represents the interest earned over the interval (t_1, t_2).

We can now examine these valuation formulas in the limiting case where the interval between two coupon payments goes to zero. This means that coupon payments are replaced by a continuous stream of cash flows with rate $c(s)$. As discussed in Chapter 15 on arbitrage pricing, a continuous cash flow rate means that

$$C = \int_{t_1}^{t_2} c(s)ds$$

is the cash received in the interval (t_1, t_2). To gain a better understanding of these valuation relationships, let's now explicitly compute the present value of a continuous cash-flow rate $c(s)$. We will arrive at the formula for the present value of a known, deterministic continuous cash flow rate $c(t)$ in two different ways. We can thus illustrate in a simple context two lines of reasoning that will be widely used later.

The first line of reasoning is the following. The cash received over the infinitesimal interval $(t, t + dt)$ is $c(t)dt$. Its value at time 0 is therefore $c(t)dte^{-it}$, if the short-term rate is constant, or, more in general,

$$c(t)dte^{-\int_0^t i(s)\ ds}$$

if the short-term rate is variable. The value at time 0 of the entire cash-flow stream is the infinite sum of all these elementary elements, that is, it is the integral

$$P_0 = \int_0^t c(s)e^{-is}ds$$

for the constant short-term rate, and:

$$P_0 = \int_0^t c(s)e^{-\int_0^s i(u)du}\ ds$$

in the general case of variable (but known) short-term interest rates. This present value has to be interpreted as the market price at which the stream of continuous cash flows would trade if arbitrage is to be avoided.

The second line of reasoning is more formal. Consider the cumulated capital $C(t)$ which is the cumulative cash flow plus the interest earned. In the interval $(t, t + dt)$, the capital increments by the cash $c(t)dt$ plus the interest $i(t)C(t)dt$ earned on the capital $C(t)$ in the elementary period dt. We can therefore write the equation

$$dC = i(t)C(t)dt + c(t)dt$$

This is a linear differential equation of the type

$$\frac{dx}{dt} = A(t)x + a(t), \, 0 \le t < \infty$$

with initial conditions $x(0) = \xi$. This is a one-dimensional case of the general d-dimensional case discussed in Chapter 10. It can be demonstrated that this equation has an absolutely continuous solution in the domain $0 \le t < \infty$; this solution can be written in the following way:

$$x(t) = \Phi(t)\left[x(0) + \int_0^t \Phi^{-1}(s)a(s)ds \right], \, 0 \le t < \infty$$

where $\Phi(t)$, called the **fundamental solution**, solves the equation

$$\frac{d\Phi}{dt} = A(t)\Phi, \, 0 \le t < \infty$$

In the case we are considering

$$x(t) = C(t), \, A(t) = i(t), \, a(t) = c(t), \, \xi = 0$$

and

$$\Phi(t) = e^{\int_0^t i(s)ds}$$

and therefore

$$C(t) = e^{\int_0^t i(s)ds} \int_0^t c(s)e^{-\int_0^s i(u)du} ds$$

If we consider that

$$P_0 = C(t)e^{-\int_0^t i(s)ds}$$

is the value at time 0 of the capital $C(t)$, we again find the formula

$$P_0 = \int_0^t c(s)e^{-\int_0^s i(u)du} ds$$

that we had previously established in a more direct way.

If the coupon payments are a continuous cash-flow stream, the sensitivity of their present value to changes in interest rates under the assumption of constant interest rates are:

$$\frac{\partial P}{\partial i} = \frac{\partial\left(\int_0^t c(s)e^{-is}ds\right)}{\partial i} = \int_0^t \frac{\partial[c(s)e^{-is}]}{\partial i}ds = -\int_0^t sc(s)e^{-is}ds$$

The above formula parallels the discrete-time formula that was established in Chapter 4.[7]

THE TERM STRUCTURE OF INTEREST RATES IN CONTINUOUS TIME

Our ultimate objective is to establish a stochastic theory of bond pricing and of bond option pricing. To do so, we will reformulate term structure theory in a continuous-time, continuous-state environment. We will subsequently develop examples on how processes can be discretized, thus going back to a discrete-state, discrete-time environment. The stochastic description of interest rates is challenging from the point of view of both mathematics and economic theory. We discussed the economic theories of interest rates earlier in this chapter.

Mathematical difficulties stem from the fact that one should consider not just one interest rate but the entire term structure of interest rates that was defined earlier. This is, in principle, a (difficult) problem of infinite dimensionality. Though attempts have been made in the academic literature to describe the stochastic behavior of a curve without any restriction, in practice models currently in use make simplifications so that the movement of the term structure curve is constrained to that of one or a small number of factors.

The term structure of interest rates is a function $U(t,s)$ of two variables t,s that represents the yield computed at time t of a zero-coupon risk-free bond with maturity s. The yield on a zero-coupon bond is called the *spot rate*. In calculating the spot rate in developed bond markets, the yields on government bonds are used. Government bonds are typically coupon-paying instruments. However, we have seen in this chapter how to obtain, from arbitrage arguments, the theoretical spot rates from a set of yields of coupon-paying bonds. The term structure of interest rates is a mathematical construct as only a finite number of spot rates can be observed. A continuous curve needs to be reconstructed from these discrete points.

---

[7] See footnote 7 in Chapter 4, p. 114. Note that in Chapter 4, V is used rather than P to denote market price.

Spot Rates: Continuous Case

Assume for the moment that the evolution of short-term interest rates is deterministic and it is known. Thus, at any time t the function $i(s)$ that describes the short-term rate is known for every moment $s \geq t$. Recall that $i(s)$ is the limit of the interest rate for an interval that tends to zero. Earlier in this chapter we established that the value at time t_1 of capital of a risk-free bond paying $B(t_2)$ at time t_2 is given by

$$B(t_1) = B(t_2)e^{-\int_{t_1}^{t_2} i(s)ds}$$

The yield over any finite interval (t_1,t_2) is the constant equivalent interest rate

$$R_{t_1}^{t_2}$$

over the same interval (t_1,t_2) which is given by the equation

$$B(t_1) = B(t_2)e^{-(t_2-t_1)R_{t_1}^{t_2}} = B(t_2)e^{-\int_{t_1}^{t_2} i(s)ds}$$

Given a short-term interest rate function $i(t)$, we can therefore define the term structure function R_t^u as the number which solves the equation

$$e^{-(u-t)R_t^u} = e^{-\int_t^u i(s)ds}$$

In a deterministic setting, we can write

$$R_t^u = \frac{1}{(u-t)}\int_t^u i(s)ds$$

This relationship does not hold in a stochastic environment, as we will see shortly. From the above it is clear that R_t^u is the yield of a risk-free bond over the interval (t,u). The function

$$\Lambda_t^u = e^{-\int_t^u i(s)ds}$$

is called the *discount function.*[8]

The term on the right side is the price at time t of a bond of face value 1 maturing at u.

Forward Rates: Continuous Case

The forward rate $f(t,u)$ is the short-term spot rate at time u contracted at time t. To avoid arbitrage, the following relationship must hold:

$$f(t, u) = \lim_{\Delta u \to 0} -\frac{\log\Lambda_t^{u + \Delta u} - \log\Lambda_t^u}{\Delta u} = -\frac{\partial\log\Lambda_t^u}{\partial u}$$

In this deterministic setting, the above relationship yields: $f(t,t) = i(t)$. Given the short-rate function $i(s)$, the term structure is completely determined and vice versa.

In a stochastic environment, short-term interest rates form a stochastic process $i_s(\omega)$. This means that for each state of the world there is a path of spot interest rates. For each path and for each interval (t,u), we can compute the discount function

$$e^{-\int_t^u i(s)ds}$$

Under a risk-neutral probability measure Q, the price at time t of a bond of face value 1 maturing at time u is the expected value of

$$e^{-\int_t^u i(s)ds}$$

computed at time t:

$$\Lambda_t^u = E_t^Q\left[e^{-\int_t^u i(s)ds}\right]$$

The term structure function can be computed from the discount function as follows as follows:

---

[8] Some authors call this function the term structure of interest rates. For example, Darrell Duffie, *Dynamic Asset Pricing Theory* (Princeton, NJ: Princeton University Press, Third Edition, 2001) and Steven Shreve, *Stochastic Calculus and Finance* (Springer, forthcoming 2004).

$$R_t^u = -\frac{1}{(u-t)}\log(\Lambda_t^u) = -\frac{1}{(u-t)}\log\left(E_t^Q\left[e^{-\int_t^u i(s)ds}\right]\right)$$

As noted above, this formula does not imply

$$(u-t)R_t^u = E_t^Q\left[\int_t^u i(s)ds\right]$$

Relationships for Bond and Option Valuation

We have established the formula

$$e^{-(u-t)R_t^u} = E_t^Q\left[e^{-\int_t^u i(s)ds}\right]$$

in a rather intuitive way as the expectation under risk-neutral probability of discounted final bond values. However, this formula can be derived formally as a particular case of the general expression for the price of a security that we determined in Chapter 15 on arbitrage pricing in continuous time:

$$S_t = E_t^Q\left[e^{\int_t^T -r_u du}S_T + \int_t^T e^{\int_t^T -r_u du}dD_s\right]$$

considering that, for zero-coupon bonds, the payoff rate is zero and that we assume $S_T = 1$.

We used risk-neutral probabilities for the following reason. The factor

$$e^{\int_t^u i(s)ds}$$

represents capital appreciation pathwise. However, the formula

$$\Lambda_t^u = e^{-\int_t^u i(s)ds}$$

which gives the price at time t of a bond of face value 1 maturing at u in a deterministic environment, does not hold pathwise in a stochastic environment. This is because bonds of longer maturities are riskier than bonds of shorter maturities. The martingale relationship holds only for risk-neutral probabilities.

We can now go back to the forward rates. The expression

$$f(t, u) = \lim_{\Delta u \to 0} -\frac{\log \Lambda_t^{u + \Delta u} - \log \Lambda_t^u}{\Delta u} = -\frac{\partial \log \Lambda_t^u}{\partial u}$$

holds in a stochastic environment when the term structure is defined as above.

We have now defined the basic terms and relationships that can be used for bond valuation and for bond option valuation and we have established a formula that relates the term structure to the short-rate process. The next step is to specify the models of the short-term interest rate process. The simplest assumption is that the short-term rate follows an Itô process of the form

$$dr_t = \mu(r_t, t)dt + \sigma(r_t, t)d\hat{B}_t$$

where $d\hat{B}_t$ is a standard Brownian motion under the equivalent martingale measure.

As explained in Chapter 15 on arbitrage pricing, it is possible to develop all calculations under the equivalent martingale measure and to revert to the real probabilities only at the end of calculations. This procedure greatly simplifies computations. Under the equivalent martingale measure all price processes S_t follow Itô processes with the same drift of the form

$$dS_t = r_t S_t dt + \sigma(r_t, t)d\hat{B}_t$$

Note that the short-term interest rate process is not a price process and therefore does not follow the previous equation. Models of the short-term rate as the above are called one-factor model because they model only one variable.

The Feynman-Kac Formula

Computing the term structure implies computing the expectation

$$\Lambda_t^u = E_t^Q \left[e^{-\int_t^u i(s)ds} \right]$$

We will now describe a mathematical technique for computing this expectation using the Feynman-Kac formula.

To understand the reasoning behind the Feynman-Kac formula, recall that there are two basic ways to represent stochastic processes. The first, which was presented in Chapter 8, is a direct representation of uncertainty pathwise through Itô processes. Itô processes can be thought of as modifications of Brownian motions. One begins by defining Brownian motions and then defines a broad class of stochastic processes, the Itô processes, as Itô integrals obtained from the Brownian motion. Discretizing an Itô process, one obtains equations that describe individual paths.

An equivalent way to represent stochastic Itô processes is through transition probabilities. Given a process X_t that starts at X_0, the transition probabilities are the conditional probability densities $p(X_t/X_0)$. Given that the process is a Markov process, these densities also describe the transition between the value of the process at time s to time t: $p(X_t | X_s)$ that we write $p(x,t,y,s)$. The Markov nature of the process means that, given any function $h(y)$, the expectation $E_s[h(X_t | X_s)]$ is the same as if the process started anew at the value X_s.

It can be demonstrated that the transition density $p(x,t,y,s)$ obeys the following partial differential equation (PDE) which is called the **forward Kolmogorov equation** or the **Fokker-Planck equation:**

$$\frac{\partial}{\partial t}p(x, t, y, s) = \frac{1}{2}\frac{\partial^2[\sigma^2(x, t)p(x, t, y, s)]}{\partial x^2} - \frac{\partial[\mu(x, t)p(x, t, y, s)]}{\partial x}$$

with boundary conditions $p(x,t,y,s) = \delta_s(y)$ where $\delta_s(y)$ is Dirac's delta function.[9] The numerical solution of this equation, after discretization, gives the required probability density.

For example, consider the Brownian motion whose stochastic differential equation is

$$dX_t = dB_t, \mu = 0, \sigma = 1$$

The associated Fokker-Planck equation is the diffusion equation in one dimension:

---

[9] Strictly speaking Dirac's delta function is not a function but a distribution. In a loose sense, it is a function that assumes value zero in all points except one where it becomes infinite. It is defined only through its integral which is finite.

$$\frac{\partial p}{\partial t} = \frac{1}{2}\sigma^2\frac{\partial^2 p}{\partial x^2}$$

As a second example, consider the geometric Brownian motion whose stochastic differential equation is

$$dX_t = \mu X_t dt + \sigma X_t dB_t, \; \mu(X_t, t) = \mu X_t, \; \sigma(X_t, t) = \sigma X_t$$

The associated Fokker-Planck equation is

$$\frac{\partial p}{\partial t} = \frac{1}{2}\sigma^2\frac{\partial^2 (x^2 p)}{\partial x^2} - \mu\frac{\partial(xp)}{\partial x}$$

The Fokker-Planck equation is a forward equation insofar it gives the probability density at a future time t starting at the present time s. Another important PDE associated with Itô diffusions is the following backward Kolmogorov equation:

$$-\frac{\partial}{\partial t}p(x, t, y, s) = \frac{1}{2}\sigma^2(x, t)\frac{\partial^2 p(x, t, y, s)}{\partial x^2} - \mu(x, t)\frac{\partial p(x, t, y, s)}{\partial x}$$

The Kolmogorov backward equation gives the probability density that we were at x,t given that we are now at y,s. Note that there is a fundamental difference between the backward and the forward Kolmogorov equations because the Itô processes are not reversible. In other words, the probability density that we were at x,t given that we are now at y,s is not the same as if we start the process at y,s and we look at density at x,t.

Thus far we have established an equivalence between stochastic differential equations and associated partial differential equations in the sense that they describe the same process. We have now to make an additional step by establishing a connection between the expectations of an Itô process and an associated PDE. The connection is provided by the Feynman-Kac formula which is obtained from a generalization of the backward Kolmogorov equation.

Consider the following PDE:

$$-\frac{\partial F(x, t)}{\partial t} = \frac{1}{2}\sigma^2(x, t)\frac{\partial^2 F(x, t)}{\partial x^2} + \mu(x, t)\frac{\partial F(x, t)}{\partial x}$$

with boundary conditions $F(x,T) = \Psi(x)$. Consider now the stochastic differential equation

$$dX_s = \mu(X_s, t)dt + \sigma(X_s, t)dB_s, \, s \in [t,T], \, X_t = x$$

There is a fundamental relationship between the two equations given by the Feynman-Kac formula, which states that

$$F(x, t) = E_t[\Psi(X_T) | X_t = x]$$

The meaning of this relationship can be summarized as follows. A PDE with the related boundary conditions $F(x,T) = \Psi(x)$ is given. The solution of this PDE is a function of two variables $F(x,t)$, which assumes the value $\Psi(x)$ for $t = T$. A stochastic differential equation (SDE) is associated to this equation. The two coefficients of the PDE are the drift and the volatility of the SDE. The solution of the SDE starts at (x,t). For each starting point (x,t), consider the expectation $E_t[\Psi(X_T)]$. This expectation coincides with $F(x,t)$.

One might wonder how it happened that a conditional expectation—which is a random variable—has become the perfectly deterministic solution of a PDE. The answer is that $F(x,t)$ associates the expectation of a given function $\Psi(X_T)$ to each starting point (x,t). This relationship is indeed deterministic while the starting point depends on the evolution of the stochastic process which solves the SDE. It is thus easy to see why the above is a consequence of the backward Kolmogorov equation which associates to each starting point (x,t) the conditional probability density of X_T.

We can now make the final step and state the Feynman-Kac equation in a more general form. In fact, it can be demonstrated that, given the following PDE:

$$\frac{\partial F(x, t)}{\partial t} + \frac{1}{2}\sigma^2(x, t)\frac{\partial^2 F(x, t)}{\partial x^2} + \mu(x, t)\frac{\partial F(x, t)}{\partial x} - f(x, t)F(x, t) = 0$$

with boundary conditions $F(x,T) = \Psi(x)$ and given the stochastic equation

$$dX_s = \mu(X_s, t)dt + \sigma(X_s, t)dB_s, \, s \in [t,T], \, X_t = x$$

the following relationship holds:

$$F(x, t) = E_t\left[e^{-\int_t^T f(X_T, s)ds}\Psi(X_T)\big|X_t = x\right]$$

We can now go back to the original problem of computing the term structure from the stochastic differential equation of the short-rate process. Recall that the term structure is given by the following conditional expectation:

$$\Lambda_t^u = E_t^Q\left[e^{\int_t^u i(s)ds}\right]$$

If we apply the Feynman-Kac formula, we see that the term structure is a function

$$\Lambda_t^u = F(i_t, t)$$

of time t and of the short-rate i_t which solves the following PDE:

$$\frac{\partial F(x, t)}{\partial t} + \frac{1}{2}\sigma^2(x, t)\frac{\partial^2 F(x, t)}{\partial x^2} + \mu(x, t)\frac{\partial F(x, t)}{\partial x} - xF(x, t) = 0$$

with boundary conditions $F(x,T) = 1$.

Note explicitly that the solution of this equation does not determine the dynamics of interest rates. In other words, given the short-term rate i_t at time t the function

$$\Lambda_t^u = F(i_t, t)$$

does not tell us what interest rate will be found at time $s > t$. It does tell, however, the price at time s of a bond with face value 1 at maturity T for every interest rate i_s. If the coefficients $\sigma = \sigma(x)$, $\mu = \mu(x)$ do not depend on time explicitly, then one single function gives the entire term structure.

Note also that the above is true in general for any asset which does not exhibit any intermediate payoff. Recall, in fact, the pricing formula:

$$S_t = E_t^Q\left[e^{-\int_t^T r_u du}S_T + \int_t^T e^{-\int_t^s r_u du}dD_s\right]$$

If intermediate payoffs are zero the previous formula becomes

$$S_t = E_t^Q\left[e^{\int_t^T -r_u du} S_T\right]$$

Given the final price S_T, there is a pricing function in the sense that

$$S_t = F(i_t, t) = E_t^Q\left[e^{\int_t^T -r_u du} S_T\right]$$

The pricing function satisfies a Feynman-Kac formula and is the solution of a PDE. It tells us that the price S_t is a function of time t and of the interest rate at time t.

Multifactor Term Structure Model

The above discussion presented the derivation of the term structure from the interest rate process. We say that, under this assumption, the term structure model is a *one-factor model* because it depends on one single process. Empirical analysis has shown that one factor is insufficient. Principal component analysis of the term structure of the U.S. Treasury market, as well as other country government bond markets, has shown that three factors are sufficient to explain 98% of the term structure fluctuations. The three factors are the level, slope, and curvature of the yield curve. Typically 90% of the term structure is explained by changes in the level of interest rates. Around 8% is explained by changes in the slope, or steepness, of the spot rate curve. Exhibit 20.4 provides a summary of these studies.[10]

Multifactor models of the term-structure have been proposed. Note that multifactor models described in the literature and currently used by practitioners might use variables such as the long-term interest rate and the short-term interest rate. This might give the impression that the short-term interest rate is not sufficient to determine the term structure. This is not true. The short-term rate is indeed sufficient to completely determine the term structure. Conversely, given the term structure,

[10] In addition to the references in Exhibit 20.4, there is the study from which the exhibit is reproduced: Lionel Martellini, Philippe Priaulet, and Stéphane Priaulet, "An Empirical Analysis of the Domestic and Euro Yield Curve Dynamics," Chapter 24 in Frank J. Fabozzi and Moorad Choudhry (eds.), *The Handbook of European Fixed Income Markets* (Hoboken, NJ: John Wiley & Sons, 2004).

EXHIBIT 20.4 Summary of Some Popular Studies of Yield Curve Dynamics

Authors	Country (Period)	Kind of Rates	Range	Factors	% of Explanation
Robert Litterman and José Scheinkman, "Common Factors Affecting Bond Returns," *Journal of Fixed Income* (June 1991), pp. 54–61.	U.S. (1984–88)	Spot Zero-Coupon (ZC)	6M–18Y	3	88.04/8.38/1.97
C. Kanony and M. Mokrane, "Reconstitution de la courbe des taux, analyse des facteurs d'évolution et couverture factorielle," *Cahiers de la Caisse Autonome de Refinancement* 1 (June 1992).	France (1989–90)	Spot ZC	1Y–25Y	2	93.7/6.1
R.L. D'Ecclesia and S.A. Zenios, "Risk Factor Analysis and Portfolio Immunization in the Italian Bond Market," *Journal of Fixed Income* 4, no. 2 (September 1994), pp. 51–58.	Italy (1988–92)	Spot ZC	6M–7Y	3	93.91/5.49/0.42
J. Kärki and C. Reyes, "Model Relationship," *Risk* 7, no. 12 (December 1994), pp. 32–35.	Germ./Switz./U.S. (1990–94)	Spot ZC	3M–10Y	3	Total: 97/98/98
J.R. Barber and M.L. Copper, "Immunization Using Principal Component Analysis," *Journal of Portfolio Management* (Fall 1996), pp. 99–105.	U.S. (1985–91)	Spot ZC	1M–20Y	3	80.93/11.85/4.36
A. Bühler and H. Zimmerman, "A Statistical Analysis of the Term Structure of Interest Rates in Switzerland and Germany," *Journal of Fixed Income* 6, no. 3 (December 1996), pp. 55–67.	Germany (1988–96) Switzerland (1988–96)	Spot ZC	1M–10Y	3	71/18/4 75/16/3
Golub, B. W., and L. M. Tilman, "Measuring Yield Curve Risk Using Principal Components Analysis, Value at Risk, and Key Rate Durations," *Journal of Portfolio Management* (Summer 1997), pp. 72–84.	RiskMetrics 09/30/96	Spot ZC	3M–30Y	3	92.8/4.8/1.27
I. Lekkos, "A Critique of Factor Analysis of Interest Rates," *Journal of Derivatives* (Fall 2000), pp. 72–83.	U.S. (1984–95) Germany (1987–95) U.K. (1987–95) Japan (1987–95)	1–Year Forward	1Y–9Y	5	56.5/17.4/9.86/8.12/4.3 50.6/17.3/13.5/8.8/5.8 63.5/6.3/7.5/8.1/5.3 42.8/25.5/17.1/6/4.9
L. Martellini and P. Priaulet, *Fixed-Income Securities: Dynamic Methods for Interest Rate Risk Pricing and Hedging* (New York: John Wiley & Sons, 2000).	France (1995–98)	Spot ZC	1M–10Y	3	66.64/20.52/6.96

Note: M stands for month and *Y* for year. For example, "88.04/8.38/1.97" means that the first factor explains 88.04% of the yield curve variations, the second 8.38%, and the third 1.97%. Sometimes, we also provide the total amount by adding up these terms.
Source: Exhibit A1 in Lionel Martellini, Philippe Priaulet, and Stéphane Priaulet, "An Empirical Analysis of the Domestic and Euro Yield Curve Dynamics," Chapter 24 in Frank J. Fabozzi and Moorad Choudhry (eds.), *The Handbook of European Fixed Income Markets* (Hoboken, NJ: John Wiley & Sons, 2004).

short-term interest rates are determined. Multiple factors model the term structure as well as the short-term rate.

In fact, a multifactor term-structure model is a model of the form: $i_t = F(X_t,t)$ where i_t is the short-rate process and X_t is an N-dimensional Itô process that obeys the following SDE:

$$dX_s = \mu(X_s, t)dt + \sigma(X_s, t)d\hat{B}_s$$

where X_s is an N-vector, i is a 1-vector, $d\hat{B}_s$ is an N-dimensional Brownian motion under an equivalent martingale measure, $\mu(X_s,t)$ is an N-vector and $\sigma(X_s,t)_s$ is a N×N matrix. The Feynman-Kac formula can be extended in a multidimensional environment in the sense that the following relationships hold:

$$F(x, t) = E_t^Q \left[e^{-\int_t^T f(X_T, s)ds} \Psi(X_T) \right]$$

and

$$\frac{\partial F(x, t)}{\partial t} + \frac{1}{2}tr\left[\sigma(x, t)\sigma^T(x, t)\frac{\partial^2 F(x, t)}{\partial x^2} \right] + \mu(x, t)\frac{\partial F(x, t)}{\partial x} - xF(x, t) = 0$$

Arbitrage-Free Models versus Equilibrium Models

Stochastic differential equations are typically used to model interest rates. There are two approaches used to implement the same SDE into a term structure model: equilibrium and no arbitrage. While these two approaches begin with a given SDE, they differ as to how each approach applies the SDE to bonds and contingent claims. *Equilibrium models* begin with an SDE model and develop pricing mechanisms for bonds under an equilibrium framework. *Arbitrage models,* also referred to as *no-arbitrage* models, start with the same or similar SDE models as the equilibrium models. However, no-arbitrage models utilize observed market prices to generate an interest rate lattice. The lattice represents the short rate in such a way as to ensure there is a no arbitrage relationship between the observed market price and the model-derived value. Practitioners prefer arbitrage-free models to value options on bonds because such models ensure that the prices observed for the underlying bonds are exact. As a result, bonds and options on those bonds will be valued in a consistent framework. Equilibrium models, in contrast, will not price bonds exactly so they do not provide a consistent framework for valuing options on bonds and the underlying bonds.

Examples of One-Factor Term Structure Models

A number of one-factor and multifactor term structure models have been proposed in the literature. We will discuss some of the more popular one-factor models here:

- The Ho-Lee model
- The Vasicek model
- The Hull-White model
- The Cox-Ingersoll-Ross model
- The Kalotay-Williams-Fabozzi model
- Black-Karasinski model
- The Black-Derman-Toy model

Our coverage is not intended to be exhaustive.[11]

Most of these models are based on a short-term process which satisfies an SDE of the following type:

$$di = \mu(i, t)dt + \sigma i^{\alpha} d\hat{B}$$

The various models differ for the choice of the drift $\mu(i,t)$ and of the exponent α.

The Ho-Lee Model

The first arbitrage-free model was introduced by Thomas Ho and Sang-Bin Lee in 1986.[12] In the Ho-Lee model $\alpha = 0$, $\mu(i,t) = \mu = $ constant.

$$di = \mu dt + \sigma d\hat{B}$$

This model is quite simple. It has the disadvantage that interest rates might drift and become negative, which is inconsistent with what is observed in financial markets. In addition, having only two free parameters, it cannot be easily fitted to the initial observed term structure.

---

[11] For a more detailed discussion of these models, see Gerald W. Buetow, Jr., Frank J. Fabozzi, and James Sochacki, "A Review of No Arbitrage Interest Rate Models," Chapter 3 in Fabozzi, *Interest Rate, Term Structure, and Valuation Modeling.*

[12] Thomas Ho and Sang Bin Lee, "Term Structure Movements and Pricing Interest Rate Contingent Claims," *Journal of Finance* (1986), pp. 1011–1029.

The Vasicek Model

In 1977, Oldrich Vasicek proposed the Ornstein-Uhlenbeck process as a model of interest rates to produce a one-factor equilibrium model.[13] In the Vasicek model $\alpha = 0$,

$$\mu(i, t) = \frac{(L - i)}{T}$$

$$di = \frac{L - i}{T}dt + \sigma d\hat{B}$$

where L and T are constants.

The Vasicek model is a mean-reverting process as interest rates are pulled back to the value L. Interest rates exhibit mean reversion properties, a fact that the Vasicek models correctly address. However, having only three free parameters, the Vasicek model is difficult to fit to the initial term structure.

The Hull-White Model

In 1990 Hull and White proposed a mean-reverting model that generalizes the Vasicek model.[14] The Hull-White model is given by the choice $\alpha = 0$,

$$\mu(i, t) = \frac{(L(t) - i)}{T(t)}$$

with time-variable volatility

$$di = \frac{L(t) - i}{T(t)}dt + \sigma(t)d\hat{B}$$

The Hull-White model has enough parameters to be fitted to any initial term structure.

---

[13] Oldrich Vasicek, "An Equilibrium Characterization of the Term Structure," *Journal of Financial Economics* (1977), pp. 177–188.

[14] J. Hull and A. White, "Pricing Interest Rate Derivative Securities," *Review of Financial Studies* 3 (1990), pp. 573–592, and, "One Factor Interest Rate Models and the Valuation of Interest Rate Derivative Securities," *Journal of Financial and Quantitative Analysis* (1993), pp. 235–254.

The Cox-Ingersoll-Ross Model

In 1985 John Cox, Jonathan Ingersoll, and Stephen Ross (CIR)[15] proposed an equilibrium model with

$$\alpha = \frac{1}{2}$$

$$\mu(i, t) = \frac{(L - i)}{T}$$

$$di = \frac{L - i}{T}dt + \sigma\sqrt{i}d\hat{B}$$

where L and T are constants. The CIR model is mean reverting but has only three free parameters to fit the initial term structure. It can be shown that in this model interest rates always remain non-negative.

Kalotay, Williams, and Fabozzi

In 1993 Andrew Kalotay, George Williams, and Frank Fabozzi (KWF)[16] proposed a model with $\alpha = 1$, $\mu = \theta(t)i$ described by the following SDE:

$$di = \theta(t)idt + \sigma idB_t$$

For θ = constant the model becomes a geometric random walk. As the model is lognormal, interest rates never become negative.

Black-Karasinski

In 1991 Fisher Black and Piotr Karasinski[17] proposed a model with $\alpha = 1$ described by the following SDE:

$$d \ln i = [\theta(t) - \phi(t)\ln i]dt + \sigma(t)dB_t$$

---

[15] John Cox, Jonathan Ingersoll, and Stephen. Ross, "A Theory of the Term Structure of Interest Rates," *Econometrica* (1985), pp. 385–408.
[16] Andrew J. Kalotay, George Williams, and Frank J. Fabozzi, "A Model for the Valuation of Bonds and Embedded Options," *Financial Analyst Journal* (May–June 1993), pp. 35–46.
[17] Fischer Black and Piotr Karasinski, "Bond and Option Pricing when Short Rates are Lognormal," *Financial Analysts Journal* (July–August 1991), pp. 2–59.

If $\phi(t) = 0$ then the Black-Karasinki model becomes the KWF model. The Black-Karasinki model is lognormal and therefore interest rates cannot be negative. The error correction term also prevents rates from diverging.

The Black-Derman-Toy Model

In 1990 Fischer Black, Emanuel Derman, and William Toy[18] proposed a lognormal arbitrage-free model with $\alpha = 1$, $\mu(i,t) = c(t)i$:

$$di = c(t)idt + \sigma(t)id\hat{B}$$

Two-Factor Models

A number of two factor models have also been proposed. Brennan and Schwarz, for example, proposed in 1979 a model based on a short rate i and a long rate y.[19] This model is written as a set of two equations,

$$di = \mu_1(i, \tau, y)dt + \sigma_1(i, \tau, y)d\hat{B}$$

$$dy = \mu_2(i, \tau, y)ydt + \sigma_2(i, \tau, y)yd\hat{B}^*$$

where the two Brownian motions are correlated.

PRICING OF INTEREST-RATE DERIVATIVES

The models of the term structure described thus far are based on deriving the arbitrage-free prices of zero-coupon bonds from the short-term rate process. In a nutshell, the methodology involves the following steps:

- *Step 1*. Assume that the short rate process i_t is a function of an N-dimensional Itô process X_t (the factors):

$$i_t = F(X_t, t)$$

---

[18] Fischer Black, Emanuel Derman, and William Toy, "A One Factor Model of Interest Rates and Its Application to the Treasury Bond Options," *Financial Analyst Journal* (January–February 1990), pp. 33–39.
[19] Michael J. Brennan. and Eduardo S. Schwartz, "A Continuous Time Approach to the Pricing of Bonds," *Journal of Banking and Finance* 3 (1979), pp. 133–155.

$$dX_s = \mu(X_s, t)dt + \sigma(X_s, t)d\hat{B}_s$$

where $d\hat{B}_s$ is a standard Brownian motion under an equivalent martingale measure Q. In the single factor case, the short rate process i_t follows an Itô process

$$di_s = \mu(i_s, t)dt + \sigma(i_s, t)d\hat{B}_s$$

■ *Step 2.* Compute the arbitrage-free price of a zero-coupon bond using the theory of arbitrage-free pricing under an equivalent martingale measure according to which the price Λ_t^u at time t of a zero-coupon bond with face-value 1 maturing at time u is

$$\Lambda_t^u = E_t^Q\left[e^{-\int_t^u i(s)\,ds}\right]$$

■ *Step 3.* Use the Feynman-Kac formula to show that $\Lambda_t^u = F(i_t, t)$, which solves the following PDE:

$$\frac{\partial F(x, t)}{\partial t} + \frac{1}{2}\sigma^2(x, t)\frac{\partial^2 F(x, t)}{\partial x^2} + \mu(x, t)\frac{\partial F(x, t)}{\partial x} - xF(x, t) = 0$$

with boundary conditions $F(x,T) = 1$.

The above methodology can be immediately extended to cover the pricing of a class of interest-rate derivatives whose payoff can be expressed as a function of short-term interest rates or, alternatively, as a function of bond prices. Consider, first, the case of a derivative security whose payoff is given by two functions $h(i_t,t)$ and $g(i_\tau,\tau)$, which specify, respectively, the continuous payoff rate and the final payoff at a specified date $\tau \le T$. This specification covers a rather broad class of derivative securities and bond optionality, including European options on zero-coupon bonds, swaps, caps and floors.

The general arbitrage pricing theory (see Chapter 15) can be immediately applied. The price at time t of a derivative security defined as above is the following extension of the bond pricing formula:

$$F(i_t, t) = E_t^Q\left[\int_t^\tau e^{-\int_t^u i(s)ds}h(i_s, s)ds + e^{-\int_t^\tau i(s)ds}g(i_\tau, \tau)\right]$$

Note that the first term under the expectation sign is the expectation under risk-neutral probabilities of the formula for the present value of a continuous cash-flow stream that we established earlier in this chapter:

$$V_0 = \int_0^t c(s)e^{-\int_0^s i(u)\,du}\,ds$$

where $c(s) = h(i_s, s)$ and the initial time is 0.

The Feynman-Kac formula can be extended to this case. In fact it can be demonstrated that the function F obeys the following PDE:

$$\frac{\partial F(x,t)}{\partial t} + \frac{1}{2}\sigma^2(x,t)\frac{\partial^2 F(x,t)}{\partial x^2} + \mu(x,t)\frac{\partial F(x,t)}{\partial x} - xF(x,t) + h(x,t) = 0$$

with boundary conditions $F(x,\tau) = g(x,\tau)$. If $h(x,t) = 0$, $g(x,\tau) \equiv 1$, we find the bond valuation formula of the previous section.

THE HEATH-JARROW-MORTON MODEL OF THE TERM STRUCTURE

In the previous sections we derived the term structure from a short-term rate process which might depend, in turn, on a number of factors. However, this is not the only possible choice. In 1992, David Heath, Robert Jarrow, and Andrew Morton introduced a methodology that recovers the term structure (i.e., bond prices) from the forward rates.[20] The key issue with this methodology is to ensure the absence of arbitrage.

Recall that the forward rate $f(t,u)$ is the short-term spot rate at time u contracted at time t. In a deterministic environment (that is, assuming that the forward rates are known) to avoid arbitrage, the following relationships must hold:

$$f(t,u) = -\frac{\partial(\log\Lambda_t^u)}{\partial u}$$

---

[20] David Heath, Robert A. Jarrow, and Andrew J. Morton, "Bond Pricing and the Term Structure of Interest Rates: A New Methodology for Contingent Claim Valuation," *Econometrica* (1992), pp. 77–105.

$$f(t,t) = i_t$$

Integrating the first relationship we obtain

$$\Lambda_t^u = e^{-\int_t^u f(t,\, s)ds}$$

Now suppose that in the interval $u \in (0,T]$ the forward rate obeys the following SDE:

$$df = \alpha(t,u)dt + \sigma(t,u)dB_t$$

Equivalently, this means that for each $u \in (0,T]$ the following relationship holds:

$$f(t, u) = f(0, u) + \int_0^t \alpha(s, u)ds + \int_0^t \sigma(s, u)d\hat{B}_s$$

Stochastic differentiation yields

$$d\left[-\int_t^u f(t, s)ds \right] = f(t, t)dt + \int_t^u df(t, s)ds$$

$$= i(t)dt - \int_t^u [\alpha(t, s)dt + \sigma(t, s)d\hat{B}_t]ds$$

$$= i(t)dt - \alpha^*(t, u)dt + \sigma^*(t, u)d\hat{B}_t$$

where

$$\alpha^*(t, u) = \int_t^u \alpha(t, s)ds$$

$$\sigma^*(t, u) = \int_t^u \sigma(t, s)ds$$

Using Itô's lemma, it can be demonstrated that the term structure process obeys the following SDE:

$$d\Lambda_t^u = \Lambda_t^u \left\{ i(t) - \alpha^*(t, u) + \frac{1}{2}[\sigma^*(t, u)]^2 \right\} dt - \sigma^*(t, u)\Lambda_t^u d\hat{B}_t$$

This process determines the bond price process in function of a forward rate process. However, to avoid arbitrage, the forward rate process must be constrained. In particular, Heath, Jarrow, and Morton (HJM) demonstrated the following theorems.

Suppose that the forward rate obeys the following SDE under the probability measure P:

$$f(t, u) = f(0, u) + \int_0^t \alpha(s, u)ds + \int_0^t \sigma(s, u)d\hat{B}_s$$

Then P is an equivalent martingale measure if and only if the coefficients $\alpha(t,u)$, $\sigma(t,u)$ obey the following relationship:

$$\alpha^*(t, u) = \frac{1}{2}[\sigma^*(t, u)]^2$$

that is,

$$\int_t^u \alpha(t, s)ds = \frac{1}{2}\left(\int_t^u \sigma(t, s)ds \right)^2$$

where $0 \le t \le u \le T$.

If P is not an equivalent martingale measure, then there is no arbitrage if and only if there is an adapted process $\theta(\tau)$ satisfying the following relationship:

$$\alpha^*(t, u) = \frac{1}{2}[\sigma^*(t, u)]^2 + \sigma^*(t, u)\theta(\tau), \quad 0 \le t \le u \le T$$

or, equivalently, differentiating both sides with respect to u:

$$\alpha(t, u) = \sigma(t, u)\sigma^*(t, u) + \sigma(t, u)\theta(t), \quad 0 \le t \le u \le T$$

Implementing the HJM methodology takes advantage of the available degrees of freedom. The initial forward rate curve $f(0,u)$ can be determined by observing the initial curve

$$f(0, T) = -\frac{\partial(\log \Lambda_0^T)}{\partial u}$$

As only a finite number of bond prices can be observed, it is necessary to use techniques to convert a number of finite observations into a smooth curve. One cannot simply fit a high-degree polynomial to the available observations as this would introduce a lot of noise. On the other hand, fitting a low-degree polynomial would create a curve that does not correspond to the true term structure. **Splines** is an approach that is often used to create a smooth initial forward curve. This technique involves fitting pieces of curves in such a way that the transition between the pieces is smooth.

Suppose that the initial forward rate curve has been fitted to empirical data. Suppose that two deterministic functions $\sigma^*(t,u)$, $\theta(t)$ have been chosen. Let's define

$$\alpha(t, u) = \sigma(t, u)\sigma^*(t, u) + \sigma(t, u)\theta(t)$$

With these definitions, the forward rate process is determined by the following equation in the risk neutral probabilities:

$$df = \sigma(t, u)\sigma^*(t, u)dt + \sigma(t, u)d\hat{B}_t$$

Solving this equation yields the forward rate process and the short-term process. The bond pricing equation then becomes

$$d\Lambda_t^u = i(t)\Lambda_t^u dt - \sigma^*(t, u)\Lambda_t^u d\hat{B}_t$$

In this equation only the volatility $\sigma^*(t,u)$ appears. This shows that, in order to implement the HJM model, only the initial term structure and the volatilities are needed.

THE BRACE-GATAREK-MUSIELA MODEL

The Brace-Gatarek-Musiela (BGM) model is a particular implementation of the HJM model which corresponds to a specific choice of the volatility.[21] The BGM model is based on defining a forward LIBOR

---

[21] Alan Brace, Dariusz Gatarek, and Marek Musiela, "The Market Model of Interest Rate Dynamics," *Mathematical Finance* 7, no. 2 (April 1997), pp 127–155.

interest rate which is a simple forward interest rate defined over a discrete time period. The BGM model, and the HJM from which it derives, form a wide class of models which has been extensively explored in the literature. Here we will only give a brief account of the BGM model.

First define $L(t,0)$ as the rate of simple interest over a discrete period δ so that an amount of $D(t,\delta)$ dollars invested at time t in a bond with maturity $(t + \delta)$ become 1 dollar at maturity:

$$D(t, \delta)[1 + \delta L(t, 0)] = 1$$

Then define the *forward LIBOR* as follows:

$$\frac{D(t, \tau + \delta)}{D(t, \tau)}[1 + \delta L(t, \tau)] = 1$$

It is possible to demonstrate that

$$L(t, \tau) = \frac{e^{\int_{\tau}^{(\tau + \delta)} f(t, u)du} - 1}{\delta}$$

where f is the continuously compounding forward rate.

Define now $\sigma^*(t,\tau)$ recursively as follows:

$$\sigma^*(t, \tau + \delta) = \sigma^*(t, \tau) + \frac{\delta L(t, \tau)\gamma(t, \tau)}{1 + \delta L(t, \tau)}$$

$$L(t, \tau)\gamma(t, \tau) = \frac{1}{\delta}[1 + \delta L(t, \tau)][\sigma^*(t, \tau + \delta) - \sigma^*(t, \tau)]$$

DISCRETIZATION OF ITÔ PROCESSES

Itô processes are stochastic differential equations that admit a forward discretization scheme similar to that of ordinary differential equations. Consider an Itô process that obeys the following SDE:

$$dX_t = \mu(X_t, t)dt + \sigma(X_t, t)dB_t$$

A natural, and simple, discretization scheme is given by the Euler approximation. The Euler approximation replaces the differentials with finite differences. If we divide the unit interval in n subintervals, the Euler approximation replaces the SDE with the following recursive scheme:

$$X_{k+1} - X_k = \mu\left(X_k, \frac{k}{n}\right)\frac{1}{n} + \sigma\left(X_k, \frac{k}{n}\right)\frac{1}{\sqrt{n}}\varepsilon_{k+1}$$

where ε_{k+1} are independent random draws from a standard normal, $N(0,1)$. A computer implementation of this scheme would start from some initial value and compute the solution recursively using a random number generator to generate the ε_{k+1}. Repeating the process many times over, one obtains many paths and many final points from which quantities such as averages can be easily computed. More complex schemes can be used in order to obtain a smaller approximation error.

As an illustration of the above, Exhibit 20.5 presents random paths generated using the Euler approximation to approximate several one-factor interest rate models described earlier in this chapter.

EXHIBIT 20.5   Ten Paths Generated from Different One-Factor Interest Rate Models

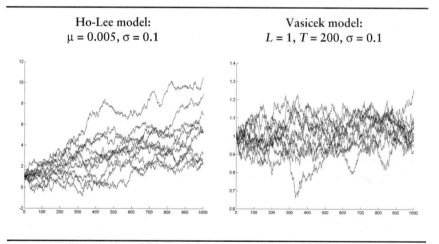

Ho-Lee model:	Vasicek model:
$\mu = 0.005, \sigma = 0.1$	$L = 1, T = 200, \sigma = 0.1$

EXHIBIT 20.5   (Continued)

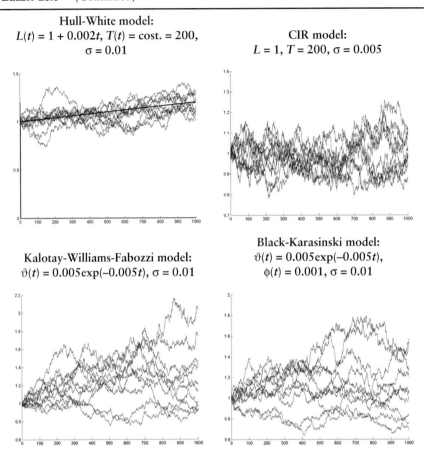

Hull-White model:
$L(t) = 1 + 0.002t, T(t) = \text{cost.} = 200,$
$\sigma = 0.01$

CIR model:
$L = 1, T = 200, \sigma = 0.005$

Kalotay-Williams-Fabozzi model:
$\vartheta(t) = 0.005\exp(-0.005t), \sigma = 0.01$

Black-Karasinski model:
$\vartheta(t) = 0.005\exp(-0.005t),$
$\phi(t) = 0.001, \sigma = 0.01$

SUMMARY

- There are different types of interest rates.
- The term structure of interest rates is a curve that associates to each future date the yield of an hypothetical risk-free zero-coupon bond maturing exactly at that date.
- The term structure of interest rates can be recovered from empirical data using the no-arbitrage principle and curve smoothing techniques.
- The term structure of interest rates is not fixed but might change with time.

- A number of classical economic theories explain the shape of the term structure.
- Mathematically, the term structure can be derived by a model of short-term interest rates.
- Multifactor models of the term structure are based on multifactor models of the short-term interest rates.
- A number of models for the short term rate as (multivariate) Itô processes have been proposed.
- The term structure of the interest rates can also be modelled starting from a model of the forward rates.
- Features of term structure models include absence of arbitrage, mean reversion, ability to fit empirical term structure.

CHAPTER 21

Bond Portfolio Management

In this chapter, we look at the more popular strategies for managing a bond portfolio. A portfolio manager will select a portfolio strategy that is consistent with the objectives and policy guidelines of the client or institution. As explained in Chapter 1, a portfolio manager's benchmark can be either a bond market index or liabilities. In this chapter, we provide an overview of strategies for managing a bond portfolio versus both benchmarks.

MANAGEMENT VERSUS A BOND MARKET INDEX

There are several bond market indexes that represent different sectors of the bond market. The wide range of bond market indexes available can be classified as *broad-based bond market indexes* and *specialized bond market indexes*. The three broad-based bond market indexes most commonly used by institutional investors are the Lehman Brothers U.S. Aggregate Index, the Salomon Smith Barney Broad Investment-Grade Bond Index, and the Merrill Lynch Domestic Market Index. There are more than 5,500 issues in each index. One study has found that the correlation of annual returns between the three broad-based bond market indexes were around 98%.[1] The three broad-based bond market indexes are computed daily and are market value weighted. This means that for each issue, the ratio of the market value of an issue relative to the market value of all issues in the index is used as the weight of the issue in all

---

[1] Frank K. Reilly and David J. Wright, "Bond Market Indexes," Chapter 7 in Frank J. Fabozzi (ed.), *The Handbook of Fixed Income Securities: Sixth Edition* (New York: McGraw-Hill, 2000).

calculations.[2] The specialized bond market indexes focus on one sector of the bond market or a subsector of the bond market.

There are risk factors associated with a bond market index which we discuss later in this chapter. The proper way to categorize bond portfolio strategies is in terms of the degree to which a manager constructs a portfolio with a risk profile that differs from the risk profile of the bond market index that is the manager's benchmark. The following general categorization of bond portfolio management strategies has been proposed by Kenneth Volpert of the Vanguard Group:[3]

- Pure bond index matching
- Enhanced indexing/matching risk factors
- Enhanced indexing/minor risk factor mismatches
- Active management/larger risk factor mismatches
- Active management/full-blown active

In terms of risk and return, a *pure bond index matching strategy* involves the least risk of underperforming a bond market index.

An *enhanced indexing strategy* can be pursued so as to construct a portfolio to match the primary risk factors associated with a bond market index without acquiring each issue in the index. While in the spectrum of strategies defined by Volpert this strategy is called an "enhanced strategy," some investors refer to this as simply an indexing strategy. Two commonly used techniques to construct a portfolio to replicate an index are cell matching (stratified sampling) and tracking error minimization using a multifactor risk model. Both techniques assume that the performance of an individual bond depends on a number of systematic factors that affect the performance of all bonds and on an unsystematic factor unique to the individual issue or issuers. With the cell matching approach the index is divided into cells representing the risk factors. The objective is then to select from all of the issues in the index one or more issues in each cell that can be used to represent that entire cell. This approach is inferior to the second approach, minimizing tracking error using a multifactor risk model discussed later.[4]

Another form of enhanced strategy is one in which the portfolio is constructed so as to have minor deviations from the risk factors that affect the performance of the index. For example, there might be a slight over-

---

[2] The securities in the SSB BIG index are all trader priced. For the two other indexes, the securities are either trader priced or model priced.
[3] Kenneth E. Volpert, "Managing Indexed and Enhanced Indexed Bond Portfolios," Chapter 3 in Frank J. Fabozzi (ed.), *Fixed Income Readings for the Chartered Financial Analyst Program: First Edition* (New Hope, PA: Frank J. Fabozzi Associates, 2000).

weighting of issues or sectors where the manager believes there is relative value. A feature of this strategy is that the duration of the constructed portfolio is matched to the duration of the benchmark index. That is, there is no duration bet for this strategy, just as with the pure index match strategy and the enhanced index with matching risk strategy.

Active bond strategies are those that attempt to outperform the bond market index by intentionally constructing a portfolio that will have a greater index mismatch than in the case of enhanced indexing. Volpert classifies two types of active strategies. In the more conservative of the two active strategies, the manager constructs the portfolio so that it has larger mismatches relative to the benchmark index in terms of risk factors. This includes minor mismatches of duration. Typically, there will be a limitation as to the degree of duration mismatch that a client will permit. In *full-blown active management*, the manager is permitted to make a significant duration bet without any constraint.

Tracking Error and Bond Portfolio Strategies

In Chapter 18, we explained forward-looking (*ex ante*) tracking error. Tracking error, or active risk, is the standard deviation of a portfolio's return relative to the return of the benchmark index.[5] Forward-looking tracking error is an estimate of how a portfolio will perform relative to a benchmark index in the future. Forward-looking tracking error is used in risk control and portfolio construction. The higher the forward-looking tracking error, the more the manager is pursuing a strategy in which the portfolio has a different risk profile than the benchmark index and there is, therefore, greater active management.

We can think of the spectrum of bond portfolio strategies relative to a bond market index in terms of forward-looking tracking error. In constructing a portfolio, a manager can estimate forward-looking tracking error. When a portfolio is constructed to have a forward-looking tracking error equal or close to zero, the manager has effectively designed the portfolio to replicate the performance of the benchmark. If the forward-looking tracking error is maintained for the entire investment period, the portfolio's return should be close to zero. Such a strategy—one with

---

[4] For a discussion and illustration of both approaches to bond indexing, see Lev Dynkin, Jay Hyman, and Vadim Konstantinovsky, "Bond Portfolio Analysis Relative to a Benchmark," Chapter 23 in Frank J. Fabozzi and Harry M. Markowitz (eds.), *The Theory and Practice of Investment Management* (Hoboken, NJ: John Wiley & Sons, 2002).

[5] There are two types of tracking error—backward-looking tracking error and forward-looking tracking error. Backward-looking tracking error is calculated based on the actual performance of a portfolio relative to a benchmark index.

a forward-looking tracking error of zero or "very small"—indicates that the manager is pursing a passive strategy relative to the benchmark index. When the forward-looking tracking error is "large" the manager is pursuing an active strategy.

Risk Factors and Portfolio Management Strategies

Since forward-looking tracking error indicates the degree of active portfolio management being pursued by a manager, it is necessary to understand what factors (referred to as "risk factors") affect the performance of a manager's benchmark index. The risk factors affecting one of the most popular broad-based bond market indexes, the Lehman Brothers U.S. Aggregate Index, have been investigated by Dynkin, Hyman, and Wu.[6] A summary of the risk factors is provided in Exhibit 21.1. They first classify the risk factors into two types: systematic risk factors and nonsystematic risk factors. *Systematic risk factors* are the common factors that affect all securities in a certain category in the benchmark bond market index. *Nonsystematic factor* risk is the risk that is not attributable to the systematic risk factors.

EXHIBIT 21.1   Summary of Risk Factors for a Benchmark

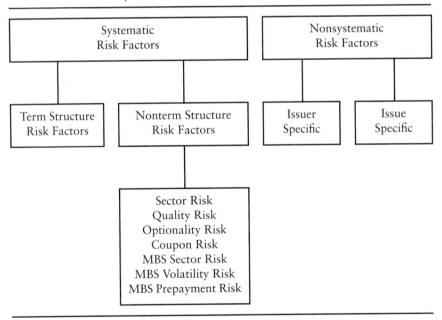

[6] Lev Dynkin, Jay Hyman, and Wei Wu, "Multi-Factor Risk Factors and Their Applications," in Frank J. Fabozzi (ed.) *Professional Perspectives on Fixed Income Portfolio Management: Volume 2* (Hoboken, NJ: John Wiley & Sons, 2001).

Systematic risk factors, in turn, are divided into two categories: term structure risk factors and nonterm structure risk factors. *Term structure risk factors* are risks associated with changes in the shape of the term structure (level and shape changes). *Nonterm structure risk factors* include the following:

- Sector risk
- Quality risk
- Optionality risk
- Coupon risk
- MBS sector risk
- MBS volatility risk
- MBS prepayment risk

Sector risk is the risk associated with exposure to the sectors of the benchmark index. For example, consider the Lehman Brothers U.S. Aggregate Index. At the macro level, these sectors include Treasury, agencies, credit (i.e., corporates), residential mortgages, commercial mortgages, and asset-backed securities (ABS). Each of these sectors is divided further. For example, the credit sector is divided into financial institutions, industrials, transportations, and utilities. In turn, each of these subsectors is further divided. For the residential mortgage market (which includes agency passthrough securities), there are a good number of subsectors based on the entity issuing the security, the coupon rate, the maturity, and the mortgage design.

Quality risk is the risk associated with exposure to the credit rating of the securities in the benchmark index. The breakdown for the Lehman Brothers U.S. Aggregate Index which includes only investment-grade credits is Aaa+, Aaa, Aa, A, Baa, and mortgage-backed securities (MBS). MBS includes credit exposure to the agency passthrough sector.

Optionality risk is the risk associated with an adverse impact on the embedded options of the securities in the benchmark index. This includes embedded options in callable and putable corporate bonds, MBS, and ABS. *Coupon risk* is the exposure of the securities in the benchmark index to different coupon rates.

The last three risks are associated with the investing in residential mortgage passthrough securities. The first is *MBS sector risk* which is the exposure to the sectors of the MBS market. The value of an MBS depends on the expected interest rate volatility and prepayments. *MBS volatility risk* is the exposure of a benchmark index to changes in expected interest rate volatility. *MBS prepayment risk* is the exposure of a benchmark index to changes in prepayments.

Nonsystematic factor risks are classified as risks associated with a particular issuer, *issuer-specific risk*, and those associated with a particular issue, *issue-specific risk*.

Determinants of Tracking Error

Using statistical techniques,[7] given the risk factors associated with a benchmark index, forward-looking tracking error can be estimated for a portfolio based on historical return data. The tracking error occurs because the portfolio constructed deviates from the exposures for the benchmark index. The tracking error for a portfolio relative to a benchmark index can be decomposed as follows:

I. Tracking error due to systematic risk factors:
   A. Tracking error due to term structure risk factor
   B. Tracking error due to nonterm structure risk factors
      1. Tracking error due to sector
      2. Tracking error due to quality
      3. Tracking error due to optionality
      4. Tracking error due to coupon
      5. Tracking error due to MBS sector
      6. Tracking error due to MBS volatility
      7. Tracking error due to MBS prepayment
II. Tracking error due to nonsystematic risk factors
   A. Tracking error due to issuer-specific risk
   B. Tracking error due to issue-specific risk

A manager provided with information about (forwarding-looking) tracking error for the current portfolio can quickly assess if (1) the risk exposure for the portfolio is one that is acceptable and (2) if the particular exposures are the ones being sought.

Illustration of the Multifactor Risk Model

We will now illustrate how a multifactor risk model is used to quantify the risk profile of a portfolio relative to a benchmark and then explain how optimization can be used to construct a portfolio. We will use the Lehman Brothers multifactor model in the illustration. The bond market index used as benchmark is the Lehman Brothers U.S. Aggregate Index.[8]

---

[7] Lev Dynkin of Lehman Brothers has described the statistical technique to the authors as follows. The risk model uses decomposition of individual bond returns into carry, yield curve, and spread components. The spread component is regressed on a certain set of systematic (or common to all bonds in a peer group) risk factors using a prespecified set of sensitivities. Residuals of this regression are used to estimate security-specific risk. Factor realizations collected over many months form the covariance matrix of systematic risk factors. The current mismatch in risk sensitivities between the portfolio and the benchmark is multiplied by this matrix to get the systematic tracking error.

[8] The illustration in this section draws from Dynkin, Hyman, and Wu, "Multi-Factor Risk Factors and Their Applications."

Exhibit 21.2 shows the sample portfolio used in the illustration. The portfolio includes 57 bonds. The analysis was performed on September 30, 1998. Summary information for the portfolio and the corresponding information for the Lehman Brothers U.S. Aggregate Index are shown in Exhibit 21.3. From the exhibit, it can be seen that the 57-bond portfolio has greater interest rate risk as measured by duration—4.82 for the portfolio versus 4.29 for the benchmark.

EXHIBIT 21.2   Portfolio Report: Composition of Sample Portfolio, 9/30/98

#	Issuer Name	Coup	Maturity	Moody	S&P	Sect	Par Val	%
1	BAKER HUGHES	8.000	05/15/04	A2	A	IND	5,000	0.87
2	BOEING CO	6.350	06/15/03	Aa3	AA	IND	10,000	1.58
3	COCA-COLA ENTERPRISES I	6.950	11/15/26	A3	A+	IND	50,000	8.06
4	ELI LILLY CO	6.770	01/01/36	Aa3	AA	IND	5,000	0.83
5	ENRON CORP	6.625	11/15/05	Baa2	BBB+	UTL	5,000	0.80
6	FEDERAL NATL MTG ASSN	5.625	03/15/01	Aaa+	AAA+	USA	10,000	1.53
7	FEDERAL NATL MTG ASSN-G	7.400	07/01/04	Aaa+	AAA+	USA	8,000	1.37
8	FHLM Gold 7-Years Balloon	6.000	04/01/26	Aaa+	AAA+	FHg	20,000	3.03
9	FHLM Gold Guar Single F.	6.500	08/01/08	Aaa+	AAA+	FHd	23,000	3.52
10	FHLM Gold Guar Single F.	7.000	01/01/28	Aaa+	AAA+	FHb	32,000	4.93
11	FHLM Gold Guar Single F.	6.500	02/01/28	Aaa+	AAA+	FHb	19,000	2.90
12	FIRST BANK SYSTEM	6.875	09/15/07	A2	A–	FIN	4,000	0.65
13	FLEET MORTGAGE GROUP	6.500	09/15/99	A2	A+	FIN	4,000	0.60
14	FNMA Conventional Long T.	8.000	05/01/21	Aaa+	AAA+	FNa	33,000	5.14
15	FNMA MTN	6.420	02/12/08	Aaa+	AAA+	USA	8,000	1.23
16	FORD MOTOR CREDIT	7.500	01/15/03	A1	A	FIN	4,000	0.65
17	FORT JAMES CORP	6.875	09/15/07	Baa2	BBB–	IND	4,000	0.63
18	GNMA I Single Family	9.500	10/01/19	Aaa+	AAA+	GNa	13,000	2.11
19	GNMA I Single Family	7.500	07/01/22	Aaa+	AAA+	GNa	30,000	4.66
20	GNMA I Single Family	6.500	02/01/28	Aaa+	AAA+	GNa	5,000	0.76
21	GTE CORP	9.375	12/01/00	Baa1	A	TEL	50,000	8.32
22	INT-AMERICAN DEV BANK-G	6.375	10/22/07	Aaa	AAA	SUP	6,000	1.00
23	INTL BUSINESS MACHINES	6.375	06/15/00	A1	A+	IND	10,000	1.55
24	LEHMAN BROTHERS INC	7.125	07/15/02	Baa1	A	FIN	4,000	0.59
25	LOCKHEED MARTIN	6.550	05/15/99	A3	BBB+	IND	10,000	1.53
26	MANITOBA PROV CANADA	8.875	09/15/21	A1	AA–	CAN	4,000	0.79
27	MCDONALDS CORP	5.950	01/15/08	Aa2	AA	IND	4,000	0.63
28	MERRILL LYNCH & CO.-GLO	6.000	02/12/03	Aa3	AA–	FIN	5,000	0.76
29	NATIONSBANK CORP	5.750	03/15/01	Aa2	A+	FIN	3,000	0.45
30	NEW YORK TELEPHONE	9.375	07/15/31	A2	A+	TEL	5,000	0.86
31	NIKE INC	6.375	12/01/03	A1	A+	IND	3,000	0.48
32	NORFOLK SOUTHERN CORP	7.800	05/15/27	Baa1	BBB+	IND	4,000	0.71
33	NORWEST FINANCIAL INC.	6.125	08/01/03	Aa3	AA–	FIN	4,000	0.62
34	ONT PROV CANADA-GLOBA	7.375	01/27/03	Aa3	AA–	CAN	4,000	0.65

EXHIBIT 21.2   (Continued)

#	Issuer Name	Coup	Maturity	Moody	S&P	Sect	Par Val	%
35	PUB SVC ELECTRIC + GAS	6.125	08/01/02	A3	A–	ELU	3,000	0.47
36	RAYTHEON CO	7.200	08/15/27	Baa1	BBB	IND	8,000	1.31
37	RESOLUTION FUNDING CORP	8.125	10/15/19	Aaa+	AAA+	USA	17,000	3.51
38	TIME WARNER ENT	8.375	03/15/23	Baa2	BBB–	IND	5,000	0.90
39	ULTRAMAR DIAMOND SHAM	7.200	10/15/17	Baa2	BBB	IND	4,000	0.63
40	US TREASURY BONDS	10.375	11/15/12	Aaa+	AAA+	UST	10,000	2.17
41	US TREASURY BONDS	10.625	08/15/15	Aaa+	AAA+	UST	14,000	3.43
42	US TREASURY BONDS	6.250	08/15/23	Aaa+	AAA+	UST	30,000	5.14
43	US TREASURY NOTES	8.875	02/15/99	Aaa+	AAA+	UST	9,000	1.38
44	US TREASURY NOTES	6.375	07/15/99	Aaa+	AAA+	UST	4,000	0.61
45	US TREASURY NOTES	7.125	09/30/99	Aaa+	AAA+	UST	17,000	2.59
46	US TREASURY NOTES	5.875	11/15/99	Aaa+	AAA+	UST	17,000	2.62
47	US TREASURY NOTES	6.875	03/31/00	Aaa+	AAA+	UST	8,000	1.23
48	US TREASURY NOTES	6.000	08/15/00	Aaa+	AAA+	UST	11,000	1.70
49	US TREASURY NOTES	8.000	05/15/01	Aaa+	AAA+	UST	9,000	1.50
50	US TREASURY NOTES	7.500	11/15/01	Aaa+	AAA+	UST	10,000	1.67
51	US TREASURY NOTES	6.625	03/31/02	Aaa+	AAA+	UST	6,000	0.96
52	US TREASURY NOTES	6.250	08/31/02	Aaa+	AAA+	UST	10,000	1.60
53	US TREASURY NOTES	5.750	08/15/03	Aaa+	AAA+	UST	1,000	0.16
54	US TREASURY NOTES	6.500	05/15/05	Aaa+	AAA+	UST	1,000	0.17
55	US TREASURY NOTES	6.125	08/15/07	Aaa+	AAA+	UST	1,000	0.17
56	WELLS FARGO + CO	6.875	04/01/06	A2	A–	FIN	5,000	0.80
57	WESTPAC BANKING CORP	7.875	10/15/02	A1	A+	FOC	3,000	0.49

Source: Exhibit 9 in Lev Dynkin, Jay Hyman, and Wei Wu, "Multi-Factor Risk Models and Their Applications," in Frank J. Fabozzi (ed.) *Professional Perspectives on Fixed Income Portfolio Management: Volume 2* (New Hope, PA: Frank J. Fabozzi Associates, 2001).

Systematic Risk Exposure

The estimated total tracking error is 52 basis points per year. Exhibit 21.3 provides a summary of the tracking error breakdown for the 57-bond portfolio. As described earlier, the systematic risk factors are broken into two parts: term structure factors and nonterm structure factors. From the first column of Exhibit 21.3 it can be seen that the three major systematic risk exposures are (1) term structure factors (i.e., exposure to changes in the term structure); (2) sector factors (i.e., changes in credit spreads of sectors); and (3) quality factors (i.e., changes in credit spreads by quality rating).

The subcomponents of the tracking error breakdown reported in Exhibit 21.3 are shown in two different ways, labeled "Isolated" and "Cumulative." In the "Isolated" column, the tracking error due to the effect of each subcomponent is considered in isolation. What is not considered in the "Isolated" calculations are the correlations between the risk factors. For example, the 14.7 basis points for the tracking error for quality considers only the mismatch between the portfolio exposure and benchmark exposure due to quality and taking into consideration the correlations only of quality exposure for the different quality ratings. The tracking error for the portfolio is 52 basis points and the tracking error for the systematic and nonsystematic risk is 45 basis points and 26.1 basis points, respectively. Because the tracking errors represent

EXHIBIT 21.3 Tracking Error Breakdown for Sample Portfolio
Sample Portfolio versus Aggregate Index, 9/30/98

	Tracking Error (bp/year)		
	Isolated	Cumulative	Change in Cumulative
Tracking error term structure	36.3	36.3	36.3
Nonterm structure	39.5		
Tracking error sector	32.0	38.3	2.0
Tracking error quality	14.7	44.1	5.8
Tracking error optionality	1.6	44.0	−0.1
Tracking error coupon	3.2	45.5	1.5
Tracking error MBS sector	4.9	43.8	−1.7
Tracking error MBS volatility	7.2	44.5	0.7
Tracking error MBS prepayment	2.5	45.0	0.4
Total systematic tracking error			45.0
Nonsystematic tracking error			
Issuer-specific	25.9		
Issue-specific	26.4		
Total	26.1		
Total tracking error			52

	Systematic	Nonsystematic	Total
Benchmark return standard deviation	417	4	417
Portfolio return standard deviation	440	27	440

Source: Exhibit 2 in Lev Dynkin, Jay Hyman, and Wei Wu, "Multi-Factor Risk Models and Their Applications," in Frank J. Fabozzi (ed.) *Professional Perspectives on Fixed Income Portfolio Management: Volume 2* (New Hope, PA: Frank J. Fabozzi Associates, 2001).

variances, it not the sum of these two risks that sum to the portfolio's tracking error, but rather the squares of these two tracking errors that will equal the square of the portfolio's tracking error. Or equivalently, the square root of the square of the two tracking errors will equal the portfolio's tracking error (i.e., $[(45.0)^2 + (26.1)^2]^{0.5} = 52.0$). Adding of variances assumes that there is zero correlation between the risk factors (i.e., the risk factors are statistically independent).

The alternative calculation for subdividing the tracking error is shown in the last two columns of Exhibit 21.3, the "Cumulative" calculation. In the second column the cumulative tracking error is computed by introducing one group of risk factors at a time and computing the resulting change in the tracking error. The analysis begins with the 36.3 basis point tracking error due to the term structure risk. The value shown in the next row of 38.3 basis points is calculated by holding the risk factors constant except for term structure risk and sector risk. The change in the cumulative tracking error from 36.3 to 38.3 basis points is shown in the last column for the row corresponding to sector risk. The 2 basis point change is interpreted as follows: given the exposure to yield curve risk, sector risk adds 2 basis points to tracking error. By continuing to add the subcomponents of the risk factors, the cumulative tracking error is determined. Because of the way in which the calculations are performed, the cumulative tracking error shown for all the systematic risk factors in the next-to-the last column is 45 basis points, the same as in the "isolated" calculation.

Exhibit 21.4 can be used to understand the difference between the "isolated" and "cumulative" calculations. For purposes of the illustration, the exhibit shows a covariance matrix for just the following three groups of risk factors: yield curve (Y), sector spreads (S), and quality spreads (Q). How the covariance matrix is used to calculate the subcomponents of the tracking error in the "isolated" case is shown in panel a. The diagonal of the covariance matrix shows the elements of the matrix that are used in the calculation for that subcomponent. The off-diagonal terms of the matrix deal with the correlations among different sets of risk factors. They are not used in calculating the tracking error and therefore do not contribute to any of the partial tracking errors. The elements of the covariance matrix used in the calculation of the "cumulative" tracking error at each stage of the calculation are shown in Panel b of Exhibit 21.4. The incremental tracking error due to sector risk takes into consideration not only the $S \times S$ variance but also the cross terms $S \times Y$ and $Y \times S$ which represent the correlation between yield curve risk and sector risk. Note that the incremental tracking error need not be positive. When the correlation is negative, the increment will be negative. This can be seen in the last column of Exhibit 21.3 which shows that the incremental risk due to the MBS sector risk is -1.7 basis points.

EXHIBIT 21.4 Illustration of "Isolated" and "Cumulative" Calculations of Tracking Error Subcomponents[a]

a. Isolated Calculation of Tracking Error Components

$Y \times Y$	$Y \times S$	$Y \times Q$
$S \times Y$	$S \times S$	$S \times Q$
$Q \times Y$	$Q \times S$	$Q \times Q$

b. Cumulative Calculation of Tracking Error Components

$Y \times Y$	$Y \times S$	$Y \times Q$
$S \times Y$	$S \times S$	$S \times Q$
$Q \times Y$	$Q \times S$	$Q \times Q$

[a] Y – Yield curve risk factors; S – Sector spread risk factors; Q – Credit Quality spread risk factors.

Source: Exhibit 12 in Lev Dynkin, Jay Hyman, and Wei Wu, "Multi-Factor Risk Models and Their Applications," in Frank J. Fabozzi (ed.), *Professional Perspectives on Fixed Income Portfolio Management: Volume 2* (New Hope, PA: Frank J. Fabozzi Associates, 2001).

The "isolated" calculation helps a portfolio manager identify the relative magnitude of each subcomponent of the tracking error. The advantage of the "cumulative" calculation is that it takes into consideration the correlations among the subcomponents of the risk factors and the sum of the tracking error components is equal to the total tracking error. The drawback of the "cumulative" calculation is that it is dependent upon the order in which the risk factors are introduced.

Another portfolio risk measure provided in Exhibit 21.3 is the volatility of returns. That is, the standard deviation of the return for each systematic risk factor and the standard deviation for the portfolio return can be computed. Similarly, the standard deviation of the benchmark return can be calculated. Note the difference between tracking error and standard deviation of returns. The former is computed by using the historical differences in return between the portfolio and the benchmark. The latter only considers the historical returns. As was computed for tracking error, there are systematic return and nonsystematic return components. The last panel in Exhibit 21.3 reports the total standard deviation for the portfolio and the benchmark and the composition of each in terms of systematic and nonsystematic risk factors. Notice that the portfolio's standard deviation (430 basis points) is greater than that of the benchmark (417 basis points).

Nonsystematic Risk Exposure

Now let's look at nonsystematic risk. The nonsystematic tracking error is divided into those that are issuer specific and those that are issue specific. As indicated in Exhibit 21.3, the tracking error associated with the 57-bond portfolio is 52 basis points per annum and there is 26 basis points per annum of nonsystematic risk. The latter risk arises from the concentration of the portfolio in individual securities or issuers. The last column of Exhibit 21.2 shows this risk. The column reports the percentage of the portfolio's market value invested in each issue. Because there are only 57 issues in the portfolio, the portfolio is relatively small in terms of issues. Consequently, each issue makes up a nontrivial fraction of the portfolio. Specifically, look at the exposure to two corporate issuers, GTE Corp. and Coca-Cola. Each is more than 8% of the portfolio. If there is a downgrade of either firm, this would cause large losses in the 57-bond portfolio, but it would not have a significant effect on the benchmark which includes 6,932 issues. Consequently, a large exposure in a portfolio to a specific corporate issuer represents a material mismatch between the exposure of the portfolio and a benchmark that must be taken into account in assessing a portfolio's risk relative to a benchmark.

Optimization Application

The multifactor risk model can be used by the portfolio manager in combination with optimization in constructing and rebalancing a portfolio to reduce tracking error. A portfolio manager using optimization, for example, can determine the single largest transaction that can be used to reduce tracking error. Or, a portfolio manager can determine using optimization a series of transactions (i.e., bond swaps) that would be necessary to alter the target tracking error at minimum cost.[9]

Suppose that the portfolio manager's objective is to minimize tracking error. From the universe of bonds selected by the portfolio manager,

---

[9] According to Lev Dynkin of Lehman Brothers, the optimization procedure is as follows. Instead of finding a complete portfolio that optimizes tracking error in the model, a step-by-step optimization algorithm is chosen based on marginal contributions of each security already in a portfolio or any buy-candidate to the portfolio risk versus the benchmark. Current portfolio holdings are then sorted in a descending order of their marginal contribution to tracking error, offering the manager an opportunity to pick a sell candidate with the most impact on tracking error, but not forcing the portfolio manager into any one choice. Once the sell candidate is selected, it is paired with any eligible buy candidate to find the highest possible tracking error improvement. Buy candidates are ranked on the tracking error that would result from having picked each specific security. This step-by-step optimization mechanism allows the portfolio manager to intervene with every transaction.

an optimizer can be employed to rank bond purchases in terms of the marginal decline in tracking error per unit of each bond purchased. A portfolio manager would then determine the bond issues that would be purchased and the optimizer would then identify potential market-value-neutral swaps of these bond issues against various bonds issues currently held in the portfolio; the optimizer would indicate the optimal transaction size for each pair of bond issues that are being swapped ranked by the potential reduction in tracking error.

Dynkin, Hyman, and Wu illustrate how this optimization process can be used to minimize the tracking error for the 57-bond portfolio. The illustration is provided in Exhibit 21.5. Look at the first trade used in the exhibit which indicates that the majority of the large position in the Coca-Cola 30-year bond can be swapped for a Treasury note. If the proposed trade (i.e., bond swap) is executed, this would result in (1) a change in the systematic exposures to term structure, sector, and quality and (2) a reduction in nonsystematic risk by cutting one of the largest issuer exposures. From this one bond swap alone that the optimizer identifies, tracking error is reduced from 52 basis points to 29 basis points. Notice that as the risk profile of the initial sample portfolio approaches that of the benchmark (Lehman Brothers U.S. Aggregate Index), the opportunity for major reductions in the tracking error declines.

If all five transactions shown in Exhibit 21.5 are executed, there is the potential to reduce the tracking error to 16 basis points. The resulting portfolio after these transactions is effectively a passive portfolio. Exhibit 21.6 provides a summary of the tracking error for the portfolio if all five transactions are executed. The systematic and nonsystematic tracking error is 10 and 13 basis points, respectively.

LIABILITY-FUNDING STRATEGIES

Liability-funding strategies are strategies whose objective is to match a given set of liabilities due at future times. These strategies provide the cash flows needed at given dates at a minimum cost and with zero or minimal interest rate risk. However, depending on the universe of bonds that are permitted to be included in the portfolio, there may be credit risk and/or call risk. Liability-funding strategies are used by (1) sponsors of defined benefit pension plans (i.e., there is a contractual liability to make payments to beneficiaries); (2) insurance companies for single premium deferred annuities (i.e., a policy in which the issuer agrees for a single premium to make payments to policyholders over time), guaranteed investment contracts (i.e., a policy in which the issuer agrees for a single premium to

EXHIBIT 21.5 Sequence of Transactions Selected by Optimizer Showing Progressively Smaller Tracking Error, $000s

Initial Tracking Error: 52.0 bp

Transaction # 1		
Sold:	31,000 of COCA-COLA ENTERPRISES	6.950 2026/11/15
Bought:	30,000 of U.S. TREASURY NOTES	8.000 2001/05/15
Cash Leftover:	−17.10	
New Tracking Error:	29.4 bp	
Cost of This Transaction:	152.500	
Cumulative Cost:	152.500	
Transaction # 2		
Sold:	10,000 of LOCKHEED MARTIN	6.550 1999/05/15
Bought:	9,000 of U.S. TREASURY NOTES	6.125 2007/08/15
Cash Leftover:	132.84	
New Tracking Error:	25.5 bp	
Cost of This Transaction:	47.500	
Cumulative Cost:	200.000	
Transaction # 3		
Sold:	4,000 of NORFOLK SOUTHERN CORP	7.800 2027/05/15
Bought:	3,000 of U.S. TREASURY BONDS	10.625 2015/08/15
Cash Leftover:	−8.12	
New Tracking Error:	23.1 bp	
Cost of This Transaction:	17.500	
Cumulative Cost:	217.500	
Transaction # 4		
Sold:	33,000 of GTE CORP	9.375 2000/12/01
Bought:	34,000 of U.S. TREASURY NOTES	6.625 2002/03/31
Cash Leftover:	412.18	
New Tracking Error:	19.8 bp	
Cost of This Transaction:	167.500	
Cumulative Cost:	385.000	
Transaction # 5		
Sold:	7,000 of COCA-COLA ENTERPRISES	6.950 2026/11/15
Bought:	8,000 of U.S. TREASURY NOTES	6.000 2000/08/15
Cash Leftover:	−304.17	
New Tracking Error:	16.4 bp	
Cost of This Transaction:	37.500	
Cumulative Cost:	422.500	

Source: Exhibit 15 in Lev Dynkin, Jay Hyman, and Wei Wu, "Multi-Factor Risk Models and Their Applications," in Frank J. Fabozzi (ed.) *Professional Perspectives on Fixed Income Portfolio Management: Volume 2* (New Hope, PA: Frank J. Fabozzi Associates, 2001).

EXHIBIT 21.6 Tracking Error Summary
Passive Portfolio versus Aggregate Index, 9/30/98

	Tracking Error (bp/year)		
	Isolated	Cumulative	Change
Tracking error term structure	7.0	7.0	7.0
Nonterm structure	9.6		
Tracking error sector	7.4	10.5	3.5
Tracking error quality	2.1	11.2	0.7
Tracking error optionality	1.6	11.5	0.3
Tracking error coupon	2.0	12.3	0.8
Tracking error MBS sector	4.9	10.2	−2.1
Tracking error MBS volatility	7.2	11.1	0.9
Tracking error MBS prepayment	2.5	10.3	−0.8
Total systematic tracking error		10.3	
Nonsystematic tracking error			
Issuer-specific	12.4		
Issue-specific	3.0		
Total	12.7		
Total tracking error return		16	

	Systematic	Nonsystematic	Total
Benchmark sigma	417	4	417
Portfolio sigma	413	13	413

Source: Exhibit 16 in Lev Dynkin, Jay Hyman, and Wei Wu, "Multi-Factor Risk Models and Their Applications," in Frank J. Fabozzi (ed.) *Professional Perspectives on Fixed Income Portfolio Management: Volume 2* (New Hope, PA: Frank J. Fabozzi Associates, 2001).

make a single payment to a policyholder at a specified date with a guaranteed interest rate); and (3) municipal governments for prerefunding municipal bond issues (i.e., creating a portfolio that replicates the payments that must be made for an outstanding municipal government bond issue), and, for states, payments that must be made to lottery winners who have agreed to accept payments over time rather than a lump sum.

There are two types of solutions to the problem of liability funding currently used by practitioners: (1) numerical/analytical solutions based on the concept of duration and convexity and (2) numerical solutions based on optimization methodologies. Ultimately, all methodologies can be cast in the framework of optimization, but duration and convexity play an important role from the practical as well as conceptual point of view. We will begin by discussing the cash-flow matching approach in a deterministic context and then successively discuss strategies based on duration and convexity and lastly a full stochastic programming approach.

Cash Flow Matching

Cash flow matching (CFM), also referred to as a *dedicated portfolio strategy*, in a deterministic environment is the problem of matching a predetermined set of liabilities with an investment portfolio that produces a deterministic stream of cash flows.[10] In this context, fluctuations of interest rates, credit risk, and other sources of uncertainty are ignored. There are, however, conditions where financial decisions have to be made. Among them we will consider:

- Reinvestment of excess cash
- Borrowing against future cash flows to match liabilities
- Trading constraints such as odd lots

To formulate the model, consider a set of m dates $\{t_0, t_1, ..., t_m\}$ and a universe U of investable assets $U = \{1, 2, ..., n\}$. Call $\{K_{i,0}, ..., K_{i,m}\}$ the stream of cash flows related to the i-th asset. We will consider only bonds but most considerations that will be developed apply to broader classes of assets with positive and negative cash flows. In the case of a bond with unit price P_i per unit par value 1, with coupon $c_{i,t}$, and with maturity k, the cash flows are

$$\{-P_i, c_{i,1}, ..., c_{i,k-1}, c_{i,k} + 1, 0, ..., 0\}$$

Let's call L_t the liability at time t. Liabilities must be met with a portfolio

$$\sum_{i \in U} \alpha_i P_i$$

where α_i is the amount of bond i in the portfolio. The CFM problem can be written, in its simplest form, in the following way:

---

[10] For an illustration of cash flow matching applied to pension fund liabilities, see Frank J. Fabozzi and Peter F. Christensen, "Dedicated Bond Portfolios," Chapter 45 in Frank J. Fabozzi (ed.), *The Handbook of Fixed Income Securities* (New York, NY: McGraw Hill, 2000).

$$\text{Minimize } \sum_{i \in U} \alpha_i P_i, \text{ subject to the constraints}$$

$$\sum_{i \in U} \alpha_i K_{i,t} \geq L_t$$

$$\alpha_i \geq 0$$

The last constraint specifies that short selling is not permitted.

The above formulation of the CFM as an optimization problem is too crude as it takes into account only the fact that it is practically impossible to create exactly the required cash flows. In fact, in this formulation at each date there will be an excess of cash not used to satisfy the liability due at that date. If borrowing and reinvesting are allowed, as is normally the case, excess cash can be reinvested and used at the next date while small cash shortcomings can be covered with borrowing.

Suppose, therefore, that it is possible to borrow in each period an amount b_t at the rate β_t and reinvest an amount r_t at the rate ρ_t. Suppose that these rates are the same for all periods. At each period we will require that the positive cash flow exactly matches liabilities. Therefore coupon payments of that period plus the amount reinvested in the previous period augmented by the interest earned on this amount plus the reinvestment of that period will be equal to the liabilities of the same period, plus the repayment of borrowing in the previous period plus the eventual new borrowing of the period. The optimization problem can be formulated as follows:

$$\text{Minimize } \sum_{i \in U} \alpha_i P_i, \text{ subject to the constraints}$$

$$\sum_{i \in U} \alpha_i K_{i,t} + (1 + \rho_t) r_{t-1} + b_t = L_t + (1 + \beta_t) b_{t-1} + r_t$$

$$b_m = 0$$

$$\alpha_i \geq 0; i \in U$$

The CFM problem formulated in this way is a linear programming (LP) problem.[11] Problems of this type can be routinely solved on desk-top computers using standard off-the-shelf software.

---

[11] The mathematical programming techniques described in this chapter are discussed in Chapter 7.

The next step is to consider trading constraints, such as the need to purchase "even" lots of assets. Under these constraints, assets can be purchased only in multiples of some minimal quantity, the even lots. For a large organization, purchasing smaller amounts, "odd" lots, might be suboptimal and might result in substantial costs and illiquidity.

The optimization problem that results from the purchase of assets in multiples of a minimal quantity is much more difficult. It is no longer a relatively simple LP problem but it becomes a much harder mixed-integer programming (MIP) problem. A MIP problem is conceptually more difficult and computationally much more expensive to solve than an LP problem.

The next step involves allowing for transaction costs. The objective of including transaction costs is to avoid portfolios made up of many assets held in small quantities. Including transaction costs, which must be divided between fixed and variable costs, will again result in a MIP problem which will, in general, be quite difficult to solve.

In the formulation of the CFM problem discussed thus far, it was implicitly assumed that the dates of positive cash flows and liabilities are the same. This might not be the case. There might be small misalignment due to the practical availability of funds or positive cash flows might be missing when liabilities are due. To cope with these problems, one could simply generate a bigger model with more dates so that all the dates corresponding to inflows and outflows are properly considered. In a number of cases, this will be the only possible solution. A simpler solution, when feasible, consists in adjusting the dates so that they match, considering the positive interest earnings or negative costs incurred to match dates.

In the above formulation of the CFM problem, the initial investment cost is the only variable to optimize: The eventual residual cash at the end of the last period is considered lost. However, it is possible to design a different model under the following scenario. One might try to maximize the final cash position, subject to the constraint of meeting all the liabilities and within the constraint of an investment budget. In other words, one starts with an investment budget which should be at least sufficient to cover all the liabilities. The optimization problem is to maximize the final cash position.

We have just described the CFM problem in a deterministic setting. This is more than an academic exercise as many practical dedication problems can be approximately cast into this framework. Generally speaking, however, a dedication problem would require a stochastic formulation, which in turn requires multistage stochastic optimization. Dahl, Meeraus, and Zenios[12] discuss the stochastic case. Later in this

---

[12] H. Dahl, A. Meeraus, and S.A. Zenios, "Some Financial Optimization Models," in S.A. Zenios (ed.), *Financial Optimization* (Cambridge: Cambridge University Press, 1993).

chapter we discuss dedication in a multistage stochastic formulation, as well as other bond portfolio optimization problems. Let's now discuss portfolio immunization, which is the numerical/analytical solution of a special dedication problem under a stochastic framework.

Portfolio Immunization

The actuary generally credited with pioneering the immunization strategy is Reddington, who defined immunization in 1952 as "the investment of the assets in such a way that the existing business is immune to a general change in the rate of interest."[13] The mathematical formulation of the immunization problem was proposed by Fisher and Weil in 1971.[14] The framework is the following in the single liability case (which we refer to as *single period immunization*): Given a predetermined liability at a fixed time horizon, create a portfolio able to satisfy the given liability even if interest rates change.

The problem would be simple to solve if investors were happy to invest in U.S. Treasury zero-coupon bonds (i.e., U.S. Treasury strips) maturing at exactly the given date of the liability. However, investors seek to earn a return greater than the risk-free rate. For example, the typical product where a portfolio immunization strategy is used is a GIC offered by an insurance company. This product is typically offered to a pension plan. The insurer receives a single premium from the pension sponsor and in turn guarantees an interest rate that will be earned such that the payment to the policyholder at a specified date is equal to the premium plus the guaranteed interest. The interest rate offered on the policy is greater than that on existing risk-free securities, otherwise a potential policy buyer can do the immunization without the need for the insurance company's service. The objective of the insurance company is to earn a higher rate than that offered on the policy (i.e., the guaranteed interest rate).[15]

The solution of the problem is based on the fact that a rise in interest rates produces a drop in bond prices but an increase in the reinvestment income on newly invested sums while a fall of interest rates increases bond prices but decreases the reinvestment income on newly invested sums. One

---

[13] F.M. Reddington, "Review of the Principle of Life-Office Valuations," *Journal of the Institute of Actuaries* 78 (1952), pp. 286–340.

[14] L. Fisher and R.L. Weil, "Coping with the Risk of Interest-Rate Fluctuations: Returns to Bondholders from Naive and Optimal Strategies," *Journal of Business* (October 1971), pp. 408–431.

[15] For a discussion of the implementation issues associated with immunization, see Frank J. Fabozzi and Peter F. Christensen, "Bond Immunization: An Asset/Liability Optimization Strategy," Chapter 44 in *The Handbook of Fixed Income Securities: Sixth Edition.*

can therefore choose an investment strategy such that the change in a portfolio's value is offset by changes in the returns earned by the reinvestment of the cash obtained through coupon payments or the repayment of the principal of bonds maturing prior to the liability date.

The principle applies in the case of multiple liabilities. To see how *multiple-period immunization* works, let's first demonstrate that—given a stream of cash flows at fixed dates—there is one instant at which the value of the stream is insensitive to small parallel shifts in interest rates. Consider a case where a sum V_0 is initially invested in a portfolio of risk-free bonds (i.e., bonds with no default risk) that produces a stream of N deterministic cash flows K_i at fixed dates t_i. At each time t_i the sum K_i is reinvested at the risk-free rate. Suppose that there is only one rate r common to all periods. The following relationship holds:

$$V_0 = \sum_{i=1}^{N} K_i e^{-rt_i}$$

where we have used the formula for the present value in continuous time.

As each intermediate payment is reinvested, the value of the portfolio at any instant t is given by the following expression:

$$V_t = \sum_{i=1}^{N} K_i e^{-r(t-t_i)} = e^{rt} V_0$$

Our objective is to determine a time t such that the value V_t at time t of the portfolio is insensitive to parallel shifts in the interest rates. The quantity V_t is a function of the interest rate r. The derivative of V_t with respect to r must be zero so that V_t is insensitive to interest rate changes. Let's compute the derivative:

$$\frac{dV_t}{dr} = \sum_{i=1}^{N} K_i (t - t_i) e^{r(t-t_i)}$$

$$= t V_t - V_t \frac{\sum_{i=1}^{N} K_i t_i e^{-rt_i}}{V_0}$$

$$= V \left[t - \sum_{i=1}^{N} t_i \left(\frac{K_i e^{-rt_i}}{V_0} \right) \right]$$

From this expression it is clear that the derivative

$$\frac{dV_t}{dr}$$

is zero at a time horizon equal to the portfolio duration. In fact, the quantity

$$\sum_{i=1}^{N} t_i \left(\frac{K_i e^{-rt_i}}{V_0} \right)$$

is the portfolio's duration expressed in continuous time.

Therefore, if the term structure of interest rates is flat, we can match a given liability with a portfolio whose duration is equal to the time of the liability and whose present value is equal to the present value of the liability. This portfolio will be insensitive to small parallel shifts of the term structure of interest rates.

We can now extend and generalize this reasoning. Consider a stream of liabilities L_t. Our objective is to match this stream of liabilities with a stream of cash flows from some initial investment insensitive to changes in interest rates. First we want to prove that the present value of liabilities and of cash flows must match. Consider the framework of CMF with reinvestment but no borrowing:

$$\sum_{i \in U} \alpha_i K_{i,t} + (1 + \rho_t) r_{t-1} = L_t + r_t$$

$$\sum_{i \in U} \alpha_i K_{i,t} - L_t \geq 0$$

$$a_i \geq 0; i \in U$$

We can recursively write the following relationships:

$$\sum_{i \in U} \alpha_i K_{i,1} - L_t = r_1$$

$$\sum_{i \in U} \alpha_i K_{i,2} + (1 + \rho_2) \sum_{i \in U} \alpha_i K_{i,1} = (1 + \rho_2) L_1 + L_2 + r_2$$

...

$$\sum_{i=1}^{n} \left[\alpha_i K_{i,1} \prod_{t=2}^{m} (1+\rho_t) + \ldots + \alpha_i K_{i,m} \right] = L_1 \prod_{t=2}^{m} (1+\rho_t) + \ldots + L_m$$

$$a_i \geq 0; i \in U$$

If we divide both sides of the last equation by

$$\prod_{t=2}^{m} (1+\rho_t)$$

we see that the present value of the portfolio's stream of cash flows must be equal to the present value of the stream of liabilities. We can rewrite the above expression in continuous-time notation as

$$\sum_{i=1}^{n} [\alpha_i K_{i,1} + \ldots + \alpha_i K_{i,m} e^{-r_m t_m}] = L_1 + \ldots + L_m e^{-r_m t_m}$$

As in the case of CFM, if cash flows and liabilities do not occur at the same dates, we can construct an enlarged model with more dates. At these dates, cash flows or liabilities can be zero.

To see under what conditions this expression is insensitive to small parallel shifts of the term structure, we perturb the term structure by a small shift r and compute the derivative with respect to r for $r = 0$. In this way, all rates are written as $r_t + r$. If we compute the derivatives we obtain the following equation:

$$\frac{d \sum_{i=1}^{n} [\alpha_i K_{i,1} + \ldots + \alpha_i K_{i,m} e^{-(r_m+r)t_m}]}{dr} = \frac{d[L_1 + \ldots + L_m e^{-(r_m+r)t_m}]}{dr}$$

$$-\sum_{i=1}^{n} [\alpha_i K_{i,1} + \ldots + \alpha_i K_{i,m} t_m e^{-(r_m+r)t_m}] = -[L_1 + \ldots + L_m t_m e^{-(r_m+r)t_m}]$$

which tells us that the first-order conditions for portfolio immunization are that the duration of the cash flows must be equal to the duration of the liabilities. This duration is intended in the sense of effective duration which allows for a shift in the term structure. This condition does not determine univocally the portfolio.

To determine the portfolio, we can proceed in two ways. The first is through optimization. Optimization calls for maximizing some function subject to constraints. In the CFM problem there are two constraints: (1) The initial present value of cash flows must match the initial present value of liabilities, and (2) the duration of cash flows must match the duration of liabilities. A typical objective function is the portfolio's return at the final date. It can be demonstrated that this problem can be approximated by an LP problem.

Optimization might not be ideal as the resulting portfolio might be particularly exposed to the risk of nonparallel shifts of the term structure. In fact, it can be demonstrated that the result of the yield maximization under immunization constraints tends to produce a barbell type of portfolio. A barbell portfolio is one in which the portfolio is concentrated at short-term and long-term maturity securities. A portfolio of this type is particularly exposed to yield curve risk, i.e., to the risk that the term structure changes its shape, as described in Chapter 20.

One way to control yield curve risk is to impose second-order convexity conditions. In fact, reasoning as above and taking the second derivative of both sides, it can be demonstrated that, in order to protect the portfolio from yield curve risk, the convexity of the cash flow stream and the convexity of the liability stream must be equal. (Recall from Chapter 4 that mathematically convexity is the derivative of duration.) This approach can be generalized[16] by assuming that changes of interest rates can be approximated as a linear function of a number of risk factors. Under this assumption we can write

$$\Delta r_t = \sum_{j=1}^{k} \beta_{j,t} \Delta f_j + \varepsilon_t$$

where the f_j are the factors and ε_t is an error term that is assumed to be normally distributed with zero mean and unitary variance. Factors here are a simple discrete-time instance of the factors we met in the description of the term structure in continuous time in Chapter 19. There we assumed that interest rates were an Itô process function of a number of other Itô processes. Here we assume that changes in interest rates, which are a discrete-time process, are a linear function of other discrete-time processes called "factors." Each path is a vector of real numbers, one for each date.

---

[16] See Stavros Zenios, *Practical Financial Optimization*, unpublished manuscript.

Ignoring the error term, changes in the present value of the stream of cash flows are therefore given by the following expression:

$$
\Delta V = -\sum_{i=1}^{n} [\alpha_i K_{i,1} + \ldots + \alpha_i K_{i,m} t_m e^{-r_m t_m} \Delta r_m]
$$

$$
= -\sum_{i=1}^{n} \left[\alpha_i K_{i,1} + \ldots + \alpha_i K_{i,m} t_m e^{-r_m t_m} \sum_{j=1}^{k} \beta_{j,t_m} \Delta f_j \right]
$$

The derivative of the present value with respect to one of the factors is therefore given by

$$
\frac{\partial V}{\partial f_j} = -\sum_{i=1}^{n} \left[\alpha_i K_{i,1} + \ldots + \alpha_i K_{i,m} t_m \beta_{j,t_m} e^{-r_m t_m} \right]
$$

The factor duration with respect to the j-th factor is defined as the relative value sensitivity to that factor:

$$
k_j = \frac{1}{V} \frac{\partial V}{\partial f_j}
$$

The second derivative represents convexity relative to a factor:

$$
Q_j = \frac{1}{V} \frac{\partial^2 V}{\partial f_j^2}
$$

First- and second-order immunization conditions become the equality of factor duration and convexity relative to cash flows and liabilities.

Scenario Optimization

The above strategies are based on perturbing the term structure of interest rates with a linear function of one or more factors. We allow stochastic behavior as rates can vary (albeit in a controlled way through factors) and impose immunization constraints. We can obtain a more general formulation of a stochastic problem in terms of scenarios.[17] Let the variables be stochastic but assume distributions are discrete. Scenar-

---

[17] Ron Dembo, "Scenario Immunization," in *Financial Optimization*.

ios are joint paths of all the relevant variables. A probability number is attached to each scenario. A path of interest rates is a scenario. If we consider corporate bonds, a scenario will be formed, for example, by a joint path of interest rates and credit ratings. How scenarios are generated will be discussed later in this chapter.

Suppose that scenarios are given. Using an LP program, one can find the optimal portfolio that (1) matches all the liabilities in each scenario and (2) minimizes initial costs or maximizes final cash positions subject to budget constraints. The CFM problem can be reformulated as follows:

$$\text{Minimize } \sum_{i \in U} \alpha_i P_i \text{, subject to the constraints}$$

$$\sum_{i \in U} \alpha_i K^s_{i,t} + (1 + \rho^s_t)r^s_{t-1} + b^s_t = L^s_t + (1 + \beta^s_t)b^s_{t-1} + r^s_t$$

$$b^s_m = 0$$

$$a_i \geq 0; i \in U$$

In this formulation, all terms are stochastic and scenario dependent except the portfolio's weights. Each scenario imposes a constraint.

Scenario optimization can also be used in a more general context. One can describe a general objective, for instance expected return or a utility function, which is scenario-dependent. Scenario-dependent constraints can be added. The optimization program maximizes or minimizes the objective function subject to the constraints.

Stochastic Programming

Strategies discussed thus far are static (or myopic) in the sense that decisions are made initially and never changed. As explained in Chapter 7, stochastic programming (or multistage stochastic optimization) is a more general, flexible framework in which decisions are made at multiple stages, under uncertainty, and on the basis of past decisions and information then available. Both immunization and CFM discussed above can be recast in the framework of stochastic programming. Indeed, multistage optimization is a general framework that allows one to formulate most problems in portfolio management, not only for bonds but also for other asset classes including stocks and derivatives.

Stochastic programming is a computerized numerical methodology to solve variational problems. A **variational principle** is a law expressed as the maximization of a functional, with a functional being a real-valued function defined over other functions. Most classical physics can be expressed equivalently through differential equations or variational principles.

Variational methodologies also have important applications in engineering, where they are used to select a path that maximizes or minimizes a functional given some exogenous dynamics. For example, one might want to find the optimal path that an airplane must follow in order to minimize fuel consumption or flying time. The given dynamics are the laws of motion and eventually specific laws that describe the atmosphere and the behavior of the airplane.

Economics and finance theory have inherited this general scheme. General equilibrium theories can be expressed as variational principles. However, financial applications generally assume that some dynamics are given. In the case of bond portfolios, for example, the dynamics of interest rates are assumed to be exogenously given. The problem is to find the optimal trading strategy that satisfies some specific objective. In the case of immunization an objective might be to match liabilities at the minimum cost with zero exposure to interest rates fluctuations. The solution is a path of the portfolio's weights. In continuous time, it would be a continuous trading strategy.

Such problems are rarely solvable analytically; numerical techniques, and in particular multistage stochastic optimization, are typically required. The key advantage of stochastic programming is its ability to optimize on the entire path followed by exogenously given quantities. In applications such as bond portfolio optimization, this is an advantage over myopic strategies which optimize looking ahead only one period. However, because stochastic programming works by creating a set of scenarios and choosing the scenario that optimizes a given objective, it involves huge computational costs. Only recently have advances in IT technology made it feasible to create the large number of scenarios required for stochastic optimization. Hence there is a renewed interest in these techniques both at academia and inside financial firms.[18]

Scenario Generation

The generation of scenarios (i.e., joint paths of the stochastic variables) is key to stochastic programming. Until recently, it was imperative to create a parsimonious system of scenarios. Complex problems could be solved only on supercomputers or massively parallel computers at costs prohibitive for most organizations. While parsimony is still a requirement, sys-

---

[18] A presentation of stochastic programming in finance can be found in Zenios, *Practical Financial Optimization*, forthcoming.

tems made of thousands of scenarios can now be solved on desk-top machines. Two well-known scenario systems in practical use are SPAN, a 16-scenario system developed by the Chicago Mercantile Exchange and New York 7, a 7-scenario system use by New York insurance regulators (National Association of Insurance Commissioner scenarios).

As a general requirement, scenarios must be both "complete" and "coherent." Completeness means that scenarios must capture the business-as-usual situations as well the extremes. Coherence means that scenarios must respect the conditions typical of many financial variables. For instance, some financial variables are perfectly anti-correlated, a condition that must be respected by scenarios. Financial and economic scenarios must also be free from anticipation of information. A natural way to make nonanticipative scenarios is the use of information structures as described in Chapter 5. Information structures require that scenarios are indistinguishable up to a given date and then part in a treelike structure.

Consider the generation of interest rates scenarios. This is a problem that can be solved starting from a model of the term structure of interest rates. Continuous-time models of interest rates were introduced in Chapter 15. To create scenarios, these models need to be discretized as discussed in Chapter 15. Recall that there are different ways of discretizing a continuous-time model. For example, a Brownian motion can be simulated as a random walk whose increments are random draws from a normal distribution. Alternatively, one can adopt a binomial approximation to the Brownian motion. The first procedure creates a random sampling from a continuous distribution while the second produces a discrete-time, discrete-state model.

If we consider only risk-free bonds, the information contained in the interest rate processes is sufficient to create scenarios. A large number of scenarios can be created either by sampling or with discrete models. If, in contrast, we want to consider bonds with default risk, then we need to generate scenarios according to a specified model of credit risk (see Chapter 22). For example, if we use a rating process, we need to simulate a rating process for each bond taking into consideration correlations. It is clear that we immediately run into computational difficulties, because the number of scenarios explodes even for a modest number of bonds. Drastic simplifications need to be made to make problems tractable. Simplifications are problem-dependent.

Multistage Stochastic Programming

After creating scenarios one can effectively optimize, taking into account that after initial decisions there will be **recourses** (i.e., new decisions eventually on a smaller set of variables) at each subsequent stage. Here we provide a brief description of multistage stochastic optimization.[19]

The key idea of stochastic programming is that at every stage a decision is made based on conditional probabilities. Scenarios form an information structure so that, at each stage, scenarios are partitioned. Conditional probabilities are evaluated on scenarios that belong to each partition. For this reason, stochastic optimization is a process that runs backwards. Optimization starts from the last period, where variables are certain, and then conditional probabilities are evaluated on each partition.

To apply optimization procedures, an equivalent deterministic problem needs to be formulated. The deterministic equivalent depends on the problem's objective. Taking expectations naturally leads to **deterministic equivalents**. A deterministic equivalent of a stochastic optimization problem might involve maximizing or minimizing the conditional expectation of some quantity at each stage.

We will illustrate stochastic optimization in the case of CFM as a two-stage stochastic optimization problem. The first decision is made under conditions of uncertainty, while the second decision at step 1 is made with certain final values. This problem could be equivalently formulated in a m-period setting, admitting perfect foresight after the first period. This two-stage setting can then be extended to a true multistage setting. At the first stage there will be a new set of variables. In this case, the new variables will be the portfolio's weights at stage 1. Call S the set of scenarios. Scenarios are generated from an interest rate model. A probability p_s, $s \in S$ is associated with each scenario s. The quantity to optimize will be the expected value of final cash. The two-stage stochastic optimization problem can be formulated as follows:

$$\text{Maximize } \sum_{s \in S} p_s h_s, \text{ subject to the constraints}$$

$$\sum_{i \in U} \alpha_i K_{i,0} + b_0 + B = r_0$$

$$\sum_{i \in U} \alpha_i K_{i,t}^s + (1 + \rho_t^s) r_{t-1}^s + b_t^s = L_t^s + (1 + \beta_t^s) b_{t-1}^s + r_t^s$$

$$\sum_{i \in U} \alpha_i P_i^s = \sum_{i \in U} \gamma_i P_i^s$$

---

[19] For a full account of stochastic programming in finance, Zenios, *Practical Financial Optimization*.

$$b^s_m = 0$$

$$r^s_m = b^s$$

$$\alpha_i, \gamma_i \geq 0;\ i \in U$$

The first condition is the initial budget constraint, which tells us that the initial investment (which has a negative sign) plus the initial borrowing plus the initial budget B is equal to the first surplus. The second condition is the liability-matching condition. The third condition is the self-financing condition. Note that as interest rates are known in each scenario, bond prices are also known in each scenario. The fifth and sixth conditions are the statements that there is no borrowing at the final stage and that the objective is the final cash. The seventh condition is the constraint that weights are nonnegative at each stage

This formulation illustrates all the basic ingredients. The problem is formulated as a deterministic equivalent problem, setting as its objective the maximization of final expected cash. The final stage is certain and the process is backward. With this objective, the stochastic optimization problem is recast as an LP problem.

This formulation can be extended to an arbitrary number of stages. Formulating in full generality a multistage stochastic optimization problem is beyond the scope of this book. In fact, there are many technical points that need a careful handling.[20]

SUMMARY

- Bond market indexes can be classified as broad-based bond market indexes and specialized bond market indexes.
- Bond management strategies range from pure bond index matching to active management.
- Pure bond index matching strategy involves the least risk of underperforming a bond market index.
- Enhanced indexing strategies involve constructing portfolios to match the primary risk factors associated with a bond market index without acquiring each issue in the index.

---

[20] See, for example, Peter Kall and Stein W. Wallace, *Stochastic Programming* (Chichester, U.K.: John Wiley & Sons, 1994).

- Active bond strategies attempt to outperform the bond market index by intentionally constructing a portfolio that will have a greater index mismatch than in the case of enhanced indexing.
- Tracking error, or active risk, is the standard deviation of a portfolio's return relative to the return of the benchmark index.
- Systematic risk factors are the common factors that affect all securities in a certain category in the benchmark bond market index.
- Nonsystematic factor risk is the risk that is not attributable to the systematic risk factors.
- Systematic risk factors are divided into term structure risk factors and nonterm structure risk factors.
- Given the risk factors associated with a benchmark index, forward-looking tracking error can be estimated.
- A multifactor risk model can be used by the portfolio manager in combination with optimization in constructing and rebalancing a portfolio to reduce tracking error.
- Optimization is generally done step-by-step based on marginal contributions of each security.
- Liability-funding strategies are strategies whose objective is to match a given set of liabilities due at future times.
- Cash flow matching in a deterministic environment is the problem of matching a predetermined set of liabilities with an investment portfolio that produces a deterministic stream of cash flows.
- Cash flow matching problems can be solved with linear programming or mixed-integer programming algorithms.
- The objective of an immunization strategy is to construct a portfolio that is insensitive to small parallel shifts of interest rates.
- A given stream of liabilities can be matched with a portfolio whose duration is equal to the duration of the liabilities and whose present value is equal to the present value of the liabilities.
- Matching duration and present value makes portfolios insensitive only to small parallel shifts of interest rates; in order to minimize the effects of nonparallel shifts, optimization procedures are needed.
- Scenario optimization optimizes on a number of representative scenarios.
- Multistage stochastic optimization deals with the problem of optimization when there is recourse, that is, when decisions are made at each stage.
- Taking expectations at each stage, stochastic optimization becomes a problem of deterministic optimization.

CHAPTER 22

Credit Risk Modeling and Credit Default Swaps*

In Chapter 2, we described the different forms of credit risk–default risk, credit spread risk, and downgrade risk. Credit derivatives are financial instruments that are designed to transfer the credit risk exposure of an underlying asset or assets between two parties. With credit derivatives, market participants can either acquire or reduce credit risk exposure. The ability to transfer credit risk and return provides a new tool for market participants to improve performance. Using credit derivatives, banks may sell concentrated credit risks in their portfolios while keeping the loans of their customers on their books; these loans are otherwise not transferable due to relationship management issues or due to legal agreements. Credit derivatives include credit default swaps, asset swaps, total return swaps, credit linked notes, credit spread options, and credit spread forwards.[1] By far the most popular credit derivatives is the credit default swap. In this chapter we describe credit risk modeling and the valuation of credit default swaps. We begin with a discussion of the basic features of credit default swaps.

CREDIT DEFAULT SWAPS

In a credit default swap, the documentation will identify the *reference entity* or the *reference obligation*. The reference entity is the issuer of

---

[1] For a discussion of each of these credit derivatives, see Mark J.P. Anson, Frank J. Fabozzi, Moorad Choudhry, and Ren-Raw Chen, *Credit Derivatives: Instruments, Applications, and Pricing* (Hoboken, NJ: John Wiley & Sons, 2003).

---

* This chapter is coauthored with Professor Ren-Raw Chen of Rutgers University.

the debt instrument. It could be a corporation, a sovereign government, or a bank loan. In contrast, a *reference obligation* is a specific obligation for which protection is being sought.

In a credit default swap, the protection buyer pays a fee, the *swap premium*, to the protection seller in return for the right to receive a payment conditional upon the default of the reference obligation or the reference entity. Collectively, the payments made by the protection buyer are called the *premium leg*; the contingent payment that might have to be made by the protection seller is called the *protection leg*.

In the documentation of a trade, a default is defined in terms of a *credit event* and we shall use the terms "default" and "credit event" interchangeably throughout this book. Should a credit event occur, the protection seller must make a payment.

Credit default swaps can be classified as follows: single-name credit default swaps and basket swaps. We'll discuss the difference between these types of swaps next.

Single-Name Credit Default Swaps

The interdealer market has evolved to where single-name credit default swaps for corporate and sovereign reference entities are standardized. The parties to the trade specify at the outset when the credit default swap will terminate. If no credit event has occurred by the maturity of the credit swap, then the swap terminates at the *scheduled termination date*—a date specified by the parties in the contract. However, the *termination date* under the contract is the earlier of the scheduled termination date or a date upon which a credit event occurs and notice is provided. Therefore, notice of a credit event terminates a credit default swap.

The *termination value* for a credit default swap is calculated at the time of the credit event, and the exact procedure that is followed to calculate the termination value will depend on the settlement terms specified in the contract. This will be either cash settlement or physical settlement.

A credit default swap contract may specify a predetermined payout value on occurrence of a credit event. This may be the nominal value of the swap contract. Alternatively, the termination value can be calculated as the difference between the nominal value of the reference obligation and its market value at the time of the credit event. This arrangement is more common with cash-settled contracts.

With *physical settlement*, on occurrence of a credit event the buyer delivers the reference obligation to the seller, in return for which the seller pays the face value of the delivered asset to the buyer. The contract may specify a number of alternative issues of the reference entity that the buyer can deliver to the seller. These are known as *deliverable obligations*.

This may apply when a credit default swap has been entered into on a reference entity rather than a specific obligation issued by that entity (i.e., when there is a reference entity rather than a reference obligation).

Where more than one deliverable obligation is specified, the protection buyer will invariably deliver the one that is the cheapest on the list of eligible deliverable obligations. This gives rise to the concept of the *cheapest-to-deliver*. In practice, the protection buyer will deliver the cheapest-to-deliver bond from the deliverable basket. This delivery option has debatable value in theory, but significant value in practice.

The standard contract for a single-name credit default swap in the interdealer market calls for a quarterly payment of the swap premium. Typically, the swap premium is paid in arrears. The quarterly payment is determined using one of the day count conventions in the bond market. A day count convention indicates the number of days in the month and the number of days in a year that will be used to determine how to prorate the swap premium to a quarter. The day count convention used for credit default swaps is actual/360. A day convention of actual/360 means that to determine the payment in a quarter, the actual number of days in the quarter are used and 360 days are assumed for the year.

Basket Default Swaps

In a basket default swap, there is more than one reference entity. Typically, in a basket default swap, there are three to five reference entities. There are different types of basket default swap. They are classified as follows:

- *Nth* to default swaps
- Subordinate basket default swaps
- Senior basket default swaps

Below we describe each type.

Nth to Default Swaps

In an N*th-to-default swap*, the protection seller makes a payment to the protection buyer only after there has been a default for the Nth reference entity and no payment for default of the first $(N - 1)$ reference entities. Once there is a payout for the Nth reference entity, the credit default swap terminates. That is, if the other reference entities that have not defaulted subsequently do default, the protection seller does not make any payout.

For example, suppose that there are five reference entities. In a *first-to-default basket swap* a payout is triggered after there is a default for only one of the reference entities. There are no other payouts made by the protection seller even if the other four reference entities subsequently have a credit event. If a payout is triggered only after there is a second default from among the reference entities, the swap is referred to as a *second-to-default basket swap*. So, if there is only one reference entity for which there is a default over the tenor of the swap, the protection seller does not make any payment. If there is a default for a second reference entity while the swap is in effect, there is a payout by the protection seller and the swap terminates. The protection seller does not make any payment for a default that may occur for the three remaining reference entities.

Subordinate and Senior Basket Credit Default Swaps

In a *subordinate basket default swap* there is (1) a maximum payout for each defaulted reference entity and (2) a maximum aggregate payout over the tenor of the swap for the basket of reference entities. For example, assume there are five reference entities and that (1) the maximum payout is $10 million for a reference entity and (2) the maximum aggregate payout is $10 million. Also assume that defaults result in the following losses over the tenor of the swap:

Loss result from default of first reference entity	=	$6 million
Loss result from default of second reference entity	=	$10 million
Loss result from default of third reference entity	=	$16 million
Loss result from default of fourth reference entity	=	$12 million
Loss result from default of fifth reference entity	=	$15 million

When there is a default for the first reference entity, there is a $6 million payout. The remaining amount that can be paid out on any subsequent defaults for the other four reference entities is $4 million. When there is a default for the second reference entity of $10 million, only $4 million will be paid out. At that point, the swap terminates.

In a *senior basket default swap* there is a maximum payout for each reference entity but the payout is not triggered until after a specified threshold is reached. To illustrate, again assume there are five reference entities and the maximum payout for an individual reference entity is $10 million. Also assume that there is no payout until the first $40 million of default losses (the threshold). Using the hypothetical losses above, the payout by the protection seller would be as follows. The losses for the first three defaults is $32 million. However, because the maximum loss for a reference entity, only $10 million of the $16 million is applied to the $40 million threshold. Consequently, after the third default, $26 million ($6 million + $10 million + $10 million) is applied toward the threshold. When the fourth reference entity defaults, only $10 million is applied to the $40 million threshold. At this point, $36 million is applied to the $40 million threshold. When the fifth reference entity defaults in our illustration, only $10 million is relevant since the maximum payout for a reference entity is $10 million. The first $4 million of the $10 million is applied to cover the threshold. Thus, there is a $6 million payout by the protection seller.

LEGAL DOCUMENTATION

Credit derivatives are privately negotiated agreements traded over the counter. The International Swaps and Derivatives Association (ISDA) has recognized the need to provide a common format for credit derivative documentation. In addition to the definitions of credit events, ISDA developed the *ISDA Master Agreement*. This is the authoritative contract used by industry participants because it established international standards governing privately negotiated derivative trades (all derivatives, not just credit derivatives).

The most important section of the documentation for a credit default swap is what the parties to the contract agree constitutes a credit event that will trigger a credit default payment. Definitions for credit events are provided by the ISDA. First published in 1999, there have been periodic supplements and revisions of these definitions

The *1999 ISDA Credit Derivatives Definitions* (referred to as the "1999 Definitions") provides a list of eight possible credit events: (1) bankruptcy; (2) credit event upon merger; (3) cross acceleration; (4) cross default; (5) downgrade; (6) failure to pay; (7) repudiation; and (8) restructuring. These eight events attempt to capture every type of situation that could cause the credit quality of the reference entity to deteriorate, or cause the value of the reference obligation to decline.

The parties to a credit default swap may include all of these events, or select only those that they believe are most relevant. There has been standardization of the credit events that are used in credit default swaps in the United States and Europe. Nevertheless, this does not preclude a credit protection buyer from including broader credit protection.

CREDIT RISK MODELING: STRUCTURAL MODELS

To value credit derivatives it is necessary to be able to model credit risk. Models for credit risks have long existed in the insurance and corporate finance literature. Those models concentrate on default rates, credit ratings, and credit risk premiums. These traditional models focus on diversification and assume that default risks are idiosyncratic and hence can be diversified away in large portfolios. Models of this kind are along the line of portfolio theory that employs the *capital asset pricing model* (CAPM). In the CAPM, only the systematic risk, or market risk, matters.

For single isolated credits, the models calculate risk premiums as mark-ups onto the risk-free rate. Since the default risk is not diversified away, a similar model to the CAPM called the security market line (described in Chapter 17) is used to compute the correct markup for bearing the default risk. The *Sharpe ratio* is commonly used to measure how credit risks are priced.[2]

Modern credit derivative models can be partitioned into two groups known as structural models and reduced form models. *Structural models* were pioneered by Black and Scholes[3] and Merton.[4] The basic idea, common to all structural-type models, is that a company defaults on its debt if the value of the assets of the company falls below a certain default point. For this reason, these models are also known as *firm-value models*. In these models it has been demonstrated that default can be modeled as an option and, as a result, researchers were able to apply the same principles used for option pricing to the valuation of risky corporate securities. The application of option pricing theory avoids the use of risk premium and tries to use other marketable securities to price the option. The use of the option pricing theory set forth by Black-Scholes-Merton (BSM) hence provides a significant improvement over traditional methods for valuing default risky bonds. It also offers not only much more accurate prices but provides information about how to hedge out the default risk which was not obtainable from traditional methods. Subsequent to the work of BSM, there have been many extensions and these extensions are described in this chapter.

The second group of credit models, known as *reduced form models*, are more recent. These models, most notably the Jarrow-Turnbull[5] and

---

[2] Robert Merton, "Option Pricing When Underlying Stock Returns Are Discontinuous," *Journal of Financial Economics* 3 (1976), pp. 125–144.

[3] Fischer Black and Myron Scholes, "The Pricing of Options and Corporate Liabilities," *Journal of Political Economy* 81, no. 3 (1973), pp. 637–654.

[4] Robert Merton, "Theory of Rational Option Pricing," *Bell Journal of Economics* (Spring 1973), pp. 141–183, and Robert Merton, "On the Pricing of Corporate Debt: The Risk Structure of Interest Rates," *Journal of Finance* 29, no. 2 (1974), pp. 449–470.

[5] Robert Jarrow and Stuart Turnbull, "Pricing Derivatives on Financial Securities Subject to Default Risk," *Journal of Finance* 50, no. 1 (1995), pp. 53–86.

Duffie-Singleton[6] models, do not look inside the firm. Instead, they model directly the likelihood of default or downgrade. Not only is the current probability of default modeled, some researchers attempt to model a "forward curve" of default probabilities which can be used to price instruments of varying maturities. Modeling a probability has the effect of making default a surprise—the default event is a random event which can suddenly occur at any time. All we know is its probability.

There is no standard model for credit. Part of the reason why this is so is that each of the models has its own set of advantages and disadvantages, making the choice of which to use depend heavily on what the model is to be used for.

The Black-Scholes-Merton Model

The earliest credit model that employed the option pricing theory can be credited to BSM. Black-Scholes, explicitly articulated that corporate liabilities can be viewed as a covered call: own the asset but short a call option. In the simplest setting, where the company has only one zero-coupon debt, at the maturity of the debt the debt holder either gets paid the face value of the debt—in such a case, the ownership of the company is transferred to the equity holder—or takes control of the company—in such a case, the equity holder receives nothing. The debt holder of the company therefore is subject to default risk for he or she may not be able to receive the face value of his or her investment. BSM effectively turned a risky debt evaluation into a covered call evaluation whereby the option pricing formulas can readily apply.

In BSM, the company balance sheet consists of issued equity with a market value at time t equal to $E(t)$. On the liability side is debt with a face value of K issued in the form of a zero-coupon bond that matures at time T. The market value of this debt at time t is denoted by $D(t,T)$. The value of the assets of the firm at time t is given by $A(t)$.

At time T (the maturity of the debt), the market value of the issued equity of the company is the amount remaining after the debts have been paid out of the firm's assets; that is,

$$E(T) = \max\{A(T) - K, 0\}$$

This payoff is identical to that of a call option on the value of the firm's assets struck at the face value of the debt. The payoff is graphed as a function of the asset value in Exhibit 22.1. The holders of the risky cor-

---

[6] Darrell Duffie and Kenneth Singleton, "Modeling the Term Structure of Defaultable Bonds," working paper, Stanford University, 1997.

porate debt get paid either the face value, K, under no default or take over the firm, A, under default. Hence the value of the debt on the maturity date is given by

$$D(T, T) = \min\{A(T), K\}$$
$$= A(T) - \max\{A(T) - K, 0\} \quad (22.1)$$
$$= K - \max\{K - A(T), 0\} \quad (22.2)$$

The equations provide two interpretations. Equation (22.1) decomposes the risky debt into the asset and a short call. This interpretation was first given by Black and Scholes that equity owners essentially own a call option of the company. If the company performs well, then the equity owners should call the company; or otherwise, the equity owners let the debt owners own the company. Equation (22.2) decomposes the risky debt into a risk-free debt and a short put. This interpretation explains the default risk of the corporate debt. The issuer (equity owners) can put the company back to the debt owner when the performance is bad.[7] The default risk hence is the put option. These relationships are shown in Exhibit 22.1. Exhibits 22.1(a) and 22.1(b) explain the relationship between equity and risky debt and Exhibits 22.1(b) and 22.1(c) explain the relationship between risky and risk-free debts.

Note that the value of the equity and debt when added together must equal the assets of the firm at all times, that is, $A(t) = E(t) + D(t,T)$. Clearly, at maturity, this is true as we have

EXHIBIT 22.1   Payoff Diagrams at Maturity for Equity, Risky Debt, and Risk-Free Debt

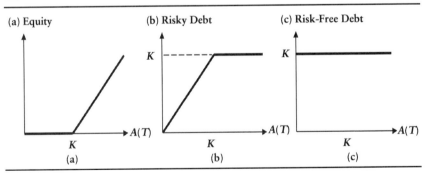

---

[7] A covered call is a combination of a selling call option and owning the same face value of the shares which might have to be delivered should the option expire in the money. If the option expires in the money, a net profit equal to the strike is made. If the option expires worthless, then the position is worth the stock price.

$$E(T) + D(T, T) = \max\{A(T) - K, 0\} + \min\{A(T), K\}$$
$$= A(T)$$

as required.

Since any corporate debt is a contingent claim on the firm's future asset value at the time the debt matures, this is what we must model in order to capture the default. BSM assumed that the dynamics of the asset value follow a lognormal stochastic process of the form

$$\frac{dA(t)}{A(t)} = r dt + \sigma dW(t) \tag{22.3}$$

where r is the instantaneous risk-free rate which is assumed constant, σ is the percentage volatility, and $W(t)$ is the Wiener process under the *risk neutral measure* (see Chapter 15).[8] This is the same process as is generally assumed within equity markets for the evolution of stock prices and has the property that the asset value of the firm can never go negative and that the random changes in the asset value increase proportionally with the asset value itself. As it is the same assumption used by Black-Scholes for pricing equity options, it is possible to use the option pricing equations developed by BSM to price risky corporate liabilities.

The company can default only at the maturity time of the debt when the payment of the debt (face value) is made. At maturity, if the asset value lies above the face value, there is no default, else the company is in bankruptcy and the recovery value of the debt is the asset value of the firm. While we shall discuss more complex cases later, for this simple one-period case, the probability of default at maturity is

$$p = \int_{-\infty}^{K} \phi[A(T)] dA(T) = 1 - N(d_2) \tag{22.4}$$

where $\phi(\cdot)$ represents the log normal density function, $N(\cdot)$ represents the cumulative normal probability, and

---

[8] The discussions of the risk neutral measure and the change of measure using the Girsanov theorem can be found in standard finance texts. See, for example, Darrell Duffie, *Dynamic Asset Pricing* (New Jersey: Princeton Press, 2000), and John Hull, *Options, Futures, and Other Derivatives* (New York: Prentice Hall, 2002).

$$d_2 = \frac{\ln A(t) - \ln K + (r - \sigma^2/2)(T-t)}{\sigma\sqrt{T-t}}$$

Equation (22.4) implies that the risk neutral probability of in the money $N(d_2)$ is also the *survival probability*. To find the current value of the debt, $D(t,T)$ (maturing at time T), we need to first use the BSM result to find the current value of the equity. As shown above, this is equal to the value of a call option:

$$E(t) = A(t)N(d_1) - e^{-r(T-t)}KN(d_2) \qquad (22.5)$$

where $d_1 = d_2 + \sigma\sqrt{T-t}$. The current value of the debt is a covered call value:

$$\begin{aligned} D(t,T) &= A(t) - E(t) \qquad (22.6)\\ &= A(t) - [A(t)N(d_1) - e^{-r(T-t)}KN(d_2)]\\ &= A(t)[1 - N(d_1)] + e^{-r(T-t)}KN(d_2) \end{aligned}$$

Note that the second term in the last equation is the present value of probability-weighted face value of the debt. It means that if default does not occur (with probability $N(d_2)$), the debt owner receives the face value K. Since the probability is risk neutral, the probability-weighted value is discounted by the risk-free rate. The first term represents the recovery value. The two values together make up the value of debt.

The yield of the debt is calculated by solving $D(t,T) = Ke^{-y(T-t)}$ for y to give

$$y = \frac{\ln K - \ln D(t,T)}{T-t} \qquad (22.7)$$

Consider the case of a company which currently has net assets worth \$140 million and has issued \$100 million in debt in the form of a zero-coupon bond which matures in one year. By looking at the equity markets, we estimate that the volatility of the asset value is 30%. The risk-free interest rate is at 5%. We therefore have

$A(t)$ = \$140 million
K = \$100 million
σ = 30%

$$T - t \;\; = \;\; 1 \text{ year}$$
$$r \quad\;\; = \;\; 5\%$$

Applying equation (22.5), the equity value based upon the above example is,

$$d_2 \;=\; \frac{\ln 140 - \ln 100 + (0.05 - 0.3^2) \times 1}{0.3\sqrt{1}} \;=\; 1.4382$$

$$d_1 \;=\; 1.4382 - 0.30 \;=\; 1.1382$$

$$E(t) \;=\; 140 \times N(1.1382) - e^{-0.05} \times 100 \times N(1.4382)$$
$$=\; \$46.48 \text{ million}$$

and market debt value, by equation (22.6) is

$$D(t, T) \;=\; A(t) - E(t) \;=\; 140 - 46.48 \;=\; \$93.52 \text{ million}$$

Hence, the yield of the debt is, by equation (22.7):

$$y \;=\; \frac{\ln 100 - \ln 93.52}{1} \;=\; 6.70\%$$

which is higher than the 5% risk-free rate by 170 basis points. This "credit spread" reflects the 1-year default probability from equation (22.4):

$$p \;=\; 1 - N(1.4382) \;=\; 12.75\%$$

and the recovery value of

$$A(t)(1 - N(d_1)) \;=\; \$17.85$$

if default occurs.

From above, we can see that, as the asset value increases, the firm is more likely to remain solvent, the default probability drops. When default is extremely unlikely, the risky debt will be surely paid off at par, the risky debt will become risk free, and yield the risk-free return (5% in our example). In contrast, when default is extremely likely (default probability approaching 1), the debt holder is almost surely to take over the company, the debt value should be the same as the asset value which approaches 0.

Implications of BSM Model

As we can see from this example, the BSM model captures some important properties of risky debt; namely, the risky yield increases with the debt-to-asset leverage of the firm and its asset value volatility. Using the above equations, one can also plot the maturity dependency of the credit spread, defined as the difference between the risky yield and the risk-free rate.

What is appealing about this model is that the shapes of the credit spread term structures resemble those observed in the market. The highly leveraged firm has a credit spread which starts high, indicating that if the debt were to mature in the short term, it would almost certainly default with almost no recovery. However as the maturity increases, the likelihood of the firm asset value increasing to the point that default does not occur increases and the credit spread falls accordingly. For the medium leveraged firm, the credit spread is small at the short end—there are just sufficient assets to cover the debt repayment. As the maturity increases, there is a rapid increase in credit spread as the likelihood of the assets falling below the debt value rises. For the low leveraged company, the initial spread is close to zero and so can only increase as the maturity increases and more time is allowed for the asset value to drop. The general downward trend of these spread curves at the long end is due to the fact that on average the asset value grows at the riskless rate and so given enough time, will always grow to cover the fixed debt.

Empirical evidence in favor of these term structure shapes has been reported by Fons who observed similar relationships between spread term structure shapes and credit quality.[9] Contrary evidence was reported by Helwege and Turner who observed that the term structure of some low-quality firms is upward sloping rather than downward sloping.[10]

Geske Compound Option Model

If the company has a series of debts (zero coupon), then it is quite easy for the BSM model to characterize default at different times. The trick is to use the compound option model by Geske.[11] A compound option is

---

[9] Jerome Fons, "Using Default Rates to Model the Term Structure of Credit Risk," *Financial Analysts Journal* (September/October 1994), pp. 25–32.

[10] Jean Helwege and Christopher Turner, "The Slope of the Credit Yield Curve for Speculative-Grade Issuers," Federal Reserve Bank of New York Working Paper no.97-25 (1997).

[11] See Geske, "The Valuation of Debt as Compound Options," and Robert Geske and Herbert Johnson, "The Valuation of Corporate Liabilities as Compound Options: A Correction," *Journal of Financial and Quantitative Analysis* 19, no. 2 (1984), pp. 231–232.

an option on another option. The main point is that defaults are a series of contingent events. Later defaults are contingent upon prior no-default. Hence, layers of contingent defaults build up a series of sequential compound options, one linking to the other.

For example, suppose there are two zero-coupon bonds expiring in one year and two years, respectively. Both bonds have a $100 face value. The asset value is $200 today and follows the diffusion process given by equation (22.3). If the asset value falls below the face value in year 1, the company is technically under default. The company may seek additional capital to keep it alive or the company may simply declare default and let the holders of the two debts liquidate the company. In this case we have

$$
\begin{aligned}
A(t) &= \$200 \text{ million} & r &= 5\% \\
K_1 &= \$100 \text{ million} & T_1 - t &= 1 \text{ year} \\
K_2 &= \$100 \text{ million} & T_2 - t &= 2 \text{ years} \\
\sigma &= 20\%
\end{aligned}
$$

The default point of a two-year model is the key to the problem. The recovery further complicates the problem. For example, the company may default when it fails to pay the first debt ($100); or the company may default if its asset value falls below the market value of the total debt, which is the face value of the first debt ($100) and the market value of the second debt. This happens at a situation where the second debt owner can audit the asset value of the firm. Furthermore, a fixed recovery of these debts simplifies the problem. But oftentimes recoveries of debts depend on claims on the assets at different priority levels.

Take a simple example where the company defaults when it fails to pay its first debt. In this case the default probability is

$$
d_2 = \frac{\ln 200 - \ln 100 + (5\% - 0.2^2/2) \times 1}{0.2\sqrt{1}} = 3.6157
$$

$$
p = 1 - N(3.6157) = 0.015\%
$$

If we further assume that the first debt has a recovery rate of 0, then the debt value is

$$
D(t, T_1) = (1 - 0.015\%)e^{-5\% \times 1} \times 100 = 95.11
$$

If we calculate the yield as before, we find that the spread to the risk-free rate is 1.5 basis points. If the recovery is the asset value, then we do need to follow equation (22.5) and the debt value is

$$d_2 = \frac{\ln 200 - \ln 100 + (0.05 - 0.2^2) \times 1}{0.2\sqrt{1}} = 3.6157$$

$$d_1 = 3.6157 + 0.2 = 3.8157$$

$$E(t) = 200 \times N(3.8157) - e^{-0.05} \times 100 \times N(3.6157)$$
$$= 104.877$$

$$D(t, T_1) = 200 - 104.8777 = 95.1223$$

The small difference in the two results is because the default probability is really small (only 0.015%). When the default probability gets bigger, the debt value difference will get larger.

The second bond is more complex to evaluate. It can be defaulted in $t = 1$ when the first debt is defaulted or $t = 2$ when only itself is defaulted. The retiring of the first debt can be viewed as the dividend of the stock. Under the lognormal model described above, we can write the firm value at the end of the two-year period as

$$A(t, T_2) = [A(t, T_1) - K_1]e^{(r-\sigma^2/2)(T_1-t)+\sigma W(T_1)}$$
$$= A(t)e^{(r-\sigma^2/2)(T_2-t)+\sigma W(T_2)}$$
$$- K_1 e^{(r-\sigma^2/2)(T_1-t)+\sigma W(T_1)}$$

where K_1 is the face value of the 1-year debt and

$$W(t) = \int_0^t dW(u)du$$

The default probability of the second debt is the sum of the first year default probability and the second year default probability as follows:

$$\Pr[A(T_1) < K_1] + \Pr[A(T_1) > K_1 \text{ and } (A(T_2) < K_2)]$$

If the company survives the first period, it has to pay off the first debt, which clearly causes the asset price to be discontinuous. The discontinuity of the asset value makes the valuation of the second debt more difficult. Geske suggests that the if the firm issues equity to pay for the first debt, then the asset value should remain continuous and a closed-form solution can be achieved. Here, we simply show the result:

$$D(t, T_1) = e^{-r(T_1 - t)} K_1 N(d_{11}^-) + A(t)[1 - N(d_{11}^+)]$$

$$\begin{aligned} D(t, T_2) = A(t)[N(d_{11}^+) - M(d_{12}^+, d_{22}^+)] \\ + e^{-r(T_2 - t)} K_2 M(d_{12}^-, d_{22}^-) \\ + e^{-r(T_1 - t)} K_1 [N(d_{12}^-) - N(d_{11}^-)] \end{aligned}$$

where

$$d_{ij}^{\pm} = \frac{\ln A(0) - \ln K_{ij} + (r \pm \sigma^2 / 2)}{\sigma \sqrt{T_{ij}}}$$

K_{12} is the internal solution to $E(T_1) = K_{11}$ which is given as the face value of the first debt (maturing at $t = 1$ year) and K_{22} is the face value of the second debt (maturing at $t = 2$). This formulation can be extended to include any number of debts, $T_{11} = T_{12} = T_1 = 1$ and $T_{22} = 2$. The correlation in the bivariate normal probability functions is the square root of the ratio of two maturity times. In this case, it is $\sqrt{\frac{1}{2}}$.

Note that the total debt values add to

$$\begin{aligned} D(t, T_1) + D(t, T_2) \\ = A(t)[1 - M(d_{12}^+, d_{22}^+)] + e^{-r(T_1 - t)} K_1 N(d_{12}^-) \\ + e^{-r(T_2 - t)} K_2 M(d_{12}^-, d_{22}^-) \end{aligned}$$

which implies that the one-year survival probability is $N(d_{12}^-)$ and two-year is $M(d_{12}^-, d_{22}^-)$ which is a bivariate normal probability function with correlation $\sqrt{T_1 / T_2}$. The equity value, which is the residual value

$$E(t) = A(t) - D(t, T_1) - D(t, T_2)$$
$$= A(t)M(d_{12}^+, d_{22}^+) - e^{-r(T_1 - t)}K_1 N(d_{12}^-)$$
$$- e^{-r(T_2 - t)}K_2 M(d_{12}^-, d_{22}^-)$$

which is precisely the compound option formula derived by Geske. The two debt values in the example are \$95.12 and \$81.27, respectively. The equity is \$23.61.

Using the information given in our earlier example, we solve for the "internal strike price"—the asset price at time 1 for $E(1) = K_{11}$ to be \$195.12. In other words, if the asset price at time 1, $A(1)$, exceeds this value, the company survives; otherwise the company defaults. As a result, we can calculate the default probability of the first year to be

$$\Pr(A(T_1) < K_{12}) = 1 - N(d_{12}) = 1 - 0.6078 = 0.3922$$

The two-year total default probability is the one whereby the company defaults in year 1 or it survives the first year but defaults the second year:

$$\Pr[A(T_1) < K_{12} \cup A(T_2) < K_{22}] = 1 - M(d_{12}^-, d_{22}^-)$$
$$= 1 - 0.6077 = 0.3923$$

The default probability therefore between the first year and the second year is only 0.0001. In other words, the Geske model indicates that the majority default probability is in the first year, and then the company can survive with almost certainty.

In general, structural models are not easy to calibrate since information regarding the size and priority of claimants on a company's assets is not readily available. Typically companies only publish details of their balance sheets at most quarterly, and some companies, particularly those facing severe financial difficulties, do not disclose the full picture. Instead, practitioners tend to take equity volatility as a proxy for the asset value volatility.[12]

Barrier Structural Models

In addition to the Geske (compound option) model, another series of models have also evolved to extend the BSM model to multiple periods.

---

[12] For example, KMV uses $\sigma_E = (A/E)N(d_1)\sigma_A$, where σ_E is the volatility of equity and σ_A is the volatility of the asset.

Pioneered by Black and Cox,[13] these models view default as a knockout (down-and-out barrier) option[14] where default occurred the moment the firm value crossed a certain threshold.

More recently Longstaff and Schwartz[15] examined the effect of stochastic interest rates as did Briys and de Varenne[16] who modeled the default as being triggered when the forward price of the firm value hits a barrier. Few studies within the structural approach of credit risk valuation have incorporated jumps in the firm value process, because of lack of analytic tractability. Zhou[17] incorporates jumps into a setting used in Longstaff and Schwartz.[18] However, this model is very computation intensive.

Huang and Huang propose a jump-diffusion structural model which allows for analytically tractable solutions for both bond prices and default probabilities and is easy to implement.[19] The presence of jumps overcomes two related limitations of the BSM approach. First, it makes it possible for default to be a surprise since the jump cannot be anticipated as the asset value process is no longer continuous. Jumps also make it more likely that firms with low leverage can suddenly default in the short term and so enable them to have wider spreads at the short end than previously possible.[20]

---

[13] Fischer Black and John Cox, "Valuing Corporate Securities: Some Effects of Bond Indenture Provisions," *Journal of Finance* 31, no. 2 (1976), pp. 351–367.

[14] A barrier option is a path dependent option. For such options both the payoff of the option and the survival of the option to the stated expiration date depends on whether the price of the underlying or the underlying reference rate reaches a specified level over the life of the option. Barrier options are also called down-and-out barrier options. Knockout options are used to describe two types of barrier options: knock-out options and knock-in options. The former is an option that is terminated once a specified price or rate level is realized by the underlying. A knock-in option is an option that is activated once a specified price or rate level is realized by the underlying.

[15] Francis Longstaff and Eduardo Schwartz, "A Simple Approach to Valuing Risky Fixed and Floating Rate Debt," *Journal of Finance* 50, no. 3 (1995), pp. 789–819.

[16] Eric Briys and Francois de Varenne, "Valuing Risky Fixed Rate Debt: An Extension," *Journal of Financial and Quantitative Analysis* 32, no. 2 (1997), pp. 239–248.

[17] Chunsheng Zhou, "An Analysis of Default Correlations and Multiple Defaults," *Review of Financial Studies* (2001), pp. 555–576.

[18] Longstaff and Schwartz, "A Simple Approach to Valuing Risky Fixed and Floating Rate Debt."

[19] Ming Huang and Jay Huang, "How Much of the Corporate-Treasury Yield Spread is Due to Credit Risk?" working paper, Stanford University (2002).

[20] For a discussion of barrier-based models, see Chapter 8 in Anson, Fabozzi, Choudhry, and Chen, *Credit Derivatives: Instruments, Applications, and Pricing.*

Advantages and Drawbacks of Structural Models

Structural models have many advantages. First, they model default on the very reasonable assumption that it is a result of the value of the firm's assets falling below the value of its debt. In the case of the BSM model, the outputs of the model show how the credit risk of a corporate debt is a function of the leverage and the asset volatility of the issuer. The term structure of spreads also appear realistic and empirical evidence argues for and against their shape. Some of the more recent structural models have addressed many of the limitations and assumptions of the original BSM model.

However structural models are difficult to calibrate and so are not suitable for the frequent marking to market of credit contingent securities. Structural models are also computationally burdensome. For instance, as we have seen, the pricing of a defaultable zero-coupon bond is as difficult as pricing an option. Just adding coupons transforms the problem into the equivalent of pricing a compound option. Pricing any subordinated debt requires the simultaneous valuation of all of the more senior debt. Consequently, structural models are not used where there is a need for rapid and accurate pricing of many credit-related securities.

Instead, the main application of structural models is in the areas of credit risk analysis and corporate structure analysis. As explained later in this chapter, a structural model is more likely to be able to predict the credit quality of a corporate security than a reduced form model. It is therefore a useful tool in the analysis of counterparty risk for banks when establishing credit lines with companies and a useful tool in the risk analysis of portfolios of securities. Corporate analysts might also use structural models as a tool for analyzing the best way to structure the debt and equity of a company.

CREDIT RISK MODELING: REDUCED FORM MODELS

The name *reduced form* was first given by Darrell Duffie to differentiate from the *structural form* models of the BSM type. Reduced form models are mainly represented by the Jarrow-Turnbull[21] and Duffie-Singleton[22] models. Both types of models are arbitrage free and employ the risk-neutral measure to price securities. The principal difference is that

[21] Robert Jarrow and Stuart Turnbull, "Pricing Derivatives on Financial Securities Subject to Default Risk," *Journal of Finance* (March 1995), pp. 53–86.
[22] Darrell Duffie and Kenneth Singleton, "Modeling the Term Structure of Defaultable Bonds" (1997), working paper, Stanford University.

default is endogenous in the BSM model while it is exogenous in the Jarrow-Turnbull and Duffie-Singleton models. As we will see, specifying defaults exogenously greatly simplifies the problem because it ignores the constraint of defining what causes default and simply looks at the default event itself. The computations of debt values of different maturities are independent, unlike in the BSM model that defaults of the later-maturity debts are contingent on defaults of earlier-maturity debts.

The Poisson Process

The theoretical framework for reduced form models is the Poisson process.[23] To see what it is, let us begin by defining a Poisson process that at time t has a value N_t. The values taken by N_t are an increasing set of integers 0, 1, 2, ... and the probability of a jump from one integer to the next occurring over a small time interval dt is given by

$$\Pr[N_{t+dt} - N_t = 1] = \lambda dt$$

where λ is known as the *intensity* parameter in the Poisson process.

Equally, the probability of no event occurring in the same time interval is simply given by

$$\Pr[N_{t+dt} - N_t = 0] = 1 - \lambda dt$$

For the time being we shall assume the intensity parameter to be a fixed constant. In later discussions and especially when pricing is covered in the next chapter, we will let it be a function of time or even a stochastic variable (known as a *Cox process*[24]). These more complex situations are beyond the scope of this chapter. It will be seen shortly that the intensity parameter represents the annualized instantaneous forward default probability at time t. As dt is small, there is a negligible probability of two jumps occurring in the same time interval.

The Poisson process can be seen as a counting process (0 or 1) for some as yet undefined sequence of events. In our case, the relationship between Poisson processes and reduced form models is that the event which causes the Poisson process to jump from zero to 1 can be viewed as being a default.

---

[23] A Poisson process is a point process. Point processes were briefly introduced in Chapter 13.

[24] David Lando, "On Cox Processes and Credit Risky Securities," *Review of Derivatives Research* 2 (1998), pp. 99–120. Cox processes were briefly covered in Chapter 13 of this book.

Another way to look at the Poisson process is to see how long it takes until the first default event occurs. This is called the *default time* distribution. It can be proven that the default time distribution obeys an *exponential distribution* as follows:

$$\Pr(T > t) = e^{-\lambda(T-t)}$$

This distribution function also characterizes the survival probability before time t:

$$Q(t, T) = \Pr(T > t) = e^{-\lambda(T-t)}$$

The Jarrow-Turnbull Model

The Jarrow-Turnbull model is a simple model of default and recovery based on the Poisson default process described above.[25] In their model, Jarrow and Turnbull assume that no matter when default occurs, the recovery payment is paid at maturity time T. Then the coupon bond value can be written as

$$B(t) = P(t, T)R(T)\int_t^T -dQ(t, u)du + \sum_{j=1}^n P(t, T_j)c_j e^{-\lambda(T_j-t)}$$

$$= P(t, T)R(T)(1 - e^{-\lambda(T-t)}) + \sum_{j=1}^n P(t, T_j)c_j e^{-\lambda(T_j-t)}$$

where:

$P(t,T)$	=	the risk-free discount factor
c_j	=	the j-th coupon
$Q(t,T)$	=	the survival probability up to time t
R	=	the recovery ratio

It is seen that the conditional default probability is integrated out and disappears from the final result. As a consequence, by assuming recovery payment to be at maturity, Jarrow and Turnbull assume away any dependency between the bond price and the conditional default probability.

It is worth noting that when the recovery rate is 0, for a zero-coupon bond the value of the intensity parameter is also the bond's forward

---

[25] Jarrow and Turnbull, "Pricing Derivatives on Financial Securities Subject to Default Risk."

yield spread. This is so because in any one-period interval in the binomial model, we have

$$
\begin{aligned}
D(t, T) &= P(t, T)e^{-\lambda(T - t)} \\
&= P(t, T)Q(t, T)
\end{aligned}
$$

This is known as the risky discount factor, which is the present value of $1 if there is no recovery (i.e., the recovery ratio is zero, $R = 0$).

The Jarrow-Turnbull model is usually modified when it is used in practice. One modification is to allow the Poisson intensity λ to be a function of time and the other is to allow recovery to be paid upon default. As a result the bond equation is modified as follows:

$$
\begin{aligned}
B(t) &= \int_t^T P(t, u)R(u)(-dQ(u)) + \sum_{j = 1}^n P(t, T_j)c_j Q(t, T_j) \\
&= \int_t^T P(t, u)R(u)\lambda(u)e^{-\int_t^u \lambda(w)dw} + \sum_{j = 1}^n P(t, T_j)c_j e^{-\int_t^{T_j} \lambda(w)dw}
\end{aligned}
$$

To actually implement this equation, it is usually assumed that λ follows a step function. That is between any two adjacent time points, λ is a constant. Furthermore, it is also, as a matter of mathematical tractability, assumed that default can occur only at coupon times.[26] As a result of this further assumption, the above equation can be simplified as

$$
B(t) = \sum_{j = 1}^n P(t, T_j)R(T_j)\lambda(T_j)e^{-\sum_{k = 1}^j \lambda(T_k)} + \sum_{j = 1}^n P(t, T_j)c_j e^{-\sum_{k = 1}^n \lambda(T_k)}
$$

The major advantage of the Jarrow-Turnbull model is calibration. Since default probabilities and recovery are exogenously specified, one can use a series of risky zero-coupon bonds to calibrate out a default probability curve and hence a spread curve.

Calibration has become a necessary first step in fixed-income trading recently for it allows traders to clearly see *relative prices* and hence be able to construct arbitrage trading strategies. The ability to quickly calibrate is the major reason why reduced form models are strongly favored by real-world practitioners in the credit derivatives markets.

---

[26] This assumption is not unreasonable because between two coupon times, if the company is not audited, the company should not have any reason to default.

The Calibration of Jarrow-Turnbull Model

Exhibit 22.2 best represents the Jarrow-Turnbull model.[27] The branches that lead to default will terminate the contract and incur a recovery payment. The branches that lead to survival will continue the contract which will then face future defaults. This is a very general framework to describe how default occurs and contract terminates. Various models differ in how the default probabilities are defined and the recovery is modeled.

Since a debt contract pays interest under survival and pays recovery upon default, the expected payment is naturally the weighted average of the two payoffs. For the ease of exposition, we shall denote the survival probability from now to any future time as $Q(0,t)$ where t is some future time. As a consequence, the difference between two survival times, $Q(0,s) - Q(0,t)$ where $s > t$, by definition, is the default probability between the two future time points t and s.

The above binomial structure can be applied to both structural models and reduced form models. The default probabilities can be easily computed by these models. The difference resides in how they specify recovery assumptions. In the Geske model, the asset value at the time is

EXHIBIT 22.2 Tree-Based Diagram of Binomial Default Process for a Debt Instrument

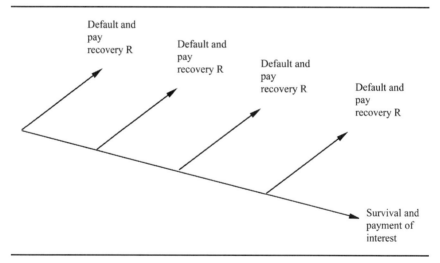

[27] As recent articles by Ren-Raw Chen and Jinzhi Huang ["Credit Spread Bonds and Their Implications for Credit Spread Modeling," Rutgers University and Penn State University (2001)] and Ren-Raw Chen ["Credit Risk Modeling: A General Framework," Rutgers University (2003)] show, the binomial process is also applicable to structural models.

recovered. In the Duffie-Singleton model, a fraction of the market debt value is recovered. And in the Jarrow-Turnbull and other barrier models, an arbitrary recovery value is assumed (it can be beta distributed).[28]

From the observed bond prices, we can easily retrieve default probabilities from bond prices. Suppose there are two bonds, a one-year bond trading at $100 with a $6 annual coupon and a two-year bond trading at $100 with a $7 annual coupon. Assuming a recovery of $50 per $100 par value, the first bond price is calculated as

$$100 = \frac{p(0, 1) \times 50 + 106 \times (1 - p(0, 1))}{1 + 5\%}$$

The default probability is then found by solving for $p(0,1)$:

$$105 = 106 - 56 \times p(0, 1)$$
$$p(0, 1) = 1.79\%$$

We use p_t to represent the forward/conditional default probability at time t. Hence, p_1 is the default probability of the first period. In the first period, the survival probability is simply 1 minus the default probability:

$$Q(0, 1) = 1 - p(0, 1) = 1 - 1.79\% = 98.21\%$$

and therefore

$$\lambda = -\ln 0.9821 = 1.8062\%$$

The second bond is priced, assuming a recovery of $20 out of $100:

$$100 = \frac{p(0, 1) \times 20 + Q(0, 1) \times \left(7 + \frac{p(1, 2) \times 20 + (1 - p(1, 2)) \times 107}{1.05}\right)}{1.05}$$

$$= \frac{1.79\% \times 20 + 98.21\% \times \left(7 + \frac{p(1, 2) \times 20 + (1 - p(1, 2)) \times 107}{1.05}\right)}{1.05}$$

---

[28] For more details, see Chen, "Credit Risk Modeling: A General Framework."

Solving for the second-period default probability one obtains $p(1,2) = 14.01\%$.

The total survival probability till two years is surviving through the first year (98.21%) *and* the second year ($1 - 14.01\% = 85.99\%$):

$$Q(0, 2) = Q(0, 1)(1 - p(1, 2)) = 98.21\% \times (1 - 14.01\%) = 84.45\%$$

$$\lambda_1 + \lambda_2 = -\ln 0.8445 = 16.9011\%$$

$$\lambda_2 = 16.9011\% - \lambda_1 = 16.9011\% - 1.8062\% = 15.0949\%$$

The total default probability is either defaulting in the first period (1.79%) *or* surviving through the first year (98.21%) *and* defaulting in the second (14.01%).

$$1.79\% + 98.21\% \times 14.01\% = 15.55\%$$

This probability can be calculated alternatively by 1 minus the two-period survival probability:

$$1 - Q(0,2) = 1 - 84.45\% = 15.55\%$$

It should be noted that any forward default probability is the difference of two survivals weighted by the previous survival as shown below:

$$p(j-1, j) = \frac{Q(0, j-1) - Q(0, j)}{Q(0, j-1)} \tag{22.8}$$

For example, the second period default probability is

$$p(0,2) = 1 - Q(0,2)/Q(0,1)$$

To express this more clearly, let us examine a two-period binomial tree shown in Exhibit 22.3. It should be clear how the recovery amount can change the default probabilities. Take the one-year bond as an example. If the recovery were higher, the default probability would be higher. This is because for a higher recovery bond to be priced at the same price (par in our example), the default probability would need to be higher to compensate for it. If the default probability remains the same, then the bond should be priced above par.

So far we have not discussed any model. We simply adopt the spirit of the reduced form models and use the market bond prices to recover

EXHIBIT 22.3 Immediate Recovery

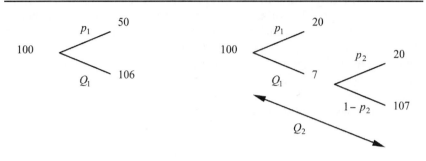

risk-neutral probabilities. This is very similar to the bootstrapping method in calibrating the yield curve. The probabilities are solved recursively.

No matter which model is used, the model has to match the default probabilities implied by the bond prices observed in the market. It can be seen in the above section that there is no closed-form solution. The reason is that the recovery amount is the liquidation value of the company and can change as time changes (so called "stochastic recovery").

Transition Matrix

The binomial structure can be extended to multinomial to incorporate various credit classes. It is as easy to specify n states (different credit ratings) instead of just two states (default and survival). The probabilities can always be given exogenously. Hence, instead of a single default for default (and survival), there can be a number of probabilities, each for the probability of moving from one credit rating to another credit rating. Based upon this idea, Jarrow, Lando, and Turnbull,[29] extend the Jarrow-Turnbull model to incorporate the so-called *migration risk*. Migration risk is different from default risk in that a downgrade in credit ratings only widens the credit spread of the debt issuer and does not cause default. No default means no recovery to worry about. This way, the Jarrow-Turnbull model can be more closely related to spread products, whereas as a model of default it can only be useful in default products. One advantage of ratings transition models is the ability to use the data published by the credit rating agencies.

---

[29] Robert Jarrow, David Lando, and Stuart Turnbull, "A Markov Model for the Term Structure of Credit Spreads," *Review of Financial Studies* 10 (1997), pp. 481–532.

For a flavor of how a rating transition model can be obtained, consider a simple three-state model. At each time interval an issuer can be upgraded, downgraded or even jump to default. This process is shown in Exhibit 22.4. This time, the tree is more complex. From a "live" state, the issuer can be upgraded or downgraded, or even jump to default. The default state, on the other hand, is an absorbing barrier which cannot become live again. In terms of Exhibit 22.4, a movement from "good rating" to "middle rating" is downgrade, and vice versa.

To best describe the situation, we can establish the following transition matrix:

$$
\begin{array}{cc}
 & \text{Future state} \\
 & \begin{array}{ccc} 2 & 1 & 0 \end{array} \\
\text{Current state}\ \begin{array}{c} 2 \\ 1 \\ 0 \end{array} & \begin{bmatrix} p_{22} & p_{21} & p_{20} \\ p_{12} & p_{11} & p_{10} \\ 0 & 0 & 1 \end{bmatrix}
\end{array}
$$

where 0 is the default state, 1 is the middle credit rating state, and 2 is good credit rating state. p_{ij} is the transition probability to move from the current state i to future state j. The sum of the probabilities of each current state should be 1, that is

$$
\sum_{j=0}^{2} p_{ij} = 1
$$

The last row of the matrix is all 0's except for the last column. This means that once the asset is in default, it cannot become live again and it will remain in default forever.

EXHIBIT 22.4　　Multistate Default Process

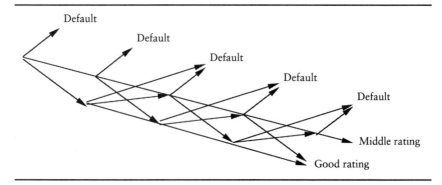

To make the model mathematically tractable, Jarrow-Lando-Turnbull assume that the transition matrix follows a Markov chain; that is, the n-period transition is the above matrix raised to the n-th power. The main purpose to derive such a matrix is that we can calibrate it to the historical transition matrix published by rating agencies. Note that the historical transition matrix consists of real probabilities which are different from the risk-neutral probabilities in the tree. Hence, Jarrow-Lando-Turnbull make a further assumption that the risk-neutral probabilities are *proportional* to the actual ones. For a risk averse investor, the risk-neutral default probabilities are larger than the actual ones because of the risk premium.

Since historical default probabilities are observable, we can then directly compute the prices of credit derivatives. For example, let the transition probability matrix for a 1-year period be

$$
\begin{array}{cc}
 & \text{Future state} \\
 & \begin{array}{ccc} 2 & 1 & 0 \end{array}
\end{array}
$$

$$
\text{Current state} \begin{array}{c} 2 \\ 1 \\ 0 \end{array} \begin{bmatrix} 0.80 & 0.15 & 0.05 \\ 0.15 & 0.70 & 0.15 \\ 0 & 0 & 1 \end{bmatrix}
$$

Then, for a one-year, 0-recovery coupon bond, if the current state is 1, it has 85% to receive the coupon and 15% to go into default in the next period. So the present value of the next coupon is

$$
\frac{0.85 \times \$6}{1.06} = \$4.81
$$

In the second period, the bond could be upgraded with probability of 15% or remain the same with probability of 70%. If it is at the good rating, then the probability of survival is 95% and if it is at the bad rating, the probability of survival is 85%. Hence, the total probability of survival is

$$
0.15 \times 0.95 + 0.7 \times 0.85 = 0.7375 = 73.75\%
$$

Therefore, the present value of the maturity cash flow (coupon and face value) is

$$
\frac{0.7375 \times 106}{1.06^2} = \$69.58
$$

The bond price today is

$$\$4.81 + \$69.58 = \$74.39$$

Similar analysis can be applied to the case where the current state is 2. In the above example, it is quite easy to include various recovery assumptions.

It is costly to include the ratings migration risk in the Jarrow-Turnbull model. It is very difficult to calibrate the model to the historical transition matrix. First of all, the historical probabilities computed by the rating agencies are *actual* probabilities while the probabilities that are used for computing prices must be *risk neutral* probabilities that we introduced in Chapter 14. The assumption by Jarrow, Lando, and Turnbull that there is a linear transformation does not necessarily provide a good fit to the data. Second, there are more variables to solve for than the available bonds. In other words, the calibration is an underidentification problem. Hence, more restrictive assumptions about the probabilities need to be made. In general, migration risk is still modeled by the traditional portfolio theory (non-option methodology). But the model by Jarrow, Lando, and Turnbull is a first attempt at using the option approach to model the rating migration risk.

The Duffie-Singleton Model

Obviously, the Jarrow-Turnbull assumption that recovery payment can occur only at maturity is too far from reality. Although it generates a closed-form solution for the bond price, it suffers from two major drawbacks in reality: recovery actually occurs upon (or soon after) default and the recovery amount can fluctuate randomly over time.[30]

Duffie and Singleton take a different approach.[31] They allow the payment of recovery to occur at any time but the amount of recovery is restricted to be the proportion of the bond price at default time as if it did not default. That is

$$R(t) = \delta D(t, T)$$

where R is the recovery ratio, δ is a fixed ratio, and $D(t,T)$ represents the debt value if default did not occur. For this reason the Duffie-Singleton model is known as a *fractional recovery model*. The rationale behind this approach is that as the credit quality of a bond deteriorates, the price falls. At default the recovery price will be some fraction of the final price

---

[30] Recovery fluctuates because it depends on the liquidation value of the firm at the time of default.

[31] Duffie and Singleton, "Modeling the Term Structure of Defaultable Bonds."

immediately prior to default. In this way we avoid the contradictory scenario which can arise in the Jarrow-Turnbull model in which the recovery rate, being an exogenously specified percentage of the default-free payoff, may actually exceed the price of the bond at the moment of default.

The debt value at time t is[32]

$$D(t, T) = \frac{1}{1 + r\Delta t}\{p\delta E[D(t + \Delta t, T)] + (1 - p)E[D(t + \Delta t, T)]\}$$

By recursive substitutions, we can write the current value of the bond as its terminal payoff if no default occurs:

$$D(t, T) = \left[\frac{1 - p\Delta t(1 - \delta)}{1 + r\Delta t}\right]^n X(T)$$

Note that the instantaneous default probability being $p\Delta t$ is consistent with the Poisson distribution,

$$\frac{-dQ}{Q} = p\Delta t$$

Hence, recognizing $\Delta t = T/n$,

$$D(t, T) = \frac{\exp(-p(1 - \delta)T)}{\exp(rT)}X(T) = \exp(-(r + s)T)X(T) \qquad (22.9)$$

When r and s are not constants, we can write the Duffie-Singleton model as

$$D(t, T) = E_t\left[\exp\left(-\int_t^T [r(u) + s(u)]du\right)\right]X(T)$$

where $s(u) = p_u(1 - \delta)$. Not only does the Duffie-Singleton model have a closed-form solution, it is possible to have a simple intuitive interpretation of their result. The product $p(1 - \delta)$ serves as a spread over the risk-free discount rate. When the default probability is small, the product is small

---

[32] The probability, p, can be time dependent in a more general case.

and the credit spread is small. When the recovery is high (i.e., $1 - \delta$ is small), the product is small and the credit spread is small.

Consider a two-year zero coupon bond. Assume that the probability of defaulting each year is 4%, conditional on surviving to the beginning of the year. If the bond defaults we assume that it loses 60% of its market value. We also assume that risk-free interest rates evolve as shown in Exhibit 22.5 where an up move and a down move have an equal probability of 50%. At any node on the tree the price is the risk-free discounted expectation of the payoff at the next time step. Therefore at the node where the risk-free rate has climbed to 7%, the value of the security is given by

$$\frac{1}{1.07}[(1 - 0.04) \times \$100 + 0.04 \times (\$100 - \$60)] = \$91.25$$

Using the relationship

EXHIBIT 22.5   Valuation of a Two-Year Defaultable Zero-Coupon Bond Using Duffie-Singleton

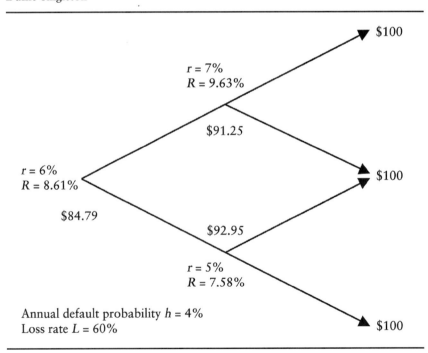

Annual default probability $h = 4\%$
Loss rate $L = 60\%$

$$\frac{1}{1+r+s} = \frac{1}{1+r}[p\delta + (1-p)]$$

this implies an effective discounting rate of $r + s = 9.63\%$ over the time step from the 7% node. In this way we can proceed to value the other nodes and roll back to calculate an initial price for the bond equal to $84.79. On each node in Exhibit 22.5 is also shown the effective discounting rate. Knowing these we can equally price the bond as though it were default free but discounted at $r + s$ rather than at the risk-free rate.

The Duffie-Singleton model has one very important advantage. The above result implies that it can be made compatible with arbitrage-free term structure models such as Cox-Ingersoll-Ross[33] and Heath-Jarrow-Morton.[34] The difference is that now the discounting is *spread adjusted*. Just like the yield curve for the risk-free term structure, the *spread curve* is added to the risk-free yield curve and we arrive at a *risky yield curve*. The spread curve is clearly based upon the *probability curve* (p_t for all t) and the recovery rate (δ).

Although the Duffie-Singleton model seems to be superior to the Jarrow-Turnbull model, it is not generic enough to be applied to all credit derivative contracts. The problem with the Duffie-Singleton model is that if a contract that has no payoff at maturity such as a credit default swap, their model implies zero value today, which is of course not true. Recall that credit default swaps pay nothing if default does not occur. If recovery is proportional to the no-default payment, then it is obvious that the contract today has no value. It is quite unfortunate that the Duffie-Singleton model is not suitable for the most popular credit derivative contracts. Hence, the proportionality recovery assumption is not very general.

The calibration of the Duffie-Singleton model is as easy as the Jarrow-Turnbull model. The two calibrations are comparable. However, there are significant differences. Note that in the Jarrow-Turnbull model, the recovery assumption is separate from the default probability. But this is not the case in the Duffie-Singleton model—the recovery and the default probability together become an instantaneous spread. While we can calibrate the spreads, we cannot separate the recovery from the default probability. On the other hand, in the Jarrow-Turnbull model, the

---

[33] John Cox, Jonathan Ingersoll, and Stephen Ross, "A Theory of the Term Structure of Interest Rates," *Econometrica* 53 (1985), pp. 385–407.
[34] David Heath, Robert Jarrow, and Andrew Morton, "Bond Pricing and the Term Structure of Interest Rates: A New Methodology," *Econometrica* 59 (February 1992), pp. 77–105.

default probability curve can be calibrated to *only if* a particular recovery assumption is adopted. Hence the default probability is a function of the assumed recovery rate.

General Observations on Reduced Form Models

While the reduced form models lay a solid theoretical foundation, as they attempt to model the underlying risk-neutral probability of default which is not a market observable, they are not as intuitive as one might like. They also suffer from the constraint that default is always a surprise. While this is true under some rare circumstances, Both Moody's and Standard & Poor's data show that there are very few defaults straight out of investment-grade quality bonds. Default is usually the end of a series of downgrades and spread widenings and so can be anticipated to a large extent. Hence, although more and more financial institutions are starting to implement the Jarrow-Turnbull and Duffie-Singleton models, spread-based diffusion models remain very popular.

The Jarrow-Turnbull and Duffie-Singleton models assume that defaults occur unexpectedly and follow the Poisson process. This assumption greatly reduces the complexity since the Poisson process has very nice mathematical properties. In order to further simplify the model, Jarrow-Turnbull and Duffie-Singleton respectively make other assumptions so that there exist closed-form solutions to the basic underlying asset.

PRICING SINGLE-NAME CREDIT DEFAULT SWAPS

There are two approaches to pricing default swaps—*static replication* and *modeling*. The former approach is based on the assumption that if one can replicate the cash flows of the structure which one is trying to price using a portfolio of tradable securities, then the price of the structure should equal the value of the replicating portfolio. This is accomplished through what is known as an asset swap; however, there are limitations of using of asset swaps for pricing.[35] In situations where either the nature of the instrument we are trying to price cannot be replicated or that we do not have access to prices for the instruments we would use in the replicating portfolio, it becomes necessary to use a modeling approach. That is the approach explained below for pricing credit default swaps.

---

[35] See Chapter 4 in Anson, Fabozzi, Choudhry, and Chen, *Credit Derivatives: Instruments, Applications, and Pricing.*

Several models have been suggested for pricing single-name credit default swaps.[36] These products (before we take into account the valuation of counterparty risk) are generally regarded as the "cash product" that can be directly evaluated off the *default probability* curves. No parametric modeling is necessary. This is just like the coupon bond valuation which is model free because the zero-coupon bond yield curve is all that is needed to price coupon bonds.

General Framework

To value credit derivatives it is necessary to be able to model credit risk. The two most commonly used approaches to model credit risk are structural models and reduced form models. The latter do not look inside the firm. Instead, they model directly the likelihood of a default occurring. Not only is the current probability of default modeled, some researchers attempt to model a "forward curve" of default probabilities which can be used to price instruments of varying maturities. Modeling a probability has the effect of making default a surprise—the default event is a random event which can suddenly occur at any time. All we know is its probability of occurrence.

Reduced form models are easy to calibrate to bond prices observed in the marketplace. Structural-based models are used more for default prediction and credit risk management.[37]

Both structural and reduced form models use risk-neutral pricing to be able to calibrate to the market. In practice, we need to determine the risk-neutral probabilities in order to reprice the market and price other instruments not currently priced. In doing so, we do not need to know or even care about the real-world default probabilities.

---

[36] See, for example, John Hull and Alan White, "Valuing Credit Default Swaps I," working paper, University of Toronto (April 2000) and "Valuing Credit Default Swaps II: Counterparty Default Risk," working paper, University of Toronto (April 2000); and Dominic O'Kane, "Credit Derivatives Explained: Markets Products and Regulations," Lehman Brothers, Structured Credit Research (March 2001) and "Introduction to Default Swaps," Lehman Brothers, Structured Credit Research (January 2000).

[37] Increasingly, investors are seeking consistency between the markets that use different modeling approaches, as the interests in seeking arbitrage opportunities across various markets grows. Ren-Raw Chen has demonstrated that all the reduced form models described above can be regarded in a non-parametric framework. This non-parametric format makes the comparison of various models possible. Furthermore, as Chen contends, the non-parametric framework focuses the difference of various models on recovery. See Ren-Raw Chen, "Credit Risk Modeling: A General Framework," working paper, Rutgers University, 2003.

Since in reality, a default can occur any time, to accurately value a default swap, we need a consistent methodology that describes the following: (1) how defaults occur; (2) how recovery is paid; and (3) how discounting is handled.

Survival Probability and Forward Default Probability: A Recap

Earlier in this chapter we introduced two important analytical constructs: survival probability and forward default probability. We recap both below since we will need them in pricing credit default swaps.

Assume the risk-neutral probabilities exist. Then we can identify a series of risk-neutral default probabilities so that the weighted average of default and no-default payoffs can be discounted at the risk-free rate.

Let $Q(t,T)$ to be the survival probability from now t till some future time T. Then $Q(t,T) - Q(t,T + \tau)$ is the default probability between T and $T + \tau$ (i.e., survive till T but default at $T + \tau$). Assume defaults can only occur at discrete points in time, $T_1, T_2, ..., T_n$. Then the total probability of default over the life of the credit default swap is the sum of all the per period default probabilities:

$$\sum_{j=0}^{n} Q(t, T_j) - Q(t, T_{j+1}) = 1 - Q(T_n) = 1 - Q(T)$$

where $t = T_0 < T_1 < ... < T_n = T$ and T is the maturity time of the credit default swap. Note that the sum of the all the per-period default probabilities should equal one minus the total survival probability.

The survival probabilities have a useful application. A \$1 "risky" cash flow received at time T has a risk-neutral expected value of $Q(t,T)$ and a present value of $P(t,T)Q(t,T)$ where P is the risk-free discount factor. A "risky" annuity of \$1 can therefore be written as

$$\sum_{j=1}^{n} P(t, T_j)Q(t, T_j)$$

A "risky" bond with no recovery upon default and a maturity of n can thus be written as

$$B(t) = \sum_{j=1}^{n} P(t, T_j)Q(t, T_j)c_j + P(t, T_n)Q(t, T_n)$$

This result is similar to the risk-free coupon bond where only risk-free discount factors are used.

The "forward" default probability is a conditional default probability for a forward interval conditional on surviving until the beginning of the interval. This probability can be expressed as

$$p(T_j) = \frac{Q(t, T_{j-1}) - Q(t, T_j)}{Q(t, T_{j-1})} \tag{22.10}$$

Credit Default Swap Value

A credit default swap takes the defaulted bond as the recovery value and pays par upon default and zero otherwise.

$$V = E\left[e^{-\int_e^\mu r(s)\,ds} 1_{\mu < T}[1 - R(\mu)] \right]$$

where μ is default time.

Hence the value of the credit default swap (V) should be the loss upon default weighted by the default probability:

$$V = \sum_{j=1}^{n} P(t, T_j)[Q(t, T_{j-1}) - Q(t, T_j)][1 - R(T_j)] \tag{22.11}$$

where $P(\cdot)$ is the risk-free discount factor and $R(\cdot)$ is the recovery rate.

In equation (22.2) it is implicitly assumed that the discount factor is independent of the survival probability. However, in reality, these two may be correlated—usually higher interest rates lead to more defaults because businesses suffer more from higher interest rates. Equation (22.2) has no easy solution.

From the value of the credit default swap, we can derive a spread (s), which is paid until default or maturity:

$$s = \frac{V}{\displaystyle\sum_{j=1}^{n} P(t, T_j)Q(t, T_j)} \tag{22.12}$$

Exhibit 22.6 depicts the general default and recovery structure. The payoff upon default of a default swap can vary. In general, the owner of

EXHIBIT 22.6   Payoff and Payment Structure of a Credit Default Swap

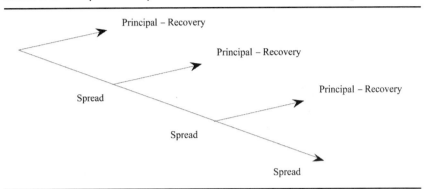

the default swap delivers the defaulted bond and in return receives principal. Many default swaps are cash settled and an estimated recovery is used. In either case, the amount of recovery is randomly dependent upon the value of the reference obligation at the time of default. Models differ in how this recovery is modeled.[38]

To illustrate how to use the above formulation of credit default swap pricing, assume (1) two "risky" zero-coupon bonds exist with one and two years to maturity and (2) no recovery upon default. From equation (22.10) we know the credit spreads of these two "risky" zeros are approximately their default probabilities. For example, assume the one-year zero has a spread of 100 basis points and the two-year has a spread of 120. The survival probabilities can be computed from equation (22.10). For the one-year bond whose yield spread is 100 basis points, the (one year) survival probability is

$$1\% = -\ln Q(0, 1)$$
$$Q(0, 1) = e^{-1\%} = 0.9900$$

For the two-year zero-coupon bond whose yield spread is 120 basis points, the (two year) survival probability is:

$$1.2\% \times 2 = -\ln Q(0, 2)$$
$$Q(0, 2) = e^{-1.2\% \times 2} = 0.9763$$

---

[38] We provide an example where the two variables are independent and the defaults follow a Poisson process. The simple solution exists under the continuous time assumption. The analysis is provided in the appendix to Chapter 10 in Anson, Fabozzi, Choudhry, and Chen, *Credit Derivatives: Instruments, Applications, and Pricing.*

These survival probabilities can then be used to compute forward default probabilities defined in equation (22.8):

$$p(1) = \frac{Q(0, 0) - Q(0, 1)}{Q(0, 0)} = \frac{1 - 99.00\%}{1} = 1.00\%$$

and

$$p(2) = \frac{Q(0, 1) - Q(0, 2)}{Q(0, 1)} = \frac{99.00\% - 97.63\%}{99.00\%} = 1.39\%$$

Since we assume a 5% flat risk-free rate for two years, the risk-free discount factors are

$$P(0, 1) = e^{-5\%}$$
$$P(0, 2) = e^{-5\% \times 2}$$

for one and two years, respectively. Assuming a 20% recovery ratio, we can then calculate, using equation (22.11), what the total protection value (V) of the default swap contract is providing

$$V = e^{-5\%}(1 - 0.99)(1 - 0.2) + e^{-5\% \times 2}(0.99 - 0.9763)(1 - 0.2)$$
$$= 0.00761 + 0.010134$$
$$= 0.017744 = 177.44 \text{ basis points}$$

As mentioned, the default swap premium is not paid in full at the inception of the swap but paid in a form of spread until either default or maturity, whichever is earlier. From equation (22.12), we can compute the spread of the default swap as follows:

$$s = \frac{0.017744}{0.99 \times \exp(-0.05) + 0.9763 \times \exp(-0.05 \times 2)}$$
$$= \frac{0.017744}{1.824838} = 0.009724$$

which is 9.724 basis points for each period, provided that default does not occur. This is a payment in arrears. That is, if default occurs in the first period, no payment is necessary. If default occurs in the second period, there is one payment; if default never occurs, there are two payments.

No Need For Stochastic Hazard Rate or Interest Rate

The analysis above demonstrates that to price a default swap, we only need a recovery rate, the risk-free yield curve (the P-curve), and the survival probability curve (the Q-curve). This implies that regardless of which model is used to justify the P-curve or the Q-curve, default swaps should be priced exactly the same. This further implies that there is no need to be concerned if the risk-free rate and the hazard rate are stochastic or not, because they do not enter into the valuation of the default swap. In other words, random interest rates and hazard rates are "calibrated out" of the valuation.[39]

Delivery Option in Default Swaps

As explained earlier in this chapter, a credit default swap trade can specify a reference entity or a reference obligation. In the former case, the protection buyer has the option to deliver one of severable deliverable obligations of the reference entity. This effectively creates a similar situation to the well-known quality option for Treasury note and bond futures contracts where more than one bond can be delivered. In this case, the value of the credit default swap is

$$V = \sum_{j=1}^{n} P(t, T_j)[Q(t, T_{j-1}) - Q(t, T_j)][1 - \min R(T_j)]$$

The difference between the above equation and equation (22.11) is the recovery. The delivery of the lowest recovery bond, $\min\{R(T_j)\}$, for all j bonds is what the payoff is.

It is natural that the worst quality bond should be delivered upon default. For a credit default swap, the one with the lowest recovery should be delivered. Unlike Treasury bond and note futures where the cheapest-to-deliver issue can change due to interest rate changes, recovery is mostly determined contractually and usually the lowest priority bond will remain the lowest priority for the life of the contract. The only uncertainty in determining the cheapest-to-deliver issue is the future introduction of new bonds. This is largely related to the capital structure of the company and beyond the scope of risk-neutral pricing. The model that can incorporate capital structure issues (i.e., using debt to optimize capital structure) needs to be a structural model with wealth maximization.[40]

---

[39] For the stochastic hazard rate model, see Daniel Lando, "On Cox Processes and Credit Risky Securities," *Review of Derivatives Research* (1998), pp. 99–120.

[40] Issues about optimal capital structure and default risk are discussed in Hayne E. Leland and Klaus Bjerre Toft, "Optimal Capital Structure, Endogenous Bankruptcy, and the Term Structure of Credit Spreads," *Journal of Finance* (July 1996), pp. 987–1019.

Default Swaps with Counterparty Risk

Counterparty risk is a major concern for credit default swap investors because major participants in the market are financial firms, which are themselves subject to default risk.[41] Most bank/dealer counterparties are single A or at most AA rated. If the reference entity name is a AAA rated company, then the default probability of the bank/dealer is so much higher than the reference entity that the bank/dealer may default well before the reference entity. In this case, the protection buyer in a credit default swap is more concerned with the counterparty default risk than the default risk of the reference entity. In this section, we shall extend the previous risk-neutral methodology to account for counter-party risk, with the assumption that the default of the reference entity and the default of the counterparty are uncorrelated.

We label the survival probability of the reference entity $Q_1(t,T)$ and that of the counterparty $Q_2(t,T)$. The default probabilities of the reference entity and counterparty in the jth period in the future are $Q_1(t,T_j) - Q_1(t,T_{j+1})$ and $Q_2(t,T_j) - Q_2(t,T_{j+1})$, respectively. The default of either one is

$$Q_1(t, T_j)Q_2(t, T_j) - Q_1(t, T_{j+1})Q_2(t, T_{j+1})$$

The above equation represents a situation that both the reference entity and counterparty jointly survive till T_j but not T_{j+1}. Hence one of them must have defaulted in the period (T_j, T_{j+1}). Subtracting the counterparty default probability from the probability of either default gives rise to the probability of the case that only the reference entity (but not the counterparty) defaults. Hence the total probability of only the reference entity defaulting is

$$\sum_{j=0}^{n} [Q_1(t,T_j)Q_2(t,T_j) - Q_1(t,T_{j+1})Q_2(t,T_{j+1})] - [Q_2(t,T_j) - Q_2(t,T_{j+1})]$$

When recovery and discounting are included, we have the credit default swap value as

$$V = \sum_{j=0}^{n} P(t, T_j)[1 - R(T_j)][Q_1(t, T_j)Q_2(t, T_j) - Q_1(t, T_{j+1})Q_2(t, T_{j+1})$$
$$-\{Q_2(t, T_j) - Q_2(t,T_{j+1})\}]$$

---

[41] See also Hull and White, "Valuing Credit Default Swaps II: Counterparty Default Risk."

The default swap valued under the counterparty risk requires two default curves, one for the reference entity and one for the counterparty. This default swap should be cheaper than the default swap with only default risk for the reference entity. The difference is the value of the default swap that protects the joint default. An investor who buys such a default swap owns a default swap on the reference entity and has implicitly sold a default swap of joint default back to the counterparty.

When the defaults of the reference entity and the counterparty are correlated, the solution becomes much more complex. When the correlation is high, it is more likely that the counterparty should default before the reference entity, and the credit default swap should have very little value. On the other hand, when the correlation is low (negative), the situation where the reference entity defaults almost guarantees the survival of the counterparty. Consequently, in such instances the counterparty risk is not a concern.

VALUING BASKET DEFAULT SWAPS

In the previous section we presented a model for valuing single-name credit default swaps. Unlike a single-name credit default swap, which provides protection for one bond, a basket default swap provides protection against a basket of bonds. As with single-name credit default swaps, the protection buyer of a basket default swap makes a stream of spread payments until either maturity or default. In the event of default, the protection buyer receives a single lump-sum payment.

Default baskets have become popular because purchasing individual basket default swaps for a collection of bonds can be very expensive, especially considering how unlikely it is that all the bonds in a given basket will default simultaneously. Buying a basket default swap, instead, provides a much cheaper solution. The most popular default basket swap contract is the first-to-default basket. In this contract, the seller pays (the default event occurs) when the first default is observed among the bonds in the basket.

In this section, we describe how to extend the model to basket default swaps. The key in the extension is estimating default correlations. We begin with the valuation model and then discuss how to model default correlations.

The Pricing Model

The number of issuers (or issues) contained in a default basket typically varies (three to five). The payoff of a default basket contract can be a fixed amount or loss based. The first-to-default basket pays principal minus the recovery value of the first defaulted bond in the basket. Hence, for pricing the default basket, we can generalize the default swap valuation as follows:

$$V = E\left\{ e^{-\int_t^{\min(u_k)} r(s)ds} \mathbf{1}_{\min(u_k) < T} [1 - R_k(u_k)] \right\} N_k \qquad (22.13)$$

where 1 is the indicator function, u_k is the default time of the k-th bond, R_k is recovery rate of the k-th bond, and N_k is the notional of the k-th bond. The basket pays when it experiences the first default, that is, $\min (u_k)$.[42]

Equation (22.13) has no easy solution when the default events (or default times, u_k) are correlated. For the sake of exposition, we assume two default processes and label the survival probabilities of the two credit names as $Q_1(t,T)$ and $Q_2(t,T)$. In the case of independence, the default probabilities at some future time t are $-dQ_1(t,T)$ and $-dQ_2(t,T)$ respectively. The default probability of either bond defaulting at time t is

$$-d[Q_1(t, T)Q_2(t, T)] \qquad (22.14)$$

The above equation represents a situation wherein both credit names jointly survive until t, but not until the next instant of time; hence one of the bonds must have defaulted instantaneously at time t. Subtracting the default probability of the first credit name from the probability of

---

[42] In either the default swap or default basket market, the premium is usually paid in a form of spreads. The spread is paid until either the default or maturity, whichever is earlier. From the total value of the default swap, we can convert it to a spread that is paid until default or maturity:

$$s = \frac{V}{\sum_{j=1}^{n} P(t, T_j)Q^*(t, T_j)}$$

where $Q^*(t,T_j)$ is the survival probability of no default of all bonds in the basket. Under independence assumption,

$$Q^*(t, T_j) = \prod_{k=1}^{N} Q_k(t, T_j)$$

where N is the number of bonds in the basket. When bonds are correlated, we need to use materials in the following section to compute Q^*.

either defaulting gives rise to the probability that only the second name (but not the first) defaults:

$$
\int_0^T - d[Q_1(0, t)Q_2(0, t)] + dQ_1(0, t)
$$
$$
= [1 - Q_1(0, T)Q_2(0, T)] - [1 - Q_1(0, T)]
$$
$$
= Q_1(0, T)[1 - Q_2(0, T)] \qquad (22.15)
$$

This probability is equal to the probability of survival of the first name and default of the second name; thus, it is with this probability that the payoff to the second name is paid. By the same token, the default probability of the first name is $1 - Q_1(0,T)$, and it is with this probability that the payoff regarding to the first name is paid.

In a basket model specified in equation (22.13), the final formula for the price of an N bond basket under independence is

$$
V = \int_0^T \sum_{k=1}^N P(0, t) \left[-d \prod_{l=1}^k Q_l(0, t) + d \prod_{l=0}^{k-1} Q_l(0, t) \right] [1 - R_k(t)] \qquad (22.16)
$$

where $Q_0(t) = 1$ and hence $dQ_0(t) = 0$. Equation (22.16) assumes that the last bond (i.e., bond N) has the highest priority in compensation, that is, if the last bond jointly defaults with any other bond, the payoff is determined by the last bond. The second to last bond has the next highest priority in a sense that if it jointly defaults with any other bond *but the last*, the payoff is determined by the second to last bond. This priority prevails recursively to the first bond in the basket.

Investment banks that sell or underwrite default baskets are themselves subject to default risks. If a basket's reference entities have a higher credit quality than their underwriting investment bank, then it is possible that the bank may default before any of the issuers. In this case, the buyer of the default basket is subject to not only the default risk of the issuers of the bonds in the basket, but also to that of the bank as well—that is, the counterparty risk. If the counterparty defaults before any of the issuers in the basket do, the buyer suffers a total loss of the whole protection (and the spreads that had been paid up to that point in time). We modify equation (22.16) to incorporate the counterparty risk by adding a new asset with zero payoff to the equation:

$$
V = \int_0^T \sum_{k=1}^{N+1} P(0, t) \left[-d \prod_{l=1}^k Q_j(0, t) + d \prod_{l=0}^{k-1} Q_l(0, t) \right] [1 - R_k(t)] \qquad (22.17)
$$

where the first asset represents the counterparty whose payoff is zero, that is,

$$1 - R_1(t) = 0 \text{ for all } t \qquad (22.18)$$

Note that the counterparty payoff has the lowest priority because the buyer will be paid if the counterparty jointly defaults with any issuer.

The default swap is a special case of the default basket with $N = 1$ discussed earlier. However, with a default swap, the counterparty risk is more pronounced than that with a basket deal. With only one issuer, equation (22.17) can be simplified to

$$
\begin{aligned}
V &= \int_0^T P(0, t)\{-dQ_1(0, t)[1 - R_1(t)] \\
&\quad + [-dQ_1(0, t)Q_2(0, t) + dQ_1(0, t)][1 - R_2(t)]\} \\
&= \int_0^T P(0, t)\{[-dQ_1(0, t)Q_2(0, t) + dQ_1(0, t)][1 - R_2(t)]\} \quad (22.19)
\end{aligned}
$$

Equation (22.19) implies that the investor who buys a default swap on the reference entity effectively sells a default swap of joint default back to the counterparty.

When the defaults of the issuers (and the counterparty) are correlated, the solution to equation (22.16) becomes very complex. When the correlations are high, issuers in the basket tend to default together. In this case, the riskiest bond will dominate the default of the basket. Hence, the basket default probability will approach the default probability of the riskiest bond. On the other hand, when the correlations are low, individual bonds in the basket may default in different situations. No bond will dominate the default in this case. Hence, the basket default probability will be closer to the sum of individual default probabilities.

To see more clearly how correlation can impact the basket value, think of a basket that contains only two bonds of different issuers. In the extreme case where the default correlation is 1, the two bonds in the basket should default together. In this case, the basket should behave like a single bond. On the other extreme, if the correlation is −1 (the bonds are perfect compliments of one another), default of one bond implies the survival of the other and vice versa. In this case, the basket should reach the maximum default probability: 100%.

How to Model Correlated Default Processes[43]

Default correlation is not an easy concept to define or measure. Put in simple terms, it is a measurement of the degree to which default of one asset makes more or less likely the default of another asset. One can think of default correlation as being jointly due to (1) a macroeconomic effect which tends to tie all industries into the common economic cycle; (2) a sector specific effect, and (3) a company specific effect.

The first contribution implies that default correlation should in general be positive even between companies in different sectors. Within the same sector we would expect companies to have an even higher default correlation since they have more in common. For example, the severe fall in oil prices during the 1980s resulted in the default of numerous oil-producing industries. On the other hand, the fall in the price of oil would have made the default of oil-using industries less likely as their energy costs fell, thereby reducing their likelihood of default and reducing the default correlation. However the sheer lack of default data means that such assumptions are difficult to verify with any degree of certainty.

It is simple enough to define pure default correlation. Basically, this number must correspond to the likelihood that should one asset default within a certain time period, how more or less likely is another asset to also default. In the case of default correlation, it is important to specify the horizon which is being considered.

The pairwise default correlation between two assets A and B is a measure of how more or less likely two assets are to default than if they were independent.

Specifying Directly Joint Default Distribution

Let two firms, A and B, follow the following joint Bernoulli distribution (letting superscripts denote complement sets):

		Firm A		
		0	1	
Firm B	0	$p(A^C \cap B^C)$	$p(A \cap B^C)$	$1-p(B)$
	1	$p(A^C \cap B)$	$p(A \cap B)$	$p(B)$
		$1-p(A)$	$p(A)$	1

[43] This discussion draws from Ren-Raw Chen and Ben J. Sopranzetti, "The Valuation of Default-Triggered Credit Derivatives," *Journal of Financial and Quantitative Analysis* (June 2003).

where

$$p(A^C \cap B) = p(B) - p(A \cap B)$$

$$p(A \cap B^C) = p(A) - p(A \cap B)$$

$$p(A^C \cap B^C) = 1 - p(B) - p(A \cap B^C)$$

The default correlation is

$$\frac{\operatorname{cov}(1_A, 1_B)}{\sqrt{\operatorname{var}(1_A)\operatorname{var}(1_B)}} = \frac{p(B|A)p(A) - p(A)p(B)}{\sqrt{p(A)(1 - p(A)p(B))(1 - p(B))}}$$

For example, suppose that A is a large automobile manufacturer and B is a small auto part supplier. Assume their joint default distribution is given as follows:

		Firm A		
		0	1	
Firm B	0	80%	0%	80%
	1	10%	10%	20%
		90%	10%	100%

In this example where A defaults should bankrupt B but not vice versa, B contains A and

$$p(A \cap B) = p(A)$$

The dependency of the part supplier on the auto manufacturer is

$$p(B|A) = \frac{p(A \cap B)}{p(A)} = \frac{p(A)}{p(A)} = 100\%$$

and the dependency of the auto manufacturer on the part supplier is

$$p(A|B) = \frac{p(A \cap B)}{p(B)} = \frac{p(A)}{p(B)} = 50\%$$

The default correlation is

$$\frac{p(B|A)p(A) - p(A)p(B)}{\sqrt{p(A)(1 - p(A)p(B))(1 - p(B))}}$$

$$= \frac{10\% - 10\% \times 20\%}{\sqrt{10\% \times 90\% \times 20\% \times 80\%}}$$

$$= \frac{0.08}{\sqrt{0.0144}} = \frac{2}{3}$$

This examples demonstrates that perfect dependency does not imply perfect correlation. To reach perfect correlation, $p(A) = p(B)$. Similarly, perfectly negative dependency does not necessarily mean perfect negative correlation. To see that, consider the following example:

		Firm A 0	Firm A 1	
Firm B	0	70%	10%	80%
	1	20%	0%	20%
		90%	10%	100%

It is clear that given A defaults, B definitely survives: $p(B^C|A) = 1$, and $p(B|A) = 0$. But the default correlation is only −0.25. To reach perfect negative correlation of −100%, $p(A) + p(B) = 1$.

The reason that perfect dependency does not result in perfect correlation is because correlation alone is not enough to identify a unique joint distribution. Only a normal distribution family can have a uniquely identified joint distribution when a correlation matrix is identified. This is not true for other distribution families.[44]

Having now defined default correlation, one can begin to show how it relates to the pricing of credit default baskets.

We represent the outcomes of the two defaultable assets A and B using a Venn diagram as shown in Exhibit 22.7. The left circle corresponds to all scenarios in which asset A defaults before time T. Its area is therefore equal to p_A, the probability of default of asset A. Similarly, the area within the circle labeled B corresponds to the probability of default of asset B and equals p_B. The area of the shaded overlap corre-

---

[44] For an extension of the above two-company analysis to multiple companies, see Chen and Sopranzetti, "The Valuation of Default-Triggered Credit Derivatives."

EXHIBIT 22.7   Venn Diagram Representation of Correlated Default for Two Assets

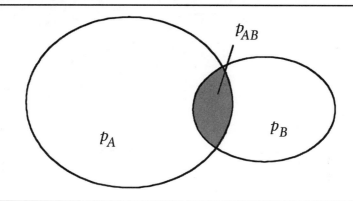

sponds to all scenarios in which both assets default before time T. Its area is the probability of joint default, p_{AB}.

The probability of either asset defaulting is

$$\Omega = p_A + p_B - p_{AB}$$

In the zero correlation limit, when the assets are independent, the probability of both assets defaulting is given by $p_{AB} = p_A p_B$. Substituting this into the above formula for the default correlation shows when the assets are independent, $\rho_D(T) = 0$ as expected (see Exhibit 22.8).

In the limit of high default correlation, the default of the stronger asset always results in the default of the weaker asset. In the limit the joint default probability is given by $p_{AB} = \min[p_A, p_B]$. This is shown in Exhibit 22.9 in the case where $p_A > p_B$. In this case we have a maximum default correlation of

$$\bar{\rho} = \frac{\sqrt{p_B(1 - p_A)}}{\sqrt{p_A(1 - p_B)}}$$

Once again, the price of a first-to-default basket is the area enclosed by the circles. In this case one circle encloses the other and the first-to-default basket price becomes the larger of the two probabilities:

$$\Omega_{\rho = \bar{\rho}} = p_A + p_B - p_{AB} = \max[p_A, p_B]$$

EXHIBIT 22.8   Independent Assets

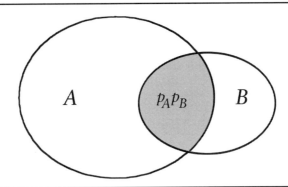

Outcome	In Venn Diagram	Probability
Both asset A and asset B default	Anywhere in overlap of both circles	p_{AB}
Asset B defaults and asset A does not default	Anywhere in B but not in overlap	$p_B - p_{AB}$
Asset A defaults and asset B does not default	Anywhere in A but not in overlap	$p_A - p_{AB}$
Neither asset defaults	Outside both circles	$1 - (p_A + p_B - p_{AB})$
Either asset A or asset B or both assets default	Anywhere within outer perimeter of circles	$p_A + p_B - p_{AB}$

EXHIBIT 22.9   Case of High Default Correlation

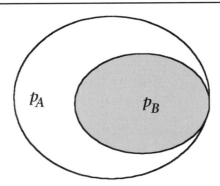

In the case default of the stronger asset is always associated with default of the weaker asset.

If p_A equals p_B then $p_{AB} = p_A$ and default of either asset results in default of the other. In this instance the correlation is at its maximum of 100%.

As correlations go negative, a point arrives at which there is zero probability of both assets defaulting together. Graphically, there is no intersection between the two circles, as shown in Exhibit 22.10, and we have $p_{AB} = 0$. The correlation becomes

$$\rho = \frac{-\sqrt{p_A p_B}}{\sqrt{1 - p_A}\sqrt{1 - p_B}}$$

A negative correlation of -100% can only occur if $p_A = 1 - p_B$—that is, for every default of asset A, asset B survives and vice versa.

The price of the first-to-default basket is simply the area of the two nonoverlapping circles

$$\Omega_{\rho = \underline{\rho}} = p_A + p_B$$

This is when the default basket is most expensive.

We have seen above the price of a basket in the limits of low, high, and zero correlation. Given that $\Omega = p_A + p_B - p_{AB}$, we can write the price of a basket in terms of the default correlation as

$$\Omega = p_A + p_B - p_A p_B - \rho \sqrt{p_A - p_A^2}\sqrt{p_B - p_B^2}$$

EXHIBIT 22.10   Negative Default Correlation Case

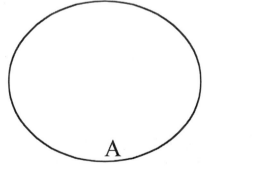

As the default correlation becomes negative, the two circles separate implying that the joint default probability has fallen to zero.

As more assets are considered, more default combinations become possible. With just three assets we have the following eight possibilities:

- No assets default
- Only asset A defaults
- Only asset B defaults
- Only asset C defaults
- Asset A and asset B default
- Asset B and asset C default
- Asset A and asset C default
- Asset A and asset B and asset C default

To price this basket we either need all of the joint probabilities or the pairwise correlations ρ_{AB}, ρ_{BC}, and ρ_{AC} (see Exhibit 22.11). The probability that the basket is triggered is given by

$$\Omega = p_A + p_B + p_C - p_{AB} - p_{BC} - p_{AC} + p_{ABC}$$

Joint Poisson Process

Recent evidence (for example, Enron, WorldCom, and Quest) demonstrated that severe economic hardship and publicity can cause chain defaults for even very large firms. Hence, incorporating default correlation is an important task in valuing credit derivatives.

As stated above, the period-end joint default probability by two reference entities is as follows:

$$\Pr(A \cap B) = E[1_{A \cap B}] = p_{AB}$$

EXHIBIT 22.11 Venn Diagram for Three Issuers

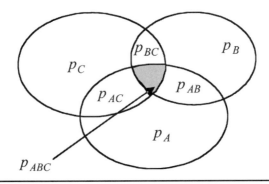

where 1 is the indicator function.[45]

The BSM model is particularly useful in modeling correlated defaults. If two firms do business together, it is likely that the two firms may have a certain relationship between their defaults. The BSM model provides an easy explanation as to how that may be modeled:

$$\Pr(A_A(T) < K_A \cap A_B(T) < K_B)$$

A bivariate diffusion of firm A and firm B can easily provide what we need. Under the BSM model, logarithm of asset price is normally distributed. Hence, the previous equation is the tail probability of a bivariate normal distribution. The correlation between the two normally distributed log asset prices characterizes the default correlation. When the correlation in the bivariate normal is 100%, the distribution becomes a univariate normal distribution and the two firms default together. When the correlation is −100%, one firm defaulting implies the survival of the other firm; so there is always one that is live and one that is dead.

While the BSM model cleverly explains how default risk is priced in the corporate debt conceptually, it remains a practical problem in that it cannot price today's complex credit derivatives. Hence, researchers recently have developed a series of reduced form models that simplify the computations of the prices.

Using Common Factors to Model Joint Defaults

There are two ways to model joint defaults in a reduced form model. One way, proposed by Duffie and Singleton, is to specify a "common factor."[46] When this common factor jumps, all firms default. Firms also can do so on their own. The model can be extended to multiple common factors: market factor, industry factor, sector factor, and so on to capture more sophisticated joint defaults.

Formally, let a firm's jump process be[47]

---

[45] Recall from Chapter 6 that for any random variable X the following relationship holds: $E[X] = \int_\Omega X dP$. If X is the indicator function of the event A, $X = 1_A$ we can write

$$E[1_A] = \int_\Omega 1_A dP = \int_A dP = P(A)$$

[46] Darrell Duffie and Kenneth Singleton, "Econometric Modeling of Term Structure of Defaultable Bonds," *Review of Financial Studies* (December 1999), pp. 687–720.

[47] Darrell Duffie and Kenneth Singleton, unpublished lecture notes on credit derivatives; and Darrell Duffie and Kenneth Singleton, "Simulating Correlated Defaults," working paper, Stanford University (September 1998).

$$J_i = a_i q_M + q_i$$

where q_M is the market jump process and q_i is the idiosyncratic jump process. The coefficient a_i is to capture different correlation levels. The joint event is then

$$\text{corr}(J_i, J_j) = a_i a_j \text{var}[q_M]$$

Correlating Default Times

Before we discuss how the default correlation is introduced, we need to discuss how single issuer default is modeled. The approach used is equivalent to the Jarrow-Turnbull model.[48] A hazard rate, $\lambda(t)$, is introduced where $\lambda(t)dt$ is the probability of defaulting in a small time interval dt. This leads to the definition of the survival probability

$$Q(0, T) = \exp\left(-\int_0^T \lambda(s)ds\right)$$

The probability of surviving to a time T and then defaulting in the next instant is therefore given by the density function:

$$-dQ = \lambda(T)\exp\left(-\int_0^T \lambda(s)ds\right)dT$$

In the simple case when the hazard rate is constant over time so that $\lambda(t) = \lambda$ we have

$$-dQ = \lambda\exp(-\lambda T)dT$$

From this we see that the probability of defaulting at time T as given by $-dQ$ shows that default times are exponentially distributed. By extension, the average time to default is given by computing

$$\langle T \rangle = \lambda\int_0^\infty T\exp(-\lambda T)dT = \frac{1}{\lambda}$$

---

[48] Robert Jarrow and Stuart Turnbull, "Pricing Derivatives on Financial Securities Subject to Default Risk," *Journal of Finance* 20, no. 1 (1995), pp. 53–86.

Knowing that defaults are normally distributed makes it easy to simulate default times for independent assets. We need to generate uniform random numbers in the range [0,1] and then given a term structure for the hazard rate, imply out the corresponding default time. For example, if we denote the uniform random draw by u, the corresponding default time T^* is given by solving

$$u = \exp(-\lambda T^*)$$

to give

$$T^* = -\frac{\log(u)}{\lambda}$$

This is an efficient method for simulating default. Every random draw produces a corresponding default time. In terms of its usefulness, the only question is whether the default time is before or after the maturity of the contract being priced.

There are many ways to introduce a default correlation between the different reference entities in a credit default basket. One way is to correlate the default times. This correlation is defined as

$$\rho(T_A, T_B) = \frac{\langle T_A T_B \rangle - \langle T_A \rangle \langle T_B \rangle}{\sqrt{\langle T_A^2 \rangle - \langle T_A \rangle^2} \sqrt{\langle T_B^2 \rangle - \langle T_B \rangle^2}}$$

It is important to stress that this is not the same as the default correlation. Although correlating default times has the effect of correlating default, there are two reasons they are not equivalent. First, there is no need to define a default horizon when correlating default times. To measure this correlation, we would observe a sample of assets over a long (infinite) period and compute the times at which each asset defaults. There is no notion of a time horizon for this correlation.

Second, since the default time correlation equals 100% when $T_j = T_i$ and when $T_j = T_i + \vartheta$, it is possible to have 100% default time correlation with assets defaulting at fixed intervals.

Under a Poisson assumption,

$$\langle T_A \rangle = \frac{1}{\lambda_A} \quad \text{and} \quad \langle T_B \rangle = \frac{1}{\lambda_B}$$

and

$$\sqrt{\langle T_A^2 \rangle - \langle T_A \rangle^2} = \frac{1}{\lambda_A} \text{ and } \sqrt{\langle T_B^2 \rangle - \langle T_B \rangle^2} = \frac{1}{\lambda_B}$$

so we have

$$\rho(T_A, T_B) = \langle T_A T_B \rangle \lambda_A \lambda_B - 1$$

Copula Function

To generate correlated default times, we use the normal Copula function methodology as proposed by Li.[49] A Copula function (see Chapter 6) is simply a specification of how the univariate marginal distributions combine to form a multivariate distribution. For example, if we have N correlated uniform random variables $U_1, U_2, ..., U_N$ then

$$C(u_1, u_2, ..., u_N) = \Pr\{U_1 < u_1, U_2 < u_2, ..., U_N < u_N\}$$

is the joint distribution function that gives the probability that all of the uniforms are in the specified range.

In a similar manner we can define the Copula function for the default times of N assets:

$$C(F_1(T_1), F_2(T_2), ..., F_N(T_N))$$
$$= \Pr\{U_1 < F_1(T_1), U_2 < F_2(T_2), ..., U_N < F_N(T_N)\}$$

where $F_i(T_i) = \Pr\{t_i < t\}$.

There are several possible choices but here we define the Copula function Θ to be the multivariate normal distribution function with correlation matrix ρ. We also define Φ^{-1} as the inverse of a univariate normal function. The Copula function is therefore given by

$$C(\mathbf{u}) = \Theta(\Phi^{-1}(u_1), \Phi^{-1}(u_2), \Phi^{-1}(u_3), \Phi^{-1}(u_4), ..., \Phi^{-1}(u_N), \boldsymbol{\rho})$$

where $\boldsymbol{\rho}$ is the correlation matrix.

What this specification says is that in order to generate correlated default times, we must first generate N correlated multivariate gaussians denoted by $u_1, u_2, u_3, ..., u_N$—one for each asset in the basket. These

---

[49] David X. Li, *Credit Metrics Monitor*, Risk Metrics Group (April 1999).

are then converted into uniform random variables by cumulative probability functions.

Once we have the vector of correlated random uniforms **u** we can calculate the corresponding default times knowing that asset i defaults in trial n at time T given by

$$T_{in} = -\frac{\ln u_{in}}{\lambda_i}$$

Comparing Default Correlation and Default Time Correlation

In addition to correlating default times, we could correlate default events. There is no simple way to do this directly. It is better to correlate the assets using some other mechanism and then measure the default correlation *a posteriori*. The question is: If we implement a model which correlates default times, how does the correlation relate to default correlation as defined above.

In common with the case of default correlation, it is only possible to have a 100% pairwise correlation in default times between two assets if both assets have the same default probabilities. Otherwise, the distributions are centered around different average default times and having equal default times and different average default times is not compatible.

If we assume that in both cases all assets have the same default probability, what is the difference between correlating default times and correlating default events? In the limit of zero correlation there is no difference as the assets default independently. In the limit of 100% correlation there is a fundamental difference: If default times have a 100% correlation, then assets must default either simultaneously or with a fixed time difference.[50] However, if there is 100% default correlation, then this means that the default of one asset within a certain horizon always coincides with the default of the other within the same horizon. In general, we would expect a 100% default correlation to imply that both assets default together, but this is not a strict requirement. In practice, the default of one asset may occur at any time and be followed by default of the other asset at the end of the horizon. Default correlation is 100%, but default times have a lower correlation.

Consider also the effect of the default horizon. Given that default times are exponentially distributed, extending the default horizon

---

[50] Since the default time correlation of 100% is preserved under translations of the form $T_j = T_i + \vartheta$.

makes it more likely for defaults to occur. Extending the default horizon therefore has the effect of increasing the measured default correlation. Indeed we must be careful to specify the horizon when we quote a default correlation. On the other hand, correlation of default times is independent of the trade horizon (i.e., the tenor of the default swap).

There is also a link between default correlation and the hazard rate. For a fixed horizon, increasing the hazard rate for all assets makes default more likely within that horizon. If the assets are correlated, the measured default correlation must increase. However, the increase in default probability makes the distribution of default times more weighted towards earlier defaults. Yet, the default time correlation can remain unchanged.

The analysis below shows that the default correlation is always lower than the default time correlation. This can be understood in qualitative terms as follows: To have the same basket price we have the same number of defaults before maturity. As default correlation is a direct measurement of the likelihood of two assets to default within a fixed horizon, it is more closely linked with the pricing of a basket default swap than a correlation of default times. Indeed, as we have shown in the one-period model above, the value of the basket default swap is a linear function of the default correlation. Though a correlation of default times introduces a tendency for assets to default within a given trade horizon, it is an indirect way to do this. As a result, a simulation of defaults with a certain default time correlation will always tend to have a lower default correlation. In other words, less default correlation is required in order to have the same effect as a correlation of default times.[51]

SUMMARY

- There are different forms of credit risk: default risk, spread risk, and downgrade risk.
- Credit derivatives are financial instruments designed to transfer credit risk between two parties.
- Credit default swaps are the most popular credit risk derivatives.
- In a credit default swap, the protection buyer pays a fee, the swap premium, to the protection seller in return for the right to receive a payment conditional upon a default, also called a credit event.

---

[51] Numerical examples for pricing credit default swap baskets in the single-period and multi-period cases are provided in Chapter 10 in Anson, Fabozzi, Choudhry, and Chen, *Credit Derivatives: Instruments, Applications, and Pricing*.

- Credit default swaps for corporate and sovereign reference entities are standardized.
- The International Swaps and Derivatives Association (ISDA) developed the ISDA Master Agreement which establishes international standards governing privately negotiated derivative trades (all derivatives).
- The 1999 ISDA Credit Derivatives Definitions provides a list of eight possible credit events.
- Credit derivative models can be partitioned into structural models and reduced form models.
- Structural-type models represent default as an option: a company defaults on its debt if the value of the assets of the company falls below a certain default point.
- Reduced form models model directly the likelihood of default or downgrade.
- Structural models use option theory.
- Structural models model default on very reasonable assumption but are difficult to calibrate and computationally burdensome.
- Structural models use Poisson processes to model the time of default.
- A transition matrix defines the probability of transition between any two credit rating states.
- Default correlation is a concept difficult to define.
- Default correlation can be modeled with copula functions that model the correlation between the times of default.

CHAPTER 23

Risk Management

Risk means uncertainty. There is risk whenever there is uncertainty about future events. There are many different notions of risk. In business, as well as in daily life, an endeavor is considered risky if it is difficult or if depends on many things that might go wrong. The notion of risk espoused by financial theory is that of pure probabilistic uncertainty, without any possibility of controlling the outcome. For example, an investor does not control market fluctuations.

Though risk cannot be individually influenced it can be managed by diversification and risk transfer. The idea of transferring and reducing risk is not new. As observed in Chapter 1, the practice of insurance and of risk reduction through diversification was already well established in the Middle Ages. Diversification is an intuitive idea, easily conveyed by the saying, "Do not put all your eggs in the same basket."

However, the modern idea of measuring risk and of selectively transferring carefully calibrated portions of risk had to wait the development of modern probability theory. As seen in Chapter 3, the foundation of probability theory as a sound mathematical discipline was achieved only around 1930.

The development of the mathematical theory of risk, initiated by Lundberg (see Chapter 3), led to the practice of modern insurance and to the development of the insurance business. Insurance is deeply rooted in the notion of diversification: Individuals protect themselves by pooling risks together. If the number of uncorrelated risks is large, individual risk becomes negligible.

In recent years, financial firms and insurance companies have taken the concept of risk management further in three different directions: (1) by recognizing that the shape of risk is an important determinant of the risk-return trade-off; (2) by engineering contracts able to transfer selected portions of risk; and (3) by trading these contracts. From a statistical point of view, a key innovation is the attention paid to the ratio between the bulk of the risk and the risk of the tails. The latter has become a key statistical determinant of risk management policies.

Within the realm of finance, one has to make a broad distinction between the management of risk in investment management and in banking and finance at large. As we have seen in the previous chapters, investment management is essentially a question of determining a probability distribution of returns and engineering the optimal trade-off between risk and return as a function of individual preferences. Therefore, risk management is intrinsic to investment management.

The risk management function, which is often associated with the investment management process, has the objective of (1) controlling risk when the investment process is not fully automated; (2) taking into consideration special risks such as the business or operational risk; and (3) controlling the global risk, especially the tails of the risk.

Banks and financial firms, however, engage in financial operations other than pure investing. Many of these operations are profitable but risky and their risk must be managed or eliminated. For instance, a financial firm offering a customized derivative instrument to a client assumes a risk that, in itself, might be suboptimal or excessive. Hence, the need to transfer all or part of this risk to the market at large. The risk management function controls this process.

The possibility of effectively controlling and managing risk depends on the availability of instruments that allow for the transfer of risk. A market is called *complete* if there are instruments able to cover any tradable risk.

In this chapter we discuss market completeness, risk measures, and the notion of coherence of risk measures, and then present risk models and their use in investment management. We begin the chapter with the concept of market completeness because it is a necessary condition for effective risk management. We first introduced this concept in Chapter 14, where we covered arbitrage pricing.

MARKET COMPLETENESS

In finance, the effectiveness of risk management is essentially related to the degree of market completeness. In a complete market any individual risky position can be completely hedged, that is, its risk can be completely eliminated by purchasing appropriate contracts. In intuitive terms, this means that any payoff, intended as a random variable, can be replicated by engineering appropriate portfolios. In other words, there is a market, and therefore a price, for every contingency.

Markets in which this hedging is not possible are called *incomplete markets*. In incomplete markets there are contingencies that are not traded and cannot be priced and replicated. An investor who "owns" one of these contingencies is stuck with them and has no assurance that a buyer will be found. An incomplete market might be completed by adding appropriate assets provided that they are tradable. If the market is completed, every contingency becomes tradable. However, there is no guarantee that an arbitrary market can be completed.

The question of market completeness is fairly complicated. There are two key aspects in the notion of market completeness: (1) the mathematics of market completeness and (2) the economic rationale as to why markets are complete or can be completed. We discuss each below.

The Mathematics of Market Completeness

The purely mathematical aspect of the completeness of a given market model is a widely studied subject. Some market models are complete while others are not. For instance, a market where stock prices evolve as geometric random walks and a risk-free asset is available is complete. On the other hand, a market represented by a stochastic volatility model is incomplete.

A market is complete if any cash flow stochastic process can be replicated by an appropriate self-financing trading strategy with some initial investment. Replication means that the self-financing trading strategy and the original cash flow process are equal processes. Recall that in Chapter 6 on probability theory we defined four notions of equality between stochastic processes. The weakest condition of equality requires that two processes have the same finite-dimensional distributions. This concept of equality is insufficient to define replication. The strongest condition of equality requires that two processes have the same paths except for a set of measure zero. Replication requires that the original cash flow process and the replicating self-financing trading strategy are equal processes in this strongest sense.

Recall also from Chapter 10 that there are two types of solutions of stochastic differential equations: strong solutions and weak solutions. Strong solutions are solutions built on given Brownian motions while weak solutions include their own Brownian motion. This notion, which might look abstract and remote, is however important from the point of view of a replicating strategy. If a replicating process is defined by a stochastic differential equation, the difference between strong and weak solutions is important.

Market completeness entails that there is a core of price processes such that any cash flow stream can be engineered as a time-varying, but self-financing, portfolio made up of the core price processes. For example, in a complete market a complex derivative instrument can be replicated by a portfolio of simpler instruments. A bank that creates a credit derivative can always hedge its positions.

As we have seen in Chapter 14 on arbitrage, in the finite-state, one-step case, market completeness means that the number of linearly independent price processes is equal to the number of states. In other words, a market is complete if there are as many linearly independent price processes as states of the world. This notion can be easily expressed in terms of linear algebra. In the finite-state, discrete-time case the above conditions must be replaced by the notion of dynamically complete markets as assets can be traded at intermediate dates. In fact, the number of linearly independent price processes can be smaller than the number of states provided that assets can be traded repeatedly. As shown by Darrell Duffie and Chi-Fu Huang[1] and Hua He,[2] what is needed, in this case, is that there are as many linearly independent price processes as there are branches leaving a node in the market information structure. Based on this, it can be demonstrated that the binomial model and its extension to multiple variables are complete.

When we proceed to the continuous-state, continuous-time case this notion looses meaning. In this case there is a continuum of states and a continuum of instants. The infinite number of trading instants allows markets to be complete even if they are formed by a finite number of securities. There are restrictions to ensure that a market model is complete. A fundamental theorem assures that, in the absence of arbitrage, market completeness is associated with the uniqueness of the equivalent martingale measure. In a complete market the equivalent martingale measure is unique, while an incomplete market is characterized by infinite martingale measures. This happens because there are contingencies that cannot be priced by arbitrage.

The condition of market completeness is violated in many important models. Two, in particular, have attracted attention: jump-diffusion models and stochastic volatility models. **Jump-diffusion models** are models formed by diffusions plus processes where finite jumps occur at random times, such as at those times represented by a Poisson process. **Stochastic**

[1] Darrell Duffie and Chi-Fu Huang, "Implementing Arrow-Debreu Equilibria by Continuous Trading of Few Long-Lived Securities," *Econometrica* 53 (1985), pp. 1337–1356

[2] Hua He, "Convergence from Discrete to Continuous Time Contingent Claims Prices," *Review of Financial Studies* 3, no. 4 (1990), pp. 523–546.

volatility models are models where prices are diffusion processes but the volatility term is driven by a separate process. In discrete time, all models make jumps while stochastic volatility models become the ARCH and GARCH models. Let's briefly discuss completeness in relation to stochastic volatility models.

A standard geometric-diffusion model is complete as there is a unique equivalent martingale measure Q (see Chapter 15) under which the model can be written as

$$dS_t = rS_t dt + \sigma S_t dB_t$$

where r is the risk-free rate, σ is the volatility constant, and B is a standard Brownian motion. If a stock price follows this model, any contingent claim can be uniquely replicated. In particular, options can be replicated as a portfolio formed with the stock and the risk-free asset. Options are redundant securities. Anyone who has underwritten an option can completely hedge its risk by constructing an appropriate self-financing replication strategy.

The same reasoning can be applied in the case of N geometric Brownian motions. In this case, there is still a unique equivalent martingale measure under which the model can be written as

$$dS_t^i = rS_t^i dt + \sum_{j=1}^{N} \sigma_j S_t^j dB_t^j$$

Suppose now that volatility is not constant but that it is a time-dependent process. The simplest two-factor, stochastic-volatility model can be written, in the physical probability measure, as

$$dS_t = \mu S_t dt + \sigma_t S_t dB_t$$

$$d\sigma_t = a(S_t, \sigma_t)dt + b(S_t, \sigma_t)B_t^\sigma$$

where B_t^σ is another standard Brownian motion eventually correlated with B_t. In this case, however, there are infinite equivalent martingale measures in which the model can be written as

$$dS_t = rS_t dt + \sigma_t S_t d\tilde{B}_t$$

$$d\sigma_t = \tilde{a}(S_t, \sigma_t)dt + b(S_t, \sigma_t)d\tilde{B}_t^{\sigma}$$

The above stochastic volatility model can be completed[3] by adding an asset $Y_t = C(t,\sigma_t,S_t)$ that follows the following process:

$$dY_t = rY_t dt + F(t, Y_t S_t)d\hat{B}_t$$

where $\hat{B}_t$ is another Brownian motion eventually correlated with the other two. Note that mathematically there is an infinite family of these models.

The question of what model applies to a new asset introduced for completing the market is an empirical one. Note that this new asset is contractually defined as a function of the stock price. In practice it is an option. The market will price the new asset according to some economic pricing principle which is not, however, a principle of absence of arbitrage. In this completed market, the underwriter of an option can completely hedge his/her position. However, the hedging will not be the same as in the case of constant volatility.

Similar considerations can be repeated for the jump-diffusion models. Suppose that a lognormal diffusion is given. Consider a Poisson point process and add a finite jump to the diffusion at every occurrence of the Poisson process. The resulting model is generally incomplete. However, it can be completed by adding appropriate contracts. What type of contracts must be added in each case is not a trivial question.

The Economics of Market Completeness

In discussing market completeness it should be kept in mind that market completeness means that any risk can be completely hedged. In modern markets, hedging is typically achieved by taking positions in appropriate contracts such as options or other derivative instruments. In this way risk is transferred to other entities and hedged. The key question is: why should there be other entities willing to take the opposite side of a risky position?

Beside the mathematical details, this is the essence of market completeness. It means that there is always someone willing to trade, at a market price, any contingent claim. It is important to reconcile this notion with that of mathematical completeness. Let's use the simple example of European stock options in a market with a risk-free asset

---

[3] M.H.A. Davis, *Complete-Market Models of Stochastic Volatility*, forthcoming in Proc. Royal Society London (A).

and where stock prices evolve as geometrical Brownian motions. This is a complete market. Therefore any European option can be perfectly replicated by a portfolio of the underlying stock plus the risk-free asset.

In this market, investors can protect themselves from excessive losses by purchasing options. However, in case of large losses someone has to foot the bill. The risk transfer process is the following. Suppose that an investor who owns a stock wants to buy protection against large price movements of the stock by purchasing an option. In this way the owner of the stock transfers the risk of eventual large movements to the underwriter of the option. The underwriter might decide to bear the risk or to transfer the risk by purchasing an appropriate self-financing strategy. In the latter case, the risk of large movements has been transferred in two steps from the initial investor to the option underwriter and then back to the market.

In case of large negative movements, there will be a transfer of money from owners of long stock positions to the original investor who sought protection. The transfer will occur through the mechanism of short positions. It would be a mistake to think that by replication everyone comes out of large negative market movement unscathed. In this case, in particular, if options are properly hedged, the final losers are those who hold stock positions without hedging them.

Suppose, now, that price processes follow stochastic volatility dynamics. In this case, markets are incomplete and options cannot be perfectly hedged. The key difference with respect to the previous case is that the underwriter of the options has to foot the bill of eventual large losses. In this case, underwriting options is a risky business, while in the previous case, ultimately the risk is borne by stock owners or stock "lenders."

In the case of stock markets, risk does not disappear in aggregate. Total market capitalization fluctuates and there is no way that this global risk can be eliminated. In fact, *on a global scale*, no one profits if markets move down or loses if markets move up. Profits and losses of short and long positions are only local relative losses. In aggregate, investors lose if markets go down and gain if markets go up.

However, the market as seen by each individual investor might be complete or not as a function of the dynamics of price processes. Completeness dictates that risk can be arbitrarily apportioned but does not change the fact that massive losses might occur in aggregate. In other markets, however, there is a level of aggregation at which risk does not exist or is very small. In this case, hedging has a different rationale as for each movement there are winners and losers. Hedging is a stabilization device as risk can be mutually exchanged. In this case, market completeness acquires a different meaning. In fact, in a complete market, risk can be eliminated by market mechanisms, while in an incomplete market this is not possible.

It should be clear that the economic rationale for risk management is different in different cases. There are essentially three possibilities. First, risk can be transferred to firms that engineer a diversification service. Insurance companies are the typical example. This means that diversification is possible; that is, in the aggregate the residual risk is very low simply because there are many uncorrelated events. For instance, the residual risk of significant short-term fluctuations of the average age of a population is very low except in exceptional cases (e.g., war or natural catastrophes). Thus life insurance is a statistically sound business.

Second, risk can be transferred to "speculators" (e.g., persons or entities who have a different risk-return profile or an information advantage). Essentially, risks exist in aggregate but there are entities willing to make bets on some portions of it. Note that if markets were not correlated, there would be no risk in aggregate.

Third, risk can be transferred because there are positions that offset each other in a true economic sense. In other words, there are "natural hedges." This means that the fluctuations of some basic variables create simultaneous gains and losses approximately of the same size. This is the case of interest rates. There are other cases, with more or less complete natural hedges.

WHY MANAGE RISK?

The basic motivation for risk management is financial optimization. In this sense, the motivation for risk management has to be found in the basic tenet of investment management: optimization of the risk-return trade-off.

Financial optimization implies that a risk return trade-off indeed exists. If some risk can be eliminated in aggregate, the market cannot remunerate it. Therefore the assumption of that risk is always suboptimal and it should be eliminated. This is the case when risk can be diversified away and when there are natural hedges, as in the case of interest rates.

As risk management means the transfer of risk from one entity to another, clearly if there is risk in aggregate there are limits to the size of the risk management business. This is the case of the stock option business. There is no natural hedge to stock market movements, at least none has been discovered thus far. No financial agent profits from market plunges, so only small optimization adjustment is possible. Therefore there are natural limits to the size of coverage that can be offered. On the other hand, in the case of interest rates if one entity loses another gains and risk transfer is effective.

In fact, the elimination of interest rate risk forms the bulk of risk management. According to the U.S. Office of the Controller of the Currency *Quarterly Derivatives Report*, interest rate derivatives made up 86% of all derivative contracts in the second quarter of 2003. Foreign-exchange contracts were the second-largest category of derivatives, making up about 11% of all derivatives in the same period while equity, commodity, and credit derivatives made up about 3% of all contracts. Note that the size of the bond and equity markets are comparable. The huge notional volume of interest rate derivatives is partially due to formal duplication of traded contracts. For instance, in a number of cases, instead of selling a swap agreement it might be easier to create a new swap agreement with opposite cash flows. Formal duplication, however, is possible just because there is no risk in aggregate.

The situation would be different for an entity that had the ability to make reliable forecasts. Banks as well as industrial firms hedge interest rates because they do not feel sufficiently comfortable with interest rate forecasts. Unable to make sufficiently safe bets they prefer to eliminate the risk. Hence the huge market for covering interest rates fluctuations.

RISK MODELS

A risk model is a mathematical model of prices, returns, rates, and eventually other quantities that allows one to determine the probability distribution of the total value of portfolios held by a financial institution. Many different models have been proposed in different areas of financial risk. Let's discuss each of them.

Market Risk

Perhaps the best known model of market risk is RiskMetrics, initially proposed by JP Morgan in 1994 and now commercialized by the RiskMetrics Group. Over 100.000 physical copies of the RiskMetrics software are now in use at banks and asset management firms.[4]

---

[4] Information on the company and technical details on the product are available and can be downloaded from the RiskMetrics Group web site www.riskmetrics.com. Since inception JPMorgan has made technical details on the product broadly available. The RiskMetrics Group has continued this practice.

The basic idea of RiskMetrics is to represent the entire set of returns and rates as a multivariate normal variable. In other words, RiskMetrics is made up of a simple linear model with some robust estimation technique. JPMorgan provided daily the estimates of volatilities and correlations essentially using empirical volatilities and correlations. Over the years the initial model has been extended to cover more complex cases, in particular derivative instruments. A suite of models for banks and asset managers is commercialized by The RiskMetrics Group.

Multifactor models are often used to evaluate the market risk of equity portfolios. Commercially available models such as Barra or APT are now in use at many asset management firms to evaluate market risk. However, if portfolios include derivative instruments, multifactor models must be completed with additional modeling tools able to capture the behavior of these instruments.

Risk models are often based on the idea of creating a relatively small number of scenarios, that is, paths of the key financial and economic variables. The Toronto-based firm Algorithmics pioneered the use of scenario-based risk management as a commercial software implementation.

Credit Risk

Credit risk models are inherently more complex than market risk models as the normal distribution is not a good approximation of default distributions. A number of models have been proposed, in particular CreditRiskMetrics from the RiskMetrics Group. This model is based on an underlying process for ratings. Credit Suisse proposed an actuarial credit risk model, Creditrisk+ that represents default distributions as a mixture of Gaussians. Models of credit risk based on option theory have been proposed by the firm KMV which is now part of Moody's. Kamakura Corporation has proposed models of credit risk based on the work of Robert Jarrow. Credit risk models were covered in Chapter 22.

Operational Risk

Operational risk can be broadly defined as risk related to processes; it generally falls under the responsibility of internal auditors or their equivalents, but in a number of instances it is under the responsibility of the risk manager. Determining its contribution to portfolio risk varies from firm to firm. Some firms attribute to human error (e.g., changing the benchmark and not informing) up to 75% of portfolio risk.

Large investment banks such as the former Bankers Trust and Credit Suisse First Boston pioneered a quantitative approach to operational risk several years ago, but the data problem is more severe in asset management than in investment banking. Many asset management firms consider the occurrence of losses due to operational risk to be irrelevant.

RISK MEASURES

Risk is embodied in a probability distribution of returns or of possible losses. From a management point of view it is interesting to collapse this probability distribution in a single number. The problem of measuring risk with a single number has received much attention, even in contexts other than finance.

Historically, the first measure of the risk contained in a distribution is its variance, or the standard deviation, which is the square root of the variance. The variance of a distribution gives an indication as to whether the distribution is concentrated around some value or spread over a large interval of values. If the standard deviation of a distribution is high, it means that there is a high probability that the variable might take values significantly different from its mean. A high standard deviation, therefore, corresponds to a high risk. In the terminology of risk management, standard deviation represents *unexpected loss* (UL).

Because risk is uncertainty (lack of information), the question of the information conveyed by a probability distribution has led to the concept of *information* and to *Information Theory*. In the case of finite probabilities, information (I) in the sense of Information Theory is defined as the average of the logarithms of probabilities (p_i):

$$I = \sum_{i=1}^{N} p_i \log p_i$$

Information reaches its maximum when the probability is concentrated in only one outcome, that is, $p_i = 1$ for $i = k$, $p_i = 0$ for $i \neq k$. In this case information is zero as the information of an outcome with probability zero is conventionally set to zero. Information reaches its minimum when all probabilities are equal, that is, when there is maximum uncertainty on the future outcome. In this case information is negative: $I = -N \log N$. There is no lower bound to information.

Information with a minus sign is well known in statistical physics as **entropy**, which is a measure of disorder: $E = -I$. The information associated with an equi-probable binary scheme, that is, the information associated with the choice between two equally probable possible outcome, is called

bit. As information is additive, it represents the number of bits necessary to characterize a choice.

This definition of information can be extended to a continuous probability distribution. However, in the continuous case, information looses its meaning.[5] For this and for other reasons, information cannot be used effectively as a measure of risk.[6]

When JP Morgan released its RiskMetrics model in 1994, it proposed a measure of risk called *Value at Risk* (VaR).[7] Defined as a confidence interval, VaR is the maximum loss that can be incurred with a given probability. Suppose we choose a confidence level of 95%. We say that a portfolio has a given VaR, say $1 million, if there is a 95% probability that losses above $1 million will not be incurred. This does not mean that the given portfolio cannot lose more than $1 million, it means only that losses above $1 million will happen with a probability of 5%. If we translate probabilities into relative frequencies, this means, in turn, that losses above $1 million will happen approximately 5 times every 100. If we measure VaR daily this means 5 days out of 100 days.

As a measure of risk, VaR has many drawbacks. It does not specify the amount of losses exceeding VaR. Different distributions might have the same VaR but totally different distributions of extreme values. For instance, in the above example of a VaR of $1 million at 95%, 5 times every 100 a portfolio might lose just above $1 million or a much larger amount. Perhaps the most serious drawback of VaR is the fact that it is not subadditive. The VaR of aggregated portfolios might be larger than the sum of individual VaRs. This is unreasonable as one expects risk to decrease in aggregate due to diversification and anticorrelations. Despite these drawbacks, and despite the fact that confidence intervals are ultimately a rather complex probabilistic concept, VaR has become extremely popular as a risk measure.

In 1998 Artzner, Delbaen, Eber, and Heath[8] published an important paper where they defined the conditions for risk measures to be coher-

---

[5] This fact is well known in statistical physics where the entropy associated with a continuous scheme is somewhat arbitrary.
[6] The pioneering work of Arnold Zellner has started a new strain of econometric literature based on Information Theory. See Arnold Zellner, "Bayesian Method of Moments (BMOM) Analysis of Mean and Regression Models," in J.C. Lee, W.D. Johnson, and A. Zellner (eds.), *Prediction and Modeling Honoring Seymour Geisser* (New York: Springer, 1994), pp. 61–74.
[7] Note that RiskMetrics and VaR are not related. The concept of VaR can be applied to any probability distribution of return and not only to RiskMetrics.
[8] Philippe Artzner, Freddy Delbaen, Jean-Marc Eber, and David Heath, "Coherent Measures of Risk," *Mathematical Finance* 9 (1999), pp. 203–228.

ent. A *coherent risk measure* must satisfy a number of properties including sub-additivity conditions, monotonicity conditions, risk-free conditions, and diversification conditions. To solve the problems inherent in the noncoherence of VaR, Artzner et al. proposed a coherent measure of risk known as *expected shortfall* (ES); Rockafellar and Uryasev[9] call the measure *conditional VaR* (CVaR). The ES at a given confidence level α is defined as the expected loss given that the loss exceeds VaR at the confidence level α. If the loss distribution is continuous, the VaR and the ES or CVaR can be written as follows.

> VaR at the $100(1 - \alpha)$ percent confidence level is the upper 100α percentile of the loss distribution. If we denote the VaR at the $100(1 - \alpha)$ percent confidence level as $\text{VaR}_\alpha(L)$, where L is the random variable of loss, then the expected shortfall at the $100(1 - \alpha)$ percent confidence level $\text{ES}_\alpha(L)$ is defined by the following equation:

$$\text{ES}_\alpha(L) = E[L \mid L \geq \text{VaR}_\alpha(L)]$$

If the distribution is not continuous, the definition of ES is slightly more complicated. Acerbi and Tasche,[10] and Rockafellar and Uryasev provide a thorough discussion of the definitions of ES and CVaR under different distributional assumptions. It can be demonstrated that at the same confidence levels, the ES and VaR are equivalent measures for normal distributions in the sense that ES can be inferred from VaR and vice versa. However other distributions, and in particular those with fat-tails, might exhibit the same VaR but different ES and vice versa. It has been demonstrated that ES is a coherent risk measure while VaR is not. Yamai and Yoshiba[11] offer a comparison of ES and VaR under a number of assumptions.

---

[9] Tyrrell R. Rockafellar and Stanislav Uryasev, "Optimization of Conditional Value-at-Risk," *Journal of Risk* 2, no. 3 (2000), pp. 21–41.

[10] Carlo Acerbi and Dirk Tasche, "On the Coherence of Expected Shortfall," working Paper, Center for Mathematical Sciences, Munich University of Technology, 2001.

[11] Yasuhiro Yamai and Toshinao Yoshiba, "On the Validity of Value-at-Risk: Comparative Analyses with Expected Shortfall," *Monetary and Economic Studies* 20, no. 1 (published by Institute for Monetary and Economic Studies, Bank of Japan, 2002), pp. 57–86. A number of papers discuss the use of ES as a risk measure in portfolio optimization. See, for example, Rockafellar and Uryasev, "Optimization of Conditional Value-at-Risk."

A different way of measuring risk consists in computing different possible scenarios and defining risk as the maximum loss that can be incurred in any of these scenarios. This technique is used in the SPAN system developed by the Chicago Mercantile Exchange which computes 16 scenarios, two of which are extreme scenarios. Risk is the largest maximum loss in the 14 scenarios or 35% of the loss in the two extreme scenarios.

The idea of analyzing risk under different scenarios is widely used in practice, often together with quantile measures such as VaR. Extreme scenarios can be computed in different ways, in particular with the use of Extreme Value Theory (EVT), which we covered in Chapter 13. As we noted in that chapter, and as we will see in the following sections, the use of EVT is still in its infancy.

Risk measures can be seen, from a different point of view, as sensitivities to given factors. In this case, rather than capture the uncertainty of a given distribution it captures the amount of fluctuation of a given quantity as a function of the fluctuations of another quantity. We have already encountered most of these measures. In the analysis of stock prices, the coefficients of factor models, the *betas*, capture the sensitivity of returns to a number of factors. As we have seen in Chapters 11 and 12 on financial econometrics, sensitivities apply to a static as well as to a dynamic framework. A dynamic framework is generally represented as a state-space model.

In the analysis of bond prices, duration captures the sensitivity of bond prices to parallel shifts in the term structure of interest rates. Convexity, which is defined as the first derivative of duration, captures the sensitivity of bond prices to the curvature of the term structure.

In the analysis of derivative instruments, a number of sensitivities are used to capture the sensitivity of their prices to changes in different parameters. These sensitivities are usually indicated with specific Greek letters. Hence, they are called the "Greeks." The most common Greeks are listed below:

Vega	Theta	Delta	Gamma
Sensitivity to a change in volatility	Sensitivity to a change in time remaining	Sensitivity to a change in the price of underlying	Linearized rate of change of delta

A concept related to risk measures is the *Sharpe ratio* developed by William Sharpe.[12] Sharpe himself called this ratio the "Reward to Vari-

---

[12] William F. Sharpe, "Mutual Fund Performance," *Journal of Business* (January 1966), pp. 119–138; and William F. Sharpe, "Adjusting for Risk in Portfolio Performance Measurement," *Journal of Portfolio Management* (Winter 1975), pp. 29–34.

ability Ratio." The Sharpe ratio is to evaluate expected returns in a risk-weighted framework. Given a portfolio, the ex ante Sharpe ratio is defined as the ratio between the expected excess return (measured relative to the risk-free rate) and volatility:

$$\text{Sharpe ratio} = \frac{\text{Expected return} - \text{Risk-free rate}}{\text{Standard deviation of return}}$$

A number of other measures similar to the Sharpe ratio have been introduced, in particular the Sortino ratio[13] which uses only downside volatility.

A variant of the Sharpe ratio commonly used to assess the performance of a portfolio manager is the *information ratio*. The information ratio is the ratio of the excess return over a designated benchmark divided by the tracking error, the standard deviation of the difference between portfolio return and the benchmark market (see Chapter 19). The excess return over the benchmark is referred to as the "alpha" or "active return." The information ratio is typically calculated on an ex post basis as follows:

$$\text{Information ratio} = \frac{\text{Portfolio return} - \text{Benchmark return}}{\text{Tracking error}}$$

RISK MANAGEMENT IN ASSET AND PORTFOLIO MANAGEMENT

Risk has different facets in asset and portfolio management. In particular, risk can be characterized as (1) market risk; (2) risk of underperformance relative to a benchmark; or (3) business risk. Ultimately, risk is market risk. The question is: Who bears it? Asset management firms define their risk as the risk of underperformance relative to a benchmark: the client assumes the market risk implicit in the portfolio; the asset manager assumes the benchmark risk. However, the asset management function is concerned essentially with market risk.

Some nuance is required. If a firm manages the assets of the parent company (e.g., an insurance company or investment bank), it is exposed to market risk as an investor. Also, volatility of returns or a loss of capital might be unacceptable to some institutional or retail investors, forc-

---

[13] See Frank Sortino and Robert Van Meer, "Downside Risk," *Journal of Portfolio Management* (Summer 1991), pp. 27–32.

ing asset managers to accept market risk as they devise guaranteed-return funds or convex strategies to protect the investor against downside risk. The type of quantitative methods used and the extent of risk modeling is largely determined by the risk—relative or absolute—that the asset management firm is exposed to; other important factors include the prevailing culture and the competitive environment.

Some asset management firms are now defining their risk more broadly as business risk. Market risk and the failure to deliver a mandate are only two facets of business risk. Others include process flows and fraud and come under the general heading of operational risk. Operational risk has been moved up on the agenda by management consultants and, more recently, by the European Commission with proposals to extend to the asset management subsidiaries of larger financial organizations the new Basel rules on capital charges to cover business risk.

Factors Driving Risk Management

One of the major contributions of quantitative methods to asset management is widely considered to be in the area of risk. For the more quantitatively-oriented firms, *ex ante* risk measurement has enabled risk-return optimization as prescribed by modern finance theory, the dynamic management of risk, and the ability to handle structured products; for others, it means the ability to "look back" on risk.

Several factors are behind the focus on risk:

- Regulatory and reporting frameworks have put risk on the agenda of institutional investors.
- Pension consultants are pressing for more measures of risk and tying performance to risk.
- Growing sophistication on the part of trustees and institutional investors is also a driver behind the demands for risk measures including VaR.
- The growing complexity of assets in portfolios (e.g., global assets, structured products) is adding to risk and the need to monitor and control it.
- The recent volatility in both asset classes and investment styles is increasing the need to monitor tracking error in an effort to limit downside risk.
- The contribution risk modeling makes in defining mandates.

Risk Measurement in Practice

In practice, as noted previously, a whole battery of risk measures are being used. A number of considerations can be made. The more complex the probability distribution, the more measures required. Over a period of several months—a typical time horizon for asset management—distributions are assumed to be Gaussian and that one risk measure suffices. But phenomena such as volatility clustering, trend reversals, large movements, and structural breaks produce distributions that are not Gaussian. There is a need to measure what might happen at the extremes. It is not infrequent that single risk measures such as variance or VaR are being complemented by scenario analysis to evaluate the risk of extreme movements.

In addition, a single measure might not be equally appropriate for all investment styles. For example, firms focused on emerging markets might use information ratios, which reflect returns on assets, to complement tracking error. Multiple measures might be required by (institutional) clients. Tracking error and information ratios or volatility are considered standard in some markets and an increasing number of clients are asking for VaR. VaR is required in managing funds for endowments and foundations with a statutory requirement to generate positive returns; in Germany, VaR measures are now regulatory for funds managing the investments of depository institutions. Multiple measures might be requested by fund managers themselves, in an attempt to improve their performance.

In some instances, it's important to understand in absolute terms how much money might be lost. This is the case with guaranteed-return funds or funds being managed for the parent company, for example, an insurance firm or investment bank. A few firms are using EVT; the objective is to ensure the ability to survive a market crash. One might want to be able to take into account different aspects or different views. VaR allows a uniform measure of risk across asset classes. Though with time horizons of 2–3 months volatility clustering phenomena disappear, ARCH-GARCH models are being used at some firms to gain an understanding of the clustering of risk.

Getting Down to the Lowest Level

Risk and performance are increasingly being measured at lower levels. Instead of looking at sector levels (e.g., geographical areas, currency or industry sector), firms are beginning to look at the single-asset level. While most firms are not there yet, this is the declared goal.

There is also a tendency at producing risk numbers daily, with daily reporting to fund managers, monthly to management, and (typically) quarterly to clients. Investment consultants and regulators consider it fundamental that asset managers be aware of the risk at all times, but not everyone agrees that crunching out the numbers daily is appropriate for all funds. Among the concerns voiced is the fact that risk measurement loses significance if the covariance matrix is changed daily. Also, if the wrong measure is used, its use on a daily basis might exacerbate the problem, leading to a too frequent rebalancing of portfolios.

Regulatory Implications of Risk Measurement

To protect the financial system and, ultimately, the broad public of investors, financial intermediation and asset management are highly regulated, though regulations governing risk management are different for banks and asset management firms. In many countries, an asset management firm's procedures are highly regulated; the firm must exhibit minimum requisites of financial prowess, the ability to process transactions, and moral qualities of its management. Asset managers are also required to demonstrate the ability to measure risk and to communicate to the investor the level of risk implied by their management.

Risk management has strong regulatory implications, especially for banks. Banks are obliged to keep an amount of liquid and safe capital to shoulder eventual adverse market movements. The amount of bank reserves is subject to strict regulation. There are many facets related to the amount of reserve capital that banks are obliged to maintain. Consider that the amount of liquid bank reserves is a fundamental quantity in the process of money creation and the management of the monetary mass. A new dimension of the reserve management process is the management of the ratio between the amount of risky capital and the amount of safe reserves. The modern view of this aspect is that regulators decide the desired ratio between risky capital and safe reserves but, under appropriate conditions, let banks measure the amount of risk they are running with internal measurement systems. This is a substantial novelty with respect to the past when banks where obliged to keep a fixed percentage in liquid reserves. The point of view of the U.S. Federal Reserve is that

> By substituting banks' internal risk measurement models for broad, uniform regulatory measures of risk exposure, [the new rule] should lead to capital charges that more accurately reflect individual banks' true risk exposures.[14]

---

[14] Darryll Hendricks and Beverly Hirtle, "Bank Capital Requirements for Market Risk: The Internal Models Approach," Federal Reserve Bank of New York, *Economic Policy Review* (December 1997).

Clearly banks must show the ability to measure risk which the Federal Reserve prescribes measuring as VaR. The Federal Reserve then controls the quality of a bank's ability to forecast adverse movements. If adverse movements occur more frequently than anticipated by a given bank's risk management system, then that bank is obliged to increase its liquid reserve. The implications of these new regulations from both the business and the macroeconomic points of view will be analyzed in the coming years.

SUMMARY

- Diversification and risk transfer through financial engineering are the key tools of risk management.
- Estimating the shape of loss distributions is central to modern financial risk management.
- A market is complete if every possible contingency can be traded.
- In a complete market, risk can be perfectly hedged.
- Multivariate geometric diffusion models are complete.
- Stochastic volatility models are not complete, but can be completed.
- If risk does not exist in aggregate, it can be eliminated; if it exists in aggregate, it can only be transferred.
- Off-the-shelf market and credit risk models are commercially available.
- Risk can be measured in numerous ways: unexpected loss, value-at-risk, expected shortfall, and sensitivities.
- Client demand and management push are behind the growing use of risk management in investment management.

Index